Finance Act 2016

CHAPTER 24

CONTENTS

PART 1

INCOME TAX

Charge and principal rates etc

1   Income tax charge and rates for 2016-17
2   Basic rate limit for 2017-18
3   Personal allowance for 2017-18

Rate structure

4   Savings allowance, and savings nil rate etc
5   Rates of tax on dividend income, and abolition of dividend tax credits etc
6   Structure of income tax rates

Employment income: taxable benefits

7   Taxable benefits: application of Chapters 5 to 7 of Part 3 of ITEPA 2003
8   Cars: appropriate percentage for 2019-20 and subsequent tax years
9   Cars which cannot emit CO2: appropriate percentage for 2017-18 and 2018-19
10 Diesel cars: appropriate percentage
11 Cash equivalent of benefit of a van
12 Tax treatment of payments from sporting testimonials
13 Exemption for trivial benefits provided by employers
14 Travel expenses of workers providing services through intermediaries
15 Taxable benefits: PAYE

Employment income: other provision

16 Employee share schemes
17 Securities options
18 Employment income provided through third parties

Pensions

19   Standard lifetime allowance from 2016-17
20   Pensions bridging between retirement and state pension
21   Dependants' scheme pensions
22   Pension flexibility
23   Netherlands Benefit Act for Victims of Persecution 1940-1945

Trading and other income

24   Fixed-rate deductions for use of home for business purposes
25   Averaging profits of farmers etc
26   Relief for finance costs related to residential property businesses
27   Individual investment plans of deceased investors

Reliefs: enterprise investment scheme, venture capital trusts etc

28   EIS, SEIS and VCTs: exclusion of energy generation
29   EIS and VCTs: definition of certain periods
30   EIS and VCTs: election
31   VCTs: requirements for giving approval

Reliefs: peer-to-peer lending

32   Income tax relief for irrecoverable peer-to-peer loans

Transactions in securities

33   Transactions in securities: company distributions
34   Transactions in securities: procedure for counteraction of advantage
35   Distributions in a winding up

Disguised fees and carried interest

36   Disguised investment management fees
37   Income-based carried interest
38   Income-based carried interest: persons coming to the UK

Deduction at source

39   Deduction of income tax at source
40   Deduction of income tax at source: intellectual property
41   Deduction of income tax at source: intellectual property - tax avoidance

Receipts from intellectual property

42   Receipts from intellectual property: territorial scope
43   Receipts from intellectual property: diverted profits tax

Supplementary welfare payments: Northern Ireland

44   Tax treatment of supplementary welfare payments: Northern Ireland

PART 2

CORPORATION TAX

Charge and rates

45 Charge for financial year 2017
46 Rate of corporation tax for financial year 2020

Research and development

47 Abolition of vaccine research relief
48 Cap on R&D aid

Loan relationships

49 Loan relationships and derivative contracts
50 Loans to participators etc: rate of tax
51 Loans to participators etc: trustees of charitable trusts

Intangible fixed assets

52 Intangible fixed assets: pre-FA 2002 assets
53 Intangible fixed assets: transfers treated as at market value

Creative industry reliefs

54 Tax relief for production of orchestral concerts
55 Television and video games tax relief: consequential amendments

Banking companies

56 Banking companies: excluded entities
57 Banking companies: restrictions on loss relief etc

Oil and gas

58 Reduction in rate of supplementary charge
59 Investment allowance: disqualifying conditions
60 Investment allowance: power to expand meaning of "relevant income"
61 Onshore allowance: disqualifying conditions
62 Cluster area allowance: disqualifying conditions
63 Cluster area allowance: power to expand meaning of "relevant income"

Exploitation of patents etc

64 Profits from the exploitation of patents etc

Miscellaneous

65 Power to make regulations about the taxation of securitisation companies
66 Hybrid and other mismatches
67 Insurance companies carrying on long-term business
68 Taking over payment obligations as lessee of plant or machinery

PART 3

INCOME TAX AND CORPORATION TAX

Capital allowances

69   Capital allowances: designated assisted areas
70   Capital allowances: anti-avoidance relating to disposals

Trade and property business profits

71   Trade and property business profits: money's worth
72   Replacement and alteration of tools

Property business deductions

73   Property business deductions: replacement of domestic items
74   Property business deductions: wear and tear allowance

Transfer pricing

75   Transfer pricing: application of OECD principles

Transactions in UK land

76   Corporation tax: territorial scope etc
77   Corporation tax: transactions in UK land
78   Income tax: territorial scope etc
79   Income tax: transactions in UK land
80   Pre-trading expenses
81   Commencement and transitional provision: sections 76, 77 and 80
82   Commencement and transitional provision: sections 78 and 79

PART 4

CAPITAL GAINS TAX

Rate

83   Reduction in rate of capital gains tax

Entrepreneurs' relief

84   Entrepreneurs' relief: associated disposals
85   Entrepreneurs' relief: disposal of goodwill
86   Entrepreneurs' relief: "trading company" and "trading group"

Investors' relief

87   Investors' relief

Employee shareholder shares

88   Employee shareholder shares: limit on exemption

89   Employee shareholder shares: disguised fees and carried interest

Other provisions

90   Disposals of UK residential property by non-residents etc
91   NRCGT returns
92   Addition of CGT to Provisional Collection of Taxes Act 1968

PART 5

INHERITANCE TAX ETC

93   Inheritance tax: increased nil-rate band
94   Inheritance tax: pension drawdown funds
95   Inheritance tax: victims of persecution during Second World War era
96   Inheritance tax: gifts for national purposes etc
97   Estate duty: objects of national, scientific, historic or artistic interest

PART 6

APPRENTICESHIP LEVY

Basic provisions

98   Apprenticeship levy
99   Charge to apprenticeship levy
100   A person's pay bill for a tax year

Connected companies and charities

101   Connected companies
102   Connected charities

Anti-avoidance

103   Anti-avoidance
104   Application of other regimes to apprenticeship levy

Payment, collection and recovery

105   Assessment, payment etc
106   Recovery from third parties
107   Real time information
108   Time limits for assessment
109   No deduction in respect of levy to be made from earnings
110   Collectors and court proceedings

Information and penalties

111   Records
112   Information and inspection powers
113   Penalties

Appeals

114   Appeals

General

115   Tax agents: dishonest conduct
116   Provisional collection of apprenticeship levy
117   Crown application
118   Charities which are "connected" with one another
119   Connection between charities: further provision
120   General interpretation
121   Regulations

PART 7

VAT

122   VAT: power to provide for persons to be eligible for refunds
123   VAT: representatives and security
124   VAT: joint and several liability of operators of online marketplaces
125   VAT: Isle of Man charities
126   VAT: women's sanitary products

PART 8

SDLT AND ATED

Stamp duty land tax

127   SDLT: calculating tax on non-residential and mixed transactions
128   SDLT: higher rates for additional dwellings etc
129   SDLT higher rate: land purchased for commercial use
130   SDLT higher rate: acquisition under regulated home reversion plan
131   SDLT higher rate: properties occupied by certain employees etc
132   SDLT: minor amendments of section 55 of FA 2003
133   SDLT: property authorised investment funds and co-ownership authorised
        contractual schemes

Annual tax on enveloped dwellings

134   ATED: regulated home reversion plans
135   ATED: properties occupied by certain employees etc
136   ATED: alternative property finance - land in Scotland

PART 9

OTHER TAXES AND DUTIES

Stamp duty and stamp duty reserve tax

137   Stamp duty: acquisition of target company's share capital
138   Stamp duty: transfers to depositaries or providers of clearance services
139   SDRT: transfers to depositaries or providers of clearance services

Petroleum revenue tax

140   Petroleum revenue tax: rate

Insurance premium tax

141   Insurance premium tax: standard rate

Landfill tax

142   Landfill tax: rates from 1 April 2017
143   Landfill tax: rates from 1 April 2018

Climate change levy

144   CCL: abolition of exemption for electricity from renewable sources
145   CCL: main rates from 1 April 2017
146   CCL: main rates from 1 April 2018
147   CCL: main rates from 1 April 2019
148   CCL: reduced rates from 1 April 2019

Air passenger duty

149   APD: rates from 1 April 2016

Vehicle excise duty

150   VED: rates for light passenger vehicles, light goods vehicles, motorcycles etc
151   VED: extension of old vehicles exemption from 1 April 2017

Other excise duties

152   Gaming duty: rates
153   Fuel duties: aqua methanol etc
154   Tobacco products duty: rates
155   Alcoholic liquor duties: rates

PART 10

TAX AVOIDANCE AND EVASION

General anti-abuse rule

156   General anti-abuse rule: provisional counteractions
157   General anti-abuse rule: binding of tax arrangements to lead arrangements
158   General anti-abuse rule: penalty

Tackling frequent avoidance

159   Serial tax avoidance
160   Promoters of tax avoidance schemes
161   Large businesses: tax strategies and sanctions for persistently unco-operative behaviour

Offshore activities

162   Penalties for enablers of offshore tax evasion or non-compliance
163   Penalties in connection with offshore matters and offshore transfers
164   Offshore tax errors etc: publishing details of deliberate tax defaulters
165   Asset-based penalties for offshore inaccuracies and failures
166   Offences relating to offshore income, assets and activities

PART 11

ADMINISTRATION, ENFORCEMENT AND SUPPLEMENTARY POWERS

Assessment and returns

167   Simple assessments
168   Time limit for self assessment tax returns
169   HMRC power to withdraw notice to file a tax return

Judgment debts

170   Rate of interest applicable to judgment debts etc: Scotland
171   Rate of interest applicable to judgment debts etc: Northern Ireland
172   Rate of interest applicable to judgment debts etc: England and Wales

Enforcement powers

173   Gift aid: power to impose penalties on charities and intermediaries
174   Proceedings under customs and excise Acts: prosecuting authority
175   Detention and seizure under CEMA 1979: notice requirements etc
176   Data-gathering powers: providers of payment or intermediary services
177   Data-gathering powers: daily penalties for extended default

Payment

178   Extension of provisions about set-off to Scotland

Raw tobacco

179   Raw tobacco approval scheme

State aids granted through provision of tax advantages

180   Powers to obtain information about certain tax advantages
181   Power to publish state aid information
182   Information powers: supplementary

Qualifying transformer vehicles

183   Qualifying transformer vehicles

PART 12

OFFICE OF TAX SIMPLIFICATION

184   Office of Tax Simplification

185　Functions of the OTS: general
186　Functions of the OTS: reviews and reports
187　Annual report
188　Review of the OTS
189　Commencement

PART 13

FINAL

190　Interpretation
191　Short title

Schedule 1 — Abolition of dividend tax credits etc
Schedule 2 — Sporting testimonial payments
Schedule 3 — Employee share schemes: minor amendments
Schedule 4 — Pensions: lifetime allowance: transitional provision
　　Part 1 — "Fixed protection 2016"
　　Part 2 — "Individual protection 2016"
　　Part 3 — Reference numbers etc
　　Part 4 — Information
　　Part 5 — Amendments in connection with protection of pre-6 April 2006 rights
　　Part 6 — Interpretation and regulations
Schedule 5 — Pension flexibility
Schedule 6 — Deduction of income tax at source
　　Part 1 — Abolition of duty to deduct tax from interest on certain investments
　　Part 2 — Deduction of tax from yearly interest: exception for deposit-takers
　　Part 3 — Amendments of or relating to Chapter 2 of Part 15 of ITA 2007
　　Part 4 — Deduction of tax from UK public revenue dividends
　　Part 5 — Commencement
Schedule 7 — Loan relationships and derivative contracts
Schedule 8 — Tax relief for production of orchestral concerts
　　Part 1 — Amendment of CTA 2009
　　Part 2 — Consequential amendments
　　Part 3 — Commencement
Schedule 9 — Profits from the exploitation of patents etc: consequential
Schedule 10 — Hybrid and other mismatches
　　Part 1 — Main provisions
　　Part 2 — Consequential amendments
　　Part 3 — Commencement
Schedule 11 — Disposals of non-UK residential property interests
Schedule 12 — Disposals of residential property interests: gains and losses
Schedule 13 — Entrepreneurs' relief: "trading company" and "trading group"
Schedule 14 — Investors' relief
Schedule 15 — Inheritance tax: increased nil-rate band
Schedule 16 — Property authorised investment funds and co-ownership authorised contractual schemes
　　Part 1 — Co-ownership authorised contractual schemes

Part 2 — Seeding relief for property authorised investment funds and
                co-ownership authorised contractual schemes
        Part 3 — Consequential amendments
        Part 4 — Commencement
Schedule 17 — Aqua methanol etc
        Part 1 — Aqua methanol
        Part 2 — Hydrocarbon oils: miscellaneous amendments
        Part 3 — Commencement
Schedule 18 — Serial tax avoidance
        Part 1 — Contents of Schedule
        Part 2 — Entry into the regime and basic concepts
        Part 3 — Annual information notices and naming
        Part 4 — Restriction of reliefs
        Part 5 — Penalty
        Part 6 — Corporate groups, associated persons and partnerships
        Part 7 — Supplemental
Schedule 19 — Large businesses: tax strategies and sanctions
        Part 1 — Interpretation
        Part 2 — Publication of tax strategies
        Part 3 — Sanctions for persistently unco-operative large businesses
        Part 4 — Supplementary
Schedule 20 — Penalties for enablers of offshore tax evasion or non-
                compliance
        Part 1 — Liability for penalty
        Part 2 — Application of Schedule 36 to FA 2008: information powers
        Part 3 — Publishing details of persons found liable to penalties
Schedule 21 — Penalties relating to offshore matters and offshore transfers
Schedule 22 — Asset-based penalty for offshore inaccuracies and failures
        Part 1 — Liability for penalty
        Part 2 — Amount of penalty
        Part 3 — Identification and valuation of assets
        Part 4 — Procedure
        Part 5 — General
Schedule 23 — Simple assessments
Schedule 24 — Tax advantages constituting the grant of state aid
        Part 1 — Tax advantages to which section 180(2)applies
        Part 2 — Tax advantages to which section 180(5) applies
Schedule 25 — Office of Tax Simplification

Finance Act 2016

2016 CHAPTER 24

An Act to grant certain duties, to alter other duties, and to amend the law relating to the National Debt and the Public Revenue, and to make further provision in connection with finance. [15th September 2016]

Most Gracious Sovereign

WE, Your Majesty's most dutiful and loyal subjects, the Commons of the United Kingdom in Parliament assembled, towards raising the necessary supplies to defray Your Majesty's public expenses, and making an addition to the public revenue, have freely and voluntarily resolved to give and to grant unto Your Majesty the several duties hereinafter mentioned; and do therefore most humbly beseech Your Majesty that it may be enacted, and be it enacted by the Queen's most Excellent Majesty, by and with the advice and consent of the Lords Spiritual and Temporal, and Commons, in this present Parliament assembled, and by the authority of the same, as follows: —

PART 1

INCOME TAX

Charge and principal rates etc

1   Income tax charge and rates for 2016-17

(1)   Income tax is charged for the tax year 2016-17.

(2)   For that tax year —
    (a)   the basic rate is 20%,
    (b)   the higher rate is 40%, and
    (c)   the additional rate is 45%.

2   Basic rate limit for 2017-18

(1)   In section 4(1)(b) of FA 2015 (basic rate limit for 2017-18) for "£32,400" substitute "£33,500".

(2)   Accordingly, omit section 6(b) of F(No.2)A 2015 (basic rate limit for 2017-18).

3   Personal allowance for 2017-18

(1)   In section 5(1)(b) of FA 2015 (personal allowance for 2017-18) for "£11,200" substitute "£11,500".

(2)   Accordingly, omit section 5(b) of F(No.2)A 2015 (personal allowance for 2017-18).

Rate structure

4   Savings allowance, and savings nil rate etc

(1)   ITA 2007 is amended in accordance with subsections (2) to (12).

(2)   In section 6(3)(a) (other rates: savings), after "starting rate for savings" insert "and savings nil rate".

(3)   In section 7 (starting rate for savings) —
      (a)   the existing text becomes subsection (1),
      (b)   after that subsection insert —

         "(2)   The savings nil rate is 0%.", and
      (c)   in the heading, after "starting rate for savings" insert "and savings nil rate".

(4)   In section 10(4) (provisions displacing charge at basic, higher and additional rates), before the entry relating to section 13 insert —
            "section 12A (savings income charged at the savings nil rate),".

(5)   After section 12 insert —

"12A   Savings income charged at the savings nil rate

      (1)   This section applies in relation to an individual if —
            (a)   the amount of the individual's Step 3 income is greater than £L, where £L is the amount of the starting rate limit for savings, and
            (b)   when the individual's Step 3 income is split into two parts —
                  (i)   one ("the individual's income up to the starting rate for savings") consisting of the lowest £L of the individual's Step 3 income, and
                  (ii)   the other ("the individual's income above the starting rate limit for savings") consisting of the rest of the individual's Step 3 income,
            some or all of the individual's income above the starting rate limit for savings consists of savings income (whether or not some or all of the individual's income up to the starting rate limit for savings consists of savings income).

      (2)   In this section —

£A is the amount of the individual's savings allowance (see section 12B),

"the excess" is so much of the individual's income above the starting rate limit for savings as consists of savings income, and

£X is the amount of the excess.

(3) If £X is less than or equal to £A, income tax is charged at the savings nil rate (rather than the basic, higher or additional rate) on the excess.

(4) If £X is more than £A, income tax is charged at the savings nil rate (rather than the basic, higher or additional rate) on the lowest £A of the excess.

(5) Subsections (3) and (4) are subject to any provisions of the Income Tax Acts (apart from section 10) which provide for income to be charged at different rates of income tax in some circumstances.

(6) Section 16 has effect for determining the extent to which the individual's income above the starting rate limit for savings consists of savings income.

(7) For the purposes of this section, an individual's "Step 3 income" is the individual's net income less allowances deducted at Step 3 of the calculation in section 23.

12B Individual's entitlement to a savings allowance

(1) Subsections (2) to (4) determine the amount of an individual's savings allowance for a tax year.

(2) If any of the individual's income for the year is additional-rate income, the individual's savings allowance for the year is nil.

(3) If —

   (a) any of the individual's income for the year is higher-rate income, and

   (b) none of the individual's income for the year is additional-rate income,

the individual's savings allowance for the year is £500.

(4) If none of the individual's income for the year is higher-rate income, the individual's savings allowance for the year is £1,000.

(5) The Treasury may by regulations substitute a different amount for the amount for the time being specified in subsection (2), (3) or (4); and regulations under this subsection that have effect for a tax year may be made at any time before the end of that tax year.

(6) If regulations under subsection (5) reduce any amount, the regulations may not be made unless a draft of the instrument containing them (whether alone or together with regulations under subsection (5) which increase any amount) has been laid before, and approved by a resolution of, the House of Commons.

(7) Section 1014(4) (negative procedure) does not apply to regulations under subsection (5) which increase any amount if —

   (a) the instrument containing them also contains regulations under subsection (5) which reduce any amount, and

      (b)   a draft of the instrument has been laid before, and approved by a resolution of, the House of Commons.

    (8)   For the purposes of this section —

      (a)   each of the following is "additional-rate income" —

        (i)   income on which income tax is charged at the additional rate or dividend additional rate,

        (ii)   income on which income tax would be charged at the additional rate but for section 12A (income charged at savings nil rate),

        (iii)   income on which income tax would be charged at the dividend additional rate but for section 13A (income charged at dividend nil rate), and

        (iv)   income of an individual who is a Scottish taxpayer or Welsh taxpayer which would, if the individual were not a Scottish taxpayer or Welsh taxpayer (as the case may be), be income on which income tax is charged at the additional rate, and

      (b)   each of the following is "higher-rate income" —

        (i)   income on which income tax is charged at the higher rate or dividend upper rate,

        (ii)   income on which income tax would be charged at the higher rate but for section 12A (income charged at savings nil rate),

        (iii)   income on which income tax would be charged at the dividend upper rate but for section 13A (income charged at dividend nil rate), and

        (iv)   income of an individual who is a Scottish taxpayer or Welsh taxpayer which would, if the individual were not a Scottish taxpayer or Welsh taxpayer (as the case may be), be income on which income tax is charged at the higher rate."

    (6)   In section 16(1) (purposes of rules about highest part of income), before the "and" at the end of paragraph (a) insert —

      "(aa)   the extent to which a person's income above the starting rate limit for savings consists of savings income,".

    (7)   In section 17 (repayment where tax paid at basic rate instead of starting rate for savings) —

      (a)   after subsection (1) insert —

      "(1A)   This section also applies if income tax at a rate greater than the savings nil rate has been paid on income on which income tax is chargeable at the savings nil rate.", and

      (b)   in the heading —

        (i)   for "basic" substitute "greater", and

        (ii)   after "savings" insert "or savings nil rate".

    (8)   In sections 55B(2)(b) and 55C(1)(c) (individual liable to tax only at certain rates), after "dividend ordinary rate" insert ", the savings nil rate".

    (9)   In section 745(1) (transfer of assets abroad: same rate of tax not to be charged twice), after "the starting rate for savings" insert "when that rate is more than 0%,".

(10) In section 828B(5) (individual liable to tax only at certain rates), after "basic rate" insert ", the savings nil rate".

(11) In section 989 (definitions for the purposes of the Income Tax Acts) —
    (a) at the appropriate places insert —
        ""savings allowance" has the meaning given by section 12B,", and
        ""savings nil rate" means the rate of income tax specified in section 7(2),", and
    (b) in the entry for "starting rate of savings", for "has the meaning given by section 7" substitute "means the rate of income tax specified in section 7(1)".

(12) In Schedule 4 (index of defined expressions), at the appropriate places insert —

    "savings allowance   section 12B", and

    "savings nil rate   section 7".

(13) In section 669(3) of ITTOIA 2005 (preventing charge to both income and inheritance tax: meaning of "extra liability"), for paragraphs (a) and (b) substitute —
    "(a) income charged at the additional rate or the higher rate were charged at the basic rate, and
    (b) income charged at the dividend additional rate or the dividend upper rate were charged at the dividend ordinary rate."

(14) In consequence of the amendment made by subsection (13) —
    (a) in Schedule 1 to ITA 2007 omit paragraph 561,
    (b) in Schedule 1 to FA 2008 omit paragraph 59, and
    (c) in Schedule 2 to FA 2009 omit paragraph 21.

(15) In section 7(6) of TMA 1970 (cases where person not required to give notice of being chargeable to income tax), after "dividend ordinary rate" insert ", the savings nil rate".

(16) In section 91(3)(c) of TMA 1970 (interest adjustments where reliefs given: when to ignore relief from higher rates on income paid subject to deduction of tax) after "basic rate" insert ", the savings nil rate".

(17) Subject to subsection (18), the amendments made by this section have effect for the tax year 2016-17 and subsequent tax years.

(18) The amendments in section 669 of ITTOIA 2005, and the repeals made by subsection (14), have effect where the tax year mentioned in section 669(1)(b) of ITTOIA 2005 is the tax year 2016-17 or a later tax year.

(19) The Treasury may, by regulations made by statutory instrument, make such provision amending, repealing or revoking any provision made by or under the Taxes Acts as the Treasury considers appropriate in consequence of the amendments made by this section; and regulations under this subsection that have effect for the tax year 2016-17 may be made at any time before the end of that tax year.

(20) In subsection (19) "the Taxes Acts" means—
  (a) the Tax Acts,
  (b) TMA 1970, and
  (c) TCGA 1992 and all other enactments relating to capital gains tax.

(21) A statutory instrument containing regulations under subsection (19) is subject to annulment in pursuance of a resolution of the House of Commons.

5   Rates of tax on dividend income, and abolition of dividend tax credits etc

(1) ITA 2007 is amended in accordance with subsections (2) to (8).

(2) In section 6(3)(b) (other rates: dividends), before "dividend ordinary rate," insert "dividend nil rate,".

(3) In section 8 (dividend ordinary, upper and additional rates)—
  (a) in the heading, after "The" insert "dividend nil rate,",
  (b) before subsection (1) insert—

  "(A1)   The dividend nil rate is 0%.",
  (c) in subsection (1) (dividend ordinary rate), for "10%" substitute "7.5%",
  and
  (d) in subsection (3) (dividend additional rate), for "37.5%" substitute "38.1%".

(4) In section 9(2) (dividend trust rate), for "37.5%" substitute "38.1%".

(5) After section 13 insert—

"13A Income charged at the dividend nil rate

  (1) Subsection (2) applies if, ignoring this section, at least some of an individual's income would be charged to income tax at the dividend ordinary rate, the dividend upper rate or the dividend additional rate.

  (2) Income tax is charged at the dividend nil rate (rather than the dividend ordinary rate, dividend upper rate or dividend additional rate) on one or more amounts of the individual's income as follows—
  Step 1
  Identify the amount ("D") of the individual's income which would, ignoring this section, be charged at the dividend ordinary rate.
  Rule 1A: If D is more than £5,000, the first £5,000 of D is charged at the dividend nil rate (rather than the dividend ordinary rate), and is the only amount charged at the dividend nil rate.
  Rule 1B: If D is equal to £5,000, D is charged at the dividend nil rate (rather than the dividend ordinary rate), and is the only amount charged at the dividend nil rate.
  Rule 1C: If D is less than £5,000 but more than nil, D is charged at the dividend nil rate (rather than the dividend ordinary rate).
  Step 2
  If D is less than £5,000, identify the amount ("U") of the individual's income which would, ignoring this section, be charged at the dividend upper rate.
  Rule 2A: If the total of D and U is more than £5,000—

      (a)   the first £M of U is charged at the dividend nil rate (rather than the dividend upper rate), where £M is the difference between £5,000 and D, and

      (b)   the amounts charged under this Rule and Rule 1C are the only amounts charged at the dividend nil rate.

Rule 2B: If the total of D and U is equal to £5,000, U is charged at the dividend nil rate (rather than the dividend upper rate), and the amounts charged under this Rule and Rule 1C are the only amounts charged at the dividend nil rate.

Rule 2C: If the total of D and U is less than £5,000 but more than nil, U is charged at the dividend nil rate (rather than the dividend upper rate).

Step 3

If the total of D and U is less than £5,000, identify the amount ("A") of the individual's income which would, ignoring this section, be charged at the dividend additional rate.

Rule 3A: If the total of D, U and A is more than £5,000, the first £X of A is charged at the dividend nil rate (rather than the dividend additional rate), where £X is the difference between —

      £5,000, and

      the total of D and U,

and the amounts charged under this Rule, and Rules 1C and 2C, are the amounts charged at the dividend nil rate.

Rule 3B: If the total of D, U and A is less than or equal to £5,000, A is charged at the dividend nil rate (rather than the dividend additional rate), and the amounts charged under this Rule, and Rules 1C and 2C, are the amounts charged at the dividend nil rate."

(6)   In section 55B(2) (transferable allowance: conditions for entitlement to tax reduction)—

      (a)   in paragraph (b) (individual liable to tax only at certain rates), after "the basic rate," insert "the dividend nil rate,", and

      (b)   after paragraph (b) insert—

            "(ba) if for the tax year the individual is liable to tax at the dividend nil rate, the individual would for that year neither be liable to tax at the dividend upper rate, nor be liable to tax at the dividend additional rate, if section 13A (dividend nil rate) were omitted,".

(7)   In section 55C(1) (transferable allowance: conditions for entitlement to elect for reduced personal allowance)—

      (a)   in paragraph (c) (individual would be liable to tax only at certain rates), after "the basic rate," insert "the dividend nil rate,", and

      (b)   before the "and" at the end of paragraph (c) insert—

            "(ca) where on that assumption the individual would for the tax year be liable to tax at the dividend nil rate, the individual on that assumption would for that year neither be liable to tax at the dividend upper rate, nor be liable to tax at the dividend additional rate, if section 13A (dividend nil rate) were omitted,".

(8)   In section 989 (definitions for the purposes of the Income Tax Acts), after the

entry for "dividend income" insert—

"'dividend nil rate" means the rate of income tax specified in section 8(A1),".

(9) In section 7 of TMA 1970 (duty to notify HMRC of liability to tax)—

    (a)   in subsection (6) (exception for net payments etc)—

        (i)   after paragraph (a) insert "or",

        (ii)   at the end of paragraph (b), for "; or" substitute a comma,

        (iii)   omit paragraph (c), and

        (iv)   in the words after paragraph (c), after "the basic rate" insert ", the dividend nil rate", and

    (b)   after subsection (6) insert—

        "(6A)   A source of income falls within this subsection in relation to any person and any year of assessment if for that year—

        (a)   all income from the source is dividend income (see section 19 of ITA 2007), and

        (b)   the person—

           (i)   is UK-resident,

           (ii)   is not liable to tax at the dividend ordinary rate,

           (iii)   is not liable to tax at the dividend upper rate,

           (iv)   is not liable to tax at the dividend additional rate, and

           (v)   is not charged to tax under section 832 of ITTOIA 2005 (relevant foreign income charged on remittance basis) on any dividend income."

(10) The amendments made by the preceding provisions of this section have effect for the tax year 2016-17 and subsequent tax years.

(11) Schedule 1 contains provision for, and connected with, the abolition of dividend tax credits etc.

6   Structure of income tax rates

(1) ITA 2007 is amended in accordance with subsections (2) to (22).

(2) Before section 10 insert—

"9A   Overview of sections 10 to 15

The general effect of sections 10 to 15 is outlined in the following table—

Type of taxpayer	*Rates payable on savings income*	*Rates payable on most dividend income*	*Rates payable on other income*
UK resident individual who is neither a Scottish taxpayer nor a Welsh taxpayer	Savings rates	Dividend rates	Main rates

Type of taxpayer	Rates payable on savings income	Rates payable on most dividend income	Rates payable on other income
Scottish taxpayer	Savings rates	Dividend rates	Scottish rates
Welsh taxpayer	Savings rates	Dividend rates	Main rates while section 11B is not in force; Welsh rates if that section is in force
Non-UK resident individual	Savings rates	Dividend rates	Default rates
Non-individual, except that some trustees in some circumstances are subject instead to the trust rate or the dividend trust rate	Default basic rate	Dividend ordinary rate	Default basic rate

Note: the table does not address the effect of some exceptions referred to in sections 10 to 15."

(3) Before section 7 insert—

   "6C The default basic, higher and additional rates

   The default basic rate, default higher rate and default additional rate for a tax year are the rates determined as such by Parliament for the tax year."

(4) After section 7 insert—

   "7A The savings basic, higher and additional rates

   The savings basic rate, savings higher rate and savings additional rate for a tax year are the rates determined as such by Parliament for the tax year."

(5) In section 6(3) (other rates)—
   (a) before paragraph (a) insert—
      "(zc) section 6C (default basic, higher and additional rates),", and
   (b) after paragraph (a) insert—
      "(aa) section 7A (savings basic, higher and additional rates),".

(6) In section 10(2) (income charged at basic rate) omit the words after "at the basic rate".

(7) In section 10(4) (provisions displacing charge at basic, higher and additional

rates), before the entry (inserted by this Act) relating to section 12A insert—

> "section 11C (income charged at the default basic, higher and additional rates: non-UK resident individuals),
>
> section 11D (savings income charged at the savings basic, higher and additional rates: individuals),
>
> section 12 (savings income charged at the starting rate for savings),".

(8) In section 11 (income charged at the basic rate: other persons)—

    (a) in the heading, for "basic rate: other persons" substitute "default basic rate: non-individuals", and

    (b) in subsection (1), before "basic" insert "default".

(9) After section 11B insert—

"11C Income charged at the default basic, higher and additional rates: non-UK resident individuals

(1) Income tax on a non-UK resident individual's income up to the basic rate limit is charged at the default basic rate.

(2) Income tax is charged at the default higher rate on a non-UK resident individual's income above the basic rate limit and up to the higher rate limit.

(3) Income tax is charged at the default additional rate on a non-UK resident individual's income above the higher rate limit.

(4) Subsections (1) to (3) are subject to—

> section 11D (savings income charged at the savings basic, higher and additional rates),
>
> section 12 (savings income charged at the starting rate for savings),
>
> section 12A (savings income charged at the savings nil rate),
>
> section 13 (income charged at the dividend ordinary, upper and additional rates: individuals), and
>
> any other provisions of the Income Tax Acts (apart from section 10) which provide for income to be charged at different rates of income tax in some circumstances.

11D Income charged at the savings basic, higher and additional rates

(1) Income tax is charged at the savings basic rate on an individual's income which—

    (a) is saving income, and

    (b) would otherwise be charged at the basic rate or the default basic rate.

(2) Income tax is charged at the savings higher rate on an individual's income which—

    (a) is savings income, and

    (b) would otherwise be charged at the higher rate or the default higher rate.

(3) Income tax is charged at the savings additional rate on an individual's income which—

        (a)   is savings income, and

        (b)   would otherwise be charged at the additional rate or the default additional rate.

(4)   Subsections (1) to (3) –

        (a)   have effect after sections 12 and 12A have been applied (so that any reference in subsections (1) to (3) to income which would otherwise be charged at a particular rate does not include income charged at the starting rate for savings or at the savings nil rate), and

        (b)   are subject to any other provisions of the Income Tax Acts (apart from sections 10 and 11C) which provide for income to be charged at different rates of income tax in some circumstances.

(5)   Section 16 has effect for determining the extent to which an individual's savings income above the starting rate limit for savings would otherwise be charged at the basic, higher or additional rate or the default basic, default higher or default additional rate.

(6)   In relation to an individual who is a Scottish taxpayer, references in this section to income which would otherwise be charged at a particular rate are to be read as references to income that would, if the individual were not a Scottish taxpayer (but were UK resident), be charged at that rate (and subsection (5) is to be read accordingly)."

(10)   In section 12(1) (income charged at the starting rate for savings) –

        (a)   omit "(rather than the basic rate)", and

        (b)   for "as is savings income" substitute "as –

                (a)   is savings income, and

                (b)   would otherwise be charged at the basic rate or the default basic rate".

(11)   In section 12A (inserted by this Act) –

        (a)   in each of subsections (3) and (4), after "rather than the basic, higher or additional rate" insert "or the default basic, default higher or default additional rate", and

        (b)   in subsection (5), for "section 10" substitute "sections 10 and 11C".

(12)   In section 12B (inserted by this Act), in subsection (8) (income charged at savings nil-rate: meaning of "additional-rate income" and "higher-rate income") –

        (a)   in paragraph (a)(i), after "at the additional rate" insert ", default additional rate",

        (b)   in paragraph (a)(ii), after "additional rate" insert ", or default additional rate,",

        (c)   in paragraph (a)(iv), after "additional rate" insert "or default additional rate",

        (d)   in paragraph (b)(i), after "at the higher rate" insert ", default higher rate",

        (e)   in paragraph (b)(ii), after "higher rate" insert ", or default higher rate,", and

        (f)   in paragraph (b)(iv), after "higher rate" insert "or default higher rate".

(13)   In section 16(1) (purposes of rules about highest part of income), before the

"and" at the end of the paragraph (aa) (inserted by this Act) insert—

> "(ab) the rate at which income tax would be charged on a person's savings income above the starting rate limit for savings apart from sections 11D and 12A,".

(14) In section 17(1) (repayment where tax paid at basic rate instead of starting rate for savings), for "at the basic rate" substitute "at a rate greater than the starting rate for savings".

(15) In section 55B (entitlement to transferable tax allowances for married couples and civil partners)—

   (a) in subsection (2)(b) as amended by section 5 of this Act, after "other than the basic rate," insert "the default basic rate, the savings basic rate,", and

   (b) in subsection (3), after "is the basic rate" insert "or default basic rate".

(16) In section 55C(1)(c) (election to reduce personal allowance conditional on not becoming subject to higher rates) as amended by section 5 of this Act, after "other than the basic rate," insert "the default basic rate, the savings basic rate,".

(17) In section 58(2) ("adjusted net income" includes grossed-up gift aid donations), after "grossed up by reference to the basic rate for the tax year" insert "if for the tax year the individual is UK resident but not a Scottish taxpayer, by reference to the default basic rate for the tax year if for the tax year the individual is non-UK resident".

(18) In section 414(2)(a) (gift aid donation treated as made after deduction of tax at the basic rate or Scottish basic rate), before the "or" at the end of sub-paragraph (i) insert—

> "(ia) at the default basic rate if for the tax year the individual is non-UK resident,".

(19) In section 415 (grossing-up rate for gift aid purposes), after "the basic rate for the tax year in which the gift is made" insert "if the gift is made by an individual who for that tax year is UK resident but not a Scottish taxpayer, by reference to the default basic rate for that tax year if the gift is made by an individual who for that tax year is non-UK resident".

(20) In section 828B(5) (exemption for non-domiciled UK residents conditional on not being subject to higher rates) as amended by section 4 of this Act, after "other than the basic rate" insert ", the savings basic rate".

(21) In section 989 (definitions for the purposes of the Income Tax Acts), at the appropriate places insert—

> ""default additional rate" means the rate of income tax of that name determined pursuant to section 6C,
>
> "default basic rate" means the rate of income tax of that name determined pursuant to section 6C,
>
> "default higher rate" means the rate of income tax of that name determined pursuant to section 6C,"

and—

> ""savings additional rate" means the rate of income tax of that name determined pursuant to section 7A,"

and —

  ""savings basic rate" means the rate of income tax of that name determined pursuant to section 7A,

  "savings higher rate" means the rate of income tax of that name determined pursuant to section 7A,".

(22) In Schedule 4 (index of defined expressions), at the appropriate places insert —

"default additional rate	section 6C (as applied by section 989)"
"default basic rate	section 6C (as applied by section 989)"
"default higher rate	section 6C (as applied by section 989)"
"savings additional rate	section 7A (as applied by section 989)"
"savings basic rate	section 7A (as applied by section 989)"
"savings higher rate	section 7A (as applied by section 989)"

(23) In sections 4(4) and (5) and 4BA(1) of TCGA 1992 (rate of capital gains tax depends on individual's liability to higher rates of income tax), after "at the higher rate" insert ", the default higher rate, the savings higher rate".

(24) Subject to any provision made by virtue of subsection (25)(b), the amendments made by this section come into force on the day appointed by the Treasury under section 13(14) of the Scotland Act 2016 and have effect —

  (a) for the tax year appointed by the Treasury under section 13(15) of the Scotland Act 2016, and

  (b) for subsequent tax years.

(25) The Treasury may by regulations make —

  (a) such consequential provision as they consider appropriate in connection with any preceding provision of this section;

  (b) such transitional or saving provision as they consider appropriate in connection with the coming into force of any provision of the preceding subsections of this section.

(26) Regulations under this section may amend, repeal or revoke an enactment, whenever passed or made (including this Act).

(27) Regulations under this section must be made by statutory instrument.

(28) A statutory instrument containing regulations under this section which includes provision amending or repealing a provision of an Act may not be made unless a draft of the instrument has been laid before and approved by a resolution of the House of Commons.

(29) Any other statutory instrument containing regulations under this section, if made without a draft having been approved by a resolution of the House of Commons, is subject to annulment in pursuance of a resolution of the House of Commons.

(30) In subsection (26) "enactment" includes an enactment contained in subordinate legislation (within the meaning of the Interpretation Act 1978).

Employment income: taxable benefits

7   **Taxable benefits: application of Chapters 5 to 7 of Part 3 of ITEPA 2003**

  (1)   Part 3 of ITEPA 2003 (employment income: earnings and benefits etc treated as earnings) is amended as follows.

  (2)   In section 97 (living accommodation to which Chapter 5 applies), after subsection (1) insert—

     "(1A)   Where this Chapter applies to any living accommodation—

        (a)   the living accommodation is a benefit for the purposes of this Chapter (and accordingly it is immaterial whether the terms on which it is provided to any of those persons constitute a fair bargain), and

        (b)   sections 102 to 108 provide for the cash equivalent of the benefit of the living accommodation to be treated as earnings."

  (3)   In section 109 (priority of Chapter 5 over Chapter 1), after subsection (3) insert—

     "(4)   In a case where the cash equivalent of the benefit of the living accommodation is nil—

        (a)   subsections (2) and (3) do not apply, and

        (b)   the full amount mentioned in subsection (1)(b) constitutes earnings from the employment for the year under Chapter 1."

  (4)   In section 114 (cars, vans and related benefits to which Chapter 6 applies), after subsection (1) insert—

     "(1A)   Where this Chapter applies to a car or van, the car or van is a benefit for the purposes of this Chapter (and accordingly it is immaterial whether the terms on which it is made available to the employee or member constitute a fair bargain)."

  (5)   For section 117 substitute—

     "117   Meaning of car or van made available by reason of employment

       (1)   For the purposes of this Chapter a car or van made available by an employer to an employee or member of an employee's family or household is to be regarded as made available by reason of the employment unless subsection (2) or (3) excludes the application of this subsection.

       (2)   Subsection (1) does not apply where—

          (a)   the employer is an individual, and

          (b)   the car or van in question is made available in the normal course of the employer's domestic, family or personal relationships.

       (3)   Subsection (1) does not apply where—

          (a)   the employer carries on a vehicle hire business under which cars or vans of the same kind are made available to members of the public for hire,

          (b)   the car or van in question is hired to the employee or member in the normal course of that business, and

    (c) in hiring that car or van the employee or member is acting as an ordinary member of the public."

 (6) In section 120 (benefit of car treated as earnings) —

   (a) in subsection (2) after "case" insert "(including a case where the cash equivalent of the benefit of the car is nil)", and

   (b) after subsection (2) insert —

    "(3) Any reference in this Act to a case where the cash equivalent of the benefit of a car is treated as the employee's earnings for a year by virtue of this section includes a case where the cash equivalent is nil."

 (7) In section 154 (benefit of van treated as earnings) —

   (a) the existing text becomes subsection (1) of that section, and

   (b) after that subsection insert —

    "(2) In such a case (including a case where the cash equivalent of the benefit of the van is nil) the employee is referred to in this Chapter as being chargeable to tax in respect of the van for that year.

    (3) Any reference in this Act to a case where the cash equivalent of the benefit of a van is treated as the employee's earnings for a year by virtue of this section includes a case where the cash equivalent is nil."

 (8) In section 173 (loans to which Chapter 7 applies), after subsection (1) insert —

   "(1A) Where this Chapter applies to a loan —

    (a) the loan is a benefit for the purposes of this Chapter (and accordingly it is immaterial whether the terms of the loan constitute a fair bargain), and

    (b) sections 175 to 183 provide for the cash equivalent of the benefit of the loan (where it is a taxable cheap loan) to be treated as earnings in certain circumstances."

 (9) The amendments made by this section have effect for the tax year 2016-17 and subsequent tax years.

8 Cars: appropriate percentage for 2019-20 and subsequent tax years

 (1) ITEPA 2003 is amended as follows.

 (2) Section 139 (car with a CO_2 figure: the appropriate percentage) is amended as set out in subsections (3) and (4).

 (3) In subsection (2) —

   (a) in paragraph (a), for "13%" substitute "16%",

   (b) in paragraph (aa), for "16%" substitute "19%", and

   (c) in paragraph (b), for "19%" substitute "22%".

 (4) In subsection (3), for "20%" substitute "23%".

 (5) Section 140 (car without a CO_2 figure: the appropriate percentage) is amended as set out in subsections (6) and (7).

 (6) In subsection (2), in the Table —

     (a)   for "20%" substitute "23%", and

     (b)   for "31%" substitute "34%".

(7)   In subsection (3)(a), for "13%" (as substituted by section 9(3)) substitute "16%".

(8)   In section 142(2) (car first registered before 1 January 1998: the appropriate percentage), in the Table —

     (a)   for "20%" substitute "23%", and

     (b)   for "31%" substitute "34%".

(9)   The amendments made by this section have effect for the tax year 2019-20 and subsequent tax years.

9   Cars which cannot emit CO_2: appropriate percentage for 2017-18 and 2018-19

(1)   In section 140(3)(a) of ITEPA 2003 (car which cannot emit CO_2: the appropriate percentage), for "7%" substitute "9%".

(2)   The amendment made by subsection (1) has effect for the tax year 2017-18.

(3)   In section 140(3)(a) of ITEPA 2003, for "9%" substitute "13%".

(4)   The amendment made by subsection (3) has effect for the tax year 2018-19.

10   Diesel cars: appropriate percentage

(1)   In section 24 of FA 2014 (cars: the appropriate percentage), omit the following ("the repealing provisions") —

     (a)   subsection (2),

     (b)   subsection (6),

     (c)   subsection (10),

     (d)   subsection (11), and

     (e)   subsection (15).

(2)   Any provision of ITEPA 2003 amended or omitted by the repealing provisions has effect for the tax year 2016-17 and subsequent tax years as if the repealing provisions had not been enacted.

11   Cash equivalent of benefit of a van

(1)   Section 155 of ITEPA 2003 (cash equivalent of the benefit of a van) is amended as follows.

(2)   In subsection (1B)(a), for "2019-20" substitute "2021-22".

(3)   In subsection (1C), for paragraphs (b) to (e) substitute —

     "(b)   20% for the tax year 2016-17;

     (c)   20% for the tax year 2017-18;

     (d)   40% for the tax year 2018-19;

     (e)   60% for the tax year 2019-20;

     (f)   80% for the tax year 2020-21;

     (g)   90% for the tax year 2021-22."

(4)   The amendments made by this section have effect for the tax year 2016-17 and subsequent tax years.

12   Tax treatment of payments from sporting testimonials

Schedule 2 contains provision about the tax treatment of payments from sporting testimonials.

13   Exemption for trivial benefits provided by employers

(1)   ITEPA 2003 is amended as follows.

(2)   After section 323 insert—

"323A Trivial benefits provided by employers

(1)   No liability to income tax arises in respect of a benefit provided by, or on behalf of, an employer to an employee or a member of the employee's family or household if—

    (a)   conditions A to D are met, or

    (b)   in a case where subsection (2) applies, conditions A to E are met.

(2)   This subsection applies where—

    (a)   the employer is a close company, and

    (b)   the employee is—

        (i)   a person who is a director or other office-holder of the employer, or

        (ii)   a member of the family or household of such a person.

(3)   Condition A is that the benefit is not cash or a cash voucher within the meaning of section 75.

(4)   Condition B is that the benefit cost of the benefit does not exceed £50.

(5)   In this section "benefit cost", in relation to a benefit, means—

    (a)   the cost of providing the benefit, or

    (b)   if the benefit is provided to more than one person and the nature of the benefit or the scale of its provision means it is impracticable to calculate the cost of providing it to each person to whom it is provided, the average cost per person of providing the benefit.

(6)   For the purposes of subsection (5)(b), the average cost per person of providing a benefit is found by dividing the total cost of providing the benefit by the number of persons to whom the benefit is provided.

(7)   Condition C is that the benefit is not provided pursuant to relevant salary sacrifice arrangements or any other contractual obligation.

(8)   "Relevant salary sacrifice arrangements", in relation to the provision of a benefit to an employee or to a member of an employee's family or household, means arrangements (whenever made, whether before or after the employment began) under which the employee gives up the right to receive an amount of general earnings or specific employment income in return for the provision of the benefit.

(9)   Condition D is that the benefit is not provided in recognition of particular services performed by the employee in the course of the employment or in anticipation of such services.

(10)   Condition E is that—

    (a)   the benefit cost of the benefit provided to the employee, or

    (b)   in a case where the benefit is provided to a member of the employee's family or household who is not an employee of the employer, the amount of the benefit cost allocated to the employee in accordance with section 323B(4),

does not exceed the employee's available exempt amount (see section 323B).

323B Section 323A: calculation of available exempt amount

(1)   The "available exempt amount", in relation to an employee of an employer, is the amount found by deducting from the annual exempt amount the aggregate of —

    (a)   the benefit cost of eligible benefits provided earlier in the tax year by, or on behalf of, the employer to the employee, and

    (b)   any amounts allocated to the employee in accordance with subsection (4) in respect of eligible benefits provided earlier in the tax year by, or on behalf of, the employer to a member of the employee's family or household who was not at that time an employee of the employer.

(2)   The annual exempt amount is £300.

(3)   For the purposes of subsection (1) "eligible benefits" means benefits in respect of which conditions A to D in section 323A are met.

(4)   The amount allocated to an employee of an employer in respect of a benefit provided to a person ("P") who —

    (a)   is a member of the employee's family or household, and

    (b)   is not an employee of the employer,

is the benefit cost of that benefit divided by the number of persons who meet the condition in subsection (5) and are members of P's family or household.

(5)   This condition is met if the person is —

    (a)   a director or other office-holder of the employer,

    (b)   an employee of the employer who is a member of the family or household of a person within paragraph (a), or

    (c)   a former employee of the employer who —

        (i)   was a director or other office-holder at any time when the employer was a close company, or

        (ii)   is a member of the family or household of such a person.

(6)   In this section "benefit cost" has the same meaning as in section 323A.

323C Power to amend sections 323A and 323B

(1)   The Treasury may by regulations amend section 323A so as to alter the conditions which must be met for the exemption conferred by section 323A(1) to apply.

(2)   Regulations under subsection (1) may include any amendment of section 323B that is appropriate in consequence of an amendment made under subsection (1).

(3) The Treasury must not make regulations under subsection (1) unless a draft of the regulations has been laid before and approved by a resolution of the House of Commons."

(3) In section 716 (alteration of amounts by Treasury order) in subsection (2), after paragraph (f) insert—

> "(fa) section 323A(4) (trivial benefits provided by employers: cost of providing benefit),
>
> (fb) section 323B(2) (trivial benefits provided by employers: annual exempt amount),".

(4) In section 717(4) (negative procedure not to apply to certain statutory instruments) after "other care: meaning of "eligible employee")," insert "section 323C(1) (trivial benefits provided by employers),".

(5) The amendments made by this section have effect for the tax year 2016-17 and subsequent tax years.

14 Travel expenses of workers providing services through intermediaries

(1) In Chapter 2 of Part 5 of ITEPA 2003 (deductions for employee's expenses), after section 339 insert—

"339A Travel for necessary attendance: employment intermediaries

(1) This section applies where an individual ("the worker")—
   (a) personally provides services (which are not excluded services) to another person ("the client"), and
   (b) the services are provided not under a contract directly between the client or a person connected with the client and the worker but under arrangements involving an employment intermediary.

This is subject to the following provisions of this section.

(2) Where this section applies, each engagement is for the purposes of sections 338 and 339 to be regarded as a separate employment.

(3) This section does not apply if it is shown that the manner in which the worker provides the services is not subject to (or to the right of) supervision, direction or control by any person.

(4) Subsection (3) does not apply in relation to an engagement if—
   (a) Chapter 8 of Part 2 applies in relation to the engagement,
   (b) the conditions in section 51, 52 or 53 are met in relation to the employment intermediary, and
   (c) the employment intermediary is not a managed service company.

(5) This section does not apply in relation to an engagement if—
   (a) Chapter 8 of Part 2 does not apply in relation to the engagement merely because the circumstances in section 49(1)(c) are not met,
   (b) assuming those circumstances were met, the conditions in section 51, 52 or 53 would be met in relation to the employment intermediary, and

      (c)   the employment intermediary is not a managed service company.

(6)   In determining for the purposes of subsection (4) or (5) whether the conditions in section 51, 52 or 53 are or would be met in relation to the employment intermediary—

      (a)   in section 51(1)—

          (i)   disregard "either" in the opening words, and

          (ii)   disregard paragraph (b) (and the preceding or), and

      (b)   read references to the intermediary as references to the employment intermediary.

(7)   Subsection (8) applies if—

      (a)   the client or a relevant person provides the employment intermediary (whether before or after the worker begins to provide the services) with a fraudulent document which is intended to constitute evidence that, by virtue of subsection (3), this section does not or will not apply in relation to the services,

      (b)   that section is taken not to apply in relation to the services, and

      (c)   in consequence, the employment intermediary does not under PAYE regulations deduct and account for an amount that would have been deducted and accounted for under those regulations if this section had been taken to apply in relation to the services.

(8)   For the purpose of recovering the amount referred to in subsection (7)(c) ("the unpaid tax")—

      (a)   the worker is to be treated as having an employment with the client or relevant person who provided the document, the duties of which consist of the services, and

      (b)   the client or relevant person is under PAYE regulations to account for the unpaid tax as if it arose in respect of earnings from that employment.

(9)   In subsections (7) and (8) "relevant person" means a person, other than the client, the worker or a person connected with the employment intermediary, who—

      (a)   is resident, or has a place of business, in the United Kingdom, and

      (b)   is party to a contract with the employment intermediary or a person connected with the employment intermediary under or in consequence of which—

          (i)   the services are provided, or

          (ii)   the employment intermediary, or a person connected with the employment intermediary, makes payments in respect of the services.

(10)   In determining whether this section applies, no regard is to be had to any arrangements the main purpose, or one of the main purposes, of which is to secure that this section does not to any extent apply.

(11)   In this section—

        "arrangements" includes any scheme, transaction or series of transactions, agreement or understanding, whether or not enforceable, and any associated operations;

"employment intermediary" means a person, other than the worker or the client, who carries on a business (whether or not with a view to profit and whether or not in conjunction with any other business) of supplying labour;

"engagement" means any such provision of service as is mentioned in subsection (1)(a);

"excluded services" means services provided wholly in the client's home;

"managed service company" means a company which—

    (a) is a managed service company within the meaning given by section 61B, or

    (b) would be such a company disregarding subsection (1)(c) of that section."

(2) In section 688A of ITEPA 2003 (managed service companies: recovery from other persons), in subsection (5), in the definition of "managed service company", after "section 61B" insert "but for the purposes of section 339A has the meaning given by subsection (11) of that section".

(3) After section 688A of ITEPA 2003 insert—

"688B Travel expenses of workers providing services through intermediaries: recovery of unpaid tax

(1) PAYE regulations may make provision for, or in connection with, the recovery from a director or officer of a company, in such circumstances as may be specified in the regulations, of amounts within any of subsections (2) to (5).

(2) An amount within this subsection is an amount that the company is to account for in accordance with PAYE regulations by virtue of section 339A(7) to (9) (persons providing fraudulent documents).

(3) An amount within this subsection is an amount which the company is to deduct and pay in accordance with PAYE regulations by virtue of section 339A in circumstances where—

    (a) the company is an employment intermediary,

    (b) on the basis that section 339A does not apply by virtue of subsection (3) of that section, the company has not deducted and paid the amount, but

    (c) the company has not been provided by any other person with evidence from which it would be reasonable in all the circumstances to conclude that subsection (3) of that section applied (and the mere assertion by a person that the manner in which the worker provided the services was not subject to (or to the right of) supervision, direction or control by any person is not such evidence).

(4) An amount within this subsection is an amount that the company is to deduct and pay in accordance with PAYE regulations by virtue of section 339A in a case where subsection (4) of that section applies (services provided under arrangements made by intermediaries).

(5) An amount within this subsection is any interest or penalty in respect of an amount within any of subsections (2) to (4) for which the company is liable.

    (6)   In this section—

        "company" includes a limited liability partnership;

        "director" has the meaning given by section 67;

        "employment intermediary" has the same meaning as in section 339A;

        "officer", in relation to a company, means any manager, secretary or other similar officer of the company, or any person acting or purporting to act as such"

    (4)   In Part 4 of the Income Tax (Pay As You Earn) Regulations 2003 (S.I. 2003/2682) (payments, returns and information), after Chapter 3A insert—

"CHAPTER 3B

CERTAIN DEBTS OF COMPANIES UNDER SECTION 339A OF ITEPA (TRAVEL EXPENSES OF WORKERS PROVIDING SERVICES THROUGH EMPLOYMENT INTERMEDIARIES)

97ZG Interpretation of Chapter 3B: "relevant PAYE debt" and "relevant date"

    (1)   In this Chapter "relevant PAYE debt", in relation to a company means an amount within any of paragraphs (2) to (5).

    (2)   An amount within this paragraph is an amount that the company is to account for in accordance with these Regulations by virtue of section 339A(7) to (9) of ITEPA (persons providing fraudulent documents).

    (3)   An amount within this paragraph is an amount which a company is to deduct and pay in accordance with these Regulations by virtue of section 339A of ITEPA in circumstances where—

        (a)   the company is an employment intermediary,

        (b)   on the basis that section 339A of ITEPA does not apply by virtue of subsection (3) of that section the company has not deducted and paid the amount, but

        (c)   the company has not been provided by any other person with evidence from which it would be reasonable in all the circumstances to conclude that subsection (3) of that section applied (and the mere assertion by a person that the manner in which the worker provided the services was not subject to (or to the right of) supervision, direction or control by any person is not such evidence).

    (4)   An amount within this paragraph is an amount that the company is to deduct and pay in accordance with these Regulations by virtue of section 339A of ITEPA in a case where subsection (4) of that section applies (services provided under arrangements made by intermediaries).

    (5)   An amount within this paragraph is any interest or penalty in respect of an amount within any of paragraphs (2) to (4) for which the company is liable.

    (6)   In this Chapter "the relevant date" in relation to a relevant PAYE debt means the date on which the first payment is due on which PAYE is not accounted for.

97ZH Interpretation of Chapter 3B: general

In this Chapter—

"company" includes a limited liability partnership;

"director" has the meaning given by section 67 of ITEPA;

"personal liability notice" has the meaning given by regulation 97ZI(2);

"the specified amount" has the meaning given by regulation 97ZI(2)(a).

97ZI Liability of directors for relevant PAYE debts

(1) This regulation applies in relation to an amount of relevant PAYE debt of a company if the company does not deduct that amount by the time by which the company is required to do so.

(2) HMRC may serve a notice (a "personal liability notice") on any person who was, on the relevant date, a director of the company—

    (a) specifying the amount of relevant PAYE debt in relation to which this regulation applies ("the specified amount"), and

    (b) requiring the director to pay to HMRC—

        (i) the specified amount, and

        (ii) specified interest on that amount.

(3) The interest specified in the personal liability notice—

    (a) is to be at the rate applicable under section 178 of the Finance Act 1989 for the purposes of section 86 of TMA, and

    (b) is to run from the date the notice is served.

(4) A director who is served with a personal liability notice is liable to pay to HMRC the specified amount and the interest specified in the notice within 30 days beginning with the day the notice is served.

(5) If HMRC serve personal liability notices on more than one director of the company in respect of the same amount of relevant PAYE debt, the directors are jointly and severally liable to pay to HMRC the specified amount and the interest specified in the notices.

97ZJ Appeals in relation to personal liability notices

(1) A person who is served with a personal liability notice in relation to an amount of relevant PAYE debt of a company may appeal against the notice.

(2) A notice of appeal must—

    (a) be given to HMRC within 30 days beginning with the day the personal liability notice is served, and

    (b) specify the grounds of the appeal.

(3) The grounds of appeal are—

    (a) that all or part of the specified amount does not represent an amount of relevant PAYE debt, of the company, to which regulation 97ZI applies, or

    (b) that the person was not a director of the company on the relevant date.

(4) But a person may not appeal on the ground mentioned in paragraph (3)(a) if it has already been determined, on an appeal by the company, that—

    (a) the specified amount is a relevant PAYE debt of the company, and

    (b) the company did not deduct, account for, or (as the case may be) pay the debt by the time by which the company was required to do so.

(5) Subject to paragraph (6), on an appeal that is notified to the tribunal, the tribunal is to uphold or quash the personal liability notice.

(6) In a case in which the ground of appeal mentioned in paragraph (3)(a) is raised, the tribunal may also reduce or increase the specified amount so that it does represent an amount of relevant PAYE debt, of the company, to which regulation 97ZI applies.

97ZK Withdrawal of personal liability notices

(1) A personal liability notice is withdrawn if the tribunal quashes it.

(2) An officer of Revenue and Customs may withdraw a personal liability notice if the officer considers it appropriate to do so.

(3) If a personal liability notice is withdrawn, HMRC must give notice of that fact to the person upon whom the notice was served.

97ZL Recovery of sums due under personal liability notice: application of Part 6 of TMA

(1) For the purposes of this Chapter, Part 6 of TMA (collection and recovery) applies as if—

    (a) the personal liability notice were an assessment, and

    (b) the specified amount, and any interest on that amount under regulation 97ZI(2)(b)(ii), were income tax charged on the director upon whom the notice is served,

and that Part of that Act applies with the modification in paragraph (2) and any other necessary modifications.

(2) Summary proceedings for the recovery of the specified amount, and any interest on that amount under regulation 97ZI(2)(b)(ii), may be brought in England and Wales or Northern Ireland at any time before the end of the period of 12 months beginning with the day after the day on which the personal liability notice is served.

97ZM Repayment of surplus amounts

(1) This regulation applies if—

    (a) one or more personal liability notices are served in respect of an amount of relevant PAYE debt of a company, and

    (b) the amounts paid to HMRC (whether by directors upon whom notices are served or the company) exceed the aggregate of the specified amount and any interest on it under regulation 97ZI(2)(b)(ii).

(2) HMRC is to repay the difference on a just and equitable basis and without unreasonable delay.

(3)   HMRC is to pay interest on any sum repaid.

(4)   The interest—

    (a)   is to be at the rate applicable under section 178 of the Finance Act 1989 for the purposes of section 824 of ICTA, and

    (b)   is to run from the date the amounts paid to HMRC come to exceed the aggregate mentioned in subsection (1)(b)."

(5)   The amendment made by subsection (4) is to be treated as having been made by the Commissioners for Her Majesty's Revenue and Customs in exercise of the power conferred by section 688B of ITEPA 2003 (inserted by subsection (3)).

(6)   The amendment made by subsection (1) has effect in relation to the tax year 2016-17 and subsequent tax years.

(7)   The amendment made by subsection (4) has effect in relation to relevant PAYE debts that are to be deducted, accounted for or paid on or after 6 April 2016.

15   Taxable benefits: PAYE

In section 684 of ITEPA 2003 (PAYE regulations), in subsection (2), in item 1ZA(a), for "Chapters 3 and 5 to 10" substitute "Chapters 3 to 10".

Employment income: other provision

16   Employee share schemes

Schedule 3 contains miscellaneous minor amendments relating to employee share schemes.

17   Securities options

(1)   In section 418 of ITEPA 2003 (provisions related to Part 7 of ITEPA 2003), in subsection (1), omit "(but not securities options)".

(2)   In that section, after subsection (1) insert—

   "(1A)   But Chapters 1 and 10 of Part 3 do not have effect in relation to—

    (a)   the acquisition of employment-related securities options (within the meaning of Chapter 5 of Part 7), or

    (b)   chargeable events (within the meaning given by section 477) occurring in relation to such options."

(3)   In section 227 of that Act (scope of Part 4), in subsection (4), before paragraph (a) insert—

   "(za)   section 418(1A) (acquisition of, and chargeable events occurring in relation to, employment-related securities options);".

(4)   The amendments made by this section come into force on 6 April 2016.

18   Employment income provided through third parties

(1)   Part 7A of ITEPA 2003 (employment income provided through third parties) is amended in accordance with subsections (2) and (3).

(2)   In section 554Z2 (value of relevant step to count as employment income) after

subsection (1) insert—

"(1A) Where the value of a relevant step would (apart from this subsection) count as employment income of more than one person—

  (a) the value of the relevant step is to be apportioned between each of those persons on a just and reasonable basis, and

  (b) subsection (1) applies as if the reference to the value of the relevant step in relation to A were a reference to so much of the value of the relevant step that is apportioned to A."

(3) In section 554Z8 (cases where consideration given for relevant step) in subsection (5), omit "and" at the end of paragraph (b) and after paragraph (c) insert ", and

  (d) there is no connection (direct or indirect) between the payment and a tax avoidance arrangement."

(4) Paragraph 59 of Schedule 2 to FA 2011 (transitional provision relating to Part 7A of ITEPA 2003) is amended in accordance with subsections (5) to (7).

(5) In sub-paragraph (2) for the words from "the earnings" to the end substitute—

  "(a) where sub-paragraph (2A) or (2B) applies, the earnings mentioned in sub-paragraph (1)(f)(i) or any return on those earnings mentioned in sub-paragraph (1)(f)(ii), and

  (b) in any other case, the earnings mentioned in sub-paragraph (1)(f)(i)."

(6) After sub-paragraph (2) insert—

  "(2A) This sub-paragraph applies where—

    (a) the agreement mentioned in sub-paragraph (1)(d)(i) is made before 1 April 2017, and

    (b) A or B pays, or otherwise accounts for, any tax as mentioned in sub-paragraph (1)(e) in accordance with that agreement.

  (2B) This sub-paragraph applies where—

    (a) the decision mentioned in sub-paragraph (1)(d)(ii) is made before 1 April 2017, and

    (b) A or B pays, or otherwise accounts for, any tax as mentioned in sub-paragraph (1)(e) before 1 April 2017."

(7) At the end insert—

  "(5) For the purposes of sub-paragraph (1)(e), a person is not to be regarded as having paid, or otherwise accounted for, any tax by reason only of making—

    (a) a payment on account of income tax,

    (b) a payment that is treated as a payment on account under section 223(3) of FA 2014 (accelerated payments), or

    (c) a payment pending determination of an appeal made in accordance with section 55 of TMA 1970."

(8) In Schedule 2 to FA 2011, omit paragraph 64 (power to make provision dealing with interactions etc.).

(9) The amendment made by subsection (3) has effect in relation to payments made on or after 16 March 2016 by way of consideration for a relevant step (as defined in section 554A(2) of ITEPA 2003) taken on or after that date.

(10) The amendment made by subsection (7) has effect in relation to chargeable steps (as defined in paragraph 59(1)(a) of Schedule 2 to FA 2011) taken on or after 16 March 2016.

Pensions

19   Standard lifetime allowance from 2016-17

(1) Section 218 of FA 2004 (pension schemes etc: lifetime allowance) is amended in accordance with subsections (2) to (5).

(2) For subsections (2) and (3) (standard lifetime allowance is £1,250,000 but may be increased by Treasury order) substitute—

"(2)   The standard lifetime allowance for the tax years 2016-17 and 2017-18 is £1,000,000.

(2A)   The standard lifetime allowance for any later tax year ("the subsequent tax year") is the same as the standard lifetime allowance for the tax year immediately preceding the subsequent tax year, unless subsection (2C) provides for it to be higher.

(2B)   Subsection (2C) applies if—
  (a)   the consumer prices index for the month of September in any tax year ("the prior tax year") is higher than it was for the previous September, and
  (b)   the prior tax year is the tax year 2017-18 or a later tax year.

(2C)   The standard lifetime allowance for the tax year following the prior tax year is the standard lifetime allowance for the prior tax year—
  (a)   increased by the percentage increase in the index, and
  (b)   if the result is not a multiple of £100, rounded up to the nearest amount which is such a multiple.

(2D)   The Treasury must before the tax year 2018-19, and before each subsequent tax year, make regulations specifying the amount given by subsections (2A) to (2C) as the standard lifetime allowance for the tax year concerned."

(3) After subsection (5BB) insert—

"(5BC)   Where the operation of a lifetime allowance enhancement factor is provided for by any of sections 220, 222, 223 and 224 and the time mentioned in the definition of SLA in the section concerned fell within the period consisting of the tax year 2014-15 and the tax year 2015-16, subsection (4) has effect as if the amount to be multiplied by LAEF were £1,250,000 if that is greater than SLA.

(5BD)   Where more than one lifetime allowance enhancement factor operates, subsection (5BC) does not apply if any of subsections (5A), (5B) and (5BA) applies."

(4) After subsection (5D) insert—

"(5E)   Where benefit crystallisation event 7 occurs on or after 6 April 2016 by reason of the payment of a relevant lump sum death benefit in respect of the death of the individual during the period consisting of the tax year 2014-15 and the tax year 2015-16, the standard lifetime allowance at the time of the benefit crystallisation event is £1,250,000."

(5) After subsection (5E) insert—

"(5F) Where—
   (a) benefit crystallisation event 5C occurs by reason of the designation on or after 6 April 2015 of sums or assets held for the purposes of an arrangement relating to the individual, and
   (b) the individual died before 6 April 2012,
   the standard lifetime allowance at the time of the benefit crystallisation event is £1,800,000.

(5G) Where—
   (a) benefit crystallisation event 5C occurs by reason of the designation on or after 6 April 2015 of sums or assets held for the purposes of an arrangement relating to the individual, and
   (b) the individual died in the period consisting of the tax year 2012-13 and the tax year 2013-14,
   the standard lifetime allowance at the time of the benefit crystallisation event is £1,500,000.

(5H) Where—
   (a) benefit crystallisation event 5C occurs by reason of the designation on or after 6 April 2016 of sums or assets held for the purposes of an arrangement relating to the individual, and
   (b) the individual died in the period consisting of the tax year 2014-15 and the tax year 2015-16,
   the standard lifetime allowance at the time of the benefit crystallisation event is £1,250,000.

(5I) Where—
   (a) benefit crystallisation event 5D occurs by reason of a person becoming entitled on or after 6 April 2016 to an annuity in respect of the individual, and
   (b) the individual died in the period beginning with 3 December 2014 and ending with 5 April 2016,
   the standard lifetime allowance at the time of the benefit crystallisation event is £1,250,000."

(6) In section 280 of FA 2004 (abbreviations and general index for Part 4), in the entry for "standard lifetime allowance" for "and (3)" substitute "to (2C)".

(7) In section 282 of FA 2004 (orders and regulations under Part 4), after subsection (2) (negative procedure applies to instruments not approved in draft) insert—

"(3) Subsection (2) does not apply to an instrument containing only regulations under section 218(2D)."

(8) The amendments made by subsections (2) to (4) have effect for the tax year 2016-17 and subsequent tax years.

(9) The amendment made by subsection (5)—
   (a) so far as it consists of the insertion of new subsections (5F) and (5G)—
      (i) is to be treated as having come into force on 6 April 2015, and

          (ii)   has effect in relation to benefit crystallisation events occurring on or after that date, and

     (b)   so far as it consists of the insertion of new subsections (5H) and (5I) —

          (i)   is to be treated as having come into force on 6 April 2016, and

          (ii)   has effect in relation to benefit crystallisation events occurring on or after that date.

(10)   Schedule 4 contains transitional and connected provision (including provision for "fixed protection 2016" and "individual protection 2016").

20   Pensions bridging between retirement and state pension

(1)   In Part 1 of Schedule 28 to FA 2004 (registered pension schemes: the pension rules), paragraph 2 (meaning of "scheme pension") is amended in accordance with subsections (2) to (4).

(2)   In sub-paragraph (4) (which specifies circumstances in which amount of scheme pension may go down and gives power to specify additional circumstances) omit paragraph (c) (reduction by reference to state retirement pensions for persons reaching pensionable age before 6 April 2016).

(3)   Omit sub-paragraphs (4B), (5) and (5A) (interpretation of sub-paragraph (4)(c)).

(4)   In sub-paragraph (8) (regulations under certain sub-paragraphs may make back-dated provision) omit "or (5)".

(5)   In consequence of the amendments made by subsections (2) and (3) —

     (a)   in FA 2006, in Schedule 23 omit paragraph 20(2) and (3), and

     (b)   in FA 2013, omit section 51(2).

(6)   Regulations under paragraph 2(4)(h) of Schedule 28 to FA 2004 (power to prescribe permitted reductions of scheme pensions, and to do so with back-dated effect) may provide for the coming into force of the amendments made by subsections (2) to (5), and —

     (a)   those amendments have effect in accordance with regulations under paragraph 2(4)(h) of that Schedule, and

     (b)   paragraph 2(8) of that Schedule (back-dating) applies for the purposes of regulations bringing the amendments into force only so as to permit the amendments to be given effect in relation to times not earlier than 6 April 2016.

21   Dependants' scheme pensions

(1)   Part 2 of Schedule 28 to Part 4 of FA 2004 (pension death benefit rules) is amended as follows.

(2)   In paragraph 16A (dependants' scheme pension: when limits in paragraphs 16B and 16C apply), after sub-paragraph (1) insert —

       "(1A)   Sub-paragraph (1) is subject to paragraphs 16AA and 16AB."

(3)   After paragraph 16A insert —

       "16AA   Paragraphs 16B and 16C do not apply if —

          (a)   each benefit crystallisation event that has occurred in relation to the member by reference to arrangements relating to the member under the scheme is benefit crystallisation event 5B (having unused funds under a money purchase arrangement at age 75), or

    (b)   paragraph 12 of Schedule 36 (enhanced protection by reference to pre-6 April 2006 rights) applies in the case of the member immediately before the member's death.

16AB(1) Paragraph 16B does not apply if, at all times in the post-death year (as defined in that paragraph), the payable annual rate is less than the limit.

    (2) Paragraph 16C does not apply in relation to a period of 12 months within paragraph (a) or (b) of paragraph 16C(1) if, at all times in that period of 12 months, the payable annual rate is less than the limit.

    (3) "The payable annual rate", at any time, is arrived at as follows—

        (a)   identify each dependants' scheme pension payable in respect of the member under the scheme to which a dependant of the member is actually entitled at that time, and

        (b)   identify the annual rate at which each pension identified at paragraph (a) is payable at that time, and

        (c)   if only one pension is identified at paragraph (a), the payable annual rate is the annual rate identified at paragraph (b), and

        (d)   if two or more pensions are identified at paragraph (a), the payable annual rate is the total of the annual rates identified at paragraph (b).

    (4) "The limit", at any time, is—

        (a)   the general limit at that time (see paragraph 16AC), or,

        (b)   if higher, the personal limit at that time (see paragraph 16AD).

16AC(1) This paragraph applies for the purposes of paragraph 16AB(4).

    (2) "The general limit" at a time in the tax year 2016-17 is £25,000.

    (3) "The general limit" at a time in a later tax year ("year T")—

        (a)   is given by—

$$G + (G \times U\%)$$

where G is the general limit at times in the tax year ("year P") that precedes year T, or

        (b)   if the amount given by paragraph (a) is not a multiple of £100, is that amount rounded up to the nearest amount that is such a multiple.

    (4) See paragraph 16AE for the meaning of U%.

16AD(1) This paragraph applies for the purposes of paragraph 16AB(4).

    (2) "The personal limit" at a time in the tax year in which the member dies is arrived at as follows—

        (a)   identify each scheme pension under the scheme to which the member is actually or prospectively entitled immediately before the member's death, and

        (b)   as regards each pension identified at paragraph (a)—

(i)   if it is one to which the member is actually entitled immediately before the member's death, identify the annual rate at which it is payable immediately before the member's death, or

(ii)   if it is one to which the member is prospectively entitled immediately before the member's death, identify the annual rate at which it would have been payable immediately before the member's death had the member been actually entitled to it immediately before the member's death, and

(c)   if only one pension is identified at paragraph (a), the personal limit is the annual rate identified at paragraph (b), and

(d)   if two or more pensions are identified at paragraph (a), the personal limit is the total of the annual rates identified at paragraph (b).

(3) "The personal limit" at a time in a tax year ("year S") later than the tax year in which the member dies —

(a)   is given by —

$$L + (L \times U\%)$$

where L is the personal limit at times in the tax year ("year P") that precedes year S, or

(b)   if the amount given by paragraph (a) is not a multiple of £100, is that amount rounded up to the nearest amount that is such a multiple.

(4) See paragraph 16AE for the meaning of U%.

(5) If the scheme is a public service pension scheme, ignore any abatement when identifying at sub-paragraph (2)(b) the annual rate of any scheme pension under the scheme.

16AE(1) In paragraphs 16AC(3) and 16AD(3), U% means the highest of —

(a)   5%,

(b)   CPI% (see sub-paragraph (2)), and

(c)   RPI% (see sub-paragraph (3)).

(2) If the consumer prices index for September in year P is higher than the consumer prices index for September in the tax year preceding year P, CPI% is the percentage increase in the index (but is otherwise 0%).

(3) If the retail prices index for September in year P is higher than the retail prices index for September in the tax year preceding year P, RPI% is the percentage increase in the index (but is otherwise 0%).

(4) In this paragraph "year P" has the same meaning as in paragraph 16AC or (as the case may be) paragraph 16AD."

(4)   In paragraph 16B (limit in post-death year) —

(a)   in sub-paragraph (3)(c), for "amounts" substitute "uprated amounts (see sub-paragraph (6))", and

(b)   after sub-paragraph (5) insert —

"(6) The "uprated amount" of a lump sum is the amount of the lump sum increased by the higher of C% and R%, where —

        (a)   if the consumer prices index for the month in which the member dies is higher than it was for the month in which the member became entitled to the lump sum, C% is the percentage increase in the index (but is otherwise 0%), and

        (b)   if the retail prices index for the month in which the member dies is higher than it was for the month in which the member became entitled to the lump sum, R% is the percentage increase in the index (but is otherwise 0%)."

(5) In paragraph 16C (limit in subsequent years) —

    (a)   in sub-paragraph (3)(a), omit "period of",

    (b)   in sub-paragraph (3)(b), for "subsection" substitute "sub-paragraph",

    (c)   for sub-paragraphs (4) and (5) substitute —

        "(4) The condition is that if the annual rate of a pension payable under the pension scheme to a dependant of the member is increased at any time in the period of 12 months in question —

           (a)   the dependant is at that time one of a group of at least 20 pensioner members of the pension scheme, and

           (b)   all the pensions being paid under the pension scheme to pensioner members of that group are at that time increased at the same rate.",

    (d)   in sub-paragraph (6) —

        (i)   for "month period" substitute "months", and

        (ii)   for the words after "increased by" substitute "the permitted margin.",

    (e)   in sub-paragraph (8)(a), for "end of the post-death year" substitute "member's death",

    (f)   in sub-paragraph (8)(b), after "first month" insert "ending after the start",

    (g)   in sub-paragraph (11), for "opening month" substitute "month in which the member died", and

    (h)   omit sub-paragraphs (13) and (14).

(6) The amendments made by this section are treated as having come into force on 6 April 2016.

(7) The amendments made by subsections (2) to (4), so far as they relate to paragraph 16B of Schedule 28 to FA 2004, have effect where the last day of "the post-death year" (see sub-paragraph (1) of that paragraph) is 6 April 2016 or any later day.

(8) The following amendments —

    (a)   the amendments made by subsections (2) to (4), so far as they relate to paragraph 16C of Schedule 28 to FA 2004, and

    (b)   the amendments made by subsection (5),

have effect where the last day of "the 12 months in question" (see sub-paragraph (1) of that paragraph) is 6 April 2016 or any later day.

22   Pension flexibility

Schedule 5 makes amendments in connection with pension flexibility.

23   Netherlands Benefit Act for Victims of Persecution 1940-1945

(1)   After section 642 of ITEPA 2003 insert—

"642A Netherlands Benefit Act for Victims of Persecution 1940-1945

No liability to income tax arises on a pension, annuity, allowance or other payment provided in accordance with the provisions of the scheme established under the law of the Netherlands and known as *Wet uitkeringen vervolgingsslachtoffers 1940-1945*."

(2)   The amendment made by this section has effect for the tax year 2016-17 and subsequent tax years.

Trading and other income

24   Fixed-rate deductions for use of home for business purposes

(1)   In Part 2 of ITTOIA 2005 (trading income), Chapter 5A (trade profits: deductions allowable at a fixed rate) is amended as follows.

(2)   Section 94H (use of home for business purposes) is amended as follows.

(3)   In subsection (1), for the words from "in respect of" to the end substitute "in respect of—
    (a)   the use of the person's home for the purposes of the trade, or
    (b)   where the person is a firm, the use of a partner's home for those purposes."

(4)   In subsection (4), for the words from "work done" to the end substitute "qualifying work".

(5)   After subsection (4) insert—

"(4A)   "Qualifying work" means—
    (a)   work done by the person, or any employee of the person, in the person's home wholly and exclusively for the purposes of the trade, or
    (b)   where the person is a firm, work done by a partner, or any employee of the firm, in the partner's home wholly and exclusively for those purposes.

(4B)   Where more than one person does qualifying work in the same home at the same time, any hour spent wholly and exclusively on that work is to be taken into account only once for the purposes of subsection (4)."

(6)   In subsection (5), after "person" insert ", or, where the person is a firm, a partner of the firm,".

(7)   After subsection (5) insert—

"(5A)   Where a firm makes a deduction for a period under this section in respect of the use of a partner's home for the purposes of a trade, the only deduction which the firm may make for the period in respect of the use of any other partner's home for those purposes is a deduction under this section."

(8)   Section 94I (premises used both as a home and as business premises) is amended as follows.

(9)   In subsection (1)(b), for "used by the person as a home," substitute "used as a home by —

      (i)   the person carrying on the trade, or

      (ii) where that person is a firm, a partner of the firm,".

(10) After subsection (6) insert—

    "(6A)   Where a person makes a deduction for a period under this section in respect of expenses incurred in relation to premises falling within subsection (1)(b), the only deduction which the person may make for the period in respect of expenses incurred in relation to any other premises falling within subsection (1)(b) is a deduction under this section."

(11) The amendments made by this section have effect for the tax year 2016-17 and subsequent tax years.

25   Averaging profits of farmers etc

(1)   Chapter 16 of Part 2 of ITTOIA 2005 (averaging profits of farmers and creative artists) is amended as specified in subsections (2) to (7).

(2)   In section 221 (claim for averaging of fluctuating profits) —

    (a)   in subsection (2), at the beginning insert "For the purposes of section 222 (two-year averaging)";

    (b)   after that subsection insert—

       "(2A)   For the purposes of section 222A (five-year averaging), a trade, profession or vocation is a "qualifying trade, profession or vocation" if it falls within subsection (2)(a) or (b).";

    (c)   in subsection (3), for "this purpose" substitute "the purpose of subsection (2)".

(3)   After section 222 insert—

"222A   Circumstances in which claim for five-year averaging may be made

(1)   An averaging claim may be made under this section in relation to five consecutive tax years in which a taxpayer is or has been carrying on the qualifying trade, profession or vocation if the volatility condition in subsection (2) is met.

(2)   The volatility condition is that—

    (a)   one of the following is less than 75% of the other —

      (i)   the average of the relevant profits of the first four tax years to which the claim relates;

      (ii) the relevant profits of the last of the tax years to which the claim relates; or

    (b)   the relevant profits of one or more (but not all) of the five tax years to which the claim relates are nil.

(3)   Any of the first four tax years to which an averaging claim under this section relates may be a tax year in relation to which an averaging claim under this section or section 222 has already been made.

(4)   An averaging claim ("the subsequent claim") may not be made under this section if an averaging claim in respect of the trade, profession or vocation has already been made under this section or section 222 in relation to a tax year which is later than the last of the tax years to which the subsequent claim relates.

(5)   An averaging claim may not be made under this section in relation to the tax year in which the taxpayer starts, or permanently ceases, to carry on the trade, profession or vocation.

(6)   An averaging claim under this section must be made on or before the first anniversary of the normal self-assessment filing date for the last of the tax years to which the claim relates.

(7)   But see section 225(4) (extended time limit if profits adjusted for some other reason)."

(4)   In section 222 (circumstances in which claim may be made)—

    (a)   in the heading, after "claim" insert "for two-year averaging";

    (b)   in subsection (1), after "made" insert "under this section";

    (c)   for subsection (2) substitute—

        "(2)   The earlier of the two years to which an averaging claim under this section relates may be a tax year in relation to which an averaging claim under this section or section 222A has already been made.";

    (d)   in subsection (3)—

        (i)   after "made", in the first place, insert "under this section";

        (ii)   after "made", in the second place, insert "under this section or section 222A";

    (e)   in subsection (4), after "made" insert "under this section";

    (f)   in subsection (5), after "averaging claim" insert "under this section".

(5)   In section 223 (adjustment of profits)—

    (a)   in subsection (2), for "second of the two tax years" substitute "last of the two or five tax years";

    (b)   for subsection (3) substitute—

        "(3)   The amount of the adjusted profits of each of the tax years to which the claim relates is the average of the relevant profits of those tax years.";

    (c)   omit subsection (4).

(6)   In section 224 (effect of adjustment)—

    (a)   in subsection (4), for "either" substitute "any";

    (b)   in subsection (6), for "second of the two tax years" substitute "last of the two or five tax years".

(7)   In section 225 (effect of later adjustment of profits), in subsection (1), for "either or both" substitute "any one or more".

(8)   In section 31C of ITTOIA 2005 (excluded provisions), in subsection (6), for "section 221" substitute "Chapter 16".

(9) In section 1025 of ITA 2007 (meaning of "modified net income"), in subsection (2)(d), for "the earlier of the tax years" substitute "any earlier tax year".

(10) In paragraph 3 of Schedule 1B to TMA 1970 (relief for fluctuating profits of farmers etc) —

    (a) in sub-paragraph (1), for the words from "for two" to the end substitute —

> "(a) in the case of a two-year claim, for two consecutive years of assessment, and
>
> (b) in the case of a five-year claim, for five consecutive years of assessment.";

    (b) in sub-paragraph (2), for "the later year" substitute "the last of the two or five years";

    (c) in sub-paragraph (3), for "the earlier year", where it occurs first, substitute "an earlier year";

    (d) in sub-paragraph (5) —

      (i) for "the earlier year" substitute "an earlier year";

      (ii) for "the later year" substitute "the last of the two or five years";

    (e) after sub-paragraph (6) insert —

> "(7) In this paragraph —
>
> "two-year claim" means a claim under section 222 of ITTOIA 2005;
>
> "five-year claim" means a claim under section 222A of ITTOIA 2005."

(11) In paragraph 4 of Schedule 1B to TMA 1970 (relief claimed by virtue of section 224(4) of ITTOIA 2005) —

    (a) in sub-paragraph (1) —

      (i) after "for two" insert "or five";

      (ii) omit "("the earlier year" and "the later year")";

      (iii) for "either" substitute "any";

    (b) in sub-paragraph (2), for "the later year" substitute "the last of the two or five years";

    (c) in sub-paragraph (3), for "the earlier year", where it occurs first, substitute "an earlier year";

    (d) in sub-paragraph (5) —

      (i) for "the earlier year" substitute "an earlier year";

      (ii) for "the later year" substitute "the last of the two or five years".

(12) The amendments made by this section have effect for the tax year 2016-17 and subsequent tax years.

26 Relief for finance costs related to residential property businesses

(1) In ITTOIA 2005, for sections 274A and 274B and the preceding italic heading (tax reductions for non-deductible costs of dwelling-related loans: individuals, and accumulated or discretionary trust income) substitute —

"Tax reductions for non-deductible costs of a dwelling-related loan

274A Reduction for individuals: entitlement

(1) If for a tax year an individual has —

        (a)   a relievable amount in respect of a property business, or

        (b)   two or more relievable amounts each in respect of a different property business,

the individual is entitled to relief under this section for that year in respect of that relievable amount or (as the case may be) each of those relievable amounts.

(2)   An individual has a relievable amount for a tax year in respect of a property business if for that year the individual has any one or more of the following in respect of that business —

        (a)   a current-year amount;

        (b)   a current-year estate amount;

        (c)   a brought-forward amount.

(3)   An individual's relievable amount for a tax year in respect of a property business is the total of —

        (a)   the individual's current-year amount (if any) for that year in respect of that business,

        (b)   the individual's current-year estate amounts (if any) for that year in respect of that business, and

        (c)   the individual's brought-forward amount (if any) for that year in respect of that business.

(4)   An individual has a current-year amount for a tax year in respect of a property business if —

        (a)   an amount ("A") would be deductible in calculating the profits for income tax purposes of that business for that year but for section 272A,

        (b)   the individual is liable for income tax on $N\%$ of those profits, where N is a number —

                (i)   greater than 0, and

                (ii)   less than or equal to 100, and

        (c)   that liability is not under Chapter 6 of Part 5 (estate income),

in which event the individual's current-year amount for that tax year in respect of that business is equal to $N\%$ of A.

(5)   An individual has a current-year estate amount for a tax year ("the current year"), in respect of a property business and a particular deceased person's estate, if —

        (a)   an amount ("A") would, but for section 272A, be deductible in calculating the profits for income tax purposes of that business for a particular tax year ("the profits year"), whether that year is the current year or an earlier tax year,

        (b)   the personal representatives of the deceased person are liable for income tax on $N\%$ of those profits, where N is a number —

                (i)   greater than 0, and

                (ii)   less than or equal to 100,

        (c)   the individual is liable for income tax on estate income treated under Chapter 6 of Part 5 as arising in the current year from an interest in the estate, and

        (d)   the basic amount of that estate income consists of, or includes, an amount representative of $E\%$ of the personal representatives'

N% of the profits of the business for the profits year, where E is a number—

  (i)   greater than 0, and

  (ii) less than or equal to 100,

in which event the individual's current-year estate amount for the current tax year, in respect of that business and estate and the profits year, is equal to E% of N% of A.

(6)   As to whether an individual has a brought-forward amount for a tax year in respect of a property business, see section 274AA(4).

(7)   In this section and section 274AA—

  "estate income", and

  "basic amount" in relation to any estate income,

have the same meaning as in Chapter 6 of Part 5 (see sections 649 and 656(4)).

274AA Reduction for individuals: calculation

(1)   This section applies if for a tax year an individual is entitled to relief under section 274A in respect of a relievable amount or in respect of each of two or more relievable amounts, and in the following subsections of this section "relievable amount" means that relievable amount or (as the case may be) any of those relievable amounts.

(2)   In respect of a relievable amount, the actual amount on which relief for the year is to be given is (subject to subsection (3)) the amount ("L") that is the lower of—

  (a)   the relievable amount, and

  (b)   the total of—

     (i)   the profits for income tax purposes of the property business concerned for the year after any deduction under section 118 of ITA 2007 ("the adjusted profits") or, if less, the share (if any) of the adjusted profits on which the individual is liable to income tax otherwise than under Chapter 6 of Part 5, and

     (ii) so much (if any) of the relievable amount as consists of current-year estate amounts.

(3)   If S is greater than the individual's adjusted total income for the year ("ATI"), the actual amount on which relief for the year is to be given in respect of a relievable amount is given by—

$$\frac{\text{ATI}}{\text{S}} \times \text{L}$$

where—

  S is the total obtained by identifying the amount that is L for each relievable amount and then finding the total of the amounts identified, and

  L has the same meaning as in subsection (2).

(4)   Where—

  (a)   a relievable amount,

  is greater than—

(b) the actual amount on which relief for the year is to be given in respect of the relievable amount,

the difference is the individual's brought-forward amount for the following tax year in respect of the property business concerned.

(5) The amount of the relief for the year in respect of a relievable amount is given by—

$$AA \times BR$$

where—

AA is the actual amount on which relief for the year is to be given in respect of the relievable amount, and

BR is the basic rate of income tax for the year,

(6) For the purposes of this section, an individual's adjusted total income for a tax year is identified as follows—

Step 1

Identify the individual's net income for the year (see Step 2 of the calculation in section 23 of ITA 2007).

Step 2

Exclude from that net income—

(a) so much of it as is within section 18(3) or (4) of ITA 2007 (income from savings), and

(b) so much of it as is dividend income.

Step 3

Reduce what is left after Step 2 of this calculation by the amount of any allowances deducted for the year in the individual's case at Step 3 of the calculation in section 23 of ITA 2007. The result is the individual's adjusted total income for the year.

274B Reduction for accumulated or discretionary trust income: entitlement

(1) If for a tax year the trustees of a settlement have—

(a) a relievable amount in respect of a property business, or

(b) two or more relievable amounts each in respect of a different property business,

the trustees of the settlement are entitled to relief under this section for that year in respect of that relievable amount or (as the case may be) each of those relievable amounts.

(2) The trustees of a settlement have a relievable amount for a tax year in respect of a property business if for that year the trustees of the settlement have a current-year amount, or brought-forward amount, in respect of that business (or have both).

(3) In the case of trustees of a settlement, their relievable amount for a tax year in respect of a property business is the total of—

(a) their current-year amount (if any) for that year in respect of that business, and

(b) their brought-forward amount (if any) for that year in respect of that business.

(4) The trustees of a settlement have a current-year amount for a tax year in respect of a property business if—

      (a)   an amount ("A") would be deductible in calculating the profits for income tax purposes of that business for that year but for section 272A,

      (b)   the trustees of the settlement are liable for income tax on N% of those profits, where N is a number −

           (i)   greater than 0, and

           (ii)   less than or equal to 100, and

      (c)   in relation to the trustees of the settlement, that N% of those profits is accumulated or discretionary income,

in which event the current-year amount of the trustees of the settlement for that tax year in respect of that business is equal to N% of A.

(5)   As to whether the trustees of a settlement have a brought-forward amount for a tax year in respect of a property business, see section 274C(3).

(6)   In this section and section 274C "accumulated or discretionary income" has the meaning given by section 480 of ITA 2007.

274C Reduction for accumulated or discretionary trust income: calculation

(1)   This section applies if for a tax year the trustees of a settlement are entitled to relief under section 274B in respect of a relievable amount or in respect of each of two or more relievable amounts, and in the following subsections of this section "relievable amount" means that relievable amount or (as the case may be) any of those relievable amounts.

(2)   The amount of the relief in respect of a relievable amount is given by −

$$L \times BR$$

where −

      BR is the basic rate of income tax for the year, and

      L is the lower of −

           (a)   the relievable amount, and

           (b)   the profits for income tax purposes of the property business concerned for the year after any deduction under section 118 of ITA 2007 ("the adjusted profits") or, if less, the share of the adjusted profits −

                (i)   on which the trustees of the settlement are liable for income tax, and

                (ii)   which, in relation to the trustees of the settlement, is accumulated or discretionary income.

(3)   Where L in the case of a relievable amount is less than the relievable amount, the difference between them is the brought-forward amount of the trustees of the settlement for the following tax year in respect of the property business concerned."

(2)   In consequence of the amendment made by subsection (1), in F(No.2)A 2015 omit section 24(5).

27   Individual investment plans of deceased investors

(1)   In Chapter 3 of Part 6 of ITTOIA 2005 (power to exempt income from

individual investment plans from income tax), after section 694 insert—

"694A Deceased investors

(1) In section 694(1) "income of an individual from investments under a plan" includes—

    (a) income (of any person) from administration-period investments under a plan, and

    (b) income (of any person) from the estate of a deceased person ("D") where the whole or any part of the income of D's personal representatives is income from administration-period investments under a plan.

(2) For the purposes of sections 694(3)(a) and (4) and 695(1) "individual", in relation to investments that are administration-period investments, includes—

    (a) the personal representatives of the deceased individual concerned, and

    (b) any other person on whose directions plan managers agree to act in relation to the investments.

(3) In sections 699 and 701 "investor" includes a person entitled to an exemption given by investment plan regulations by virtue of subsection (1) of this section.

(4) Investments are "administration-period investments" if—

    (a) an individual dies, and

    (b) immediately before the individual's death—

        (i) the investments were held under a plan,

        (ii) the individual was entitled to the income from the investments, and

        (iii) as a result of investment plan regulations, the individual's income from investments under the plan was exempt from income tax (either wholly or to an extent specified in the regulations).

(5) Investments are also "administration-period investments" if (directly or indirectly) they represent investments that are administration-period investments as a result of subsection (4).

(6) Investment plan regulations may provide that investments are administration-period investments as a result of subsection (4) or (5) only at times specified in, or ascertained in accordance with, the regulations.

(7) Provision under subsection (6) may (in particular) be framed by reference to the completion of the administration of a deceased individual's estate.

(8) In the application of subsection (7) in relation to Scotland, the reference to the completion of the administration is to be read in accordance with section 653(2)."

(2) In section 151(2) of TCGA 1992 (Chapter 3 of Part 6 of ITTOIA 2005 applies with modifications in relation to regulations giving relief from capital gains tax in respect of investments under plans)—

   (a)   in the words before paragraph (a), for "section 694(1) to (2)" substitute "sections 694(1) to (2) and 694A(1)", and

   (b)   after paragraph (a) insert—

      "(aa)   section 694A(2) applies also for the purposes of subsection (1) of this section,

      (ab)   the reference in section 694A(3) to section 694A(1) is to be read as a reference to paragraph (aa) of this subsection,

      (ac)   the reference in section 694A(4)(b)(iii) to the individual's income from investments under the plan being exempt from income tax is to be read as a reference to the individual being entitled to relief from capital gains tax in respect of the investments,".

(3)   In section 62 of TCGA 1992 (death: general provisions), after subsection (4) (acquisition of asset as legatee) insert—

   "(4A)   The Treasury may by regulations make provision having effect in place of subsection (4)(b) above in a case where there has been a time when the personal representatives—

      (a)   held the asset acquired by the legatee, and

      (b)   would, if they had disposed of the asset at that time—

         (i)   by way of a bargain at arm's length, and

         (ii)   otherwise than to a legatee,

      have been entitled as a result of regulations under section 151 (investments under plans) to relief from capital gains tax in respect of any chargeable gain accruing on the disposal.

   (4B)   Provision made by regulations under subsection (4A) above may (in particular) treat a person who acquires an asset as legatee as doing so at a time or for a consideration, or at a time and for a consideration, ascertained as specified by the regulations."

(4)   In consequence of subsection (2)(a), in FA 2011 omit section 40(6)(a).

Reliefs: enterprise investment scheme, venture capital trusts etc

28   EIS, SEIS and VCTs: exclusion of energy generation

(1)   In section 192(1) of ITA 2007 (meaning of "excluded activities": EIS and SEIS), for paragraphs (ka) to (kc) substitute—

   "(ka)   generating or exporting electricity or making electricity generating capacity available,

   (kb)   generating heat,

   (kc)   generating any form of energy not within paragraph (ka) or (kb),

   (kd)   producing gas or fuel, and".

(2)   In section 303(1) of ITA 2007 (meaning of "excluded activities": VCTs), for paragraphs (ka) to (kc) substitute—

   "(ka)   generating or exporting electricity or making electricity generating capacity available,

   (kb)   generating heat,

       (kc)   generating any form of energy not within paragraph (ka) or (kb),

       (kd)   producing gas or fuel, and".

(3)   In consequence of subsection (1), ITA 2007 is amended as follows—

     (a)   in section 192(2)—

        (i)   for paragraph (g) substitute "and

              (g)   section 198A (export of electricity).";

        (ii) omit paragraph (h);

     (b)   in section 198A—

        (i)   in the heading, omit "subsidised generation or";

        (ii) omit subsections (3) to (9);

     (c)   omit section 198B.

(4)   In consequence of subsection (2), ITA 2007 is amended as follows—

     (a)   in section 303(2)—

        (i)   for paragraph (g) substitute "and

              (g)   section 309A (export of electricity).";

        (ii) omit paragraph (h);

     (b)   in section 309A—

        (i)   in the heading, omit "subsidised generation or";

        (ii) omit subsections (3) to (9);

     (c)   omit section 309B.

(5)   The amendments made by subsections (1) and (3) have effect in relation to shares issued on or after 6 April 2016.

(6)   The amendments made by subsections (2) and (4) have effect in relation to relevant holdings issued on or after 6 April 2016.

29   EIS and VCTs: definition of certain periods

(1)   In section 175A of ITA 2007 (EIS: the permitted maximum age requirement)—

     (a)   in subsection (7) for the words from "five" to the end substitute "relevant five year period.";

     (b)   after that subsection insert—

       "(7A) Subject to subsection (7B), the relevant five year period is the five year period which ends immediately before the beginning of the last accounts filing period.

       (7B) If the last accounts filing period ends more than 12 months before the issue date, the relevant five year period is the five year period which ends 12 months before the issue date."

(2)   In section 252A of ITA 2007 (EIS: meaning of "knowledge-intensive company")—

     (a)   in subsection (4), in the definition of "the relevant three preceding years", for the words from "means" to the end substitute "means, subject to subsection (4A), the three consecutive years the last of which ends immediately before the beginning of the last accounts filing period.";

      (b)   after that subsection insert—

          "(4A)   If the last accounts filing period ends more than 12 months before the date on which the relevant shares are issued, the relevant three preceding years are the three consecutive years the last of which ends 12 months before the date on which the relevant shares are issued."

  (3)   In section 280C of ITA 2007 (VCTs: the permitted maximum age condition)—

      (a)   in subsection (8) for the words from "five" to the end substitute "relevant five year period.";

      (b)   after that subsection insert—

          "(8A)   Subject to subsection (8B), the relevant five year period is the five year period which ends immediately before the beginning of the last accounts filing period.

          (8B)   If the last accounts filing period ends more than 12 months before the investment date, the relevant five year period is the five year period which ends 12 months before the investment date."

  (4)   In section 294A of ITA 2007 (VCTs: the permitted company age requirement)—

      (a)   in subsection (7) for the words from "five" to the end substitute "relevant five year period.";

      (b)   after that subsection insert—

          "(7A)   Subject to subsection (7B), the relevant five year period is the five year period which ends immediately before the beginning of the last accounts filing period.

          (7B)   If the last accounts filing period ends more than 12 months before the investment date, the relevant five year period is the five year period which ends 12 months before the investment date."

  (5)   In section 331A of ITA 2007 (VCTs: meaning of "knowledge-intensive company")—

      (a)   in subsection (5), in the definition of "the relevant three preceding years", for the words from "means" to the end substitute "means, subject to subsection (5A), the three consecutive years the last of which ends immediately before the beginning of the last accounts filing period.";

      (b)   after that subsection insert—

          "(5A)   If the last accounts filing period ends more than 12 months before the applicable time, the relevant three preceding years are the three consecutive years the last of which ends 12 months before the applicable time."

  (6)   The amendments made by this section are to be treated as always having had effect; but this is subject to section 30.

30   EIS and VCTs: election

  (1)   If a company ("the relevant company") makes an election for this section to apply, then—

(a) the amendments made by subsection (1) of section 29 do not apply in relation to shares issued by the relevant company in the material period,

(b) the amendments made by subsection (2) of that section do not apply for the purposes of determining whether, at the date of issue of any shares issued by the company in the material period, the company is a knowledge-intensive company for the purposes of Part 5 of ITA 2007,

(c) the amendments made by subsection (3) of that section do not apply in relation to investments made in the relevant company in the material period,

(d) the amendments made by subsection (4) of that section do not apply for the purposes of determining whether the requirement of section 294A of ITA 2007 is met in relation to any holding of shares or securities issued by the relevant company in the material period, and

(e) the amendments made by subsection (5) of that section do not apply for the purposes of determining whether, at any time in the material period which is the applicable time within the meaning given by section 331A of ITA 2007, the relevant company is a knowledge-intensive company for the purposes of Part 6 of ITA 2007.

(2) Amendments that by reason of an election under this section do not apply in relation to particular shares or investments or for particular purposes are also to be treated as never having applied in relation to those shares or investments or for those purposes.

(3) Any election under this section must be made in writing and signed by a director of the relevant company.

(4) Where a company has made an election under this section —

(a) it must include a statement that the election has been made in any compliance statement subsequently provided by it under section 204(2) of ITA 2007 in respect of an issue of shares made by it in the material period, and

(b) it must provide a copy of the election to each company to which it has issued shares or securities in the material period.

(5) An election under this section is irrevocable.

(6) In this section "the material period" means the period beginning with 18 November 2015 (the date when F(No. 2)A 2015 was passed) and ending with 5 April 2016.

31 VCTs: requirements for giving approval

(1) Section 274 of ITA 2007 (requirements for the giving of approval) is amended as follows.

(2) In the table in subsection (2), after the entry beginning "The 70% eligible shares

condition" insert—

"The non-qualifying investments condition	The company has not made and will not make, in the relevant period, an investment which is neither of the following— (a) an investment that on the date it is made is included in the company's qualifying holdings; (b) an investment falling within subsection (3A)."

(3)   In subsection (3), in each of paragraphs (f), (g) and (h), for "(3A)" substitute "(3ZA)".

(4)   After subsection (3) insert—

"(3ZA)   In the second column of the table in subsection (2), in the entries for the investment limits condition, the permitted maximum age condition and the no business acquisition condition, any reference to an investment made by the company in a company does not include an investment falling within subsection (3A)."

(5)   In subsection (3A)—

(a)   for the words from "In the second" to "does not include" substitute "An investment made by a company ("the investor") falls within this subsection if it is";

(b)   in paragraph (c) for "the company" substitute "the investor";

(c)   after paragraph (c) insert—

"(d)   money in the investor's possession;

(e)   a sum owed to the investor which—

(i)   under section 285(4)(b) (read with section 285(5) and (6)) is to be regarded as an investment of the investor, and

(ii)   is such that the investor's right mentioned in section 285(5)(a) may be exercised on 7 days' notice given by the investor."

(6)   After subsection (3A) insert—

"(3B)   In subsection (3A), any reference to a thing which may be done on 7 days' notice includes a case where that thing may be done—

(a)   on less than 7 days' notice, or

(b)   without notice."

(7)   In subsection (5)—

(a)   after paragraph (b) insert—

"(ba)   amend or repeal subsection (3B) in consequence of any provision made under paragraph (b),";

(b)   in paragraph (c) for the words from "made by" to "(3A)" substitute "falling within subsection (3A) may be held by the company".

(8) The amendments made by this section have effect in relation to investments made on or after 6 April 2016.

Reliefs: peer-to-peer lending

32   Income tax relief for irrecoverable peer-to-peer loans

(1) ITA 2007 is amended as follows.

(2) After section 412 insert—

"**CHAPTER 1A**

IRRECOVERABLE PEER-TO-PEER LOANS

The relief

412A Relief for irrecoverable peer-to-peer loans

(1) A person ("L") is entitled to relief under this section if—
    (a) L has made a peer-to-peer loan ("the relevant loan"),
    (b) the loan was made through an operator,
    (c) L has not assigned the right to recover the principal of the loan, and
    (d) any outstanding amount of the principal of the loan has, on or after 6 April 2015, become irrecoverable.

(2) But if the outstanding amount became irrecoverable before 6 April 2016 L is entitled to relief under this section only on the making of a claim.

(3) The relief is given by deducting the outstanding amount in calculating L's net income for the tax year in which the amount became irrecoverable (see Step 2 of the calculation in section 23).

(4) The deduction under this section is to be made only from income arising from the payment to L of interest on—
    (a) the relevant loan, and
    (b) any other loan within subsection (5) or (6).

(5) A loan is within this subsection if—
    (a) it is a peer-to-peer loan made by L, and
    (b) it was made through the operator through whom the relevant loan was made.

(6) A loan is within this subsection if—
    (a) the loan was made by someone other than L,
    (b) the right to receive interest on the loan has been assigned to L,
    (c) the right was assigned through the operator through whom the relevant loan was made, and
    (d) either—
        (i) L is a person within paragraph (a), (b) or (c) of section 412I(4), or
        (ii) the recipient of the loan is a person within one of those paragraphs and the loan is a personal or small loan.

(7) The amount deducted under this section is limited in accordance with section 25(4) and (5).

(8) In this section "irrecoverable" means irrecoverable other than by legal proceedings or by the exercise of any right granted by way of security for the loan.

412B Claims for additional relief: sideways relief

(1) A person ("L") may make a claim for relief under this section if —
   (a) L is entitled to relief under section 412A in respect of any outstanding amount of the principal of a loan ("the relevant loan"), but
   (b) in the tax year in relation to which L is entitled to that relief ("the relevant year") —
      (i) L has no income of the kind mentioned in section 412A(4) from which to deduct the outstanding amount, or
      (ii) L has insufficient income of that kind to enable the outstanding amount to be deducted in full under that section.

(2) The claim is for the outstanding amount or (in a case within subsection (1)(b)(ii)) the part of the outstanding amount not capable of being deducted under section 412A to be deducted under this section in calculating L's net income for the relevant year.

(3) The deduction under this section is to be made only from income arising from the payment to L of interest on loans within subsection (4) or (5).

(4) A loan is within this subsection if —
   (a) it is a peer-to-peer loan made by L, and
   (b) it was made through an operator who is not the operator through whom the relevant loan was made.

(5) A loan is within this subsection if —
   (a) the loan was made by someone other than L,
   (b) the right to receive interest on the loan has been assigned to L,
   (c) that right was assigned through an operator who is not the operator through whom the relevant loan was made, and
   (d) either —
      (i) L is a person within paragraph (a), (b) or (c) of section 412I(4), or
      (ii) the recipient of the loan is a person within one of those paragraphs and the loan is a personal or small loan.

(6) The amount deducted under this section is limited in accordance with section 25(4) and (5).

412C Claims for additional relief: carry-forward relief

(1) A person ("L") may make a claim for relief under this section if —
   (a) L is entitled to relief under section 412A in respect of any outstanding amount of the principal of a loan ("the relevant loan"), but

      (b)   in the tax year in relation to which L is entitled to that relief ("the relevant year") —

          (i)   L has no income of the kind mentioned in section 412A(4) or section 412B(3) from which to deduct the outstanding amount, or

          (ii) L has insufficient income of that kind to enable the outstanding amount to be deducted in full under those sections.

(2)   The claim is for the outstanding amount or (in a case within subsection (1)(b)(ii)) the part of the outstanding amount not capable of being deducted under sections 412A and 412B to be deducted under this section in calculating L's net income for the four tax years following the relevant year.

(3)   The deduction under this section is to be made only from income arising from the payment to L of interest on—

      (a)   the relevant loan, and

      (b)   any other loan within subsection (4) or (5).

(4)   A loan is within this subsection if—

      (a)   it is a peer-to-peer loan made by L, and

      (b)   it was made through an operator (whether or not that operator is the operator through whom the relevant loan was made).

(5)   A loan is within this subsection if—

      (a)   the loan was made by someone other than L,

      (b)   the right to receive interest on the loan has been assigned to L,

      (c)   that right was assigned through an operator (whether or not that operator is the operator through whom the relevant loan was made), and

      (d)   either—

          (i)   L is a person within paragraph (a), (b) or (c) of section 412I(4), or

          (ii) the recipient of the loan is a person within one of those paragraphs and the loan is a personal or small loan.

(6)   This section needs to be read with section 412D (how relief works).

412D How carry-forward relief works

(1)   This subsection explains how deductions are to be made under section 412C.

The amount to be deducted at any step is limited in accordance with section 25(4) and (5).

Step 1 Deduct the outstanding amount or (in a case within section 412C(1)(b)(ii)) the part of the outstanding amount not capable of being deducted under sections 412A and 412B from the lending income for the first tax year following the relevant year.

Step 2 Deduct from the lending income for the second tax year following the relevant year any part of the outstanding amount not previously deducted.

Step 3 Apply Step 2 in relation to the lending income for the third and fourth tax years following the relevant year, stopping if all of the outstanding amount is deducted.

(2) In this section—

"lending income" means income of a kind mentioned in section 412C(3);

"relevant year" has the meaning given by section 412C(1)(b).

Supplementary provisions

412E Subsequent recovery of peer-to-peer loans

(1) This section applies where—

  (a) any amount of the principal of a loan has been deducted under this Chapter in calculating a person's net income for a tax year, and

  (b) the person subsequently recovers that amount or any part of it.

(2) The amount recovered is to be treated for the purposes of this Act as if it were interest on the loan paid to the person at the time it was recovered.

(3) For the purposes of this section, a person is to be treated as recovering an amount if the person (or any other person at his or her direction) receives any money or money's worth—

  (a) in satisfaction of the person's right to recover that amount, or

  (b) in consideration of the person's assignment of the right to recover it;

and where a person assigns such a right otherwise than by way of a bargain made at arm's length the person shall be treated as receiving money or money's worth equal to the market value of the right at the time of the assignment.

412F Assigned loans treated as made by the assignee etc

(1) This section applies where—

  (a) a person ("A") is assigned the right to recover the principal of a loan,

  (b) the right is assigned through an operator ("O"),

  (c) A makes a payment in consideration of the assignment, and

  (d) A does not further assign the right.

(2) The loan is to be treated for the purposes of section 412A(1) as—

  (a) having been made by A, and

  (b) having been made through O.

(3) The amount (if any) of the principal of the loan which is treated as irrecoverable may not exceed the amount which is arrived at by—

  (a) taking the amount of the payment mentioned in subsection (1)(c), and

  (b) deducting any amount of the principal of the loan previously recovered by A.

412G Nominees etc

For the purposes of this Chapter—

  (a) a loan or a payment made by or to a nominee or bare trustee for a person is treated as made by or to that person, and

    (b)   a right assigned by or to a nominee or bare trustee for a person is treated as assigned by or to that person.

412H Interaction with other reliefs

(1)   Subsection (2) applies in relation to a loan if any person has obtained income tax relief (other than under this Chapter) which is properly attributable to the loan.

(2)   The amount (if any) of the principal of the loan which is treated as irrecoverable may not exceed the amount which is arrived at by —
    (a)   taking the amount of the principal of the loan, and
    (b)   deducting the amount of the relief mentioned in subsection (1).

Interpretation

412I Meaning of "loan", "peer-to-peer loan" and related terms

(1)   This section applies for the purposes of this Chapter.

(2)   "Loan" means a loan of money which—
    (a)   is made on genuine commercial terms, and
    (b)   is not part of a scheme or arrangement the main purpose or one of the main purposes of which is to obtain a tax advantage (within the meaning given by section 208 of the FA 2013).

(3)   A loan is a "peer-to-peer loan" only if it meets—
    (a)   Condition A or B, and
    (b)   Condition C.

(4)   Condition A is that the person who made the loan is—
    (a)   an individual,
    (b)   a partnership which consists of—
        (i)   two or three persons, and
        (ii)   at least one person who is not a body corporate, or
    (c)   an unincorporated body of persons which—
        (i)   is not a partnership, and
        (ii)   consists of at least one person who is not a body corporate.

(5)   Condition B is that—
    (a)   the recipient of the loan is a person within paragraph (a), (b) or (c) of subsection (4), and
    (b)   the loan is a personal or small loan.

(6)   Condition C is that, assuming interest were paid on the loan, the person who made the loan would (except for this Chapter) be liable for income tax charged on the interest.

(7)   "Personal loan" means a loan which is not used wholly or predominantly for the purposes of a business carried on, or intended to be carried on, by the recipient of the loan.

(8)   "Small loan" means a loan of £25,000 or less.

412J Meaning of "operator" and related terms

(1) This section applies for the purposes of this Chapter.

(2) "Operator" means a person who —

    (a) has permission under Part 4A of FISMA 2000 to carry on a regulated activity specified in Article 36H of the Financial Services and Markets Act 2000 (Regulated Activities) Order 2001 (S.I. 2001/544) (operating an electronic system in relation to lending), or

    (b) has been granted equivalent permission under the law of a territory outside the United Kingdom that is within the European Economic Area.

(3) A loan is "made through" an operator if the person who makes the loan and the recipient of the loan enter the agreement under which the loan is made at the invitation of the operator.

(4) A right is "assigned through" an operator if the person who assigns the right and the person to whom the right is assigned enter the agreement under which the assignment takes effect at the invitation of the operator.

(5) A person is not to be treated as having entered an agreement at the invitation of an operator if the operator made the invitation otherwise than in the course of carrying on the activity to which the permission mentioned in subsection (2)(a) or (b) relates."

(3) In section 24(1) (list of reliefs deductible at Step 2 of the calculation of income tax liability), in paragraph (b), at the appropriate place insert —

    "Chapter 1A of Part 8 (irrecoverable peer-to-peer loans),".

(4) In section 25(3) (list of provisions requiring reliefs to be deducted from particular components of income etc) at the appropriate place insert —

    "sections 412A(4), 412B(3) and 412C(3) (relief for irrecoverable peer-to-peer loans only against interest on certain loans),".

Transactions in securities

33 Transactions in securities: company distributions

(1) Chapter 1 of Part 13 of ITA 2007 (transactions in securities) is amended as follows.

(2) In section 684 (person liable to counteraction), in subsection (1) —

    (a) in the opening words, after "a person" insert "("the party")";

    (b) in paragraph (c), omit "the person in being a party to";

    (c) in paragraph (d), for "the person" substitute "the party or any other person".

(3) In that section, in subsection (2) —

    (a) in paragraph (c), omit the final "and";

    (b) after paragraph (d) insert —

        "(e) a repayment of share capital or share premium, and

        (f) a distribution in respect of securities in a winding up."

(4) In section 685 (receipt of consideration in connection with distribution by or assets of close company) —

    (a) in subsection (2) —

        (i) in the opening words, for "the person" substitute "a relevant person";

        (ii) in the words after paragraph (c), after "and" insert "the relevant person";

    (b) in subsection (3) —

        (i) in paragraph (a), for "the person" substitute "a relevant person";

        (ii) in paragraph (c), for "the person" substitute "the relevant person";

    (c) after subsection (3) insert —

        "(3A) In subsections (2) and (3) "relevant person" means —

            (a) the party, or

            (b) any person other than the party in relation to whom the condition in section 684(1)(d) is met."

    (d) omit subsection (6);

    (e) after subsection (7) insert —

        "(7A) The references in subsection (4)(a)(i) and (ii) to assets do not include assets shown to represent return of sums paid by subscribers on the issue of securities merely because the law of the country in which the company is incorporated allows assets of that description to be available for distribution by way of dividend.

        (7B) The references in subsections (4)(a)(i) and (5)(a) to assets which are available for distribution by way of dividend by the company include assets which are available for distribution to the company by way of dividend by any other company it controls."

(5) In section 686 (excluded circumstances: fundamental change of ownership) —

    (a) in subsection (1)(a), for the words from "the person" to "party")" substitute "the party";

    (b) for subsections (2) to (5) substitute —

        "(2) There is a fundamental change of ownership of the close company if, as a result of the transaction or transactions in securities, the condition in subsection (3) is met.

        (3) The condition in this subsection is that the original shareholder or original shareholders taken together with any associate or associates —

            (a) do not directly or indirectly hold more than 25% of the ordinary share capital of the close company,

            (b) do not directly or indirectly hold shares in the close company carrying an entitlement to more than 25% of the distributions which may be made by the close company, and

            (c) do not directly or indirectly hold shares in the close company carrying more than 25% of the total voting rights in the close company.

    (4)   In this section "original shareholder" means a person who, immediately before the transaction in securities (or the first of the transactions in securities), held any ordinary share capital of the close company.

    (5)   For the purposes of this section, shares of or share capital in the close company which are held by a person controlled by an original shareholder, or by two or more original shareholders taken together, count as shares or share capital held by that original shareholder or those original shareholders."

(6)   In section 687 (income tax advantage)—

    (a)   in subsection (1), in the opening words, for "the person" substitute "a person";

    (b)   in subsection (2)—

        (i)   after "to the person" insert "or an associate of the person";

        (ii)   for "the relevant consideration is received" substitute "Condition A or B in section 685 is met".

(7)   In section 713 (interpretation), at the appropriate place insert—

    ""associate" is to be construed in accordance with section 681DL, but as if subsection (4) of that section also included, as persons associated with each other, a person as trustee of a settlement and an individual, where one or more beneficiaries of the settlement are connected or associated with the individual;".

(8)   The amendments made by this section have effect in relation to—

    (a)   a transaction occurring on or after 6 April 2016, or

    (b)   a series of transactions any one or more of which occurs on or after that date.

(9)   Accordingly, Chapter 1 of Part 13 of ITA 2007 has effect without the amendments made by this section in relation to a tax advantage obtained on or after 6 April 2016 in consequence of—

    (a)   a transaction occurring before that date, or

    (b)   a series of transactions all of which occur before that date.

(10)   Where—

    (a)   before 6 April 2016 a person provides particulars to the Commissioners for Her Majesty's Revenue and Customs under section 701 of ITA 2007 in respect of a transaction or transactions,

    (b)   on the basis of Chapter 1 of Part 13 of ITA 2007 as it has effect apart from this section, notification is given under section 701 of that Act that no counteraction notice ought to be served about the transaction or transactions,

    (c)   the transaction, or any one or more of the transactions, occurs on or after 6 April 2016, and

    (d)   the person would, but for the notification, be liable for counteraction of an income tax advantage from the transaction or transactions under Chapter 1 of Part 13 of ITA 2007 as amended by this section,

the notification is void and section 702(2) of ITA 2007 does not apply in relation to the transaction or transactions.

34   Transactions in securities: procedure for counteraction of advantage

(1)   Chapter 1 of Part 13 of ITA 2007 (transactions in securities) is amended as follows.

(2)   For section 695 (preliminary notification) substitute—

> **"695   Notice of enquiry**
>
> (1)   An officer of Revenue and Customs may enquire into a transaction or transactions if—
>> (a)   the officer has reason to believe that section 684 (person liable to counteraction of income tax advantage) may apply to a person ("the taxpayer") in respect of the transaction or transactions, and
>> (b)   the officer notifies the taxpayer of his intention to do so.
>
> (2)   The notification may be given at any time not more than 6 years after the end of the tax year to which the income tax advantage in question relates."

(3)   Omit sections 696 and 697 (opposed notifications).

(4)   In section 698 (counteraction notices), for subsection (1) substitute—

> "(1)   If on an enquiry under section 695 an officer of Revenue and Customs determines that section 684 applies to the taxpayer, the income tax advantage in question is to be counteracted by adjustments, unless the officer is of the opinion that no counteraction is required."

(5)   In that section, for subsection (5) substitute—

> "(5)   An assessment may be made in accordance with a counteraction notice at any time (without regard to any time limit on making the assessment that would otherwise apply)."

(6)   After that section insert—

> **"698A   No-counteraction notices**
>
> (1)   If on an enquiry under section 695 an officer of Revenue and Customs is of the opinion that no counteraction is required, the officer must serve notice on the person (a "no-counteraction notice") stating that no counteraction is required and why.
>
> (2)   The taxpayer may apply to the tribunal for a direction requiring an officer of Revenue and Customs to issue one of the following within a specified period—
>> (a)   a counteraction notice;
>> (b)   a no-counteraction notice.
>
> (3)   Any such application is to be subject to the relevant provisions of Part 5 of TMA 1970 (see, in particular, section 48(2)(b) of that Act).
>
> (4)   The tribunal must give the direction applied for unless satisfied that there are reasonable grounds for not serving either a counteraction notice or a no-counteraction notice within a specified period."

(7) In section 684 (person liable to counteraction), for subsection (4) substitute—

"(4) This section is subject to no-counteraction notices issued under section 698A."

(8) The amendments made by this section have effect in relation to—

(a) a transaction occurring on or after 6 April 2016, or

(b) a series of transactions any one or more of which occurs on or after that date.

(9) Accordingly, Chapter 1 of Part 13 of ITA 2007 has effect without the amendments made by this section in relation to a tax advantage obtained on or after 6 April 2016 in consequence of—

(a) a transaction occurring before that date, or

(b) a series of transactions all of which occur before that date.

35 Distributions in a winding up

(1) In Chapter 3 of Part 4 of ITTOIA 2005 (dividends and other distributions from UK resident companies), after section 396A insert—

"396B Distributions in a winding up

(1) For the purposes of this Chapter, a distribution made to an individual in respect of share capital in the winding up of a UK resident company is a distribution of the company if—

(a) Conditions A to D are met, and

(b) the distribution is not excluded (see subsection (7)).

(2) Condition A is that, immediately before the winding up, the individual has at least a 5% interest in the company.

(3) Condition B is that the company—

(a) is a close company when it is wound up, or

(b) was a close company at any time in the period of two years ending with the start of the winding up.

(4) Condition C is that, at any time within the period of two years beginning with the date on which the distribution is made—

(a) the individual carries on a trade or activity which is the same as, or similar to, that carried on by the company or an effective 51% subsidiary of the company,

(b) the individual is a partner in a partnership which carries on such a trade or activity,

(c) the individual, or a person connected with him or her, is a participator in a company in which he or she has at least a 5% interest and which at that time—

(i) carries on such a trade or activity, or

(ii) is connected with a company which carries on such a trade or activity, or

(d) the individual is involved with the carrying on of such a trade or activity by a person connected with the individual.

(5) Condition D is that it is reasonable to assume, having regard to all the circumstances, that—

        (a)   the main purpose or one of the main purposes of the winding up is the avoidance or reduction of a charge to income tax, or

        (b)   the winding up forms part of arrangements the main purpose or one of the main purposes of which is the avoidance or reduction of a charge to income tax.

  (6)   The circumstances referred to in subsection (5) include in particular the fact that Condition C is met.

  (7)   A distribution to an individual is excluded if or to the extent that—

        (a)   the amount of the distribution does not exceed the amount that would result in no gain accruing for the purposes of capital gains tax, or

        (b)   the distribution is a distribution of irredeemable shares.

  (8)   In this section—

        "arrangements" includes any agreement, understanding, scheme, transaction or series of transactions, whether or not legally enforceable;

        "effective 51% subsidiary" has the meaning given by section 170(7) of TCGA 1992;

        "participator" has the meaning given by section 454 of CTA 2010.

  (9)   For the purposes of this section, an individual has at least a 5% interest in a company if—

        (a)   at least 5% of the ordinary share capital of the company is held by the individual, and

        (b)   at least 5% of the voting rights in the company are exercisable by the individual by virtue of that holding.

  (10)   For the purposes of subsection (9) if an individual holds any shares in a company jointly or in common with one or more other persons, he or she is to be treated as sole holder of so many of them as is proportionate to the value of his or her share (and as able to exercise voting rights by virtue of that holding)."

(2)   In Chapter 4 of Part 4 of ITTOIA 2005 (dividends from non-UK resident companies), after section 404 insert—

"404A Distributions in a winding up

  (1)   For the purposes of this Chapter, a distribution made to an individual in respect of share capital in a winding up of a non-UK resident company is a dividend of the company if—

        (a)   Conditions A to D are met, and

        (b)   the distribution is not excluded (see subsection (7)).

  (2)   Condition A is that, immediately before the winding up, the individual has at least a 5% interest in the company.

  (3)   Condition B is that the company—

        (a)   is a close company when it is wound up, or

        (b)   was a close company at any time in the period of two years ending with the start of the winding up.

  (4)   Condition C is that, at any time within the period of two years beginning with the date on which the distribution is made—

     (a)   the individual carries on a trade or activity which is the same as, or similar to, that carried on by the company or an effective 51% subsidiary of the company,

     (b)   the individual is a partner in a partnership which carries on such a trade or activity,

     (c)   the individual, or a person connected with him or her, is a participator in a company in which he or she has at least a 5% interest and which at that time—

         (i)   carries on such a trade or activity, or

         (ii)   is connected with a company which carries on such a trade or activity, or

     (d)   the individual is involved with the carrying on of such a trade or activity by a person connected with the individual.

(5)   Condition D is that it is reasonable to assume, having regard to all the circumstances, that—

     (a)   the main purpose or one of the main purposes of the winding up is the avoidance or reduction of a charge to income tax, or

     (b)   the winding up forms part of arrangements the main purpose or one of the main purposes of which is the avoidance or reduction of a charge to income tax.

(6)   The circumstances referred to in subsection (5) include in particular the fact that Condition C is met.

(7)   A distribution to an individual is excluded if or to the extent that—

     (a)   the amount of the distribution does not exceed the amount that would result in no gain accruing for the purposes of capital gains tax, or

     (b)   the distribution is a distribution of irredeemable shares.

(8)   In this section—

       "arrangements" includes any agreement, understanding, scheme, transaction or series of transactions, whether or not legally enforceable;

       "close company" includes a company which would be a close company if it were a UK resident company;

       "effective 51% subsidiary" has the meaning given by section 170(7) of TCGA 1992;

       "participator" has the meaning given by section 454 of CTA 2010.

(9)   For the purposes of this section, a person has at least a 5% interest in a company if—

     (a)   at least 5% of the ordinary share capital of the company is held by the individual, and

     (b)   at least 5% of the voting rights in the company are exercisable by the individual by virtue of that holding.

(10)   For the purposes of subsection (9) if an individual holds any shares in a company jointly or in common with one or more other persons, he or she is to be treated as sole holder of so many of them as is proportionate to the value of his or her share (and as able to exercise voting rights by virtue of that holding)."

(3) The amendments made by this section have effect in relation to distributions made on or after 6 April 2016.

Disguised fees and carried interest

36 Disguised investment management fees

(1) Section 809EZA of ITA 2007 (disguised investment management fees: charge to income tax) is amended as specified in subsections (2) and (3).

(2) In subsection (3)—

    (a) in paragraph (a), for "performs" substitute "at any time performs or is to perform";

    (b) omit paragraph (b);

    (c) in paragraph (c), for "the scheme" substitute "an investment scheme".

(3) After subsection (6) insert—

    "(7) The reference in subsection (6)(a) to a collective investment scheme includes—

        (a) arrangements which permit an external investor to participate in investments acquired by the collective investment scheme without participating in the scheme itself, and

        (b) arrangements under which sums arise to an individual performing investment management services in respect of the collective investment scheme without those sums arising from the scheme itself."

(4) In section 809EZE of that Act (interpretation), in subsection (1), in paragraph (a) of the definition of "external investor", for "performs" substitute "at any time performs or is to perform".

(5) The amendments made by this section have effect in relation to sums arising on or after 6 April 2016 (whenever the arrangements under which the sums arise were made).

37 Income-based carried interest

(1) In Chapter 5E of Part 13 of ITA 2007 (tax avoidance: disguised investment management fees), in section 809EZB(1) (meaning of "management fee"), for paragraph (c) substitute—

    "(c) carried interest which is not income-based carried interest (see sections 809EZC and 809EZD for carried interest, and Chapter 5F for income-based carried interest)."

(2) After Chapter 5E of Part 13 of ITA 2007 insert—

"CHAPTER 5F

INCOME-BASED CARRIED INTEREST

Income-based carried interest

809FZA Overview

(1) This Chapter determines when carried interest arising to an individual from an investment scheme is "income-based carried interest" for the purposes of Chapter 5E (and, in particular, section 809EZB(1)(c)).

(2) Section 809FZB contains the general rule, under which the extent to which carried interest is income-based carried interest depends on the average holding period of the investment scheme.

(3) Sections 809FZC to 809FZP contain further provision relating to average holding periods.

(4) Sections 809FZQ and 809FZR contain a particular rule for direct lending funds.

(5) Sections 809FZS and 809FZT contain an exception to the general rule for carried interest which is conditionally exempt from income tax.

(6) Sections 809FZU to 809FZZ contain supplementary and interpretative provision.

(7) Nothing in this Chapter affects the liability to any tax of—
    (a) the investment scheme, or
    (b) external investors in the investment scheme.

809FZB Income-based carried interest: general rule

(1) "Income-based carried interest" is the relevant proportion of a sum of carried interest arising to an individual from an investment scheme.

(2) The relevant proportion is determined by reference to the investment scheme's average holding period as follows.

Average holding period	Relevant proportion
Less than 36 months	100%
At least 36 months but less than 37 months	80%
At least 37 months but less than 38 months	60%
At least 38 months but less than 39 months	40%
At least 39 months but less than 40 months	20%
40 months or more	0%

(3) This section is subject to the following provisions of this Chapter.

Average holding period

809FZC Average holding period

(1) The average holding period of an investment scheme, in relation to a sum of carried interest, is the average length of time for which relevant investments have been held for the purposes of the scheme.

(2) In this section, "relevant investments" means investments —
   (a) which are made for the purposes of the scheme, and
   (b) by reference to which the carried interest is calculated.

(3) The average holding period is calculated by reference to the time the carried interest arises.

(4) It is calculated as follows.
   Step 1
   For each relevant investment, multiply the value invested at the time the investment was made by the length of time for which the investment has been held.
   Step 2
   Add together the amounts produced under *step 1* in respect of all relevant investments.
   Step 3
   Divide the amount produced under *step 2* by the total value invested in all relevant investments.

(5) Disregard intermediate holdings or intermediate holding structures (including intermediate investment schemes) by or through which investments are made or held —
   (a) when identifying, for the purpose of determining the average holding period of an investment scheme, what relevant investments are held for the purposes of an investment scheme, and
   (b) for any other purpose relating to the determination of the average holding period.
   This is subject to the following provisions of this Chapter.

(6) In this section, references to the length of time for which a relevant investment has been held are —
   (a) in the case of an investment which has been disposed of before the carried interest arises, references to the time for which it was held before being disposed of, and
   (b) in any other case, references to the time for which it has been held up to the time the carried interest arises.

(7) For the purposes of this Chapter, carried interest which is deferred carried interest in relation to a person within the meaning of section 103KG of TCGA 1992 is to be treated as arising to that person at the time it would have arisen had it not been deferred as specified in section 103KG(3)(a) or (b) of that Act.

(8) Sections 809FZD to 809FZP apply for the purposes of determining the average holding period of an investment scheme.

Average holding period: disposals

809FZD Disposals

(1) An investment or part of an investment is disposed of where —
  (a) there is a disposal of the investment or the part of the investment for the purposes of the investment scheme,
  (b) there is a disposal for the purposes of the investment scheme of an intermediate holding or intermediate holding structure (including an intermediate investment scheme) by or through which the investment is held, or
  (c) in any other case, there is a deemed disposal under subsection (2).

(2) There is a deemed disposal of an investment or part of an investment under this subsection where —
  (a) under any arrangements —
    (i)   the scheme in substance closes its position on the investment or the part of the investment, or
    (ii) the scheme ceases to be exposed to risks and rewards in the respect of the investment or the part of the investment, and
  (b) it is reasonable to suppose that the arrangements were designed to secure that result.

(3) In the case of a disposal of part of a holding of securities in a company which are of the same class, suppose for the purposes of determining which investments have been disposed of that the disposal affects the securities in the order in which they were acquired (that is, on a first in first out basis).

(4) The references in subsection (1)(a) and (b) to a disposal are to something which is a disposal for the purposes of TCGA 1992; but for the purposes of subsection (1)(a) disregard section 116 of TCGA 1992 (which disapplies sections 127 to 130 of that Act in relation to qualifying corporate bonds).

809FZE Part disposals

(1) Where there is a disposal of part of an investment, the part disposed of and the part not disposed of are to be treated as two separate investments which were made at the same time.

(2) The value of each of those two separate investments is the appropriate proportion of the value first invested in the whole investment.

(3) The appropriate proportion is the proportion of the value of the part in question to the value of the whole investment at the time of the disposal.

(4) The disposal of part of an asset includes the disposal of an interest in or right over the asset (and "part disposed of" is to be construed accordingly).

809FZF Unwanted short-term investments

(1) The making and disposal of an investment for the purposes of an investment scheme are to be disregarded if —

        (a) the investment is an unwanted short-term investment, and

        (b) the unwanted short-term investment is excludable.

(2)   An investment is an unwanted short-term investment where—

        (a) the investment is made as part of a transaction under which one or more other investments are made for the purposes of the scheme,

        (b) the value of the investment does not exceed that of the other investments taken together,

        (c) it is reasonable to suppose that the investment had to be made in order for the other investments to be made,

        (d) at the time the investment is made, managers of the scheme have a firm, settled and evidenced intention to dispose of the investment for the purposes of the scheme within the relevant period,

        (e) the investment is disposed of for the purposes of the scheme within the relevant period, and

        (f) any profit resulting from the disposal has no bearing on whether a sum of carried interest arises or on the amount of any sum of carried interest which does arise.

(3)   An unwanted short-term investment is excludable if it constitutes—

        (a) an investment in land,

        (b) an investment in securities in an unlisted company,

        (c) the making of a direct loan where the other investments specified in subsection (2)(b) are shares or other securities in an unlisted company, or

        (d) the making of a direct loan which is a qualifying loan within the meaning given by section 809FZR(2).

(4)   In subsection (2)(e) "relevant period" means—

        (a) for an investment within subsection (3)(a), 12 months;

        (b) for an investment within subsection (3)(b) or (c), 6 months;

        (c) for an investment within subsection (3)(d), 120 days.

(5)   But if at any time it becomes reasonable to suppose that, when the scheme ceases to invest, 25% or more of the capital of the investment scheme will have been invested in unwanted short-term investments which are excludable, subsection (1) does not apply to any investment made subsequently for the purposes of the scheme.

Average holding period: derivatives and hedging

809FZG Derivatives

(1)   A derivative contract entered into for the purposes of an investment scheme is an investment, subject to the following provisions of this section.

(2)   The value invested in the derivative contract is—

        (a) where the contract is an option, the cost of acquiring the option (whether from the grantor or another person),

        (b) where the contract is a future, the price specified in the contract for the underlying subject matter, or

    (c)   where the contract is a contract for differences, the notional principal of the contract.

(3)   But where entering into a derivative contract constitutes a deemed disposal of an investment or part of an investment by virtue of section 809FZD(2)(a)(ii) —

    (a)   the derivative contract is not an investment, and

    (b)   the subsequent disposal of the derivative contract without a corresponding disposal of the investment or part investment is to be regarded as the making of a new investment to the extent that the scheme becomes materially exposed to risks and rewards in respect of the investment or part investment.

(4)   For the purposes of this Chapter, references to disposal, in the case of a derivative contract, include any of the following events (to the extent that the event is not otherwise a disposal under section 809FZD(1) or (2)) —

    (a)   the expiry of the contract,

    (b)   the termination of the contract (whether or not in accordance with its terms),

    (c)   the disposal, substantial variation, loss or cancellation of the investment scheme's rights under the contract, and

    (d)   in the case of a derivative contract which is an option, the exercise of the option,

but do not include the renewal of the contract with the same counterparty on substantially the same terms.

(5)   The substantial variation of an investment scheme's rights under a derivative contract constitutes (in addition to the disposal of the contract as originally entered into (see subsection (4)(c)) a new investment consisting of the contract as varied.

809FZH Hedging: exchange gains and losses

(1)   This section applies where —

    (a)   an investment scheme has a hedging relationship between a relevant instrument and a relevant investment, and

    (b)   the hedging relationship relates to exchange gains or losses.

(2)   In this section —

    "relevant instrument" means a derivative contract or a liability representing a loan relationship, and

    "relevant investment" means —

        (a)   where the relevant instrument is a derivative contract, an investment made for the purposes of the scheme or a liability representing a loan relationship;

        (b)   where the relevant instrument is a liability representing a loan relationship, an investment made for the purposes of the scheme.

(3)   An investment scheme has a hedging relationship between a relevant instrument and a relevant investment if or to the extent that —

    (a)   the instrument and the investment are designated by the scheme as a hedge, or

(b) in any other case, the instrument is intended to act as a hedge of exposure to —
    (i) changes in fair value of the investment or an identified portion of the investment, or
    (ii) variability in cash flows,
    where the exposure is attributable to exchange gains or losses and could affect profit or loss of the investment scheme.

(4) Entering into the hedging relationship is not a deemed disposal of the relevant investment under section 809FZD(2).

(5) The relevant instrument is not an investment for the purposes of the investment scheme to the extent that the conditions in subsection (3)(a) and (b) are met.

(6) But the termination of the hedging relationship is the making of an investment constituting the relevant instrument if or to the extent that that instrument continues to subsist.

809FZI Hedging: interest rates

(1) This section applies where an investment scheme has a hedging relationship between —
    (a) an interest rate contract, and
    (b) a qualifying investment held for the purposes of the fund.

(2) An investment scheme has a hedging relationship between an interest rate contract and a qualifying investment if or to the extent that —
    (a) the interest rate contract and the investment are designated by the scheme as a hedge, or
    (b) in any other case, the interest rate contract is intended to act as a hedge of exposure to —
        (i) changes in fair value of the investment or an identified portion of the investment, or
        (ii) variability in cash flows,
    where the exposure is attributable to interest rates and could affect profit or loss of the investment scheme.

(3) Entering into the hedging relationship is not a deemed disposal of the relevant investment under section 809FZD(2).

(4) The interest rate contract is not an investment for the purposes of the investment scheme to the extent that the conditions in subsection (2)(a) and (b) are met.

(5) But the termination of the hedging relationship is the making of an investment constituting the interest rate contract if or to the extent that the interest rate contract continues to subsist.

(6) In this section "qualifying investment" means —
    (a) money placed at interest,
    (b) securities (excluding shares issued by companies),
    (c) alternative finance arrangements, and
    (d) a liability representing a loan relationship.

Average holding period: aggregation of acquisitions and disposals

809FZJ Significant interests

(1) Where an investment scheme has a controlling interest in a trading company or the holding company of a trading group—

    (a) any investment made for the purposes of the scheme in that company after the time when the controlling interest was acquired is to be regarded as having been made at that time, and

    (b) any disposal for the purposes of the scheme of an investment in the company after the time the controlling interest was acquired is to be regarded as not being made until a relevant disposal is made.

(2) In subsection (1)(b) "relevant disposal", in relation to a company, means a disposal which (apart from subsection (1)) has the effect that the investment scheme ceases to have a 40% interest in the company.

(3) For the purposes of this section, in determining whether an investment scheme has a controlling interest or a 40% interest in a company, any share capital of the company which is held for the purposes of an associated investment scheme is to be regarded as held for the purposes of the investment scheme.

809FZK Venture capital funds

(1) Where a venture capital fund has a relevant interest in a trading company or the holding company of a trading group—

    (a) any venture capital investment made for the purposes of the scheme in the company after the time the relevant interest was acquired (and before a relevant disposal) is to be regarded as having been made at the time the relevant interest was acquired, and

    (b) any disposal for the purposes of the scheme of a venture capital investment in the company after that time is to be regarded as not being made until—

        (i) a relevant disposal is made, or

        (ii) the scheme director condition ceases to be met.

(2) For the purposes of subsection (1) a venture capital fund has a relevant interest in a company if—

    (a) by virtue of its venture capital investments the fund has at least a 5% interest in the company, or

    (b) venture capital investments held for the purposes of the scheme in the company have a value of more than £1 million.

(3) For the purposes of subsection (1) "relevant disposal" means a disposal which (apart from subsection (1)) has the effect that the venture capital fund has disposed of more than 80% of the greatest amount invested at any one time in the company for the purposes of the fund.

(4) In this Chapter, "venture capital fund" means an investment scheme in relation to which the condition in subsection (5) is met.

(5) The condition is that when the scheme starts to invest it is reasonable to suppose that over the investing life of the scheme—

     (a)   at least two-thirds of the total value invested for the purposes of the scheme will be invested in venture capital investments, and

     (b)   at least two-thirds of the total value invested for the purposes of the scheme will be invested in investments which are held for 40 months or more.

(6) In determining whether subsection (5)(b) is met in relation to an investment scheme, apply the rule in subsection (1) to the scheme.

(7) In this section, "venture capital investment", in relation to an investment scheme, means an investment in a trading company or the holding company of a trading group where—

     (a)   at the time the investment is made the company is unlisted and is likely to remain so,

     (b)   at least 75% of the total value of the investment is invested in—

         (i)   newly issued shares or

         (ii)   newly issued securities convertible into shares,

     (c)   the investment is used in a trade carried on by the trading company or the trading group—

         (i)   to support its growth, or

         (ii)   for the development of new products or services,

        and is not used directly or indirectly to acquire shares in the company which are not newly issued,

     (d)   if the investment is the first investment made in the company for the purposes of the scheme, the trading company or group has not carried on that trade for more than 7 years, and

     (e)   the scheme director condition is met.

(8) In this Chapter, the scheme director condition, in relation to an investment scheme and a company, is that—

     (a)   the scheme (or the scheme and one or more investment schemes acting together) are entitled to appoint a director ("the scheme director") of—

         (i)   the company, or

         (ii)   a company which controls the company, and

     (b)   the scheme director is entitled to exercise rights within subsection (9).

(9) Those rights are rights which—

     (a)   are rights conferred under contractual arrangements—

         (i)   to which some or all of the investors in the company are parties, and

         (ii)   which it would be reasonable to suppose would not otherwise be capable of being exercised by the scheme director,

     (b)   relate to the conduct of the business and affairs of the company, and

     (c)   are at least equivalent to the rights which it is reasonable to suppose a prudent investor would have obtained on making an investment in the company at arm's length of the same size and nature as that held in the company for the purposes of the investment scheme.

(10) In determining whether the condition in subsection (2)(a) or (b) is met in relation to a venture capital fund, any share capital of a company which is held for the purposes of an associated investment scheme is to be regarded as held for the purposes of the venture capital fund.

809FZL Significant equity stake funds

(1) Where a significant equity stake fund has a significant equity stake investment in a trading company or the holding company of a trading group —

    (a) any investment made for the purposes of the fund in that company made after the time the significant equity stake investment was acquired is to be regarded as having been made at that time, and

    (b) any disposal for the purposes of the fund of an investment in the company after that time is to be regarded as not being made until —

        (i) a relevant disposal is made, or

        (ii) the scheme director condition ceases to be met.

(2) In subsection (1)(b) "relevant disposal" means a disposal which (apart from subsection (1)) has the effect that the significant equity stake fund ceases to have a 15% interest in the company.

(3) In this Chapter, "significant equity stake fund" means an investment scheme —

    (a) which is not a venture capital fund, and

    (b) in relation to which the condition in subsection (4) is met.

(4) The condition is that when the scheme starts to invest it is reasonable to suppose that over the investing life of the scheme —

    (a) more than 50% of the total value invested for the purposes of the scheme will be invested in investments which are significant equity stake investments, and

    (b) more than 50% of that value will be invested in investments which are held for 40 months or more.

(5) In determining whether subsection (4)(b) is met in relation to an investment scheme, apply the rule in subsection (1) to the scheme.

(6) In this section, "significant equity stake investment", in relation to an investment scheme, means an investment in a trading company or the holding company of a trading group where —

    (a) at the time the investment is made, the company is unlisted and likely to remain so,

    (b) by virtue of the investment (on its own or with other investments) the scheme has a 20% interest in the company, and

    (c) the scheme director condition is met.

(7) For the purposes of this section, in determining whether a significant equity stake fund has an interest of a particular percentage in a company, any share capital of the company which is held for the purposes of an associated investment scheme is to be regarded as held for the purposes of the significant equity stake fund.

809FZM Controlling equity stake funds

(1) Where a controlling equity stake fund has a 25% interest in a trading company or the holding company of a trading group—

    (a) any investment made for the purposes of the controlling equity stake fund in the company after the time the 25% interest was acquired is to be regarded as having been made at that time, and

    (b) any disposal for the purposes of the controlling equity stake fund of an investment in the company after that time is to be regarded as not being made until a relevant disposal is made.

(2) In subsection (1)(b), "relevant disposal", in relation to a company, means a disposal which (apart from subsection (1)) has the effect that the controlling equity stake fund ceases to have a 25% interest in the company.

(3) In this Chapter, "controlling equity stake fund" means an investment scheme—

    (a) which is not a venture capital fund or significant equity stake fund, and

    (b) in relation to which the condition in subsection (4) is met.

(4) The condition is that when the scheme starts to invest it is reasonable to suppose that, over the investing life of the scheme—

    (a) more than 50% of the total value invested for the purposes of the scheme will be invested in investments which are controlling interests in trading companies or holding companies of trading groups, and

    (b) more than 50% of the total value invested for the purposes of the scheme will be invested in investments which are held for 40 months or more.

(5) In determining whether subsection (4)(b) is met in relation to an investment scheme, apply the rule in subsection (1) to the scheme.

(6) For the purposes of this section, in determining whether a controlling equity stake fund has a controlling interest or an interest of a particular percentage in a company, any share capital of the company which is held for the purposes of an associated investment scheme is to be regarded as held for the purposes of the controlling equity stake fund.

809FZN Real estate funds

(1) Where a real estate fund has a major interest in any land—

    (a) any investment made for the purposes of the fund in that land after the time the major interest was acquired is to be regarded as having been made at that time, and

    (b) any disposal for the purposes of the fund of an investment in the land after that time is to be regarded as not being made until a relevant disposal is made.

(2) In subsection (1)(b) "relevant disposal" means a disposal which (apart from subsection (1)) has the effect that the real estate fund has disposed of more than 50% of the greatest amount invested at any one time in the land for the purposes of the real estate fund.

(3) Where a real estate fund has a major interest in any land ("the original land") and subsequently acquires a major interest in any adjacent land—

    (a) the acquisition is an investment in the original land for the purposes of subsection (1)(a), and

    (b) after the acquisition, the adjacent land is to be regarded as part of the original land for the purposes of subsections (1) and (2).

(4) In this Chapter, "real estate fund" means an investment scheme—

    (a) which is not a venture capital fund, significant equity stake fund or controlling equity stake fund, and

    (b) in relation to which the condition in subsection (5) is met.

(5) The condition is that when the scheme starts to invest it is reasonable to suppose that over the investing life of the scheme—

    (a) more than 50% of the total value invested for the purposes of the scheme will be invested in land, and

    (b) more than 50% of the total value invested for the purposes of the scheme will be invested in investments which are held for 40 months or more.

(6) In determining whether subsection (5)(b) is met in relation to an investment scheme, apply the rule in subsection (1) to the scheme.

809FZO Funds of funds

(1) Section 809FZC(5) (disregard of intermediate holdings and holding structures) does not apply to an investment made for the purposes of a fund of funds in a collective investment scheme (and, accordingly, such an investment is regarded as an investment in the collective investment scheme itself).

(2) Subsection (1) does not apply in relation to a fund of funds in relation to a collective investment scheme if it is reasonable to suppose that the main purpose or one of the main purposes of the making of any investment in any collective investment scheme for the purposes of the fund of funds is to reduce the proportion of carried interest arising to any person which is income-based carried interest.

(3) Where by virtue of subsection (1) a fund of funds has a significant investment in a collective investment scheme ("the underlying scheme")—

    (a) any qualifying investment made for the purposes of the fund in the underlying scheme after the time the significant investment was acquired is to be regarded as having been made at that time, and

    (b) any disposal for the purposes of the fund of a qualifying investment in the underlying scheme after that time is to be regarded as not being made until a relevant disposal is made.

(4) In subsection (3)(b) "relevant disposal", in relation to an underlying scheme, means a disposal which (apart from subsection (3)) has the effect that—

    (a) the fund of funds has (by virtue of disposals of its interest in the underlying scheme) disposed of at least 50% of the greatest amount invested for its purposes at any one time in the underlying scheme, or

      (b)   the fund of fund's investment in the underlying scheme is worth less than whichever is the greater of —

           (i)   £1 million, or

           (ii) 5% of the total value of the investments made before the disposal for the purposes of the fund of funds in the underlying scheme.

(5)   In this Chapter, "fund of funds" means an investment scheme in relation to which the condition in subsection (6) is met.

(6)   The condition is that when the scheme starts to invest it is reasonable to suppose that over the investing life of the scheme —

      (a)   substantially all of the total value invested for the purposes of the scheme will be invested in collective investment schemes of which the scheme holds less than 50% by value,

      (b)   more than 50% of the total value invested for the purposes of the scheme will be invested in investments which are held for 40 months or more, and

      (c)   more than 75% of the total value invested in the scheme will be invested by external investors.

(7)   In determining whether subsection (6)(b) is met in relation to an investment scheme, apply the rule in subsection (3) to the scheme.

(8)   In this section, "significant investment", in relation to a collective investment scheme, means —

      (a)   an investment of a least £1 million in the scheme, or

      (b)   an investment of at least 5% of the total amounts raised or to be raised from external investors in the scheme.

(9)   In this section, "qualifying investment" means an investment made for the purposes of an investment scheme in a collective investment scheme ("the underlying scheme") where —

      (a)   the investment is held on the same terms as other investments made by external investors in the underlying scheme,

      (b)   the fund of funds, together with any connected funds, does not hold more than 30% by value of the underlying scheme,

      (c)   the underlying scheme has not made an investment in the fund of funds,

      (d)   no person providing investment management services to the underlying scheme provides investment management services to the fund of funds, and

      (e)   it is reasonable to suppose that the investment in the underlying scheme is not part of arrangements the main purpose or one of the main purposes of which is to reward any person involved in providing investment management services to the underlying scheme or a scheme connected with that underlying scheme.

809FZP Secondary funds

(1)   Section 809FZC(5) (disregard of intermediate holdings and holding structures) does not apply to investments acquired for the purposes of a secondary fund in a collective investment scheme (and, accordingly,

such an investment is regarded as an investment in the collective investment scheme itself).

(2) Subsection (1) does not apply in relation to a secondary fund in relation to a collective investment scheme if it is reasonable to suppose that the main purpose or one of the main purposes of the making of any investment in any collective investment scheme for the purposes of the secondary fund is to reduce the proportion of carried interest arising to any person which is income-based carried interest.

(3) Where by virtue of subsection (1) a secondary fund has a significant investment in a collective investment scheme ("the underlying scheme")—

    (a) any qualifying investment acquired for the purposes of the fund in the underlying scheme after the time when the significant investment is acquired is to be regarded as having been made at that time, and

    (b) any disposal for the purposes of the fund of a qualifying investment in the underlying scheme after that time is to be regarded as not being made until a relevant disposal is made.

(4) In subsection (3)(b) "relevant disposal" means a disposal which (apart from subsection (3)) has the effect that—

    (a) the secondary fund has (by virtue of disposals of its interest in the underlying scheme) disposed of at least 50% of the greatest amount invested for its purposes at any one time in the underlying scheme, or

    (b) the secondary fund's investment in the underlying scheme is worth less than whichever is the greater of—

        (i) £1 million, or

        (ii) 5% of the total value of the investments held immediately before the disposal for the purposes of the secondary fund in the underlying scheme.

(5) In this Chapter, "secondary fund" means an investment scheme in relation to which the condition in subsection (6) is met.

(6) The condition is that when the scheme starts to invest it is reasonable to suppose that over the investing life of the scheme—

    (a) substantially all of the total value invested for the purposes of the scheme will be in the acquisition of investments in, or the acquisition of portfolios of investments from, unconnected collective investment schemes,

    (b) more than 50% of the total value invested for the purposes of the scheme will be invested in investments which are held for 40 months or more, and

    (c) more than 75% of the total amount invested in the scheme will be invested by external investors.

(7) In determining whether subsection (6)(b) is met in relation to an investment scheme, apply the rule in subsection (3) to the scheme.

(8) In this section, "significant interest", in relation to a collective investment scheme, means—

    (a) an investment of at least £1 million in the scheme, or

      (b)   an investment of at least 5% of the total amounts raised or to be raised from external investors in the scheme.

  (9)   In this section, "qualifying investment" means an investment in a collective investment scheme ("the underlying scheme") acquired for the purposes of a secondary fund where—

      (a)   the investment acquired was originally made on the same terms as investments in the underlying scheme made by external investors,

      (b)   the terms on which the investment was acquired or investments made in the underlying scheme were made by external investors have not significantly changed since the investment was acquired,

      (c)   the secondary fund, together with any connected funds, does not hold more than 30% by value of the underlying scheme,

      (d)   no person providing investment management services to the underlying scheme provides investment management services to the secondary fund, and

      (e)   it is reasonable to suppose that the investment in the underlying scheme is not part of arrangements the main purpose or one of the main purposes of which is to reward any person involved in providing investment management services to the underlying scheme or a scheme connected with that underlying scheme.

Direct lending funds

809FZQ Direct lending funds

  (1)   Carried interest arising from an investment scheme which is a direct lending fund is income-based carried interest in its entirety.

       Subsections (2) to (4) apply for the purposes of this Chapter.

  (2)   A direct lending fund is an investment scheme—

      (a)   which is not a venture capital fund, significant equity stake fund, controlling equity stake fund or real estate fund, and

      (b)   in relation to which it is reasonable to suppose that, when the scheme ceases to invest, a majority of the investments made for the purposes of the scheme (calculated by reference to value invested) will have been direct loans made by the scheme.

  (3)   An investment scheme makes a direct loan if for the purposes of the scheme money is advanced at interest or for any other return determined by reference to the time value of money.

  (4)   The acquisition of a direct loan is to be regarded as the making of a direct loan if the loan is acquired within the period of 120 days beginning with the day on which the money is first advanced.

809FZR Direct lending funds: exception

  (1)   Section 809FZQ does not apply to carried interest arising from a direct lending fund if—

      (a)   the fund is a limited partnership,

      (b)   the carried interest is a sum falling within section 809EZD(2) or (3), and

     (c)   it is reasonable to suppose that, when investments cease to be made for the purposes of the fund, at least 75% of the direct loans made by the fund (calculated by reference to value advanced) will have been qualifying loans.

(2)   In this section "qualifying loan" means a direct loan made by an investment scheme where—

     (a)   the borrower is not connected with the investment scheme,

     (b)   the money is advanced under a genuine commercial loan agreement negotiated at arm's length,

     (c)   repayments are fixed and determinable,

     (d)   maturity is fixed,

     (e)   the scheme has the positive intention and ability to hold the loan to maturity, and

     (f)   the relevant term of the loan is at least four years.

(3)   In this section "relevant term", in relation to a loan, means the period which—

     (a)   begins with the time when the money is advanced, and

     (b)   ends with the time by which, under the terms of the loan, at least 75% of the principal due under the loan must be repaid.

(4)   For the purposes of determining the average holding period of a scheme, where—

     (a)   a qualifying loan made by an investment scheme is repaid by the borrower to any extent before the end of 40 months from the time the loan is made, and

     (b)   it is reasonable to suppose that the borrower's decision to repay was not affected by considerations relating to the application of this Chapter,

the loan is, to the extent it is repaid by the borrower before the end of 40 months from the time it is made, to be treated as held for 40 months.

(5)   In determining for the purposes of subsection (1)(b) whether a sum falls within section 809EZD(2) or (3), read section 809EZD(4)(b) as if the reference to 6% were to 4%.

(6)   Section 809FZB applies to carried interest to which, by virtue of subsection (1), section 809FZQ does not apply.

Conditionally exempt carried interest

809FZS Conditionally exempt carried interest

(1)   Carried interest which—

     (a)   arises to an individual from an investment scheme, and

     (b)   is conditionally exempt from income tax,

is to be treated as if it were not income-based carried interest to any extent.

(2)   Carried interest is conditionally exempt from income tax if Conditions A to D are met.

(3)   Condition A is that the carried interest arises to the individual in the period of—

      (a)   four years beginning with the day on which the scheme starts to invest, or

      (b)   ten years beginning with that day if the carried interest is calculated on the realisation model.

(4)   Condition B is that the carried interest would, apart from this section, be income-based carried interest to any extent.

(5)   Condition C is that it is reasonable to suppose that, were the carried interest to arise to the individual at the relevant time (but by reference to the same relevant investments), it would not be income-based carried interest to any extent.

(6)   The "relevant time" is whichever is the earliest of—

      (a)   the time when it is reasonable to suppose that the investment scheme will be wound up;

      (b)   the end of the period of four years beginning with the time when it is reasonable to suppose that the scheme will cease to invest;

      (c)   the end of the period of—

           (i)   four years beginning with the day on which the sum of carried interest arises to the individual, or

           (ii)   ten years beginning with that day if the carried interest was calculated on the realisation model;

      (d)   the end of the period of four years beginning with the end of the period by reference to which the amount of the carried interest was determined.

(7)   Subsection (5) does not affect what would otherwise be the time at which an investment is disposed of for the purposes of this Chapter.

(8)   Condition D is that the individual makes a claim under this section for the carried interest to be conditionally exempt from income tax.

809FZT Carried interest which ceases to be conditionally exempt

(1)   Carried interest which is conditionally exempt from income tax ceases to be conditionally exempt from income tax at whichever is the earliest of—

      (a)   the time when the investment scheme is wound up;

      (b)   the end of the period of four years beginning with the time the scheme ceases to invest;

      (c)   the end of the period of—

           (i)   four years beginning with the day on which the sum of carried interest arises to the individual, or

           (ii)   ten years beginning with that day if the carried interest was calculated on the realisation model;

      (d)   the end of the period of four years beginning with the end of the period by reference to which the amount of the carried interest is determined;

      (e)   the time at which Condition C in section 809FZS(5) ceases to be met.

(2)   Carried interest which ceases to be conditionally exempt from income tax is to be treated as having been income-based carried interest at the

time it arose to the individual if or to the extent that, had it arisen to the individual at the time it ceased to be conditionally exempt (but in relation to the same relevant investments) it would have been income-based carried interest.

(3) All such assessments and adjustments of assessments are to be made as are necessary to give effect to subsection (2).

(4) Any amount paid by way of capital gains tax in respect of carried interest which is conditionally exempt from income tax is to be treated as if it had been paid in respect of any income tax liability arising under subsection (2).

Supplementary

809FZU Employment-related securities

This Chapter does not apply in relation to carried interest arising to an individual in respect of employment-related securities as defined by section 421B(8) of ITEPA 2003.

809FZV "Loan to own" investments

(1) This section applies where—
   (a) an investment scheme acquires a debt,
   (b) the debt is to any extent uncollectable or otherwise impaired,
   (c) the debt is acquired at a discount with a view to securing direct or indirect ownership of any assets which are—
       (i) owned by a company which is the debtor in respect of the debt, or
       (ii) subject to a security interest in respect of the debt, and
   (d) the fund acquires ownership of the assets within three months of the acquisition of the debt.

(2) For the purposes of this Chapter—
   (a) the debt and the assets are to be treated as a single investment, and
   (b) the value invested in that single investment is the amount paid for the debt.

(3) In this section "security interest" means an interest or right (other than a rentcharge) held for the purpose of securing the payment of money or the performance of any obligation.

809FZW Anti-avoidance

(1) For the purposes mentioned in subsection (2), no regard is to be had to any arrangements the main purpose of which, or one of the main purposes of which, is to reduce the proportion of carried interest which is income-based carried interest.

(2) The purposes referred to in subsection (1) are—
   (a) determining the average holding period, or
   (b) determining whether an investment scheme is a venture capital fund, significant equity stake fund, controlling equity stake fund, real estate fund, fund of funds or secondary fund.

(3) In determining to what extent carried interest is income-based carried interest, no regard is to be had to any arrangements the main purpose, or one of the main purposes, of which is to secure that section 809EZA(1) (charge to income tax) does not apply in relation to some or all of the carried interest.

809FZX Treasury regulations

(1) The Treasury may by regulations make—

    (a) provision relating to the calculation of the average holding period in some or all cases;

    (b) provision repealing, or restricting the application of, section 809FZU (employment-related securities).

(2) The provision referred to in subsection (1)(a) includes in particular—

    (a) provision for a method of calculating that period which is different from that in section 809FZC;

    (b) provision as to what is and is not to be regarded as an investment;

    (c) provision as to when an investment is to be regarded as made or disposed of;

    (d) anti-avoidance provision.

(3) Regulations under this section may—

    (a) amend this Chapter;

    (b) make different provision for different purposes;

    (c) contain incidental, supplemental, consequential and transitional provision and savings.

809FZY "Reasonable to suppose"

(1) For the purposes of this Chapter, in determining what it is reasonable to suppose in relation to an investment scheme, regard is to be had to all the circumstances.

(2) Those circumstances include in particular any prospectus or other document which—

    (a) is made available to external investors in the investment scheme, and

    (b) on which external investors may reasonably be supposed to have relied or been able to rely.

Interpretation

809FZZ Interpretation of Chapter 5F

(1) In this Chapter—

    "5% interest", "15% interest", "20% interest", "25% interest" and "40% interest" are to be construed in accordance with subsection (4);

    "act together": two or more investment schemes act together in relation to a company if—

        (a) they enter into contractual arrangements (with or without other persons) in relation to the conduct of the company's affairs,

(b)   the arrangements are negotiated on arm's length terms, and

(c)   the investment schemes act together to secure greater control or influence over the company's affairs than they would be able to secure individually;

"alternative finance arrangements" has the same meaning as in Part 6 of CTA 2009 (see section 501(2) of that Act);

"arrangements" has the same meaning as in Chapter 5E (see section 809EZE);

"associated": two (or more) investment schemes are "associated" if—

(a)   the same or substantially the same individuals provide investment management services to both schemes;

(b)   the investment schemes have the same or substantially the same investments, and

(c)   the schemes act together in relation to all or substantially all of the investments they acquire;

"carried interest" has the same meaning as in section 809EZB (see sections 809EZC and 809EZD);

"collective investment scheme" has the same meaning as in Chapter 5E (see section 809EZE);

"connected" and "unconnected" are to be construed in accordance with subsections (6) and (7);

"contract for differences" has the same meaning as in Part 7 of CTA 2009 (see section 582 of that Act);

"controlling equity stake fund" has the meaning given in section 809FZM;

"controlling interest" has the meaning given in subsection (3);

"derivative contract" has the same meaning as in Part 7 of CTA 2009 (but see below);

"designated" has the same meaning as for accounting purposes;

"direct lending fund" and "direct loan" have the meanings given in section 809FZQ;

"exchange gain or loss" is to be construed in accordance with section 475 of CTA 2009;

"external investor" has the same meaning as in Chapter 5E (see section 809EZE);

"fund of funds" has the meaning given in section 809FZO;

"future" has the same meaning as in Part 7 of CTA 2009 (see section 581 of that Act);

"interest rate contract" means—

(a)   a derivative contract whose underlying subject-matter is, or includes, interest rates, or

(b)   a swap contract in which payments fall to be made by reference to a rate of interest;

"investing life" is to be construed in accordance with subsection (2);

"investment" does not include—

(a)   cash awaiting investment, or

     (b)   cash representing the proceeds of the disposal of an investment, where the cash is to be distributed as soon as reasonably practicable to investors in the scheme;

"investment scheme" has the same meaning as in Chapter 5E (see section 809EZA(6));

"limited partnership" means—

     (a)   a limited partnership registered under the Limited Partnerships Act 1907,

     (b)   a limited liability partnership formed under the Limited Liability Partnerships Act 2000 or the Limited Liability Partnerships Act (Northern Ireland) 2002 (c.12 (N.I.)), or

     (c)   a firm or entity of a similar character to any of those mentioned in paragraph (a) or (b) formed under the law of a country or territory outside the United Kingdom;

"loan relationship" has the meaning given by section 302 of CTA 2009 (but see below);

"major interest", in relation to land, has the meaning given by section 96 of the Value Added Tax Act 1994;

"option" has the same meaning as in Part 7 of CTA 2009, disregarding section 580(2) of that Act;

"real estate fund" has the meaning given by section 809FZN;

"realisation model": a sum of carried interest is calculated on the "realisation model" if it falls within section 809EZD(2) or (3) (disregarding section 809EZD(2)(b) and (3)(b));

"scheme director condition" has the meaning given by section 809FZK(8) and (9);

"secondary fund" has the meaning given by section 809FZP;

"significant equity stake fund" has the meaning given by section 809FZL;

"sum" has the same meaning as in Chapter 5E (see section 809EZB(3));

"trading company" and "trading group" have the meanings given by paragraphs 20 and 21 of Schedule 7AC to TCGA 1992;

"underlying subject matter" has the same meaning as in Part 7 of CTA 2009;

"unlisted": a company is unlisted if—

     (a)   no shares of any class issued by the company are listed on any stock exchange, and

     (b)   there are no other trading arrangements in place in respect of shares of any class issued by the company;

"venture capital fund" has the meaning given by section 809FZK.

(2) In this Chapter—

     (a)   references to when a scheme starts or ceases to invest are to the time when investments start or cease to be made for the purposes of the scheme, and

     (b)   references to the investing life of the scheme are to the time between when a scheme starts and ceases to invest.

(3) For the purposes of this Chapter, an investment scheme has a controlling interest in a company if share capital of the company is held for the purposes of the scheme which—

       (a)   amounts to more than 50% of the ordinary share capital of the company, and

       (b)   carries an entitlement to more than 50% of —

           (i)   voting rights in the company,

           (ii) profits available for distribution to shareholders, and

           (iii) assets of the company available for distribution to shareholders in a winding-up.

(4) For the purposes of this Chapter, an investment scheme has an interest of a particular percentage in a company (for example, a 40% interest) if share capital of the company is held for the purposes of the scheme which —

       (a)   amounts to at least that percentage of the ordinary share capital of the company, and

       (b)   carries an entitlement to at least that percentage of —

           (i)   voting rights in the company,

           (ii) profits available for distribution to shareholders, and

           (iii) assets of the company available for distribution to shareholders in a winding-up.

(5) For the purposes of subsections (3) and (4) any share capital held by a company controlled by an investment scheme is to be regarded as held for the purposes of the investment scheme.

(6) For the purposes of this Chapter, an investment scheme (A) is connected with another investment scheme or person (B) if —

       (a)   A directly or indirectly has control of B, or

       (b)   the same person, directly or indirectly, has control of A and B.

(7) For the purposes of subsection (6) "control" —

       (a)   in the case of control of a company, is to be read in accordance with sections 450 and 451 of CTA 2010;

       (b)   in the case of control of a partnership, has the meaning given in section 995(3);

       (c)   in the case of control of an investment scheme which is not a company or partnership, or of any other person which is not a company or partnership, means the ability to secure that the affairs of that scheme or other person are conducted in accordance with one's wishes.

(8) For the purposes of the definition of "derivative contract", read Part 7 of CTA 2009 as if —

       (a)   references to a company were references to an investment scheme, and

       (b)   references to a contract of a company were references to a contract for the purposes of an investment scheme.

(9) For the purposes of the definition of "loan relationship", read Part 5 of CTA 2009 as if —

       (a)   references to a company were references to an investment scheme, and

       (b)   references to a loan relationship of a company were references to a loan relationship for the purposes of an investment scheme."

(3) In section 2 of ITA 2007 (overview), in subsection (13), after paragraph (hb) insert—

"(hc)   income-based carried interest (Chapter 5F),".

(4) The amendments made by this section have effect in relation to sums of carried interest arising on or after 6 April 2016 (whenever the arrangements under which the sums arise were made).

38   Income-based carried interest: persons coming to the UK

(1) In section 809EZA of ITA 2007 (disguised investment management fees: charge to income tax), after subsection (2) insert—

"(2A)   Subsection (2B) applies instead of subsections (1) and (2) where—
  (a)   one or more disguised fees arise to an individual in a tax year ("the relevant tax year") from one or more investment schemes (whether or not by virtue of the same arrangements),
  (b)   the disguised fees consist of carried interest which is income-based carried interest,
  (c)   the individual is UK resident in the relevant tax year,
  (d)   before the relevant tax year, the individual was not UK resident for a period of at least five consecutive tax years ("the period of non-residence"), and
  (e)   either—
      (i)   the relevant tax year is the first tax year immediately after the end of the period of non-residence, or
      (ii)   the relevant tax year is the second, third, or fourth tax year after the end of that period and the individual has been UK resident in all the intervening tax years.

(2B)   To the extent that the income-based carried interest arises by virtue of pre-arrival services, the individual is liable for income tax for the relevant tax year in respect of it as if—
  (a)   in relation to pre-arrival services performed in the United Kingdom—
      (i)   the individual were carrying on a trade for the relevant year consisting of the performance of those services,
      (ii)   the income-based carried interest, so far as arising by virtue of those services, were profits of that trade, and
      (iii)   the individual were the person receiving or entitled to those profits, and
  (b)   in relation to pre-arrival services performed outside the United Kingdom—
      (i)   the individual were carrying on a trade for the relevant tax year consisting of the performance of those services,
      (ii)   the income-based carried interest, so far as arising by virtue of those services, were profits of that trade, and
      (iii)   the individual were the person receiving or entitled to those profits.

(2C)   In subsection (2B) "pre-arrival services" means investment management services performed before the end of the period of non-residence."

(2) The amendment made by this section has effect in relation to sums of carried interest arising on or after 6 April 2016 (whenever the arrangements under which the sums arise were made).

Deduction at source

39 Deduction of income tax at source

Schedule 6 contains provisions about deduction of income tax at source.

40 Deduction of income tax at source: intellectual property

(1) Part 15 of ITA 2007 (deduction from other payments connected with intellectual property) is amended as specified in subsections (2) and (3).

(2) In section 906 (certain royalties etc where usual place of abode of owner is abroad), for subsections (1) to (3) substitute—

   "(1) This section applies to any payment made in a tax year where condition A or condition B is met.

   (2) Condition A is that—
      (a) the payment is a royalty, or a payment of any other kind, for the use of, or the right to use, intellectual property (see section 907),
      (b) the usual place of abode of the owner of the intellectual property is outside the United Kingdom, and
      (c) the payment is charged to income tax or corporation tax.

   (3) Condition B is that—
      (a) the payment is a payment of sums payable periodically in respect of intellectual property,
      (b) the person entitled to those sums ("the assignor") assigned the intellectual property to another person,
      (c) the usual place of abode of the assignor is outside the United Kingdom, and
      (d) the payment is charged to income tax or corporation tax."

(3) For section 907 substitute—

"907 Meaning of "intellectual property"

   (1) In section 906 "intellectual property" means—
      (a) copyright of literary, artistic or scientific work,
      (b) any patent, trade mark, design, model, plan, or secret formula or process,
      (c) any information concerning industrial, commercial or scientific experience, or
      (d) public lending right in respect of a book.

   (2) In this section "copyright of literary, artistic or scientific work" does not include copyright in—
      (a) a cinematographic film or video recording, or
      (b) the sound-track of a cinematographic film or video recording, except so far as it is separately exploited."

(4) The amendments made by subsections (2) and (3) have effect in respect of payments made on or after 28 June 2016.

(5) In determining whether section 906 of ITA 2007 applies to a payment, no regard is to be had to any arrangements the main purpose of which, or one of the main purposes of which, is to avoid the effect of the amendments made by this section.

(6) Where arrangements are disregarded under subsection (5) in relation to a payment which—
    (a) is made before 28 June 2016, and
    (b) is due on or after that day,
the payment is to be regarded for the purposes of section 906 of ITA 2007 as made on the date on which it is due.

(7) In determining the date on which a payment is due for the purposes of subsection (6), disregard the arrangements referred to in that subsection.

(8) In this section "arrangements" includes any agreement, understanding, scheme, transaction or series of transactions (whether or not legally enforceable and whether entered into before, or on or after, 28 June 2016).

41 Deduction of income tax at source: intellectual property - tax avoidance

(1) In Part 15 of ITA 2007 (deduction of income tax at source), after section 917 insert—

"Tax avoidance

917A Tax avoidance arrangements

    (1) This section applies if and to the extent that—
        (a) a person ("the payer") makes an intellectual property royalty payment,
        (b) the payment is received by a person ("the payee") who is connected with the payer, and
        (c) the payment is made under DTA tax avoidance arrangements.

    (2) Any duty under Chapter 6 or 7 to deduct a sum representing income tax at any rate applies without regard to any double taxation arrangements.

    (3) Any income tax deducted by virtue of subsection (2) may not be set off under section 967 or 968 of CTA 2010.

    (4) In this section—
        "arrangements" (except in the phrase "double taxation arrangements") includes any agreement, understanding, scheme, transaction or series of transactions, whether or not legally enforceable;
        "DTA tax avoidance arrangements" means arrangements where, having regard to all the circumstances, it is reasonable to conclude that—
            (a) the main purpose, or one of the main purposes, of the arrangements was to obtain a tax advantage by virtue of any provisions of a double taxation arrangement, and

        (b)   obtaining that tax advantage is contrary to the object and purpose of those provisions;

    "intellectual property royalty payment" means a payment referred to in section 906(2)(a) or (3)(a);

    "receive" means receive—

        (a)   directly or indirectly;

        (b)   by one payment or by a series of payments;

    "tax advantage" is to be construed in accordance with section 208 of FA 2013.

    (5)   For the purposes of this section the payer is connected with the payee if the participation condition is met as between them.

    (6)   Section 148 of TIOPA 2010 (when the participation condition is met) applies for the purposes of subsection (5) as for the purposes of section 147(1)(b) of that Act, but as if references to the actual provision were to the provision made or imposed between the payer and the payee in respect of the arrangements under which the payment is made."

(2)   The amendment made by this section has effect in respect of a payment made on or after 17 March 2016 under arrangements entered into at any time (including arrangements entered into before that date).

(3)   In relation to payments made (under any such arrangements) on or after 17 March 2016 and on or before the day on which this Act is passed, section 917A of ITA 2007 as inserted by subsection (1) has effect as if the definition of "intellectual property royalty payment" in that section were as follows—

    ""intellectual property royalty payment" means—

        (a)   a payment of a royalty or other sum in respect of the use of a patent,

        (b)   a payment specified in section 906(1)(a) (as originally enacted), or

        (c)   a payment which is a "qualifying annual payment" for the purposes of Chapter 6 by virtue of section 899(3)(a)(ii) (royalties etc from intellectual property);".

(4)   In relation to payments made (under any such arrangements) on or after 28 June 2016 and on or before the day on which this Act is passed, section 917A of ITA 2007 as inserted by subsection (1) has effect as if "intellectual property royalty payment" also included (so far as it would not otherwise do so) any payments referred to in section 906(2)(a) or (3)(a) of ITA 2007 as substituted by section 40.

Receipts from intellectual property

42   Receipts from intellectual property: territorial scope

    (1)   In section 577 of ITTOIA 2005 (territorial scope of Part 5 charges), at the end insert—

    "(5)   See also section 577A (territorial scope of Part 5 charges: receipts from intellectual property)."

(2)   After that section insert—

"577A   Territorial scope of Part 5 charges: receipts from intellectual property

   (1)   References in section 577 to income which is from a source in the United Kingdom include income arising where—

      (a)   a royalty or other sum is paid in respect of intellectual property by a person who is non-UK resident, and

      (b)   the payment is made in connection with a trade carried on by that person through a permanent establishment in the United Kingdom.

   (2)   Subsection (3) applies where a royalty or other sum is paid in respect of intellectual property by a person who is non-UK resident in connection with a trade carried on by that person only in part through a permanent establishment in the United Kingdom.

   (3)   The payment referred to in subsection (2) is to be regarded for the purposes of subsection (1)(b) as made in connection with a trade carried on through a permanent establishment in the United Kingdom to such extent as is just and reasonable, having regard to all the circumstances.

   (4)   In determining for the purposes of section 577 whether income arising is from a source in the United Kingdom, no regard is to be had to arrangements the main purpose of which, or one of the main purposes of which, is to avoid the effect of the rule in subsection (1).

   (5)   In this section—

      "arrangements" includes any agreement, understanding, scheme, transaction or series of transactions (whether or not legally enforceable);

      "intellectual property" has the same meaning as in section 579;

      "permanent establishment"—

         (a)   in relation to a company, is to be read (by virtue of section 1007A of ITA 2007) in accordance with Chapter 2 of Part 24 of CTA 2010, and

         (b)   in relation to any other person, is to be read in accordance with that Chapter but as if references in that Chapter to a company were references to that person."

(3)   The amendments made by subsections (1) and (2) have effect in relation to royalties or other sums paid in respect of intellectual property on or after 28 June 2016.

(4)   It does not matter for the purposes of subsection (4) of section 577A of ITTOIA 2005 (as inserted by this section) whether the arrangements referred to in that subsection are entered into before, or on or after, 28 June 2016.

(5)   Where arrangements are disregarded under subsection (4) of section 577A of ITTOIA 2005 (as inserted by this section) in relation to a payment of a royalty or other sum which—

   (a)   is made before 28 June 2016, but

   (b)   is due on or after that day,

the payment is to be regarded for the purposes of subsection (1) of that section as made on the date on which it is due.

(6) In determining the date on which a payment is due for the purposes of subsection (5), disregard the arrangements referred to in that subsection.

(7) Where—

    (a) an intellectual property royalty payment within the meaning of section 917A of ITA 2007 is made on or after 28 June 2016,

    (b) the payment is made under arrangements (within the meaning of that section) entered into before that day,

    (c) the arrangements are not DTA tax avoidance arrangements for the purposes of that section,

    (d) it is reasonable to conclude that the main purpose, or one of the main purposes, of the arrangements was to obtain a tax advantage by virtue of any provisions of a foreign double taxation arrangement, and

    (e) obtaining that tax advantage is contrary to the object and purpose of those provisions,

the arrangements are to be regarded as DTA tax avoidance arrangements for the purposes of section 917A of ITA 2007 in relation to the payment.

(8) In subsection (7)—

    "foreign double taxation arrangement" means an arrangement made by two or more territories outside the United Kingdom with a view to affording relief from double taxation in relation to tax chargeable on income (with or without other tax relief);

    "tax advantage" is to be construed in accordance with section 208 of FA 2013 but as if references in that section to "tax" were references to tax chargeable on income under the law of a territory outside the United Kingdom.

(9) Where—

    (a) a royalty is paid on or after 28 June 2016,

    (b) the right in respect of which the royalty is paid was created or assigned before that day,

    (c) section 765(2) of ITTOIA 2005 does not apply in relation to the payment, and

    (d) it is reasonable to conclude that the main purpose, or one of the main purposes, of any person connected with the creation or assignment of the right was to take advantage, by means of that creation or assignment, of the law of any territory giving effect to Council Directive 2003/49/EC of 3rd June 2003 on a common system of taxation applicable to interest and royalty payments made between associated companies of different member States,

section 758 of ITTOIA 2005 does not apply in relation to the payment.

43   Receipts from intellectual property: diverted profits tax

(1) Part 3 of FA 2015 (diverted profits tax) is amended as follows.

(2) In section 79 (charge to tax), at the end insert—

    "(6) But banking surcharge profits and notional banking surcharge profits, to the extent that they are determined by reference to notional PE profits (or what would have been notional PE profits) for an accounting period, do not include any amount which is (or would have been) included in notional PE profits for that period by virtue of section 88(5)(b)."

(3) In section 88 (which relates to the calculation of taxable diverted profits), for subsection (5) substitute—

"(5) "Notional PE profits", in relation to an accounting period, means an amount equal to the sum of—

(a) the amount of profits (if any) which would have been the chargeable profits of the foreign company for that period, attributable (in accordance with sections 20 to 32 of CTA 2009) to the avoided PE, had the avoided PE been a permanent establishment in the United Kingdom through which the foreign company carried on the trade mentioned in section 86(1)(b), and

(b) an amount equal to the total of royalties or other sums which are paid by the foreign company during that period in connection with that trade in circumstances where the payment avoids the application of section 906 of ITA 2007 (duty to deduct tax).

(5A) For the purposes of subsection (5)(b) a payment of a royalty or other sum avoids the application of section 906 of ITA 2007 if—

(a) that section does not apply in relation to the payment, but

(b) that section would have applied in relation to the payment had the avoided PE been a permanent establishment in the United Kingdom through which the foreign company carried on the trade mentioned in section 86(1)(b)."

(4) In section 100 (credit for UK or foreign tax on same profits), for the heading substitute "Credits for tax on the same profits".

(5) In section 100, after subsection (2) insert—

"(2A) Subsection (2)(b) does not allow a credit against a liability to diverted profits tax if or to the extent that the liability arises by virtue of section 88(5)(b) (payments of royalties etc)."

(6) In section 100, after subsection (4) insert—

"(4A) Subsection (4B) applies where—

(a) a company's notional PE profits for an accounting period include an amount under section 88(5)(b) determined by reference to a royalty or other sum,

(b) the company's liability to diverted profits tax for the accounting period is determined by reference to taxable diverted profits calculated under section 91(4) or (5), and

(c) those taxable diverted profits include an amount of relevant taxable income referred to in section 91(4)(b) or (5)(b) determined by reference to the same royalty or other sum.

(4B) A credit equal to the company's liability to diverted profits tax for that accounting period which arises by virtue of section 88(5)(b) in respect of the royalty or other sum, to the extent that it is included in relevant taxable income for the purposes of section 91(4)(b) or (5)(b), is allowed against the company's total liability to diverted profits tax for that period.

    (4C)   Subsection (4D) applies where—

        (a)   by reason of the payment of a royalty or other sum a company's liability to diverted profits tax for an accounting period includes liability arising by virtue of section 88(5)(b),

        (b)   the royalty or other sum is paid to a person who is resident in a country or territory outside the United Kingdom, and

        (c)   under any relevant provision relief would have been due to that person had the avoided PE been a permanent establishment in the United Kingdom through which the company carried on the trade mentioned in section 86(1)(b).

    (4D)   Such credit as is just and reasonable having regard to the amount of the relief referred to in subsection (4C)(c) is allowed against the company's liability to diverted profits tax.

    (4E)   In subsection (4C)(c) "relevant provision" means—

        (a)   the provision of a double taxation arrangement (as defined by section 2(4) of TIOPA 2010), or

        (b)   section 758 of ITTOIA 2005 (exemption for certain interest and royalty payments)."

    (7)   The amendments made by this section have effect in relation to accounting periods ending on or after 28 June 2016.

    (8)   For the purposes of section 88(5)(b) of FA 2015 as substituted by this section, a royalty or other sum which would not otherwise be regarded as paid during an accounting period ending on or after 28 June 2016 is to be regarded as so paid if—

        (a)   for the purposes of section 906 of ITA 2007 it is regarded as paid on a date during that period by virtue of section 40(6), or

        (b)   for the purposes of section 577A(1) of ITTOIA 2005 it is regarded as paid on a date during that period by virtue of section 42(5).

Supplementary welfare payments: Northern Ireland

44   Tax treatment of supplementary welfare payments: Northern Ireland

    (1)   In this section "supplementary welfare payment" means a payment made under regulations under—

        (a)   Article 135(1)(a) of the Welfare Reform (Northern Ireland) Order 2015 (S.I. 2015/2006 (N.I. 1)) ("the Order") (discretionary support),

        (b)   Article 137 of the Order (payments to persons suffering financial disadvantage), or

        (c)   any provision (including future provision) of the Order which enables provision to be made for payments to persons who suffer financial disadvantage as a result of relevant housing benefit changes.

    (2)   In subsection (1)(c) "relevant housing benefit changes" means changes to social security benefits consisting of or including changes contained in the Housing Benefit (Amendment) Regulations (Northern Ireland) 2016 (S.R. (N.I.) 2016 No. 258).

    (3)   The Treasury may by regulations amend any provision of Chapters 1 to 5 of Part 10 of ITEPA 2003 so as to—

    (a)   provide that no liability to income tax arises on supplementary welfare payments of a specified description;

    (b)   impose a charge to income tax under Part 10 of ITEPA 2003 on payments of a specified description made under regulations under Article 137 of the Order (payments to persons suffering financial disadvantage).

(4)   The regulations may make—

    (a)   different provision for different cases;

    (b)   incidental or supplementary provision;

    (c)   consequential provision (which may include provision amending any provision made by or under the Income Tax Acts).

(5)   Regulations made before 6 April 2017 may, so far as relating to the tax year 2016-17, have effect in relation to times before they are made.

(6)   Regulations under this section are to be made by statutory instrument.

(7)   A statutory instrument containing regulations under this section is subject to annulment in pursuance of a resolution of the House of Commons.

(8)   In section 655(2) of ITEPA 2003 (other provisions about the taxation of social security payments) after the entry relating to section 782 of ITTOIA 2005 insert
";

       section 44 of FA 2016 (tax treatment of supplementary welfare payments: Northern Ireland)."

PART 2

CORPORATION TAX

Charge and rates

45   Charge for financial year 2017

Corporation tax is charged for the financial year 2017.

46   Rate of corporation tax for financial year 2020

In section 7(2) of F(No.2)A 2015 (main rate of corporation tax for the financial year 2020) for "18%" substitute "17%".

Research and development

47   Abolition of vaccine research relief

(1)   CTA 2009 is amended in accordance with subsections (2) to (9).

(2)   Omit Chapter 7 of Part 13 (vaccine research relief).

(3)   In section 1039 (overview of Part 13) omit—

    (a)   subsection (6), and

    (b)   in subsection (8) "or 7".

(4)   In section 1042 (meaning of "relevant research and development") omit subsection (3).

(5)   In section 1113 (cap on aid under Chapters 2 and 7) –
        (a)   in the heading omit "or 7", and
        (b)   in subsection (4) omit –
                (i)   the "or" at the end of paragraph (a), and
                (ii)   paragraph (b).

(6)   In section 1118(2) (meaning of "qualifying expenditure") omit –
        (a)   the "or" at the end of paragraph (a), and
        (b)   paragraph (b).

(7)   In section 1133(3) (sub-contractor payments) omit "and section 1102(2)."

(8)   In section 1137(1)(b) (accounting periods) omit "or qualifying Chapter 7 expenditure".

(9)   In Schedule 4 (index of defined expressions) omit the entries for –
        (a)   qualifying Chapter 7 expenditure (in Part 13), and
        (b)   qualifying R&D activity (in Chapter 7 of Part 13).

(10)   CTA 2010 is amended in accordance with subsections (11) to (13).

(11)   In section 357P (research and development expenditure: introduction and interpretation) –
        (a)   in subsection (1) omit –
                (i)   the "and" at the end of paragraph (b), and
                (ii)   paragraph (c), and
        (b)   omit subsection (2)(d) and (e).

(12)   Omit section 357PF (additional deduction under section 1087 CTA 2009).

(13)   In Schedule 4 (index of defined expressions) omit the entries for –
        (a)   Northern Ireland qualifying Chapter 7 expenditure (in Chapter 9 of Part 8B), and
        (b)   qualifying Chapter 7 expenditure (in Chapter 9 of Part 8B).

(14)   In consequence of the amendments made by subsections (1) to (13) –
        (a)   in Schedule 3 to FA 2012 omit paragraphs 7, 12 to 14, 16(2), 17, 20 to 30, and 31(2), and
        (b)   in FA 2015 omit section 28(4)(o) and (p).

(15)   The amendments made by this section have effect in relation to expenditure incurred on or after 1 April 2017.

48   Cap on R&D aid

(1)   CTA 2009 is amended as follows.

(2)   In section 1114 (calculation of total R&D aid) –
        (a)   in the formula for "(N x CT)" substitute "N", and
        (b)   in the definition of "N" for "relief" substitute "R&D expenditure credit".

(3)   In section 1118(1) (meaning of "notional relief") –

    (a)   for "relief" in the first two places it occurs substitute "R&D expenditure credit",

    (b)   for "Chapter 5 (relief for large companies)" substitute "Chapter 6A of Part 3 (trade profits: R&D expenditure credits)", and

    (c)   in the heading for "relief" substitute "R&D expenditure credit".

(4)   The amendments made by this section have effect in relation to expenditure incurred on or after 1 April 2016.

Loan relationships

49   Loan relationships and derivative contracts

Schedule 7 contains amendments relating to loan relationships and derivative contracts.

50   Loans to participators etc: rate of tax

(1)   In section 455 of CTA 2010 (charge to tax in case of loan to participator), in subsection (2), for "25% of the amount of the loan or advance" substitute "such percentage of the amount of the loan or advance as corresponds to the dividend upper rate specified in section 8(2) of ITA 2007 for the tax year in which the loan or advance is made".

(2)   The amendment made by subsection (1) has effect in relation to a loan or advance made on or after 6 April 2016.

(3)   In section 464A of CTA 2010 (charge to tax: arrangements conferring benefit on participator), in subsection (3), for "25% of the value of the benefit conferred" substitute "such percentage of the value of the benefit conferred as corresponds to the dividend upper rate specified in section 8(2) of ITA 2007 for the tax year in which the benefit is conferred".

(4)   The amendment made by subsection (3) has effect in relation to a benefit conferred on or after 6 April 2016.

51   Loans to participators etc: trustees of charitable trusts

(1)   In section 456 of CTA 2010 (exceptions to the charge to tax in case of loan to participator), after subsection (2) insert—

    "(2A)   Section 455 does not apply to a loan or advance made to a trustee of a charitable trust if the loan or advance is applied to the purposes of the charitable trust only."

(2)   The amendment made by subsection (1) has effect in relation to a loan or advance made on or after 25 November 2015.

Intangible fixed assets

52   Intangible fixed assets: pre-FA 2002 assets

(1)   Chapter 16 of Part 8 of CTA 2009 (pre-FA 2002 assets) is amended as follows.

(2)   In section 882 (application of Part 8 to assets created or acquired on or after 1

April 2002), after subsection (5) insert—

"(5A)   References in this section to one person being (or not being) a related party in relation to another person are to be read as including references to the participation condition being met (or, as the case may be, not met) as between those persons.

(5B)   References in subsection (5A) to a person include a firm in a case where, for section 1259 purposes, references in this section to a company are read as references to the firm.

(5C)   In subsection (5B) "section 1259 purposes" means the purposes of determining under section 1259 the amount of profits or losses to be allocated to a partner in a firm.

(5D)   Section 148 of TIOPA 2010 (when the participation condition is met) applies for the purposes of subsection (5A) as it applies for the purposes of section 147(1)(b) of TIOPA 2010."

(3)   In section 894 (preserved status condition etc), after subsection (6) insert—

"(6A)   Section 882(5A) to (5D) applies for the purposes of section 893 and this section."

(4)   In section 895 (assets acquired in connection with disposals of pre-FA 2002 assets), at the end insert—

"(5)   Section 882(5A) to (5D) applies for the purposes of this section."

(5)   The amendments made by this section have effect in relation to accounting periods beginning on or after 25 November 2015.

(6)   For the purposes of subsection (5), an accounting period beginning before and ending on or after 25 November 2015 is to be treated as if so much of the accounting period as falls before that date, and so much of the accounting period as falls on or after that date, were separate accounting periods.

(7)   An apportionment for the purposes of subsection (6) must be made—
    (a)   in accordance with section 1172 of CTA 2010 (time basis), or
    (b)   if that method produces a result that is unjust or unreasonable, on a just and reasonable basis.

53   Intangible fixed assets: transfers treated as at market value

(1)   In section 845 of CTA 2009 (transfer between company and related party treated as at market value), after subsection (4) insert—

"(4A)   References in subsection (1) to a related party in relation to a company are to be read as including references to a person in circumstances where the participation condition is met as between that person and the company.

(4B)   References in subsection (4A) to a company include a firm in a case where, for section 1259 purposes, references in subsection (1) to a company are read as references to the firm.

(4C)   Section 148 of TIOPA 2010 (when the participation condition is met) applies for the purposes of subsection (4A) as it applies for the purposes of section 147(1)(b) of TIOPA 2010.

(4D) Subsection (4E) applies where—
   (a) a gain on the disposal of an intangible asset by a firm is a gain to be taken into account for section 1259 purposes, and
   (b) for those purposes, references in subsection (1) to a company are read as references to the firm.

(4E) Where this subsection applies, the gain referred to in subsection (4D)(a) is to be treated for the purposes of this section as if it were a chargeable realisation gain for the purposes of section 741(1) (meaning of "chargeable intangible asset").

(4F) In this section, "section 1259 purposes" means the purposes of determining under section 1259 the amount of profits or losses to be allocated to a partner in a firm."

(2) The amendment made by this section applies in relation to a transfer which takes place on or after 25 November 2015, unless it takes place pursuant to an obligation, under a contract, that was unconditional before that date.

(3) For the purposes of subsection (2), an obligation is "unconditional" if it may not be varied or extinguished by the exercise of a right (whether under the contract or otherwise).

Creative industry reliefs

54 Tax relief for production of orchestral concerts

Schedule 8 contains provision about relief in respect of the production of orchestral concerts.

55 Television and video games tax relief: consequential amendments

In the following provisions, for "section 1218" substitute "section 1218B"—
   (a) paragraph 8(2)(c) of Schedule 7A to TCGA 1992,
   (b) section 63(1) of CTA 2010, and
   (c) section 729 of CTA 2010.

Banking companies

56 Banking companies: excluded entities

(1) Section 133F of CTA 2009 ("excluded company") has effect, and is to be deemed always to have had effect, with the amendments set out in subsections (2) to (4).

(2) After subsection (2) insert—

"(2A) A company is also an "excluded company" at any time (in an accounting period) if—
   (a) the company would fall within a relevant relieving provision but for one (and only one) line of business which it carries on,
   (b) that line of business does not involve the relevant regulated activity described in the provision mentioned in section 133G(1)(a), and

        (c)   the company's activities in that line of business would not, on their own, result in it being both a 730k firm and a full scope investment firm.

    (2B)   For the purposes of subsection (2A) the "relevant relieving provisions" are paragraphs (b), (c), (e), (g) and (h) of subsection (2)."

(3)   In subsection (7), before the definition of "authorised corporate director" insert—

        ""730k firm"—

           (a)   in relation to any time on or after 1 January 2014, means an IFPRU 730k firm,

           (b)   in relation to any time before that date, means a BIPRU 730k firm;".

(4)   In subsection (7), at the appropriate places insert—

        ""BIPRU 730k firm" and "full scope BIPRU investment firm" have the same meaning as in subsections (2) to (4) of section 133H;"

        ""IFPRU 730k firm" and full scope IFPRU investment firm" have the meaning given by the FCA Handbook at the time in question;"

        ""full scope investment firm"—

           (a)   in relation to any time on or after 1 January 2014, means a full scope IFPRU investment firm,

           (b)   in relation to any time before that date, means a full scope BIPRU investment firm;".

(5)   Section 133M of CTA 2009 has effect, and is to be deemed always to have had effect, with the amendment set out in subsection (6).

(6)   For subsection (5)(b)(ii) substitute—

        "(ii)   the firm would not (if references in section 133F(2) and (3) to companies included firms) be an excluded company for the purposes of section 133E."

(7)   Part 7A of CTA 2010 has effect, and is to be deemed always to have had effect, with the amendments set out in subsections (8) and (9).

(8)   In section 269BA (excluded entities), after subsection (1) insert—

    "(1A)   For the purposes of section 269B an entity is also an "excluded entity" if—

        (a)   the entity would fall within a relevant relieving provision but for one (and only one) line of business which it carries on,

        (b)   that line of business does not involve the relevant regulated activity described in the provision mentioned in section 269BB(a), and

        (c)   the entity's activities in that line of business would not, on their own, result in it being both an IFPRU 730k firm and a full scope IFPRU investment firm.

    (1B)   For the purposes of subsection (1A) the "relevant relieving provisions" are paragraphs (b), (c), (e), (g) and (h) of subsection (1)."

(9)   In section 269DO (interpretation)—

(a) after subsection (5) insert—

"(5A) For the purposes of section 269BA(1A) (extension of certain exclusions under subsection (1) of that section) a line of business carried on by a company is not regarded as involving the relevant regulated activity described in the provision mentioned in section 269BB(a) if—

(a) the carrying on of that activity is ancillary to asset management activities the company carries on, and

(b) the company would not carry that activity on but for the fact that it carries on asset management activities.";

(b) in subsection (6) for "subsection (5)" substitute "subsections (5) and (5A)".

(10) In Schedule 19 to FA 2011 (the bank levy), paragraph 73 is amended in accordance with subsections (11) and (12).

(11) In sub-paragraph (1), omit "or" at the end of paragraph (j) and after paragraph (k) insert ", or

(l) an entity falling within sub-paragraph (1A)."

(12) After sub-paragraph (1) insert—

"(1A) An entity falls within this sub-paragraph if—

(a) it would fall within a relevant relieving provision but for one (and only one) line of business which it carries on,

(b) that line of business does not involve the relevant regulated activity described in the provision mentioned in paragraph 79(a), and

(c) the entity's activities in that line of business would not, on their own, result in it being both an IFPRU 730k firm and a full scope IFPRU investment firm.

(1B) For the purposes of sub-paragraph (1A) the "relevant relieving provisions" are paragraphs (b), (c), (e), (g) and (h) of sub-paragraph (1)."

(13) Subsections (10) to (12) have effect in relation to chargeable periods beginning on or after the day on which this Act is passed.

(14) But for the purposes of determining what groups and entities must be listed under subsection (4) of section 285 of FA 2014 (Code of Practice on Taxation for Banks: HMRC reports) in any relevant report under that section—

(a) subsection (13) is to be disregarded, and

(b) Schedule 19 to FA 2011 is to be deemed to have effect, and always to have had effect, with the amendments set out in subsections (10) to (12).

(15) In subsection (14) "relevant report" means a report for the reporting period beginning with 1 April 2015 or any subsequent reporting period.

57 Banking companies: restrictions on loss relief etc

(1) Chapter 3 of Part 7A of CTA 2010 (restrictions on banking companies obtaining certain deductions) is amended as follows.

(2) In section 269CA (restriction on deductions for trading losses), in subsection (2), for "50%" substitute "25%".

(3) In section 269CB (restriction on deductions for non-trading deficits from loan relationships), in subsection (2), for "50%" substitute "25%".

(4) In section 269CC (restriction on deductions for management expenses etc), in step 1 in subsection (7), for "50%" substitute "25%".

(5) The amendments made by this section have effect for the purposes of determining the taxable total profits of companies for accounting periods beginning on or after 1 April 2016.

(6) For the purposes of subsection (5), where a company has an accounting period beginning before 1 April 2016 and ending on or after that date ("the straddling period")—

    (a) so much of the straddling period as falls before 1 April 2016, and so much of that period as falls on or after that date, are treated as separate accounting periods, and

    (b) profits or losses of the company for the straddling period are apportioned to the two separate accounting periods—

        (i) in accordance with section 1172 of CTA 2010 (time basis), or

        (ii) if that method would produce a result that is unjust or unreasonable, on a just and reasonable basis.

Oil and gas

58 Reduction in rate of supplementary charge

(1) In section 330 of CTA 2010 (supplementary charge in respect of ring fence trades), in subsection (1), for "20%" substitute "10%".

(2) The amendment made by subsection (1) has effect in relation to accounting periods beginning on or after 1 January 2016 (but see also subsection (3)).

(3) Subsections (4) and (5) apply where a company has an accounting period beginning before 1 January 2016 and ending on or after that date ("the straddling period").

(4) For the purpose of calculating the amount of the supplementary charge on the company for the straddling period—

    (a) so much of that period as falls before 1 January 2016, and so much of that period as falls on or after that date, are treated as separate accounting periods, and

    (b) the company's adjusted ring fence profits for the straddling period are apportioned to the two separate accounting periods in proportion to the number of days in those periods.

(5) The amount of the supplementary charge on the company for the straddling period is the sum of the amounts of supplementary charge that would, in accordance with subsection (4), be chargeable on the company for those separate accounting periods.

(6) In this section—

    "adjusted ring fence profits" has the same meaning as in section 330 of CTA 2010;

    "supplementary charge" means any sum chargeable under section 330(1) of CTA 2010 as if it were an amount of corporation tax.

59   Investment allowance: disqualifying conditions

(1)   Section 332D of CTA 2010 (expenditure on acquisition of asset: disqualifying conditions) is amended as follows.

(2)   In subsection (1) after "an asset" insert "("the acquisition concerned")".

(3)   In subsection (2) —
    (a)   for "acquisition," substitute "acquisition concerned," and
    (b)   after "acquiring," insert "leasing,".

(4)   In subsection (3)(b) —
    (a)   for "acquisition," substitute "acquisition concerned,", and
    (b)   after "acquiring," insert "leasing,".

(5)   After subsection (4) insert —

    "(5)   In subsection (3)(c) "this Chapter" means the provisions of this Chapter, and of any regulations made under this Chapter, as those provisions have effect at the time when the investment expenditure mentioned in subsection (1) is incurred.

    (6)   Subsections (7) and (8) apply where investment expenditure mentioned in subsection (1) would, in the absence of this section, be relievable under section 332C by reason of section 332CA (treatment of expenditure incurred before field is determined).

    (7)   Where this subsection applies —
        (a)   subsection (2) is to be read as if after "was" there were inserted ", or has become,", and
        (b)   in determining for the purposes of subsection (2) or (3)(b) whether particular expenditure was incurred "before" the acquisition concerned —
            (i)   paragraph (b) of section 332CA(3) is to be ignored, and
            (ii)   accordingly, that expenditure is to be taken (for the purposes of determining whether it was incurred before the acquisition concerned) to have been incurred when it was actually incurred.

    (8)   Where this subsection applies, in determining whether the second disqualifying condition applies to the asset —
        (a)   the reference in subsection (3)(a)(i) to a qualifying oil field is to be read as including an area which, at the time of the acquisition concerned, had not been determined to be an oil field but which has subsequently become a qualifying oil field,
        (b)   the reference in subsection (3)(a)(ii) to a qualifying oil field is to be read as including an area which, at the time of the transfer, had not been determined to be an oil field but which has subsequently become a qualifying oil field,
        (c)   the reference in subsection (3)(c)(i) to "the qualifying oil field" is to be read accordingly, and
        (d)   the following sub-paragraph is to be treated as substituted for subsection (3)(c)(ii) —
                "(ii)   would have been relievable under section 332C if this Chapter had been fully in force and had applied to expenditure incurred at the time

when that expenditure was actually incurred and the area in question had been a qualifying oil field at that time."

(9) In subsection (8)(a) and (b) "determined" means determined under Schedule 1 to OTA 1975.

(10) In this section any reference to expenditure which was incurred by a company in "leasing" an asset is to expenditure incurred by the company under an agreement under which the asset was leased to the company."

(6) The amendments made by this section have effect for the purposes of determining whether any expenditure—

    (a) incurred by a company on or after 16 March 2016 on the acquisition of an asset, or

    (b) treated under section 332CA of CTA 2010 as so incurred,

is relievable expenditure for the purposes of section 332C of CTA 2010.

60 Investment allowance: power to expand meaning of "relevant income"

(1) Section 332F of CTA 2010 (activation of investment allowance) is amended as follows.

(2) In subsection (2)(b) before "the company's relevant income" insert "the total amount of".

(3) For subsection (3) substitute—

"(3) For the purposes of this Chapter, income is relevant income of a company from a qualifying oil field for an accounting period if it is—

    (a) production income of the company from any oil extraction activities carried on in that oil field that is taken into account in calculating the company's adjusted ring fence profits for the accounting period, or

    (b) income that—

        (i) is income of such description (whether or not relating to the oil field) as may be prescribed by the Treasury by regulations, and

        (ii) is taken into account as mentioned in paragraph (a).

(4) The Treasury may by regulations make such amendments of this Chapter as the Treasury consider appropriate in consequence of, or in connection with, any provision contained in regulations under subsection (3)(b).

(5) Regulations under subsection (3)(b) or (4) may provide for any of the provisions of the regulations to have effect in relation to accounting periods ending before (or current when) the regulations are made.

(6) But subsection (5) does not apply to—

    (a) any provision of amending or revoking regulations under subsection (3)(b) which has the effect that income of any description is to cease to be treated as relevant income of a company from a qualifying oil field for an accounting period, or

   (b) provision made under subsection (4) in consequence of or in connection with provision within paragraph (a).

(7) Regulations under this section may make transitional provision or savings.

(8) Regulations under this section may not be made unless a draft of the instrument containing them has been laid before, and approved by a resolution of, the House of Commons."

61 Onshore allowance: disqualifying conditions

(1) CTA 2010 is amended as follows.

(2) In section 356C after subsection (4) insert—

   "(4A) Subsections (1) to (4) are subject to section 356CAA (which prevents expenditure on the acquisition of an asset from being relievable in certain circumstances)."

(3) After section 356CA insert—

"356CAA Expenditure on acquisition of asset: further disqualifying conditions

(1) Capital expenditure incurred by a company ("the acquiring company") on the acquisition of an asset ("the acquisition concerned") is not relievable capital expenditure for the purposes of section 356C if subsection (2), (3) or (8) applies to the asset.

(2) This subsection applies to the asset if capital expenditure incurred before the acquisition concerned, by the acquiring company or another company, in acquiring, bringing into existence or enhancing the value of the asset was relievable under section 356C.

(3) This subsection applies to the asset if—
   (a) the asset—
      (i) is the whole or part of the equity in a qualifying site, or
      (ii) is acquired in connection with a transfer to the acquiring company of the whole or part of the equity in a qualifying site,
   (b) capital expenditure was incurred before the acquisition concerned, by the acquiring company or another company, in acquiring, bringing into existence or enhancing the value of the asset, and
   (c) any of that expenditure—
      (i) related to the qualifying site, and
      (ii) would have been relievable under section 356C if this Chapter had been fully in force and had applied to expenditure incurred at that time.

(4) For the purposes of subsection (3)(a)(ii) it does not matter whether the asset is acquired at the time of the transfer.

(5) In subsection (3)(c) "this Chapter" means the provisions of this Chapter as those provisions have effect at the time when the capital expenditure mentioned in subsection (1) is incurred.

(6) The reference in subsection (3)(c)(i) to the qualifying site includes an area that, although not a qualifying site when the expenditure mentioned in subsection (3)(b) was incurred, subsequently became the qualifying site.

(7) Where expenditure mentioned in subsection (3)(b) related to an area which subsequently became the qualifying site, the following sub-paragraph is to be treated as substituted for subsection (3)(c)(ii) —

"(ii) would have been relievable under section 356C if the area in question had been a qualifying site when the expenditure was incurred, or if the area in question had been such a site at that time and this Chapter had been fully in force and had applied to expenditure incurred at that time."

(8) This subsection applies to the asset if —

(a) capital expenditure mentioned in subsection (1) would, in the absence of this section, be relievable under section 356C by reason of an election under section 356CB (treatment of expenditure not related to an established site), and

(b) capital expenditure which was incurred before the acquisition concerned, by the acquiring company or another company, in acquiring, bringing into existence or enhancing the value of the asset, either —

(i) has become relievable under section 356C by reason of an election under section 356CB, or

(ii) would be so relievable if such an election were made in respect of that expenditure.

(9) In determining for the purposes of subsection (8)(b) whether particular expenditure was incurred "before" the acquisition concerned —

(a) paragraph (b) of section 356CB(6) is to be ignored, and

(b) accordingly, that expenditure is to be taken (for the purposes of determining whether it was incurred before the acquistion concerned) to have been incurred when it was actually incurred.

(10) For the purposes of subsection (8)(b)(ii) it does not matter if an election is not in fact capable of being made."

(4) The amendments made by this section have effect for the purposes of determining whether any expenditure —

(a) incurred by a company on or after 16 March 2016 on the acquisition of an asset, or

(b) treated by reason of an election under section 356CB as so incurred,

is relievable expenditure for the purposes of section 356C of CTA 2010.

62 Cluster area allowance: disqualifying conditions

(1) Section 356JFA of CTA 2010 (expenditure on acquisition of asset: disqualifying conditions) is amended as follows.

(2) In subsection (2) after "acquiring," insert "leasing,".

(3) In subsection (3)(b) after "acquiring," insert "leasing,".

(4) After subsection (4) insert—

"(5) In this section any reference to expenditure which was incurred by a company in "leasing" an asset is to expenditure incurred by the company under an agreement under which the asset was leased to the company."

(5) The amendments made by this section have effect for the purposes of determining whether any expenditure incurred by a company on or after 16 March 2016 on the acquisition of an asset is relievable expenditure for the purposes of section 356JF of CTA 2010.

63 Cluster area allowance: power to expand meaning of "relevant income"

(1) Section 356JH of CTA 2010 (activation of cluster area allowance) is amended as follows.

(2) In subsection (2)(b) before "the company's relevant income" insert "the total amount of".

(3) For subsection (3) substitute—

"(3) For the purposes of this Chapter, income is relevant income of a company from a cluster area for an accounting period if it is—
  (a) production income of the company from any oil extraction activities carried on in that area that is taken into account in calculating the company's adjusted ring fence profits for the accounting period, or
  (b) income that—
    (i) is income of such description (whether or not relating to the cluster area) as may be prescribed by the Treasury by regulations, and
    (ii) is taken into account as mentioned in paragraph (a).

(4) The Treasury may by regulations make such amendments of this Chapter as the Treasury consider appropriate in consequence of, or in connection with, any provision contained in regulations under subsection (3)(b).

(5) Regulations under subsection (3)(b) or (4) may provide for any of the provisions of the regulations to have effect in relation to accounting periods ending before (or current when) the regulations are made.

(6) But subsection (5) does not apply to—
  (a) any provision of amending or revoking regulations under subsection (3)(b) which has the effect that income of any description is to cease to be treated as relevant income of a company from a cluster area for an accounting period, or
  (b) provision made under subsection (4) in consequence of or in connection with provision within paragraph (a).

(7) Regulations under this section may make transitional provision or savings.

(8) Regulations under this section may not be made unless a draft of the instrument containing them has been laid before, and approved by a resolution of, the House of Commons."

Exploitation of patents etc

64   Profits from the exploitation of patents etc

(1)   Part 8A of CTA 2010 (profits arising from the exploitation of patents etc) is amended as follows.

(2)   In section 357A (election for special treatment of profits from patents etc) —

    (a)   for subsections (6) and (7) substitute —

        "(6)   Chapter 2A makes provision for determining the relevant IP profits or relevant IP losses of a trade of a company for an accounting period in a case where —

            (a)   the accounting period begins on or after 1 July 2021, or

            (b)   the company is a new entrant (see subsection (11)).

        (7)   Chapters 2B, 3 and 4 make provision for determining the relevant IP profits or relevant IP losses of a trade of a company for an accounting period in various cases where —

            (a)   the accounting period begins before 1 July 2021, and

            (b)   the company is not a new entrant.", and

    (b)   after subsection (10) insert —

        "(11)   A company is a "new entrant" for the purposes of this Part if —

            (a)   the first accounting period for which the company's election (or most recent election) under subsection (1) has effect begins on or after 1 July 2016, or

            (b)   the company elects to be treated as a new entrant for the purposes of this Part."

(3)   After section 357BE insert —

"CHAPTER 2A

RELEVANT IP PROFITS: CASES MENTIONED IN SECTION 357A(6)

Steps for calculating relevant IP profits of a trade

357BF   Relevant IP profits

(1)   This section applies for the purposes of determining the relevant IP profits of a trade of a company for an accounting period in a case where —

    (a)   the accounting period begins on or after 1 July 2021, or

    (b)   the company is a new entrant (see section 357A(11)).

(2)   To determine the relevant IP profits —

Step 1

Take any amounts which are brought into account as credits in calculating the profits of the trade for the accounting period, other than any amounts of finance income (see section 357BG), and divide them into two "streams", amounts of relevant IP income (see sections 357BH to 357BHC) and amounts that are not amounts of relevant IP income.

The stream consisting of relevant IP income is "the relevant IP income stream"; the other stream is the "standard income stream".

Step 2

Divide the relevant IP income stream into "relevant IP income sub-streams" so that each sub-stream is—

    (a)   a sub-stream consisting of income properly attributable to a particular qualifying IP right (an "individual IP right sub-stream"),

    (b)   a sub-stream consisting of income properly attributable to a particular kind of IP item (a "product sub-stream"), or

    (c)   a sub-stream consisting of income properly attributable to a particular kind of IP process (a "process sub-stream").

See subsection (5) for the meaning of "IP item" and "IP process" and see subsections (6) and (7) for further provision in connection with product sub-streams and process sub-streams.

Step 3

Take any amounts which are brought into account as debits in calculating the profits of the trade for the accounting period, other than any excluded debits (see section 357BI), and allocate them on a just and reasonable basis between the standard income stream and each of the relevant IP income sub-streams.

Step 4

Deduct from each relevant IP income sub-stream—

    (a)   the amounts allocated to the sub-stream at Step 3, and

    (b)   the routine return figure for the sub-stream (see section 357BJ).

But see section 357BIA (which provides that certain amounts allocated to a relevant IP income sub-stream at Step 3 are not to be deducted from the sub-stream at this Step).

Step 5

Deduct from each relevant IP income sub-stream which is greater than nil following Step 4 the marketing assets return figure for the sub-stream (see section 357BK).

Step 6

Multiply the amount of each relevant IP income sub-stream (following the deductions required at Steps 4 and 5) by the R&D fraction for the sub-stream (see section 357BL).

Step 7

Add together the amounts of the relevant IP income sub-streams (following Step 6).

Step 8

If the company has made an election under section 357BM (which provides in certain circumstances for profits arising before the grant of a right to be treated as relevant IP profits), add to the amount given by Step 7 any amount determined in accordance with subsection (3) of that section.

(3)   If the amount given by subsection (2) is greater than nil, that amount is the relevant IP profits of the trade for the accounting period.

(4)   If the amount given by subsection (2) is less than nil, that amount is the relevant IP losses of the trade for the accounting period (see Chapter 5).

(5)   In this section—

        "IP item" means—

   (a) an item in respect of which a qualifying IP right held by the company has been granted, or

   (b) an item which incorporates one or more items within paragraph (a);

  "IP process" means—

   (a) a process in respect of which a qualifying IP right held by the company has been granted, or

   (b) a process which incorporates one or more processes within paragraph (a).

(6) For the purposes of this section two or more IP items, or two or more IP processes, may be treated as being of a particular kind if they are intended to be, or are capable of being, used for the same or substantially the same purposes.

(7) Income may be allocated at Step 2 of subsection (2) to a product sub-stream or process sub-stream only if—

  (a) it would not be reasonably practicable to apportion the income between individual IP right sub-streams, or

  (b) it would be reasonably practicable to do that but doing so would result in it not being reasonably practicable to apply any of the remaining steps in subsection (2).

(8) Any reference in this section to a qualifying IP right held by the company includes a reference to a qualifying IP right in respect of which the company holds an exclusive licence.

Finance income

357BG Finance income

(1) For the purposes of this Part "finance income", in relation to a trade of a company, means—

  (a) any credits which are treated as receipts of the trade by virtue of—

   (i) section 297 of CTA 2009 (credits in respect of loan relationships), or

   (ii) section 573 of CTA 2009 (credits in respect of derivative contracts),

  (b) any amount which in accordance with generally accepted accounting practice falls to be recognised as arising from a financial asset, and

  (c) any return, in relation to an amount, which—

   (i) is produced for the company by an arrangement to which it is a party, and

   (ii) is economically equivalent to interest.

(2) In subsection (1)—

  "economically equivalent to interest" is to be construed in accordance with section 486B(2) and (3) of CTA 2009, and

  "financial asset" means a financial asset as defined for the purposes of generally accepted accounting practice.

(3) For the purposes of subsection (1)(c), the amount of a return is the amount which by virtue of the return would, in calculating the company's chargeable profits, be treated under section 486B of CTA 2009 (disguised interest to be regarded as profit from loan relationship) as profit arising to the company from a loan relationship.

But, in calculating that profit for the purposes of this subsection, sections 486B(7) and 486C to 486E of that Act are to be ignored.

Relevant IP income

357BH Relevant IP income

(1) For the purposes of this Part "relevant IP income" means income falling within any of the Heads set out in—

    (a) subsection (2) (sales income),

    (b) subsection (6) (licence fees),

    (c) subsection (7) (proceeds of sale etc),

    (d) subsection (8) (damages for infringement), and

    (e) subsection (9) (other compensation).

This is subject to section 357BHB (excluded income).

(2) Head 1 is income arising from the sale by the company of any of the following items—

    (a) items in respect of which a qualifying IP right held by the company has been granted ("qualifying items");

    (b) items incorporating one or more qualifying items;

    (c) items that are wholly or mainly designed to be incorporated into items within paragraph (a) or (b).

(3) For the purposes of this Part an item and its packaging are not to be treated as a single item, unless the packaging performs a function that is essential for the use of the item for the purposes for which it is intended to be used.

(4) In subsection (3) "packaging", in relation to an item, means any form of container or other packaging used for the containment, protection, handling, delivery or presentation of the item, including by way of attaching the item to, or winding the item round, some other article.

(5) In a case where a qualifying item and an item that is designed to incorporate that item ("the parent item") are sold together as, or as part of, a single unit for a single price, the reference in subsection (2)(b) to an item incorporating a qualifying item includes a reference to the parent item.

(6) Head 2 is income consisting of any licence fee or royalty which the company receives under an agreement granting another person any of the following rights only—

    (a) a right in respect of any qualifying IP right held by the company,

    (b) any other right in respect of a qualifying item or process, and

    (c) in the case of an agreement granting any right within paragraph (a) or (b), a right granted for the same purposes as those for which that right was granted.

In this subsection "qualifying process" means a process in respect of which a qualifying IP right held by the company has been granted.

(7) Head 3 is any income arising from the sale or other disposal of a qualifying IP right or an exclusive licence in respect of such a right.

(8) Head 4 is any amount received by the company in respect of an infringement, or alleged infringement, of a qualifying IP right held by the company at the time of the infringement or alleged infringement.

(9) Head 5 is any amount of damages, proceeds of insurance or other compensation, other than an amount in respect of an infringement or alleged infringement of a qualifying IP right, which is received by the company in respect of an event and —

    (a) is paid in respect of any items that fell within subsection (2) at the time of that event, or

    (b) represents a loss of income which would, if received by the company at the time of that event, have been relevant IP income.

(10) But income is not relevant IP income by virtue of subsection (8) or (9) unless the event in respect of which the income is received, or any part of that event, occurred at a time when —

    (a) the company was a qualifying company, and

    (b) an election under section 357A(1) had effect in relation to it.

(11) In a case where the whole of that event does not occur at such a time, subsection (8) or (9) (as the case may be) applies only to so much of the amount received by the company in respect of the event as on a just and reasonable apportionment is properly attributable to such a time.

(12) Any reference in this section to a qualifying IP right held by the company includes a reference to a qualifying IP right in respect of which the company holds an exclusive licence.

357BHA Notional royalty

(1) This section applies where —

    (a) a company holds a qualifying IP right or an exclusive licence in respect of a qualifying IP right,

    (b) the qualifying IP right falls within paragraph (a), (b) or (c) of section 357BB(1), and

    (c) the income of a trade of the company for an accounting period includes income ("IP-derived income") which —

        (i) arises from things done by the company that involve the exploitation by the company of the qualifying IP right, and

        (ii) is not relevant IP income, finance income or excluded income.

(2) The company may elect that the appropriate percentage of the IP-derived income is to be treated for the purposes of this Part as if it were relevant IP income.

(3) The "appropriate percentage" is the proportion of the IP-derived income which the company would pay another person ("P") for the

right to exploit the qualifying IP right in the accounting period concerned if the company were not otherwise able to exploit it.

(4) For the purposes of determining the appropriate percentage under this section, assume that—

    (a) the company and P are dealing at arm's length,

    (b) the company, or the company and persons authorised by it, will have the right to exploit the qualifying IP right to the exclusion of any other person (including P),

    (c) the company will have the same rights in relation to the qualifying IP right as it actually has,

    (d) the right to exploit the qualifying IP right is conferred on the relevant day,

    (e) the appropriate percentage is determined at the beginning of the accounting period concerned,

    (f) the appropriate percentage will apply for each succeeding accounting period for which the company will have the right to exploit the qualifying IP right, and

    (g) no income other than IP-derived income will arise from anything done by the company that involves the exploitation by the company of the qualifying IP right.

(5) In subsection (4)(d) "the relevant day" means—

    (a) the first day of the accounting period concerned, or

    (b) if later, the day on which the company first began to hold the qualifying IP right or licence.

(6) In determining the appropriate percentage, the company must act in accordance with—

    (a) Article 9 of the OECD Model Tax Convention, and

    (b) the OECD transfer pricing guidelines.

(7) In this section "excluded income" means any income falling within either of the Heads in section 357BHB.

357BHB Excluded income

(1) For the purposes of this Part income falling within either of the Heads set out in the following subsections is not relevant IP income—

    (a) subsection (2) (ring fence income),

    (b) subsection (3) (income attributable to non-exclusive licences).

(2) Head 1 is income arising from oil extraction activities or oil rights.

In this subsection "oil extraction activities" and "oil rights" have the same meaning as in Part 8 (see sections 272 and 273).

(3) Head 2 is income which on a just and reasonable apportionment is properly attributable to a licence (a "non-exclusive licence") held by the company which—

    (a) is a licence in respect of an item or process, but

    (b) is not an exclusive licence in respect of a qualifying IP right.

(4) In a case where—

    (a) a company holds an exclusive licence in respect of a qualifying IP right, and

    (b)   the licence also confers on the company (or on the company and persons authorised by it) any right in respect of the invention otherwise than to the exclusion of all other persons,

the licence is to be treated for the purposes of this Part as if it were two separate licences, one an exclusive licence that does not confer any such rights, and the other a non-exclusive licence conferring those rights.

357BHC Mixed sources of income

  (1)   This section applies to any income that—

      (a)   is mixed income, or

      (b)   is paid under a mixed agreement.

  (2)   "Mixed income" means the proceeds of sale where an item falling within subsection (2) of section 357BH and an item not falling within that subsection are sold together as, or as part of, a single unit for a single price.

  (3)   A "mixed agreement" is an agreement providing for—

      (a)   one or more of the matters in paragraphs (a) to (c) of subsection (4), and

      (b)   one or more of the matters in paragraphs (d) to (g) of that subsection.

  (4)   The matters are—

      (a)   the sale of an item falling within section 357BH(2),

      (b)   the grant of any right falling within paragraph (a), (b) or (c) of section 357BH(6),

      (c)   a sale or disposal falling within section 357BH(7),

      (d)   the sale of any other item,

      (e)   the grant of any other right,

      (f)   any other sale or disposal,

      (g)   the provision of any services.

  (5)   So much of the income as on a just and reasonable apportionment is properly attributable to—

      (a)   the sale of an item falling within section 357BH(2),

      (b)   the grant of any right falling within paragraph (a), (b) or (c) of section 357BH(6), or

      (c)   a sale or disposal falling within section 357BH(7),

is to be regarded for the purposes of this Part as relevant IP income.

  (6)   But where the amount of income that on such an apportionment is properly attributable to any of the matters in paragraphs (d) to (g) of subsection (4) is a trivial proportion of the income to which this section applies, all of that income is to be regarded for the purposes of this Part as relevant IP income.

Excluded debits etc

357BI Excluded debits

For the purposes of this Part "excluded debits" means—

    (a)   the amount of any debits which are treated as expenses of a trade by virtue of—

      (i)   section 297 of CTA 2009 (debits in respect of loan relationships), or

      (ii)   section 573 of CTA 2009 (debits in respect of derivative contracts),

   (b)   the amount of any additional deduction for an accounting period obtained by a company under Part 13 of CTA 2009 for expenditure on research and development in relation to a trade,

   (c)   the amount of any additional deduction for an accounting period obtained by a company under Part 15A of CTA 2009 in respect of qualifying expenditure on a television programme,

   (d)   the amount of any additional deduction for an accounting period obtained by a company under Part 15B of CTA 2009 in respect of qualifying expenditure on a video game, and

   (e)   the amount of any additional deduction for an accounting period obtained by a company under Part 15C of CTA 2009 in respect of qualifying expenditure on a theatrical production.

357BIA Certain amounts not to be deducted from sub-streams at Step 4 of section 357BF

(1)   This section applies where a company enters into an arrangement with a person under which—

   (a)   the person assigns to the company a qualifying IP right or grants or transfers to the company an exclusive licence in respect of a qualifying IP right, and

   (b)   the company makes to the person an income-related payment.

(2)   A payment is an "income-related payment" for the purposes of subsection (1) if—

   (a)   the obligation to make the payment arises under the arrangement by reason of the amount of income the company has accrued which is properly attributable to the right or licence, or

   (b)   the amount of the payment is determined under the arrangement by reference to the amount of income the company has accrued which is so attributable.

(3)   If the amount of the income-related payment is allocated to a relevant IP income sub-stream at Step 3 of section 357BF(2), the amount is not to be deducted from the sub-stream at Step 4 of section 357BF(2) unless the payment will not affect the R&D fraction for the sub-stream."

Routine return figure

357BJ Routine return figure

(1)   This section applies for the purpose of calculating the routine return figure for a relevant IP income sub-stream established at Step 2 in section 357BF(2) in determining the relevant IP profits of a trade of a company for an accounting period.

(2)   The routine return figure for the sub-stream is 10% of the aggregate of any routine deductions which—

   (a)   have been made by the company in calculating the profits of the trade for the accounting period, and

      (b)   have been allocated to the sub-stream at Step 3 in section 357BF(2).

For the meaning of "routine deductions", see sections 357BJA and 357BJB.

(3)   In a case where—

      (a)   the company ("C") is a member of a group,

      (b)   another member of the group has incurred expenses on behalf of C,

      (c)   had they been incurred by C, C would have made a deduction in respect of the expenses in calculating the profits of the trade for the accounting period,

      (d)   the deduction would have been a routine deduction, and

      (e)   the deduction would have been allocated to the sub-stream at Step 3 in section 357BF(2),

C is to be treated for the purposes of subsection (2) as having made such a routine deduction and as having allocated the deduction to the sub-stream.

(4)   Where expenses have been incurred by any member of the group on behalf of C and any other member of the group, subsection (3) applies in relation to so much of the amount of the expenses as on a just and reasonable apportionment may properly be regarded as incurred on behalf of C.

357BJA Routine deductions

(1)   For the purposes of this Part, "routine deductions" means deductions falling within any of the Heads set out in—

      (a)   subsection (2) (capital allowances),

      (b)   subsection (3) (costs of premises),

      (c)   subsection (4) (personnel costs),

      (d)   subsection (5) (plant and machinery costs),

      (e)   subsection (6) (professional services), and

      (f)   subsection (7) (miscellaneous services).

This is subject to section 357BJB (deductions that are not routine deductions).

(2)   Head 1 is any allowances under CAA 2001.

(3)   Head 2 is any deductions made by the company in respect of any premises occupied by the company.

(4)   Head 3 is any deductions made by the company in respect of—

      (a)   any director or employee of the company, or

      (b)   any externally provided workers.

(5)   Head 4 is any deductions made by the company in respect of any plant or machinery used by the company.

(6)   Head 5 is any deductions made by the company in respect of any of the following services—

      (a)   legal services, other than IP-related services;

      (b)   financial services, including—

            (i)   insurance services, and

       (ii)   valuation or actuarial services;

    (c)   services provided in connection with the administration or management of the company's directors and employees;

    (d)   any other consultancy services.

(7)   Head 6 is any deductions made by the company in respect of any of the following services —

    (a)   the supply of water, fuel or power;

    (b)   telecommunications services;

    (c)   computing services, including computer software;

    (d)   postal services;

    (e)   the transportation of any items;

    (f)   the collection, removal and disposal of refuse.

(8)   In this section —

    "externally provided worker" has the same meaning as in Part 13 of CTA 2009 (see section 1128 of that Act),

    "IP-related services" means services provided in connection with —

        (a)   any application for a right to which this Part applies, or

        (b)   any proceedings relating to the enforcement of any such right,

    "premises" includes any land,

    "telecommunications service" means any service that consists in the provision of access to, and of facilities for making use of, any telecommunication system (whether or not one provided by the person providing the service), and

    "telecommunication system" means any system (including the apparatus comprised in it) which exists for the purpose of facilitating the transmission of communications by any means involving the use of electrical or electromagnetic energy.

(9)   The Treasury may by regulations amend this section.

357BJB Deductions that are not routine deductions

(1)   For the purposes of this Part a deduction is not a "routine deduction" if it falls within any of the Heads set out in —

    (a)   subsection (2) (loan relationships and derivative contracts),

    (b)   subsection (3) (R&D expenses),

    (c)   subsection (4) (capital allowances for R&D or patents),

    (d)   subsection (5) (R&D-related employee share acquisitions),

    (e)   subsection (8) (television production expenditure),

    (f)   subsection (9) (video games development expenditure).

(2)   Head 1 is any debits which are treated as expenses of the trade by virtue of —

    (a)   section 297 of CTA 2009 (debits in respect of loan relationships), or

    (b)   section 573 of CTA 2009 (debits in respect of derivative contracts).

(3)   Head 2 is —

      (a)   the amount of any expenditure on research and development in relation to the trade—

          (i)   for which an additional deduction for the accounting period is obtained by the company under Part 13 of CTA 2009, or

          (ii)   in respect of which the company is entitled to an R&D expenditure credit for the accounting period under Chapter 6A of Part 3 of CTA 2009, and

      (b)   where the company obtains an additional deduction as mentioned in paragraph (a)(i), the amount of that additional deduction.

(4)   Head 3 is any allowances under—

      (a)   Part 6 of CAA 2001 (research and development allowances), or

      (b)   Part 8 of CAA 2001 (patent allowances).

(5)   Head 4 is the appropriate proportion of any deductions allowed under Part 12 of CTA 2009 (relief for employee share acquisitions) in a case where—

      (a)   shares are acquired by an employee or another person because of the employee's employment by the company, and

      (b)   the employee is wholly or partly engaged directly and actively in relevant research and development (within the meaning of section 1042 of CTA 2009).

(6)   In subsection (5) "the appropriate proportion", in relation to a deduction allowed in respect of an employee, is the proportion of the staffing costs in respect of the employee which are attributable to relevant research and development for the purposes of Part 13 of CTA 2009 (see section 1124 of that Act).

"Staffing costs" has the same meaning as in that Part (see section 1123 of that Act).

(7)   Subsections (5) and (6) of section 1124 of CTA 2009 apply for the purposes of subsection (5)(b) as they apply for the purposes of that section.

(8)   Head 5 is—

      (a)   the amount of any qualifying expenditure on a television programme for which an additional deduction for the accounting period is obtained by the company under Part 15A of CTA 2009, and

      (b)   the amount of that additional deduction.

(9)   Head 6 is—

      (a)   the amount of any qualifying expenditure on a video game for which an additional deduction for the accounting period is obtained by the company under Part 15B of CTA 2009, and

      (b)   the amount of that additional deduction.

(10)   The Treasury may by regulations amend this section.

Marketing assets return figure

357BK Marketing assets return figure

(1) The marketing assets return figure for a relevant IP income sub-stream is—

$$NMR - AMR$$

where—

NMR is the notional marketing royalty in respect of the sub-stream (see section 357BKA), and

AMR is the actual marketing royalty in respect of the sub-stream (see section 357BKB).

(2) Where—

(a) AMR is greater than NMR, or

(b) the difference between NMR and AMR is less than 10% of the amount of the relevant IP income sub-stream following the deductions required by Step 4 in section 357BF(2),

the marketing assets return figure for the sub-stream is nil.

357BKA Notional marketing royalty

(1) The notional marketing royalty in respect of a relevant IP income sub-stream is the appropriate percentage of the income allocated to that sub-stream at Step 2 in section 357BF(2).

(2) The "appropriate percentage" is the proportion of that income which the company would pay another person ("P") for the right to exploit the relevant marketing assets in the accounting period concerned if the company were not otherwise able to exploit them.

(3) For the purposes of this section a marketing asset is a "relevant marketing asset" in relation to a relevant IP income sub-stream if the sub-stream includes any income arising from things done by the company that involve the exploitation by the company of that marketing asset.

(4) For the purpose of determining the appropriate percentage under this section, assume that—

(a) the company and P are dealing at arm's length,

(b) the company, or the company and persons authorised by it, will have the right to exploit the relevant marketing assets to the exclusion of any other person (including P),

(c) the company will have the same rights in relation to the relevant marketing assets as it actually has,

(d) the right to exploit the relevant marketing assets is conferred on the relevant day,

(e) the appropriate percentage is determined at the beginning of the accounting period concerned,

(f) the appropriate percentage will apply for each succeeding accounting period for which the company will have the right to exploit the relevant marketing assets, and

(g) no income other than income within the relevant IP income sub-stream will arise from anything done by the company that involves the exploitation by the company of the relevant marketing assets.

(5) In subsection (4)(d) "the relevant day", in relation to a relevant marketing asset, means —

    (a) the first day of the accounting period concerned, or

    (b) if later, the day on which the company first acquired the relevant marketing asset or the right to exploit the asset.

(6) In determining the appropriate percentage, the company must act in accordance with —

    (a) Article 9 of the OECD Model Tax Convention, and

    (b) the OECD transfer pricing guidelines.

(7) In this section "marketing asset" means any of the following (whether or not capable of being transferred or assigned) —

    (a) anything in respect of which proceedings for passing off could be brought, including a registered trade mark (within the meaning of the Trade Marks Act 1994),

    (b) anything that corresponds to a marketing asset within paragraph (a) and is recognised under the law of a country or territory outside the United Kingdom,

    (c) any signs or indications (so far as not falling within paragraph (a) or (b)) which may serve, in trade, to designate the geographical origin of goods or services, and

    (d) any information which relates to customers or potential customers of the company, or any other member of a group of which the company is a member, and is intended to be used for marketing purposes.

357BKB Actual marketing royalty

(1) The actual marketing royalty for a relevant IP income sub-stream is the aggregate of any sums which —

    (a) were paid by the company for the purposes of acquiring any relevant marketing assets or the right to exploit any such assets, and

    (b) have been allocated to the sub-stream at Step 3 in section 357BF(2).

(2) In this section "relevant marketing asset" has the same meaning as in section 357BKA.

R&D fraction

357BL Introduction

(1) Sections 357BLA to 357BLH apply for the purpose of determining the R&D fraction for a relevant IP income sub-stream established at Step 2 in section 357BF(2) in determining the relevant IP profits of a trade of a company for an accounting period.

(2) In sections 357BLA to 357BLH, references to "the sub-stream", "the trade", "the company" and "the accounting period" are to the relevant IP income sub-stream, the trade, the company and the accounting period referred to in subsection (1).

357BLA The R&D fraction

(1) The R&D fraction for the sub-stream is the lesser of 1 and —

$$\frac{(D + S1) \times 1.3}{D + S1 + S2 + A}$$

where —

> D is the company's qualifying expenditure on relevant R&D undertaken in-house (see section 357BLB),
>
> S1 is the company's qualifying expenditure on relevant R&D sub-contracted to unconnected persons (see section 357BLC),
>
> S2 is the company's qualifying expenditure on relevant R&D sub-contracted to connected persons (see section 357BLD), and
>
> A is the company's qualifying expenditure on the acquisition of relevant qualifying IP rights (see section 357BLE).

(2) This section is subject to section 357BLH (R&D fraction: increase for exceptional circumstances).

357BLB Qualifying expenditure on relevant R&D undertaken in-house

(1) In section 357BLA, the company's "qualifying expenditure on relevant R&D undertaken in-house" means the expenditure incurred by the company during the relevant period which meets conditions A and B.

(2) Condition A is that the expenditure is —

(a) incurred on staffing costs,

(b) incurred on software or consumable items,

(c) qualifying expenditure on externally provided workers, or

(d) incurred on relevant payments to the subjects of clinical trials.

(3) Condition B is that the expenditure is attributable to relevant research and development undertaken by the company itself.

(4) If an election made by the company under section 18A of CTA 2009 (election for exemption for profits or losses of company's foreign permanent establishments) applies to the relevant period, expenditure incurred by the company during the period which meets conditions A and B —

(a) is not "qualifying expenditure on relevant R&D undertaken in-house", but

(b) is "qualifying expenditure on relevant R&D sub-contracted to connected persons",

so far as it is expenditure brought into account in calculating a relevant profits amount, or a relevant losses amount, aggregated at section 18A(4)(a) or (b) of CTA 2009 in calculating the company's foreign permanent establishments amount for the period.

(5) In this section and sections 357BLC and 357BLD, "relevant research and development" means research and development (within the meaning of section 1138) which —

(a) in a case where the sub-stream is an individual IP right sub-stream, relates to the qualifying IP right to which the income in the sub-stream is attributable,

(b) in a case where the sub-stream is a product sub-stream, relates to a qualifying IP right granted in respect of any item —

       (i)   to which income in the sub-stream is attributable, or

       (ii) which is incorporated in an item to which income in the sub-stream is attributable, or

  (c) in a case where the sub-stream is a process sub-stream, relates to a qualifying IP right granted in respect of any process—

       (i)   to which income in the sub-stream is attributable, or

       (ii) which is incorporated in a process to which income in the sub-stream is attributable.

(6) Research and development "relates" to a qualifying IP right for the purposes of subsection (5) if—

  (a) it creates, or contributes to the creation of, the invention,

  (b) it is undertaken for the purpose of developing the invention,

  (c) it is undertaken for the purpose of developing ways in which the invention may be used or applied, or

  (d) it is undertaken for the purpose of developing any item or process incorporating the invention.

(7) The following provisions of CTA 2009 apply for the purposes of this section—

  (a) section 1123 (meaning of "staffing costs"),

  (b) section 1124 (when staffing costs are attributable to relevant research and development),

  (c) section 1125 (meaning of "software or consumable items"),

  (d) sections 1126 to 1126B (when software or consumable items are attributable to relevant research and development),

  (e) sections 1127 to 1131 (meaning of "qualifying expenditure on externally provided workers"),

  (f) section 1132 (when qualifying expenditure on externally provided workers is attributable to relevant research and development), and

  (g) section 1140 (meaning of "relevant payments to the subjects of clinical trials"),

and in the application of those provisions for the purposes of this section any reference to "relevant research and development" is to be read as a reference to relevant research and development within the meaning given by subsection (5).

357BLC Qualifying expenditure on relevant R&D sub-contracted to unconnected persons

(1) In section 357BLA, the company's "qualifying expenditure on relevant R&D sub-contracted to unconnected persons" means the expenditure incurred by the company during the relevant period in making payments within subsection (2).

(2) A payment is within this subsection if—

  (a) it is made to a person in respect of relevant research and development contracted out by the company to the person, and

  (b) the company and the person are not connected (within the meaning given by section 1122).

(3) If an election made by the company under section 18A of CTA 2009 (election for exemption for profits or losses of company's foreign

permanent establishments) applies to the relevant period, expenditure incurred by the company during the period in making payments within subsection (2)—

    (a)   is not "qualifying expenditure on relevant R&D sub-contracted to unconnected persons", but

    (b)   is "qualifying expenditure on relevant R&D sub-contracted to connected persons",

so far as it is expenditure brought into account in calculating a relevant profits amount, or a relevant losses amount, aggregated at section 18A(4)(a) or (b) of CTA 2009 in calculating the company's foreign permanent establishments amount for the period.

(4)   Where a payment is made to a person in respect of relevant research and development contracted out to the person and in respect of other matters, so much of the payment as is properly attributable to other matters is to be disregarded for the purposes of this section.

357BLD Qualifying expenditure on relevant R&D sub-contracted to connected persons

(1)   In section 357BLA, the company's "qualifying expenditure on relevant R&D sub-contracted to connected persons" means the total of—

    (a)   any expenditure which is "qualifying expenditure on relevant R&D sub-contracted to connected persons" as a result of section 357BLB(4) or 357BLC(3) (certain expenditure attributed to company's foreign permanent establishments), and

    (b)   the expenditure incurred by the company during the relevant period in making payments within subsection (2).

(2)   A payment is within this subsection if—

    (a)   it is made to a person in respect of relevant research and development contracted out by the company to the person, and

    (b)   the company and the person are connected (within the meaning given by section 1122).

(3)   Where a payment is made to a person in respect of relevant research and development contracted out to the person and in respect of other matters, so much of the payment as is properly attributable to other matters is to be disregarded for the purposes of this section.

357BLE Qualifying expenditure on acquisition of relevant qualifying IP rights

(1)   In section 357BLA, the company's "qualifying expenditure on the acquisition of relevant qualifying IP rights" means the expenditure incurred by the company in making during the relevant period payments within any of subsections (2), (3) and (4).

(2)   A payment is within this subsection if it is made to a person in respect of the assignment by that person to the company of a relevant qualifying IP right.

(3)   A payment is within this subsection if it is made to a person in respect of the grant or transfer by that person to the company of an exclusive licence in respect of a relevant qualifying IP right.

(4)   A payment is within this subsection if—

    (a)   it is made to a person in respect of the disclosure by that person to the company of any item or process, and

    (b)   the company applies for and is granted a relevant qualifying IP right in respect of that item or process (or any item or process derived from it).

(5)   Where the company has incurred expenditure in making a series of payments to a person in respect of a single assignment, grant, transfer or disclosure, each of the payments in the series is to be treated for the purposes of this section as having been made on the date on which the first payment in the series was made.

(6)   "Relevant qualifying IP right" means —

    (a)   in a case where the sub-stream is an individual IP right sub-stream, the qualifying IP right to which the income in the sub-stream is attributable,

    (b)   in a case where the sub-stream is a product sub-stream, a qualifying IP right granted in respect of an item —

        (i)   to which income in the sub-stream is attributable, or

        (ii) which is incorporated in an item to which income in the sub-stream is attributable, or

    (c)   in a case where the sub-stream is a process sub-stream, a qualifying IP right granted in respect of a process —

        (i)   to which income in the sub-stream is attributable, or

        (ii) which is incorporated in a process to which income in the sub-stream is attributable.

357BLF Meaning of the "relevant period" etc

(1)   Subsections (2) to (6) define "the relevant period" for the purposes of sections 357BLB to 357BLE.

(2)   The "relevant period" is the period which —

    (a)   ends with the last day of the accounting period, and

    (b)   begins on the relevant day or such earlier day as the company may elect.

This is subject to subsection (6).

(3)   The "relevant day" is 1 July 2013 in a case where —

    (a)   the accounting period begins before 1 July 2021, and

    (b)   the company is a new entrant (see section 357A(11)).

(4)   The "relevant day" is 1 July 2016 in any other case.

(5)   A day elected under subsection (2)(b) must not be more than 20 years before the last day of the accounting period.

(6)   If the last day of the accounting period is, or is after, 1 July 2036 the "relevant period" is the period of 20 years ending with that day.

(7)   Expenditure incurred by the company is to be treated for the purposes of sections 357BLB to 357BLD as incurred during the relevant period if (and only if) the expenditure is allowable as a deduction in calculating for corporation tax purposes the profits of the trade for an accounting period which falls, in whole or in part, within the relevant period.

357BLG Cases where the company is a new entrant with insufficient information about pre-enactment expenditure

(1) This section applies if —

   (a) the accounting period begins before 1 July 2021 and the company is a new entrant (so that subsection (3) of section 357BLF applies), and

   (b) the company has insufficient information about its expenditure in the period which begins with 1 July 2013 and ends with 30 June 2016 to be able to calculate the R&D fraction for the sub-stream.

(2) If the accounting period begins on or after 1 July 2019, the company may elect that, for the purposes of enabling it to determine the R&D fraction for the sub-stream, section 357BLF is to have effect as if in subsection (3) for "1 July 2013" there were substituted "1 July 2016".

(3) If the accounting period begins before 1 July 2019 the company may elect that, for the purposes of enabling it to determine the R&D fraction for the sub-stream, sections 357BL to 357BLE are to have effect as if —

   (a) any reference in those sections to the relevant period were to the period of three years ending with the last day of the accounting period,

   (b) in section 357BLB, for subsections (5) and (6) there were substituted —

   "(5) In this section and sections 357BLC and 357BLD, "relevant research and development" means research and development (within the meaning of section 1138) which relates to the trade.", and

   (c) in section 357BLE —

      (i) in each of subsections (2), (3) and (4) the word "relevant" were omitted, and

      (ii) subsection (6) were omitted.

357BLH R&D fraction: increase for exceptional circumstances

(1) The company may elect to increase the R&D fraction for the sub-stream by the amount mentioned in subsection (2) if (but for the increase) —

   (a) it would not be less than 0.325, and

   (b) it would, because of exceptional circumstances, be less than the value fraction for the sub-stream (see subsection (3)).

(2) The amount of the increase referred to in subsection (1) is the amount which is equal to the difference between the R&D fraction (before the increase) and the value fraction.

(3) The "value fraction" for the sub-stream is the fraction which, on a just and reasonable assessment, represents the proportion of the value of the relevant qualifying IP rights which is properly attributable to research and development undertaken at any time —

   (a) by the company itself, or

   (b) on behalf of the company by persons not connected with it.

(4) An election under subsection (1) is made by the company giving notice to an officer of Revenue and Customs.

(5) The notice must be given on or before the last day on which an amendment of the company's tax return for the accounting period could be made under paragraph 15 of Schedule 18 to FA 1998.

(6) In this section —

"relevant qualifying IP rights" has the same meaning as in section 357BLE, and

"research and development" has the meaning given by section 1138.

(7) Section 1122 (meaning of "connected" persons") applies for the purposes of this section.

Profits arising before grant of right

357BM Profits arising before grant of right

(1) This section applies where a company —

   (a) holds a right mentioned in paragraph (a), (b) or (c) of section 357BB(1) (rights to which this Part applies) or an exclusive licence in respect of such a right, or

   (b) would hold such a right or licence but for the fact that the company disposed of any rights in the invention or (as the case may be) the licence before the right was granted.

(2) The company may elect that, for the purposes of determining the relevant IP profits of a trade of the company for the accounting period in which the right is granted, there is to be added the amount determined in accordance with subsection (3) (the "additional amount").

(3) The additional amount is the difference between —

   (a) the aggregate of the relevant IP profits of the trade for each relevant accounting period, and

   (b) the aggregate of what the relevant IP profits of the trade for each relevant accounting period would have been if the right had been granted on the relevant day.

(4) For the purposes of determining the additional amount, the amount of any relevant IP profits to which section 357A does not apply by virtue of Chapter 5 (relevant IP losses) is to be disregarded.

(5) In this section "relevant accounting period" means —

   (a) the accounting period of the company in which the right is granted, and

   (b) any earlier accounting period of the company which meets the conditions in subsection (6).

(6) The conditions mentioned in subsection (5)(b) are —

   (a) that it is an accounting period for which an election made by the company under section 357A(1) has effect,

   (b) that it is an accounting period for which the company is a qualifying company, and

   (c) that it ends on or after the relevant day.

(7) In this section "the relevant day" is the later of —

      (a)   the first day of the period of 6 years ending with the day on which the right is granted, and

      (b)   the day on which—

            (i)   the application for the grant of the right was filed, or

            (ii)   in the case of a company that holds an exclusive licence in respect of the right, the licence was granted.

(8)   Where the company would be a qualifying company for an accounting period but for the fact that the right had not been granted at any time during that accounting period, the company is to be treated for the purposes of this section as if it were a qualifying company for that accounting period.

(9)   Where the company would be a qualifying company for the accounting period in which the right was granted but for the fact that the company disposed of the rights or licence mentioned in subsection (1)(b) before the right was granted, the company is to be treated for the purposes of section 357A as if it were a qualifying company for that accounting period.

Small claims treatment

357BN Small claims treatment

(1)   This section applies where—

      (a)   a company carries on only one trade during an accounting period,

      (b)   section 357BF applies for the purposes of determining the relevant IP profits of the trade for the accounting period, and

      (c)   the qualifying residual profit of the trade for the accounting period does not exceed whichever is the greater of—

            (i)   £1,000,000, and

            (ii)   the relevant maximum for the accounting period.

(2)   The company may make any of the following elections for the accounting period—

      (a)   a notional royalty election (see section 357BNA),

      (b)   a small claims figure election (see section 357BNB), and

      (c)   a global streaming election (see section 357BNC).

This is subject to subsections (3) and (4).

(3)   The company may not make a notional royalty election, a small claims figure election or a global streaming election for the accounting period if—

      (a)   the qualifying residual profit of the trade for the accounting period exceeds £1,000,000,

      (b)   section 357BF applied for the purposes of determining the relevant IP profits of the trade for any previous accounting period beginning within the relevant 4-year period, and

      (c)   the company did not make a notional royalty election, a small claims figure election or (as the case may be) a global streaming election for that previous accounting period.

(4)   The company may not make a small claims figure election for the accounting period if—

    (a)   the qualifying residual profit of the trade for the accounting period exceeds £1,000,000,

    (b)   section 357C or 357DA applied for the purposes of determining the relevant IP profits of the trade for any previous accounting period beginning within the relevant 4-year period, and

    (c)   the company did not make an election under section 357CL for small claims treatment for that previous accounting period.

(5) In subsections (3) and (4) "the relevant 4-year period" means the period of 4 years ending with the beginning of the accounting period mentioned in subsection (1)(a).

(6) For the purposes of this section, the "qualifying residual profit" of a trade of a company for an accounting period is the amount which (assuming the company did not make an election under this section) would be equal to the aggregate of the relevant IP income sub-streams established at Step 2 in section 357BF(2) in determining the relevant IP profits of the trade for the accounting period, following the deductions from those sub-streams required by Step 4 in section 357BF(2) (ignoring the amount of any sub-stream which is not greater than nil following those deductions).

(7) For the purposes of this section, the "relevant maximum" for an accounting period of a company is—

    (a)   in a case where no company is a related 51% group company of the company in the accounting period, £3,000,000;

    (b)   in a case where one or more companies are related 51% group companies of the company in the accounting period, the amount given by the formula—

$$\frac{£3,000,000}{1+N}$$

        where N is the number of those related 51% group companies in relation to which an election under section 357A(1) has effect for the accounting period.

(8) For an accounting period of less than 12 months, the relevant maximum is proportionally reduced.

357BNA Notional royalty election

(1) Subsection (2) applies where a company has made a notional royalty election for an accounting period under section 357BN(2)(a).

(2) In its application for the purposes of determining the relevant IP profits of the trade of the company for the accounting period, section 357BHA (notional royalty) has effect as if—

    (a)   in subsection (2) for "the appropriate percentage" there were substituted "75%", and

    (b)   subsections (3) to (6) were omitted.

357BNB Small claims figure election

(1) Subsection (2) applies where a company has made a small claims figure election for an accounting period under section 357BN(2)(b).

(2) In its application for the purposes of determining the relevant IP profits of the trade of the company for the accounting period, section 357BF(2) (steps for calculating relevant IP profits) has effect as if in Step 5—

    (a) for "marketing assets return figure" there was substituted "small claims figure", and

    (b) for "(see section 357BK)" there was substituted "(see section 357BNB(3))".

(3) Subsections (4) to (9) apply for the purpose of calculating the small claims figure for a relevant IP income sub-stream established at Step 2 in section 357BF(2) in determining the relevant IP profits of a trade of a company for an accounting period.

(4) If 75% of the qualifying residual profit of the trade for the accounting period is lower than the small claims threshold, the small claims figure for the sub-stream is 25% of the amount of the sub-stream following Step 4 in section 357BF(2).

(5) If 75% of the qualifying residual profit of the trade for the accounting period is higher than the small claims threshold, the small claims figure for the sub-stream is the amount given by—

$$A - \left(\frac{A}{QRP} \times SCT \right)$$

where—

    A is the amount of the sub-stream following the deductions required by Step 4 in section 357BF(2),

    QRP is the qualifying residual profit of the trade of the company for the accounting period, and

    SCT is the small claims threshold.

(6) If no company is a related 51% group company of the company in the accounting period, the small claims threshold is £1,000,000.

(7) If one or more companies are related 51% group companies of the company in the accounting period, the small claims threshold is—

$$\frac{£1,000,000}{1 + N}$$

where N is the number of those related 51% group companies in relation to which an election under section 357A(1) has effect for the accounting period.

(8) For an accounting period of less than 12 months, the small claims threshold is proportionately reduced.

(9) Subsection (6) of section 357BN (meaning of "qualifying residual profit") applies for the purposes of subsection (4) and (5) of this section.

357BNC Global streaming election

(1) Subsection (2) applies where a company has made a global streaming election for an accounting period under section 357BN(2)(c).

(2) In its application for the purpose of determining the relevant IP profits of the trade of the company for the accounting period, this Chapter has effect with the following modifications.

(3) In subsection (2) of section 357BF (relevant IP profits) —

    (a) omit Step 2,

    (b) in Step 3 for "each of the relevant IP income sub-streams" substitute "the relevant IP income stream",

    (c) in Step 4 —

        (i) in the words before paragraph (a), for "each" substitute "the",

        (ii) for "sub-stream", in each place it occurs, substitute "stream",

    (d) in Step 5 —

        (i) at the beginning insert "If the relevant IP income stream is greater than nil following Step 4,",

        (ii) for the words from "each" to "Step 4" substitute "the stream",

        (iii) for "sub-stream", in the second place it occurs, substitute "stream",

    (e) in Step 6 —

        (i) for "each relevant IP income sub-stream" substitute "the relevant IP income stream",

        (ii) for "sub-stream", in the second place it occurs, substitute "stream",

    (f) omit Step 7, and

    (g) in Step 8 for "given by Step 7" substitute "of the relevant IP income stream following Step 6".

(4) In subsection (3) of that section for "given by" substitute "of the relevant IP income stream following the Steps in".

(5) In subsection (4) of that section for "given by" substitute "of the relevant IP income stream following the Steps in".

(6) Omit subsections (5) to (7) of that section.

(7) In section 357BIA(3) (certain amounts not to be deducted from sub-streams at Step 4 of section 357BF) —

    (a) for "a relevant IP income sub-stream" substitute "the relevant IP income stream";

    (b) for "sub-stream", in the second and third places it occurs, substitute "stream".

(8) In section 357BJ (routine return figure) —

    (a) for "sub-stream", in each place it occurs, substitute "stream", and

    (b) in subsection (1) for "Step 2" substitute "Step 1".

(9) In section 357BK (marketing asset return figure) for "sub-stream", in each place it occurs, substitute "stream".

(10) In section 357BKA (notional marketing royalty) —

    (a) for "sub-stream", in each place it occurs, substitute "stream", and

    (b) in subsection (1) for "Step 2" substitute "Step 1".

(11) In section 357BKB (actual marketing royalty) for "sub-stream", in each place it occurs, substitute "stream".

(12) In section 357BL (R&D fraction: introduction)—
   (a) for "sub-stream" (in each place it occurs) substitute "stream", and
   (b) in subsection (1) for "Step 2" substitute "Step 1".

(13) In section 357BLA(1) (R&D fraction) for "sub-stream" substitute "stream".

(14) In section 357BLB(5) (qualifying expenditure on relevant R&D undertaken in-house) for the words after "1138)" substitute "which relates to a qualifying IP right to which income in the stream is attributable".

(15) In section 357BLE(6) (qualifying expenditure on acquisition of relevant qualifying IP rights) for the words from "means" to the end substitute "means a qualifying IP right to which income in the stream is attributable".

(16) In section 357BLG (cases where the company is a new entrant with insufficient information about pre-enactment expenditure) for "sub-stream", in each place it occurs, substitute "stream".

(17) In section 357BLH (R&D fraction: increase for exceptional circumstances) for "sub-stream", in each place it occurs, substitute "stream".

(18) In section 357BNB (small claims figure election)—
   (a) for "sub-stream", in each place it occurs, substitute "stream", and
   (b) in subsection (3) for "Step 2" substitute "Step 1".

CHAPTER 2B

RELEVANT IP PROFITS: CASES MENTIONED IN SECTION 357A(7): INCOME FROM NEW IP

357BO Relevant IP profits

(1) Section 357BF applies, with the modifications set out in section 357BQ, for the purposes of determining the relevant IP profits of a trade of a company for an accounting period in a case where—
   (a) the accounting period begins before 1 July 2021,
   (b) the company is not a new entrant (see section 357A(11)), and
   (c) any amount of relevant IP income brought into account as a credit in calculating the profits of the trade for the accounting period is properly attributable to a new qualifying IP right (see section 357BP).

(2) Where it is necessary for the purposes of section 357BF, as applied by this section, to determine the R&D fraction for a relevant IP income sub-stream, the company concerned is to be treated for the purposes of sections 357BLF and 357BLG as if it were a new entrant.

(3) Where section 357BF applies by reason of this section for the purposes of determining the relevant IP profits of a trade of a company for an accounting period, the company may not make a global streaming election for the accounting period under section 357BN(2)(c).

357BP Meaning of "new qualifying IP right" and "old qualifying IP right"

(1) This section applies for the purposes of this Part.

(2) "New qualifying IP right", in relation to a company, means a qualifying IP right which meets condition A, B or C.

(3) "Old qualifying IP right", in relation to a company, means a qualifying IP right which does not meet any of those conditions.

(4) Condition A is that the right was granted or issued to the company in response to an application filed on or after the relevant date.

(5) Condition B is that the right was assigned to the company on or after the relevant date.

(6) Condition C is that an exclusive licence in respect of the right was granted to the company on or after the relevant date.

(7) The "relevant date" for the purposes of subsections (4), (5) and (6) is 1 July 2016; but this is subject to subsection (8).

(8) The "relevant date" for the purposes of subsections (5) and (6) is 2 January 2016 if—

    (a) the company and the person who assigned the right or granted the licence were connected at the time of the assignment or grant,

    (b) the main purpose, or one of the main purposes, of the assignment of the right or the grant of the licence was the avoidance of a foreign tax,

    (c) the person who assigned the right or granted the licence was not within the charge to corporation tax at the time of the assignment or grant, and

    (d) the person who assigned the right or granted the licence was not liable at the time of the assignment or grant to a foreign tax which is designated for the purposes of this section by regulations made by the Treasury.

(9) Regulations may be made under subsection (8)(d) which designate a foreign tax only if it appears to the Treasury that the tax may be charged at a reduced rate under provisions of the law of the country or territory concerned which correspond to the provisions of this Part.

(10) Regulations may not be made under subsection (8)(d) after 31 December 2016.

(11) In this section "foreign tax" means a tax under the law of a country or territory outside the United Kingdom.

(12) Section 1122 (meaning of "connected" persons) applies for the purposes of this section.

357BQ The modifications

(1) The modifications of section 357BF referred to in section 357BO(1) are as follows.

(2) Omit subsection (1).

(3) In subsection (2) —

    (a) in Step 2 —

        (i) before paragraph (a) insert —

            "(aa) a sub-stream consisting of income properly attributable to old qualifying IP rights ("an old IP rights sub-stream"),",

        (ii) in paragraph (a) before "qualifying IP right" insert "new",

        (iii) in the words after paragraph (c) for "and (7)" substitute "to (7E)",

    (b) in Step 6, for "relevant IP income sub-stream" substitute "individual IP right sub-stream, each product sub-stream and each process sub-stream", and

    (c) for Step 7 substitute —

        "*Step 7*

        Add together —

            (a) the amount of any old IP rights sub-stream (following Steps 4 and 5), and

            (b) the amount of each of the individual IP right sub-streams, each of the product sub-streams and each of the process sub-streams (following Step 6)."

(4) In subsection (7) for paragraph (a) substitute —

    "(a) it would not be reasonably practicable to apportion the income between —

        (i) individual IP rights sub-streams, or

        (ii) individual IP rights sub-streams and an old IP rights sub-stream, or".

(5) After subsection (7) insert —

    "(7A) Subsections (7B) to (7E) apply where —

        (a) income which is properly attributable to an IP item or IP process may in accordance with subsection (7) be allocated at Step 2 of subsection (2) to a product sub-stream or process sub-stream, and

        (b) the IP item or IP process incorporates —

            (i) at least one item or process in respect of which an old qualifying IP right held by the company has been granted, and

            (ii) at least one item or process in respect of which a new qualifying IP right held by the company has been granted.

    (7B) If —

      (a)   the value of the IP item or IP process is wholly or mainly attributable to the incorporation in it of the items or processes referred to in subsection (7A)(b)(i), or

      (b)   the old IP percentage for the IP item or IP process is 80% or more,

the income properly attributable to the IP item or IP process may be treated as if it were properly attributable to old qualifying IP rights only; and, accordingly, the income may be allocated at Step 2 of subsection (2) to an old qualifying IP rights sub-stream (rather than to a product sub-stream or process sub-stream).

(7C)   If the old IP percentage for the IP item or IP process is less than 80% but not less than 20%, that percentage of the income which is properly attributable to the IP item or IP process may be treated as if it were properly attributable to old qualifying IP rights only; and, accordingly, that percentage of the income may be allocated at Step 2 of subsection (2) to an old IP rights sub-stream (and the remainder is to be allocated to a product sub-stream or process sub-stream).

(7D)   Where by reason of subsection (7C) only part of the income properly attributable to the IP item or IP process is allocated to a product sub-stream or process sub-stream, the IP item or IP process is to be treated, in determining the R&D fraction for the sub-stream, as if it did not incorporate the items or processes referred to in subsection (7A)(b)(i).

(7E)   For the purposes of subsection (7B) and (7C), the "old IP percentage" for an IP item or IP process is the percentage found by the following calculation −

$$\frac{O}{T} \times 100$$

Where −

O is the number of items or processes incorporated in the IP item or IP process in respect of which an old qualifying IP right held by the company has been granted, and

T is the number of items or processes incorporated in the IP item or IP process in respect of which an old or a new qualifying IP right held by the company has been granted.""

(4)   In section 357FB (tax advantage schemes) −

    (a)   in subsection (2)(b) (list of ways by which deductions can be inflated) −

       (i)   omit "or" at the end of sub-paragraph (ii), and

      (ii)   after sub-paragraph (iii) insert ", or

              (iv)   an R&D fraction (see subsection (4A)) being greater than it would be but for the scheme.", and

    (b)   after subsection (4) insert −

"(4A)   The reference in subsection (2)(b)(iv) to an R&D fraction is a reference to such a fraction as is mentioned at Step 6 of section 357BF(2)."

(5)   After section 357GC insert—

"Transferred trades

357GCA Application of this Part in relation to transferred trades

(1)   Where—

    (a)   a company ("the transferor") ceases to carry on a trade which involves the exploitation of a qualifying IP right ("the relevant qualifying IP right"),

    (b)   the transferor assigns the relevant qualifying IP right, or grants or transfers an exclusive licence in respect of it, to another company ("the transferee"), and

    (c)   the transferee begins to carry on the trade,

the following provisions apply in determining under this Part the relevant IP profits of the trade carried on by the transferee.

(2)   The transferee is to be treated as not being a new entrant if—

    (a)   an election under section 357A(1) has effect in relation to the transferor on the date of the assignment, grant or transfer mentioned in subsection (1)(b) ("the transfer date"), and

    (b)   the first accounting period of the transferor for which that election had effect began before 1 July 2016.

(3)   The relevant qualifying IP right is to be treated as being an old qualifying IP right in relation to the transferee if by reason of section 357BP it is an old qualifying IP right in relation to the transferor.

(4)   Expenditure incurred prior to the transfer date by the transferor which is attributable to relevant research and development undertaken by the transferor is to be treated for the purposes of section 357BLB as if it is expenditure incurred by the transferee which is attributable to relevant research and development undertaken by the transferee.

(5)   Expenditure incurred prior to the transfer date by the transferor in making a payment to a person in respect of relevant research and development contracted out by the transferor to that person is to be treated for the purposes of sections 357BLC and 357BLD as if it is expenditure incurred by the transferee in making a payment to that person in respect of relevant research and development contracted out by the transferee to that person.

(6)   Expenditure incurred prior to the transfer date by the transferor in making a payment in connection with the relevant qualifying IP right which is within subsection (2), (3) or (4) of section 357BLE is to be treated for the purposes of that section as if it is expenditure incurred by the transferee in making a payment in connection with that right which is within one of those subsections.

(7)   Expenditure incurred by the transferee in making a payment to the transferor in respect of the assignment, grant or transfer mentioned in subsection (1)(b) is to be ignored for the purposes of section 357BLE.

(8)   In this section—

      "trade" includes part of a trade, and

           "relevant research and development" means research and development which relates to the relevant qualifying IP right.

    (9)   For the purposes of this section research and development "relates" to the relevant qualifying IP right if—

        (a)   it creates, or contributes to the creation of the invention,

        (b)   it is undertaken for the purpose of developing the invention,

        (c)   it is undertaken for the purpose of developing ways in which the invention may be used or applied, or

        (d)   it is undertaken for the purpose of developing any item or process incorporating the invention."

  (6)   Schedule 9 contains amendments consequential on this section.

  (7)   The amendments made by this section have effect in relation to accounting periods beginning on or after 1 July 2016.

  (8)   Subsection (9) applies where a company has an accounting period ("the straddling period") which begins before, and ends on or after, 1 July 2016 or 1 July 2021 ("the relevant date").

  (9)   For the purposes of this section and Part 8A of CTA 2010—

        (a)   so much of the straddling period as falls before the relevant date, and so much of that period as falls on or after that date, are treated as separate accounting periods, and

        (b)   any amounts brought into account for the purposes of calculating for corporation tax purposes the profits of any trade of the company for the straddling period are apportioned to the two separate accounting periods on such basis as is just and reasonable.

 (10)   Subsection (11) applies if—

        (a)   an election is made by a company under section 357A(1) of CTA 2010, and

        (b)   the notice under section 357G of that Act specifies the accounting period of the company which ends on 30 June 2016, or any earlier accounting period, as being the first accounting period for which the election is to have effect.

 (11)   Nothing in section 357GA(5) prevents the election having effect in relation to the accounting period of the company which ends on 30 June 2016 or any subsequent accounting period.

 (12)   Subsection (13) applies to an amount of relevant IP income of a company if—

        (a)   the company is not a new entrant,

        (b)   the income is properly attributable to a new qualifying IP right which was assigned to the company, or in respect of which an exclusive licence was granted to the company, during the period beginning on 2 January 2016 and ending on 1 July 2016, and

        (c)   the income accrued to the company during the period beginning on 1 July 2016 and ending on 1 January 2017.

 (13)   The income is to be treated for the purposes of Part 8A of CTA 2010 as being properly attributable to an old qualifying IP right.

 (14)   Expressions used in subsections (12) and (13) and in Part 8A of CTA 2010 have the meaning they have in that Part.

Miscellaneous

65 Power to make regulations about the taxation of securitisation companies

(1) Section 624 of CTA 2010 (power to make regulations about the application of the Corporation Tax Acts in relation to securitisation companies) is amended in accordance with subsections (2) to (4).

(2) In subsection (1), for "Corporation Tax Acts" substitute "Taxes Acts".

(3) In subsection (2), for "Corporation Tax Acts" substitute "Taxes Acts".

(4) In subsection (9), after "section" insert "—
    "the Taxes Acts" has the meaning given by section 118(1) of TMA 1970, and".

(5) In section 625 of CTA 2010 (regulations: supplementary provision) in subsection (3) (power to include retrospective provision) after "may" insert ", insofar as they concern the application of the Corporation Tax Acts in relation to a securitisation company,".

66 Hybrid and other mismatches

Schedule 10 contains provision that counteracts, for corporation tax purposes, hybrid and other mismatches that would otherwise arise.

67 Insurance companies carrying on long-term business

(1) Part 2 of FA 2012 (insurance companies carrying on long-term business) is amended as follows.

(2) In section 73 (the I-E basis), in step 4—
    (a) for "(but not below nil) by the" substitute "by the relievable", and
    (b) at the end of the step insert—
    "In this step, "the relievable amount" of a non-trading deficit means so much of the deficit as does not exceed the total of—
        (a) the amount given by the calculation required by step 1,
        (b) the amount given by the calculation required by step 2, and
        (c) any amount of an I-E receipt under section 92 brought into account under step 3."

(3) In section 88 (loan relationships, derivative contracts and intangible fixed assets), in subsection (6), for "excess—" and paragraphs (a) and (b), substitute "excess is treated for the purposes of section 76 as a deemed BLAGAB management expense for that period."

(4) In section 126 (restrictions in respect of non-trading deficit), in subsection (2), for "would have under section 388" to the end substitute "has, calculated by reference only to credits and debits—
    (a) arising in respect of such of the company's loan relationships as are debtor relationships (see section 302(6) of CTA 2009), and
    (b) referable, in accordance with Chapter 4, to the company's basic life assurance and general annuity business."

(5) The amendments made by this section have effect in relation to accounting periods beginning on or after the day on which this Act is passed.

68   Taking over payment obligations as lessee of plant or machinery

(1)   In Part 20 of CTA 2010 (tax avoidance involving leasing plant or machinery), after section 894 insert—

"CHAPTER 3

CONSIDERATION FOR TAKING OVER PAYMENT OBLIGATIONS AS LESSEE TREATED AS INCOME

"894A Consideration for taking over payment obligations as lessee treated as income

(1)   This section applies where under any arrangements—
    (a)   a company chargeable to corporation tax (C) agrees to take over obligations of another person (D) as lessee under a lease of plant or machinery,
    (b)   as a result of that agreement C, or a person connected with C, becomes entitled to income deductions (whether deductions in calculating income or from total profits), and
    (c)   a payment is payable to C, or a person connected with C, by way of consideration for that agreement.

(2)   The payment is treated for the purposes of corporation tax as income received by C in the period of account in which C takes over the obligations mentioned in subsection (1)(a).

(3)   Subsection (2) does not apply if and to the extent that the payment is (apart from this section)—
    (a)   charged to tax on C, or a person connected with C, as an amount of income,
    (b)   brought into account in calculating for tax purposes any income of C or a person connected with C, or
    (c)   brought into account for the purposes of any provision of CAA 2001 as a disposal receipt, or proceeds from a balancing event or disposal event, of C or a person connected with C.

(4)   It does not matter how C takes over the obligations of D (whether by assignment, novation, variation or replacement of the contract, by operation of law or otherwise).

(5)   In this section—
        "arrangements" include any scheme, arrangement, understanding, transaction or series of transactions (whether or not legally enforceable);
        "lease of plant or machinery" means any kind of agreement or arrangement under which sums are paid for the use of, or otherwise in respect of, plant or machinery;
        "payment" includes the provision of any benefit, the assumption of any liability or the transfer of money or money's worth (and "payable" is to be construed accordingly);
        "payment by way of consideration" means any payment made, directly or indirectly, in consequence of or otherwise in connection with, the agreement mentioned in subsection (1)(a), where it is reasonable to assume the agreement would not have

been made unless the arrangements included provision for the payment.

(6) Any priority rule (other than section 212(1) of FA 2013 (general anti-abuse rule to have priority over other rules)) has effect subject to this section, despite the terms of the priority rule.

(7) For that purpose "priority rule" is a rule (however expressed) to the effect that particular provisions have effect to the exclusion of, or otherwise in priority to, anything else.

(8) Examples of priority rules are section 464 of CTA 2009 (priority of loan relationships rules) and section 6(1) of TIOPA 2010 (effect to be given to double taxation arrangements despite anything in any enactment)."

(2) In Chapter 6 of Part 13 of ITA 2007 (avoidance involving leases of plant or machinery), after section 809ZF insert—

"809ZFA Consideration for taking over payment obligations as lessee treated as income

(1) This section applies where under any arrangements—
   (a) a person within the charge to income tax (P) agrees to take over obligations of another person (Q) as lessee under a lease of plant or machinery,
   (b) as a result of that agreement P, or a person connected with P, becomes entitled to income deductions (whether deductions in calculating income or from total profits), and
   (c) a payment is payable to P, or a person connected with P, by way of consideration for that agreement.

(2) The payment is treated for the purposes of income tax as income received by P in the tax year in which P takes over the obligations mentioned in subsection (1)(a).

(3) Subsection (2) does not apply if and to the extent that the consideration is (apart from this section)—
   (a) charged to tax on P, or a person connected with P, as an amount of income,
   (b) brought into account in calculating for tax purposes any income of P or a person connected with P, or
   (c) brought into account for the purposes of any provision of CAA 2001 as a disposal receipt, or proceeds from a balancing event or disposal event, of P or a person connected with P.

(4) It does not matter how P takes over the obligations of Q (whether by assignment, novation, variation or replacement of the contract, by operation of law or otherwise).

(5) In this section—
   "arrangements" include any scheme, arrangement, understanding, transaction or series of transactions (whether or not legally enforceable);
   "lease of plant or machinery" means any kind of agreement or arrangement under which sums are paid for the use of, or otherwise in respect of, plant or machinery;

> > "payment" includes the provision of any benefit, the assumption of any liability or the transfer of money or money's worth (and "payable" is to be construed accordingly),;
> >
> > "payment by way of consideration" includes a payment made, directly or indirectly, in consequence of or otherwise in connection with, the agreement mentioned in subsection (1)(a), where it is reasonable to assume the agreement would not have been made unless the arrangements included provision for the payment.

> (6) Any priority rule (other than section 212(1) of FA 2013 (general anti-abuse rule to have priority over other rules)) has effect subject to this section, despite the terms of the priority rule.

> (7) For that purpose "priority rule" is a rule (however expressed) to the effect that particular provisions have effect to the exclusion of, or otherwise in priority to, anything else.

> (8) An example of a priority rule is section 6(1) of TIOPA 2010 (effect to be given to double taxation arrangements despite anything in any enactment)."

(3) This section applies to agreements of the kind mentioned in section 894A(1)(a) of CTA 2010 or section 809ZFA of ITA 2007 that are made on or after 25 November 2015.

PART 3

INCOME TAX AND CORPORATION TAX

Capital allowances

69 Capital allowances: designated assisted areas

In section 45K of CAA 2001 (expenditure on plant and machinery for use in designated assisted area), in subsection (1)(b) (condition that expenditure is incurred in the period of 8 years beginning with 1 April 2012), for "1 April 2012" substitute "the date on which the area is (or is treated as) designated under subsection (2)(a)".

70 Capital allowances: anti-avoidance relating to disposals

(1) Part 2 of CAA 2001 (plant and machinery allowances) is amended as follows.

(2) Section 213 (relevant transactions: sale, hire purchase etc. and assignment) is amended in accordance with subsections (3) and (4).

(3) In subsection (1) for the words from "enters" to "("S")" substitute "and another person ("S") enter into a relevant transaction".

(4) After subsection (3) insert—

> "(4) For the purposes of this Chapter, references to the disposal value of the plant or machinery under a relevant transaction are references to the disposal value that is to be brought into account by S as a result of the sale, contract or assignment in question."

(5) Section 215 (transactions to obtain tax advantages) is amended in accordance with subsections (6) to (8).

(6) In subsection (1)—

    (a) after "restricted" insert ", and balancing charges are imposed or increased,", and

    (b) for the words from "B" to "S" substitute "B and S enter into a relevant transaction".

(7) In subsection (4)—

    (a) after "includes" insert "—

        (a)   ", and

    (b) at end insert ", and

        (b)   avoiding liability for the whole or part of a balancing charge to which a person would otherwise be liable."

(8) After subsection (4) insert—

"(4A) If the tax advantage relates to the disposal value of the plant or machinery under the relevant transaction (whether by obtaining a more favourable allowance or by avoiding the whole or part of a balancing charge) then—

    (a) the applicable section is section 218ZB, and

    (b) the tax advantage is to be disregarded for the purposes of subsection (6) and (8)(b)."

(9) After section 218ZA (restrictions on writing down allowances: section 215) insert—

"218ZB Disposal values: section 215

    (1) If—

        (a) this section applies as a result of section 215,

        (b) a payment is payable to any person under the transaction, scheme or arrangement mentioned in that section,

        (c) some or all of the payment would not (apart from this section) be taken into account in determining the disposal value of the plant or machinery under the relevant transaction, and

        (d) as a result of the matters mentioned in paragraphs (b) and (c) S would otherwise obtain a tax advantage as mentioned in section 215(3) and (4),

the disposal value of the plant or machinery under the relevant transaction is to be adjusted in a just and reasonable manner so as to include an amount representing so much of the payment as would or would in effect cancel out the tax advantage.

    (2) In subsection (1) "payment" includes the provision of any benefit, the assumption of any liability and any other transfer of money or money's worth, and "payable" is to be construed accordingly."

(10) In section 66 (list of provisions outside Chapter 5 about disposal values) insert at the appropriate place—

"section 218ZB   disposal of plant or machinery in avoidance cases".

(11)   The amendments made by this section have effect in relation to transactions mentioned in section 213(1)(a), (b) or (c) of CAA 2001 that take place on or after 25 November 2015.

Trade and property business profits

71   Trade and property business profits: money's worth

(1)   ITTOIA 2005 is amended in accordance with subsections (2) and (3).

(2)   In Chapter 3 of Part 2 (trade profits: basic rules), after section 28 insert—

"28A   Money's worth

     (1)   Subsection (2) applies—

         (a)   for the purpose of bringing into account an amount arising in respect of a transaction involving money's worth entered into in the course of a trade, and

         (b)   if an amount at least equal to the amount that would be brought into account under that subsection is not otherwise brought into account as a receipt in calculating the profits of a trade under a provision of this Part other than a provision mentioned in subsection (3).

     (2)   For the purpose of calculating the profits of the trade, an amount equal to the value of the money's worth is brought into account as a receipt if, had the transaction involved money, an amount would have been brought into account as a receipt in respect of it.

     (3)   But where another provision of this Part makes express provision for the bringing into account of an amount in respect of money's worth as a receipt in calculating the profits of a trade (however expressed), that other provision applies instead of subsection (2)."

(3)   In Chapter 3 of Part 3 (profits of property businesses), in section 272 (application of trading income rules), in the Table in subsection (2), at the appropriate place insert—

                   "section 28A   money's worth".

(4)   CTA 2009 is amended in accordance with subsections (5) and (6).

(5)   In Chapter 3 of Part 3 (trade profits: basic rules), after section 49 insert—

"49A   Money's worth

     (1)   Subsection (2) applies—

         (a)   for the purpose of bringing into account an amount arising in respect of a transaction involving money's worth entered into in the course of a trade, and

         (b)   if an amount at least equal to the amount that would be brought into account under that subsection is not otherwise brought into account as a receipt in calculating the profits of a trade under a provision of this Part other than a provision mentioned in subsection (3).

(2) For the purpose of calculating the profits of the trade, an amount equal to the value of the money's worth is brought into account as a receipt if, had the transaction involved money, an amount would have been brought into account as a receipt in respect of it.

(3) But where another provision of this Part makes express provision for the bringing into account of an amount in respect of money's worth as a receipt in calculating the profits of a trade (however expressed), that other provision applies instead of subsection (2)."

(6) In Chapter 3 of Part 4 (profits of property businesses), in section 210 (application of trading income rules), in the Table in subsection (2), at the appropriate place insert—

"section 49A   money's worth".

(7) The amendments made by this section have effect in relation to transactions entered into on or after 16 March 2016.

72 Replacement and alteration of tools

(1) Omit the following provisions (replacement and alteration of trade tools)—
   (a) section 68 of ITTOIA 2005 and the italic heading before that section, and
   (b) section 68 of CTA 2009 and the italic heading before that section.

(2) In consequence of subsection (1)(a), in ITTOIA 2005—
   (a) in subsection (1) of section 56A (cash basis accounting), omit the entry relating to section 68, and
   (b) in section 272 (profits of a property business: application of trading income rules), in subsection (2), omit the entry in the table relating to section 68.

(3) In consequence of subsection (1)(b), in section 210 of CTA 2009 (profits of a property business: application of trading income rules), in subsection (2), omit the entry in the table relating to section 68.

(4) The amendments made by this section have effect in relation to expenditure incurred on or after the date in subsection (5).

(5) The date is—
   (a) for corporation tax purposes, 1 April 2016, and
   (b) for income tax purposes, 6 April 2016.

Property business deductions

73 Property business deductions: replacement of domestic items

(1) In Chapter 5 of Part 3 of ITTOIA 2005 (property income), after section 311

insert—

"Deduction for replacement of domestic items

311A Replacement domestic items relief

(1) This section applies if conditions A to D are met.

(2) Condition A is that a person ("P") carries on a property business in relation to land which consists of or includes a dwelling-house.

(3) Condition B is that—

    (a) a domestic item has been provided for use in the dwelling-house ("the old item"),

    (b) P incurs expenditure on a domestic item for use in the dwelling-house ("the new item"),

    (c) the new item is provided solely for the use of the lessee,

    (d) the new item replaces the old item, and

    (e) following that replacement, the old item is no longer available for use in the dwelling-house.

(4) Condition C is that a deduction for the expenditure is not prohibited by the wholly and exclusively rule but would otherwise be prohibited by the capital expenditure rule (see subsection (15)).

(5) Condition D is that no allowance under CAA 2001 may be claimed in respect of the expenditure.

(6) In calculating the profits of the business, a deduction for the expenditure is allowed.
But this is subject to subsections (7) and (8).

(7) No deduction is allowed for expenditure in a tax year if—

    (a) the business consists of or includes the commercial letting of furnished holiday accommodation (see Chapter 6), and

    (b) the dwelling-house constitutes some or all of that accommodation for the tax year.

(8) No deduction is allowed for expenditure in a tax year if—

    (a) the person has rent-a-room receipts in respect of the dwelling-house for the tax year, and

    (b) section 793 or 797 (rent-a-room relief) applies in relation to those receipts.

(9) The basic amount of the deduction is as follows—

    (a) where the new item is the same or substantially the same as the old item, the deduction is equal to the expenditure incurred by P on the new item;

    (b) where the new item is not the same or substantially the same as the old item, the deduction is equal to so much of the expenditure incurred by P on the new item as does not exceed the expenditure which P would have incurred on an item which is the same or substantially the same as the old item.

Subsections (10) to (13) make further provision about the calculation of the deduction in certain cases.

(10) If P incurs incidental expenditure of a capital nature in connection with the disposal of the old item or the purchase of the new item, the deduction is increased by the amount of the incidental expenditure.

(11) If the old item is disposed of in part-exchange for the new item—
    (a) the expenditure incurred by P on the new item is treated as including an amount equal to the value of the old item, and
    (b) the deduction is reduced by that amount.

(12) If the old item is disposed of other than in part-exchange for the new item, the deduction is reduced by the amount or value of any consideration in money or money's worth which P or a person connected with P receives, or is entitled to receive, in respect of the disposal.

(13) For the purposes of subsection (12), where the old item is disposed of together with other consideration, the consideration in respect of the disposal mentioned in that subsection is taken not to include the amount of, or an amount equal to the value of, that other consideration.

(14) In this section, "domestic item" means an item for domestic use (such as furniture, furnishings, household appliances and kitchenware), and does not include anything that is a fixture.
"Fixture"—
    (a) means any plant or machinery that is so installed or otherwise fixed in or to a dwelling-house as to become, in law, part of that dwelling-house, and
    (b) includes any boiler or water-filled radiator installed in a dwelling-house as part of a space or water heating system.
"Plant or machinery" here has the same meaning as in Part 2 of CAA 2001.

(15) In this section—
"the capital expenditure rule" means the rule in section 33 (capital expenditure), as applied by section 272;
"lessee" means the person who is entitled to the use of the dwelling-house under a lease or other arrangement under which a sum is payable in respect of the use of the dwelling-house;
"the wholly and exclusively rule" means the rule in section 34 (expenses not wholly and exclusively for trade and unconnected losses), as applied by section 272."

(2) In Chapter 5 of Part 4 of CTA 2009 (property income), after section 250 insert—

"Deduction for replacement of domestic items

250A Replacement domestic items relief

(1) This section applies if conditions A to D are met.

(2) Condition A is that a company ("C") carries on a property business in relation to land which consists of or includes a dwelling-house.

(3) Condition B is that—

      (a)   a domestic item has been provided for use in the dwelling-house ("the old item"),

      (b)   C incurs expenditure on a domestic item for use in the dwelling-house ("the new item"),

      (c)   the new item is provided solely for the use of the lessee,

      (d)   the new item replaces the old item, and

      (e)   following that replacement, the old item is no longer available for use in the dwelling-house.

(4)   Condition C is that a deduction for the expenditure is not prohibited by the wholly and exclusively rule but would otherwise be prohibited by the capital expenditure rule (see subsection (14)).

(5)   Condition D is that no allowance under CAA 2001 may be claimed in respect of the expenditure.

(6)   In calculating the profits of the business, a deduction for the expenditure is allowed.

(7)   But no deduction is allowed for expenditure in an accounting period if −

      (a)   the business consists of or includes the commercial letting of furnished holiday accommodation (see Chapter 6), and

      (b)   the dwelling-house constitutes some or all of that accommodation for the accounting period.

(8)   The basic amount of the deduction is as follows −

      (a)   where the new item is the same or substantially the same as the old item, the deduction is equal to the expenditure incurred by C on the new item;

      (b)   where the new item is not the same or substantially the same as the old item, the deduction is equal to so much of the expenditure incurred by C on the new item as does not exceed the expenditure which C would have incurred on an item which is the same or substantially the same as the old item.

Subsections (9) to (12) make further provision about the calculation of the deduction in certain cases.

(9)   If C incurs incidental expenditure of a capital nature in connection with the disposal of the old item or the purchase of the new item, the deduction is increased by the amount of the incidental expenditure.

(10)   If the old item is disposed of in part-exchange for the new item −

      (a)   the expenditure incurred by C on the new item is treated as including an amount equal to the value of the old item, and

      (b)   the deduction is reduced by that amount.

(11)   If the old item is disposed of other than in part-exchange for the new item, the deduction is reduced by the amount or value of any consideration in money or money's worth which C or a person connected with C receives, or is entitled to receive, in respect of the disposal.

(12)   For the purposes of subsection (11), where the old item is disposed of together with other consideration, the consideration in respect of the

disposal mentioned in that subsection is taken not to include the amount of, or an amount equal to the value of, that other consideration.

(13) In this section, "domestic item" means an item for domestic use (such as furniture, furnishings, household appliances and kitchenware), and does not include anything that is a fixture.

"Fixture"—

    (a) means any plant or machinery that is so installed or otherwise fixed in or to a dwelling-house as to become, in law, part of that dwelling-house, and

    (b) includes any boiler or water-filled radiator installed in a dwelling-house as part of a space or water heating system.

"Plant or machinery" here has the same meaning as in Part 2 of CAA 2001.

(14) In this section—

"the capital expenditure rule" means the rule in section 53 (capital expenditure), as applied by section 210;

"lessee" means the person who is entitled to the use of the dwelling-house under a lease or other arrangement under which a sum is payable in respect of the use of the dwelling-house;

"the wholly and exclusively rule" means the rule in section 54 (expenses not wholly and exclusively for trade and unconnected losses), as applied by section 210."

(3) In section 41 of TCGA 1992 (restriction of losses by reference to capital allowances and renewals allowances), in subsection (4), after paragraph (a) insert—

"(aa) any deduction under section 311A of ITTOIA 2005 or section 250A of CTA 2009 (replacement domestic items relief),".

(4) In section 308 of ITTOIA 2005 (furnished lettings), in subsection (1)(b), after "expenses" insert "of a revenue nature".

(5) In section 322 of ITTOIA 2005 (commercial letting of furnished holiday accommodation), after paragraph (za) in subsections (2) and (2A) insert—

"(zb) section 311A (replacement domestic items relief: see subsection (7)),".

(6) In section 248 of CTA 2009 (furnished lettings), in subsection (1)(b), after "expenses" insert "of a revenue nature".

(7) In section 264 of CTA 2009 (commercial letting of furnished holiday accommodation), before paragraph (a) in subsections (2) and (2A) insert—

"(za) section 250A (replacement domestic items relief: see subsection (7)),".

(8) The amendments made by this section have effect in relation to expenditure incurred on or after the date in subsection (9).

(9) The date is—

    (a) for corporation tax purposes, 1 April 2016, and

    (b) for income tax purposes, 6 April 2016.

74   Property business deductions: wear and tear allowance

(1)   In Part 3 of ITTOIA 2005 (property income) —

    (a)   omit sections 308A to 308C and the italic heading before section 308A (wear and tear allowance), and

    (b)   in section 327 (capital allowances and loss relief: UK property business), in subsection (2), omit paragraph (c) and the "or" before that paragraph.

(2)   The amendments made by subsection (1) have effect for the tax year 2016-17 and subsequent tax years.

(3)   In Part 4 of CTA 2009 (property income) —

    (a)   omit sections 248A to 248C of CTA 2009 and the italic heading before section 248A (wear and tear allowance), and

    (b)   in section 269 (capital allowances and loss relief: UK property business), in subsection (2), omit paragraph (c) and the "or" before that paragraph.

(4)   The amendments made by subsection (3) have effect in relation to accounting periods beginning on or after 1 April 2016.

(5)   For the purposes of subsection (3), where a company has an accounting period beginning before 1 April 2016 and ending on or after that date ("the straddling period") —

    (a)   so much of the straddling period as falls before 1 April 2016, and so much of that period as falls on or after that date, are treated as separate accounting periods, and

    (b)   any amounts brought into account for the purposes of calculating for corporation tax purposes the profits of a property business for the straddling period are apportioned to the two separate accounting periods in accordance with section 1172 of CTA 2010 (time basis) or, if that method produces a result that is unjust or unreasonable, on a just and reasonable basis.

Transfer pricing

75   Transfer pricing: application of OECD principles

(1)   In section 164(4) of TIOPA 2010 (Part to be interpreted in accordance with OECD principles) —

    (a)   in paragraph (a) after "2010" insert "as revised by the report, Aligning Transfer Pricing Outcomes with Value Creation, Actions 8-10 - 2015 Final Reports, published by the OECD on 5 October 2015", and

    (b)   in the words after paragraph (b) —

        (i)   for "such material" substitute "material which is", and

        (ii)   for "as may be so designated" substitute "and which is designated for the time being by order made by the Treasury".

(2)   In section 357GE(1) of CTA 2010 (other interpretation), in the definition of "the OECD transfer pricing guidelines", for the words from "means" to the end substitute "has the same meaning as "the transfer pricing guidelines" in section 164 of TIOPA 2010".

(3) The amendments made by subsection (1) have effect (in relation to provision made or imposed at any time)—

    (a) for corporation tax purposes, in relation to accounting periods beginning on or after 1 April 2016, and

    (b) for income tax purposes, in relation to the tax year 2016-17 and subsequent tax years.

(4) The amendment made by subsection (2) has effect in relation to accounting periods beginning on or after 1 April 2016.

Transactions in UK land

76 Corporation tax: territorial scope etc

(1) Section 5 of CTA 2009 (territorial scope of charge) is amended in accordance with subsections (2) to (4).

(2) For subsection (2) substitute—

"(2) A non-UK resident company is within the charge to corporation tax only if—

    (a) it carries on a trade of dealing in or developing UK land (see section 5B), or

    (b) it carries on a trade in the United Kingdom (other than a trade of dealing in or developing UK land) through a permanent establishment in the United Kingdom."

(3) After subsection (2) insert—

"(2A) A non-UK resident company which carries on a trade of dealing in or developing UK land is chargeable to corporation tax on all its profits wherever arising that are profits of that trade."

(4) In subsection (4), after "(1)" insert ", (2A)".

(5) After section 5 of CTA 2009 insert—

"5A Arrangements for avoiding tax

(1) Subsection (3) applies if a company has entered into an arrangement the main purpose or one of the main purposes of which is to obtain a relevant tax advantage for the company.

(2) In subsection (1) the reference to obtaining a relevant tax advantage includes obtaining a relevant tax advantage by virtue of any provisions of double taxation arrangements, but only in a case where the relevant tax advantage is contrary to the object and purpose of the provisions of the double taxation arrangements (and subsection (3) has effect accordingly, regardless of section 6(1) of TIOPA 2010).

(3) The relevant tax advantage is to be counteracted by means of adjustments.

(4) For this purpose adjustments may be made (whether by an officer of Revenue and Customs or by the company) by way of an assessment, the modification of an assessment, amendment or disallowance of a claim, or otherwise.

(5)   In this section "relevant tax advantage" means a tax advantage in relation to corporation tax to which the company is chargeable (or would without the tax advantage be chargeable) by virtue of section 5(2A).

(6)   In this section—

"arrangement" (except in the phrase "double taxation arrangements") includes any agreement, understanding, scheme, transaction or series of transactions, whether or not legally enforceable;

"double taxation arrangements" means arrangements which have effect under section 2(1) of TIOPA 2010 (double taxation relief by agreement with territories outside the United Kingdom);

"tax advantage" has the meaning given by section 1139 of CTA 2010.

5B   Trade of dealing in or developing UK land

(1)   A non-UK resident company's "trade of dealing in or developing UK land" consists of —

(a)   any activities falling within subsection (2) which it carries on, and

(b)   any activities from which profits, gains or losses arise which are treated under Part 8ZB of CTA 2010 as profits or losses of the company's trade of dealing in or developing UK land.

(2)   The activities within this subsection are—

(a)   dealing in UK land;

(b)   developing UK land for the purpose of disposing of it.

(3)   In this section "land" includes—

(a)   buildings and structures,

(b)   any estate, interest or right in or over land, and

(c)   land under the sea or otherwise covered by water.

(4)   In this section—

"disposal" is to be interpreted in accordance with section 356OQ of CTA 2010;

"UK land" means land in the United Kingdom."

(6)   In section 3 of CTA 2009 (exclusion of charge to income tax), in subsection (1), for paragraph (b) substitute—

"(b)   the company is not UK resident and—

(i)   the income is profits of a trade of dealing in or developing UK land, or

(ii)   the income is within its chargeable profits as defined by section 19."

(7)   In section 18A of CTA 2009 (exemption for profits or losses of foreign permanent establishments), after subsection (2) insert—

"(2A)   But profits and losses are not to be left out of account as mentioned in subsection (2) so far as they are, or would if the company were non-UK resident be, profits of the company's trade of dealing in or developing UK land (as defined in section 5B)."

(8)   In section 19 of CTA 2009 (chargeable profits) —

    (a)   in subsection (2) for "company's chargeable profits" substitute "company's "chargeable profits"";

    (b)   after subsection (2) insert —

       "(2A)   But the company's "chargeable profits" do not include profits of a trade of dealing in or developing UK land (and accordingly such profits are not attributable to any permanent establishment of the company)."

(9)   In section 189 of CTA 2009 (post-cessation receipts: extent of charge to tax), in subsection (4), at the end insert "other than a company's trade of dealing in or developing UK land".

(10)   In section 107 of CTA 2010 (restrictions on losses etc surrenderable by non-UK resident), in subsection (1), for the words from "non-UK resident" to the end substitute "non-UK resident company —

    (a)   carrying on a trade of dealing in or developing UK land, or

    (b)   carrying on a trade in the United Kingdom through a permanent establishment."

(11)   In section 1119 of CTA 2010 (definitions for purposes of Corporation Tax Acts), at the appropriate place insert —

       ""trade of dealing in or developing UK land", in relation to a non-UK resident company, has the meaning given by section 5B of CTA 2009,".

77   Corporation tax: transactions in UK land

(1)   In CTA 2010, after Part 8ZA insert —

"PART 8ZB

TRANSACTIONS IN UK LAND

Introduction

356OA Overview of Part

This Part contains provision about the corporation tax treatment of certain profits and gains realised from disposals concerned with land in the United Kingdom.

Amounts treated as profits of a trade

356OB Disposals of land in the United Kingdom

(1)   Section 356OC(1) applies (subject to subsection (3) of that section) if —

    (a)   a person within subsection (2)(a), (b) or (c) realises a profit or gain from a disposal of any land in the United Kingdom, and

    (b)   any of conditions A to D is met in relation to the land.

(2)   The persons referred to in subsection (1) are —

    (a)   the person acquiring, holding or developing the land,

    (b)   a person who is associated with the person in paragraph (a) at a relevant time, and

    (c)   a person who is a party to, or concerned in, an arrangement within subsection (3).

(3)   An arrangement is within this subsection if —

    (a)   it is effected with respect to all or part of the land, and

    (b)   it enables a profit or gain to be realised —

        (i)   by any indirect method, or

        (ii)   by any series of transactions.

(4)   Condition A is that the main purpose, or one of the main purposes, of acquiring the land was to realise a profit or gain from disposing of the land.

(5)   Condition B is that the main purpose, or one of the main purposes, of acquiring any property deriving its value from the land was to realise a profit or gain from disposing of the land.

(6)   Condition C is that the land is held as trading stock.

(7)   Condition D is that (in a case where the land has been developed) the main purpose, or one of the main purposes, of developing the land was to realise a profit or gain from disposing of the land when developed.

(8)   In this section "relevant time" means any time in the period beginning when the activities of the project begin and ending 6 months after the disposal mentioned in subsection (1).

(9)   In this section "the project" means all activities carried out for any of the following purposes —

    (a)   the purposes of dealing in or developing the land, and

    (b)   any other purposes mentioned in Conditions A to D.

(10)   For the purposes of this section a person ("A") is associated with another person ("B") if —

    (a)   A is connected with B by virtue of any of subsections (5) to (7) of section 1122 (read in accordance with section 1123), or

    (b)   A is related to B (see section 356OT).

356OC Disposals of land: profits treated as trading profits

(1)   The profit or gain is to be treated for corporation tax purposes as profits of a trade carried on by the chargeable company (see section 356OG).

(2)   If the chargeable company is non-UK resident, that trade is the company's trade of dealing in or developing UK land (as defined in section 5B of CTA 2009).

(3)   But subsection (1) does not apply to a profit or gain so far as it would (apart from this section) be brought into account as income in calculating profits (of any person) —

    (a)   for corporation tax purposes, or

    (b)   for income tax purposes.

(4)   The profits are treated as arising in the accounting period of the chargeable company in which the profit or gain is realised.

(5)   This section applies in relation to gains which are capital in nature as it applies in relation to other gains.

356OD Disposals of property deriving its value from land in the United Kingdom

(1)   Section 356OE applies (subject to subsection (3) of that section) if—

    (a)   a person realises a profit or gain from a disposal of any property which (at the time of the disposal) derives at least 50% of its value from land in the United Kingdom,

    (b)   the person is a party to, or concerned in, an arrangement concerning some or all of the land mentioned in paragraph (a) ("the project land"), and

    (c)   the arrangement meets the condition in subsection (2).

(2)   The condition is that the main purpose, or one of the main purposes, of the arrangement is to—

    (a)   deal in or develop the project land, and

    (b)   realise a profit or gain from a disposal of property deriving the whole or part of its value from that land.

356OE Disposals within section 356OD: profits treated as trading profits

(1)   The relevant amount is to be treated for corporation tax purposes as profits of a trade carried on by the chargeable company.

(2)   If the chargeable company is non-UK resident, that trade is the company's trade of dealing in or developing UK land.

(3)   But subsection (1) does not apply to an amount so far as it would (apart from this section) be brought into account as income in calculating profits (of any person)—

    (a)   for corporation tax purposes, or

    (b)   for income tax purposes.

(4)   The profits are treated as arising in the accounting period of the chargeable company in which the profit or gain is realised.

(5)   In this section the "relevant amount" means so much (if any) of the profit or gain mentioned in section 356OD(1) as is attributable, on a just and reasonable apportionment, to the relevant UK assets.

(6)   In this section "the relevant UK assets" means any land in the United Kingdom from which the property mentioned in section 356OD(1) derives any of its value (at the time of the disposal mentioned in that subsection).

(7)   This section applies in relation to gains which are capital in nature as it applies in relation to other gains.

356OF Profits and losses

(1)   Sections 356OB to 356OE have effect as if they included provision about losses corresponding to the provision they make about profits and gains.

(2)   Accordingly, in the following sections of this Part references to a "profit or gain" include a loss.

Person to whom profits attributed

356OG The chargeable company

(1) For the purposes of sections 356OC and 356OE the general rule is that the "chargeable company" is the company ("C") that realises the profit or gain (as mentioned in section 356OB(1) or 356OD(1)).

(2) The general rule in subsection (1) is subject to the special rules in subsections (4) to (6).

(3) But those special rules do not apply in relation to a profit or gain to which section 356OH(3) (fragmented activities) applies.

(4) If all or any part of the profit or gain accruing to C is derived from value provided directly or indirectly by another person ("B") which is a company, B is the "chargeable company".

(5) Subsection (4) applies whether or not the value is put at the disposal of C.

(6) If all or any part of the profit or gain accruing to C is derived from an opportunity of realising a profit or gain provided directly or indirectly by another person ("D") which is a company, D is "the chargeable company" (unless the case falls within subsection (4)).

(7) For the meaning of "another person" see section 356OO.

Anti-fragmentation

356OH Fragmented activities

(1) Subsection (3) applies if—
    (a) a company ("C") disposes of any land in the United Kingdom,
    (b) any of conditions A to D in section 356OB is met in relation to the land, and
    (c) a person ("R") who is associated with C at a relevant time has made a relevant contribution to activities falling within subsection (2).

(2) The following activities fall within this subsection—
    (a) the development of the land,
    (b) any other activities directed towards realising a profit or gain from the disposal of the land.

(3) For the purposes of this Part, the profit or gain (if any) realised by C from the disposal is to be taken to be what that profit or gain would be if R were not a distinct person from C (and, accordingly, as if everything done by or in relation to R had been done by or in relation to C).

(4) Subsection (5) applies to any amount which is paid (directly or indirectly) by R to C for the purposes of meeting or reimbursing the cost of corporation tax which C is liable to pay as a result of the application of subsection (3) in relation to R and C.

(5) The amount—

      (a)   is not to be taken into account in calculating profits or losses of either R or C for the purposes of income tax or corporation tax, and

      (b)   is not for any purpose of the Corporation Tax Acts to be regarded as a distribution.

(6)   In subsection (1) "relevant time" means any time in the period beginning when the activities of the project begin and ending 6 months after the disposal.

(7)   For the purposes of this section any contribution made by R to activities falling within subsection (2) is a "relevant contribution" unless the profit made or to be made by R in respect of the contribution is insignificant having regard to the size of the project.

(8)   In this section "contribution" means any kind of contribution, including, for example—

      (a)   the provision of professional or other services, or

      (b)   a financial contribution (including the assumption of a risk).

(9)   For the purposes of this section R is "associated" with C if—

      (a)   R is connected with C by virtue of any of subsections (5) to (7) of section 1122 (read in accordance with section 1123), or

      (b)   R is related to C (see section 356OT).

(10)   In this section "the project" means all activities carried out for any of the following purposes—

      (a)   the purposes of dealing in or developing the land, and

      (b)   any other purposes mentioned in Conditions A to D in section 356OB.

Calculation of profit or gain on disposal

356OI Calculation of profit or gain on disposal

For the purposes of this Part, the profit or gain (if any) from a disposal of any property is to be calculated according to the principles applicable for calculating the profits of a trade under Part 3 of CTA 2009, subject to any modifications that may be appropriate (and for this purpose the same rules are to apply in calculating losses from a disposal as apply in calculating profits).

356OJ Apportionments

Any apportionment (whether of expenditure, consideration or any other amount) that is required to be made for the purposes of this Part is to be made on a just and reasonable basis.

Arrangements for avoiding tax

356OK Arrangements for avoiding tax

(1)   Subsection (3) applies if an arrangement has been entered into the main purpose or one of the main purposes of which is to enable a company to obtain a relevant tax advantage.

(2) In subsection (1) the reference to obtaining a relevant tax advantage includes obtaining a relevant tax advantage by virtue of any provisions of double taxation arrangements, but only in a case where the relevant tax advantage is contrary to the object and purpose of the provisions of the double taxation arrangements (and subsection (3) has effect accordingly, regardless of anything in section 6(1) of TIOPA 2010).

(3) The tax advantage is to be counteracted by means of adjustments.

(4) For this purpose adjustments may be made (whether by an officer of Revenue and Customs or by the company) by way of an assessment, the modification of an assessment, amendment or disallowance of a claim, or otherwise.

(5) In this section "relevant tax advantage" means a tax advantage in relation to corporation tax charged (or which would, if the tax advantage were not obtained, be charged) in respect of amounts treated as profits of a trade by virtue of this Part.

(6) In this section—

"double taxation arrangements" means arrangements which have effect under section 2(1) of TIOPA 2010 (double taxation relief by agreement with territories outside the United Kingdom);

"tax advantage" has the meaning given by section 1139.

Exemption

356OL Profits attributable to period before relevant activities etc began

(1) Subsection (2) applies if—

    (a) subsection (1) of section 356OC applies because Condition D in section 356OB is met (land developed with purpose of realising a gain from its disposal when developed), and

    (b) part of the profit or gain mentioned in that subsection is fairly attributable to a period before the intention to develop was formed.

(2) Section 356OC(1) has effect as if the person mentioned in section 356OB(1) had not realised that part of the profit or gain.

(3) Subsection (4) applies if—

    (a) section 356OE(1) applies, and

    (b) part of the profit or gain mentioned in section 356OE(5) is fairly attributable to a period before the person mentioned in section 356OD(1) was a party to, or concerned in, the arrangement in question.

(4) Section 356OE has effect as if the person had not realised that part of the profit or gain.

(5) In applying this section account must be taken of the treatment under Part 3 of CTA 2009 (trading income) of a company which appropriates land as trading stock.

Other supplementary provisions

356OM Tracing value

(1) This section applies if it is necessary to determine the extent to which the value of any property or right is derived from any other property or right for the purposes of this Part.

(2) Value may be traced through any number of companies, partnerships, trusts and other entities or arrangements.

(3) The property held by a company, partnership or trust must be attributed to the shareholders, partners, beneficiaries or other participants at each stage in whatever way is appropriate in the circumstances.

(4) In this section —

"partnership" includes an entity established under the law of a country or territory outside the United Kingdom of a similar nature to a partnership; and "partners", in relation to such arrangements, is to be construed accordingly;

"trust" includes arrangements —

    (a) which have effect under the law of a country or territory outside the United Kingdom; and

    (b) under which persons acting in a fiduciary capacity hold and administer property on behalf of other persons,

and "beneficiaries", in relation to such arrangements, is to be construed accordingly.

356ON Relevance of transactions, arrangements, etc

(1) In determining whether section 356OC(1) or 356OE(1) applies, account is to be taken of any method, however indirect, by which —

    (a) any property or right is transferred or transmitted, or

    (b) the value of any property or right is enhanced or diminished.

(2) Accordingly —

    (a) the occasion of the transfer or transmission of any property or right, however indirect, and

    (b) the occasion when the value of any property or right is enhanced,

may be an occasion on which section 356OC(1) or 356OE(1) applies.

(3) Subsections (1) and (2) apply in particular —

    (a) to sales, contracts and other transactions made otherwise than for full consideration or for more than full consideration,

    (b) to any method by which any property or right, or the control of any property or right, is transferred or transmitted by assigning —

        (i) share capital or other rights in a company,

        (ii) rights in a partnership, or

        (iii) an interest in settled property,

    (c) to the creation of an option affecting the disposition of any property or right and the giving of consideration for granting it,

  (d) to the creation of a requirement for consent affecting such a disposition and the giving of consideration for granting it,

  (e) to the creation of an embargo affecting such a disposition and the giving of consideration for releasing it, and

  (f) to the disposal of any property or right on the winding up, dissolution or termination of a company, partnership or trust.

Interpretation

356OO "Another person"

 (1) In this Part references to "other" persons are to be interpreted in accordance with subsections (2) to (4).

 (2) A partnership or partners in a partnership may be regarded as a person or persons distinct from the individuals or other persons who are for the time being partners.

 (3) The trustees of settled property may be regarded as persons distinct from the individuals or other persons who are for the time being the trustees.

 (4) Personal representatives may be regarded as persons distinct from the individuals or other persons who are for the time being personal representatives.

356OP "Arrangement"

 (1) In this Part "arrangement" (except in the phrase "double taxation arrangements") includes any agreement, understanding, scheme, transaction or series of transactions, whether or not legally enforceable).

 (2) For the purposes of this Part any number of transactions may be regarded as constituting a single arrangement if—

  (a) a common purpose can be discerned in them, or

  (b) there is other sufficient evidence of a common purpose.

356OQ "Disposal"

 (1) In this Part references to a "disposal" of any property include any case in which the property is effectively disposed of (whether wholly or in part, as mentioned in subsection (2))—

  (a) by one or more transactions, or

  (b) by any arrangement.

 (2) For the purposes of this Part—

  (a) references to a disposal of land or any other property include a part disposal of the property, and

  (b) there is a part disposal of property ("the asset") where on a person making a disposal, any form of property derived from the asset remains undisposed of (including in cases where an interest or right in or over the asset is created by the disposal, as well as where it subsists before the disposal).

356OR "Land" and related expressions

 (1) In this Part "land" includes—

      (a)   buildings and structures,

      (b)   any estate, interest or right in or over land, and

      (c)   land under the sea or otherwise covered by water.

(2)   In this Part references to property deriving its value from land include—

      (a)   any shareholding in a company deriving its value directly or indirectly from land,

      (b)   any partnership interest deriving its value directly or indirectly from land,

      (c)   any interest in settled property deriving its value directly or indirectly from land, and

      (d)   any option, consent or embargo affecting the disposition of land.

356OS References to realising a gain

(1)   For the purposes of sections 356OB(1) and 356OD(1) it does not matter whether the person ("P") realising the profit or gain in question realises it for P or another person.

(2)   For the purposes of subsection (1), if, for example by a premature sale, a person ("A") directly or indirectly transmits the opportunity of realising a profit or gain to another person ("B"), A realises B's profit or gain for B.

356OT Related parties

(1)   For the purposes of this Part a person ("A") is related to another person ("B")—

      (a)   throughout any period for which A and B are consolidated for accounting purposes,

      (b)   on any day on which the participation condition is met in relation to them, or

      (c)   on any day on which the 25% investment condition is met in relation to them.

(2)   A and B are consolidated for accounting purposes for a period if—

      (a)   their financial results for a period are required to be comprised in group accounts,

      (b)   their financial results for the period would be required to be comprised in group accounts but for the application of an exemption, or

      (c)   their financial results for a period are in fact comprised in group accounts.

(3)   In subsection (2) "group accounts" means accounts prepared under—

      (a)   section 399 of the Companies Act 2006, or

      (b)   any corresponding provision of the law of a territory outside the United Kingdom.

(4)   The participation condition is met in relation to A and B ("the relevant parties") on a day if, within the period of 6 months beginning with that day—

      (a)   one of the relevant parties directly or indirectly participates in the management, control or capital of the other, or

   (b) the same person or persons directly or indirectly participate in the management, control or capital of each of the relevant parties.

  (5) The 25% investment condition is met in relation to A and B if—

   (a) one of them has a 25% investment in the other, or

   (b) a third person has a 25% investment in each of them.

  (6) Section 259NC of TIOPA 2010 applies for the purposes of determining whether a person has a "25% investment" in another person for the purposes of this section as it applies for the purposes of section 259NB(2) of that Act.

  (7) In Chapter 2 of Part 4 of TIOPA 2010, sections 157(2), 158(4), 159(2) and 160(2) (which are about the interpretation of references to direct and indirect participation) apply in relation to subsection (4) as they apply in relation to subsection (4) of section 259NA of that Act."

 (2) In section 1 of CTA 2010 (overview), in subsection (4), omit paragraph (e).

 (3) In section 481 of CTA 2010 (exemption from charges under provisions to which section 1173 applies), in subsection (2) omit paragraph (a).

 (4) In CTA 2010 omit Part 18 (transactions in land).

 (5) In section 1173 of CTA 2010 (miscellaneous charges), in Part 2 of the table in subsection (2), omit the entry relating to section 818(1) of CTA 2010.

 (6) In section 14B of TCGA 1992 (meaning of "non-resident CGT disposal")—

   (a) in subsection (1) for "subsection (5)" substitute "subsections (5) and (6)";

   (b) after subsection (5) insert—

    "(6) A disposal of a UK residential property interest is not a non-resident CGT disposal if section 356OC(1) of CTA 2010 (gains etc on certain disposals treated as trading profits for corporation tax purposes) or section 517C of ITA 2007 (gains etc on certain disposals treated as trading profits for income tax purposes) applies in relation to it."

 (7) In section 37 of TCGA 1992 (consideration chargeable to tax on income), in subsection (5A)(a), for the words from "821(3)" to "not" substitute "356OG(4) or (6) of CTA 2010 (transactions in land: the chargeable company) applies, an amount is charged to corporation tax as profits of a person other than".

 (8) In section 39 of TCGA 1992 (exclusion of expenditure by reference to tax on income), in subsection (5)(a), for the words from "821(3)" to "not" substitute "356OG(4) or (6) of CTA 2010 (transactions in land: the chargeable company) applies, an amount is charged to corporation tax as profits of a person other than".

 (9) In section 161 of TCGA 1992 (appropriations to and from stock), in subsection (6), for paragraph (a) substitute—

    "(a) any person is charged to corporation tax by virtue of sections 356OB and 356OC of CTA 2010 (certain profits or gains on a disposal of land treated as trading profits) on the realisation of a profit or gain because the condition in section 356OB(7) of that Act is met, and".

(10) In section 188A of TCGA 1992 (election for pooling), in subsection (4), at the end insert "or section 14B(6) (gains on certain disposals treated as trading profits)".

78 Income tax: territorial scope etc

(1) In section 6 of ITTOIA 2005 (territorial scope of charge to tax) —

    (a) after subsection (1) insert —

        "(1A) Profits of a trade of dealing in or developing UK land arising to a non-UK resident are chargeable to tax under this Chapter wherever the trade is carried on.";

    (b) in subsection (2), after "Profits of a trade" insert "other than a trade of dealing in or developing UK land".

(2) After section 6 of ITTOIA 2005 insert —

"6A Arrangements for avoiding tax

(1) Subsection (3) applies if a person has entered into an arrangement the main purpose or one of the main purposes of which is to obtain a relevant tax advantage for the person.

(2) In subsection (1) the reference to obtaining a relevant tax advantage includes obtaining a relevant tax advantage by virtue of any provisions of double taxation arrangements, but only in a case where the relevant tax advantage is contrary to the object and purpose of the provisions of the double taxation arrangements (and subsection (3) has effect accordingly, regardless of anything in section 6(1) of TIOPA 2010).

(3) The relevant tax advantage is to be counteracted by means of adjustments.

(4) For this purpose adjustments may be made (whether by an officer of Revenue and Customs or by the person) by way of an assessment, the modification of an assessment, amendment or disallowance of a claim, or otherwise.

(5) In this section "relevant tax advantage" means a tax advantage in relation to income tax to which the person is chargeable (or would without the tax advantage be chargeable) by virtue of section 6(1A).

(6) In this section "tax advantage" includes —

    (a) a relief or increased relief from tax,

    (b) repayment or increased repayment of tax,

    (c) avoidance or reduction of a charge to tax or an assessment to tax,

    (d) avoidance of a possible assessment to tax,

    (e) deferral of a payment of tax or advancement of a repayment of tax, and

    (f) avoidance of an obligation to deduct or account for tax.

(7) In this section —

        "arrangement" (except in the phrase "double taxation arrangements") includes any agreement, understanding, scheme, transaction or series of transactions, whether or not legally enforceable;

"double taxation arrangements" means arrangements which have effect under section 2(1) of TIOPA 2010 (double taxation relief by agreement with territories outside the United Kingdom).

6B   Trade of dealing in or developing UK land

(1) A non-UK resident person's "trade of dealing in or developing UK land" consists of —

    (a) any activities falling within subsection (2) which the person carries on, and

    (b) any activities from which profits arise which are treated under Part 9A of ITA 2007 as profits of the person's trade of dealing in or developing UK land.

(2) The activities within this subsection are—

    (a) dealing in UK land;

    (b) developing UK land for the purpose of disposing of it.

(3) In this section "land" includes—

    (a) buildings and structures,

    (b) any estate, interest or right in or over land, and

    (c) land under the sea or otherwise covered by water.

(4) In this section—

    "disposal" is to be interpreted in accordance with section 517R of ITA 2007;

    "UK land" means land in the United Kingdom."

(3) In section 3 of ITTOIA 2005 (overview of Part 2), in subsection (4) for "6(2)" substitute "6(1A), (2)".

(4) In section 243 of ITTOIA 2005 (post-cessation receipts: extent of charge to tax), in subsection (4), at the end insert ", other than a person's trade of dealing in or developing UK land".

(5) In section 989 of ITA 2007 (definitions for purposes of Income Tax Acts), at the appropriate place insert—

    ""trade of dealing in or developing UK land", in relation to a non-UK resident person, has the meaning given by section 6B of ITTOIA 2005,".

79   Income tax: transactions in UK land

(1) In ITA 2007, after Part 9 insert—

"PART 9A

TRANSACTIONS IN UK LAND

Introduction

517A Overview of Part

This Part contains provision about the income tax treatment of certain profits and gains realised from disposals concerned with land in the United Kingdom.

Amounts treated as profits of a trade

517B   Disposals of land in the United Kingdom

(1)   Section 517C(1) applies (subject to subsection (3) of that section) if—

    (a)   a person within subsection (2)(a), (b) or (c) realises a profit or gain from a disposal of any land in the United Kingdom, and

    (b)   any of conditions A to D is met in relation to the land.

(2)   The persons referred to in subsection (1) are—

    (a)   the person acquiring, holding or developing the land,

    (b)   a person who is associated with the person in paragraph (a) at a relevant time, and

    (c)   a person who is a party to, or concerned in, an arrangement within subsection (3).

(3)   An arrangement is within this subsection if—

    (a)   it is effected with respect to all or part of the land, and

    (b)   it enables a profit or gain to be realised—

        (i)   by any indirect method, or

        (ii)   by any series of transactions.

(4)   Condition A is that the main purpose, or one of the main purposes, of acquiring the land was to realise a profit or gain from disposing of the land.

(5)   Condition B is that the main purpose, or one of the main purposes, of acquiring any property deriving its value from the land was to realise a profit or gain from disposing of the land.

(6)   Condition C is that the land is held as trading stock.

(7)   Condition D is that (in a case where the land has been developed) the main purpose, or one of the main purposes, of developing the land was to realise a profit or gain from disposing of the land when developed.

(8)   In this section "relevant time" means any time in the period beginning when the activities of the project begin and ending 6 months after the disposal mentioned in subsection (1).

(9)   In this section "the project" means all activities carried out for any of the following purposes—

    (a)   the purposes of dealing in or developing the land, and

    (b)   any other purposes mentioned in Conditions A to D.

(10)   For the purposes of this section a person ("A") is associated with another person ("B") if—

    (a)   A is connected with B by virtue of any of subsections (2) to (4) of section 993 (read in accordance with section 994), or

    (b)   A is related to B (see section 517U).

517C   Disposals of land: profits treated as trading profits

(1)   The profit or gain is to be treated for income tax purposes as profits of a trade carried on by the chargeable person.

(2) If the chargeable person is non-UK resident, that trade is the person's trade of dealing in or developing UK land (as defined in section 6B of ITTOIA 2005).

(3) But subsection (1) does not apply to a profit or gain so far as it would (apart from this section) be brought into account as income in calculating profits (of any person) —

    (a) for income tax purposes, or

    (b) for corporation tax purposes.

(4) The profits are treated as arising in the tax year in which the profit or gain is realised.

(5) This section applies in relation to gains which are capital in nature as it applies in relation to other gains.

517D Disposals of property deriving its value from land in the United Kingdom

(1) Section 517E(1) applies (subject to subsection (3) of that section) if —

    (a) a person realises a profit or gain from a disposal of any property which (at the time of the disposal) derives at least 50% of its value from land in the United Kingdom,

    (b) the person is a party to, or concerned in, an arrangement concerning some or all of the land mentioned in paragraph (a) ("the project land"), and

    (c) the arrangement meets the condition in subsection (2).

(2) The condition is that the main purpose, or one of the main purposes, of the arrangement is to —

    (a) deal in or develop the project land, and

    (b) realise a profit or gain from a disposal of property deriving the whole or part of its value from that land.

517E Disposals within section 517D: profits treated as trading profits

(1) The relevant amount is to be treated for income tax purposes as profits of a trade carried on by the chargeable person.

(2) If the chargeable person is non-UK resident, that trade is the chargeable person's trade of dealing in or developing UK land.

(3) But subsection (1) does not apply to an amount so far as it would (apart from this section) be brought into account as income in calculating profits (of any person) —

    (a) for income tax purposes, or

    (b) for corporation tax purposes.

(4) The profits are treated as arising in the tax year in which the profit or gain is realised.

(5) In this section the "relevant amount" means so much (if any) of the profit or gain mentioned in section 517D(1) as is attributable, on a just and reasonable apportionment, to the relevant UK assets.

(6) In this section "the relevant UK assets" means any land in the United Kingdom from which the property mentioned in section 517D(1)

derives any of its value (at the time of the disposal mentioned in that subsection).

(7) This section applies in relation to gains which are capital in nature as it applies in relation to other gains.

517F   Profits and losses

(1) Sections 517B to 517E have effect as if they included provision about losses corresponding to the provision they make about profits and gains.

(2) Accordingly, in the following sections of this Part references to a "profit or gain" include a loss.

Person to whom profits attributed

517G   The chargeable person

(1) For the purposes of sections 517C and 517E the general rule is that the "chargeable person" is the person ("P") that realises the profit or gain (as mentioned in section 517B(1) or 517D(1)).

(2) The general rule in subsection (1) is subject to the special rules in subsections (4) to (6).

(3) But those special rules do not apply in relation to a profit or gain to which section 517H(3) (fragmented activities) applies.

(4) If all or any part of the profit or gain accruing to P is derived from value provided directly or indirectly by another person ("B"), B is the "chargeable person".

(5) Subsection (4) applies whether or not the value is put at the disposal of P.

(6) If all or any part of the profit or gain accruing to P is derived from an opportunity of realising a profit or gain provided directly or indirectly by another person ("D"), D is "the chargeable person" (unless the case falls within subsection (4)).

(7) For the meaning of "another person" see section 517P.

Anti-fragmentation

517H   Fragmented activities

(1) Subsection (3) applies if —
   (a) a person ("P") disposes of any land in the United Kingdom,
   (b) any of conditions A to D in section 517B is met in relation to the land, and
   (c) a person ("R") who is associated with P at a relevant time has made a relevant contribution to activities falling within subsection (2).

(2) The following activities fall within this subsection —
   (a) the development of the land,

     (b)   any other activities directed towards realising a profit or gain from the disposal of the land.

(3)   For the purposes of this Part, the profit or gain (if any) realised by P from the disposal is to be taken to be what that profit or gain would be if R were not a distinct person from P (and, accordingly, as if everything done by or in relation to R had been done by or in relation to P).

(4)   Subsection (5) applies to any amount which is paid (directly or indirectly) by R to P for the purposes of meeting or reimbursing the cost of income tax which P is liable to pay as a result of the application of subsection (3) in relation to R and P.

(5)   The amount—

    (a)   is not to be taken into account in calculating profits or losses of either R or P for the purposes of income tax or corporation tax, and

    (b)   is not for any purpose of the Corporation Tax Acts to be regarded as a distribution.

(6)   In subsection (1) "relevant time" means any time in the period beginning when the activities of the project begin and ending 6 months after the disposal.

(7)   For the purposes of this section any contribution made by P to activities falling within subsection (2) is a "relevant contribution" unless the profit made or to be made by P in respect of the contribution is insignificant having regard to the size of the project.

(8)   In this section "contribution" means any kind of contribution, including, for example—

    (a)   the provision of professional or other services, or

    (b)   a financial contribution (including the assumption of a risk).

(9)   For the purposes of this section R is "associated" with P if—

    (a)   R is connected with P by virtue of any of subsections (2) to (4) of section 993 (read in accordance with section 994), or

    (b)   R is related to P (see section 517U).

(10)   In this section "the project" means all activities carried out for any of the following purposes—

    (a)   the purposes of dealing in or developing the land, and

    (b)   any other purposes mentioned in Conditions A to D in section 517B.

Calculation of profit or gain on disposal

517I   Calculation of surplus on a disposal of land

For the purposes of this Part, the profit or gain (if any) from a disposal of any property is to be calculated according to the principles applicable for calculating the profits of a trade under Part 2 of ITTOIA 2005, subject to any modifications that may be appropriate (and for this purpose the same rules are to apply in calculating losses from a disposal as apply in calculating profits).

517J Apportionments

Any apportionment (whether of expenditure, consideration or any other amount) that is required to be made for the purposes of this Part is to be made on a just and reasonable basis.

Arrangements for avoiding tax

517K Arrangements for avoiding tax

(1) Subsection (3) applies if an arrangement has been entered into the main purpose or one of the main purposes of which is to enable a person to obtain a relevant tax advantage.

(2) In subsection (1) the reference to obtaining a relevant tax advantage includes obtaining a relevant tax advantage by virtue of any provisions of double taxation arrangements, but only in a case where the relevant tax advantage is contrary to the object and purpose of the provisions of the double taxation arrangements (and subsection (3) has effect accordingly, regardless of anything in section 6(1) of TIOPA 2010).

(3) The tax advantage is to be counteracted by means of adjustments.

(4) For this purpose adjustments may be made (whether by an officer of Revenue and Customs or by the person) by way of an assessment, the modification of an assessment, amendment or disallowance of a claim, or otherwise.

(5) In this section "relevant tax advantage" means an advantage in relation to income tax charged (or which would, if the tax advantage were not obtained, be charged) in respect of amounts treated as profits of a trade by virtue of this Part.

(6) In this section "advantage" includes —
   (a) a relief or increased relief from tax,
   (b) repayment or increased repayment of tax,
   (c) avoidance or reduction of a charge to tax or an assessment to tax,
   (d) avoidance of a possible assessment to tax,
   (e) deferral of a payment of tax or advancement of a repayment of tax, and
   (f) avoidance of an obligation to deduct or account for tax.

Exemptions

517L Gain attributable to period before intention to develop formed

(1) Subsection (2) applies if —
   (a) subsection (1) of section 517C applies because Condition D in section 517B is met (land developed with purpose of realising a gain from its disposal when developed), and
   (b) part of the profit or gain mentioned in that subsection is fairly attributable to a period before the intention to develop was formed.

(2) Section 517C(1) has effect as if the person mentioned in section 517B(1) had not realised that part of the profit or gain.

(3) Subsection (4) applies if—

    (a) section 517E(1) applies, and

    (b) part of the profit or gain mentioned in section 517E(5) is fairly attributable to a period before the person mentioned in section 517D(1) was a party to, or concerned in, the arrangement in question.

(4) Section 517E has effect as if the person had not realised that part of the profit or gain.

(5) In applying this section account must be taken of the treatment under Part 2 of ITTOIA 2005 (trading income) of a person who appropriates land as trading stock.

517M Private residences

No liability to income tax arises under this Part in respect of a gain accruing to an individual if—

    (a) the gain is exempt from capital gains tax as a result of sections 222 to 226 of TCGA 1992 (private residences), or

    (b) it would be so exempt but for section 224(3) of that Act (residences acquired partly with a view to making a gain).

Other supplementary provisions

517N Tracing value

(1) This section applies if it is necessary to determine the extent to which the value of any property or right is derived from any other property or right for the purposes of this Part.

(2) Value may be traced through any number of companies, partnerships, trusts and other entities or arrangements.

(3) The property held by a company, partnership or trust must be attributed to the shareholders, partners, beneficiaries or other participants at each stage in whatever way is appropriate in the circumstances.

(4) In this section—

    "partnership" includes an entity established under the law of a country or territory outside the United Kingdom of a similar nature to a partnership; and "partners", in relation to such arrangements, is to be construed accordingly;

    "trust" includes arrangements—

        (a) which have effect under the law of a country or territory outside the United Kingdom; and

        (b) under which persons acting in a fiduciary capacity hold and administer property on behalf of other persons,

    and "beneficiaries", in relation to such arrangements, is to be construed accordingly.

517O Relevance of transactions, arrangements, etc

(1) In determining whether section 517C(1) or 517E(1) applies, account is to be taken of any method, however indirect, by which—

    (a) any property or right is transferred or transmitted, or

    (b) the value of any property or right is enhanced or diminished.

(2) Accordingly—

    (a) the occasion of the transfer or transmission of any property or right, however indirect, and

    (b) the occasion when the value of any property or right is enhanced,

may be an occasion on which section 517C(1) or 517E(1) applies.

(3) Subsections (1) and (2) apply in particular—

    (a) to sales, contracts and other transactions made otherwise than for full consideration or for more than full consideration,

    (b) to any method by which any property or right, or the control of any property or right, is transferred or transmitted by assigning—

        (i) share capital or other rights in a company,

        (ii) rights in a partnership, or

        (iii) an interest in settled property,

    (c) to the creation of an option affecting the disposition of any property or right and the giving of consideration for granting it,

    (d) to the creation of a requirement for consent affecting such a disposition and the giving of consideration for granting it,

    (e) to the creation of an embargo affecting such a disposition and the giving of consideration for releasing it, and

    (f) to the disposal of any property or right on the winding up, dissolution or termination of a company, partnership or trust.

Interpretation

517P "Another person"

(1) In this Part references to "other" persons are to be interpreted in accordance with subsections (2) to (4).

(2) A partnership or partners in a partnership may be regarded as a person or persons distinct from the individuals or other persons who are for the time being partners.

(3) The trustees of settled property may be regarded as persons distinct from the individuals or other persons who are for the time being the trustees.

(4) Personal representatives may be regarded as persons distinct from the individuals or other persons who are for the time being personal representatives.

517Q "Arrangement"

(1) In this Part "arrangement" (except in the phrase "double taxation arrangements") includes any agreement, understanding, scheme, transaction or series of transactions, whether or not legally enforceable.

(2) For the purposes of this Part any number of transactions may be regarded as constituting a single arrangement if—

    (a) a common purpose can be discerned in them, or

    (b) there is other sufficient evidence of a common purpose.

517R "Disposal"

(1) In this Part references to a "disposal" of any property include any case in which the property is effectively disposed of (whether wholly or in part, as mentioned in subsection (2))—

    (a) by one or more transactions, or

    (b) by any arrangement.

(2) For the purposes of this Part—

    (a) references to a disposal of land or any other property include a part disposal of the property, and

    (b) there is a part disposal of property ("the asset") where on a person making a disposal, any form of property derived from the asset remains undisposed of (including in cases where an interest or right in or over the asset is created by the disposal, as well as where it subsists before the disposal).

517S "Land" and related expressions

(1) In this Part "land" includes—

    (a) buildings and structures,

    (b) any estate, interest or right in or over land, and

    (c) land under the sea or otherwise covered by water.

(2) In this Part references to property deriving its value from land include—

    (a) any shareholding in a company deriving its value directly or indirectly from land,

    (b) any partnership interest deriving its value directly or indirectly from land,

    (c) any interest in settled property deriving its value directly or indirectly from land, and

    (d) any option, consent or embargo affecting the disposition of land.

517T References to realising a gain

(1) For the purposes of sections 517B(1) and 517D(1) it does not matter whether the person ("P") realising the profit or gain in question realises it for P or another person.

(2) For the purposes of subsection (1), if, for example by a premature sale, a person ("A") directly or indirectly transmits the opportunity of realising a profit or gain to another person ("B"), A realises B's profit or gain for B.

517U Related parties

(1) For the purposes of this Part a person ("A") is related to another person ("B")—

        (a)   throughout any period for which A and B are consolidated for accounting purposes,

        (b)   on any day on which the participation condition is met in relation to them, or

        (c)   on any day on which the 25% investment condition is met in relation to them.

(2)   A and B are consolidated for accounting purposes for a period if—

        (a)   their financial results for a period are required to be comprised in group accounts,

        (b)   their financial results for the period would be required to be comprised in group accounts but for the application of an exemption, or

        (c)   their financial results for a period are in fact comprised in group accounts.

(3)   In subsection (2) "group accounts" means accounts prepared under—

        (a)   section 399 of the Companies Act 2006, or

        (b)   any corresponding provision of the law of a territory outside the United Kingdom.

(4)   The participation condition is met in relation to A and B ("the relevant parties") on a day if, within the period of 6 months beginning with that day—

        (a)   one of the relevant parties directly or indirectly participates in the management, control or capital of the other, or

        (b)   the same person or persons directly or indirectly participate in the management, control or capital of each of the relevant parties.

(5)   The 25% investment condition is met in relation to A and B if—

        (a)   one of them has a 25% investment in the other, or

        (b)   a third person has a 25% investment in each of them.

(6)   Section 259NC of TIOPA 2010 applies for the purposes of determining whether a person has a "25% investment" in another person for the purposes of this section as it applies for the purposes of section 259NB(2) of that Act.

(7)   In Chapter 2 of Part 4 of TIOPA 2010, sections 157(2), 158(4), 159(2) and 160(2) (which are about the interpretation of references to direct and indirect participation) apply in relation to subsection (4) as they apply in relation to subsection (4) of section 259NA of that Act."

(2)   In section 2 of ITA 2007 (overview of Act)—

    (a)   after subsection (9) insert—

        "(9A)   Part 9A is about the treatment of certain transactions in UK land.", and

    (b)   in subsection (13), omit paragraph (c).

(3)   In section 482 of ITA 2007 (types of amount to be charged at special rates for trustees), in the words relating to Type 11, for "Chapter 3 of Part 13 of this Act (tax avoidance: transactions in land)" substitute "Part 9A of this Act (transactions in land)".

(4)   In section 527 of ITA 2007 (exemption from charges under provisions to which section 1016 applies), in subsection (2) —

    (a)   insert "and" at the end of paragraph (d), and

    (b)   omit paragraph (e).

(5)   In Part 13 of ITA 2007, omit Chapter 3 (transactions in land).

(6)   In section 944 of ITA 2007 (tax avoidance: directions for duty to deduct to apply), in subsection (1) —

    (a)   omit paragraph (a), and

    (b)   in paragraph (b) for "that Part" substitute "Part 13".

(7)   In section 1016 of ITA 2007 (table of provisions to which that section applies), in Part 2 of the table in subsection (2), omit the entry relating to Chapter 3 of Part 13 of that Act.

(8)   In section 37 of TCGA 1992 (consideration chargeable to tax on income), in subsection (5)(a), for the words from "759(4)" to "is" substitute "517G(4) or (6) of ITA 2007 (transactions in land: the chargeable person) applies, an amount is charged to income tax as income of"

(9)   In section 39 of TCGA 1992 (exclusion of expenditure by reference to tax on income), in subsection (4)(a), for the words from "759(4)" to "is" substitute "517G(4) or (6) of ITA 2007 (transactions in land: the chargeable person) applies, an amount is charged to income tax as income of".

(10)   In section 161 of TCGA 1992 (appropriations to and from stock), in subsection (5), for paragraph (a) substitute —

    "(a)   any person is charged to income tax by virtue of sections 517B and 517C of CTA 2010 (certain profits or gains on a disposal of land treated as trading profits) on the realisation of a profit or gain because the condition in section 517B(7) of that Act is met, and".

(11)   In section 830 of ITTOIA 2005, in subsection (3), for the words from "of" to the end substitute "of —

    (a)   section 844 (unremittable income: income charged on withdrawal of relief after source ceases), or

    (b)   section 517C or 517E of ITA 2007 (profits on certain disposals concerned with land in the United Kingdom treated as trading profits)."

80   Pre-trading expenses

(1)   Subsection (2) has effect if —

    (a)   a particular time ("T") is the time when a company ("C") is first within the charge to corporation tax by virtue of subsection (2)(a) of section 5 of CTA 2009 (territorial scope of charge),

    (b)   immediately before time T, C was within the charge to corporation tax as a result of carrying on the relevant trade in the United Kingdom through a permanent establishment in the United Kingdom, and

    (c)   expenses which the company has incurred for the purposes of the trade meet the conditions in subsection (3) and (4).

"The relevant trade" means the trade of dealing in or developing UK land mentioned in subsection (2)(a) of section 5 of CTA 2009.

(2) Section 61 of CTA 2009 (pre-trading expenses) has effect in relation to those expenses as if the company had started to carry on the relevant trade at time T.

(3) The condition in this subsection is that—

    (a) no deduction would be allowed for the expenses in calculating the profits of the relevant trade for corporation tax purposes (ignoring subsection (2)), but

    (b) a deduction would be allowed for them (in accordance with sections 41 and section 61 of CTA 2009) if the company had not been within the charge to corporation tax in respect of the relevant trade immediately before time T.

(4) The condition in this subsection is that no relief has been obtained for the expenses under the law of any country or territory outside the United Kingdom.

81 Commencement and transitional provision: sections 76, 77 and 80

(1) The amendments made by sections 76, 77 and 80 have effect in relation to disposals on or after 5 July 2016.

(2) In subsection (1) of section 5A of CTA 2009 (tax avoidance in relation to section 5(2A) of that Act) "arrangement" does not include an arrangement (as defined in section 5A(6) of that Act) entered into before 16 March 2016.

(3) In subsection (1) of section 356OK of CTA 2010 (tax avoidance in relation to Part 8ZB of CTA 2010) "arrangement" does not include an arrangement (as defined in section 356OP of that Act) entered into before 16 March 2016.

(4) Subsection (6) applies if—

    (a) a person disposes of a relevant asset to a person who is associated with that person at the relevant time,

    (b) the disposal is made on or after 16 March 2016 and before 5 July 2016, and

    (c) a company obtains a relevant tax advantage as a result of the disposal.

(5) In subsection (4) the reference to obtaining a relevant tax advantage includes obtaining a relevant tax advantage by virtue of any provisions of double taxation arrangements, but only in a case where the relevant tax advantage is contrary to the object and purpose of the provisions of the double taxation arrangements (and subsection (6) has effect accordingly, regardless of anything in section 6(1) of TIOPA 2010).

(6) The tax advantage is to be counteracted by means of adjustments.

(7) Adjustments for the purposes of subsection (6) may be made (whether by an officer of Revenue and Customs or by the company) by way of an assessment, the modification of an assessment, amendment or disallowance of a claim, or otherwise.

(8) In subsection (4)(c) "relevant tax advantage" means a tax advantage in relation to tax to which the company in question is charged or chargeable (or would, if the tax advantage were not obtained, be charged or chargeable)—

    (a) by virtue of section 5(2A) of CTA 2009, or

    (b) in respect of amounts treated as profits of a trade by virtue of Part 8ZB of CTA 2010.

(9) For the purposes of this section, where any property is disposed of under a contract, the time at which the disposal is made is the time the contract is made (and not, if different, the time at which the property is conveyed or transferred).

(10) In subsection (9) "contract" includes a conditional contract.

(11) In this section—

"arrangement" includes any scheme, agreement or understanding (whether or not legally enforceable);

"disposal" is to be interpreted in accordance with section 356OQ of CTA 2010;

"relevant asset" means land, or property deriving the whole or part of its value from land;

"tax advantage" has the meaning given by section 1139 of CTA 2010.

(12) For the purposes of this section a person ("A") is "associated" with another person ("B") if—

   (a) A is connected with B by virtue of any of subsections (5) to (7) of section 1122 of CTA 2010 (read in accordance with section 1123 of that Act), or

   (b) A is related to B.

(13) In subsection (12) "related to" is to be interpreted in accordance with section 356OT of CTA 2010.

(14) In subsection (4) "the relevant time"—

   (a) in a case within subsection (8)(a), means the time of the disposal mentioned in subsection (4)(a).

   (b) in a case within subsection (8)(b), means any time in the period beginning when the activities of the project began and ending 6 months after the disposal mentioned in section 356OB(1) or 356OD(1) of CTA 2010.

(15) In subsection (14) "the project" means (as the case requires) the project described in section 356OB(9) of CTA 2010 or the activities mentioned in section 356OD(2)(a) of that Act.

82 Commencement and transitional provision: sections 78 and 79

(1) The amendments made by sections 78 and 79 have effect in relation to disposals on or after 5 July 2016.

(2) In subsection (1) of section 6A of ITA 2007 (tax avoidance arrangements in relation to section 6(1A) of that Act) "arrangement" does not include an arrangement (as defined in section 6A(7) of that Act) entered into before 16 March 2016.

(3) In subsection (1) of section 517K of ITA 2007 (tax avoidance in relation to Part 9A of that Act) "arrangement" does not include an arrangement (as defined in section 517Q of that Act) entered into before 16 March 2016.

(4) Subsection (6) applies if—

   (a) a person disposes of a relevant asset to a person who is associated with that person at the relevant time,

   (b) the disposal is made on or after 16 March 2016 and before 5 July 2016, and

        (c)   a person obtains a relevant tax advantage as a result of the disposal.

(5)   In subsection (4) the reference to obtaining a relevant tax advantage includes obtaining a relevant tax advantage by virtue of any provisions of double taxation arrangements, but only in a case where the relevant tax advantage is contrary to the object and purpose of the provisions of the double taxation arrangements (and subsection (6) has effect accordingly, regardless of anything in section 6(1) of TIOPA 2010).

(6)   The tax advantage is to be counteracted by means of adjustments.

(7)   Adjustments for the purposes of subsection (6) may be made (whether by an officer of Revenue and Customs or by the person) by way of an assessment, the modification of an assessment, amendment or disallowance of a claim, or otherwise.

(8)   In subsection (4)(c) "relevant tax advantage" means a tax advantage in relation to tax to which the person in question is charged or chargeable (or would, if the tax advantage were not obtained, be charged or chargeable) —

        (a)   by virtue of section 6(1A) of ITTOIA 2005, or

        (b)   in respect of amounts treated as profits of a trade by virtue of Part 9A of ITA 2007.

(9)   For the purposes of this section, where any property is disposed of under a contract, the time at which the disposal is made is the time the contract is made (and not, if different, the time at which the property is conveyed or transferred).

(10)   In subsection (9) "contract" includes a conditional contract.

(11)   In this section—

        "arrangement" includes any scheme, agreement or understanding (whether or not legally enforceable);

        "disposal" is to be interpreted in accordance with section 517R of ITA2007;

        "relevant asset" means land, or property deriving the whole or part of its value from land;

        "tax advantage" has the same meaning as in section 6A of ITTOIA 2005.

(12)   For the purposes of this section a person ("A") is "associated" with another person ("B") if—

        (a)   A is connected with B by virtue of any of subsections (2) to (4) of section 993 of ITA 2007 (read in accordance with section 994 of that Act), or

        (b)   A is related to B.

(13)   In subsection (12) "related to" is to be interpreted in accordance with section 517U of ITA 2007.

(14)   In subsection (4), "the relevant time"—

        (a)   in a case within subsection (8)(a), means the time when the disposal was made,

        (b)   in a case within subsection (8)(b), means any time in the period beginning when the activities of the project began and ending 6 months after the disposal mentioned in section 517B(1) or 517D(1) of ITA 2007.

(15)   In subsection (14) "the project" means (as the case requires) the project described in section 517B(9) of ITA 2007 or the activities mentioned in section 517D(2)(a) of that Act.

PART 4

CAPITAL GAINS TAX

Rate

83   Reduction in rate of capital gains tax

(1)   Section 4 of TCGA 1992 (rates of capital gains tax) is amended as set out in subsections (2) to (12).

(2)   In subsection (1) after "entrepreneurs' relief)" insert "and section 169VC (rate in case of claim for investors' relief)".

(3)   In subsection (2) —

    (a)   after "section" insert "and section 4BA", and

    (b)   for the words from "in respect" to the end substitute —

        "(a)   in respect of upper rate gains accruing to a person in a tax year, is 18%, and

        (b)   in respect of gains accruing to a person in a tax year which are not upper rate gains, is 10%."

(4)   After subsection (2) insert —

    "(2A)   In this section "upper rate gains" means —

        (a)   residential property gains (see section 4BB),

        (b)   NRCGT gains (see section 14D), and

        (c)   carried interest gains (see subsections (12) and (13))."

(5)   For subsection (3) substitute —

    "(3)   The rate of capital gains tax in respect of gains accruing in a tax year to the trustees of a settlement or the personal representatives of a deceased person —

        (a)   in respect of upper rate gains, is 28%, and

        (b)   in respect of gains which are not upper rate gains, is 20%."

(6)   In subsection (4), for the words from the second "in respect" to the end substitute —

        "(a)   in respect of upper rate gains accruing to the individual in the tax year, is 28%, and

        (b)   in respect of gains accruing to the individual in the tax year which are not upper rate gains, is 20%."

(7)   In subsection (5) for "28%" substitute "(subject to section 4BA) 20%".

(8)   For subsection (6) substitute —

    "(6)   Subsection (6A) applies for the purposes of subsection (5) where —

        (a)   there is an excess as mentioned in that subsection ("the higher-rate excess"), and

        (b)   the amount on which the individual is chargeable to capital gains tax for the tax year includes any special rate gains, that is, gains which are —

> > (i) chargeable to capital gains tax at the rate in section 169N(3), or
> >
> > (ii) chargeable to capital gains tax at the rate in section 169VC(2).
>
> (6A) Where this subsection applies—
>
> > (a) if the total amount of the special rate gains exceeds the unused part of the individual's basic rate band, the higher-rate excess is to be treated as reduced by the amount by which the special rate gains exceed that unused part;
> >
> > (b) if not, the higher-rate excess is to be treated as consisting of gains other than the special rate gains."

(9) In subsection (7) for "The reference in subsection (5)" substitute "Any reference in this section".

(10) In subsection (9) after "this section" insert "and section 4BA".

(11) In subsection (10) after "and (5)" insert "and section 4BA(1)".

(12) After subsection (11) insert—

> "(12) In subsection (2A)(c) "carried interest gains" means—
>
> > (a) gains treated as accruing under section 103KA(2) or (3), and
> >
> > (b) gains accruing to an individual as a result of carried interest arising to the individual where—
> >
> > > (i) the individual performs investment management services directly or indirectly in respect of an investment scheme under arrangements not involving a partnership,
> > >
> > > (ii) the carried interest arises to the individual under the arrangements, and
> > >
> > > (iii) the carried interest does not constitute a co-investment repayment or return.
>
> (13) For the purposes of subsection (12)(b)—
>
> > (a) "carried interest", in relation to any arrangements, has the same meaning as in section 809EZB of ITA 2007 (see sections 809EZC and 809EZD of that Act);
> >
> > (b) carried interest "arises" to an individual if it arises to him or her for the purposes of Chapter 5E of Part 13 of ITA 2007;
> >
> > (c) "arrangements", "investment management services" and "investment scheme" have the same meanings as in that Chapter (see sections 809EZA(6) and 809EZE of that Act);
> >
> > (d) "co-investment repayment or return" has the same meaning as in section 103KA."

(13) In section 4A of TCGA 1992 (special cases), in subsection (5) after "and (5)" insert "and section 4BA(1)".

(14) After section 4B of TCGA 1992 insert—

"4BA Rates, and use of unused basic rate band, in certain cases

> (1) This section applies where an individual is chargeable to capital gains tax in respect of gains accruing in a tax year and—

      (a)   no income tax is chargeable at the higher rate, the Welsh higher rate or the dividend upper rate in respect of the income of the individual for the tax year,

      (b)   the amount on which the individual is chargeable to capital gains tax for the tax year ("the chargeable gains amount") exceeds the unused part of the individual's basic rate band, and

      (c)   all or part of the chargeable gains amount consists of upper rate gains.

(2)   In the following provisions of this section "the available gains" means the gains on which the individual is chargeable to capital gains tax for the tax year, excluding any special rate gains.

(3)   The available gains not used by the individual under subsection (4) are to be charged to capital gains tax—

      (a)   to the extent that they consist of upper rate gains, at the rate in section 4(4)(a);

      (b)   to the extent that they consist of gains which are not upper rate gains, at the rate in section 4(5).

(4)   The individual may, subject to subsection (5) (which limits the overall amount that can be used under this subsection)—

      (a)   use any of the available gains that are upper rate gains to be charged at the rate in section 4(2)(a);

      (b)   use any of the available gains that are not upper rate gains to be charged at the rate in section 4(2)(b).

(5)   The total amount of gains used under subsection (4) must equal the qualifying amount.

(6)   The "qualifying amount" is the unused part of the individual's basic rate band less the total amount of any special rate gains.

(7)   If special rate gains are included in the chargeable gains amount, subsection (4) applies only if the unused part of the individual's basic rate band exceeds the total amount of the special rate gains.

(8)   In this section—

      "upper rate gains" has the same meaning as in section 4;

      "special rate gains" has the same meaning as in section 4(6);

      "the unused part of the individual's basic rate band" has the same meaning as in section 4.

4BB   Residential property gain or loss

(1)   For the purposes of the charge to capital gains tax, a residential property gain or loss is a gain or loss which accrues on the disposal of a residential property interest.

(2)   But a residential property gain or loss does not accrue on a non-resident CGT disposal.

(3)   In this Act "disposal of a residential property interest" means—

      (a)   a disposal of a UK residential property interest, or

      (b)   a disposal of a non-UK residential property interest.

    (4)   Schedule B1 gives the meaning in this Act of "disposal of a UK residential property interest".

    (5)   Schedule BA1 gives the meaning in this Act of "disposal of a non-UK residential property interest".

    (6)   See section 57C and Schedule 4ZZC for how to compute—
        (a)   the residential property gain or loss accruing on the disposal of a residential property interest, and
        (b)   the gain or loss accruing on the disposal of a residential property interest which is not a residential property gain or loss."

  (15) Schedule 11 inserts Schedule BA1 in TCGA 1992 and makes related amendments.

  (16) Schedule 12 inserts section 57C and Schedule 4ZZC in TCGA 1992 and makes related amendments.

  (17) The amendments made by this section and Schedules 11 and 12 have effect in relation to gains accruing on or after 6 April 2016.

  (18) In relation to a time before the tax year appointed under section 14(3)(b) of the Wales Act 2014 in relation to the provision inserted by section 9(14) of that Act, subsection (1) of section 4BA of TCGA 1992 (inserted by subsection (14) of this section) has effect as if the words ", the Welsh higher rate" were omitted.

  (19) In relation to a time before the tax year appointed under section 13(15) of the Scotland Act 2016, subsection (1) of section 4BA of TCGA 1992 (inserted by subsection (14) of this section) has effect as if before "or the dividend upper rate" there were inserted ", the Scottish higher rate".

Entrepreneurs' relief

84   Entrepreneurs' relief: associated disposals

    (1)   Section 169K of TCGA 1992 (disposal associated with relevant material disposal) is amended as follows.

    (2)   In subsection (1)—
        (a)   in paragraph (a), after "A1," insert "A1A,", and
        (b)   in paragraph (b), for "and C" substitute ", C and D".

    (3)   After subsection (1A) insert—

  "(1AA) Condition A1A is that P makes a material disposal of business assets which consists of the disposal of the whole of P's interest in the assets of a partnership, and—
        (a)   that interest is an interest of less than 5%,
        (b)   P holds at least a 5% interest in the partnership's assets throughout a continuous period of at least 3 years in the 8 years ending with the date of the disposal, and
        (c)   at the date of the disposal, no partnership purchase arrangements exist.

   (1AB) Subject to subsection (6A), for the purposes of conditions A1 and A1A, in relation to the disposal of an interest in the assets of a partnership,

"partnership purchase arrangements" means arrangements (other than the material disposal itself) under which P or a person connected with P is entitled to acquire any interest in, or increase that person's interest in, the partnership (including a share of the profits or assets of the partnership or an interest in such a share)."

(4)   In subsection (1E), in the words before paragraph (a)—

    (a)   at the beginning insert "Subject to subsection (6A),", and

    (b)   after "means arrangements" insert "(other than the material disposal itself)".

(5)   After subsection (3A) insert—

  "(3AA)   Subject to subsection (6A), for the purposes of condition B, in relation to a disposal mentioned in that condition and a partnership, "partnership purchase arrangements" means arrangements under which P or a person connected with P is entitled to acquire any interest in, or increase that person's interest in, the partnership (including a share of the profits or assets of the partnership or an interest in such a share), but does not include any arrangements in connection with a material disposal in relation to which condition A1 or A1A is met."

(6)   In subsection (3B), for "arrangements" to the end substitute "share purchase arrangements".

(7)   After subsection (3B) insert—

  "(3BA)   Subject to subsection (6A), for the purposes of condition B, in relation to a disposal mentioned in that condition and company A, "share purchase arrangements" means arrangements under which P or a person connected with P is entitled to acquire shares in or securities of—

    (a)   company A, or

    (b)   a company which is a member of a trading group of which company A is a member,

but does not include any arrangements in connection with a material disposal in relation to which condition A2 or A3 is met."

(8)   In subsection (3C), for "(3B)" substitute "(3BA)".

(9)   After subsection (4) insert—

  "(4A)   Condition D is that the disposal mentioned in condition B is of an asset which P owns throughout the period of 3 years ending with the date of that disposal."

(10)   Omit subsection (6).

(11)   Before subsection (7) insert—

  "(6A)   For the purposes of this section, in relation to a material disposal of business assets and a disposal mentioned in condition B, arrangements are not partnership purchase arrangements or share purchase arrangements if they were made before both disposals and without regard to either of them."

(12)   In subsection (9), after "entitled to share in the" insert "capital".

(13)   The amendments made by subsections (2)(a), (3) to (8) and (10) to (12) have effect in relation to disposals made on or after 18 March 2015.

(14)   The amendments made by subsections (2)(b) and (9) have effect in relation to disposals of assets which are acquired on or after 13 June 2016.

85   Entrepreneurs' relief: disposal of goodwill

(1)   Section 169LA of TCGA 1992 (relevant business assets: goodwill transferred to a related party etc) is amended as follows.

(2)   In subsection (1) –

    (a)   at the beginning insert "Subject to subsection (1A),",

    (b)   at the end of paragraph (a) insert "and",

    (c)   after paragraph (a) insert –

        "(aa)   immediately after the disposal –

            (i)   P and any relevant connected person together own 5% or more of the ordinary share capital of C or of any company which is a member of a group of companies of which C is a member, or

            (ii)   P and any relevant connected person together hold 5% or more of the voting rights in C or in any company which is a member of a group of companies of which C is a member.", and

    (d)   omit paragraphs (b) and (c).

(3)   After subsection (1) insert –

"(1A)   Where –

    (a)   subsection (1)(aa) applies by virtue of P's ownership, or any relevant connected person's ownership, of C's ordinary share capital, and

    (b)   the conditions mentioned in subsection (1B) are met,

subsection (4) does not apply.

(1B)   The conditions referred to in subsection (1A)(b) are –

    (a)   P and any relevant connected person dispose of C's ordinary share capital to another company ("A") such that, immediately before the end of the relevant period, neither P nor any relevant connected person own any of C's ordinary share capital, and

    (b)   where A is a close company, immediately before the end of the relevant period –

        (i)   P and any relevant connected person together own less than 5% of the ordinary share capital of A or of any company which is a member of a group of companies of which A is a member, and

        (ii)   P and any relevant connected person together hold less than 5% of the voting rights in A or in any company which is a member of a group of companies of which A is a member.

(1C)   In subsection (1B) "the relevant period" means the period of 28 days beginning with the date of the qualifying business disposal, or such longer period as the Commissioners for Her Majesty's Revenue and Customs may by notice allow."

(4)   Omit subsections (2) and (3).

(5)   In subsection (5), omit the words from "(including" to the end.

(6)   In subsection (7), omit paragraph (b) and the "or" at the end of paragraph (a).

(7)   In subsection (8)—
       (a)   after the definition of "arrangements" insert—
                       ""group" is to be construed in accordance with section
                       170;", and

       (b)   for the definition of "associate", "control", "major interest" and
              "participator" substitute—
                       ""relevant connected person" means—
                               (a)   a company connected with P, and
                               (b)   trustees connected with P."

(8)   In the heading, for "related party etc" substitute "close company".

(9)   The amendments made by this section have effect in relation to disposals made
       on or after 3 December 2014.

86   Entrepreneurs' relief: "trading company" and "trading group"

Schedule 13 contains provision about the meaning of "trading company" and
"trading group" for the purposes of Chapter 3 of Part 5 of TCGA 1992
(entrepreneurs' relief).

Investors' relief

87   Investors' relief

Schedule 14 contains provision relating to investors' relief.

Employee shareholder shares

88   Employee shareholder shares: limit on exemption

(1)   Section 236B of TCGA 1992 (exemption for employee shareholder shares) is
       amended in accordance with subsections (2) and (3).

(2)   After subsection (1) insert—

       "(1A)   Where a gain accrues to a person ("P") on the first disposal of a post-16
               March 2016 exempt employee shareholder share (the "relevant
               disposal"), subsection (1) applies only to so much of the gain as, when
               added to the total amount of previous potentially chargeable gains,
               does not exceed £100,000.

       (1B)   For the purposes of subsection (1A), "previous potentially chargeable
               gain" means a gain accruing to P on the first disposal of a post-16 March
               2016 exempt employee shareholder share at any time before the
               relevant disposal.

(1C) Where a single transaction disposes of more than one post-16 March 2016 exempt employee shareholder share, the reference in subsection (1A) to the first disposal of a share is to be treated as a reference to the disposal of all of the post-16 March 2016 exempt employee shareholder shares first disposed of by that transaction."

(3) After subsection (3) insert—

"(3A) In this section, "post-16 March 2016 exempt employee shareholder share" means an exempt employee shareholder share acquired in consideration of an employee shareholder agreement entered into after 16 March 2016."

(4) Section 236F of TCGA 1992 (reorganisation of share capital involving employee shareholder shares) is amended in accordance with subsections (5) and (6).

(5) After subsection (1) insert—

"(1A) Subsection (1B) applies where—
    (a) an exempt employee shareholder share ("the original EES share") is held by a person ("P") before, and is concerned in, a reorganisation, and
    (b) the original EES share is disposed of on the reorganisation.

(1B) P is to be treated as if the original EES share were disposed of for consideration of an amount determined in accordance with subsections (1D) to (1H) (the "relevant amount").

(1C) In this section "notional gain" means the gain, if any, that would accrue to P if the original EES share were disposed of on the reorganisation for consideration of an amount equal to the market value of the share.

(1D) Subsections (1E) to (1G) apply where a notional gain would accrue to P on the disposal of the original EES share.

(1E) Where the whole of the notional gain would be a chargeable gain by virtue of section 236B(1A), the relevant amount is the amount that would secure that on the disposal neither a gain nor a loss would accrue to P.

(1F) Where part (but not the whole) of the notional gain would be a chargeable gain by virtue of section 236B(1A), the relevant amount is the maximum amount, not exceeding the market value of the share, that would secure that on the disposal no chargeable gain would accrue to P.

(1G) Where no part of the notional gain would be a chargeable gain by virtue of section 236B(1A), the relevant amount is equal to the market value of the original EES share at the time of the disposal.

(1H) Where no notional gain would accrue to P on the disposal of the original EES share, the relevant amount is the amount that would secure that on the disposal neither a gain nor a loss would accrue to P.

(1I) In determining for the purposes of this section whether any part of a notional gain is a chargeable gain by virtue of section 236B(1A), subsection (1B) is to be disregarded.

(1J) Where more than one original EES share is disposed of by P on a reorganisation, references in this section to the disposal of the original EES share are to be treated as references to the disposal of all of the original EES shares disposed of on the reorganisation.

(1K) In this section "reorganisation" has the same meaning as in section 127."

(6) In subsection (2) for "reference in subsection (1) to section 127 includes" substitute "references in this section to section 127 include".

(7) Section 58 of TCGA 1992 (spouses and civil partners) is amended in accordance with subsections (8) and (9).

(8) In subsection (2)(c) after "disposal is" insert "a relevant disposal".

(9) After subsection (2) insert—

"(3) For the purposes of subsection (2) a disposal of exempt employee shareholder shares is a "relevant disposal" if (apart from this section)—
(a) a gain would accrue on the disposal, and
(b) no part of the gain would be a chargeable gain.

(4) Subsection (5) applies where the disposal is of exempt employee shareholder shares and (apart from this section)—
(a) a gain would accrue on the disposal, and
(b) part (but not the whole) of the gain would be a chargeable gain by virtue of section 236B(1A).

(5) Where this subsection applies, subsection (1) has effect in relation to the disposal as if—
(a) for "such amount as" there were substituted "the maximum amount, not exceeding the market value of the asset, that", and
(b) for "neither a gain nor a loss" there were substituted "no chargeable gain"."

(10) The amendments made by this section have effect in relation to disposals made after 16 March 2016.

89 Employee shareholder shares: disguised fees and carried interest

(1) In section 236B of TCGA 1992 (exemption for employee shareholder shares), after subsection (2) insert—

"(2A) Subsection (1) does not apply in relation to a gain accruing on a disposal where the proceeds of the disposal, in relation to any individual, constitute—
(a) a disguised fee for the purposes of Chapter 5E of Part 13 of ITA 2007 (see section 809EZA(3) of that Act), or
(b) carried interest within the meaning given by section 809EZC of that Act."

(2) The amendment made by this section has effect in relation to gains accruing on or after 6 April 2016.

Other provisions

90   Disposals of UK residential property by non-residents etc

(1) In Schedule 4ZZA to TCGA 1992 (relevant high value disposals: gains and losses), in paragraph 2(1), for "paragraph 6" substitute "paragraph 6A".

(2) In Schedule 4ZZB to TCGA 1992 (non-resident CGT disposals: gains and losses), in paragraph 17—
   (a) omit sub-paragraph (2), and
   (b) in sub-paragraph (3), omit the words from "If" to "applies".

(3) The amendment made by subsection (1) has effect in relation to disposals made on or after 6 April 2015.

(4) The amendment made by subsection (2) has effect in relation to disposals made on or after 26 November 2015.

91   NRCGT returns

In TMA 1970, after section 12ZB (NRCGT return) insert—

"12ZBA Elective NRCGT return

(1) A person is not required to make and deliver an NRCGT return under section 12ZB(1), but may do so, in circumstances to which this section applies.

(2) The circumstances to which this section applies are where the disposal referred to in section 12ZB(1) is—
   (a) a disposal on or after 6 April 2015 where, by virtue of any of the no gain/no loss provisions, neither a gain nor a loss accrues, or
   (b) the grant of a lease on or after 6 April 2015 which is—
      (i) for no premium,
      (ii) to a person who is not connected with the grantor, and
      (iii) under a bargain made at arm's length.

(3) For the purposes of subsection (2)—
   "connected" is to be construed in accordance with section 286 of 1992 Act;
   "no gain/no loss provisions" has the meaning given by section 288(3A) of the 1992 Act;
   "lease" and premium" have the meanings given by paragraph 10 of Schedule 8 to the 1992 Act.

(4) The Treasury may by regulations made by statutory instrument add or remove circumstances to which this section applies.

(5) Regulations under subsection (4) may—
   (a) amend this section or any other enactment;
   (b) make consequential provision.

(6) A statutory instrument containing regulations under subsection (4) is subject to annulment in pursuance of a resolution of the House of Commons.

(7) Paragraph 1 of Schedule 55 to the Finance Act 2009 (penalty for late returns) does not apply in relation to an NRCGT return which is made and delivered by virtue of this section."

92 Addition of CGT to Provisional Collection of Taxes Act 1968

In section 1 of the Provisional Collection of Taxes Act 1968 (temporary statutory effect of House of Commons resolutions affecting income tax etc), in subsection (1), after "income tax," insert "capital gains tax,".

PART 5

INHERITANCE TAX ETC

93 Inheritance tax: increased nil-rate band

Schedule 15 contains provision in connection with the increased nil-rate band provided for by section 8D of IHTA 1984 (extra nil-rate band on death if interest in home goes to descendants etc).

94 Inheritance tax: pension drawdown funds

(1) IHTA 1984 is amended as follows.

(2) In the italic heading before section 10, at the end insert "(and omissions that do not give rise to deemed dispositions)".

(3) In section 12(2G) (interpretation of section 12(2ZA)), in the definition of "entitled", for "166(2)" substitute "167(1A), or section 166(2),".

(4) After section 12 insert—

"12A Pension drawdown fund not used up: no deemed disposition

(1) Where a person has a drawdown fund, section 3(3) above does not apply in relation to any omission that results in the fund not being used up in the person's lifetime.

(2) For the purposes of subsection (1) above, a person has a drawdown fund if the person has—

    (a) a member's drawdown pension fund,

    (b) a member's flexi-access drawdown fund,

    (c) a dependant's drawdown pension fund,

    (d) a dependant's flexi-access drawdown fund,

    (e) a nominee's flexi-access drawdown fund, or

    (f) a successor's flexi-access drawdown fund, and

in respect of a money purchase arrangement under a registered pension scheme.

(3) For the purposes of subsection (1) above, a person also has a drawdown fund if sums or assets held for the purposes of a money purchase arrangement under a corresponding scheme would, if that scheme were a registered pension scheme, be the person's—

    (a) member's drawdown pension fund,

    (b) member's flexi-access drawdown fund,

(c) dependant's drawdown pension fund,

(d) dependant's flexi-access drawdown fund,

(e) nominee's flexi-access drawdown fund, or

(f) successor's flexi-access drawdown fund,

in respect of the arrangement.

(4) In this section—

"corresponding scheme" means—

(a) a qualifying non-UK pension scheme (see section 271A below), or

(b) a section 615(3) scheme that is not a registered pension scheme;

"money purchase arrangement" has the same meaning as in Part 4 of the Finance Act 2004 (see section 152 of that Act);

"member's drawdown pension fund", "member's flexi-access drawdown fund", "dependant's drawdown pension fund", "dependant's flexi-access drawdown fund", "nominee's flexi-access drawdown fund" and "successor's flexi-access drawdown fund" have the meaning given, respectively, by paragraphs 8, 8A, 22, 22A, 27E and 27K of Schedule 28 to that Act."

(5) The amendment made by subsection (4)—

(a) so far as relating to a fund within the new section 12A(2)(a) or (c) (drawdown pension funds), or to a fund within the new section 12A(3) that corresponds to a fund within the new section 12A(2)(a) or (c)—

(i) has effect where the person who has the fund dies on or after 6 April 2011, and

(ii) is to be treated as having come into force on 6 April 2011, and

(b) so far as relating to a fund mentioned in the new section 12A(2)(b), (d), (e) or (f) (flexi-access drawdown funds), or to a fund within the new section 12A(3) that corresponds to a fund within the new section 12A(2)(b), (d), (e) or (f)—

(i) has effect where the person who has the fund dies on or after 6 April 2015, and

(ii) is to be treated as having come into force on 6 April 2015.

(6) Where an amount paid by way of—

(a) inheritance tax, or

(b) interest on inheritance tax,

is repayable as a result of the amendment made by subsection (4), section 241(1) of IHTA 1984 applies as if the last date for making a claim for repayment of the amount were 5 April 2020 if that is later than what would otherwise be the last date for that purpose.

95   **Inheritance tax: victims of persecution during Second World War era**

(1)   After section 153 of IHTA 1984 insert—

"Payments to victims of persecution during Second World War era

153ZA Qualifying payments

(1)   This section applies where a qualifying payment has at any time been received by a person ("P"), or by the personal representatives of P.

(2)   The tax chargeable on the value transferred by the transfer made on P's death (the "value transferred") is to be reduced by an amount equal to—

     (a)   the relevant percentage of the amount of the qualifying payment, or

     (b)   if lower, the amount of tax that would, apart from this section, be chargeable on the value transferred.

(3)   In subsection (2) "relevant percentage" means the percentage specified in the last row of the third column of the Table in Schedule 1.

(4)   For the purposes of this section, a "qualifying payment" is a payment that meets Condition A, B or C.

(5)   Condition A is that the payment—

     (a)   is of a kind specified in Part 1 of Schedule 5A, and

     (b)   is made to a person, or the personal representatives of a person, who was—

          (i)   a victim of National-Socialist persecution, or

          (ii)   the spouse or civil partner of a person within sub-paragraph (i).

(6)   Condition B is that the payment is of a kind listed in Part 2 of Schedule 5A.

(7)   Condition C is that the payment—

     (a)   is of a kind specified in regulations made by the Treasury, and

     (b)   is made to a person, or the personal representatives of a person, who was—

          (i)   held as a prisoner of war, or a civilian internee, during the Second World War, or

          (ii)   the spouse or civil partner of a person within sub-paragraph (i).

(8)   The Treasury may by regulations add a payment of a specified kind to the list in Part 1 of Schedule 5A.

(9)   Regulations under this section are to be made by statutory instrument.

(10)   A statutory instrument containing regulations under this section is subject to annulment in pursuance of a resolution of the House of Commons."

(2)   After Schedule 5 to IHTA 1984 insert—

"SCHEDULE 5A

Section 153ZA

QUALIFYING PAYMENTS: VICTIMS OF PERSECUTION DURING SECOND WORLD WAR ERA

PART 1

COMPENSATION PAYMENTS

1   A payment of a fixed amount from the German foundation known as "Remembrance, Responsibility and Future" (*Stiftung EVZ*) in respect of a person who was a slave or forced labourer.

2   A payment of a fixed amount in accordance with the arrangements made under the Swiss Bank Settlement (Holocaust Victim Assets Litigation) in respect of the slave or forced labourers qualifying for compensation under the Remembrance, Responsibility and Future scheme.

3   A payment of a fixed amount from the Hardship Fund established by the Government of the Federal Republic of Germany.

4   A payment of a fixed amount from the National Fund of the Republic of Austria for Victims of National-Socialism under the terms of the scheme as at June 1995.

5   A payment of a fixed amount in respect of a slave or forced labourer from the Austrian Reconciliation Fund.

6   A payment of a fixed amount by the Swiss Refugee Programme in accordance with the arrangements made under the Swiss Bank Settlement (Holocaust Victim Assets Litigation) in respect of refugees.

7   A payment of a fixed amount under the foundation established in the Netherlands and known as the Dutch Maror Fund (*Stichting Maror-Gelden Overheid*).

8   A one-off payment of a fixed amount from the scheme established by the Government of the French Republic and known as the French Orphan Scheme.

9   A payment of a fixed amount from the Child Survivor Fund established by the Government of the Federal Republic of Germany.

PART 2

EX-GRATIA PAYMENTS

10   A payment of a fixed amount made from the scheme established by the United Kingdom Government and known as the Far Eastern Prisoners of War Ex Gratia Scheme."

(3)   The amendments made by this section have effect in relation to deaths occurring on or after 1 January 2015.

96　　Inheritance tax: gifts for national purposes etc

(1)　The Schedule 3 IHTA approval function is transferred to the Treasury.

(2)　The "Schedule 3 IHTA approval function" is the function of approval conferred by Schedule 3 to IHTA 1984 in the entry beginning "Any other similar national institution" (and which was initially conferred on the Treasury but, along with other functions, transferred to the Commissioners of Inland Revenue under section 95 of FA 1985).

(3)　Subsection (1) does not affect any approval given under Schedule 3 to IHTA 1984 before this Act is passed.

(4)　In Schedule 3 to IHTA 1984 (gifts for national purposes, etc), in the entry beginning "Any museum", after "and is" insert "or has been".

97　　Estate duty: objects of national, scientific, historic or artistic interest

(1)　Section 40 of FA 1930 and section 2 of the Finance Act (Northern Ireland) 1931 (exemption from death duties of objects of national etc interest), so far as continuing to have effect, have effect as if after subsection (2) there were inserted—

"(2A)　In the event of the loss of any objects to which this section applies, estate duty shall become chargeable on the value of those objects in respect of the last death on which the objects passed at the rate appropriate to the principal value of the estate passing on that death upon which estate duty is leviable, and with which the objects would have been aggregated if they had not been objects to which this section applies.

(2B)　Where subsection (2A) applies, any owner of the objects—
　　(a)　shall be accountable for the estate duty, and
　　(b)　shall deliver an account for the purposes thereof.

(2C)　The account under subsection (2B)(b) must be delivered within the period of one month beginning with—
　　(a)　in the case of a loss occurring before the coming into force of subsection (2A)—
　　　　(i)　the coming into force of subsection (2A), or
　　　　(ii)　if later, the date when the owner became aware of the loss;
　　(b)　in the case of a loss occurring after the coming into force of subsection (2A)—
　　　　(i)　the date of the loss, or
　　　　(ii)　if later, the date when the owner became aware of the loss.
　　This is subject to subsection (2E).

(2D)　Subsection (2E) applies if—
　　(a)　no account has been delivered under subsection (2B),
　　(b)　the Commissioners for Her Majesty's Revenue and Customs have by notice required an owner of the objects to confirm that the objects have not been lost,
　　(c)　the owner has not so confirmed by the end of—

           (i)   the period of three months beginning with the day on which the notice was sent, or

           (ii)   such longer period as the Commissioners may allow, and

     (d)   the Commissioners are satisfied that the objects are lost.

(2E)   Where this subsection applies—

     (a)   the objects are to be treated as lost for the purposes of subsection (2A) on the day on which the Commissioners are satisfied as specified in subsection (2D)(d), and

     (b)   the account under subsection (2B)(b) must be delivered within the period of one month beginning with that date.

(2F)   The reference in subsection (2A) to the value of objects is to their value at the time they are lost (or treated as lost).

(2G)   Subsection (2A) does not apply in relation to a loss notified to the Commissioners before the coming into force of that subsection.

(2H)   In this section "owner", in relation to any objects, means a person who, if the objects were sold, would be entitled to receive (whether for their own benefit or not) the proceeds of sale or any income arising therefrom.

(2I)   In this section references to the loss of objects include their theft or destruction; but do not include a loss which the Commissioners are satisfied was outside the owner's control."

(2)   Section 48 of FA 1950, so far as continuing to have effect, has effect as if—

    (a)   after subsection (3) there were inserted—

        "(3A)   But where the value of any objects is chargeable with estate duty under subsection (2A) of the said section forty (loss of objects), no estate duty shall be chargeable under this section on that value.";

    (b)   after subsection (4) there were inserted—

        "(5)   Where any objects are lost (within the meaning of the said section forty) after becoming chargeable with estate duty under this section in respect of any death, the value of those objects shall not be chargeable with estate duty under subsection (2A) of the said section forty."

(3)   Section 39 of FA 1969, so far as continuing to have effect, has effect as if—

    (a)   in subsection (1)—

        (i)   after "subsection (2)" there were inserted "or (2A)";

        (ii)   after "other disposal" there were inserted "or loss";

    (b)   in subsection (2), after "subsection (2)" there were inserted ", (2A)";

    (c)   in subsection (3)—

        (i)   after "subsection (2)" there were inserted ", (2A)";

        (ii)   for the words from "the amount" to the end there were substituted "the amount in respect of which estate duty is chargeable under the said subsection".

(4)   Section 6 of the Finance Act (Northern Ireland) 1969, so far as continuing to have effect as originally enacted, has effect as if—

     (a)   in subsection (1) —

        (i)   after "subsection (2)" there were inserted "or (2A)";

        (ii)   after "sale" there were inserted "or loss";

     (b)   in subsection (2) —

        (i)   for "sale" there were substituted "event";

        (ii)   after "subsection (2)" there were inserted "or (2A)";

     (c)   in subsection (3) —

        (i)   for "sale" there were substituted "event";

        (ii)   after "subsection (2)" there were inserted "or (2A)";

        (iii)   for "the amount of the proceeds of sale" there were substituted "the amount in respect of which estate duty is chargeable under the said subsection".

(5)   Section 6 of the Finance Act (Northern Ireland) 1969, so far as continuing to have effect as amended by Article 7 of the Finance (Northern Ireland) Order 1972 (S.I. 1972/1100 (N.I.11)) (deaths occurring after the making of that Order), has effect as if —

     (a)   in subsection (1) —

        (i)   after "subsection (2)" there were inserted "or (2A)";

        (ii)   after "sale" there were inserted "or loss";

     (b)   in subsection (2), after "subsection (2)" there were inserted "or (2A)";

     (c)   in subsection (3) —

        (i)   in the opening words, after "subsection (2)" there were inserted "or (2A)";

        (ii)   in paragraphs (a) and (b), after "otherwise than on sale" there were inserted "or at the time of the loss".

(6)   In section 35 of IHTA 1984 (conditional exemption on death before 7th April 1976), in subsection (2), for paragraphs (a) and (b) substitute —

        "(a)   tax shall be chargeable under section 32 or 32A (as the case may be), or

        (b)   tax shall be chargeable under Schedule 5,

        as the Board may elect,".

(7)   In Schedule 6 to IHTA 1984 (transition from estate duty), in paragraph 4 (objects of national etc interest left out of account on death) —

     (a)   in sub-paragraph (2), for paragraphs (a) and (b) substitute —

        "(a)   tax shall be chargeable under section 32 or 32A of this Act (as the case may be), or

        (b)   estate duty shall be chargeable under those provisions,

        as the Board may elect,", and

     (b)   in sub-paragraph (4), after "40(2)" insert "or (2A)".

(8)   Subsections (6) and (7) have effect in relation to a chargeable event where the conditionally exempt transfer referred to in section 35(2) of or paragraph 4(2) of Schedule 6 to IHTA 1984 occurred after 16 March 2016.

PART 6

APPRENTICESHIP LEVY

Basic provisions

98 Apprenticeship levy

(1) A tax called apprenticeship levy is to be charged in accordance with this Part.

(2) The Commissioners are responsible for the collection and management of apprenticeship levy.

99 Charge to apprenticeship levy

(1) Apprenticeship levy is charged if—
   (a) a person has a pay bill for a tax year, and
   (b) the relevant percentage of that pay bill exceeds the amount of the person's levy allowance (if any) for that tax year.

(2) The amount charged for the tax year is equal to—

$$N - A$$

where—
N is the relevant percentage of the pay bill for the tax year, and
A is the amount of the levy allowance (if any) to which the person is entitled for the tax year.

(3) The person mentioned in subsection (1) is liable to pay the amount charged.

(4) Except so far as section 103 provides otherwise, a person who has a pay bill for a tax year is entitled to a levy allowance for the tax year.

(5) The amount of the levy allowance is £15,000 (except where section 101 or 102 provides otherwise).

(6) For the purposes of this section the "relevant percentage" is 0.5%.

100 A person's pay bill for a tax year

(1) A person has a pay bill for a tax year if, in the tax year—
   (a) the person is the secondary contributor in relation to payments of earnings to, or for the benefit of, one or more employed earners, and
   (b) in consequence, the person incurs liabilities to pay secondary Class 1 contributions.

(2) The amount of the person's pay bill for the tax year is equal to the total amount of the earnings in respect of which the liabilities mentioned in subsection (1)(b) are incurred.

(3) For the purposes of this section a person is treated as incurring, in respect of any earnings, any liabilities which the person would incur but for the condition in section 6(1)(b) of the Contributions and Benefits Act.

(4) The Treasury may by regulations provide for persons specified in certificates in force under section 120(4) of the Social Security Contributions and Benefits Act 1992 (employment at sea: continental shelf operations) to be treated for the purposes of this section as the secondary contributor in relation to payments of earnings to which the certificate relates and as liable to pay secondary Class 1 contributions to which the certificate relates.

(5) For the purposes of this section—
   (a) references to "payments of earnings" are to be interpreted as they would be interpreted for the purposes of determining liability to pay secondary Class 1 contributions under the Contributions and Benefits Act;
   (b) the amount of any earnings is to be calculated in the same manner and on the same basis as for the purpose of calculating the liabilities mentioned in subsection (1)(b).

(6) In this section references to liability to pay secondary Class 1 contributions are to liability to pay secondary Class 1 contributions under Part 1 of the Contributions and Benefits Act (and are therefore to be interpreted in accordance with sections 9A(6) and 9B(3) of that Act).

Connected companies and charities

101 Connected companies

(1) Two or more companies which are not charities form a "company unit" for a tax year (and are the "members" of that unit) if—
   (a) they are connected with one another at the beginning of the tax year, and
   (b) each of them is entitled to a levy allowance for the tax year.

(2) The members of a company unit must determine what amount of levy allowance each of them is to be entitled to for the tax year (and the determination must comply with subsections (3) and (4)).
But see subsections (6) and (11).

(3) A member's levy allowance for a tax year may be zero (but not a negative amount).

(4) The total amount of the levy allowances to which the members of a company unit are entitled for a tax year must equal £15,000.

(5) A determination made under subsection (2) (with respect to a tax year) cannot afterwards be altered by the members concerned (but this does not prevent the correction of a failure to comply with subsection (4)).

(6) If subsection (8) applies—
   (a) HMRC must determine in accordance with subsection (7) what amount of levy allowance each of the relevant members (see subsection (8)(a)) of the unit concerned is to be entitled to for the tax year, and
   (b) accordingly subsection (2) is treated as never having applied in relation to that company unit and that tax year.

(7) The determination is to be made by multiplying the amount of levy allowance set out in each relevant return (see subsection (8)(a)) by —

$$\frac{15{,}000}{T}$$

where T is the total of the amounts of levy allowance set out in the relevant returns.

The result is, in each case, the amount of the levy allowance to which the relevant member in question is entitled for the tax year (but amounts may be rounded up or down where appropriate provided that subsection (4) is complied with).

(8) This subsection applies if —
  (a) HMRC is aware —
    (i) that two or more members of a company unit ("the relevant members") have made apprenticeship levy returns ("the relevant returns") on the basis mentioned in subsection (9), and
    (ii) that those returns, together, imply that the total mentioned in subsection (4) is greater than £15,000,
  (b) HMRC has notified the relevant members in writing that HMRC is considering taking action under subsection (6), and
  (c) the remedial action specified in the notice has not been taken within the period specified in the notice.

(9) The basis in question is that the member making the return is entitled to a levy allowance (whether or not of zero) for the tax year concerned.

(10) If any member of the company unit mentioned in subsection (8)(a) is not a relevant member, that member is entitled to a levy allowance of zero for the tax year.

(11) If subsection (13) applies —
  (a) HMRC must determine in accordance with subsection (12) what amount of levy allowance each of the members of the unit concerned is to be entitled to for the tax year, and
  (b) accordingly subsection (2) is treated as never having applied in relation to that company unit and that tax year.

(12) Each member of the unit is to be entitled to a levy allowance for the tax year equal to —

$$\frac{£15{,}000}{N}$$

where N is the number of the members of the company unit for the tax year.

Amounts determined in accordance with the formula in this subsection may be rounded up or down where appropriate provided that subsection (4) is complied with.

(13) This subsection applies if —

    (a)   the total amount paid by the members of a company unit in respect of apprenticeship levy for a tax year or any period in a tax year is less than the total of the amounts due and payable by them for the tax year or other period concerned,

    (b)   either the members of the unit have made no apprenticeship levy returns for any period in the tax year concerned or the returns that have been made do not contain sufficient information to enable HMRC to determine how the whole of the £15,000 mentioned in subsection (4) is to be used by the members of the unit for the tax year,

    (c)   HMRC has notified all the members of the unit in writing that HMRC is considering taking action under subsection (11), and

    (d)   the remedial action specified in the notice has not been taken within the period specified in the notice.

(14)   Subsection (4) is to be taken into account in calculating the total of the amounts due and payable as mentioned in subsection (13)(a).

(15)   The Commissioners may by regulations provide that in circumstances specified in the regulations the members of a company unit may alter a determination made under subsection (2) (despite subsection (5)).

(16)   In this section "apprenticeship levy return" means a return under regulations under section 105(4).

(17)   Part 1 of Schedule 1 to the National Insurance Contributions Act 2014 (rules for determining whether companies are "connected" with one another) applies for the purposes of subsection (1) as it applies for the purposes of section 3(1) of that Act.

(18)   In this Part "company" has the meaning given by section 1121(1) of CTA 2010 and includes a limited liability partnership.

(19)   See section 102 for the meaning of "charity".

102 Connected charities

(1)   Two or more charities form a "charities unit" for a tax year (and are the "members" of that unit) if—

    (a)   they are connected with one another at the beginning of the tax year, and

    (b)   each of them is entitled to a levy allowance for the tax year.

(2)   The members of a charities unit must determine what amount of levy allowance each of them is to be entitled to for the tax year (and the determination must comply with subsections (3) and (4)).
But see subsections (6) and (11).

(3)   A member's levy allowance for a tax year may be zero (but not a negative amount).

(4)   The total amount of the levy allowances to which the members of a charities unit are entitled for a tax year must equal £15,000.

(5)   A determination made under subsection (2) (with respect to a tax year) cannot afterwards be altered by the members concerned (but this does not prevent the correction of a failure to comply with subsection (4)).

(6)   If subsection (8) applies—

    (a)   HMRC must determine in accordance with subsection (7) what amount of levy allowance each of the relevant members (see subsection (8)(a)) of the unit concerned is to be entitled to for the tax year, and

    (b)   accordingly subsection (2) is treated as never having applied in relation to that charities unit and that tax year.

(7)   The determination is to be made by multiplying the amount of levy allowance set out in each relevant return (see subsection (8)(a)) by —

$$\frac{15,000}{T}$$

where T is the total of the amounts of levy allowance set out in the relevant returns.

The result is, in each case, the amount of the levy allowance to which the relevant member in question is entitled for the tax year (but amounts may be rounded up or down where appropriate provided that subsection (4) is complied with).

(8)   This subsection applies if —

    (a)   HMRC is aware —

        (i)   that two or more members of a charities unit ("the relevant members") have made apprenticeship levy returns ("the relevant returns") on the basis mentioned in subsection (9), and

        (ii)   that those returns, together, imply that the total mentioned in subsection (4) is greater than £15,000,

    (b)   HMRC has notified the relevant members in writing that HMRC is considering taking action under subsection (6), and

    (c)   the remedial action specified in the notice has not been taken within the period specified in the notice.

(9)   The basis in question is that the member making the return is entitled to a levy allowance (whether or not of zero) for the tax year concerned.

(10)   If any member of the charities unit mentioned in subsection (8)(a) is not a relevant member, that member is entitled to a levy allowance of zero for the tax year.

(11)   If subsection (13) applies —

    (a)   HMRC must determine in accordance with subsection (12) what amount of levy allowance each of the members of the unit concerned is to be entitled to for the tax year, and

    (b)   accordingly subsection (2) is treated as never having applied in relation to that charities unit and that tax year.

(12)   Each member of the unit is to be entitled to a levy allowance for the tax year equal to —

$$\frac{£15,000}{N}$$

where N is the number of the members of the charities unit for the tax year.

Amounts determined in accordance with the formula in this subsection may be rounded up or down where appropriate provided that subsection (4) is complied with.

(13) This subsection applies if —

    (a) the total amount paid by the members of a charities unit in respect of apprenticeship levy for a tax year or any period in a tax year is less than the total of the amounts due and payable by them for the tax year or other period concerned,

    (b) either the members of the unit have made no apprenticeship levy returns for any period in the tax year concerned or the returns that have been made do not contain sufficient information to enable HMRC to determine how the whole of the £15,000 mentioned in subsection (4) is to be used by the members of the unit for the tax year,

    (c) HMRC has notified all the members of the unit in writing that HMRC is considering taking action under subsection (11), and

    (d) the remedial action specified in the notice has not been taken within the period specified in the notice.

(14) Subsection (4) is to be taken into account in calculating the total of the amounts due and payable as mentioned in subsection (13)(a).

(15) The Commissioners may by regulations provide that in circumstances specified in the regulations the members of a charities unit may alter a determination made under subsection (2) (despite subsection (5)).

(16) In this section "apprenticeship levy return" means a return under regulations under section 105(4).

(17) In this Part "charity" means —

    (a) a charity within the meaning of Part 1 of Schedule 6 to FA 2010;

    (b) the Trustees of the National Heritage Memorial Fund;

    (c) the Historic Buildings and Monuments Commission for England;

    (d) a registered club within the meaning of Chapter 9 of Part 13 of CTA 2010 (community amateur sports clubs).

(18) Subsection (17) is subject to section 118(5).

(19) See sections 118 and 119 for provision about the meaning of "connected" in subsection (1).

Anti-avoidance

103 Anti-avoidance

(1) For the purposes of this section "avoidance arrangements" are arrangements the main purpose, or one of the main purposes, of which is to secure that a person —

    (a) benefits, or further benefits, from an entitlement to a levy allowance for a tax year, or

    (b) otherwise obtains an advantage in relation to apprenticeship levy.

(2) Subsection (3) applies where, in consequence of avoidance arrangements within subsection (1)(a) or (b), a person incurs a liability to pay secondary Class 1 contributions in a particular tax year (as opposed to another tax year).

(3) If the person would (apart from this subsection) obtain an advantage in relation to apprenticeship levy as a result of incurring the liability at the time mentioned in subsection (2), section 100 has effect as if the liability had been incurred when it would have been incurred but for the avoidance arrangements.

(4) Subsection (6) applies where (apart from this section) a person ("P") —

    (a) would be in a position to use or make greater use of a levy allowance for a tax year, in consequence of avoidance arrangements within subsection (1)(a), or

    (b) would otherwise obtain an advantage in relation to apprenticeship levy in consequence of avoidance arrangements within subsection (1)(a).

(5) But subsection (6) only applies so far as the advantage in relation to apprenticeship levy cannot be counteracted under subsection (3).

(6) P is not entitled to a levy allowance for the tax year.

(7) In this section "arrangements" includes any agreement, understanding, scheme, transaction or series of transactions (whether or not legally enforceable).

(8) In this section a reference to "an advantage in relation to apprenticeship levy" includes a reference to —

    (a) repayment or increased repayment of apprenticeship levy,

    (b) avoidance or reduction of a charge, or an assessment, to the levy,

    (c) avoidance of a possible assessment to the levy,

    (d) deferral of a payment of, or advancement of a repayment of, the levy, and

    (e) avoidance of an obligation to account for the levy.

(9) Sections 101 and 102 are to be ignored for the purpose of determining under subsection (4) what the position would be apart from this section.

(10) In subsection (2) the reference to "a particular tax year" is to be read as including a reference to the period of 12 months beginning with 6 April 2016.

104 Application of other regimes to apprenticeship levy

(1) In section 318(1) of FA 2004 (disclosure of tax avoidance schemes: interpretation), in the definition of "tax", after paragraph (d) insert —
      "(da) apprenticeship levy,".

(2) In section 206(3) of FA 2013 (taxes to which the general anti-abuse rule applies), after paragraph (da) insert —
      "(db) apprenticeship levy,".

(3) Part 4 of FA 2014 (follower notices and accelerated payments) is amended in accordance with subsections (4) and (5).

(4) In section 200 (meaning of "relevant tax"), after paragraph (c) insert —
      "(ca) apprenticeship levy,".

(5)   In section 203 (meaning of "tax appeal"), after paragraph (e) insert—

        "(ea)   an appeal under section 114 of FA 2016 (apprenticeship levy: appeal against an assessment),".

(6)   Part 5 of FA 2014 (promoters of tax avoidance schemes) is amended in accordance with subsections (7) and (8).

(7)   In section 253(6) (duty to notify the Commissioners: meaning of "tax return"), after paragraph (d) insert—

        "(da)   a return under regulations made under section 105 of FA 2016 (apprenticeship levy);".

(8)   In section 283(1) (interpretation), in the definition of "tax", after paragraph (d) insert—

        "(da)   apprenticeship levy,".

Payment, collection and recovery

105   Assessment, payment etc

(1)   The Commissioners may by regulations make provision about the assessment, payment, collection and recovery of apprenticeship levy.

(2)   Regulations under subsection (1) may include—

    (a)   provision which applies, with or without modifications, provisions of PAYE regulations;

    (b)   provision for combining any arrangements under the regulations with arrangements under PAYE regulations.

(3)   Regulations under subsection (1) may—

    (a)   require payments to be made on account of apprenticeship levy;

    (b)   determine periods ("tax periods") by reference to which payments are to be made;

    (c)   make provision about the times at which payments are to be made and methods of payment;

    (d)   require the amounts payable by reference to tax periods to be calculated (and levy allowance to be taken into account) in the manner and on the basis determined by or under the regulations;

    (e)   make provision for dealing with cases where such calculations lead to overpayment of levy (by repayment or otherwise);

    (f)   make other provision about the recovery of overpayments of levy.

(4)   Regulations under subsection (1) may make provision requiring persons to make returns, including provision about—

    (a)   the periods by reference to which returns are to be made,

    (b)   the information to be included in returns,

    (c)   timing, and

    (d)   the form of, and method of making, returns.

(5)   Regulations under subsection (1) may—

    (a)   authorise HMRC to assess to the best of their judgement amounts payable by a person in respect of apprenticeship levy;

      (b)   make provision about the treatment of amounts so assessed, including provision for treating such amounts as apprenticeship levy payable by the person;

      (c)   make provision about the process of assessments.

(6)   Regulations under subsection (1) may make, in relation to amounts of apprenticeship levy which have been repaid to a person and ought not to have been repaid, any provision which may be made in relation to apprenticeship levy payable by a person.

(7)   Where—

      (a)   a repayment of apprenticeship levy has been increased in accordance with section 102 of FA 2009 (repayment interest), and

      (b)   the whole or part of the repayment has been paid to any person but ought not to have been paid to the person,

any amount by which the repayment paid to the person ought not to have been increased is to be treated for the purposes of regulations made by virtue of subsection (6) as if it were an amount of apprenticeship levy repaid to the person which ought not to have been repaid.

(8)   Regulations under subsection (1) may make provision for enabling the repayment or remission of interest under section 101 of FA 2009.

(9)   The provision that may be made under subsection (1) includes—

      (a)   provision for the making of decisions (other than relevant assessments) by HMRC as to any matter required to be decided for the purposes of the regulations and for appeals against such decisions;

      (b)   provision for appeals with respect to matters arising under the regulations which would otherwise not be the subject of an appeal;

      (c)   provision for the way in which any matters provided for by the regulations are to be proved.

(10)   In subsection (9) "relevant assessment" means an assessment of amounts payable by a person in respect of apprenticeship levy.

(11)   Regulations under subsection (1) must not affect any right of appeal to the tribunal which a person would have apart from the regulations.

(12)   In this section (except where the context requires otherwise) references to payments are to payments of, or on account of, apprenticeship levy.

106   Recovery from third parties

(1)   Regulations under section 105(1) may make corresponding provision for the recovery of amounts in respect of apprenticeship levy from persons other than the person liable to pay the amounts by virtue of section 99(3).

(2)   In subsection (1) "corresponding provision" means provision which corresponds to provision made by regulations under the Contributions and Benefits Act for secondary Class 1 contributions in respect of any earnings to be recovered from a person other than the secondary contributor.

107   Real time information

(1)   Regulations under section 105(1) may make provision—

     (a)   for authorising or requiring relevant service providers to supply to HMRC information about payments of apprenticeship levy with respect to which their service is provided, or any information the Commissioners may request about features of the service provided or to be provided with respect to particular payments of apprenticeship levy;

     (b)   for requiring clients to provide relevant service providers with information about payments of apprenticeship levy;

     (c)   for prohibiting or restricting the disclosure, otherwise than to HMRC, of information by a person to whom it was supplied pursuant to a requirement imposed under paragraph (b);

     (d)   for conferring power on the Commissioners to specify by directions circumstances in which provision made by virtue of paragraph (a) or (b) is not to apply in relation to a payment;

     (e)   for requiring relevant service providers to take steps for facilitating the meeting by clients of obligations imposed under paragraph (b);

     (f)   for requiring compliance with any directions the Commissioners may give—

         (i)   specifying, or further specifying, steps for the purposes of paragraph (e), or

        (ii)   specifying information that a person making payments of apprenticeship levy must provide about the method by which the payments are made.

(2)   Directions made under the regulations may make different provision for different cases or different classes of case.

(3)   In this section—

     "client", in relation to a relevant service provider, means a person to whom that relevant service provider provides or is to provide a service with respect to a payment of apprenticeship levy;

     "payment of apprenticeship levy" includes a payment on account of apprenticeship levy;

     "relevant service provider" means a person who provides or is to provide with respect to payments of apprenticeship levy a service that is specified, or of a description specified, by the regulations.

108 Time limits for assessment

(1)   The general rule is that no assessment under regulations under section 105 may be made more than 4 years after the end of the tax year to which it relates.

(2)   An assessment on a person in a case of loss of apprenticeship levy brought about carelessly by the person may be made at any time not more than 6 years after the end of the tax year to which it relates.

(3)   An assessment on a person in a case falling within subsection (4) may be made at any time not more than 20 years after the end of the tax year to which it relates.

(4)   A case falls within this subsection if it involves a loss of apprenticeship levy—

     (a)   brought about deliberately by the person,

     (b)   attributable to arrangements in respect of which the person has failed to comply with an obligation under section 309, 310 or 313 of FA 2004 (obligation of parties to tax avoidance schemes to provide information to HMRC), or

  (c) attributable to arrangements which were expected to give rise to a tax advantage in respect of which the person was under an obligation to notify the Commissioners under section 253 of FA 2014 (duty to notify Commissioners of promoter reference number) but failed to do so.

(5) An assessment made by virtue of section 105(6) (amounts of levy repaid which ought not to have been repaid etc) is not out of time as a result of subsection (1) if it is made before the end of the tax year following that in which the amount assessed was repaid or paid (as the case may be).

(6) Subsections (2), (3) and (5) do not limit one another's application.

(7) An objection to the making of an assessment on the ground that the time limit for making it has expired may only be made on an appeal against the assessment.

(8) In subsections (2) and (4) references to a loss brought about by a person include a loss brought about by another person acting on behalf of that person.

109 No deduction in respect of levy to be made from earnings

(1) A person ("P") must not—
  (a) make from any payment of earnings any deduction in respect of apprenticeship levy for which P (or any other person) is liable,
  (b) otherwise recover the cost, or any part of the cost, of P's (or any other person's) liability to apprenticeship levy from any person who is or has been a relevant earner, or
  (c) enter into any agreement with any person to do anything prohibited by paragraph (a) or (b).

(2) In this section "relevant earner" means an earner in respect of whom P is or has been liable to pay any secondary Class 1 contributions under Part 1 of the Contributions and Benefits Act.

110 Collectors and court proceedings

(1) The following provisions of Part 6 of TMA 1970 apply in relation to apprenticeship levy as they apply in relation to income tax—
  (a) section 60 (issue of demand notes and receipts);
  (b) section 61 (distraint by collectors: Northern Ireland);
  (c) sections 65 to 68 (court proceedings).

(2) See also Chapter 5 of Part 7 of FA 2008 (which makes general provision about payment and enforcement).

Information and penalties

111 Records

(1) The Commissioners may by regulations require persons—
  (a) to keep for purposes connected with apprenticeship levy records of specified matters, and
  (b) to preserve the records for a specified period.

(2) A duty under regulations under this section to preserve records may be discharged—

    (a) by preserving them in any form and by any means, or

    (b) by preserving the information contained in them in any form and by any means, subject to any conditions or exceptions specified in writing by the Commissioners.

(3) In this section "specified" means specified or described in the regulations.

112 Information and inspection powers

In Schedule 36 to FA 2008 (information and inspection powers), in paragraph 63(1), after paragraph (ca) insert—

    "(cb) apprenticeship levy,".

113 Penalties

(1) Schedule 24 to FA 2007 (penalties for errors) is amended in accordance with subsections (2) to (4).

(2) In the Table in paragraph 1, after the entry relating to accounts in connection with a partnership return insert—

"Apprenticeship levy	Return under regulations under section 105 of FA 2016."

(3) In paragraph 13—

    (a) in sub-paragraph (1ZA), after "CIS returns," insert "or for two or more penalties relating to apprenticeship levy returns,";

    (b) in sub-paragraph (1ZD), after the entry relating to "a CIS return" insert—

        ""an apprenticeship levy return" means a return under regulations under section 105 of FA 2016;".

(4) In paragraph 21C, after "capital gains tax)" insert "and amounts payable on account of apprenticeship levy".

(5) Schedule 55 to FA 2009 (penalty for failure to make returns etc) is amended in accordance with subsections (6) to (8).

(6) In the Table in paragraph 1, after item 4 insert—

"4A	Apprenticeship levy	Return under regulations under section 105 of FA 2016"

(7) In paragraph 6B, after "item 4" insert "or 4A".

(8) In the italic heading before paragraph 6B, at the end insert "and apprenticeship levy".

(9) Schedule 56 to FA 2009 (penalty for failure to make payments on time) is amended in accordance with subsections (10) to (15).

(10) In the Table in paragraph 1, after item 4 insert—

"4A	Apprenticeship levy	Amount payable under regulations under section 105 of FA 2016	The date determined by or under regulations under section 105 of FA 2016"

(11) In paragraph 3(1)—
    (a) in paragraph (b) after "within" insert "item 4A or";
    (b) after paragraph (c) insert—
        "(ca) an amount in respect of apprenticeship levy falling within item 4A which is payable by virtue of regulations under section 106 of FA 2016 (recovery from third parties)."

(12) In paragraph 5(1), for "or 4" substitute ", 4 or 4A".

(13) In paragraph 5(2), for "or (c)" substitute ", (c) or (ca)."

(14) In paragraph 6(2), after paragraph (b) insert—
        "(ba) a payment under regulations under section 105 of FA 2016 of an amount in respect of apprenticeship levy payable in relation to the tax year;".

(15) In the italic heading before paragraph 5, at the end insert "etc.".

(16) The amendments made by subsections (1) to (4) of this section come into force in accordance with provision made by the Treasury by regulations.

(17) In subsections (2) and (4) of section 106 of FA 2009 (penalties for failure to make returns: commencement etc) references to Schedule 55 to that Act have effect as references to that Schedule as amended by subsections (5) to (8) of this section.

(18) Schedule 56 to FA 2009, as amended by this section, is taken to come into force for the purposes of apprenticeship levy on the date on which this Act is passed.

Appeals

114 Appeals

(1) An appeal may be brought against an assessment of apprenticeship levy or other amounts under regulations under section 105.

(2) Notice of appeal must be given—
    (a) in writing,
    (b) within the period of 30 days beginning with the date on which notice of the assessment was given,
    (c) to the officer of Revenue and Customs by whom notice of the assessment was given.

(3) Part 5 of TMA 1970 (appeals and other proceedings) applies in relation to an appeal under this section as it applies in relation to an appeal against an assessment to income tax.

General

115 Tax agents: dishonest conduct

In Schedule 38 to FA 2012 (tax agents: dishonest conduct), in paragraph 37(1), after paragraph (l) insert—

"(la) apprenticeship levy,".

116 Provisional collection of apprenticeship levy

In section 1 of the Provisional Collection of Taxes Act 1968 (temporary statutory effect of House of Commons resolutions), in subsection (1), after "diverted profits tax," insert "the apprenticeship levy,".

117 Crown application

This Part binds the Crown.

118 Charities which are "connected" with one another

(1) Two charities are connected with one another for the purposes of section 102(1) if—

   (a) they are connected with one another in accordance with section 993 of ITA 2007 (meaning of "connected persons"), and

   (b) their purposes and activities are the same or substantially similar.

(2) In the application of section 993 of ITA 2007 for the purposes of subsection (1)(a)—

   (a) a charity which is a trust is to be treated as if it were a company (and accordingly a person), including in this subsection;

   (b) a charity which is a trust has "control" of another person if the trustees (in their capacity as trustees of the charity) have, or any of them has, control of the person;

   (c) a person (other than a charity regulator) has "control" of a charity which is a trust if—

      (i) the person is a trustee of the charity and some or all of the powers of the trustees of the charity could be exercised by the person acting alone or by the person acting together with any other persons who are trustees of the charity and who are connected with the person,

      (ii) the person, alone or together with other persons, has power to appoint or remove a trustee of the charity, or

      (iii) the person, alone or together with other persons, has any power of approval or direction in relation to the carrying out by the trustees of any of their functions.

(3) For the purposes of section 102(1) a charity which is a trust is also connected with another charity which is a trust if at least half of the trustees of one of the charities are—

      (a)   trustees of the other charity,

      (b)   persons who are connected with persons who are trustees of the other charity, or

      (c)   a combination of both,

and the charities' purposes and activities are the same or substantially similar.

(4)   In determining if a person is connected with another person for the purposes of subsection (2)(c)(i) or (3)(b), apply section 993 of ITA 2007 with the omission of subsection (3) of that section (and without the modifications in subsection (2) above).

(5)   If a charity ("A") controls a company ("B") which, apart from this subsection, would not be a charity—

      (a)   B is to be treated as if it were a charity for the purposes of this Part, and

      (b)   A and B are connected with one another for the purposes of section 102(1).

(6)   In subsection (5) "control" has the same meaning as in Part 10 of CTA 2010 (see sections 450 and 451 of that Act) (and a limited liability partnership is to be treated as a company for the purposes of that Part as applied by this subsection).

(7)   For this purpose, where under section 450 of that Act "C" is a limited liability partnership, subsection (3) of that section has effect as if before (a) there were inserted—

      "(za)   rights to a share of more than half the assets, or of more than half the income, of C,".

119   Connection between charities: further provision

(1)   This section applies if—

      (a)   a charity ("A") is connected with another charity ("B") for the purposes of section 102(1), and

      (b)   B is connected with another charity ("C") for the purposes of section 102(1).

(2)   A and C are also connected with one another for the purposes of section 102(1) (if that would not otherwise be the case).

(3)   In subsection (1)—

      (a)   in paragraph (a) the reference to a charity being connected with another charity for the purposes of section 102(1) is to that charity being so connected by virtue of section 118 or this section, and

      (b)   in paragraph (b) the reference to a charity being connected with another charity for the purposes of section 102(1) is to that charity being so connected by virtue of section 118.

120   General interpretation

(1)   In this Part (except where the contrary is indicated, expressly or by implication), expressions which are also used in Part 1 of the Contributions and Benefits Act have the same meaning as in that Part.

(2)   In this Part—

      "charity" has the meaning given by section 102(17) and (18);

> "the Commissioners" means the Commissioners for Her Majesty's Revenue and Customs;
>
> "company" has the meaning given by section 101(18);
>
> "the Contributions and Benefits Act" means the Social Security Contributions and Benefits Act 1992 or (as the case requires) the Social Security Contributions and Benefits (Northern Ireland) Act 1992;
>
> "HMRC" means Her Majesty's Revenue and Customs;
>
> "tax year" means the 12 months beginning with 6 April in 2017 or any subsequent year;
>
> "tribunal" means the First-tier Tribunal or, where determined by or under Tribunal Procedure Rules, the Upper Tribunal.

121 Regulations

(1) Regulations under this Part—

   (a) may make different provision for different purposes;

   (b) may include incidental, consequential, supplementary or transitional provision.

(2) Regulations under this Part are to be made by statutory instrument.

(3) A statutory instrument containing regulations under this Part is subject to annulment in pursuance of a resolution of the House of Commons.

(4) Subsection (3) does not apply to a statutory instrument containing only regulations under section 113(16).

PART 7

VAT

122 VAT: power to provide for persons to be eligible for refunds

In Part 2 of VATA 1994 (reliefs, exemptions and repayments), after section 33D insert—

> **"33E Power to extend refunds of VAT to other persons**
>
> (1) This section applies where—
>
>   (a) VAT is chargeable on—
>
>   (i) the supply of goods or services to a specified person,
>
>   (ii) the acquisition of any goods from another member State by a specified person, or
>
>   (iii) the importation of any goods from a place outside the member States by a specified person, and
>
>   (b) the supply, acquisition or importation is not for the purpose of—
>
>   (i) any business carried on by the person, or
>
>   (ii) a supply by the person which, by virtue of section 41A, is treated as a supply in the course or furtherance of a business.
>
> (2) If and to the extent that the Treasury so direct, the Commissioners shall, on a claim made by the specified person at such time and in such form

and manner as the Commissioners may determine, refund to the person the amount of the VAT so chargeable.

This is subject to subsection (3) below.

(3)   A specified person may not make a claim under subsection (2) above unless it has been agreed with the Treasury that, in the circumstances specified in the agreement, the amount of the person's funding is to be reduced by all or part of the amount of the VAT so chargeable.

(4)   A claim under subsection (2) above in respect of a supply, acquisition or importation must be made on or before the relevant day.

(5)   The "relevant day" is—

(a)   in the case of a person who is registered, the last day on which the person may make a return under this Act for the prescribed accounting period containing the last day of the financial year in which the supply is made or the acquisition or importation takes place;

(b)   in the case of a person who is not registered, the last day of the period of 3 months beginning immediately after the end of the financial year in which the supply is made or the acquisition or importation takes place.

(6)   Subsection (7) applies where goods or services supplied to, or acquired or imported by, a specified person otherwise than for the purpose of—

(a)   any business carried on by the person, or

(b)   a supply falling within subsection (1)(b)(ii) above,

cannot be conveniently distinguished from goods or services supplied to, or acquired or imported by, the person for such a purpose.

(7)   The amount to be refunded under this section is such amount as remains after deducting from the whole of the VAT chargeable on any supply to, or acquisition or importation by, the specified person such proportion of that VAT as appears to the Commissioners to be attributable to the carrying on of the business or (as the case may be) the making of the supply.

(8)   In this section, "specified person" means a person specified in an order made by the Treasury.

(9)   An order under subsection (8) may make transitional provision or savings.

(10)   References in this section to VAT do not include any VAT which, by virtue of an order under section 25(7), is excluded from credit under section 25."

123   VAT: representatives and security

(1)   Section 48 of VATA 1994 (VAT representatives) is amended in accordance with subsections (2) to (11).

(2)   In the heading, at the end insert "and security".

(3)   In subsection (1)—

(a)   for "Where" substitute "Subsection (1ZA) applies where",

(b)   in paragraph (c) after "residence" insert "or permanent address", and

      (c)   omit the words after paragraph (c).

(4)   After subsection (1) insert—

    "(1ZA)   The Commissioners may direct the person to secure that there is a UK-established person who is—
        (a)   appointed to act on the person's behalf in relation to VAT, and
        (b)   registered against the name of the person in accordance with any regulations under subsection (4)."

(5)   In subsection (1B) for paragraphs (a) and (b) substitute—
        "(a)   section 87 of the Finance Act 2011 (mutual assistance for recovery of taxes etc) and Schedule 25 to that Act;
        (b)   section 173 of the Finance Act 2006 (international tax enforcement arrangements);".

(6)   In subsection (2)—
        (a)   in paragraph (a), for the words from "required" to "VAT" substitute "given a direction under subsection (1ZA)",
        (b)   in paragraph (b) for "that subsection" substitute "subsection (1)", and
        (c)   in the words after paragraph (b), for "another" substitute "a UK-established".

(7)   In subsection (2A) for "(1)" substitute "(1ZA)".

(8)   In subsection (4)—
        (a)   omit the "and" at the end of paragraph (a), and
        (b)   after paragraph (b) insert—
            "(c)   give the Commissioners power to refuse to register a person as a VAT representative, or to cancel a person's registration as a VAT representative, in such circumstances as may be specified in the regulations."

(9)   In subsection (7) for the words from the beginning to the first "him" substitute "The Commissioners may require a person in relation to whom the conditions specified in paragraphs (a), (b) and (c) of subsection (1) are satisfied".

(10)   After subsection (7A) insert—

    "(7B)   A direction under subsection (1ZA)—
        (a)   may specify a time by which it (or any part of it) must be complied with;
        (b)   may be varied;
        (c)   continues to have effect (subject to any variation) until it is withdrawn or the conditions specified in subsection (1) are no longer satisfied.

    (7C)   A requirement under subsection (7)—
        (a)   may specify a time by which it (or any part of it) must be complied with;
        (b)   may be varied;
        (c)   continues to have effect (subject to any variation) until it is withdrawn."

(11) After subsection (8) insert—

"(8A) For the purposes of subsections (1ZA) and (2)—

(a) a person is UK-established if the person is established, or has a fixed establishment, in the United Kingdom, and

(b) an individual is also UK-established if the person's usual place of residence or permanent address is in the United Kingdom."

(12) In paragraph 19 of Schedule 3B to VATA 1994 for "(1)" substitute "(1ZA)".

124 VAT: joint and several liability of operators of online marketplaces

(1) VATA 1994 is amended in accordance with subsections (2) to (4).

(2) After section 77A insert—

"77B Joint and several liability: operators of online marketplaces

(1) This section applies where a person ("P") who is not UK-established—

(a) makes taxable supplies of goods through an online marketplace, and

(b) fails to comply with any requirement imposed on P by or under this Act (whether or not it relates to those supplies).

(2) The Commissioners may give the person who is the operator of the online marketplace ("the operator") a notice—

(a) stating that, unless the operator secures the result mentioned in subsection (3), subsection (5) will apply, and

(b) explaining the effect of subsection (5).

(3) The result referred to in subsection (2)(a) is that P does not offer goods for sale through the online marketplace at any time between—

(a) the end of such period as may be specified in the notice, and

(b) the notice ceasing to have effect.

(4) If the operator does not secure the result mentioned in subsection (3), subsection (5) applies.

(5) The operator is jointly and severally liable to the Commissioners for the amount of VAT payable by P in respect of all taxable supplies of goods made by P through the online marketplace in the period for which the notice has effect.

(6) A notice under subsection (2) ("the liability notice") has effect for the period beginning with the day after the day on which it is given, and ending—

(a) with the day specified in a notice given by the Commissioners under subsection (7), or

(b) in accordance with subsection (8).

(7) The Commissioners may at any time give the operator a notice stating that the period for which the liability notice has effect ends with the day specified in the notice.

(8) If the person to whom the liability notice is given ceases to be the operator of the online marketplace, the liability notice ceases to have effect at the end of—

       (a)   the day on which the person ceases to be the operator, or

       (b)   (if later) the day on which the person notifies the Commissioners that the person is no longer the operator.

   (9)   In this section—

          "online marketplace" means a website, or any other means by which information is made available over the internet, through which persons other than the operator are able to offer goods for sale (whether or not the operator also does so);

          "operator", in relation to an online marketplace, means the person who controls access to, and the contents of, the online marketplace.

  (10)   For the purposes of this section a person is "UK-established" if the person is established in the United Kingdom within the meaning of Article 10 of Implementing Regulation (EU) No 282/2011.

  (11)   The Treasury may by regulations provide that supplies made or goods offered for sale in circumstances specified in the regulations are, or are not, to be treated for the purposes of this section as having been made or offered through an online marketplace.

  (12)   The Treasury may by regulations amend this section so as to alter the meaning of—

          "online marketplace",

          "operator", and

          "UK-established".

77C   Joint and several liability under section 77B: assessments

   (1)   The Commissioners may assess the amount of VAT due from the operator of an online marketplace by virtue of section 77B to the best of their judgment and notify it to the operator.

   (2)   Subject to subsections (3) to (6), an assessment may be made for such period or periods as the Commissioners consider appropriate.

   (3)   An assessment for any month may not be made after the end of—

       (a)   2 years after the end of that month, or

       (b)   (if later) one year after evidence of facts, sufficient in the opinion of the Commissioners to justify the making of an assessment for that month, comes to their knowledge.

   (4)   Subsection (5) applies if, after the Commissioners have made an assessment for a period, evidence of facts sufficient in the opinion of the Commissioners to justify the making of a further assessment for that period comes to their knowledge.

   (5)   The Commissioners may, no later than one year after that evidence comes to their knowledge, make a further assessment for that period (subject to subsection (6)).

   (6)   An assessment or further assessment for a month may not be made more than 4 years after the end of the month.

   (7)   An amount which has been assessed and notified to a person under this section is deemed to be an amount of VAT due from the person and

may be recovered accordingly (unless, or except to the extent that, the assessment is subsequently withdrawn or reduced).

(8) Subsection (7) is subject to the provisions of this Act as to appeals.

(9) Expressions used in this section and in section 77B have the same meaning in this section as in section 77B.

77D Joint and several liability under section 77B: interest

(1) If an amount assessed under section 77C is not paid before the end of the period of 30 days beginning with the day on which notice of the assessment is given, the amount assessed carries interest from the day on which the notice of assessment is given until payment.

(2) Interest under this section is payable at the rate applicable under section 197 of the Finance Act 1996.

(3) Where the operator of an online marketplace is liable for interest under this section the Commissioners may assess the amount due and notify it to the operator.

(4) A notice of assessment under this section must specify a date (not later than the date of the notice) to which the interest is calculated.

(5) A further assessment or assessments may be made under this section in respect of any interest accrued after that date.

(6) An amount of interest assessed and notified to the operator of an online marketplace under this section is recoverable as if it were VAT due from the operator (unless, or except to the extent that, the assessment is withdrawn or reduced).

(7) Interest under this section is to be paid without any deduction of income tax.

(8) Expressions used in this section and in section 77B have the same meaning in this section as in section 77B."

(3) In section 83(1) (appeals) after paragraph (ra) insert—

"(rb) an assessment under section 77C or the amount of such an assessment;".

(4) In section 84 (further provision relating to appeals)—
   (a) in subsection (3) after "(ra)" insert ", (rb)", and
   (b) in subsection (5) after "83(1)(p)" insert "or (rb)".

125 VAT: Isle of Man charities

In Schedule 6 to FA 2010 (charities etc), in paragraph 2(2) (jurisdiction condition: meaning of "a relevant UK court"), after paragraph (c) (and on a new line) insert "(and, for enactments relating to value added tax, includes the High Court of the Isle of Man)."

126 VAT: women's sanitary products

(1) VATA 1994 is amended as follows.

(2) In Schedule 7A (reduced rate)—

      (a)   in Part 1 (index), omit the entry relating to women's sanitary products;

      (b)   in Part 2 (the Groups), omit Group 4 (women's sanitary products).

(3)   In Schedule 8 (zero-rating), in Part 1 (index), at the end insert—

"Women's sanitary products   Group 19".

(4)   In Schedule 8, in Part 2 (the Groups), after Group 18 insert—

"GROUP 19 - WOMEN'S SANITARY PRODUCTS

Item No.

1   The supply of women's sanitary products.

NOTES

    (1) In this Group "women's sanitary products" means women's sanitary products of any of the following descriptions—

        (a)   subject to Note (2), products that are designed, and marketed, as being solely for use for absorbing, or otherwise collecting, lochia or menstrual flow;

        (b)   panty liners, other than panty liners that are designed as being primarily for use as incontinence products;

        (c)   sanitary belts.

    (2) Note (1)(a) does not include protective briefs or any other form of clothing."

(5)   The amendments made by this section have effect in relation to supplies made, and acquisitions and importations taking place, on or after such day as the Treasury may by regulations made by statutory instrument appoint.

(6)   The date appointed under subsection (5) must not be after the later of—

      (a)   1 April 2017, and

      (b)   the earliest date that may be appointed consistently with the United Kingdom's EU obligations.

PART 8

SDLT AND ATED

Stamp duty land tax

127   SDLT: calculating tax on non-residential and mixed transactions

(1)   Section 55 of FA 2003 (general rules on calculating the amount of stamp duty land tax chargeable) is amended in accordance with subsections (2) to (7).

(2)   In subsection (1) for ", (1C) and (2)" substitute "and (1C)".

(3)   In subsection (1B)—

      (a)   omit the words from "the relevant land" to "and",

      (b)   in Step 1—

       (i)   for "Table A" substitute "the appropriate table",

      (ii)   for "that Table" substitute "the appropriate table",

     (iii)   at the end insert—

         "The "appropriate table" is—

          (a)   Table A, if the relevant land consists entirely of residential property, and

          (b)   Table B, if the relevant land consists of or includes land that is not residential property.", and

  (c)   after Table A insert—

    "Table B: Non-residential or mixed

Relevant consideration	Percentage
So much as does not exceed £150,000	0%
So much as exceeds £150,000 but does not exceed £250,000	2%
The remainder (if any)	5%".

(4)   In subsection (1C)—

  (a)   omit the words from "the relevant land" to "and" (in the first place it occurs),

  (b)   in Step 1—

       (i)   for "Table A" substitute "the appropriate table",

      (ii)   for "that Table" substitute "the appropriate table",

     (iii)   at the end insert—

         "The "appropriate table" is—

          (a)   Table A, if the relevant land consists entirely of residential property, and

          (b)   Table B, if the relevant land consists of or includes land that is not residential property."

(5)   Omit subsection (2).

(6)   In subsection (3)—

  (a)   in the words before paragraph (a), for "subsections (1B) and (2)" substitute "subsection (1B)", and

  (b)   in paragraph (b) omit ", subject as follows".

(7)   In subsection (4)—

  (a)   in the words before paragraph (a), for the words from "subsections (1C)" to "linked transactions" substitute "subsection (1C)", and

  (b)   in paragraph (a) for "those" substitute "the linked".

(8)   Schedule 5 to FA 2003 (rules on calculating the amount of stamp duty land tax chargeable in respect of transactions for which the consideration consists of or includes rent) is amended in accordance with subsections (9) to (11).

(9)   In paragraph 2(3) (calculation of tax chargeable in respect of rent) in Table B (bands and percentages for non-residential or mixed property) for the final entry substitute—

"Over £150,000 but not over £5 million	1%
Over £5 million	2%"

(10) In paragraph 9 (tax chargeable in respect of consideration other than rent: general), in sub-paragraph (1), omit "(but see paragraph 9A)".

(11) Omit paragraph 9A (calculation of tax chargeable in respect of consideration other than rent: 0% band) and the cross-heading preceding it.

(12) The amendments made by this section have effect in relation to any land transaction of which the effective date is, or is after, 17 March 2016.

(13) But those amendments do not have effect in relation to a transaction if the purchaser so elects and either —

    (a) the transaction is effected in pursuance of a contract entered into and substantially performed before 17 March 2016, or

    (b) the transaction is effected in pursuance of a contract entered into before that date and is not excluded by subsection (15).

(14) An election under subsection (13) —

    (a) must be included in the land transaction return made in respect of the transaction or in an amendment of that return, and

    (b) must comply with any requirements specified by the Commissioners for Her Majesty's Revenue and Customs as to its form or the manner of its inclusion.

(15) A transaction effected in pursuance of a contract entered into before 17 March 2016 is excluded by this subsection if —

    (a) there is any variation of the contract, or assignment of rights under the contract, on or after 17 March 2016,

    (b) the transaction is effected in consequence of the exercise on or after that date of any option, right of pre-emption or similar right, or

    (c) on or after that date there is an assignment, subsale or other transaction relating to the whole or part of the subject-matter of the contract as a result of which a person other than the purchaser under the contract becomes entitled to call for a conveyance.

(16) In this section —

    "land transaction return", in relation to a transaction, means the return under section 76 of FA 2003 in respect of that transaction;

    "purchaser" has the same meaning as in Part 4 of that Act (see section 43(4) of that Act);

    "substantially performed", in relation to a contract, has the same meaning as in that Part (see section 44(5) of that Act).

128 SDLT: higher rates for additional dwellings etc

(1) FA 2003 is amended in accordance with subsections (2) to (4).

(2) In section 55 (amount of tax chargeable: general) after subsection (4) insert—

"(4A) Schedule 4ZA (higher rates for additional dwellings and dwellings purchased by companies) modifies this section as it applies for the purpose of determining the amount of tax chargeable in respect of certain transactions involving major interests in dwellings."

(3) After Schedule 4 insert—

"SCHEDULE 4ZA

STAMP DUTY LAND TAX: HIGHER RATES FOR ADDITIONAL DWELLINGS AND DWELLINGS PURCHASED BY COMPANIES

PART 1

HIGHER RATES

1 (1) In its application for the purpose of determining the amount of tax chargeable in respect of a chargeable transaction which is a higher rates transaction, section 55 (amount of tax chargeable: general) has effect with the modification in sub-paragraph (2).

(2) In subsection (1B) of section 55, for Table A substitute—
"Table A: Residential

Relevant consideration	*Percentage*
So much as does not exceed £125,000	3%
So much as exceeds £125,000 but does not exceed £250,000	5%
So much as exceeds £250,000 but does not exceed £925,000	8%
So much as exceeds £925,000 but does not exceed £1,500,000	13%
The remainder (if any)	15%"

PART 2

MEANING OF "HIGHER RATES TRANSACTION"

Meaning of "higher rates transaction" etc

2   (1) This paragraph explains how to determine whether a chargeable transaction is a "higher rates transaction" for the purposes of paragraph 1.

(2) In the case of a transaction where there is only one purchaser, determine whether the transaction falls within any of paragraphs 3 to 7; if it does fall within any of those paragraphs it is a "higher rates transaction" (otherwise it is not).

(3) In the case of a transaction where there are two or more purchasers—
     (a) take one of the purchasers and determine, having regard to that purchaser only, whether the transaction falls within any of paragraphs 3 to 7, and
     (b) do the same with each of the other purchasers.
     If the transaction falls within any of those paragraphs when having regard to any one of the purchasers it is a "higher rates transaction" (otherwise it is not).

(4) For the purposes of this Schedule any term of years absolute or leasehold estate is not a "major interest" if its term does not exceed 7 years on the date of its grant.

Single dwelling transactions

3   (1) A chargeable transaction falls within this paragraph if—
     (a) the purchaser is an individual,
     (b) the main subject-matter of the transaction consists of a major interest in a single dwelling ("the purchased dwelling"), and
     (c) Conditions A to D are met.

(2) Condition A is that the chargeable consideration for the transaction is £40,000 or more.

(3) Condition B is that on the effective date of the transaction the purchased dwelling—
     (a) is not subject to a lease upon which the main subject-matter of the transaction is reversionary, or
     (b) is subject to such a lease but the lease has an unexpired term of no more than 21 years.

(4) Condition C is that at the end of the day that is the effective date of the transaction—
     (a) the purchaser has a major interest in a dwelling other than the purchased dwelling,
     (b) that interest has a market value of £40,000 or more, and
     (c) that interest is not reversionary on a lease which has an unexpired term of more than 21 years.

(5) Condition D is that the purchased dwelling is not a replacement for the purchaser's only or main residence.

(6) For the purposes of sub-paragraph (5) the purchased dwelling is a replacement for the purchaser's only or main residence if—

    (a) on the effective date of the transaction ("the transaction concerned") the purchaser intends the purchased dwelling to be the purchaser's only or main residence,

    (b) in another land transaction ("the previous transaction") whose effective date was during the period of three years ending with the effective date of the transaction concerned, the purchaser or the purchaser's spouse or civil partner at the time disposed of a major interest in another dwelling ("the sold dwelling"),

    (c) at any time during that period of three years the sold dwelling was the purchaser's only or main residence, and

    (d) at no time during the period beginning with the effective date of the previous transaction and ending with the effective date of the transaction concerned has the purchaser or the purchaser's spouse or civil partner acquired a major interest in any other dwelling with the intention of it being the purchaser's only or main residence.

(7) For the purposes of sub-paragraph (5) the purchased dwelling may become a replacement for the purchaser's only or main residence if—

    (a) on the effective date of the transaction ("the transaction concerned") the purchaser intended the purchased dwelling to be the purchaser's only or main residence,

    (b) in another land transaction whose effective date is during the period of three years beginning with the day after the effective date of the transaction concerned, the purchaser or the purchaser's spouse or civil partner disposes of a major interest in another dwelling ("the sold dwelling"), and

    (c) at any time during the period of three years ending with the effective date of the transaction concerned the sold dwelling was the purchaser's only or main residence.

4   A chargeable transaction falls within this paragraph if—

    (a) the purchaser is not an individual,

    (b) the main subject-matter of the transaction consists of a major interest in a single dwelling, and

    (c) Conditions A and B in paragraph 3 are met.

Multiple dwelling transactions

5   (1) A chargeable transaction falls within this paragraph if—

    (a) the purchaser is an individual,

    (b) the main subject-matter of the transaction consists of a major interest in two or more dwellings ("the purchased dwellings"), and

    (c) at least two of the purchased dwellings meet conditions A, B and C.

(2) A purchased dwelling meets condition A if the amount of the chargeable consideration for the transaction which is attributable on

a just and reasonable basis to the purchased dwelling is £40,000 or more.

(3) A purchased dwelling meets condition B if on the effective date of the transaction the purchased dwelling—

    (a) is not subject to a lease upon which the main subject-matter of the transaction is reversionary, or

    (b) is subject to such a lease but the lease has an unexpired term of no more than 21 years.

(4) A purchased dwelling meets condition C if it is not subsidiary to any of the other purchased dwellings.

(5) One of the purchased dwellings ("dwelling A") is subsidiary to another of the purchased dwellings ("dwelling B") if—

    (a) dwelling A is situated within the grounds of, or within the same building as, dwelling B, and

    (b) the amount of the chargeable consideration for the transaction which is attributable on a just and reasonable basis to dwelling B is equal to, or greater than, two thirds of the amount of the chargeable consideration for the transaction which is attributable on a just and reasonable basis to the following combined—

        (i) dwelling A,

        (ii) dwelling B, and

        (iii) each of the other purchased dwellings (if any) which are situated within the grounds of, or within the same building as, dwelling B.

6   (1) A chargeable transaction falls within this paragraph if—

    (a) the purchaser is an individual,

    (b) the main subject-matter of the transaction consists of a major interest in two or more dwellings ("the purchased dwellings"),

    (c) only one of the purchased dwellings meets conditions A, B and C,

    (d) the purchased dwelling which meets those conditions is not a replacement for the purchaser's only or main residence, and

    (e) at the end of the day that is the effective date of the transaction—

        (i) the purchaser has a major interest in a dwelling other than one of the purchased dwellings,

        (ii) that interest has a market value of £40,000 or more, and

        (iii) that interest is not reversionary on a lease which has an unexpired term of more than 21 years.

(2) Sub-paragraphs (2) to (5) of paragraph 5 apply for the purposes of sub-paragraph (1)(c) of this paragraph as they apply for the purposes of sub-paragraph (1)(c) of that paragraph.

(3) Sub-paragraphs (6) and (7) of paragraph 3 apply for the purposes of sub-paragraph (1)(d) of this paragraph as they apply for the purposes of sub-paragraph (5) of that paragraph.

7   (1) A chargeable transaction falls within this paragraph if —

    (a)   the purchaser is not an individual,

    (b)   the main subject-matter of the transaction consists of a major interest in two or more dwellings ("the purchased dwellings"), and

    (c)   at least one of the purchased dwellings meets conditions A and B.

  (2) Sub-paragraphs (2) and (3) of paragraph 5 apply for the purposes of sub-paragraph (1)(c) of this paragraph as they apply for the purposes of sub-paragraph (1)(c) of that paragraph.

PART 3

SUPPLEMENTARY PROVISIONS

Further provision in connection with paragraph 3(6) and (7)

8   (1) This paragraph applies where by reason of paragraph 3(7) a chargeable transaction ("the transaction concerned") ceases to be a higher rates transaction for the purposes of paragraph 1.

  (2) The land transaction ("the subsequent transaction") by reference to which the condition in paragraph 3(7)(b) was met may not be taken into account for the purposes of paragraph 3(6)(b) in determining whether any other chargeable transaction is a higher rates transaction.

  (3) A land transaction return in respect of the transaction concerned may be amended, to take account of its ceasing to be a higher rates transaction, at any time within whichever of the following periods expires later —

    (a)   the period of 3 months beginning within the effective date of the subsequent transaction, and

    (b)   the period of 12 months beginning with the filing date for the return.

  (4) Where a land transaction return in respect of the transaction concerned is amended to take account of its ceasing to be a higher rates transaction (and not for any other reason), paragraph 6(2A) of Schedule 10 (notice of amendment of return to be accompanied by the contract for the transaction etc) does not apply in relation to the amendment.

Spouses and civil partners purchasing alone

9   (1) Sub-paragraph (2) applies in relation to a chargeable transaction if —

    (a)   the purchaser (or one of them) is married or in a civil partnership on the effective date,

    (b)   the purchaser and the purchaser's spouse or civil partner are living together on that date, and

    (c)   the purchaser's spouse or civil partner is not a purchaser in relation to the transaction.

    (2) The transaction is to be treated as being a higher rates transaction for the purposes of paragraph 1 if it would have been a higher rates transaction had the purchaser's spouse or civil partner been a purchaser.

    (3) Persons who are married to, or are civil partners of, each other are treated as living together for the purposes of this paragraph if they are so treated for the purposes of the Income Tax Acts (see section 1011 of the Income Tax Act 2007).

Settlements and bare trusts

10   (1) Sub-paragraph (3) applies in relation to a land transaction if—

        (a) the main subject-matter of the transaction consists of a major interest in one or more dwellings,

        (b) the purchaser (or one of them) is acting as trustee of a settlement, and

        (c) under the terms of the settlement a beneficiary will be entitled to—

            (i) occupy the dwelling or dwellings for life, or

            (ii) income earned in respect of the dwelling or dwellings.

    (2) Sub-paragraph (3) also applies in relation to a land transaction if—

        (a) the main subject-matter of the transaction consists of a term of years absolute in a dwelling, and

        (b) the purchaser (or one of them) is acting as a trustee of a bare trust.

    (3) Where this sub-paragraph applies in relation to a land transaction the beneficiary of the settlement or bare trust (rather than the trustee) is to be treated for the purposes of this Schedule as the purchaser (or as one of them).

    (4) Paragraphs 3(3) and 4 of Schedule 16 (trustees to be treated as the purchaser) have effect subject to sub-paragraph (3).

11   (1) Sub-paragraph (3) applies where—

        (a) a person is a beneficiary under a settlement,

        (b) a major interest in a dwelling forms part of the trust property, and

        (c) under the terms of the settlement, the beneficiary is entitled to—

            (i) occupy the dwelling for life, or

            (ii) income earned in respect of the dwelling.

    (2) Sub-paragraph (3) also applies where—

        (a) a person is a beneficiary under a bare trust, and

        (b) a term of years absolute in a dwelling forms part of the trust property.

    (3) Where this sub-paragraph applies—

        (a) the beneficiary is to be treated for the purposes of this Schedule as holding the interest in the dwelling, and

      (b)   if the trustee of the settlement or bare trust disposes of the interest, the beneficiary is to be treated for the purposes of this Schedule as having disposed of it.

12   (1) This paragraph applies where, by reason of paragraph 10 or 11 or paragraph 3(1) of Schedule 16, the child of a person ("P") would (but for this paragraph) be treated for the purposes of this Schedule as—

      (a)   being the purchaser in relation to a land transaction,

      (b)   holding an interest in a dwelling, or

      (c)   having disposed of an interest in a dwelling.

    (2) Where this paragraph applies—

      (a)   P and any spouse or civil partner of P are to be treated for the purposes of this Schedule as being the purchaser, holding the interest or (as the case may be) having disposed of the interest, and

      (b)   the child is not to be so treated.

    (3) But sub-paragraph (2)(a) does not apply in relation to a spouse or civil partner of P if the two of them are not living together.

    (4) Sub-paragraph (3) of paragraph 9 applies for the purposes of this paragraph as it applies for the purposes of that paragraph.

    (5) "Child" means a person under the age of 18.

13   (1) This paragraph applies in relation to a land transaction if—

      (a)   the main subject-matter of the transaction consists of a major interest in one or more dwellings,

      (b)   the purchaser (or one of them) is acting as trustee of a settlement,

      (c)   that purchaser is an individual, and

      (d)   under the terms of the settlement a beneficiary is not entitled to—

         (i)   occupy the dwelling or dwellings for life, or

        (ii)   income earned in respect of the dwelling or dwellings.

    (2) In determining whether the transaction falls within paragraph 4 or paragraph 7—

      (a)   if the purchaser mentioned in sub-paragraph (1) is the only purchaser, ignore paragraph (a) of those paragraphs, and

      (b)   if that purchaser is not the only purchaser, ignore paragraph (a) of those paragraphs when having regard to that purchaser.

Partnerships

14   (1) Sub-paragraph (2) applies in relation to a chargeable transaction whose subject-matter consists of a major interest in one or more dwellings if—

      (a)   the purchaser (or one of them) is a partner in a partnership, but

      (b)   the purchaser does not enter into the transaction for the purposes of the partnership.

(2) For the purposes of determining whether the transaction falls within paragraph 3 or 6 any major interest in any other dwelling that is held by or on behalf of the partnership for the purposes of a trade carried on by the partnership is not to be treated as held by or on behalf of the purchaser.

(3) Paragraph 2(1)(a) of Schedule 15 (chargeable interests held by partnerships treated as held by the partners) has effect subject to sub-paragraph (2).

Alternative finance arrangements

15 (1) This paragraph applies in relation to a chargeable transaction which is the first transaction under an alternative finance arrangement entered into between a person and a financial institution.

(2) The person (rather than the institution) is to be treated for the purposes of this Schedule as the purchaser in relation to the transaction.

(3) In this paragraph—

"alternative finance arrangement" means an arrangement of a kind mentioned in section 71A(1) or 73(1);

"financial institution" has the meaning it has in those sections (see section 73BA);

"first transaction", in relation to an alternative finance arrangement, has the meaning given by section 71A(1)(a) or (as the case may be) section 73(1)(a)(i).

Major interests in dwellings inherited jointly

16 (1) This paragraph applies where by virtue of an inheritance—

    (a) a person ("P") becomes jointly entitled with one or more other persons to a major interest in a dwelling, and

    (b) P's beneficial share in the interest does not exceed 50% (see sub-paragraph (4)).

(2) P is not to be treated for the purposes of paragraph 3(4)(a) or 6(1)(e) as having the major interest at any time during the period of three years beginning with the date of the inheritance.

(3) But if at any time during that period of three years P becomes the only person beneficially entitled to the whole of the interest or P's beneficial share in the interest exceeds 50% P is, from that time, to be treated as having the major interest for the purposes of paragraph 3(4)(a) and 6(1)(e) (subject to any disposal by P).

(4) P's share in the interest exceeds 50% if—

    (a) P is beneficially entitled as a tenant in common or coparcener to more than half the interest,

    (b) P and P's spouse or civil partner taken together are beneficially entitled as tenants in common or coparceners to more than half the interest, or

    (c) P and P's spouse or civil partner are beneficially entitled as joint tenants to the interest and there is no more than one other joint tenant who is so entitled.

(5) In this section "inheritance" means the acquisition of an interest in or towards satisfaction of an entitlement under or in relation to the will of a deceased person, or on the intestacy of a deceased person.

Dwellings outside England, Wales and Northern Ireland

17 (1) In the provisions of this Schedule specified in sub-paragraph (3), references to a "dwelling" include references to a dwelling situated in a country or territory outside England, Wales and Northern Ireland.

(2) In the application of those provisions in relation to a dwelling situated in a country or territory outside England, Wales and Northern Ireland —

   (a) references to a "major interest" in the dwelling are to an equivalent interest in the dwelling under the law of that country or territory,

   (b) references to persons being beneficially entitled as joint tenants, tenants in common or coparceners to an interest in the dwelling are to persons having an equivalent entitlement to the interest in the dwelling under the law of that country or territory,

   (c) references to a "land transaction" in relation to the dwelling are to the acquisition of an interest in the dwelling under the law of that country or territory,

   (d) references to the "effective date" of a land transaction in relation to the dwelling are to the date on which the interest in the dwelling is acquired under the law of that country or territory,

   (e) references to "inheritance" are to the acquisition of an interest from a deceased person's estate in accordance with the laws of that country or territory concerning the inheritance of property.

(3) The provisions of this Schedule referred to in sub-paragraphs (1) and (2) are —

   (a) paragraph 3(4), (6)(b), (c) and (d) and (7)(b) and (c),

   (b) paragraph 6(1)(e),

   (c) paragraph 11,

   (d) paragraph 14(2), and

   (e) paragraph 16.

(4) Where the child of a person ("P") has an interest in a dwelling which is situated in a country or territory outside England, Wales and Northern Ireland, P and any spouse or civil partner of P are to be treated for the purposes of this Schedule as having that interest.

(5) But sub-paragraph (4) does not apply in relation to a spouse or civil partner of P if the two of them are not living together.

(6) Sub-paragraph (3) of paragraph 9 applies for the purposes of sub-paragraph (5) of this paragraph as it applies for the purposes of that paragraph.

What counts as a dwelling

18   (1) This paragraph sets out rules for determining what counts as a dwelling for the purposes of this Schedule.

(2) A building or part of a building counts as a dwelling if—
   (a) it is used or suitable for use as a single dwelling, or
   (b) it is in the process of being constructed or adapted for such use.

(3) Land that is, or is to be, occupied or enjoyed with a dwelling as a garden or grounds (including any building or structure on that land) is taken to be part of that dwelling.

(4) Land that subsists, or is to subsist, for the benefit of a dwelling is taken to be part of that dwelling.

(5) The main subject-matter of a transaction is also taken to consist of or include an interest in a dwelling if—
   (a) substantial performance of a contract constitutes the effective date of that transaction by virtue of a relevant deeming provision,
   (b) the main subject-matter of the transaction consists of or includes an interest in a building, or a part of a building, that is to be constructed or adapted under the contract for use as a single dwelling, and
   (c) construction or adaptation of the building, or part of a building, has not begun by the time the contract is substantially performed.

(6) In sub-paragraph (5)—
   "contract" includes any agreement;
   "relevant deeming provision" means any of sections 44 to 45A or paragraph 5(1) or (2) of Schedule 2A or paragraph 12A of Schedule 17A;
   "substantially performed" has the same meaning as in section 44.

(7) A building or part of a building used for a purpose specified in section 116(2) or (3) is not used as a dwelling for the purposes of sub-paragraph (2) or (5).

(8) Where a building or part of a building is used for a purpose mentioned in sub-paragraph (7), no account is to be taken for the purposes of sub-paragraph (2) of its suitability for any other use.

Power to modify this Schedule

19   (1) The Treasury may by regulations amend or otherwise modify this Schedule for the purpose of preventing certain chargeable transactions from being higher rates transactions for the purposes of paragraph 1.

(2) The provision which may be included in regulations under this paragraph by reason of section 114(6)(c) includes incidental or

consequential provision which may cause a chargeable transaction to be a higher rates transaction for the purposes of paragraph 1."

(4) In paragraph 5 of Schedule 6B (relief for transfers involving multiple dwellings) after sub-paragraph (6) insert—

"(6A) In the application of sub-paragraph (1), account is to be taken of paragraph 1 of Schedule 4ZA if the relevant transaction is a higher rates transaction for the purposes of that paragraph."

(5) The amendments made by this section have effect in relation to any land transaction of which the effective date is, or is after, 1 April 2016.

(6) But those amendments do not have effect in relation to a transaction—
   (a) effected in pursuance of a contract entered into and substantially performed before 26 November 2015, or
   (b) effected in pursuance of a contract entered into before that date and not excluded by subsection (7).

(7) A transaction effected in pursuance of a contract entered into before 26 November 2015 is excluded by this subsection if—
   (a) there is any variation of the contract, or assignment of rights under the contract, on or after 26 November 2015,
   (b) the transaction is effected in consequence of the exercise on or after that date of any option, right of pre-emption or similar right, or
   (c) on or after that date there is an assignment, subsale or other transaction relating to the whole or part of the subject-matter of the contract as a result of which a person other than the purchaser under the contract becomes entitled to call for a conveyance.

(8) Subsection (9) applies in relation to a land transaction of which the effective date is or is before 26 November 2018.

(9) In its application for the purpose of determining whether a land transaction to which this subsection applies is a higher rates transaction, paragraph 3(6) of Schedule 4ZA to FA 2003 has effect with the following modifications—
   (a) in paragraph (b) for "during the period of three years ending with" substitute "the same as or before",
   (b) in paragraph (c) for "during that period of three years" substitute "before the effective date of the transaction concerned".

(10) Paragraph 15 of Schedule 4ZA to FA 2003 does not apply in relation to a land transaction of which the effective date is, or is before, the date on which this Act is passed if the effect of its application would be that the transaction is a higher rates transaction for the purposes of paragraph 1 of that Schedule.

129 SDLT higher rate: land purchased for commercial use

(1) Schedule 4A to FA 2003 (SDLT: higher rate for certain transactions) is amended in accordance with subsections (2) to (4).

(2) In paragraph 5—
   (a) in sub-paragraph (1)—
      (i) after paragraph (a) insert—
         "(aa) use as business premises for the purposes of a qualifying property rental business (other

than one which gives rise to income consisting wholly or mainly of excluded rents);

    (ab)   use for the purposes of a relievable trade;";

  (ii)   for paragraph (b) substitute—

    "(b)   development or redevelopment and—

       (i)   resale in the course of a property development trade, or

      (ii)   exploitation falling within paragraph (a) or use falling within paragraph (aa) or (ab);";

  (b)   in sub-paragraph (2), for "the dwelling" substitute "a dwelling on the land";

  (c)   in sub-paragraph (3), at the appropriate place insert—

    ""relievable trade" means a trade that is run on a commercial basis and with a view to profit."

(3)   In paragraph 5G, in sub-paragraph (3)(c) for "the dwelling" substitute "any dwelling on the land".

(4)   In paragraph 6D(3)(b), for "the dwelling" substitute "any dwelling on the land concerned".

(5)   The amendments made by this section have effect in relation to any land transaction of which the effective date is on or after 1 April 2016.

130 SDLT higher rate: acquisition under regulated home reversion plan

(1)   Schedule 4A to FA 2003 (SDLT: higher rate for certain transactions) is amended as follows.

(2)   After paragraph 5C insert—

"Acquisition under a regulated home reversion plan

5CA (1)   Paragraph 3 does not apply to a chargeable transaction if (and so far as) the purchaser—

    (a)   is an authorised plan provider, and

    (b)   acquires the subject-matter of the chargeable transaction as a plan provider.

   (2)   For the purposes of this paragraph the purchaser acquires the subject-matter of the chargeable transaction "as a plan provider" so far as the purchaser acquires it under a regulated home reversion plan which the purchaser enters into as plan provider.

   (3)   In this paragraph—

    "authorised plan provider" means a person authorised under the Financial Services and Markets Act 2000 to carry on in the United Kingdom the regulated activity specified in article 63B(1) of the Regulated Activities Order (entering into regulated home reversion plan as plan provider);

    "the Regulated Activities Order" means the Financial Services and Markets (Regulated Activities) Order 2001 (S.I. 2001/544);

"regulated home reversion plan" means an arrangement which is a regulated home reversion plan for the purposes of Chapter 15A of Part 2 of the Regulated Activities Order.

(4) In this section references to entering into a regulated home reversion plan "as plan provider" are to be interpreted as if the references were in the Regulated Activities Order."

(3) After paragraph 5I insert—

"5IA(1) This paragraph applies where relief under paragraph 5CA (acquisition under a regulated home reversion plan) has been allowed in respect of a higher threshold interest forming the whole or part of the subject-matter of a chargeable transaction.

(2) The relief is withdrawn if at any time in the period of three years beginning with the effective date of the chargeable transaction the purchaser holds the higher threshold interest otherwise than for the purposes of the regulated home reversion plan (as defined in paragraph 5CA).

(3) But sub-paragraph (2) does not apply if—

(a) after ceasing to hold the higher threshold interest for the purposes of the regulated home reversion plan, the purchaser sells the higher threshold interest without delay (except so far as delay is justified by commercial considerations or cannot be avoided), and

(b) at no time when the higher threshold interest is held by the purchaser as mentioned in sub-paragraph (2) is the dwelling (or any part of the dwelling) occupied by a non-qualifying individual.

(4) In this paragraph—

"the dwelling" means the dwelling to which the relief under paragraph 5CA relates;

"non-qualifying individual" is to be interpreted in accordance with paragraph 5A."

(4) The amendments made by this section have effect in relation to any land transaction of which the effective date is on or after 1 April 2016.

131   SDLT higher rate: properties occupied by certain employees etc

(1) Schedule 4A to FA 2003 (SDLT: higher rate for certain transactions) is amended as follows.

(2) In paragraph 5D (dwellings for occupation by certain employees etc)—

(a) in sub-paragraph (1), for "trade" substitute "business";

(b) in sub-paragraph (2)(b) for "trade" substitute "business";

(c) for sub-paragraph (4) substitute—

"(4) "Relievable business" means a trade or property rental business that is run on a commercial basis and with a view to profit."

(3) The heading before paragraph 5D becomes "*Dwellings for occupation by certain employees etc of a relievable business*".

(4)   After paragraph 5E insert—

"Acquisition by management company of flat for occupation by caretaker

5EA (1) Paragraph 3 does not apply to a chargeable transaction so far as its
subject-matter consists of a higher threshold interest in or over a flat
which—

(a)   is one of at least three flats contained in the same premises,
and

(b)   is acquired by a tenants' management company for the
purpose of making the flat available for use as caretaker
accommodation.

(2) For the purposes of this paragraph a tenants' management company
makes a flat available for use "as caretaker accommodation" if it
makes it available to an individual for use as living accommodation
in connection with the individual's employment as caretaker of the
premises.

(3) In relation to the acquisition of a flat, a company is a "tenants'
management company" if—

(a)   the tenants of two or more other flats contained in the
premises are members of the company, and

(b)   the company owns, or it is intended that the company will
acquire, the freehold of the premises;

but a company which carries on a relievable business is not a tenants'
management company.

(4) In this paragraph "premises" means premises constituting the whole
or part of a building."

(5)   After paragraph 5J insert—

"5JA(1) This paragraph applies where relief under paragraph 5EA
(acquisition by management company of flat for occupation by
caretaker) has been allowed in respect of a higher threshold interest
forming the whole or part of the subject-matter of a chargeable
transaction.

(2) The relief is withdrawn if at any time in the period of three years
beginning with the effective date of the chargeable transaction the
purchaser holds the higher threshold interest otherwise than for the
purpose of making the flat available for use as caretaker
accommodation.

(3) For the purposes of this paragraph a tenants' management company
makes a flat available for use "as caretaker accommodation" if it
makes it available to an individual for use as living accommodation
in connection with the individual's employment as caretaker of the
premises."

(6)   In paragraph 5E (meaning of "qualifying partner", "qualifying employee"
etc)—

(a)   in sub-paragraph (1) for "trade" substitute "business";

(b)   in sub-paragraph (2) for "qualifying trade" substitute "relievable
business";

      (c)   in sub-paragraph (4) —

          (i)   in the words before paragraph (a), for "trade" substitute "relievable business";

         (ii)   in paragraph (a)(i), for "trade" substitute "relievable business".

(7)   In paragraph 5J (withdrawal of relief under paragraph 5D), in sub-paragraph (3) —

      (a)   in paragraph (a), for the words from "trade" to the end substitute "relievable business";

      (b)   in paragraph (c), for the words from "trade" to the end substitute "relievable business".

(8)   In paragraph 6G (withdrawal of relief under paragraph 5D in cases involving alternative finance arrangements), in sub-paragraph (4) —

      (a)   in paragraph (a), for "qualifying trade" substitute "relievable business";

      (b)   in paragraph (c) for "trade" substitute "relievable business".

(9)   In paragraph 9 (interpretation), at the appropriate place insert —

            ""relievable business" has the meaning given by paragraph 5D(4)."

(10)   The amendments made by this section have effect in relation to any land transaction of which the effective date is on or after 1 April 2016.

132   SDLT: minor amendments of section 55 of FA 2003

In section 55 of FA 2003 (general rules on calculating the amount of stamp duty land tax chargeable), in subsection (5) —

      (a)   for "74(2) and (3)" substitute "74(1B)", and

      (b)   for "rate" substitute "amount".

133   SDLT: property authorised investment funds and co-ownership authorised contractual schemes

Schedule 16 contains provision about —

      (a)   the stamp duty land tax treatment of co-ownership authorised contractual schemes, and

      (b)   relief from stamp duty land tax for certain acquisitions by such schemes and by property authorised investment funds.

Annual tax on enveloped dwellings

134   ATED: regulated home reversion plans

(1)   Part 3 of FA 2013 (annual tax on enveloped dwellings) is amended as follows.

(2)   After section 144 insert —

"144A Regulated home reversion plans

(1)   A day in a chargeable period is relievable in relation to a single dwelling interest held by a person ("P") who is an authorised plan provider if —

      (a)   P has, as plan provider, entered into a regulated home reversion plan relating to the single dwelling interest, and

      (b)   the occupation condition is met on that day.

(2)   If no qualifying termination event has occurred, the "occupation condition" is that a person who was originally entitled to occupy the dwelling (or any part of it) under the regulated home reversion plan is still entitled to do so.

(3)   If a qualifying termination event has occurred, the "occupation condition" is that—

      (a)   the single dwelling interest is being held with the intention that it will be sold without delay (except so far as delay is justified by commercial considerations or cannot be avoided), and

      (b)   no non-qualifying individual is permitted to occupy the dwelling (or any part of it).

(4)   In this section—

    "authorised plan provider" means a person authorised under the Financial Services and Markets Act 2000 to carry on in the United Kingdom the regulated activity specified in article 63B(1) of the Regulated Activities Order (entering into regulated home reversion plan as plan provider);

    "qualifying termination event" is to be interpreted in accordance with article 63B of the Regulated Activities Order;

    "the Regulated Activities Order" means the Financial Services and Markets (Regulated Activities) Order 2001 (S.I. 2001/544);

    "regulated home reversion plan" means an arrangement which is a regulated home reversion plan for the purposes of Chapter 15A of Part 2 of the Regulated Activities Order (but see also subsection (6)).

(5)   In this section references to entering into a regulated home reversion plan "as plan provider" are to be interpreted as if the references were in the Regulated Activities Order (but see also subsection (6)).

(6)   For the purposes of this section—

      (a)   an arrangement which P entered into before 6 April 2007 is treated for the purposes of this section as a regulated home reversion plan entered into by P as plan provider if that arrangement would have been so treated for the purposes of article 63B(1) of the Regulated Activities Order had P entered into that arrangement on the day mentioned in subsection (1);

      (b)   an arrangement in relation to which P acquired rights or obligations before 6 April 2007 is treated for the purposes of this section as a regulated home reversion plan entered into by P as plan provider if that arrangement would have been so treated for the purposes of article 63B(1) of the Regulated Activities Order had P acquired those rights or obligations on the day mentioned in subsection (1).

(7)   Section 136 (meaning of "non-qualifying individual") applies in relation to this section as in relation to sections 133 and 135."

(3)   In section 116 (dwelling in grounds of another dwelling), in the list in

subsection (6), at the appropriate place insert—
    "section 144A (regulated home reversion plans);".

(4) In section 117 (dwellings in the same building), in the list in subsection (5), at the appropriate place insert—
    "section 144A (regulated home reversion plans);".

(5) In section 132 (effect of reliefs under sections 133 to 150), in the list in subsection (3), at the appropriate place insert—
    "section 144A (regulated home reversion plans);".

(6) In section 159A (relief declaration returns), in the table in subsection (9), at the appropriate place insert—

"144A (regulated home reversion plans)	5A".

(7) The amendments made by this section have effect for chargeable periods beginning on or after 1 April 2016.

135 ATED: properties occupied by certain employees etc

(1) Part 3 of FA 2013 (annual tax on enveloped dwellings) is amended as follows.

(2) Section 145 (occupation by certain employees or partners) is amended in accordance with subsections (3) to (5).

(3) In subsection (1)—
    (a) in paragraph (b), after "qualifying trade" insert "or qualifying property rental business";
    (b) in paragraph (d) for "trade" substitute "qualifying trade or qualifying property rental business".

(4) After subsection (4) insert—
    "(5) For the meaning of "qualifying property rental business" see section 133(3)."

(5) The heading of that section becomes "**Occupation by employees or partners of a qualifying trade or property rental business**".

(6) In section 146 (meaning of "qualifying employee" and "qualifying partner" in section 145)—
    (a) in subsection (1), after "trade" insert "or property rental business";
    (b) in subsection (2)—
        (i) in the words before paragraph (a), after "qualifying trade" insert "or qualifying property rental business", and
        (ii) in paragraph (a)(i), after "trade" insert "or (as the case may be) property rental business".

(7) After section 147 insert—

"147A Caretaker flat owned by management company

(1) A day in a chargeable period is relievable in relation to a single-dwelling interest if the dwelling in question is a flat in relation to which the conditions in subsection (2) are met.

(2) The conditions are that on that day—

(a) a company ("the management company") holds the single-dwelling interest for the purpose of making the flat available as caretaker accommodation,

(b) the flat is contained in premises which also contain two or more other flats,

(c) the tenants of at least two of the other flats in the premises are members of the management company,

(d) the management company owns the freehold of the premises, and

(e) the management company is not carrying on a trade or property rental business.

(3) For the purposes of subsection (2), the management company makes a flat available "as caretaker accommodation" if it makes it available to an individual for use as living accommodation in connection with the individual's employment as caretaker of the premises.

(4) In this section "premises" means premises constituting the whole or part of a building."

(8) In section 116 (dwelling in grounds of another dwelling), in the list in subsection (6)—

(a) in the entry relating to section 145, for "certain employees or partners" substitute "employees or partners of a qualifying trade or property rental business";

(b) at the appropriate place insert—

"section 147A (caretaker flat owned by management company);".

(9) In section 117 (dwellings in the same building), in the list in subsection (5)—

(a) in the entry relating to section 145, for "certain employees or partners" substitute "employees or partners of a qualifying trade or property rental business";

(b) at the appropriate place insert—

"section 147A (caretaker flat owned by management company);".

(10) In section 132 (effect of reliefs under sections 133 to 150), in the list in subsection (3)—

(a) in the entry relating to section 145, for "certain employees or partners" substitute "employees or partners of a qualifying trade or property rental business";

(b) at the appropriate place insert—

"section 147A (caretaker flat owned by management company);".

(11) In section 159A (relief declaration returns), in the table in subsection (9), in the entry relating to section 145, for "(dwellings used for trade purposes: occupation by certain employees or partners)" substitute "or 147A (occupation by certain employees etc)".

(12) The amendments made by this section have effect for chargeable periods beginning on or after 1 April 2016.

136 ATED: alternative property finance - land in Scotland

(1) Part 3 of FA 2013 (annual tax on enveloped dwellings) is amended as follows.

(2) Section 157 (land sold to financial institution and leased to person) is amended in accordance with subsections (3) to (6).

(3) In subsection (1)—
  (a) in paragraph (a), omit "or section 72 of that Act (land in Scotland sold to financial institution and leased to person)";
  (b) in paragraph (b), after "transaction" insert "is in England, Wales or Northern Ireland and".

(4) In subsection (7)—
  (a) in the definition of "the first transaction" omit "or (as the case requires) 72";
  (b) in the definition of "the second transaction" omit "or (as the case requires) 72".

(5) Omit subsection (10).

(6) The heading of that section becomes "**Land in England, Wales or Northern Ireland sold to financial institution and leased to person**".

(7) After section 157 insert—

"157A Land in Scotland sold to financial institution and leased to person

(1) This section applies where Conditions A and B are met.

(2) Condition A is that arrangements are entered into between a person ("the lessee") and a financial institution under which the institution—
  (a) purchases a major interest in land ("the first transaction"),
  (b) grants to the lessee out of that interest a lease (if the interest acquired is the interest of the owner) or a sub-lease (if the interest acquired is the tenant's right over or interest in a property subject to a lease) ("the second transaction"), and
  (c) enters into an agreement under which the lessee has a right to require the institution to transfer the major interest purchased by the institution under the first transaction.

(3) Condition B is that the land in which the institution purchases a major interest under the first transaction is in Scotland and consists of or includes one or more dwellings or parts of a dwelling.

(4) If the lessee is a company, this Part has effect in relation to times when the arrangements are in operation (see subsection (5)) as if—
  (a) the interest held by the financial institution as mentioned in subsection (5)(b) were held by the lessee (and not by the financial institution), and

        (b)   the lease or sub-lease granted under the second transaction had not been granted.

(5)   The reference in subsection (4) to times when the arrangements are in operation is to times when—

        (a)   the lessee holds the interest granted to it under the second transaction, and

        (b)   the interest purchased under the first transaction is held by a financial institution.

(6)   A company treated under subsection (4)(a) as holding an interest at a particular time is treated as holding it as a member of a partnership if at the time in question the company holds the interest granted to it under the second transaction as a member of the partnership (and this Part has effect accordingly in relation to the other members of the partnership).

(7)   In relation to times when the arrangements operate for the benefit of a collective investment scheme (see subsection (8)), this Part has effect as if—

        (a)   the interest held by the financial institution as mentioned in subsection (8)(b) were held by the lessee for the purposes of a collective investment scheme (and were not held by the financial institution), and

        (b)   the lease or sub-lease granted under the second transaction had not been granted.

(8)   The reference in subsection (7) to times when the arrangements operate for the benefit of a collective investment scheme is to times when—

        (a)   the lessee holds the interest granted to it under the second transaction for the purposes of a collective investment scheme, and

        (b)   the interest purchased under the first transaction is held by a financial institution.

(9)   In this section "financial institution" has the same meaning as in section 71A of FA 2003 (see section 73BA of that Act).

(10)   References in this section to a "major interest" in land are to—

        (a)   ownership of land, or

        (b)   the tenant's right over or interest in land subject to a lease.

(11)   Where the lessee is an individual, references in subsections (7) and (8) to the lessee are to be read, in relation to times after the death of the lessee, as references to the lessee's personal representatives."

(8)   The amendments made by this section have effect for chargeable periods beginning on or after 1 April 2016.

PART 9

OTHER TAXES AND DUTIES

Stamp duty and stamp duty reserve tax

137 Stamp duty: acquisition of target company's share capital

(1) Section 77 of FA 1986 (acquisition of target company's share capital) is amended as follows.

(2) In subsection (3), omit the "and" at the end of paragraph (g) and after paragraph (h) insert ", and

      (i) at the time the instrument mentioned in subsection (1) is executed there are no disqualifying arrangements, within the meaning given by section 77A, in existence."

(3) In subsection (3A) for "(3)" substitute "(3)(b) to (h)".

(4) In subsection (4) after "this section" insert "and section 77A".

(5) After section 77 of FA 1986 insert—

"77A Disqualifying arrangements

(1) This section applies for the purposes of section 77(3)(i).

(2) Arrangements are "disqualifying arrangements" if it is reasonable to assume that the purpose, or one of the purposes, of the arrangements is to secure that—

      (a) a particular person obtains control of the acquiring company, or

      (b) particular persons together obtain control of that company.

(3) But neither of the following are disqualifying arrangements—

      (a) the arrangements for the issue of shares in the acquiring company which is the consideration for the acquisition mentioned in section 77(3);

      (b) any relevant merger arrangements.

(4) In subsection (3) "relevant merger arrangements" means arrangements for the issue of shares in the acquiring company to the shareholders of a company ("company B") other than the target company ("company A") in a case where—

      (a) that issue of shares to the shareholders of company B would be the only consideration for the acquisition by the acquiring company of the whole of the issued share capital of company B,

      (b) the conditions in section 77(3)(c) and (e) would be met in relation to that acquisition (if that acquisition were made in accordance with the arrangements), and

      (c) the conditions in paragraphs (f) to (h) of section 77(3) would be met in relation to that acquisition if—

            (i) that acquisition were made in accordance with the arrangements, and

            (ii) the shares in the acquiring company issued as consideration for the acquisition of the share capital of company A were ignored for the purposes of those paragraphs;

and in section 77(3)(e) to (h) and (3A) as they apply by virtue of this subsection, references to the target company are to be read as references to company B.

(5) Where—

    (a) arrangements within any paragraph of subsection (3) are part of a wider scheme or arrangement, and

    (b) that scheme or arrangement includes other arrangements which—

        (i) fall within subsection (2), and

        (ii) do not fall within any paragraph of subsection (3),

    those other arrangements are disqualifying arrangements despite anything in subsection (3).

(6) In this section—

"the acquiring company" has the meaning given by section 77(1);

"arrangements" includes any agreement, understanding or scheme (whether or not legally enforceable);

"control" is to be read in accordance with section 1124 of the Corporation Tax Act 2010;

"the target company" has the meaning given by section 77(1)."

(6) The amendments made by this section have effect in relation to any instrument executed on or after 29 June 2016 (and references to arrangements in any provision inserted by this section include arrangements entered into before that date).

138 Stamp duty: transfers to depositaries or providers of clearance services

(1) Part 3 of FA 1986 (stamp duty) is amended as follows.

(2) In section 67 (depositary receipts)—

    (a) in subsection (2), for the words from "1.5% of" to the end substitute "1.5% of—

        (a) the amount or value of the consideration for the sale to which the instrument gives effect, or

        (b) where subsection (2A) applies—

            (i) the amount or value of the consideration for the sale to which the instrument gives effect, or

            (ii) if higher, the value of the securities at the date the instrument is executed.",

    (b) after subsection (2) insert—

"(2A) This subsection applies where the instrument transferring the securities is executed pursuant to—

    (a) the exercise of an option to buy or to sell the securities, and

    (b) either—

        (i) a term of the option which provides for the securities to be transferred to the person falling within subsection (6), (7) or (8), or

               (ii)   a direction, given by or on behalf of the person entitled or bound to acquire the securities pursuant to the exercise of the option, for the securities to be so transferred.", and

    (c)   in subsection (3), for "In any other case" substitute "If stamp duty is not chargeable on the instrument under Part 1 of Schedule 13 to the Finance Act 1999 (transfer on sale)".

(3)   In section 69 (depositary receipts: supplementary), in subsection (4), for "section 67(3)" substitute "section 67(2)(b)(ii) and (3)".

(4)   In section 70 (clearance services) –

    (a)   in subsection (2), for the words from "1.5% of" to the end substitute "1.5% of –

        (a)   the amount or value of the consideration for the sale to which the instrument gives effect, or

        (b)   where subsection (2A) applies –

            (i)   the amount or value of the consideration for the sale to which the instrument gives effect, or

            (ii)   if higher, the value of the securities at the date the instrument is executed.",

    (b)   after subsection (2) insert –

    "(2A)   This subsection applies where the instrument transferring the securities is executed pursuant to –

        (a)   the exercise of an option to buy or to sell the securities, and

        (b)   either –

            (i)   a term of the option which provides for the securities to be transferred to the person falling within subsection (6), (7) or (8), or

            (ii)   a direction, given by or on behalf of the person entitled or bound to acquire the securities pursuant to the exercise of the option, for the securities to be so transferred.", and

    (c)   in subsection (3), for "In any other case" substitute "If stamp duty is not chargeable on the instrument under Part 1 of Schedule 13 to the Finance Act 1999 (transfer on sale)".

(5)   In section 72 (clearance services: supplementary), in subsection (2), for "section 70(3)" substitute "section 70(2)(b)(ii) and (3)".

(6)   The amendments made by this section have effect in relation to an instrument which transfers securities pursuant to the exercise of an option where –

    (a)   the option was granted on or after 25 November 2015, and

    (b)   the option was exercised on or after 23 March 2016.

139   SDRT: transfers to depositaries or providers of clearance services

(1)   Part 4 of FA 1986 (stamp duty reserve tax) is amended as follows.

(2)   In section 93 (depositary receipts) –

    (a)   in subsection (4)(b), for the words from "worth," to the end substitute "worth—

  (i) the amount or value of the consideration, or

  (ii) where subsection (4A) applies, the amount or value of the consideration or, if higher, the value of the securities;", and

(b) after subsection (4) insert—

"(4A) This subsection applies where the transfer of the securities is pursuant to—

  (a) the exercise of an option to buy or to sell the securities, and

  (b) either—

    (i) a term of the option which provides for the securities to be transferred to the person falling within subsection (2) or (3), or

    (ii) a direction, given by or on behalf of the person entitled or bound to acquire the securities pursuant to the exercise of the option, for the securities to be so transferred."

(3) In section 94 (depositary receipts: supplementary), in subsection (4), for "section 93(4)(c)" substitute "section 93(4)(b)(ii) and (c)".

(4) In section 96 (clearance services)—

(a) in subsection (2)(b), for the words from "worth," to the end substitute "worth—

  (i) the amount or value of the consideration, or

  (ii) where subsection (2A) applies, the amount or value of the consideration or, if higher, the value of the securities;",

(b) after subsection (2) insert—

"(2A) This subsection applies where the transfer of the securities is pursuant to—

  (a) the exercise of an option to buy or to sell the securities, and

  (b) either—

    (i) a term of the option which provides for the securities to be transferred to A or (as the case may be) to the person whose business is or includes holding chargeable securities as nominee for A, or

    (ii) a direction, given by or on behalf of the person entitled or bound to acquire the securities pursuant to the exercise of the option, for the securities to be so transferred.", and

(c) in subsection (10), for "subsection (2)(c)" substitute "subsection (2)(b)(ii) and (c)".

(5) The amendments made by this section have effect in relation to a transfer pursuant to the exercise of an option where—

(a) the option was granted on or after 25 November 2015, and

(b) the option was exercised on or after 23 March 2016.

Petroleum revenue tax

140 Petroleum revenue tax: rate

(1) In section 1(2) of OTA 1975 (rate of petroleum revenue tax) for "35" substitute "0".

(2) In paragraph 17 of Schedule 2 to that Act (cap on interest on repayments of tax), in sub-paragraph (5)(b) omit the words from "if that" to the end.

(3) In paragraph 2 of Schedule 19 to FA 1982 (duty to pay instalments based on amount of tax payable in previous chargeable period), after sub-paragraph (4) insert—

"(4A) In sub-paragraph (1) the reference to any chargeable period for an oil field ending on or after 30th June 1983 does not include a chargeable period ending on 31st December 2015."

(4) The amendment made by subsection (1) has effect with respect to chargeable periods ending after 31 December 2015.

Insurance premium tax

141 Insurance premium tax: standard rate

(1) In section 51(2)(b) of FA 1994 (standard rate of insurance premium tax), for "9.5 per cent" substitute "10 per cent".

(2) The amendment made by subsection (1) has effect in relation to a premium falling to be regarded for the purposes of Part 3 of FA 1994 as received under a taxable insurance contract by an insurer on or after 1 October 2016.

(3) The amendment made by subsection (1) does not have effect in relation to a premium which—
   (a) is in respect of a contract made before 1 October 2016, and
   (b) falls to be regarded for the purposes of Part 3 of FA 1994 as received under the contract by the insurer before 1 February 2017 by virtue of regulations under section 68 of that Act (special accounting schemes).

(4) Subsection (3) does not apply in relation to a premium which—
   (a) is an additional premium under a contract,
   (b) falls to be regarded for the purposes of Part 3 of FA 1994 as received under the contract by the insurer on or after 1 October 2016 by virtue of regulations under section 68 of that Act, and
   (c) is in respect of a risk which was not covered by the contract before that date.

(5) In the application of sections 67A to 67C of FA 1994 (announced increase in rate) in relation to the increase made by this section—
   (a) the announcement for the purposes of sections 67A(1) and 67B(1) is to be taken to have been made on 16 March 2016,
   (b) the date of the change is 1 October 2016, and
   (c) the concessionary date is 1 February 2017.

Landfill tax

142   Landfill tax: rates from 1 April 2017

(1)   Section 42 of FA 1996 (amount of landfill tax) is amended as follows.

(2)   In subsection (1)(a) (standard rate), for "£84.40" substitute "£86.10".

(3)   In subsection (2) (reduced rate for certain disposals)—
   (a)   for "£84.40" substitute "£86.10", and
   (b)   for "£2.65" substitute "£2.70".

(4)   The amendments made by this section have effect in relation to disposals made (or treated as made) on or after 1 April 2017.

143   Landfill tax: rates from 1 April 2018

(1)   Section 42 of FA 1996 (amount of landfill tax) (as amended by section 142) is amended as follows.

(2)   In subsection (1)(a) (standard rate), for "£86.10" substitute "£88.95".

(3)   In subsection (2) (reduced rate for certain disposals)—
   (a)   for "£86.10" substitute "£88.95", and
   (b)   for "£2.70" substitute "£2.80".

(4)   The amendments made by this section have effect in relation to disposals made (or treated as made) on or after 1 April 2018.

Climate change levy

144   CCL: abolition of exemption for electricity from renewable sources

(1)   In Schedule 6 to FA 2000 (climate change levy), in paragraph 19(1) (exemption for electricity from renewable sources)—
   (a)   in paragraph (c), omit the final "and";
   (b)   after paragraph (d) insert ", and
         (e)   the electricity is actually supplied before 1 April 2018."

(2)   In that Schedule omit the following—
   (a)   in paragraph 5(3), "20(6)(a),";
   (b)   paragraphs 19 and 20;
   (c)   paragraph 24(2).

(3)   The repeals made by subsection (2) come into force on the day appointed by the Treasury by regulations made by statutory instrument.

145   CCL: main rates from 1 April 2017

(1)   In paragraph 42(1) of Schedule 6 to FA 2000 (climate change levy: amount payable by way of levy) for the table substitute—

"TABLE

Taxable commodity supplied	Rate at which levy payable if supply is not a reduced-rate supply
Electricity	£0.00568 per kilowatt hour
Gas supplied by a gas utility or any gas supplied in a gaseous state that is of a kind supplied by a gas utility	£0.00198 per kilowatt hour
Any petroleum gas, or other gaseous hydrocarbon, supplied in a liquid state	£0.01272 per kilogram
Any other taxable commodity	£0.01551 per kilogram".

(2)   The amendment made by this section has effect in relation to supplies treated as taking place on or after 1 April 2017.

146   CCL: main rates from 1 April 2018

(1)   In paragraph 42(1) of Schedule 6 to FA 2000 (climate change levy: amount payable by way of levy) for the table substitute—

"TABLE

Taxable commodity supplied	Rate at which levy payable if supply is not a reduced-rate supply
Electricity	£0.00583 per kilowatt hour
Gas supplied by a gas utility or any gas supplied in a gaseous state that is of a kind supplied by a gas utility	£0.00203 per kilowatt hour
Any petroleum gas, or other gaseous hydrocarbon, supplied in a liquid state	£0.01304 per kilogram
Any other taxable commodity	£0.01591 per kilogram".

(2)   The amendment made by this section has effect in relation to supplies treated as taking place on or after 1 April 2018.

147   CCL: main rates from 1 April 2019

(1)   In paragraph 42(1) of Schedule 6 to FA 2000 (climate change levy: amount payable by way of levy) for the table substitute—

"TABLE

Taxable commodity supplied	Rate at which levy payable if supply is not a reduced-rate supply
Electricity	£0.00847 per kilowatt hour
Gas supplied by a gas utility or any gas supplied in a gaseous state that is of a kind supplied by a gas utility	£0.00339 per kilowatt hour
Any petroleum gas, or other gaseous hydrocarbon, supplied in a liquid state	£0.02175 per kilogram
Any other taxable commodity	£0.02653 per kilogram".

(2) The amendment made by this section has effect in relation to supplies treated as taking place on or after 1 April 2019.

148 CCL: reduced rates from 1 April 2019

(1) In paragraph 42(1) of Schedule 6 to FA 2000 (climate change levy: amount payable by way of levy)—

    (a) in paragraph (ba) (reduced-rate supplies of electricity), for "10" substitute "7";

    (b) in paragraph (c) (other reduced-rate supplies), for "35" substitute "22".

(2) The amendments made by this section have effect in relation to supplies treated as taking place on or after 1 April 2019.

Air passenger duty

149 APD: rates from 1 April 2016

(1) In section 30 of FA 1994 (air passenger duty: rates of duty) in subsection (4A) (long haul rates of duty)—

    (a) in paragraph (a), for "£71" substitute "£73", and

    (b) in paragraph (b), for "£142" substitute "£146".

(2) The amendments made by this section have effect in relation to the carriage of passengers beginning on or after 1 April 2016.

Vehicle excise duty

150 VED: rates for light passenger vehicles, light goods vehicles, motorcycles etc

(1) Schedule 1 to VERA 1994 (annual rates of duty) is amended as follows.

(2) In paragraph 1(2) (vehicle not covered elsewhere in Schedule with engine cylinder capacity exceeding 1,549cc), for "£230" substitute "£235".

(3) In paragraph 1B (graduated rates of duty for light passenger vehicles)—

    (a) for the tables substitute—

"TABLE 1

RATES PAYABLE ON FIRST VEHICLE LICENCE FOR VEHICLE

CO_2 emissions figure		Rate	
(1)	*(2)*	*(3)*	*(4)*
Exceeding	*Not exceeding*	*Reduced rate*	*Standard rate*
g/km	*g/km*	£	£
130	140	120	130
140	150	135	145
150	165	175	185
165	175	290	300
175	185	345	355
185	200	490	500
200	225	640	650
225	255	875	885
255	–	1110	1120

TABLE 2

RATES PAYABLE ON ANY OTHER VEHICLE LICENCE FOR VEHICLE

CO_2 emissions figure		Rate	
(1)	*(2)*	*(3)*	*(4)*
Exceeding	*Not exceeding*	*Reduced rate*	*Standard rate*
g/km	*g/km*	£	£
100	110	10	20
110	120	20	30
120	130	100	110
130	140	120	130
140	150	135	145
150	165	175	185
165	175	200	210

CO_2 emissions figure		Rate	
(1)	(2)	(3)	(4)
Exceeding	Not exceeding	Reduced rate	Standard rate
g/km	g/km	£	£
175	185	220	230
185	200	260	270
200	225	285	295
225	255	490	500
255	—	505	515”;

(b)   in the sentence immediately following the tables, for paragraphs (a) and (b) substitute—

> "(a)   in column (3), in the last two rows, "285" were substituted for "490" and "505", and
>
> (b)   in column (4), in the last two rows, "295" were substituted for "500" and "515"."

(4)   In paragraph 1J (VED rates for light goods vehicles), in paragraph (a), for "£225" substitute "£230".

(5)   In paragraph 2(1) (VED rates for motorcycles)—

   (a)   in paragraph (b), for "£38" substitute "£39",

   (b)   in paragraph (c), for "£59" substitute "£60", and

   (c)   in paragraph (d), for "£81" substitute "£82".

(6)   The amendments made by this section have effect in relation to licences taken out on or after 1 April 2016.

151   VED: extension of old vehicles exemption from 1 April 2017

(1)   Paragraph 1A of Schedule 2 to VERA 1994 (exemption for old vehicles) is amended as follows.

(2)   In sub-paragraph (1) for the words from "if" to the end substitute "during the period of 12 months beginning with 1 April in any year if it was constructed more than 40 years before 1 January in that year."

(3)   After that sub-paragraph insert—

> "(1A)   But nothing in sub-paragraph (1) has the effect that a nil licence is required to be in force in respect of a vehicle while a vehicle licence is in force in respect of it."

(4)   The amendments made by this section come into force on 1 April 2017.

Other excise duties

152 Gaming duty: rates

(1)   In section 11(2) of FA 1997 (rates of gaming duty), for the table substitute—

"TABLE

Part of gross gaming yield	Rate
The first £2,370,500	15 per cent
The next £1,634,000	20 per cent
The next £2,861,500	30 per cent
The next £6,040,000	40 per cent
The remainder	50 per cent".

(2)   The amendment made by this section has effect in relation to accounting periods beginning on or after 1 April 2016.

153 Fuel duties: aqua methanol etc

(1)   Schedule 17 contains provision relating to fuel duties.

(2)   Part 1 of the Schedule provides for charging excise duty on aqua methanol.

(3)   Part 2 of the Schedule contains miscellaneous amendments.

(4)   Part 3 of the Schedule makes provision about commencement.

154 Tobacco products duty: rates

(1)   For the table in Schedule 1 to TPDA 1979 substitute—
"TABLE

1. Cigarettes	An amount equal to 16.5% of the retail price plus £196.42 per thousand cigarettes
2. Cigars	£245.01 per kilogram
3. Hand-rolling tobacco	£198.10 per kilogram
4. Other smoking tobacco and chewing tobacco	£107.71 per kilogram".

(2)   The amendment made by this section is treated as having come into force at 6pm on 16 March 2016.

155 Alcoholic liquor duties: rates

(1)   ALDA 1979 is amended as follows.

(2) In section 62(1A)(a) (rate of duty on sparkling cider of a strength exceeding 5.5%) for "£264.61" substitute "£268.99".

(3) For Part 1 of the table in Schedule 1 substitute—

"PART 1

WINE OR MADE-WINE OF A STRENGTH NOT EXCEEDING 22%

Description of wine or made-wine	Rates of duty per hectolitre £
Wine or made-wine of a strength not exceeding 4%	£85.60
Wine or made-wine of a strength exceeding 4% but not exceeding 5.5%	£117.72
Wine or made-wine of a strength exceeding 5.5% but not exceeding 15% and not being sparkling	£277.84
Sparkling wine or sparkling made-wine of a strength exceeding 5.5% but less than 8.5%	£268.99
Sparkling wine or sparkling made-wine of a strength of at least 8.5% but not exceeding 15%	£355.87
Wine or made-wine of a strength exceeding 15% but not exceeding 22%	£370.41".

(4) The amendments made by this section are treated as having come into force on 21 March 2016.

PART 10

TAX AVOIDANCE AND EVASION

General anti-abuse rule

156 General anti-abuse rule: provisional counteractions

(1) In Part 5 of FA 2013 (general anti-abuse rule), after section 209 insert—

"209A Effect of adjustments specified in a provisional counteraction notice

(1) Adjustments made by an officer of Revenue and Customs which—

  (a) are specified in a provisional counteraction notice given to a person by the officer (and have not been cancelled: see sections 209B to 209E),

  (b) are made in respect of a tax advantage that would (ignoring this Part) arise from tax arrangements that are abusive, and

    (c)   but for section 209(6)(a), would have effected a valid counteraction of that tax advantage under section 209,

are treated for all purposes as effecting a valid counteraction of the tax advantage under that section.

(2)   A "provisional counteraction notice" is a notice which—

    (a)   specifies adjustments (the "notified adjustments") which the officer reasonably believes may be required under section 209(1) to counteract a tax advantage that would (ignoring this Part) arise to the person from tax arrangements;

    (b)   specifies the arrangements and the tax advantage concerned, and

    (c)   notifies the person of the person's rights of appeal with respect to the notified adjustments (when made) and contains a statement that if an appeal is made against the making of the adjustments—

        (i)   no steps may be taken in relation to the appeal unless and until the person is given a notice referred to in section 209F(2), and

        (ii)   the notified adjustments will be cancelled if HMRC fails to take at least one of the actions mentioned in section 209B(4) within the period specified in section 209B(2).

(3)   It does not matter whether the notice is given before or at the same time as the making of the adjustments.

(4)   In this section "adjustments" includes adjustments made in any way permitted by section 209(5).

209B Notified adjustments: 12 month period for taking action if appeal made

(1)   This section applies where a person (the "taxpayer") to whom a provisional counteraction notice has been given appeals against the making of the notified adjustments.

(2)   The notified adjustments are to be treated as cancelled with effect from the end of the period of 12 months beginning with the day on which the provisional counteraction notice is given unless an action mentioned in subsection (4) is taken before that time.

(3)   For the purposes of subsection (2) it does not matter whether the action mentioned in subsection (4)(c), (d) or (e) is taken before or after the provisional counteraction notice is given (but if that action is taken before the provisional counteraction notice is given subsection (5) does not have effect).

(4)   The actions are—

    (a)   an officer of Revenue and Customs notifying the taxpayer that the notified adjustments are cancelled;

    (b)   an officer of Revenue and Customs giving the taxpayer written notice of the withdrawal of the provisional counteraction notice (without cancelling the notified adjustments);

    (c)   a designated HMRC officer giving the taxpayer a notice under paragraph 3 of Schedule 43 which—

        (i)   specifies the arrangements and the tax advantage which are specified in the provisional counteraction notice, and

        (ii) specifies the notified adjustments (or lesser adjustments) as the counteraction that the officer considers ought to be taken (see paragraph 3(2)(c) of that Schedule);

    (d) a designated HMRC officer giving the taxpayer a pooling notice or a notice of binding under Schedule 43A which—

        (i)   specifies the arrangements and the tax advantage which are specified in the provisional counteraction notice, and

        (ii) specifies the notified adjustments (or lesser adjustments) as the counteraction that the officer considers ought to be taken;

    (e) a designated HMRC officer giving the taxpayer a notice under paragraph 1(2) of Schedule 43B which—

        (i)   specifies the arrangements and the tax advantage which are specified in the provisional counteraction notice, and

        (ii) specifies the notified adjustments (or lesser adjustments) as the counteraction that the officer considers ought to be taken.

(5)   In a case within subsection (4)(c), (d) or (e), if—

    (a) the notice under paragraph 3 of Schedule 43, or

    (b) the pooling notice or notice of binding, or

    (c) the notice under paragraph 1(2) of Schedule 43B,

(as the case may be) specifies lesser adjustments the officer must modify the notified adjustments accordingly.

(6)   The officer may not take the action in subsection (4)(b) unless the officer was authorised to make the notified adjustments otherwise than under this Part.

(7)   In this section "lesser adjustments" means adjustments which assume a smaller tax advantage than was assumed in the provisional counteraction notice.

209C Notified adjustments: case within section 209B(4)(c)

(1)   This section applies if the action in section 209B(4)(c) (notice to taxpayer of proposed counteraction of tax advantage) is taken.

(2)   If the matter is not referred to the GAAR Advisory Panel, the notified adjustments are to be treated as cancelled with effect from the date of the designated HMRC officer's decision under paragraph 6(2) of Schedule 43 unless the notice under paragraph 6(3) of Schedule 43 states that the adjustments are not to be treated as cancelled under this section.

(3)   A notice under paragraph 6(3) of Schedule 43 may not contain the statement referred to in subsection (2) unless HMRC would have been authorised to make the adjustments if the general anti-abuse rule did not have effect.

(4) If the taxpayer is given a notice under paragraph 12 of Schedule 43 which states that the specified tax advantage is not to be counteracted under the general anti-abuse rule, the notified adjustments are to be treated as cancelled unless that notice states that those adjustments are not to be treated as cancelled under this section.

(5) A notice under paragraph 12 of Schedule 43 may not contain the statement referred to in subsection (4) unless HMRC would have been authorised to make the adjustments if the general anti-abuse rule did not have effect.

(6) If the taxpayer is given a notice under paragraph 12 of Schedule 43 stating that the specified tax advantage is to be counteracted—

  (a) the notified adjustments are confirmed only so far as they are specified in that notice as adjustments required to give effect to the counteraction, and

  (b) so far as they are not confirmed, the notified adjustments are to be treated as cancelled.

209D Notified adjustments: case within section 209B(4)(d)

(1) This section applies if the action in section 209B(4)(d) (pooling notice or notice of binding) is taken.

(2) If the taxpayer is given a notice under paragraph 8(2) or 9(2) of Schedule 43A which states that the specified tax advantage is not to be counteracted under the general anti-abuse rule, the notified adjustments are to be treated as cancelled, unless that notice states that those adjustments are not to be treated as cancelled under this section.

(3) A notice under paragraph 8(2) or 9(2) of Schedule 43A may not contain the statement referred to in subsection (2) unless HMRC would have been authorised to make the adjustments if the general anti-abuse rule did not have effect.

(4) If the taxpayer is given a notice under paragraph 8(2) or 9(2) of Schedule 43A stating that the specified tax advantage is to be counteracted—

  (a) the notified adjustments are confirmed only so far as they are specified in that notice as adjustments required to give effect to the counteraction, and

  (b) so far as they are not confirmed, the notified adjustments are to be treated as cancelled.

209E Notified adjustments: case within section 209B(4)(e)

(1) This section applies if the action in section 209B(4)(e) (notice of proposal to make generic referral) is taken.

(2) If the notice under paragraph 1(2) of Schedule 43B is withdrawn, the notified adjustments are to be treated as cancelled unless the notice of withdrawal states that the adjustments are not to be treated as cancelled under this section.

(3) The notice of withdrawal may not contain the statement referred to in subsection (2) unless HMRC was authorised to make the notified adjustments otherwise than under this Part.

(4) If the taxpayer is given a notice under paragraph 8(2) of Schedule 43B, which states that the specified tax advantage is not to be counteracted under the general anti-abuse rule, the notified adjustments are to be treated as cancelled, unless that notice states that those adjustments are not to be treated as cancelled under this section.

(5) A notice under paragraph 8(2) of Schedule 43B may not contain the statement referred to in subsection (4) unless HMRC was authorised to make the adjustments otherwise than under this Part.

(6) If the taxpayer is given a notice under paragraph 8(2) of Schedule 43B stating that the specified tax advantage is to be counteracted—

    (a) the notified adjustments are confirmed only so far as they are specified in that notice as adjustments required to give effect to the counteraction, and

    (b) so far as they are not confirmed, the notified adjustments are to be treated as cancelled.

209F Appeals against provisional counteractions: further provision

(1) Subsections (2) to (5) have effect in relation to an appeal by a person ("the taxpayer") against the making of adjustments which are specified in a provisional counteraction notice.

(2) No steps after the initial notice of appeal are to be taken in relation to the appeal unless and until the taxpayer is given—

    (a) a notice under section 209B(4)(b),

    (b) a notice under paragraph 6(3) of Schedule 43 (notice of decision not to refer matter to GAAR advisory panel) containing the statement described in section 209C(2) (statement that adjustments are not to be treated as cancelled),

    (c) a notice under paragraph 12 of Schedule 43,

    (d) a notice under paragraph 8(2) or 9(2) of Schedule 43A, or

    (e) a notice under paragraph 8 of Schedule 43B,

in respect of the tax arrangements concerned.

(3) The taxpayer has until the end of the period mentioned in subsection (4) to comply with any requirement to specify the grounds of appeal.

(4) The period mentioned in subsection (3) is the 30 days beginning with the day on which the taxpayer receives the notice mentioned in subsection (2).

(5) In subsection (2) the reference to "steps" does not include the withdrawal of the appeal."

(2) In section 214(1) of FA 2013 (interpretation of Part 5), at the appropriate place insert—

        ""notified adjustments", in relation to a provisional counteraction notice, has the meaning given by section 209A(2);"

        ""provisional counteraction notice" has the meaning given by section 209A(2);".

(3) The amendments made by this section have effect in relation to tax arrangements (within the meaning of Part 5 of FA 2013) entered into at any time (whether before or on or after the day on which this Act is passed).

157 General anti-abuse rule: binding of tax arrangements to lead arrangements

(1) Part 5 of FA 2013 (general anti-abuse rule) is amended in accordance with subsections (2) to (11).

(2) After Schedule 43 insert—

"SCHEDULE 43A

PROCEDURAL REQUIREMENTS: POOLING NOTICES AND NOTICES OF BINDING

Pooling notices

1   (1) This paragraph applies where a person has been given a notice under paragraph 3 of Schedule 43 in relation to any tax arrangements (the "lead arrangements") and the condition in sub-paragraph (2) is met.

(2) The condition is that the period of 45 days mentioned in paragraph 4(1) of Schedule 43 has expired but no notice under paragraph 12 of Schedule 43 or paragraph 8 of Schedule 43B has yet been given in respect of the matter.

(3) If a designated HMRC officer considers—

   (a) that a tax advantage has arisen to another person ("R") from tax arrangements that are abusive,

   (b) that those tax arrangements ("R's arrangements") are equivalent to the lead arrangements, and

   (c) that the advantage ought to be counteracted under section 209,

   the officer may give R a notice (a "pooling notice") which places R's arrangements in a pool with the lead arrangements.

(4) There is one pool for any lead arrangements, so all tax arrangements placed in a pool with the lead arrangements (as well as the lead arrangements themselves) are in one and the same pool.

(5) Tax arrangements which have been placed in a pool do not cease to be in the pool except where that is expressly provided for by this Schedule (regardless of whether or not the lead arrangements or any other tax arrangements remain in the pool).

(6) The officer may not give R a pooling notice if R has been given in respect of R's arrangements a notice under paragraph 3 of Schedule 43.

Notice of proposal to bind arrangements to counteracted arrangements

2   (1) This paragraph applies where a counteraction notice has been given to a person in relation to any tax arrangements (the "counteracted arrangements") which are in a pool created under paragraph 1.

(2) If a designated HMRC officer considers—

   (a) that a tax advantage has arisen to another person ("R") from tax arrangements that are abusive,

   (b) that those tax arrangements ("R's arrangements") are equivalent to the counteracted arrangements, and

    (c)   that the advantage ought to be counteracted under section 209,

the officer may give R a notice (a "notice of binding") in relation to R's arrangements.

(3)   The officer may not give R a notice of binding if R has been given in respect of R's arrangements a notice under—

    (a)   paragraph 1, or

    (b)   paragraph 3 of Schedule 43.

(4)   In this paragraph "counteraction notice" means a notice such as is mentioned in sub-paragraph (2) of paragraph 12 of Schedule 43 or sub-paragraph (3) of paragraph 8 of Schedule 43B (notice of final decision to counteract).

3   (1)   The decision whether or not to give R a pooling notice or notice of binding must be taken, and any notice must be given, as soon as is reasonably practicable after HMRC becomes aware of the relevant facts.

    (2)   A pooling notice or notice of binding must—

        (a)   specify the tax arrangements in relation to which the notice is given and the tax advantage,

        (b)   explain why the officer considers R's arrangements to be equivalent to the lead arrangements or the counteracted arrangements (as the case may be),

        (c)   explain why the officer considers that a tax advantage has arisen to R from tax arrangements that are abusive,

        (d)   set out the counteraction that the officer considers ought to be taken, and

        (e)   explain the effect of—

            (i)   paragraphs 4 to 10,

            (ii)   subsection (9) of section 209, and

            (iii)   section 212A.

    (3)   A pooling notice or notice of binding may set out steps that R may (subject to subsection (9) of section 209) take to avoid the proposed counteraction.

Corrective action by a notified taxpayer

4   (1)   If a person to whom a pooling notice or notice of binding has been given takes the relevant corrective action in relation to the tax arrangements and tax advantage specified in the notice before the beginning of the closed period mentioned in section 209(9), the person is to be treated for the purposes of paragraphs 8 and 9 and Schedule 43B (generic referral of tax arrangements) as not having been given the notice in question (and accordingly the tax arrangements in question are no longer in the pool).

    (2)   For the purposes of this Schedule the "relevant corrective action" is taken if (and only if) the person takes the steps set out in sub-paragraphs (3) and (4).

    (3)   The first step is that—

    (a) the person amends a return or claim to counteract the tax advantage specified in the pooling notice or notice of binding, or

    (b) if the person has made a tax appeal (by notifying HMRC or otherwise) on the basis that the tax advantage specified in the pooling notice or notice of binding arises from the tax arrangements specified in that notice, the person takes all necessary action to enter into an agreement with HMRC (in writing) for the purpose of relinquishing that advantage.

(4) The second step is that the person notifies HMRC—

    (a) that the first step has been taken, and

    (b) of any additional amount which has or will become due and payable in respect of tax by reason of the first step being taken.

(5) Where a person takes the first step described in sub-paragraph (3)(b), HMRC may proceed as if the person had not taken the relevant corrective action if the person fails to enter into the written agreement.

(6) In determining the additional amount which has or will become due and payable in respect of tax for the purposes of sub-paragraph (4)(b), it is to be assumed that, where the person takes the necessary action as mentioned in sub-paragraph (3)(b), the agreement is then entered into.

(7) No enactment limiting the time during which amendments may be made to returns or claims operates to prevent the person taking the first step mentioned in sub-paragraph (3)(a) before the tax enquiry is closed.

(8) No appeal may be brought, by virtue of a provision mentioned in sub-paragraph (9), against an amendment made by a closure notice in respect of a tax enquiry to the extent that the amendment takes into account an amendment made by the taxpayer to a return or claim in taking the first step mentioned in sub-paragraph (3)(a).

(9) The provisions are—

    (a) paragraph 35(1)(b) of Schedule 33,

    (b) section 31(1)(b) or (c) of TMA 1970,

    (c) paragraph 9 of Schedule 1A to TMA 1970,

    (d) paragraph 34(3) of Schedule 18 to FA 1998, and

    (e) paragraph 35(1)(b) of Schedule 10 to FA 2003.

Corrective action by lead taxpayer

5   If the person mentioned in paragraph 1(1) takes the relevant corrective action (as defined in paragraph 4A of Schedule 43) before the end of the period of 75 days beginning with the day on which the notice mentioned in paragraph 1(1) was given to that person, the lead arrangements are treated as ceasing to be in the pool.

Opinion notices and right to make representations

6   (1) Sub-paragraph (2) applies where—

    (a)   a pooling notice is given to a person in relation to any tax arrangements, and

    (b)   an opinion notice (or opinion notices) under paragraph 11(2) of Schedule 43 about another set of tax arrangements in the pool ("the referred arrangements") is subsequently given to a designated HMRC officer.

(2) The officer must give the person a pooled arrangements opinion notice.

(3) No more than one pooled arrangements opinion notice may be given to a person in respect of the same tax arrangements.

(4) Where a designated HMRC officer gives a person a notice of binding, the officer must, at the same time, give the person a bound arrangements opinion notice.

7   (1) In relation to a person who is, or has been, given a pooling notice, "pooled arrangements opinion notice" means a written notice which—

    (a)   sets out a report prepared by HMRC of any opinion of the GAAR Advisory Panel about the referred arrangements,

    (b)   explains the person's right to make representations falling within sub-paragraph (3), and

    (c)   sets out the period in which those representations may be made.

(2) In relation to a person who is given a notice of binding "bound arrangements opinion notice" means a written notice which—

    (a)   sets out a report prepared by HMRC of any opinion of the GAAR Advisory Panel about the counteracted arrangements (see paragraph 2(1)),

    (b)   explains the person's right to make representations falling within sub-paragraph (3), and

    (c)   sets out the period in which those representations may be made.

(3) A person who is given a pooled arrangements opinion notice or a bound arrangements opinion notice has 30 days beginning with the day on which the notice is given to make representations in any of the following categories—

    (a)   representations that no tax advantage has arisen to the person from the arrangements to which the notice relates;

    (b)   representations as to why the arrangements to which the notice relates are or may be materially different from—

        (i)   the referred arrangements (in the case of a pooled arrangements opinion notice), or

        (ii)   the counteracted arrangements (in the case of a bound arrangements opinion notice).

(4) In sub-paragraph (3)(b) references to "arrangements" include any circumstances which would be relevant in accordance with section 207 to a determination of whether the tax arrangements in question are abusive.

Notice of final decision

8   (1) This paragraph applies where—

(a)   any tax arrangements have been placed in a pool by a notice given to a person under paragraph 1, and

(b)   a designated HMRC officer has given a notice under paragraph 12 of Schedule 43 in relation to any other arrangements in the pool (the "referred arrangements").

(2) The officer must, having considered any opinion of the GAAR Advisory Panel about the referred arrangements and any representations made under paragraph 7(3) in relation to the arrangements mentioned in sub-paragraph (1)(a), give the person a written notice setting out whether the tax advantage arising from those arrangements is to be counteracted under the general anti-abuse rule.

9   (1) This paragraph applies where—

(a)   a person has been given a notice of binding under paragraph 2, and

(b)   the period of 30 days for making representations under paragraph 7(3) has expired.

(2) A designated HMRC officer must, having considered any opinion of the GAAR Advisory Panel about the counteracted arrangements and any representations made under paragraph 7(3) in relation to the arrangements specified in the notice of binding, give the person a written notice setting out whether the tax advantage arising from the arrangements specified in the notice of binding is to be counteracted under the general anti-abuse rule.

10   If a notice under paragraph 8(2) or 9(2) states that a tax advantage is to be counteracted, it must also set out—

(a)   the adjustments required to give effect to the counteraction, and

(b)   if relevant, any steps the person concerned is required to take to give effect to it.

"Equivalent arrangements"

11   (1) For the purposes of paragraph 1, tax arrangements are "equivalent" to one another if they are substantially the same as one another having regard to—

(a)   their substantive results,

(b)   the means of achieving those results, and

(c)   the characteristics on the basis of which it could reasonably be argued, in each case, that the arrangements are abusive tax arrangements under which a tax advantage has arisen to a person.

Notices may be given on assumption that tax advantage does arise

12   (1) A designated HMRC officer may give a notice, or do anything else, under this Schedule where the officer considers that a tax advantage might have arisen to the person concerned.

(2) Accordingly, any notice given by a designated HMRC officer under this Schedule may be expressed to be given on the assumption that a tax advantage does arise (without conceding that it does).

Power to amend

13 (1) The Treasury may by regulations amend this Schedule (apart from this paragraph).

(2) Regulations under sub-paragraph (1) may include —
   (a) any amendment of this Part that is appropriate in consequence of an amendment by virtue of sub-paragraph (1);
   (b) transitional provision.

(3) Regulations under sub-paragraph (1) are to be made by statutory instrument.

(4) A statutory instrument containing regulations under sub-paragraph (1) is subject to annulment in pursuance of a resolution of the House of Commons."

(3) After Schedule 43A insert —

"SCHEDULE 43B

PROCEDURAL REQUIREMENTS: GENERIC REFERRAL OF TAX ARRANGEMENTS

Notice of proposal to make generic referral of tax arrangements

1 (1) Sub-paragraph (2) applies if —
   (a) pooling notices given under paragraph 1 of Schedule 43A have placed one or more sets of tax arrangements in a pool with the lead arrangements,
   (b) the lead arrangements (see paragraph 1(1) of Schedule 43A) have ceased to be in the pool, and
   (c) no referral under paragraph 5 or 6 of Schedule 43 has been made in respect of any arrangements in the pool.

(2) A designated HMRC officer may determine that, in respect of each of the tax arrangements that are in the pool, there is to be given (to the person to whom the pooling notice in question was given) a written notice of a proposal to make a generic referral to the GAAR Advisory Panel in respect of the arrangements in the pool.

(3) Only one determination under sub-paragraph (2) may be made in relation to any one pool.

(4) The persons to whom those notices are given are "the notified taxpayers".

(5) A notice given to a person ("T") under sub-paragraph (2) must —
   (a) specify the arrangements (the "specified arrangements") and the tax advantage (the "specified advantage") to which the notice relates,
   (b) inform T of the period under paragraph 2 for making a proposal.

2   (1) T has 30 days beginning with the day on which the notice under paragraph 1 is given to propose to HMRC that it—

    (a) should give T a notice under paragraph 3 of Schedule 43 in respect of the arrangements to which the notice under paragraph 1 relates, and

    (b) should not proceed with the proposal to make a generic referral to the GAAR Advisory Panel in respect of those arrangements.

    (2) If a proposal is made in accordance with sub-paragraph (1) a designated HMRC officer must consider it.

Generic referral

3   (1) This paragraph applies where a designated HMRC officer has given notices to the notified taxpayers in accordance with paragraph 1(2).

    (2) If none of the notified taxpayers has made a proposal under paragraph 2 by the end of the 30 day period mentioned in that paragraph, the officer must make a referral to the GAAR Advisory Panel in respect of the notified taxpayers and the arrangements which are specified arrangements in relation to them.

    (3) If at least one of the notified taxpayers makes a proposal in accordance with paragraph 2, the designated HMRC officer must, after the end of that 30 day period, decide whether to—

    (a) give a notice under paragraph 3 of Schedule 43 in respect of one set of tax arrangements in the relevant pool, or

    (b) make a referral to the GAAR Advisory Panel in respect of the tax arrangements in the relevant pool.

    (4) A referral under this paragraph is a "generic referral".

4   (1) If a generic referral is made to the GAAR Advisory Panel, the designated HMRC officer must at the same time provide it with—

    (a) a general statement of the material characteristics of the specified arrangements, and

    (b) a declaration that—

        (i) the statement under paragraph (a) is applicable to all the specified arrangements, and

        (ii) as far as HMRC is aware, nothing which is material to the GAAR Advisory Panel's consideration of the matter has been omitted.

    (2) The general statement under sub-paragraph (1)(a) must—

    (a) contain a factual description of the tax arrangements;

    (b) set out HMRC's view as to whether the tax arrangements accord with established practice (when the arrangements were entered into);

    (c) explain why it is the designated HMRC officer's view that a tax advantage of the nature described in the statement and arising from tax arrangements having the characteristics described in the statement would be a tax advantage arising from arrangements that are abusive;

   (d)   set out any matters the designated officer is aware of which may suggest that any view of HMRC or the designated HMRC officer expressed in the general statement is not correct;

   (e)   set out any other matters which the designated officer considers are required for the purposes of the exercise of the GAAR Advisory Panel's functions under paragraph 6.

5   If a generic referral is made the designated HMRC officer must at the same time give each of the notified taxpayers a notice which—

   (a)   specifies that a generic referral is being made, and

   (b)   is accompanied by a copy of the statement given to the GAAR Advisory Panel in accordance with paragraph 4(1)(a).

Decision of GAAR Advisory Panel and opinion notices

6   (1)   If a generic referral is made to the GAAR Advisory Panel under paragraph 3, the Chair must arrange for a sub-panel consisting of 3 members of the GAAR Advisory Panel (one of whom may be the Chair) to consider it.

   (2)   The sub-panel must produce—

     (a)   one opinion notice stating the joint opinion of all the members of the sub-panel, or

     (b)   two or three opinion notices which taken together state the opinions of all the members.

   (3)   The sub-panel must give a copy of the opinion notice or notices to the designated HMRC officer.

   (4)   An opinion notice is a notice which states that in the opinion of the members of the sub-panel, or one or more of those members—

     (a)   the entering into and carrying out of tax arrangements such as are described in the general statement under paragraph 4(1)(a) is a reasonable course of action in relation to the relevant tax provisions,

     (b)   the entering into or carrying out of such tax arrangements is not a reasonable course of action in relation to the relevant tax provisions, or

     (c)   it is not possible, on the information available, to reach a view on that matter,

and the reasons for that opinion.

   (5)   In forming their opinions for the purposes of sub-paragraph (4) members of the sub-panel must—

     (a)   have regard to all the matters set out in the statement under paragraph 4(1)(a),

     (b)   assume (unless the contrary is stated in the statement under paragraph 4(1)(a)) that the tax arrangements do not form part of any other arrangements,

     (c)   have regard to the matters mentioned in paragraphs (a) to (c) of section 207(2), and

     (d)   take account of subsections (4) to (6) of section 207.

(6) For the purposes of the giving of an opinion under this paragraph, the arrangements are to be assumed to be tax arrangements.

(7) In this Part, a reference to any opinion of the GAAR Advisory Panel in respect of a generic referral of any tax arrangements is a reference to the contents of any opinion notice given in relation to a generic referral in respect of the arrangements.

Notice of right to make representations

7 (1) Where a designated HMRC officer is given an opinion notice (or opinion notices) under paragraph 6, the officer must give each of the notified taxpayers a copy of the opinion notice (or notices) and a written notice which—

  (a) explains the notified taxpayer's right to make representations falling within sub-paragraph (2), and

  (b) sets out the period in which those representations may be made.

  (2) A notified taxpayer ("T") who is given a notice under sub-paragraph (1) has 30 days beginning with the day on which the notice is given to make representations in any of the following categories—

  (a) representations that no tax advantage has arisen from the specified arrangements;

  (b) representations that T has already been given a notice under paragraph 6 of Schedule 43A in relation to the specified arrangements;

  (c) representations that any matter set out in the statement under paragraph 4(1)(a) is materially inaccurate as regards the specified arrangements (having regard to all circumstances which would be relevant in accordance with section 207 to a determination of whether the tax arrangements in question are abusive).

Notice of final decision after considering opinion of GAAR Advisory Panel

8 (1) A designated HMRC officer who has received a copy of a notice or notices under paragraph 6(3) in respect of a generic referral must consider the case of each notified taxpayer in accordance with sub-paragraph (2).

  (2) The officer must, having considered—

  (a) any opinion of the GAAR Advisory Panel about the matters referred to it, and

  (b) any representations made by the notified taxpayer under paragraph 7,

  give to the notified taxpayer a written notice setting out whether the specified advantage is to be counteracted under the general anti-abuse rule.

  (3) If the notice states that a tax advantage is to be counteracted, it must also set out—

  (a) the adjustments required to give effect to the counteraction, and

        (b)   if relevant, any steps that the taxpayer is required to take to give effect to it.

Notices may be given on assumption that tax advantage does arise

9   (1) A designated HMRC officer may give a notice, or do anything else, under this Schedule where the officer considers that a tax advantage might have arisen to the person concerned.

      (2) Accordingly, any notice given by a designated HMRC officer under this Schedule may be expressed to be given on the assumption that a tax advantage does arise (without conceding that it does).

Power to amend

10   (1) The Treasury may by regulations amend this Schedule (apart from this paragraph).

      (2) Regulations under sub-paragraph (1) may include —
         (a)   any amendment of this Part that is appropriate in consequence of an amendment by virtue of sub-paragraph (1);
         (b)   transitional provision.

      (3) Regulations under sub-paragraph (1) are to be made by statutory instrument.

      (4) A statutory instrument containing regulations under sub-paragraph (1) is subject to annulment in pursuance of a resolution of the House of Commons."

(4)   In section 209 (counteracting tax advantages), in subsection (6)(a), after "Schedule 43" insert ", 43A or 43B".

(5)   In section 210 (consequential relieving adjustments), in subsection (1)(b), after "Schedule 43," insert "paragraph 8 or 9 of Schedule 43A or paragraph 8 of Schedule 43B,".

(6)   In section 211 (proceedings before a court or tribunal), in subsection (2)(b), for the words from "Panel" to the end substitute "Panel given —
         (i)   under paragraph 11 of Schedule 43 about the arrangements or any tax arrangements which are, as a result of a notice under paragraph 1 or 2 of Schedule 43A, the referred or (as the case may be) counteracted arrangements in relation to the arrangements, or
        (ii)   under paragraph 6 of Schedule 43B in respect of a generic referral of the arrangements."

(7)   Section 214 (interpretation of Part 5) is amended in accordance with subsections (8) to (10).

(8)   Renumber section 214 as subsection (1) of section 214.

(9)   In subsection (1) (as renumbered), at the appropriate places insert —
        ""designated HMRC officer" has the meaning given by paragraph 2 of Schedule 43;".

           ""notice of binding" has the meaning given by paragraph 2(2) of Schedule 43A;

           ""pooling notice" has the meaning given by paragraph 1(4) of Schedule 43A;"

           ""tax appeal" has the meaning given by paragraph 1A of Schedule 43;"

           ""tax enquiry" has the meaning given by section 202(2) of FA 2014."

(10)   After subsection (1) insert—

    "(2)   In this Part references to any "opinion of the GAAR Advisory Panel" about any tax arrangements are to be interpreted in accordance with paragraph 11(5) of Schedule 43.

    (3)   In this Part references to tax arrangements which are "equivalent" to one another are to be interpreted in accordance with paragraph 11 of Schedule 43A."

(11)   In Schedule 43 (general anti-abuse rule: procedural requirements), in paragraph 6, after sub-paragraph (2) insert—

    "(3)   The officer must, as soon as reasonably practicable after deciding whether or not the matter is to be referred to the GAAR Advisory Panel, give the taxpayer written notice of the decision."

(12)   Section 10 of the National Insurance Contributions Act 2014 (GAAR to apply to national insurance contributions) is amended in accordance with subsections (13) to (16).

(13)   In subsection (4), at the end insert ", paragraph 8 or 9 of Schedule 43A to that Act (pooling of tax arrangements: notice of final decision) or paragraph 8 of Schedule 43B to that Act (generic referral of arrangements: notice of final decision)".

(14)   After subsection (6) insert—

    "(6A)   Where, by virtue of this section, a case falls within paragraph 4A of Schedule 43 to the Finance Act 2013 (referrals of single schemes: relevant corrective action) or paragraph 4 of Schedule 43A to that Act (pooled schemes: relevant corrective action)—

        (a)   the person ("P") mentioned in sub-paragraph (1) of that paragraph takes the "relevant corrective action" for the purposes of that paragraph if (and only if)—

            (i)   in a case in which the tax advantage in question can be counteracted by making a payment to HMRC, P makes that payment and notifies HMRC that P has done so, or

            (ii)   in any case, P takes all necessary action to enter into an agreement in writing with HMRC for the purpose of relinquishing the tax advantage, and

        (b)   accordingly, sub-paragraphs (2) to (8) of that paragraph do not apply."

(15)   In subsection (11)—

        (a)   for "and HMRC" substitute ", "HMRC" and "tax advantage"";

        (b)   after "2013" insert "(as modified by this section)".

(16)   After subsection (11) insert—

"(12)   See section 10A for further modifications of Part 5 of the Finance Act 2013."

(17)   After section 10 of the National Insurance Contributions Act 2014 insert—

"10A   Application of GAAR in relation to penalties

(1)   For the purposes of this section a penalty under section 212A of the Finance Act 2013 is a "relevant NICs-related penalty" so far as the penalty relates to a tax advantage in respect of relevant contributions.

(2)   A relevant NICs-related penalty may be recovered as if it were an amount of relevant contributions which is due and payable.

(3)   Section 117A of the Social Security Administration Act 1992 or (as the case may be) section 111A of the Social Security Administration (Northern Ireland) Act 1992 (issues arising in proceedings: contributions etc) has effect in relation to proceedings before a court for recovery of a relevant NICs-related penalty as if the assessment of the penalty were a NICs decision as to whether the person is liable for the penalty.

(4)   Accordingly, paragraph 5(4)(b) of Schedule 43C to the Finance Act 2013 (assessment of penalty to be enforced as if it were an assessment to tax) does not apply in relation to a relevant NICs-related penalty.

(5)   In the application of Schedule 43C to the Finance Act 2013 in relation to a relevant NICs-related penalty, paragraph 9(5) has effect as if the reference to an appeal against an assessment to the tax concerned were to an appeal against a NICs decision.

(6)   In paragraph 8 of that Schedule (aggregate penalties), references to a "relevant penalty provision" include—

(a)   any provision mentioned in sub-paragraph (5) of that paragraph, as applied in relation to any class of national insurance contributions by regulations (whenever made);

(b)   section 98A of the Taxes Management Act 1970, as applied in relation to any class of national insurance contributions by regulations (whenever made);

(c)   any provision in regulations made by the Treasury under which a penalty can be imposed in respect of any class of national insurance contributions.

(7)   The Treasury may by regulations—

(a)   disapply, or modify the effect of, subsection (6)(a) or (b);

(b)   modify paragraph 8 of Schedule 43C to the Finance Act 2013 as it has effect in relation to a relevant penalty provision by virtue of subsection (6)(b) or (c).

(8)   Section 175(3) to (5) of SSCBA 1992 (various supplementary powers) applies to a power to make regulations conferred by subsection (7).

(9)   Regulations under subsection (7) must be made by statutory instrument.

(10) A statutory instrument containing regulations under subsection (7) is subject to annulment in pursuance of a resolution of either House of Parliament.

(11) In this section "NICs decision" means a decision under section 8 of the Social Security Contributions (Transfer of Functions, etc) Act 1999 or Article 7 of the Social Security Contributions (Transfer of Functions, etc) (Northern Ireland) Order 1999 (SI 1999/671).

(12) In this section "relevant contributions" means the following contributions under Part 1 of SSCBA 1992 or Part 1 of SSCB(NI)A 1992—

    (a) Class 1 contributions;

    (b) Class 1A contributions;

    (c) Class 1B contributions;

    (d) Class 2 contributions which must be paid but in relation to which section 11A of the Act in question (application of certain provisions of the Income Tax Acts in relation to Class 2 contributions under section 11(2) of that Act) does not apply."

(18) Section 219 of FA 2014 (circumstances in which an accelerated payment notice may be given) is amended in accordance with subsections (19) and (20).

(19) In subsection (4), after paragraph (c) insert—

"(d) a notice has been given under paragraph 8(2) or 9(2) of Schedule 43A to FA 2013 (notice of final decision after considering Panel's opinion about referred or counteracted arrangements) in relation to the asserted advantage or part of it and the chosen arrangements (or is so given at the same time as the accelerated payment notice) in a case where the stated opinion of at least two of the members of the sub-panel of the GAAR Advisory Panel about the other arrangements (see subsection (8)) was as set out in paragraph 11(3)(b) of Schedule 43 to FA 2013;

(e) a notice under paragraph 8(2) of Schedule 43B to FA 2013 (GAAR: generic referral of tax arrangements) has been given in relation to the asserted advantage or part of it and the chosen arrangements (or is so given at the same time as the accelerated payment notice) in a case where the stated opinion of at least two of the members of the sub-panel of the GAAR Advisory Panel which considered the generic referral in respect of those arrangements under paragraph 6 of Schedule 43B to FA 2013 was as set out in paragraph 6(4)(b) of that Schedule."

(20) After subsection (7) insert—

"(8) In subsection (4)(d) "other arrangements" means—

    (a) in relation to a notice under paragraph 8(2) of Schedule 43A to FA 2013, the referred arrangements (as defined in that paragraph);

    (b) in relation to a notice under paragraph 9(2) of that Schedule, the counteracted arrangements (as defined in paragraph 2 of that Schedule).

(21) In section 220 of FA 2014 (content of notice given while a tax enquiry is in progress)—

    (a) in subsection (4)(c), after "219(4)(c)" insert ", (d) or (e)";

    (b)   in subsection (5)(c), after "219(4)(c)" insert ", (d) or (e)";

    (c)   in subsection (7), for the words from "under" to the end substitute "under —

        (a)   paragraph 12 of Schedule 43 to FA 2013,

        (b)   paragraph 8 or 9 of Schedule 43A to that Act, or

        (c)   paragraph 8 of Schedule 43B to that Act,

    as the case may be."

(22)   Section 287 of FA 2014 (Code of Practice on Taxation for Banks) is amended in accordance with subsections (23) to (25).

(23)   In subsection (4), after "(5)" insert "or (5A)".

(24)   In subsection (5)(b), after "Schedule" insert "or paragraph 8 or 9 of Schedule 43A to that Act".

(25)   After subsection (5) insert—

    "(5A)   This subsection applies to any conduct—

        (a)   in relation to which there has been given—

            (i)   an opinion notice under paragraph 6(4)(b) of Schedule 43B to FA 2013 (GAAR advisory panel: opinion that such conduct unreasonable) stating the joint opinion of all the members of a sub-panel arranged under that paragraph, or

           (ii)   one or more such notices stating the opinions of at least two members of such a sub-panel, and

        (b)   in relation to which there has been given a notice under paragraph 8 of that Schedule (HMRC final decision on tax advantage) stating that a tax advantage is to be counteracted.

    (5B)   For the purposes of subsection (5), any opinions of members of the GAAR advisory panel which must be considered before a notice is given under paragraph 8 or 9 of Schedule 43A to FA 2013 (opinions about the lead arrangements) are taken to relate to the conduct to which the notice relates."

(26)   In Schedule 32 to FA 2014 (accelerated payments and partnerships), paragraph 3 is amended in accordance with subsections (27) and (28).

(27)   In sub-paragraph (5), after paragraph (c) insert—

    "(d)   the relevant partner in question has been given a notice under paragraph 8(2) or 9(2) of Schedule 43A to FA 2013 (notice of final decision after considering Panel's opinion about referred or counteracted arrangements) in respect of any tax advantage resulting from the asserted advantage or part of it and the chosen arrangements (or is given such a notice at the same time as the partner payment notice) in a case where the stated opinion of at least two of the members of the sub-panel of the GAAR Advisory Panel about the other arrangements (see sub-paragraph (7)) was as set out in paragraph 11(3)(b) of Schedule 43 to FA 2013;

    (e)   the relevant partner in question has been given a notice under paragraph 8(2) of Schedule 43B to FA 2013 (GAAR: generic referral of arrangements) in respect of any tax advantage resulting from the asserted advantage or part of it and the chosen arrangements (or is given such a notice at the same time as the partner payment notice) in a case where the stated opinion of at least two of the members of the sub-panel of the GAAR Advisory Panel which considered the generic referral in respect of those arrangements was as set out in paragraph 6(4)(b) of that Schedule."

(28) After sub-paragraph (6) insert—

"(7) "Other arrangements" means—

(a) in relation to a notice under paragraph 8(2) of Schedule 43A to FA 2013, the referred arrangements (as defined in that paragraph);

(b) in relation to a notice under paragraph 9(2) of that Schedule, the counteracted arrangements (as defined in paragraph 2 of that Schedule)."

(29) In Schedule 34 to FA 2014 (promoters of tax avoidance schemes: threshold conditions), in paragraph 7—

(a) in paragraph (a), at the end insert "(referrals of single schemes) or are in a pool in respect of which a referral has been made to that Panel under Schedule 43B to that Act (generic referrals),";

(b) in paragraph (b)—

(i) for "in relation to the arrangements" substitute "in respect of the referral";

(ii) after "11(3)(b)" insert "or (as the case may be) 6(4)(b)";

(c) in paragraph (c)(i) omit "paragraph 10 of".

(30) The amendments made by this section have effect in relation to tax arrangements (within the meaning of Part 5 of FA 2013) entered into at any time (whether before or on or after the day on which this Act is passed).

158 General anti-abuse rule: penalty

(1) Part 5 of FA 2013 (general anti-abuse rule) is amended as follows.

(2) After section 212 insert—

"212A Penalty

(1) A person (P) is liable to pay a penalty if—

(a) P has been given a notice under—

(i) paragraph 12 of Schedule 43,

(ii) paragraph 8 or 9 of Schedule 43A, or

(iii) paragraph 8 of Schedule 43B,

stating that a tax advantage arising from particular tax arrangements is to be counteracted,

(b) a tax document has been given to HMRC on the basis that the tax advantage arises to P from those arrangements,

(c) that document was given to HMRC—

(i) by P, or

(ii) by another person in circumstances where P knew, or ought to have known, that the other person gave the document on the basis mentioned in paragraph (c), and

    (d)   the tax advantage has been counteracted by the making of adjustments under section 209.

  (2)   The penalty is 60% of the value of the counteracted advantage.

  (3)   Schedule 43C —

    (a)   gives the meaning of "the value of the counteracted advantage", and

    (b)   makes other provision in relation to penalties under this section.

  (4)   In this section "tax document" means any return, claim or other document submitted in compliance (or purported compliance) with any provision of, or made under, an Act.

  (5)   In this section the reference to giving a tax document to HMRC is to be interpreted in accordance with paragraph 11(g) and (h) of Schedule 43C.

(3)   After Schedule 43B insert —

"SCHEDULE 43C

Penalty under section 212A: supplementary provision

Value of the counteracted advantage: introduction

1   Paragraphs 2 to 4 set out how to calculate the "value of the counteracted advantage" for the purposes of section 212A.

Value of the counteracted advantage: basic rule

2 (1)   The "value of the counteracted advantage" is the additional amount due or payable in respect of tax as a result of the counteraction mentioned in section 212A(1)(c).

  (2)   The reference in sub-paragraph (1) to the additional amount due and payable includes a reference to —

    (a)   an amount payable to HMRC having erroneously been paid by way of repayment of tax, and

    (b)   an amount which would be repayable by HMRC if the counteraction were not made.

  (3)   The following are ignored in calculating the value of the counteracted advantage —

    (a)   group relief, and

    (b)   any relief under section 458 of CTA 2010 (relief in respect of repayment etc of loan) which is deferred under subsection (5) of that section.

  (4)   For the purposes of this paragraph consequential adjustments under section 210 are regarded as part of the counteraction in question.

  (5)   If the counteraction affects the person's liability to two or more taxes, the taxes concerned are to be considered together for the purpose of determining the value of the counteracted advantage.

  (6)   This paragraph is subject to paragraphs 3 and 4.

Value of counteracted advantage: losses

3   (1) To the extent that the tax advantage mentioned in section 212A(1)(b) ("the tax advantage") resulted in the wrong recording of a loss for the purposes of direct tax and the loss has been wholly used to reduce the amount due or payable in respect of tax, the value of the counteracted advantage is determined in accordance with paragraph 2.

(2) To the extent that the tax advantage resulted in the wrong recording of a loss for purposes of direct tax and the loss has not been wholly used to reduce the amount due or payable in respect of tax, the value of the counteracted advantage is −

   (a) the value under paragraph 2 of so much of the tax advantage as results (or would in the absence of the counteraction result) from the part (if any) of the loss which was used to reduce the amount due or payable in respect of tax, plus

   (b) 10% of the part of the loss not so used.

(3) Sub-paragraphs (1) and (2) apply both −

   (a) to a case where no loss would have been recorded but for the tax advantage, and

   (b) to a case where a loss of a different amount would have been recorded (but in that case sub-paragraphs (1) and (2) apply only to the difference between the amount recorded and the true amount).

(4) To the extent that the tax advantage creates or increases (or would in the absence of the counteraction create or increase) an aggregate loss recorded for a group of companies −

   (a) the value of the counteracted advantage is calculated in accordance with this paragraph, and

   (b) in applying paragraph 2 in accordance with sub-paragraphs (1) and (2), group relief may be taken into account (despite paragraph 2(3)).

(5) To the extent that the tax advantage results (or would in the absence of the counteraction result) in a loss, the value of it is nil where, because of the nature of the loss or the person's circumstances, there was no reasonable prospect of the loss being used to support a claim to reduce a tax liability (of any person).

Value of counteracted advantage: deferred tax

4   (1) To the extent that the tax advantage mentioned in section 212A is a deferral of tax, the value of the counteracted advantage is −

   (a) 25% of the amount of the deferred tax for each year of the deferral, or

   (b) a percentage of the amount of the deferred tax, for each separate period of deferral of less than a year, equating to 25% per year,

   or, if less, 100% of the amount of the deferred tax.

(2) This paragraph does not apply to a case to the extent that paragraph 3 applies.

Assessment of penalty

5   (1) Where a person is liable for a penalty under section 212A, HMRC must assess the penalty.

     (2) Where HMRC assess the penalty, HMRC must—
         (a) notify the person who is liable for the penalty, and
         (b) state in the notice a tax period in respect of which the penalty is assessed.

     (3) A penalty under this paragraph must be paid before the end of the period of 30 days beginning with the day on which notification of the penalty is issued.

     (4) An assessment—
         (a) is to be treated for procedural purposes as if it were an assessment to tax,
         (b) may be enforced as if it were an assessment to tax, and
         (c) may be combined with an assessment to tax.

     (5) An assessment of a penalty under this paragraph must be made before the end of the period of 12 months beginning with—
         (a) the end of the appeal period for the assessment which gave effect to the counteraction mentioned in section 212A(1)(b), or
         (b) if there is no assessment within paragraph (a), the date (or the latest of the dates) on which that counteraction becomes final.

     (6) The reference in sub-paragraph (5)(b) to the counteraction becoming final is to be interpreted in accordance with section 210(8).

Alteration of assessment of penalty

6   (1) After notification of an assessment has been given to a person under paragraph 5(2), the assessment may not be altered except in accordance with this paragraph or paragraph 7, or on appeal.

     (2) A supplementary assessment may be made in respect of a penalty if an earlier assessment operated by reference to an underestimate of the value of the counteracted advantage.

     (3) An assessment may be revised as necessary if it operated by reference to an overestimate of the value of the counteracted advantage.

Revision of assessment following consequential relieving adjustment

7   (1) Sub-paragraph (2) applies where a person—
         (a) is notified under section 210(7) of a consequential adjustment relating to a counteraction under section 209, and
         (b) an assessment to a penalty in respect of that counteraction of which the person has been notified under paragraph 5(2) does not take account of that consequential adjustment.

(2) HMRC must make any alterations of the assessment that appear to HMRC to be just and reasonable in connection with the consequential amendment.

(3) Alterations under this paragraph may be made despite any time limit imposed by or under an enactment.

Aggregate penalties

8   (1) Sub-paragraph (3) applies where—
     (a) two or more penalties are incurred by the same person and fall to be determined by reference to an amount of tax to which that person is chargeable,
     (b) one of those penalties is incurred under section 212A, and
     (c) one or more of the other penalties are incurred under a relevant penalty provision.

   (2) But sub-paragraph (3) does not apply if section 212(2) of FA 2014 (follower notices: aggregate penalties) applies in relation to the amount of tax in question.

   (3) The aggregate of the amounts of the penalties mentioned in subsection (1)(b) and (c), so far as determined by reference to that amount of tax, must not exceed—
     (a) the relevant percentage of that amount, or
     (b) in a case where at least one of the penalties is under paragraph 5(2)(b) of, or sub-paragraph (3)(b), (4)(b) or (5)(b) of paragraph 6 of, Schedule 55 to FA 2009, £300 (if greater).

   (4) In the application of section 97A of TMA 1970 (multiple penalties) no account shall be taken of a penalty under section 212A.

   (5) "Relevant penalty provision" means—
     (a) Schedule 24 to FA 2007 (penalties for errors),
     (b) Schedule 41 to FA 2008 (penalties: failure to notify etc),
     (c) Schedule 55 to FA 2009 (penalties for failure to make returns etc), or
     (d) Part 5 of Schedule 18 to FA 2016 (penalty under serial tax avoidance regime).

   (6) "The relevant percentage" means—
     (a) 200% in a case where at least one of the penalties is determined by reference to the percentage in—
        (i) paragraph 4(4)(c) of Schedule 24 to FA 2007,
        (ii) paragraph 6(4)(a) of Schedule 41 to FA 2008, or
        (iii) paragraph 6(3A)(c) of Schedule 55 to FA 2009,
     (b) 150% in a case where paragraph (a) does not apply and at least one of the penalties is determined by reference to the percentage in—
        (i) paragraph 4(3)(c) of Schedule 24 to FA 2007,
        (ii) paragraph 6(3)(a) of Schedule 41 to FA 2008, or
        (iii) paragraph 6(3A)(b) of Schedule 55 to FA 2009,

    (c)   140% in a case where neither paragraph (a) nor paragraph (b) applies and at least one of the penalties is determined by reference to the percentage in—

        (i)   paragraph 4(4)(b) of Schedule 24 to FA 2007,

        (ii)   paragraph 6(4)(b) of Schedule 41 to FA 2008, or

        (iii)   paragraph 6(4A)(c) of Schedule 55 to FA 2009,

    (d)   105% in a case where at none of paragraphs (a), (b) and (c) applies and at least one of the penalties is determined by reference to the percentage in—

        (i)   paragraph 4(3)(b) of Schedule 24 to FA 2007,

        (ii)   paragraph 6(3)(b) of Schedule 41 to FA 2008, or

        (iii)   paragraph 6(4A)(b) of Schedule 55 to FA 2009, and

    (e)   in any other case, 100%.

Appeal against penalty

9   (1)   A person may appeal against—

    (a)   the imposition of a penalty under section 212A, or

    (b)   the amount assessed under paragraph 5.

    (2)   An appeal under sub-paragraph (1)(a) may only be made on the grounds that the arrangements were not abusive or there was no tax advantage to be counteracted.

    (3)   An appeal under sub-paragraph (1)(b) may only be made on the grounds that the assessment was based on an overestimate of the value of the counteracted advantage (whether because the estimate was made by reference to adjustments which were not just and reasonable or for any other reason).

    (4)   An appeal under this paragraph must be made within the period of 30 days beginning with the day on which notification of the penalty is given under paragraph 5(2).

    (5)   An appeal under this paragraph is to be treated in the same way as an appeal against an assessment to the tax concerned (including by the application of any provision about bringing the appeal by notice to HMRC, about HMRC's review of the decision or about determination of the appeal by the First-tier Tribunal or Upper Tribunal).

    (6)   Sub-paragraph (5) does not apply—

    (a)   so as to require a person to pay a penalty before an appeal against the assessment of the penalty is determined, or

    (b)   in respect of any other matter expressly provided for by this Part.

    (7)   On an appeal against the penalty the tribunal may affirm or cancel HMRC's decision.

    (8)   On an appeal against the amount of the penalty the tribunal may—

    (a)   affirm HMRC's decision, or

    (b)   substitute for HMRC's decision another decision that HMRC has power to make.

(9) In this paragraph "tribunal" means the First-tier Tribunal or Upper Tribunal (as appropriate by virtue of sub-paragraph (5)).

Mitigation of penalties

10 (1) The Commissioners may in their discretion mitigate a penalty under section 212A, or stay or compound any proceedings for such a penalty.

(2) They may also, after judgment, further mitigate or entirely remit the penalty.

Interpretation

11 In this Schedule—

(a) a reference to an "assessment" to tax is to be interpreted, in relation to inheritance tax, as a reference to a determination;

(b) "direct tax" means—

(i) income tax,

(ii) capital gains tax,

(iii) corporation tax (including any amount chargeable as if it were corporation tax or treated as corporation tax),

(iv) petroleum revenue tax, and

(v) diverted profits tax;

(c) a reference to a loss includes a reference to a charge, expense, deficit and any other amount which may be available for, or relied on to claim, a deduction or relief;

(d) a reference to a repayment of tax includes a reference to allowing a credit against tax or to a payment of a corporation tax credit;

(e) "corporation tax credit" means—

(i) an R&D tax credit under Chapter 2 or 7 of Part 13 of CTA 2009,

(ii) an R&D expenditure credit under Chapter 6A of Part 3 of CTA 2009,

(iii) a land remediation tax credit or life assurance company tax credit under Chapter 3 or 4 respectively of Part 14 of CTA 2009,

(iv) a film tax credit under Chapter 3 of Part 15 of CTA 2009,

(v) a television tax credit under Chapter 3 of Part 15A of CTA 2009,

(vi) a video game tax credit under Chapter 3 of Part 15B of CTA 2009,

(vii) a theatre tax credit under section 1217K of CTA 2009,

(viii) an orchestra tax credit under Chapter 3 of Part 15D of CTA 2009, or

(ix) a first-year tax credit under Schedule A1 to CAA 2001;

(f) "tax period" means a tax year, accounting period or other period in respect of which tax is charged;

    (g)   a reference to giving a document to HMRC includes a reference to communicating information to HMRC in any form and by any method (whether by post, fax, email, telephone or otherwise),

    (h)   a reference to giving a document to HMRC includes a reference to making a statement or declaration in a document."

(4)   In section 209 (counteracting the tax advantages), after subsection (7) insert—

"(8)   Where a matter is referred to the GAAR Advisory Panel under paragraph 5 or 6 of Schedule 43, the taxpayer (as defined in paragraph 3 of that Schedule) must not make any GAAR-related adjustments in relation to the taxpayer's tax affairs in the period (the "closed period") which—

    (a)   begins with the 31st day after the end of the 45 day period mentioned in paragraph 4(1) of that Schedule, and

    (b)   ends immediately before the day on which the taxpayer is given the notice under paragraph 12 of Schedule 43 (notice of final decision after considering opinion of GAAR Advisory Panel).

(9)   Where a person has been given a pooling notice or a notice of binding under Schedule 43A in relation to any tax arrangements, the person must not make any GAAR-related adjustments in the period ("the closed period") that—

    (a)   begins with the 31st day after that on which that notice is given, and

    (b)   ends—

        (i)   in the case of a pooling notice, immediately before the day on which the person is given a notice under paragraph 8(2) or 9(2) of Schedule 43A, or a notice under paragraph 8(2) of Schedule 43B, in relation to the tax arrangements (notice of final decision after considering opinion of GAAR Advisory Panel), or

        (ii)   in the case of a notice of binding, with the 30th day after the day on which the notice is given.

(10)   In this section "GAAR-related adjustments" means—

    (a)   for the purposes of subsection (8), adjustments which give effect (wholly or in part) to the proposed counteraction set out in the notice under paragraph 3 of Schedule 43;

    (b)   for the purposes of subsection (9), adjustments which give effect (wholly or partly) to the proposed counteraction set out in the notice of pooling or binding (as the case may be)."

(5)   Schedule 43 (general anti-abuse rule: procedural requirements) is amended in accordance with subsections (6) to (9).

(6)   After paragraph 1 insert—

"Meaning of "tax appeal"

1A   In this Part "tax appeal" means—

    (a)   an appeal under section 31 of TMA 1970 (income tax: appeals against amendments of self-assessment, amendments made by closure notices under section 28A or 28B of that Act, etc), including an appeal under that section by virtue of regulations under Part 11 of ITEPA 2003 (PAYE),

 (b) an appeal under paragraph 9 of Schedule 1A to TMA 1970 (income tax: appeals against amendments made by closure notices under paragraph 7(2) of that Schedule, etc),

 (c) an appeal under section 705 of ITA 2007 (income tax: appeals against counteraction notices),

 (d) an appeal under paragraph 34(3) or 48 of Schedule 18 to FA 1998 (corporation tax: appeals against amendment of a company's return made by closure notice, assessments other than self-assessments, etc),

 (e) an appeal under section 750 of CTA 2010 (corporation tax: appeals against counteraction notices),

 (f) an appeal under section 222 of IHTA 1984 (appeals against HMRC determinations) other than an appeal made by a person against a determination in respect of a transfer of value at a time when a tax enquiry is in progress in respect of a return made by that person in respect of that transfer,

 (g) an appeal under paragraph 35 of Schedule 10 to FA 2003 (stamp duty land tax: appeals against amendment of self-assessment, discovery assessments, etc),

 (h) an appeal under paragraph 35 of Schedule 33 to FA 2013 (annual tax on enveloped dwellings: appeals against amendment of self-assessment, discovery assessments, etc),

 (i) an appeal under paragraph 14 of Schedule 2 to the Oil Taxation Act 1975 (petroleum revenue tax: appeal against assessment, determination etc),

 (j) an appeal under section 102 of FA 2015 (diverted profits tax: appeal against charging notice etc),

 (k) an appeal under section 114 of FA 2016 (apprenticeship levy: appeal against an assessment), or

 (l) an appeal against any determination of—

  (i) an appeal within paragraphs (a) to (k), or

  (ii) an appeal within this paragraph."

(7) In paragraph 3(2)(e), for "of paragraphs 5 and 6" substitute "of—

  (i) paragraphs 5 and 6, and

  (ii) sections 209(8) and (9) and 212A."

(8) After paragraph 4 insert—

"Corrective action by taxpayer

4A (1) If the taxpayer takes the relevant corrective action before the beginning of the closed period mentioned in section 209(8), the matter is not to be referred to the GAAR Advisory Panel.

 (2) For the purposes of this Schedule the "relevant corrective action" is taken if (and only if) the taxpayer takes the steps set out in sub-paragraphs (3) and (4).

 (3) The first step is that—

      (a)   the taxpayer amends a return or claim to counteract the tax advantage specified in the notice under paragraph 3, or

      (b)   if the taxpayer has made a tax appeal (by notifying HMRC or otherwise) on the basis that the tax advantage specified in the notice under paragraph 3 arises from the tax arrangements specified in that notice, the taxpayer takes all necessary action to enter into an agreement with HMRC (in writing) for the purpose of relinquishing that advantage.

(4)   The second step is that the taxpayer notifies HMRC—

      (a)   that the taxpayer has taken the first step, and

      (b)   of any additional amount which has or will become due and payable in respect of tax by reason of the first step being taken.

(5)   Where the taxpayer takes the first step described in sub-paragraph (3)(b), HMRC may proceed as if the taxpayer had not taken the relevant corrective action if the taxpayer fails to enter into the written agreement.

(6)   In determining the additional amount which has or will become due and payable in respect of tax for the purposes of sub-paragraph (4)(b), it is to be assumed that, where the taxpayer takes the necessary action as mentioned in sub-paragraph (3)(b), the agreement is then entered into.

(7)   No enactment limiting the time during which amendments may be made to returns or claims operates to prevent the taxpayer taking the first step mentioned in sub-paragraph (3)(a) before the tax enquiry is closed (whether or not before the specified time).

(8)   No appeal may be brought, by virtue of a provision mentioned in sub-paragraph (9), against an amendment made by a closure notice in respect of a tax enquiry to the extent that the amendment takes into account an amendment made by the taxpayer to a return or claim in taking the first step mentioned in sub-paragraph (3)(a).

(9)   The provisions are—

      (a)   section 31(1)(b) or (c) of TMA 1970,

      (b)   paragraph 9 of Schedule 1A to TMA 1970,

      (c)   paragraph 34(3) of Schedule 18 to FA 1998,

      (d)   paragraph 35(1)(b) of Schedule 10 to FA 2003, and

      (e)   paragraph 35(1)(b) of Schedule 33 to FA 2013."

(9)   Before paragraph 5 (but after the heading "Referral to GAAR Advisory Panel") insert—

   "4B   Paragraphs 5 and 6 apply if the taxpayer does not take the relevant corrective action (see paragraph 4A) by the beginning of the closed period mentioned in section 209(8)."

(10)   In section 103ZA of TMA 1970 (disapplication of sections 100 to 103 in the case of certain penalties)—

      (a)   omit "or" at the end of paragraph (g), and

      (b)   after paragraph (g) insert

          "(ga)   section 212A of the Finance Act 2013 (general anti-abuse rule), or"

(11)   In section 212 of FA 2014 (follower notices: aggregate penalties) (as amended by Schedule 18), in subsection (4) –

      (a)   omit "or" at the end of paragraph (c), and

      (b)   after paragraph (d) insert ", or

          (e)   section 212A of FA 2013 (general anti-abuse rule)."

(12)   FA 2015 is amended in accordance with subsections (13) and (14).

(13)   In section 120 (penalties in connection with offshore matters and offshore transfers), in subsection (1), omit "and" before paragraph (c) and after paragraph (c) insert – ", and

          (d)   Schedule 43C to FA 2013 (as amended by FA 2016)."

(14)   In Schedule 20 to that Act, after paragraph 19 insert –

"General anti-abuse rule: aggregate penalties

   20   (1)   In Schedule 43C to FA 2013 (general anti-abuse rule: supplementary provision about penalty), sub-paragraph (6) of paragraph 8 is amended as follows.

        (2)   After paragraph (b) insert –

          "(ba)   125% in a case where neither paragraph (a) nor paragraph (b) applies and at least one of the penalties is determined by reference to the percentage in –

             (i)   paragraph 4(2)(c) of Schedule 24 to FA 2007,

             (ii)   paragraph 6(2)(a) of Schedule 41 to FA 2008,

             (iii)   paragraph 6(3A)(a) of Schedule 55 to FA 2009,".

        (3)   In sub-paragraph (c) for "neither paragraph (a) nor paragraph (b) applies" substitute "none of paragraphs (a) to (ba) applies.

        (4)   In sub-paragraph (d) for "none of paragraphs (a), (b) and (c) applies" substitute "none of paragraphs (a) to (c) applies".

(15)   The amendments made by this section have effect in relation to tax arrangements (within the meaning of Part 5 of FA 2013) entered into on or after the day on which this Act is passed.

Tackling frequent avoidance

159   Serial tax avoidance

Schedule 18 contains provision about the issue of warning notices to, and further sanctions for, persons who incur a relevant defeat in relation to arrangements.

160   Promoters of tax avoidance schemes

(1)   Part 5 of FA 2014 (promoters of tax avoidance schemes) is amended as follows.

(2)   After section 237 insert—

"237A Duty to give conduct notice: defeat of promoted arrangements

    (1)   If an authorised officer becomes aware at any time ("the relevant time") that a person ("P") who is carrying on a business as a promoter meets any of the conditions in subsections (11) to (13), the officer must determine whether or not P's meeting of that condition should be regarded as significant in view of the purposes of this Part.
But see also subsection (14).

    (2)   An authorised officer must make the determination set out in subsection (3) if the officer becomes aware at any time ("the section 237A(2) relevant time") that—

        (a)   a person meets a condition in subsection (11), (12) or (13), and

        (b)   at the section 237A(2) relevant time another person ("P"), who is carrying on a business as a promoter, meets that condition by virtue of Part 4 of Schedule 34A (meeting the section 237A conditions: bodies corporate and partnerships).

    (3)   The authorised officer must determine whether or not—

        (a)   the meeting of the condition by the person as mentioned in subsection (2)(a), and

        (b)   P's meeting of the condition as mentioned in subsection (2)(b),

    should be regarded as significant in view of the purposes of this Part.

    (4)   Subsections (1) and (2) do not apply if a conduct notice or monitoring notice already has effect in relation to P.

    (5)   Subsection (1) does not apply if, at the relevant time, an authorised officer is under a duty to make a determination under section 237(5) in relation to P.

    (6)   Subsection (2) does not apply if, at the section 237A(2) relevant time, an authorised officer is under a duty to make a determination under section 237(5) in relation to P.

    (7)   But in a case where subsection (1) does not apply because of subsection (5), or subsection (2) does not apply because of subsection (6), subsection (5) of section 237 has effect as if—

        (a)   the references in paragraph (a) of that subsection to "subsection (1)", and "subsection (1)(a)" included subsection (1) of this section, and

        (b)   in paragraph (b) of that subsection the reference to "subsection (1A)(a)" included a reference to subsection (2)(a) of this section and the reference to subsection (1A)(b) included a reference to subsection (2)(b) of this section.

    (8)   If the authorised officer determines under subsection (1) that P's meeting of the condition in question should be regarded as significant, the officer must give P a conduct notice, unless subsection (10) applies.

    (9)   If the authorised officer determines under subsection (3) that—

        (a)   the meeting of the condition by the person as mentioned in subsection (2)(a), and

        (b)   P's meeting of the condition as mentioned in subsection (2)(b), should be regarded as significant in view of the purposes of this Part, the officer must give P a conduct notice, unless subsection (10) applies.

(10) This subsection applies if the authorised officer determines that, having regard to the extent of the impact that P's activities as a promoter are likely to have on the collection of tax, it is inappropriate to give P a conduct notice.

(11) The condition in this subsection is that in the period of 3 years ending with the relevant time at least 3 relevant defeats have occurred in relation to P.

(12) The condition in this subsection is that at least two relevant defeats have occurred in relation to P at times when a single defeat notice under section 241A(2) or (6) had effect in relation to P.

(13) The condition in this subsection is that at least one relevant defeat has occurred in relation to P at a time when a double defeat notice under section 241A(3) had effect in relation to P.

(14) A determination that the condition in subsection (12) or (13) is met cannot be made unless —

  (a) the defeat notice in question still has effect when the determination is made, or

  (b) the determination is made on or before the 90th day after the day on which the defeat notice in question ceased to have effect.

(15) Schedule 34A sets out the circumstances in which a "relevant defeat" occurs in relation to a person and includes provision limiting what can amount to a further relevant defeat in relation to a person (see paragraph 6).

237B Duty to give further conduct notice where provisional notice not complied with

(1) An authorised officer must give a conduct notice to a person ("P") who is carrying on a business as a promoter if—

  (a) a conduct notice given to P under section 237A(8) —

    (i) has ceased to have effect otherwise than as a result of section 237D(2) or 241(3) or (4), and

    (ii) was provisional immediately before it ceased to have effect,

  (b) the officer determines that P had failed to comply with one or more conditions in the conduct notice,

  (c) the conduct notice relied on a Case 3 relevant defeat,

  (d) since the time when the conduct notice ceased to have effect, one or more relevant defeats falling within subsection (2) have occurred in relation to—

    (i) P, and

    (ii) any arrangements to which the Case 3 relevant defeat also relates, and

  (e) had that relevant defeat or (as the case may be) those relevant defeats, occurred before the conduct notice ceased to have effect, an authorised officer would have been required to notify the person under section 237C(3) that the notice was no longer provisional.

(2) A relevant defeat falls within this subsection if it occurs by virtue of Case 1 or Case 2 in Schedule 34A.

(3) Subsection (1) does not apply if the authorised officer determines that, having regard to the extent of the impact that the person's activities as a promoter are likely to have on the collection of tax, it is inappropriate to give the person a conduct notice.

(4) Subsection (1) does not apply if a conduct notice or monitoring notice already has effect in relation to the person.

(5) For the purposes of this Part a conduct notice "relies on a Case 3 relevant defeat" if it could not have been given under the following condition.

The condition is that paragraph 9 of Schedule 34A had effect with the substitution of "100% of the tested arrangements" for "75% of the tested arrangements".

237C When a conduct notice given under section 237A(8) is "provisional"

(1) This section applies to a conduct notice which—
   (a) is given to a person under section 237A(8), and
   (b) relies on a Case 3 relevant defeat.

(2) The notice is "provisional" at all times when it has effect, unless an authorised officer notifies the person that the notice is no longer provisional.

(3) An authorised officer must notify the person that the notice is no longer provisional if subsection (4) or (5) applies.

(4) This subsection applies if—
   (a) the condition in subsection (5)(a) is not met, and
   (b) a full relevant defeat occurs in relation to P.

(5) This subsection applies if—
   (a) two, or all three, of the relevant defeats by reference to which the conduct notice is given would not have been relevant defeats if paragraph 9 of Schedule 34A had effect with the substitution of "100% of the tested arrangements" for "75% of the tested arrangements", and
   (b) the same number of full relevant defeats occur in relation to P.

(6) A "full relevant defeat" occurs in relation to P if—
   (a) a relevant defeat occurs in relation to P otherwise than by virtue of Case 3 in paragraph 9 of Schedule 34A, or
   (b) circumstances arise which would be a relevant defeat in relation to P by virtue of paragraph 9 of Schedule 34A if that paragraph had effect with the substitution of "100% of the tested arrangements" for "75% of the tested arrangements".

(7) In determining under subsection (6) whether a full relevant defeat has occurred in relation to P, assume that in paragraph 6 of Schedule 34A (provision limiting what can amount to a further relevant defeat in relation to a person) the first reference to a "relevant defeat" does not include a relevant defeat by virtue of Case 3 in paragraph 9 of Schedule 34A.

237D Judicial ruling upholding asserted tax advantage: effect on conduct notice which is provisional

(1) Subsection (2) applies if at any time −

    (a) a conduct notice which relies on a Case 3 relevant defeat (see section 237B(5)) is provisional, and

    (b) a court or tribunal upholds a corresponding tax advantage which has been asserted in connection with any of the related arrangements to which that relevant defeat relates (see paragraph 5(2) of Schedule 34A).

(2) The conduct notice ceases to have effect when that judicial ruling becomes final.

(3) An authorised officer must give the person to whom the conduct notice was given a written notice stating that the conduct notice has ceased to have effect.

(4) For the purposes of this section, a tax advantage is "asserted" in connection with any arrangements if a person makes a return, claim or election on the basis that the tax advantage arises from those arrangements.

In relation to the arrangements mentioned in paragraph (b) of subsection (1) "corresponding tax advantage" means a tax advantage corresponding to any tax advantage the counteraction of which contributed to the relevant defeat mentioned in that paragraph.

(5) For the purposes of this section a court or tribunal "upholds" a tax advantage if −

    (a) the court or tribunal makes a ruling to the effect that no part of the tax advantage is to be counteracted, and

    (b) that judicial ruling is final.

(6) For the purposes of this Part a judicial ruling is "final" if it is −

    (a) a ruling of the Supreme Court, or

    (b) a ruling of any other court or tribunal in circumstances where −

        (i) no appeal may be made against the ruling,

        (ii) if an appeal may be made against the ruling with permission, the time limit for applications has expired and either no application has been made or permission has been refused,

        (iii) if such permission to appeal against the ruling has been granted or is not required, no appeal has been made within the time limit for appeals, or

        (iv) if an appeal was made, it was abandoned or otherwise disposed of before it was determined by the court or tribunal to which it was addressed.

(7) In this section references to "counteraction" include anything referred to as a counteraction in any of Conditions A to F in paragraphs 11 to 16 of Schedule 34A."

(3)   After section 241 insert —

241A Defeat notices

(1)   This section applies in relation to a person ("P") only if P is carrying on a business as a promoter.

(2)   An authorised officer, or an officer of Revenue and Customs with the approval of an authorised officer, may give P a notice if the officer concerned has become aware of one (and only one) relevant defeat which has occurred in relation to P in the period of 3 years ending with the day on which the notice is given.

(3)   An authorised officer, or an officer of Revenue and Customs with the approval of an authorised officer, may give P a notice if the officer concerned has become aware of two (but not more than two) relevant defeats which have occurred in relation to P in the period of 3 years ending with the day on which the notice is given.

(4)   A notice under this section must be given by the end of the 90 days beginning with the day on which the matters mentioned in subsection (2) or (as the case may be) (3) come to the attention of HMRC.

(5)   Subsection (6) applies if —
    (a)   a single defeat notice which had been given to P (under subsection (2) or (6)) ceases to have effect as a result of section 241B(1), and
    (b)   in the period when the defeat notice had effect a relevant defeat ("the further relevant defeat") occurred in relation to P.

(6)   An authorised officer or an officer of Revenue and Customs with the approval of an authorised officer may give P a notice in respect of the further relevant defeat (regardless of whether or not it occurred in the period of 3 years ending with the day on which the notice is given).

(7)   In this Part —
    (a)   "single defeat notice" means a notice under subsection (2) or (6);
    (b)   "double defeat notice" means a notice under subsection (3);
    (c)   "defeat notice" means a single defeat notice or a double defeat notice.

(8)   A defeat notice must —
    (a)   set out the dates on which the look-forward period for the notice begins and ends;
    (b)   in the case of a single defeat notice, explain the effect of section 237A(12);
    (c)   in the case of a double defeat notice, explain the effect of section 237A(13).

(9)   HMRC may specify what further information must be included in a defeat notice.

(10) "Look-forward period" —

       (a)   in relation to a defeat notice under subsection (2) or (3), means the period of 5 years beginning with the day after the day on which the notice is given;

       (b)   in relation to a defeat notice under subsection (6), means the period beginning with the day after the day on which the notice is given and ending at the end of the period of 5 years beginning with the day on which the further relevant defeat mentioned in subsection (6) occurred in relation to P.

(11)   A defeat notice has effect throughout its look-forward period unless it ceases to have effect earlier in accordance with section 241B(1) or (4).

241B Judicial ruling upholding asserted tax advantage: effect on defeat notice

(1)   If the relevant defeat to which a single defeat notice relates is overturned (see subsection (5)), the notice has no further effect on and after the day on which it is overturned.

(2)   Subsection (3) applies if one (and only one) of the relevant defeats in respect of which a double defeat notice was given is overturned.

(3)   The notice is to be treated for the purposes of this Part (including this section) as if it had always been a single defeat notice given (in respect of the other of the two relevant defeats) on the date on which the notice was in fact given.

The look-forward period for the notice is accordingly unchanged.

(4)   If both the relevant defeats to which a double defeat notice relates are overturned (on the same date), that notice has no further effect on and after that date.

(5)   A relevant defeat specified in a defeat notice is "overturned" if—

       (a)   the notice could not have specified that relevant defeat if paragraph 9 of Schedule 34A had effect with the substitution of "100% of the tested arrangements" for "75% of the tested arrangements", and

       (b)   at a time when the notice has effect a court or tribunal upholds a corresponding tax advantage which has been asserted in connection with any of the related arrangements to which the relevant defeat relates (see paragraph 5(2) of Schedule 34A).

Accordingly the relevant defeat is overturned on the day on which the judicial ruling mentioned in paragraph (b) becomes final.

(6)   If a defeat notice ceases to have effect as a result of subsection (1) or (4) an authorised officer, or an officer of Revenue and Customs with the approval of an authorised officer, must notify the person to whom the notice was given that it has ceased to have effect.

(7)   If subsection (3) has effect in relation to a defeat notice, an authorised officer, or an officer of Revenue and Customs with the approval of an authorised officer, must notify the person of the effect of that subsection.

(8)   For the purposes of this section, a tax advantage is "asserted" in connection with any arrangements if a person makes a return, claim or election on the basis that the tax advantage arises from those arrangements.

(9) In relation to the arrangements mentioned in paragraph (b) of subsection (5) "corresponding tax advantage" means a tax advantage corresponding to any tax advantage the counteraction of which contributed to the relevant defeat mentioned in that paragraph.

(10) For the purposes of this section a court or tribunal "upholds" a tax advantage if—

    (a) the court or tribunal makes a ruling to the effect that no part of the tax advantage is to be counteracted, and

    (b) that judicial ruling is final.

(11) In this section references to "counteraction" include anything referred to as a counteraction in any of Conditions A to F in paragraphs 11 to 16 of Schedule 34A."

(4) In section 242 (monitoring notices: duty to apply to tribunal), after subsection (5) insert—

"(6) At a time when a notice given under section 237A is provisional, no determination is to be made under subsection (1) in respect of the notice.

(7) If a promoter fails to comply with conditions in a conduct notice at a time when the conduct notice is provisional, nothing in subsection (6) prevents those failures from being taken into account under subsection (1) at any subsequent time when the conduct notice is not provisional."

(5) After Schedule 34 insert—

"SCHEDULE 34A

PROMOTERS OF TAX AVOIDANCE SCHEMES: DEFEATED ARRANGEMENTS

PART 1

INTRODUCTION

1   In this Schedule—

    (a) Part 2 is about the meaning of "relevant defeat";

    (b) Part 3 contains provision about when a relevant defeat is treated as occurring in relation to a person;

    (c) Part 4 contains provision about when a person is treated as meeting a condition in subsection (11), (12) or (13) of section 237A;

    (d) Part 5 contains definitions and other supplementary provisions.

PART 2

MEANING OF "RELEVANT DEFEAT"

"Related" arrangements

2   (1) For the purposes of this Part of this Act, separate arrangements which persons have entered into are "related" to one another if (and only if) they are substantially the same.

(2) Sub-paragraphs (3) to (6) set out cases in which arrangements are to be treated as being "substantially the same" (if they would not otherwise be so treated under sub-paragraph (1)).

(3) Arrangements to which the same reference number has been allocated under Part 7 of FA 2004 (disclosure of tax avoidance schemes) are treated as being substantially the same.

For this purpose arrangements in relation to which information relating to a reference number has been provided in compliance with section 312 of FA 2004 are treated as arrangements to which that reference number has been allocated under Part 7 of that Act.

(4) Arrangements to which the same reference number has been allocated under paragraph 9 of Schedule 11A to VATA 1994 (disclosure of avoidance schemes) are treated as being substantially the same.

(5) Any two or more sets of arrangements which are the subject of follower notices given by reference to the same judicial ruling are treated as being substantially the same.

(6) Where a notice of binding has been given in relation to any arrangements ("the bound arrangements") on the basis that they are, for the purposes of Schedule 43A to FA 2013, equivalent arrangements in relation to another set of arrangements (the "lead arrangements")—

    (a) the bound arrangements and the lead arrangements are treated as being substantially the same, and

    (b) the bound arrangements are treated as being substantially the same as any other arrangements which, as a result of this sub-paragraph, are treated as substantially the same as the lead arrangements.

"Promoted arrangements"

3   (1) For the purposes of this Schedule arrangements are "promoted arrangements" in relation to a person if—

    (a) they are relevant arrangements or would be relevant arrangements under the condition stated in sub-paragraph (2), and

    (b) the person is carrying on a business as a promoter and—

        (i) the person is or has been a promoter in relation to the arrangements, or

        (ii) that would be the case if the condition in sub-paragraph (2) were met.

(2) That condition is that the definition of "tax" in section 283 includes, and has always included, value added tax.

Relevant defeat of single arrangements

4   (1) A defeat of arrangements (entered into by any person) which are promoted arrangements in relation to a person ("the promoter") is a "relevant defeat" in relation to the promoter if the condition in sub-paragraph (2) is met.

(2) The condition is that the arrangements are not related to any other arrangements which are promoted arrangements in relation to the promoter.

(3) For the meaning of "defeat" see paragraphs 10 to 16.

Relevant defeat of related arrangements

5   (1) This paragraph applies if arrangements (entered into by any person) ("Set A") –

      (a)   are promoted arrangements in relation to a person ("P"), and

      (b)   are related to other arrangements which are promoted arrangements in relation to P.

    (2) If Case 1, 2 or 3 applies (see paragraphs 7 to 9) a relevant defeat occurs in relation to P and each of the related arrangements.

    (3) "The related arrangements" means Set A and the arrangements mentioned in sub-paragraph (1)(b).

Limit on number of separate relevant defeats in relation to the same, or related, arrangements

6   In relation to a person, if there has been a relevant defeat of arrangements (whether under paragraph 4 or 5) there cannot be a further relevant defeat of –

      (a)   those particular arrangements, or

      (b)   arrangements which are related to those arrangements.

Case 1: counteraction upheld by judicial ruling

7   (1) Case 1 applies if –

      (a)   any of Conditions A to E is met in relation to any of the related arrangements, and

      (b)   in the case of those arrangements the decision to make the relevant counteraction has been upheld by a judicial ruling (which is final).

    (2) In sub-paragraph (1) "the relevant counteraction" means the counteraction mentioned in paragraph 11(d), 12(1)(b), 13(1)(d), 14(1)(d) or 15(1)(d) (as the case requires).

Case 2: judicial ruling that avoidance-related rule applies

8   Case 2 applies if Condition F is met in relation to any of the related arrangements.

Case 3: proportion-based relevant defeat

9   (1) Case 3 applies if –

      (a)   at least 75% of the tested arrangements have been defeated, and

      (b)   no final judicial ruling in relation to any of the related arrangements has upheld a corresponding tax advantage which has been asserted in connection with any of the related arrangements.

(2) In this paragraph "the tested arrangements" means so many of the related arrangements (as defined in paragraph 5(3)) as meet the condition in sub-paragraph (3) or (4).

(3) Particular arrangements meet this condition if a person has made a return, claim or election on the basis that a tax advantage results from those arrangements and —

    (a) there has been an enquiry or investigation by HMRC into the return, claim or election, or

    (b) HMRC assesses the person to tax on the basis that the tax advantage (or any part of it) does not arise, or

    (c) a GAAR counteraction notice has been given in relation to the tax advantage or part of it and the arrangements.

(4) Particular arrangements meet this condition if HMRC takes other action on the basis that a tax advantage which might be expected to arise from those arrangements, or is asserted in connection with them, does not arise.

(5) For the purposes of this paragraph a tax advantage has been "asserted" in connection with particular arrangements if a person has made a return, claim or election on the basis that the tax advantage arises from those arrangements.

(6) In sub-paragraph (1)(b) "corresponding tax advantage" means a tax advantage corresponding to any tax advantage the counteraction of which is taken into account by HMRC for the purposes of sub-paragraph (1)(a).

(7) For the purposes of this paragraph a court or tribunal "upholds" a tax advantage if —

    (a) the court or tribunal makes a ruling to the effect that no part of the tax advantage is to be counteracted, and

    (b) that judicial ruling is final.

(8) In this paragraph references to "counteraction" include anything referred to as a counteraction in any of Conditions A to F in paragraphs 11 to 16.

(9) In this paragraph "GAAR counteraction notice" means —

    (a) a notice such as is mentioned in sub-paragraph (2) of paragraph 12 of Schedule 43 to FA 2013 (notice of final decision to counteract),

    (b) a notice under paragraph 8(2) or 9(2) of Schedule 43A to that Act (pooling or binding of arrangements) stating that the tax advantage is to be counteracted under the general anti-abuse rule, or

    (c) a notice under paragraph 8(2) of Schedule 43B to that Act (generic referrals) stating that the tax advantage is to be counteracted under the general anti-abuse rule.

"Defeat" of arrangements

10   For the purposes of this Part of this Act a "defeat" of arrangements occurs if any of Conditions A to F (in paragraphs 11 to 16) is met in relation to the arrangements.

11   Condition A is that—

    (a)   a person has made a return, claim or election on the basis that a tax advantage arises from the arrangements,

    (b)   a notice given to the person under paragraph 12 of Schedule 43 to, paragraph 8(2) or 9(2) of Schedule 43A to or paragraph 8(2) of Schedule 43B to FA 2013 stated that the tax advantage was to be counteracted under the general anti-abuse rule,

    (c)   the tax advantage has been counteracted (in whole or in part) under the general anti-abuse rule, and

    (d)   the counteraction is final.

12   (1) Condition B is that a follower notice has been given to a person by reference to the arrangements (and not withdrawn) and—

    (a)   the person has complied with subsection (2) of section 208 of FA 2014 by taking the action specified in subsections (4) to (6) of that section in respect of the denied tax advantage (or part of it), or

    (b)   the denied tax advantage has been counteracted (in whole or in part) otherwise than as mentioned in paragraph (a) and the counteraction is final.

   (2) In this paragraph "the denied tax advantage" is to be interpreted in accordance with section 208(3) of FA 2014.

   (3) In this Schedule "follower notice" means a follower notice under Chapter 2 of Part 4 of FA 2014.

13   (1) Condition C is that—

    (a)   the arrangements are DOTAS arrangements,

    (b)   a person ("the taxpayer") has made a return, claim or election on the basis that a relevant tax advantage arises,

    (c)   the relevant tax advantage has been counteracted, and

    (d)   the counteraction is final.

   (2) For the purposes of sub-paragraph (1) "relevant tax advantage" means a tax advantage which the arrangements might be expected to enable the taxpayer to obtain.

   (3) For the purposes of this paragraph the relevant tax advantage is "counteracted" if adjustments are made in respect of the taxpayer's tax position on the basis that the whole or part of that tax advantage does not arise.

14   (1) Condition D is that—

    (a)   the arrangements are disclosable VAT arrangements to which a taxable person is a party,

    (b)   the taxable person has made a return or claim on the basis that a relevant tax advantage arises,

    (c)   the relevant tax advantage has been counteracted, and

      (d)   the counteraction is final.

  (2) For the purposes of sub-paragraph (1) "relevant tax advantage" means a tax advantage which the arrangements might be expected to enable the taxable person to obtain.

  (3) For the purposes of this paragraph the relevant tax advantage is "counteracted" if adjustments are made in respect of the taxable person's tax position on the basis that the whole or part of that tax advantage does not arise.

15 (1) Condition E is that the arrangements are disclosable VAT arrangements to which a taxable person ("T") is a party and —

      (a)   the arrangements relate to the position with respect to VAT of a person other than T ("S") who has made supplies of goods or services to T,

      (b)   the arrangements might be expected to enable T to obtain a tax advantage in connection with those supplies of goods or services,

      (c)   the arrangements have been counteracted, and

      (d)   the counteraction is final.

  (2) For the purposes of this paragraph the arrangements are "counteracted" if —

      (a)   HMRC assess S to tax or take any other action on a basis which prevents T from obtaining (or obtaining the whole of) the tax advantage in question, or

      (b)   adjustments are made on a basis such as is mentioned in paragraph (a).

16 (1) Condition F is that —

      (a)   a person has made a return, claim or election on the basis that a relevant tax advantage arises,

      (b)   the tax advantage, or part of the tax advantage would not arise if a particular avoidance-related rule (see paragraph 25) applies in relation to the person's tax affairs,

      (c)   it is held in a judicial ruling that the relevant avoidance-related rule applies in relation to the person's tax affairs, and

      (d)   the judicial ruling is final.

  (2) For the purposes of sub-paragraph (1) "relevant tax advantage" means a tax advantage which the arrangements might be expected to enable the person to obtain.

PART 3

RELEVANT DEFEATS: ASSOCIATED PERSONS

Attribution of relevant defeats

17 (1) Sub-paragraph (2) applies if —

      (a)   there is (or has been) a person ("Q"),

      (b)   arrangements ("the defeated arrangements") have been entered into,

      (c)   an event occurs such that either —

           (i)   there is a relevant defeat in relation to Q and the defeated arrangements, or

           (ii)   the condition in sub-paragraph (i) would be met if Q had not ceased to exist,

     (d)   at the time of that event a person ("P") is carrying on a business as a promoter (or is carrying on what would be such a business under the condition in paragraph 3(2)), and

     (e)   Condition 1 or 2 is met in relation to Q and P.

   (2) The event is treated for all purposes of this Part of this Act as a relevant defeat in relation to P and the defeated arrangements (whether or not it is also a relevant defeat in relation to Q, and regardless of whether or not P existed at any time when those arrangements were promoted arrangements in relation to Q).

   (3) Condition 1 is that—

     (a)   P is not an individual,

     (b)   at a time when the defeated arrangements were promoted arrangements in relation to Q—

           (i)   P was a relevant body controlled by Q, or

           (ii)   Q was a relevant body controlled by P, and

     (c)   at the time of the event mentioned in sub-paragraph (1)(c)—

           (i)   Q is a relevant body controlled by P,

           (ii)   P is a relevant body controlled by Q, or

           (iii)   P and Q are relevant bodies controlled by a third person.

   (4) Condition 2 is that—

     (a)   P and Q are relevant bodies,

     (b)   at a time when the defeated arrangements were promoted arrangements in relation to Q, a third person ("C") controlled Q, and

     (c)   C controls P at the time of the event mentioned in sub-paragraph (1)(c).

   (5) For the purposes of sub-paragraphs (3)(b) and (4)(b), the question whether arrangements are promoted arrangements in relation to Q at any time is to be determined on the assumption that the reference to "design" in paragraph (b) of section 235(3) (definition of "promoter" in relation to relevant arrangements) is omitted.

Deemed defeat notices

18   (1) This paragraph applies if—

     (a)   an authorised officer becomes aware at any time ("the relevant time") that a relevant defeat has occurred in relation to a person ("P") who is carrying on a business as a promoter,

     (b)   there have occurred, more than 3 years before the relevant time—

           (i)   one third party defeat, or

           (ii)   two third party defeats, and

      (c)   conditions A1 and B1 (in a case within paragraph (b)(i)), or conditions A2 and B2 (in a case within paragraph (b)(ii)), are met.

(2)   Where this paragraph applies by virtue of sub-paragraph (1)(b)(i), this Part of this Act has effect as if an authorised officer had (with due authority), at the time of the time of the third party defeat, given P a single defeat notice under section 241A(2) in respect of it.

(3)   Where this paragraph applies by virtue of sub-paragraph (1)(b)(ii), this Part of this Act has effect as if an authorised officer had (with due authority), at the time of the second of the two third party defeats, given P a double defeat notice under section 241A(3) in respect of the two third party defeats.

(4)   Section 241A(8) has no effect in relation to a notice treated as given as mentioned in sub-paragraph (2) or (3).

(5)   Condition A1 is that—

      (a)   a conduct notice or a single or double defeat notice has been given to the other person (see sub-paragraph (9)) in respect of the third party defeat,

      (b)   at the time of the third party defeat an authorised officer would have had power by virtue of paragraph 17 to give P a defeat notice in respect of the third party defeat, had the officer been aware that it was a relevant defeat in relation to P, and

      (c)   so far as the authorised officer mentioned in sub-paragraph (1)(a) is aware, the conditions for giving P a defeat notice in respect of the third party defeat have never been met (ignoring this paragraph).

(6)   Condition A2 is that—

      (a)   a conduct notice or a single or double defeat notice has been given to the other person (see sub-paragraph (9)) in respect of each, or both, of the third party defeats,

      (b)   at the time of the second third party defeat an authorised officer would have had power by virtue of paragraph 17 to give P a double defeat notice in respect of the third party defeats, had the officer been aware that either of the third party defeats was a relevant defeat in relation to P, and

      (c)   so far as the authorised officer mentioned in sub-paragraph (1)(a) is aware, the conditions for giving P a defeat notice in respect of those third party defeats (or either of them) have never been met (ignoring this paragraph).

(7)   Condition B1 is that, had an authorised officer given P a defeat notice in respect of the third party defeat at the time of that relevant defeat, that defeat notice would still have effect at the relevant time (see sub-paragraph (1)).

(8)   Condition B2 is that, had an authorised officer given P a defeat notice in respect of the two third party defeats at the time of the second of those relevant defeats, that defeat notice would still have effect at the relevant time.

(9) In this paragraph "third party defeat" means a relevant defeat which has occurred in relation to a person other than P.

Meaning of "relevant body" and "control"

19 (1) In this Part of this Schedule "relevant body" means—

    (a) a body corporate, or

    (b) a partnership.

  (2) For the purposes of this Part of this Schedule a person controls a body corporate if the person has power to secure that the affairs of the body corporate are conducted in accordance with the person's wishes—

    (a) by means of the holding of shares or the possession of voting power in relation to the body corporate or any other relevant body,

    (b) as a result of any powers conferred by the articles of association or other document regulating the body corporate or any other relevant body, or

    (c) by means of controlling a partnership.

  (3) For the purposes of this Part of this Schedule a person controls a partnership if the person is a controlling member or the managing partner of the partnership.

  (4) In this paragraph "controlling member" has the same meaning as in Schedule 36 (partnerships).

  (5) In this paragraph "managing partner", in relation to a partnership, means the member of the partnership who directs, or is on a day-to-day level in control of, the management of the business of the partnership.

PART 4

MEETING SECTION 237A CONDITIONS: BODIES CORPORATE AND PARTNERSHIPS

Treating persons under another's control as meeting section 237A condition

20 (1) A relevant body ("RB") is treated as meeting a section 237A condition at the section 237A(2) relevant time if—

    (a) that condition was met by a person ("C") at a time when—

      (i) C was carrying on a business as a promoter, or

      (ii) RB was carrying on a business as a promoter and C controlled RB, and

    (b) RB is controlled by C at the section 237A(2) relevant time.

  (2) Sub-paragraph (1) does not apply if C is an individual.

  (3) For the purposes of determining whether the requirements of sub-paragraph (1) are met by reason of meeting the requirement in sub-paragraph (1)(a)(i), it does not matter whether RB existed at the time when C met the section 237A condition.

Treating persons in control of others as meeting section 237A condition

21 (1) A person other than an individual is treated as meeting a section 237A condition at the section 237A(2) relevant time if—

    (a) a relevant body ("A") met the condition at a time when A was controlled by the person, and

    (b) at the time mentioned in paragraph (a) A, or another relevant body ("B") which was also at that time controlled by the person, carried on a business as a promoter.

  (2) For the purposes of determining whether the requirements of sub-paragraph (1) are met it does not matter whether A or B (or neither) exists at the section 237A(2) relevant time.

Treating persons controlled by the same person as meeting section 237A condition

22 (1) A relevant body ("RB") is treated as meeting a section 237A condition at the section 237A(2) relevant time if—

    (a) another relevant body met that condition at a time ("time T") when it was controlled by a person ("C"),

    (b) at time T, there was a relevant body controlled by C which carried on a business as a promoter, and

    (c) RB is controlled by C at the section 237A(2) relevant time.

  (2) For the purposes of determining whether the requirements of sub-paragraph (1) are met it does not matter whether—

    (a) RB existed at time T, or

    (b) any relevant body (other than RB) by reason of which the requirements of sub-paragraph (1) are met exists at the section 237A(2) relevant time.

Interpretation

23 (1) In this Part of this Schedule—

    "control" has the same meaning as in Part 3 of this Schedule;

    "relevant body" has the same meaning as in Part 3 of this Schedule;

    "section 237A(2) relevant time" means the time referred to in section 237A(2);

    "section 237A condition" means any of the conditions in section 237A(11), (12) and (13).

  (2) For the purposes of paragraphs 20(1)(a), 21(1)(a) and 22(1)(a), the condition in section 237A(11) (occurrence of 3 relevant defeats in the 3 years ending with the relevant time) is taken to have been met by a person at any time if at least 3 relevant defeats have occurred in relation to the person in the period of 3 years ending with that time.

PART 5

SUPPLEMENTARY

"Adjustments"

24   In this Schedule "adjustments" means any adjustments, whether by way of an assessment, the modification of an assessment or return, the amendment or disallowance of a claim, the entering into of a contract settlement or otherwise (and references to "making" adjustments accordingly include securing that adjustments are made by entering into a contract settlement).

Meaning of "avoidance-related rule"

25   (1)   In this Schedule "avoidance-related rule" means a rule in Category 1 or 2.

    (2)   A rule is in Category 1 if—
       (a)   it refers (in whatever terms) to the purpose or main purpose or purposes of a transaction, arrangements or any other action or matter, and
       (b)   to whether or not the purpose in question is or involves the avoidance of tax or the obtaining of any advantage in relation to tax (however described).

    (3)   A rule is also in Category 1 if it refers (in whatever terms) to—
       (a)   expectations as to what are, or may be, the expected benefits of a transaction, arrangements or any other action or matter, and
       (b)   whether or not the avoidance of tax or the obtaining of any advantage in relation to tax (however described) is such a benefit.

For the purposes of paragraph (b) it does not matter whether the reference is (for instance) to the "sole or main benefit" or "one of the main benefits" or any other reference to a benefit.

    (4)   A rule falls within Category 2 if as a result of the rule a person may be treated differently for tax purposes depending on whether or not purposes referred to in the rule (for instance the purposes of an actual or contemplated action or enterprise) are (or are shown to be) commercial purposes.

    (5)   For example, a rule in the following form would fall within Category 1 and within Category 2—

"Example rule

Section X does not apply to a company in respect of a transaction if the company shows that the transaction meets Condition A or B.

Condition A is that the transaction is effected—
          (a) for genuine commercial reasons, or
          (b) in the ordinary course of managing investments.

Condition B is that the avoidance of tax is not the main object or one of the main objects of the transaction."

"DOTAS arrangements"

26 (1) For the purposes of this Schedule arrangements are "DOTAS arrangements" at any time if at that time a person−

    (a) has provided, information in relation to the arrangements under section 308(3), 309 or 310 of FA 2004, or

    (b) has failed to comply with any of those provisions in relation to the arrangements.

  (2) But for the purposes of this Schedule "DOTAS arrangements" does not include arrangements in respect of which HMRC has given notice under section 312(6) of FA 2004 (notice that promoters not under duty to notify client of reference number).

  (3) For the purposes of sub-paragraph (1) a person who would be required to provide information under subsection (3) of section 308 of FA 2004−

    (a) but for the fact that the arrangements implement a proposal in respect of which notice has been given under subsection (1) of that section, or

    (b) but for subsection (4A), (4C) or (5) of that section,

is treated as providing the information at the end of the period referred to in subsection (3) of that section.

"Disclosable VAT arrangements"

27 For the purposes of this Schedule arrangements are "disclosable VAT arrangements" at any time if at that time−

    (a) a person has complied with paragraph 6 of Schedule 11A to VATA 1994 in relation to the arrangements (duty to notify Commissioners),

    (b) a person under a duty to comply with that paragraph in relation to the arrangements has failed to do so, or

    (c) a reference number has been allocated to the scheme under paragraph 9 of that Schedule (voluntary notification of avoidance scheme which is not a designated scheme).

Paragraphs 26 and 27: supplementary

28 (1) A person "fails to comply" with any provision mentioned in paragraph 26(1)(a) or 27(b) if and only if any of the conditions in sub-paragraphs (2) to (4) is met.

  (2) The condition in this sub-paragraph is that−

    (a) the tribunal has determined that the person has failed to comply with the provision concerned,

    (b) the appeal period has ended, and

    (c) the determination has not been overturned on appeal.

  (3) The condition in this sub-paragraph is that−

    (a)   the tribunal has determined for the purposes of section 118(2) of TMA 1970 that the person is to be deemed not to have failed to comply with the provision concerned as the person had a reasonable excuse for not doing the thing required to be done,

    (b)   the appeal period has ended, and

    (c)   the determination has not been overturned on appeal.

(4) The condition in this sub-paragraph is that the person admitted in writing to HMRC that the person has failed to comply with the provision concerned.

(5) In this paragraph "the appeal period" means—

    (a)   the period during which an appeal could be brought against the determination of the tribunal, or

    (b)   where an appeal mentioned in paragraph (a) has been brought, the period during which that appeal has not been finally determined, withdrawn or otherwise disposed of.

"Final" counteraction

29   For the purposes of this Schedule the counteraction of a tax advantage or of arrangements is "final" when the assessment or adjustments made to effect the counteraction, and any amounts arising as a result of the assessment or adjustments, can no longer be varied, on appeal or otherwise.

Inheritance tax, stamp duty reserve tax, VAT and petroleum revenue tax

30 (1) In this Schedule, in relation to inheritance tax, each of the following is treated as a return—

    (a)   an account delivered by a person under section 216 or 217 of IHTA 1984 (including an account delivered in accordance with regulations under section 256 of that Act);

    (b)   a statement or declaration which amends or is otherwise connected with such an account produced by the person who delivered the account;

    (c)   information or a document provided by a person in accordance with regulations under section 256 of that Act;

and such a return is treated as made by the person in question.

(2) In this Schedule references to an assessment to tax, in relation to inheritance tax, stamp duty reserve tax and petroleum revenue tax, include a determination.

(3) In this Schedule an expression used in relation to VAT has the same meaning as in VATA 1994.

Power to amend

31 (1) The Treasury may by regulations amend this Schedule (apart from this paragraph).

      (2) An amendment by virtue of sub-paragraph (1) may, in particular, add, vary or remove conditions or categories (or otherwise vary the meaning of "avoidance-related rule").

      (3) Regulations under sub-paragraph (1) may include any amendment of this Part of this Act that is appropriate in consequence of an amendment made by virtue of sub-paragraph (1)."

(6) In section 241 (duration of conduct notice), after subsection (4) insert—

    "(5) See also section 237D(2) (provisional conduct notice affected by judicial ruling)."

(7) After section 281 insert—

"281A VAT

    (1) In the provisions mentioned in subsection (2)—
        (a) "tax" includes value added tax, and
        (b) "tax advantage" has the meaning given by section 234(3) and also includes a tax advantage as defined in paragraph 1 of Schedule 11A to VATA 1994.

    (2) Those provisions are—
        (a) section 237D;
        (b) section 241B;
        (c) Schedule 34A.

    (3) Other references in this Part to "tax" are to be read as including value added tax so far as that is necessary for the purposes of sections 237A to 237D, 241A and 241B and Schedule 34A; but "tax" does not include value added tax in section 237A(10) or 237B(3)."

(8) In section 282 (regulations), in subsection (3), after paragraph (b) insert—
    "(ba) paragraph 31 of Schedule 34A,".

(9) In section 283(1) (interpretation of Part 5)—
    (a) in the definition of "conduct notice", after paragraph (a) insert—
            "(aa) section 237A(8),
            (ab) section 237B(1),";
    (b) in the definition of "tax", after ""tax"" insert "(except in provisions to which section 281A applies)";
    (c) in the definition of ""tax advantage"", after "234(3)" insert "(but see also section 281A)";
    (d) at the appropriate places insert—
            ""contract settlement" means an agreement in connection with a person's liability to make a payment to the Commissioners under or by virtue of an enactment;"
            ""defeat", in relation to arrangements, has the meaning given by paragraph 10 of Schedule 34A;"
            ""defeat notice" has the meaning given by section 241A(7);"
            ""double defeat notice" has the meaning given by section 241A(7);"
            ""final", in relation to a judicial ruling, is to be interpreted in accordance with section 237D(6);"

""judicial ruling" means a ruling of a court or tribunal on one or more issues;"

""look-forward period, in relation to a defeat notice, has the meaning given by section 241A(10);"

""provisional", in relation to a conduct notice given under section 237A(8), is to be interpreted in accordance with section 237C;"

""relevant defeat", in relation to a person, is to be interpreted in accordance with Schedule 34A;"

""related", in relation to arrangements, is to be interpreted in accordance with paragraph 2 of Schedule 34A;"

""relies on a Case 3 relevant defeat" is to be interpreted in accordance section 237B(5);"

""single defeat notice" has the meaning given by section 241A(7)."

(10) Schedule 36 (promoters of tax avoidance schemes: partnerships) is amended in accordance with subsections (11) to (16).

(11) In Part 2, before paragraph 5 insert—

"Defeat notices

4A   A defeat notice that is given to a partnership must state that it is a partnership defeat notice.".

(12) In paragraph 7(1)(b) after "a" insert "defeat notice,".

(13) In paragraph 7(2) after "the" insert "defeat notice,".

(14) After paragraph 7 insert—

"Persons leaving partnership: defeat notices

7A (1) Sub-paragraphs (2) and (3) apply where—
      (a) a person ("P") who was a controlling member of a partnership at the time when a defeat notice ("the original notice") was given to the partnership has ceased to be a member of the partnership,
      (b) the defeat notice had effect in relation to the partnership at the time of that cessation, and
      (c) P is carrying on a business as a promoter.

    (2) An authorised officer may give P a defeat notice.

    (3) If P is carrying on a business as a promoter in partnership with one or more other persons and is a controlling member of that partnership ("the new partnership"), an authorised officer may give a defeat notice to the new partnership.

    (4) A defeat notice given under sub-paragraph (3) ceases to have effect if P ceases to be a member of the new partnership.

    (5) A notice under sub-paragraph (2) or (3) may not be given after the original notice has ceased to have effect.

(6) A defeat notice given under sub-paragraph (2) or (3) is given in respect of the relevant defeat or relevant defeats to which the original notice relates."

(15) In paragraph 10—

   (a) in sub-paragraph (1)(b) for "conduct notice or a" substitute ", defeat notice, conduct notice or";

   (b) in sub-paragraph (3), after "partner—" insert—

       "(za) a defeat notice (if the original notice is a defeat notice);".

   (c) in sub-paragraph (4), after "("the new partnership")—" insert—

       "(za) a defeat notice (if the original notice is a defeat notice);"

   (d) after sub-paragraph (5) insert—

       "(5A) A notice under sub-paragraph (3)(za) or (4)(za) may not be given after the end of the look-forward period of the original notice."

(16) After paragraph 11 insert—

   "11A   The look-forward period for a notice under paragraph 7A(2) or (3) or 10(3)(za) or (4)(za)—

       (a) begins on the day after the day on which the notice is given, and

       (b) continues to the end of the look-forward period for the original notice (as defined in paragraph 7A(1)(a) or 10(2), as the case may be)."

(17) Part 2 of Schedule 2 to the National Insurance Contributions Act 2015 (application of Part 5 of FA 2014 to national insurance contributions) is amended in accordance with subsections (18) and (19).

(18) After paragraph 30 insert—

"Threshold conditions

   30A (1) In paragraph 5 of Schedule 34 (non-compliance with Part 7 of FA 2004), in sub-paragraph (4)—

       (a) paragraph (a) includes a reference to a decision having been made for corresponding NICs purposes that P is to be deemed not to have failed to comply with the provision concerned as P had a reasonable excuse for not doing the thing required to be done, and

       (b) the reference in paragraph (c) to a determination is to be read accordingly.

     (2) In this paragraph "corresponding NICs purposes" means the purposes of any provision of regulations under section 132A of SSAA 1992.

Relevant defeats

   30B (1) Schedule 34A (promoters of tax avoidance schemes: defeated arrangements) has effect with the following modifications.

     (2) References to an assessment (or an assessment to tax) include a NICs decision relating to a person's liability for relevant contributions.

(3) References to adjustments include a payment in respect of a liability to pay relevant contributions (and the definition of "adjustments" in paragraph 24 accordingly has effect as if such payments were included in it).

(4) In paragraph 9(3) the reference to an enquiry into a return includes a relevant contributions dispute (as defined in paragraph 6 of this Schedule).

(5) In paragraph 28(3)—

    (a) paragraph (a) includes a reference to a decision having been made for corresponding NICs purposes that the person is to be deemed not to have failed to comply with the provision concerned as the person had a reasonable excuse for not doing the thing required to be done, and

    (b) the reference in paragraph (c) to a determination is to be read accordingly.

"Corresponding NICs purposes" means the purposes of any provision of regulations under section 132A of SSAA 1992."

(19) In paragraph 31 (interpretation)—

    (a) before paragraph (a) insert—

        "(za) "NICs decision" means a decision under section 8 of SSC(TF)A 1999 or Article 7 of the Social Security Contributions (Transfer of Functions, etc) (Northern Ireland) Order 1999 (SI 1999/671);"

    (b) in paragraph (b), for "are to sections of" substitute "or Schedules are to sections of, or Schedules to".

(20) For the purposes of sections 237A and 241A of FA 2014, a defeat (by virtue of any of Conditions A to F in Schedule 34A to that Act) of arrangements is treated as not having occurred if—

    (a) there has been a final judicial ruling on or before the day on which this Act is passed as a result of which the counteraction referred to in paragraph 11(d), 12(1)(b), 13(1)(d), 14(1)(d) or 15(1)(d) (as the case may be) is final for the purposes of Schedule 34A of that Act, or

    (b) (in the case of a defeat by virtue of Condition F in Schedule 34A) the judicial ruling mentioned in paragraph 16(1)(d) of that Schedule becomes final on or before the day on which this Act is passed.

(21) Subsection (20) does not apply in relation to a person (who is carrying on a business as a promoter) if at any time after 17 July 2014 that person or an associated person takes action as a result of which the person taking the action—

    (a) becomes a promoter in relation to the arrangements, or arrangements related to those arrangements, or

    (b) would have become a promoter in relation to arrangements mentioned in paragraph (a) had the person not already been a promoter in relation to those arrangements.

(22) For the purposes of sections 237A and 241A of FA 2014, a defeat of arrangements is treated as not having occurred if it would (ignoring this sub-paragraph) have occurred—

    (a) on or before the first anniversary of the day on which this Act is passed, and

      (b)   by virtue of any of Conditions A to E in Schedule 34A to FA 2014, but otherwise than as a result of a final judicial ruling.

(23)   For the purposes of subsection (21) a person ("Q") is an "associated person" in relation to another person ("P") at any time when any of the following conditions is met—

      (a)   P is a relevant body which is controlled by Q;

      (b)   Q is a relevant body, P is not an individual and Q is controlled by P;

      (c)   P and Q are relevant bodies and a third person controls P and Q.

(24)   In subsection (23) "relevant body" and "control" are to be interpreted in accordance with paragraph 19 of Schedule 34A to FA 2014.

(25)   In subsections (20) to (22) expressions used in Part 5 of FA 2014 (as amended by this section) have the same meaning as in that Part.

161 Large businesses: tax strategies and sanctions for persistently unco-operative behaviour

(1)   Schedule 19 contains provisions relating to—

      (a)   the publication of tax strategies by bodies which are or are part of a large business,

      (b)   the imposition of sanctions for such bodies where there has been persistent unco-operative behaviour.

(2)   That Schedule, so far as relating to the publication of a tax strategy for a financial year of a relevant body or other entity, has effect only where the financial year begins on or after the day on which this Act is passed.

(3)   An officer of HMRC may not give a warning notice under Part 3 of that Schedule to a relevant body or other entity before the beginning of its first financial year beginning on or after the day on which this Act is passed.

(4)   In this section and Schedule 19 "HMRC" means Her Majesty's Revenue and Customs.

Offshore activities

162 Penalties for enablers of offshore tax evasion or non-compliance

(1)   Schedule 20 makes provision for penalties for persons who enable offshore tax evasion or non-compliance by other persons.

(2)   Subsection (1) and that Schedule come into force on such day as the Treasury may appoint by regulations made by statutory instrument.

(3)   Regulations under this section may—

      (a)   commence a provision generally or only for specified purposes,

      (b)   appoint different days for different purposes, and

      (c)   make supplemental, incidental and transitional provision in connection with the coming into force of any provision of the Schedule.

163 Penalties in connection with offshore matters and offshore transfers

(1)   Schedule 21 contains provisions amending—

296   *Finance Act 2016 (c. 24)*

Part 10 — Tax avoidance and evasion

    (a) Schedule 24 to FA 2007 (penalties for errors in tax returns etc),

    (b) Schedule 41 to FA 2008 (penalties for failure to notify etc), and

    (c) Schedule 55 to FA 2009 (penalties for failure to make return etc).

 (2) That Schedule comes into force on such day as the Treasury may by regulations made by statutory instrument appoint.

 (3) Regulations under this section may—

    (a) commence a provision generally or only for specified purposes,

    (b) appoint different days for different provisions or for different purposes, and

    (c) make supplemental, incidental and transitional provision.

164 Offshore tax errors etc: publishing details of deliberate tax defaulters

 (1) Section 94 of FA 2009 (publishing details of deliberate tax defaulters) is amended as follows.

 (2) After subsection (4), insert—

  "(4A) Subsection (4B) applies where a person who is a body corporate or a partnership has incurred—

    (a) a penalty under paragraph 1 of Schedule 24 to FA 2007 in respect of a deliberate inaccuracy which involves an offshore matter or an offshore transfer (within the meaning of paragraph 4A of that Schedule), or

    (b) a penalty under paragraph 1 of Schedule 41 to FA 2008 in respect of a deliberate failure which involves an offshore matter or an offshore transfer (within the meaning of paragraph 6A of that Schedule).

  (4B) The Commissioners may publish the information mentioned in subsection (4) in respect of any individual who—

    (a) controls the body corporate or the partnership (within the meaning of section 1124 of CTA 2010), and

    (b) has obtained a tax advantage as a result of the inaccuracy or failure.

  (4C) Subsection (4D) applies where one or more trustees of a settlement have incurred—

    (a) a penalty under paragraph 1 of Schedule 24 to FA 2007 in respect of a deliberate inaccuracy which involves an offshore matter or an offshore transfer (within the meaning of paragraph 4A of that Schedule), or

    (b) a penalty under paragraph 1 of Schedule 41 to FA 2008 in respect of a deliberate failure which involves an offshore matter or an offshore transfer (within the meaning of paragraph 6A of that Schedule).

  (4D) The Commissioners may publish the information mentioned in subsection (4) in respect of any trustee who is an individual and who has obtained a tax advantage as a result of the inaccuracy or failure."

 (3) In subsection (6), after "information" insert "about a person under subsection (1),".

(4) After subsection (6), insert—

"(6A) Before publishing any information about an individual under subsection (4B) or (4D), the Commissioners—

(a) must inform the individual that they are considering doing so, and

(b) afford the individual reasonable opportunity to make representations about whether it should be published."

(5) In subsection (10)—

(a) omit the word "or" at the end of paragraph (a), and after that paragraph insert—

"(aa) paragraph 10A of that Schedule to the full extent permitted following an unprompted disclosure,";

(b) after paragraph (b) insert ", or

(c) paragraph 13A of that Schedule to the full extent permitted following an unprompted disclosure."

(6) For subsection (16) substitute—

"(16) In this section—

"the Commissioners" means the Commissioners for Her Majesty's Revenue and Customs;

"tax advantage" has the meaning given by section 208 of FA 2013."

(7) The amendments made by this section come into force on such day as the Treasury may by regulations made by statutory instrument appoint.

165 Asset-based penalties for offshore inaccuracies and failures

(1) Schedule 22 contains provision imposing asset-based penalties on certain taxpayers who have been charged a penalty for deliberate offshore inaccuracies and failures.

(2) That Schedule comes into force on such day as the Treasury may by regulations made by statutory instrument appoint.

(3) Regulations under subsection (2) may—

(a) commence a provision generally or only for specified purposes,

(b) appoint different days for different provisions or for different purposes, and

(c) make supplemental, incidental and transitional provision.

166 Offences relating to offshore income, assets and activities

(1) After section 106A of TMA 1970 insert—

"Offshore income, assets and activities

106B Offence of failing to give notice of being chargeable to tax

(1) A person who is required by section 7 to give notice of being chargeable to income tax or capital gains tax (or both) for a year of assessment and who has not given that notice by the end of the notification period commits an offence if—

      (a)   the tax in question is chargeable (wholly or in part) on or by reference to offshore income, assets or activities, and

      (b)   the total amount of income tax and capital gains tax that is chargeable for the year of assessment on or by reference to offshore income, assets or activities exceeds the threshold amount.

(2)   It is a defence for a person accused of an offence under this section to prove that the person had a reasonable excuse for failing to give the notice required by section 7.

(3)   In this section "the notification period" has the same meaning as in section 7 (see subsection (1C) of that section).

106C Offence of failing to deliver return

(1)   A person who is required by a notice under section 8 to make and deliver a return for a year of assessment commits an offence if—

      (a)   the return is not delivered by the end of the withdrawal period,

      (b)   an accurate return would have disclosed liability to income tax or capital gains tax (or both) that is chargeable for the year of assessment on or by reference to offshore income, assets or activities, and

      (c)   the total amount of income tax and capital gains tax that is chargeable for the year of assessment on or by reference to offshore income, assets or activities exceeds the threshold amount.

(2)   It is a defence for a person accused of an offence under this section to prove that the person had a reasonable excuse for failing to deliver the return.

(3)   In this section "the withdrawal period" has the same meaning as in section 8B (see subsection (6) of that section).

106D Offence of making inaccurate return

(1)   A person who is required by a notice under section 8 to make and deliver a return for a year of assessment commits an offence if, at the end of the amendment period—

      (a)   the return contains an inaccuracy the correction of which would result in an increase in the amount of income tax or capital gains tax (or both) that is chargeable for the year of assessment on or by reference to offshore income, assets or activities, and

      (b)   the amount of that increase exceeds the threshold amount.

(2)   It is a defence for a person accused of an offence under this section to prove that the person took reasonable care to ensure that the return was accurate.

(3)   In this section "the amendment period" means the period for amending the return under section 9ZA.

106E Exclusions from offences under sections 106B to 106D

(1)   A person is not guilty of an offence under section 106B, 106C or 106D if the capacity in which the person is required to give the notice or make and deliver the return is—

    (a)   as a relevant trustee of a settlement, or

    (b)   as the executor or administrator of a deceased person.

(2)   The Treasury may by regulations provide that a person is not guilty of an offence under section 106B, 106C or 106D if—

    (a)   conditions specified in the regulations are met, or

    (b)   circumstances so specified exist.

(3)   The conditions may (in particular) include conditions in relation to the income, assets or activities on or by reference to which the tax in question is chargeable.

106F Offences under sections 106B to 106D: supplementary provision

(1)   Where a period of time is extended under subsection (2) of section 118 by HMRC, the tribunal or an officer (but not where a period is otherwise extended under that subsection), any reference in section 106B, 106C or 106D to the end of the period is to be read as a reference to the end of the period as so extended.

(2)   The Treasury may by regulations specify the amount (which must not be less than £25,000) that is to be the threshold amount for the purposes of sections 106B to 106D.

(3)   The Treasury may by regulations make provision as to the calculation for the purposes of sections 106B to 106D of—

    (a)   the amount of tax that is chargeable on or by reference to offshore income, assets or activities, and

    (b)   the increase in the amount of tax that is so chargeable as a result of correcting an inaccuracy.

(4)   In sections 106B to 106D and this section "offshore income, assets or activities" means—

    (a)   income arising from a source in a territory outside the United Kingdom,

    (b)   assets situated or held in a territory outside the United Kingdom, or

    (c)   activities carried on wholly or mainly in a territory outside the United Kingdom.

(5)   In subsection (4), "assets" has the meaning given in section 21(1) of the 1992 Act, but also includes sterling.

106G Penalties for offences under sections 106B to 106D

(1)   A person guilty of an offence under section 106B, 106C or 106D is liable on summary conviction—

    (a)   in England and Wales, to a fine or to imprisonment for a term not exceeding 51 weeks or to both, and

    (b)   in Scotland or Northern Ireland, to a fine not exceeding level 5 on the standard scale or to imprisonment for a term not exceeding 6 months or to both.

(2)   In relation to an offence committed before the coming into force of section 281(5) of the Criminal Justice Act 2003, the reference in subsection (1)(a) to 51 weeks is to be read as a reference to 6 months.

106H Regulations under sections 106E and 106F

(1) This section makes provision about regulations under sections 106E and 106F.

(2) If the regulations contain a reference to a document or any provision of a document and it appears to the Treasury that it is necessary or expedient for the reference to be construed as a reference to that document or that provision as amended from time to time, the regulations may make express provision to that effect.

(3) The regulations—
    (a) may make different provision for different cases, and
    (b) may include incidental, supplemental, consequential and transitional provision and savings.

(4) The regulations are to be made by statutory instrument.

(5) An instrument containing the regulations is subject to annulment in pursuance of a resolution of the House of Commons."

(2) The amendment made by this section comes into force on such day as the Treasury may by regulations made by statutory instrument appoint.

(3) The regulations—
    (a) may appoint different days for different purposes, and
    (b) may include incidental, supplemental, consequential and transitional provision and savings.

(4) The amendment made by this section does not have effect in relation to—
    (a) a failure to give a notice required by section 7 of TMA 1970,
    (b) a failure to make and deliver a return required by section 8 of TMA 1970, or
    (c) a return required by section 8 that contains an inaccuracy,

if the notice or return relates to a tax year before that in which the amendment comes into force.

PART 11

ADMINISTRATION, ENFORCEMENT AND SUPPLEMENTARY POWERS

Assessment and returns

167 Simple assessments

(1) Schedule 23 contains provisions about simple assessments by HMRC.

(2) Paragraphs 1 to 8 of that Schedule have effect in relation to the 2016-17 tax year and subsequent years.

(3) Paragraph 9 of that Schedule comes into force on such day as the Treasury may appoint by regulations made by statutory instrument.

(4) Regulations under subsection (3) may—
    (a) commence paragraph 9 generally or only for specified purposes, and
    (b) appoint different days for different purposes.

168   Time limit for self assessment tax returns

(1)   TMA 1970 is amended as follows.

(2)   In section 34 (ordinary time limit of 4 years for assessments), after subsection (2) insert—

"(3)   In this section "assessment" does not include a self-assessment."

(3)   After that section insert—

"34A   Ordinary time limit for self-assessments

(1)   Subject to subsections (2) and (3), a self assessment contained in a return under section 8 or 8A may be made and delivered at any time not more than 4 years after the end of the year of assessment to which it relates.

(2)   Nothing in subsection (1) prevents—
   (a)   a person who has received a notice under section 8 or 8A within that period of 4 years from delivering a return including a self-assessment within the period of 3 months beginning with the date of the notice,
   (b)   a person in respect of whom a determination under section 28C has been made from making a self-assessment in accordance with that section within the period allowed by subsection (5)(a) or (b) of that section.

(3)   Subsection (1) has effect subject to the following provisions of this Act and to any other provisions of the Taxes Acts allowing a longer period in any particular class of case.

(4)   This section has effect in relation to self-assessments for a year of assessment earlier than 2012-13 as if—
   (a)   in subsection (1) for the words from "not more" to the end there were substituted "on or before 5 April 2017", and
   (b)   in subsection (2)(a) for the words "within that period of 4 years" there were substituted "on or before 5 April 2017.""

169   HMRC power to withdraw notice to file a tax return

(1)   Section 8B of TMA 1970 (withdrawal of notice under section 8 or 8A) is amended as follows.

(2)   In subsection (2) for the words from "the person" to the end substitute "HMRC may withdraw the notice (whether at the request of the person or otherwise)".

(3)   In subsection (3) for "no request may be made" substitute "the notice may not be withdrawn".

(4)   In subsection (4) omit ", on receiving a request,".

(5)   In subsection (6)(b) for "agree with the person" substitute "determine".

(6)   In paragraph 17A of Schedule 55 to the Finance Act 2009 (penalty for failure to make returns etc), in sub-paragraph (1)(b) for the words from the beginning to "withdraw" substitute "HMRC decide to give P a notice under section 8B withdrawing".

(7) The amendments made by this section have effect in relation to any notice under section 8 or 8A of TMA 1970 given in relation to the 2014-15 tax year or any subsequent year (and it is immaterial whether the notice was given before or after the passing of this Act).

Judgment debts

170 Rate of interest applicable to judgment debts etc: Scotland

(1) This section applies if—

    (a) a sum is payable to or by the Commissioners under a decree or extract issued in any court proceedings relating to a taxation matter (a "tax-related judgment debt"), and

    (b) interest in relation to the tax-related judgment debt is included in or payable under the decree or extract.

(2) In a case where the rate of interest in relation to the tax-related judgment debt is stated in the decree or extract, the rate stated in relation to that debt may not exceed (and may not be capable of exceeding)—

    (a) in the case of a sum payable to the Commissioners, the late payment interest rate, and

    (b) in the case of a sum payable by the Commissioners, the special repayment rate.

(3) In a case where the rate of interest in relation to the tax-related judgment debt is not stated in the decree or extract but provided for by an enactment or rule of court (whenever passed or made), that enactment or rule is to have effect in relation to the debt as if for the rate for which it provides there were substituted—

    (a) in the case of a sum payable to the Commissioners, the late payment interest rate, and

    (b) in the case of a sum payable by the Commissioners, the special repayment rate.

(4) This section has effect in relation to interest for periods beginning on or after the day on which this Act is passed, regardless of—

    (a) the date of the decree or extract in question, and

    (b) whether interest begins to run on or after the day on which this Act is passed, or began to run before that date.

(5) In this section—

"the Commissioners" means the Commissioners for Her Majesty's Revenue and Customs;

"enactment" includes an Act of the Scottish Parliament or an instrument made under such an Act;

"late payment interest rate" means the rate provided for in regulations made by the Treasury under section 103(1) of FA 2009;

"special repayment rate" has the same meaning as in section 52 of F(No.2)A 2015 (and subsections (7) to (10) of that section apply for the purposes of this section as they apply for the purposes of that section);

"taxation matter" means anything the collection and management of which is the responsibility of the Commissioners (or was the responsibility of the Commissioners of Inland Revenue or Commissioners of Customs and Excise);

        "working day" means any day other than a non-business day as defined in section 92 of the Bills of Exchange Act 1882.

(6)   This section extends to Scotland only.

171   Rate of interest applicable to judgment debts etc: Northern Ireland

(1)   This section applies if a sum payable to or by the Commissioners under a judgment or order given or made in any court proceedings relating to a taxation matter (a "tax-related judgment debt") carries interest.

(2)   In a case where the rate of interest is specified in the judgment (in the case of the High Court) or directed by the judge (in the case of a county court), the rate specified or directed in relation to that debt may not exceed (and may not be capable of exceeding) —

    (a)   in the case of a sum payable to the Commissioners, the late payment interest rate, and

    (b)   in the case of a sum payable by the Commissioners, the special repayment rate.

(3)   In a case where the rate of interest in relation to the tax-related judgment debt is not specified in the judgment or directed by the judge but provided for by an enactment or rule of court (whenever passed or made), that enactment or rule is to have effect in relation to the debt as if for the rate for which it provides there were substituted —

    (a)   in the case of a sum payable to the Commissioners, the late payment interest rate, and

    (b)   in the case of a sum payable by the Commissioners, the special repayment rate.

(4)   This section has effect in relation to interest for periods beginning on or after the day on which this Act is passed, regardless of —

    (a)   the date of the judgment or order in question, and

    (b)   whether interest begins to run on or after the day on which this Act is passed, or began to run before that date.

(5)   In this section —

    "the Commissioners" means the Commissioners for Her Majesty's Revenue and Customs;

    "enactment" includes Northern Ireland legislation or an instrument made under such legislation;

    "late payment interest rate" means the rate provided for in regulations made by the Treasury under section 103(1) of FA 2009;

    "special repayment rate" has the same meaning as in section 52 of F(No.2)A 2015 (and subsections (7) to (10) of that section apply for the purposes of this section as they apply for the purposes of that section);

    "taxation matter" means anything the collection and management of which is the responsibility of the Commissioners (or was the responsibility of the Commissioners of Inland Revenue or Commissioners of Customs and Excise);

    "working day" means any day other than a non-business day as defined in section 92 of the Bills of Exchange Act 1882.

(6)   This section extends to Northern Ireland only.

172 Rate of interest applicable to judgment debts etc: England and Wales

(1) In section 52 of F(No. 2)A 2015 (rates of interest applicable to judgment debts etc in taxation matters: England and Wales), in subsection (15), in the definition of "taxation matter" omit ", other than national insurance contributions,".

(2) This section has effect in relation to interest for periods beginning on or after the day on which this Act is passed, regardless of—

    (a) the date of the judgment or order in question, and

    (b) whether interest begins to run on or after the day on which this Act is passed, or began to run before that date.

(3) This section extends to England and Wales only.

Enforcement powers

173 Gift aid: power to impose penalties on charities and intermediaries

(1) At the end of section 428 of ITA 2007 insert—

    "(5) The regulations may also make provision—

        (a) for the imposition of a penalty of a specified amount (which must not exceed £3000) for a failure to comply with a specified requirement imposed by the regulations,

        (b) for the assessment and recovery of the penalty (which may include provision about the reduction of the penalty in specified circumstances), and

        (c) conferring a right of appeal against a decision that a penalty is payable."

(2) The amendment made by this section comes into force on such day as the Treasury may by regulations made by statutory instrument appoint.

174 Proceedings under customs and excise Acts: prosecuting authority

(1) Part 11 of CEMA 1979 (arrest of persons, forfeiture and legal proceedings) is amended as set out in subsections (2) and (3).

(2) In section 146A(7) (definition of prosecuting authority)—

    (a) in the opening words, for "prosecution" substitute "prosecuting";

    (b) in paragraph (b), omit "the Commissioners or";

    (c) in paragraph (c), for "the Commissioners" substitute "the Director of Public Prosecutions for Northern Ireland".

(3) In section 150(1) (joint and several liability), for the words from "the Director" to "Ireland)" substitute "prosecuting authority (within the meaning of section 146A)".

(4) In consequence of subsection (3), in Schedule 4 to the Commissioners for Revenue and Customs Act 2005, omit paragraph 25.

(5) The amendments made by this section apply in relation to proceedings commenced on or after the day on which this Act is passed.

175 Detention and seizure under CEMA 1979: notice requirements etc

(1) CEMA 1979 is amended as follows.

(2) Schedule 2A (detention of things as liable to forfeiture) is amended as set out in subsections (3) and (4).

(3) In paragraph 3(2) (exceptions to requirement of notice of detention) —

    (a) omit the "or" at the end of paragraph (b), and after that paragraph insert —

        "(ba) a person who has (or appears to have) possession or control of the thing being detained,";

    (b) in paragraph (c), after "on" insert "or from";

    (c) at the end insert ", or

        (d) in the case of any thing detained on or from a vehicle, the driver of the vehicle."

(4) In paragraph 4(2) (unauthorised removal or disposal of things detained: definition of "responsible person"), for paragraphs (a) and (b) substitute —

    "(a) the person whose offence or suspected offence occasioned the detention,

    (b) the owner or any of the owners of the thing detained or any servant or agent of such an owner,

    (c) a person who has (or appears to have) possession or control of the thing being detained,

    (d) in the case of any thing detained on a ship or aircraft, the master or commander,

    (e) in the case of any thing detained on a vehicle, the driver of the vehicle, or

    (f) a person whom the person who detains the thing reasonably believes to be a person within any of paragraphs (a) to (e)."

(5) In Schedule 3 (seizure and forfeiture), in paragraph 1(2) (exceptions to requirement of notice of seizure) —

    (a) after paragraph (b) insert —

        "(ba) a person who has (or appears to have) possession or control of the thing being seized; or";

    (b) in paragraph (c), for "in" substitute "on or from";

    (c) at the end insert "; or

        (d) in the case of any thing seized on or from a vehicle, the driver of the vehicle."

(6) The amendments made by this section have effect in relation to things detained or seized on or after the day on which this Act is passed.

176 Data-gathering powers: providers of payment or intermediary services

(1) In Part 2 of Schedule 23 to FA 2011 (data-gathering powers: relevant data-holders), after paragraph 13A insert —

"Providers of electronic stored-value payment services

    13B (1) A person who provides electronic stored-value payment services is a relevant data-holder.

(2) In this paragraph "electronic stored-value payment services" means services by means of which monetary value is stored electronically for the purpose of payments being made in respect of transactions to which the provider of those services is not a party.

Business intermediaries

13C (1) A person who—

    (a) provides services to enable or facilitate transactions between suppliers and their customers or clients (other than services provided solely to enable payments to be made), and

    (b) receives information about such transactions in the course of doing so,

is a relevant data-holder.

(2) In this paragraph "suppliers" means persons supplying goods or services in the course of business.

(3) For the purposes of this paragraph, information about transactions includes information that is capable of indicating the likely quantity or value of transactions."

(2) This section applies in relation to relevant data with a bearing on any period (whether before, on or after the day on which this Act is passed).

177 Data-gathering powers: daily penalties for extended default

(1) Part 4 of Schedule 23 to FA 2011 (data-gathering powers: penalties) is amended as follows.

(2) In paragraph 38 (increased daily default penalty)—

    (a) in sub-paragraphs (1)(c) and (2), for "imposed" substitute "assessable";

    (b) for sub-paragraphs (3) and (4) substitute—

        "(3) If the tribunal decides that an increased daily penalty should be assessable—

        (a) the tribunal must determine the day from which the increased daily penalty is to apply and the maximum amount of that penalty ("the new maximum amount");

        (b) from that day, paragraph 31 has effect in the data-holder's case as if "the new maximum amount" were substituted for "£60".

        (4) The new maximum amount may not be more than £1,000.";

    (c) in sub-paragraph (5), for "the amount" substitute "the new maximum amount".

(3) In paragraph 39—

    (a) in sub-paragraph (1), for "a data-holder becomes liable to a penalty" substitute "the tribunal makes a determination";

    (b) in sub-paragraph (2), for "the day from which the increased penalty is to apply" substitute "new maximum amount and the day from which it applies";

    (c) omit sub-paragraph (3).

(4) In paragraph 40 (enforcement of penalties), in sub-paragraph (2)(a) omit "or 39".

(5) At the end of paragraph 36 (right to appeal against penalty), the existing text of which becomes sub-paragraph (1), insert—

"(2) But sub-paragraph (1)(b) does not give a right of appeal against the amount of an increased daily penalty payable by virtue of paragraph 38."

Payment

178 Extension of provisions about set-off to Scotland

(1) Sections 130 and 131 of FA 2008 (which deal with the availability of set-off in England and Wales and Northern Ireland) extend also to Scotland.

(2) Accordingly, those sections are amended as follows.

(3) In section 130—
   (a) omit subsection (10), and
   (b) in the heading omit ": England and Wales and Northern Ireland".

(4) In section 131—
   (a) in subsection (5), in paragraph (a), after "winding up order" insert "or award of sequestration",
   (b) in that subsection, omit the "or" at the end of paragraph (d) and after paragraph (e) insert ", or
      (f) that person's estate becomes vested in any other person as that person's trustee under a trust deed (within the meaning of the Bankruptcy (Scotland) Act 1985).", and
   (c) omit subsection (9).

Raw tobacco

179 Raw tobacco approval scheme

(1) After section 8J of TPDA 1979 insert—

"8K Raw tobacco: definitions

(1) The following definitions apply for the purposes of sections 8L to 8U.

(2) "Raw tobacco" means the leaves or any other part of a plant of the genus *Nicotiana* but does not include—
   (a) any part of a living plant, or
   (b) a tobacco product.

(3) "Controlled activity" means any activity involving raw tobacco.

8L Raw tobacco: requirement for approval

(1) A person may not carry on a controlled activity otherwise than in accordance with an approval given by the Commissioners under this section.

(2)   The Commissioners may approve a person to carry on a controlled activity only if satisfied that—

    (a)   the person is a fit and proper person to carry on the activity, and

    (b)   the activity will not be carried on for the purpose of, or with a view to, the fraudulent evasion of the duty of excise charged on tobacco products under section 2(1).

(3)   An approval may—

    (a)   specify the period of approval, and

    (b)   be subject to conditions or restrictions.

(4)   The Commissioners may at any time for reasonable cause revoke or vary the terms of an approval.

8M   Regulations about approval etc.

The Commissioners may, by or under regulations, make provision—

    (a)   regulating the approval of persons under section 8L,

    (b)   about the form, manner and content of an application for approval,

    (c)   specifying conditions or restrictions to which an approval is subject,

    (d)   regulating the variation or revocation of an approval, or of any condition or restriction to which an approval is subject, and

    (e)   about the surrender or transfer of an approval.

8N   Exemptions from requirement for approval

(1)   The Commissioners may by regulations provide that section 8L(1) does not apply in relation to a person (an "exempt person") who—

    (a)   carries on any controlled activity, or a controlled activity of a specified description, and

    (b)   meets the conditions (if any) specified by or under the regulations.

(2)   The regulations may require an exempt person to comply with specified requirements or restrictions relating to the carrying on of a controlled activity.

(3)   The regulations may, in particular—

    (a)   specify the maximum quantity of raw tobacco that may be involved in a controlled activity carried on by an exempt person;

    (b)   require an exempt person to keep records relating to the activity.

8O   Raw tobacco: penalties

(1)   A person who contravenes section 8L(1) is liable to a penalty of an amount equal to the amount of duty that would be charged on the relevant quantity of smoking tobacco.

(2)   A person who contravenes a requirement or restriction imposed by regulations under section 8N is liable to a penalty of—

    (a)   £250, or

        (b)   if less, an amount equal to the amount of duty that would be charged on the relevant quantity of smoking tobacco.

(3)   The relevant quantity of smoking tobacco is equal to the quantity by weight of the raw tobacco in respect of which the controlled activity contravening section 8L(1) or (as the case may be) regulations under section 8N has been carried on.

(4)   In this section a reference to "smoking tobacco" is a reference to tobacco products within section 1(1)(d) ("other smoking tobacco").

8P   Penalties under section 8O: special reduction

(1)   If the Commissioners think it right because of special circumstances, they may reduce a penalty under section 8O.

(2)   In subsection (1) "special circumstances" does not include ability to pay.

(3)   In subsection (1) the reference to reducing a penalty includes a reference to—
        (a)   staying a penalty, and
        (b)   agreeing a compromise in relation to proceedings for a penalty.

8Q   Penalties under section 8O: assessment of penalty

(1)   Where a person becomes liable for a penalty under section 8O—
        (a)   the Commissioners may assess the penalty, and
        (b)   if they do so, they must notify the person liable.

(2)   A notice under subsection (1)(b) must state the contravention in respect of which the penalty is assessed.

(3)   A penalty payable under section 8O must be paid before the end of the period of 30 days beginning with the day on which the notification of the penalty is issued.

(4)   An assessment is to be treated as an amount of duty due from the person liable for the penalty and may be recovered accordingly.

(5)   An assessment may not be made later than one year after evidence of facts sufficient in the opinion of the Commissioners to indicate the contravention comes to their knowledge.

(6)   Two or more contraventions may be treated by the Commissioners as a single contravention for the purposes of assessing a penalty payable under section 8O.

8R   Penalties under section 8O: reasonable excuse

(1)   A person is not liable to a penalty under section 8O in respect of a contravention if—
        (a)   the contravention is not deliberate, and
        (b)   the person satisfies the Commissioners that there is a reasonable excuse for the contravention.

(2)   For the purposes of subsection (1)(b)—

    (a)   where the person relies on another person to do anything, that is not a reasonable excuse unless the first person took reasonable care to avoid the contravention;

    (b)   where the person had a reasonable excuse for the relevant act or failure but the excuse has ceased, the person is to be treated as having continued to have the excuse if the contravention is remedied without unreasonable delay after the excuse has ceased.

8S   Penalties under section 8O: double jeopardy

A person is not liable to a penalty under section 8O in respect of a contravention in respect of which the person has been convicted of an offence.

8T   Forfeiture of raw tobacco

Where a person carries on a controlled activity in relation to raw tobacco in contravention of section 8L(1) or a requirement or restriction imposed by regulations under section 8N, the raw tobacco is liable to forfeiture.

8U   Raw tobacco: application of Customs and Excise Management Act 1979

The Commissioners may by regulations provide that specified provisions of the Customs and Excise Management Act 1979 apply (with or without modification)—

    (a)   in relation to persons who carry on controlled activities as they apply in relation to revenue traders whose trade or business relates to tobacco products, and

    (b)   in relation to raw tobacco as they apply in relation to tobacco products."

(2)   In section 9 of TPDA 1979 (regulations)—

    (a)   in subsection (1), after "statutory instrument and" insert ", subject to subsection (1A),", and

    (b)   after subsection (1) insert—

    "(1A)   A statutory instrument containing regulations under section 8M, 8N or 8U is subject to annulment in pursuance of a resolution of the House of Commons."

(3)   In section 13A(2) of FA 1994 (customs and excise reviews and appeals: "relevant decisions"), after paragraph (g) insert—

    "(gb)   any decision by HMRC that a person is liable to a penalty, or as to the amount of the person's liability, under section 8O of the Tobacco Products Duty Act 1979;".

(4)   In Schedule 5 to FA 1994 (decisions subject to review and appeal) after paragraph 5 insert—

    "5A   Any decision—

        (a)   to refuse an approval under section 8L of the Tobacco Products Duty Act 1979 (raw tobacco: approval to carry on a controlled activity);

        (b)   to impose a condition or restriction on, or to revoke or vary the terms of, an approval under that section."

(5) The amendments made by this section come into force on such day as the Commissioners for Her Majesty's Revenue and Customs may by regulations made by statutory instrument appoint.

(6) Regulations under subsection (5) may appoint different days for different purposes.

State aids granted through provision of tax advantages

180 Powers to obtain information about certain tax advantages

(1) The powers conferred by this section are only exercisable for the purpose of complying (or enabling another person to comply) with relevant EU obligations.

(2) The Commissioners may determine that claims made for a tax advantage of a description listed in Part 1 of Schedule 24 must include (or be accompanied by) such information, presented in such form, as the determination may specify.

(3) For the purposes of subsection (2) "information" includes –
   (a) information about the claimant (or the claimant's activities),
   (b) information about the subject-matter of the claim, and
   (c) other information which relates to the grant of state aid through the provision of the tax advantage in question.

(4) A determination under subsection (2) –
   (a) may make different provision for different descriptions of tax advantages or for different cases or circumstances, and
   (b) may be revoked or amended by another determination.

(5) Subsection (6) applies where it appears to the Commissioners that a tax advantage of a description listed in Part 2 of Schedule 24 –
   (a) has been given, or
   (b) may be given in the future.

(6) The Commissioners may give the relevant person a notice requiring the person –
   (a) to supply the Commissioners with the information specified in the request, and
   (b) if the notice so provides, to present it in the form specified in the request.

(7) The relevant person must comply with those requirements within the period specified in the notice.

(8) In subsections (6) and (7) "the relevant person", in relation to a tax advantage of any description, means the person mentioned in the third column of the entry for that tax advantage in Part 2 of Schedule 24.

(9) For the purposes of subsection (6) "information" includes –
   (a) information about –
      (i) the person to whom the request is given (or their activities),
      (ii) any other person who is the beneficiary of the tax advantage,
   (b) information about the tax advantage (including the circumstances in which it was obtained), and

    (c)   any other information which relates to the grant of state aid through the provision of the tax advantage in question.

(10)   A determination under subsection (2) may not apply to claims made before 1 July 2016.

(11)   A notice under subsection (6) may relate to any information required by the Commissioners for the purpose mentioned in subsection (1) (including information which relates to matters arising before this Act is passed).

181   Power to publish state aid information

(1)   The Commissioners may publish any state aid information for the purpose of securing compliance with any relevant EU obligation which requires the publication of that information.

(2)   That power includes power to disclose state aid information to another person for the purpose of securing its publication.

(3)   In this section "state aid information" means information which relates to the grant of state aid through the provision of a tax advantage and includes (but is not limited to) any information mentioned in section 180(3) or (9).

(4)   This section applies to any state aid information (including information which relates to a tax advantage given before the passing of this Act).

182   Information powers: supplementary

(1)   In sections 180 and 181 —

    "the Commissioners" means the Commissioners for Her Majesty's Revenue and Customs;

    "relevant EU obligations" means —

        (a)   obligations under the General Block Exemption Regulation that relate to the grant of state aid through the provision of a tax advantage, or

        (b)   any corresponding obligations under EU law that apply to the grant of a notified state aid through the provision of a tax advantage.

(2)   The "General Block Exemption Regulation" is Commission Regulation (EU) No 651/2014 declaring certain categories of aid to be compatible with the internal market in application of Articles 107 and 108 of the Treaty establishing the European Union (which relate to state aids granted by Member States).

(3)   The Treasury may by regulations made by statutory instrument amend Part 1 or Part 2 of Schedule 24 by adding, omitting or varying an entry for any description of tax advantage.

(4)   Regulations under subsection (3) may include incidental or supplemental provision.

(5)   A statutory instrument containing regulations under subsection (3) is subject to annulment in pursuance of a resolution of the House of Commons.

(6)   The powers under sections 180 and 181 are in addition to any other powers of the Commissioners to acquire, disclose or publish information.

Qualifying transformer vehicles

183 Qualifying transformer vehicles

(1) In this section "qualifying transformer vehicle" means a transformer vehicle which meets conditions which are specified in regulations made by the Treasury.

(2) The Treasury may by regulations make provision about the treatment for the purposes of any enactment relating to taxation of —

   (a) qualifying transformer vehicles;

   (b) investors in qualifying transformer vehicles;

   (c) transactions involving qualifying transformer vehicles.

(3) Regulations under subsection (2) may, in particular, disapply, apply (with or without modification) or modify the application of any enactment.

(4) Without limiting the generality of subsection (2), regulations under that subsection may in particular include —

   (a) provision for profits or other amounts to be calculated with any adjustments, or on any basis, set out in the regulations;

   (b) provision conferring, altering or removing an exemption or relief;

   (c) provision about the treatment of arrangements the purpose, or one of the main purposes, of which is to secure a tax advantage;

   (d) provision about collection and enforcement (including the withholding of tax);

   (e) in relation to qualifying transformer vehicles, requirements with regard to the provision of information to investors;

   (f) in relation to qualifying transformer vehicles or investors in qualifying transformer vehicles, requirements with regard to —

      (i) the provision of information to Her Majesty's Revenue and Customs,

      (ii) the preparation of accounts,

      (iii) the keeping of records, or

      (iv) other administrative matters.

(5) Regulations under this section —

   (a) may provide for Her Majesty's Revenue and Customs to exercise a discretion in dealing with any matter;

   (b) may make provision by reference to rules, guidance or other documents issued by any person (as they have effect from time to time).

(6) Regulations under this section may —

   (a) make different provision for different cases or different purposes (including different provision in relation to different descriptions of qualifying transformer vehicle or, as the case may be, transformer vehicle);

   (b) contain incidental, supplementary, consequential and transitional provision and savings.

(7) Regulations under this section are to be made by statutory instrument.

(8) A statutory instrument containing regulations under subsection (1) is subject to annulment in pursuance of a resolution of the House of Commons.

(9)   But the first set of regulations under subsection (1) may not be made unless a draft has been laid before, and approved by a resolution of, the House of Commons.

(10)   A statutory instrument containing regulations under subsection (2) may not be made unless a draft has been laid before, and approved by a resolution of, the House of Commons.

(11)   In this section—

        "enactment" includes subordinate legislation (as defined in section 21 of the Interpretation Act 1978);

        "investors" in relation to a qualifying transformer vehicle means holders of investments issued by the qualifying transformer vehicle; and for this purpose "investment" includes any asset, right or interest;

        "tax advantage" has the meaning given by section 1139 of CTA 2010;

        "transformer vehicle" has the same meaning as in section 284A of the Financial Services and Markets Act 2000.

PART 12

OFFICE OF TAX SIMPLIFICATION

184   Office of Tax Simplification

(1)   There continues to be an Office of Tax Simplification (referred to in this Act as the "OTS").

(2)   Schedule 25 contains provision about the OTS.

185   Functions of the OTS: general

(1)   The OTS must provide advice to the Chancellor of the Exchequer, on request or as the OTS considers appropriate, on the simplification of the tax system.

(2)   For the purposes of this section and section 186—

    (a)   "the tax system" means the law relating to, and the administration of, relevant taxes,

    (b)   "relevant taxes" means taxes that the Commissioners for Her Majesty's Revenue and Customs are responsible for collecting and managing, and

    (c)   a reference to "taxes" includes a reference to duties and national insurance contributions.

(3)   References in this section and section 186 (however expressed) to the simplification of the tax system include references to improving the efficiency of the administration of relevant taxes.

186   Functions of the OTS: reviews and reports

(1)   At the request of the Chancellor of the Exchequer, the OTS must conduct a review of an aspect of the tax system for the purpose of identifying whether, and if so how, that aspect of the tax system could be simplified.

(2)   The OTS must prepare a report—

    (a)   setting out the results of the review, and

      (b)   making such recommendations (if any) as the OTS consider appropriate.

(3)   The OTS must send a copy of the report to the Chancellor of the Exchequer.

(4)   The Chancellor of the Exchequer must—
    (a)   publish the report, and
    (b)   lay a copy of the report before Parliament.

(5)   The Chancellor of the Exchequer must prepare and publish a response to the report.

187 Annual report

(1)   The OTS must prepare a report of the performance of its functions in each financial year.

(2)   The report relating to a financial year must be prepared as soon as reasonably practicable after the end of the financial year.

(3)   The OTS must—
    (a)   send a copy of the report to the Chancellor of the Exchequer, and
    (b)   publish the report.

(4)   The Chancellor of the Exchequer must lay a copy of the report before Parliament.

(5)   For the purposes of this paragraph, each of the following is a "financial year"—
    (a)   the period beginning with the day on which this section comes into force and ending with the following 31 March, and
    (b)   each successive period of 12 months.

188 Review of the OTS

(1)   The Treasury must, before the end of each review period, conduct a review of the effectiveness of the OTS in performing its functions.

(2)   The "review period" means—
    (a)   in relation to the first review, the period of 5 years beginning with the day on which this section comes into force, and
    (b)   in relation to subsequent reviews, the period of 5 years beginning with the day on which the previous review was completed.

(3)   The Treasury must prepare and publish a report of each review.

189 Commencement

Sections 184 to 188 and Schedule 25 come into force on such day as the Treasury may by regulations made by statutory instrument appoint.

PART 13

FINAL

190   Interpretation

In this Act—

"ALDA 1979" means the Alcoholic Liquor Duties Act 1979;

"CAA 2001" means the Capital Allowances Act 2001;

"CEMA 1979" means the Customs and Excise Management Act 1979;

"CTA 2009" means the Corporation Tax Act 2009;

"CTA 2010" means the Corporation Tax Act 2010;

"FA", followed by a year, means the Finance Act of that year;

"F(No.2)A, followed by a year means the Finance (No.2) Act of that year;

"F(No.3)A, followed by a year, means the Finance (No.3) Act of that year;

"HODA 1979" means the Hydrocarbon Oil Duties Act 1979;

"ICTA" means the Income and Corporation Taxes Act 1988;

"IHTA 1984" means the Inheritance Tax Act 1984;

"ITA 2007" means the Income Tax Act 2007;

"ITEPA 2003" means the Income Tax (Earnings and Pensions) Act 2003;

"ITTOIA 2005" means the Income Tax (Trading and Other Income) Act 2005;

"OTA 1975" means the Oil Taxation Act 1975;

"TCGA 1992" means the Taxation of Chargeable Gains Act 1992;

"TIOPA 2010" means the Taxation (International and Other Provisions) Act 2010;

"TMA 1970" means the Taxes Management Act 1970;

"TPDA 1979" means the Tobacco Products Duty Act 1979;

"VATA 1994" means the Value Added Tax Act 1994;

"VERA 1994" means the Vehicle Excise and Registration Act 1994.

191   Short title

This Act may be cited as the Finance Act 2016.

SCHEDULES

SCHEDULE 1

Section 5

ABOLITION OF DIVIDEND TAX CREDITS ETC

Main repeals

1   (1) In ITTOIA 2005 omit sections 397 to 398, 400, 414 and 421 (distributions: tax credits, and tax treated as paid).

     (2) In CTA 2010 omit section 1109 (tax credits for certain distributions).

Further amendments in ITTOIA 2005

2   ITTOIA 2005 is further amended as follows.

3   In the heading of Chapter 3 of Part 4, for "credits etc" substitute "treated as paid".

4   In section 382(2) (other contents of Chapter 3 of Part 4) —
     (a) omit "tax credits,", and
     (b) for "397" substitute "399".

5   Omit section 384(3) (which refers to section 398).

6   Omit section 393(5) (determining entitlement to tax credit).

7   In section 394 (which deems a distribution to be made) —
     (a) omit subsection (5) (determining entitlement to tax credit), and
     (b) in subsection (6), for "But for" substitute "For".

8   In section 395(3) (interpretation of section 395(2)) omit the words from "after" to the end.

9   For section 396A(2)(b) (alternative receipt treated as qualifying distribution for the purposes of sections 397 and 399 and for the purposes of section 1100 of CTA 2010) substitute —
     "(b) for the purposes of sections 1100 to 1103 of CTA 2010 (statements and returns of details of distributions) it is treated as a distribution that —
          (i)   is so made, and
          (ii) is one to which section 1100 of CTA 2010 applies."

10   In the italic heading before section 397, omit "Tax credits and".

11   (1) Section 399 (qualifying distribution received by person not entitled to tax credits) is amended as follows.

(2) For subsection (1) substitute—

"(1) This section applies if—

(a) a person's income for a tax year includes a distribution of a company, and

(b) the person is non-UK resident."

(3) In subsection (2) omit "(but see subsection (7))".

(4) Omit subsections (3) to (5) (amount of dividend received by non-UK resident to be treated as its grossed-up amount).

(5) Omit subsection (5A) (amounts treated as qualifying distributions for purposes of the section).

(6) Omit subsection (7) (which provides for subsection (2) to be subject to repealed provisions).

(7) For the heading substitute "Tax treated as paid on distributions received by non-UK resident persons".

12 (1) Section 401 (relief: qualifying distribution after linked non-qualifying distribution) is amended as follows.

(2) For subsections (1) to (6) substitute—

"(1) Where a person is liable to income tax on a CD distribution, the person's liability to income tax on a subsequent non-CD distribution is reduced in accordance with this section if the non-CD distribution consists of a repayment of—

(a) the share capital, or

(b) the principal of the security,

which constituted the CD distribution.

(1A) The reduction is—

(a) the amount of income tax to which the person is liable on the CD distribution, or

(b) if lower, the amount of income tax to which the person is liable on the non-CD distribution.

(1B) For the purposes of calculating the amounts mentioned in subsection (1A)(a) and (b) assume—

(a) that the CD distribution is the lowest part of the person's dividend income in the tax year ("year 1") in which it is made,

(b) that the non-CD distribution, if it is made in year 1, is the part of the person's dividend income in year 1 that is next lowest after the CD distribution, and

(c) that the non-CD distribution, if it is made after year 1, is the lowest part of the person's dividend income in the tax year in which it is made."

(3) In subsection (7) (interpretation), for ""security"" substitute "—

"CD distribution" means a distribution which is a distribution for the purposes of the Corporation Tax Acts only because it falls within paragraph C or D in section 1000(1) of CTA 2010 (redeemable share capital or security issued as bonus in respect of shares in, or securities of, the company), "non-CD distribution" means a distribution which is not a CD distribution, and

"security"".

(4) In the heading, for "qualifying distribution after linked non-qualifying distribution" substitute "distribution repaying shares or security issued in earlier distribution".

13   Omit section 401A (recovery of overpaid tax credit etc).

14   In section 401B (power to obtain information for the purposes of section 397), for "section 397", in each place it occurs, substitute "this Chapter".

15   Omit sections 406(4A) and 407(4A) (determining entitlement to tax credit).

16   In section 408(2A) (interpretation of section 408(2)) omit the words from "after" to the end.

17   In section 411(2) (stock dividends: amount on which tax charged) omit ", grossed up by reference to the dividend ordinary rate for the tax year".

18   In section 416 (released debts: amount on which tax charged) —
        (a)   in subsection (1) (tax charged on gross amount) omit "gross", and
        (b)   omit subsection (2) (meaning of "gross amount").

19   In section 418(3) (release of loan: tax only on grossed-up amount of excess where part previously charged) omit ", grossed up by reference to the dividend ordinary rate".

20   In section 651 (meaning of "UK estate" and "foreign estate") —
        (a)   in subsection (4), for "680(3) or (4) (sums" substitute "664(2)(c) or (d) or 680(4) (sums not liable to tax and sums", and
        (b)   in subsection (5), for "680(3) or (4)" substitute "664(2)(c) or (d) or 680(4)".

21   In section 657 (tax charged on estate income from foreign estates), for "680(3) or (4)", in both places, substitute "680(4)".

22   In section 663 (applicable rate for purposes of grossing-up under sections 656 and 657), after subsection (4) insert—

        "(5)   The aggregate income of the estate, so far as it consists of income within section 664(2)(c) or (d), is treated for the purposes of this section as bearing income tax at 0%."

23   In section 670 (applicable rate for purposes of Step 2 in section 665(1)), after subsection (4) insert—

        "(4A) The aggregate income of the estate, so far as it consists of income within section 664(2)(c) or (d), is treated for the purposes of this section as bearing income tax at 0%."

24   In section 680 (income of an estate that is treated as bearing income tax) —
        (a)   in subsection (2) omit "(3) or", and
        (b)   omit subsection (3) (sums treated as bearing tax at the dividend ordinary rate).

25   In section 680A (estate income treated as dividend income), in each of subsections (1)(a) and (4)(a), after "at the dividend ordinary rate" insert "or as bearing tax at 0% because of section 663(5)".

26   In section 854(6) (carrying on by partner of notional business: meaning of "untaxed income")—

    (a)   omit the "or" at the end of paragraph (b), and

    (b)   after paragraph (c) insert—

        "(d)   income chargeable under Chapter 5 of Part 4 (stock dividends from UK resident companies), or

        (e)   income chargeable under Chapter 6 of Part 4 (release of loan to participator in closed company)."

27   Omit section 858(3) (partnerships with foreign element: entitlement to tax credit).

Further amendments in CTA 2010

28   CTA 2010 is further amended as follows.

29   (1) Section 279F (ring fence profits: related 51% group company) is amended as follows.

    (2) In subsection (7)(c) (conditions to be met by a company's dividend income in order for company to be a passive company), in sub-paragraph (ii) (dividends must be franked investment income) for "franked investment income" substitute "exempt ABGH distributions".

    (3) After subsection (9) insert—

      "(10) In subsection (7)(c) "exempt ABGH distribution" means a distribution which—

        (a)   is a distribution for the purposes of the Corporation Tax Acts only because it falls within paragraph A, B, G or H in section 1000(1), and

        (b)   is exempt for the purposes of Part 9A of CTA 2009 (company distributions)."

30   (1) Section 279G (ring fence profits: meaning of "augmented profits") is amended as follows.

    (2) In subsection (1)(b) (franked investment income is part of augmented profits unless excluded)—

        (a)   for "franked investment income" substitute "exempt ABGH distributions", and

        (b)   for "is" substitute "are".

    (3) In subsection (3) (exclusion of franked investment income received from certain subsidiaries etc), for "franked investment income" substitute "exempt ABGH distribution".

    (4) After subsection (4) insert—

      "(5) In this section "exempt ABGH distribution" means a distribution which—

       (a)   is a distribution for the purposes of the Corporation Tax Acts only because it falls within paragraph A, B, G or H in section 1000(1), and

       (b)   is exempt for the purposes of Part 9A of CTA 2009 (company distributions)."

31   For section 463(7) (loan to trustees of settlement which has ended: amount on which debtor taxed when all or part of loan released or written off) substitute —

      "(7)   The amount which Y is treated as receiving is equal to the amount released or written off."

32   (1) Section 549 (distributions: supplementary) is amended as follows.

     (2) Omit subsection (2) (which excludes entitlement to tax credits).

     (3) In subsection (2A) (which disapplies sections 409 to 414 of ITTOIA 2005), for "414" substitute "413A".

33   (1) Section 751 (interpretation of Part 15 (transactions in securities)) is amended as follows.

     (2) The existing text becomes subsection (1).

     (3) In that subsection, in the definition of "dividends", omit "qualifying".

     (4) After that subsection insert —

     "(2)   In the definition of "dividends" given by subsection (1), "other distributions" does not include a distribution which is a distribution for the purposes of the Corporation Tax Acts only because it falls within paragraph C or D in section 1000(1) (redeemable share capital or security issued as bonus in respect of shares in, or securities of, the company)."

34   Omit section 814D(8) (which excludes entitlement to tax credits).

35   Omit section 997(5) (which introduces sections 1109 to 1111).

36   In sections 1026(1)(b) and 1027(2)(b) (cases where amount paid up in respect of bonus shares does not fall to be treated as a qualifying distribution) omit "qualifying".

37   (1) Section 1070 (distributions by company carrying on mutual business) is amended as follows.

     (2) In subsection (2) (provisions about distributions apply to company's distributions only where made out of taxed profits or franked investment income), for paragraph (b) (franked investment income) substitute —

        "(b)   income of the company consisting of exempt ABGH distributions."

     (3) After subsection (5) insert —

     "(5A) In subsection (2) "exempt ABGH distribution" means a distribution which —

        (a)   is a distribution for the purposes of the Corporation Tax Acts only because it falls within paragraph A, B, G or H in section 1000(1), and

    (b)   is exempt for the purposes of Part 9A of CTA 2009 (company distributions)."

38   (1) Section 1071 (company not carrying on business) is amended as follows.

    (2) In subsection (5) (provisions about distributions apply to company's distributions only where made out of taxed profits or franked investment income), for paragraph (b) (franked investment income) substitute —

        "(b)   income of the company consisting of exempt ABGH distributions."

    (3) After subsection (5) insert —

      "(5A) In subsection (5) "exempt ABGH distribution" means a distribution which —

        (a)   is a distribution for the purposes of the Corporation Tax Acts only because it falls within paragraph A, B, G or H in section 1000(1), and

        (b)   is exempt for the purposes of Part 9A of CTA 2009 (company distributions)."

39   (1) Section 1100 (qualifying distribution: right to request a statement) is amended as follows.

    (2) In subsection (1) (requests for statement) —

        (a)   for "qualifying distribution" substitute "distribution to which this section applies", and

        (b)   omit paragraph (b) (amount of any tax credit), and the "and" preceding it.

    (3) After subsection (4) insert —

      "(4A) This section applies to any distribution other than one which is a distribution for the purposes of the Corporation Tax Acts only because it falls within paragraph C or D in section 1000(1) (redeemable share capital or security issued as bonus in respect of shares in, or securities of, the company)."

    (4) Omit subsections (2) and (5) (interpretation of subsection (1)(b)).

    (5) In subsection (7) (section to be read with section 396A(2) of ITTOIA 2005) —

        (a)   for "needs" substitute ", and sections 1101 to 1103, need", and

        (b)   for "as "qualifying distributions" for the purposes of this section" substitute "as distributions to which this section applies".

    (6) In the heading, for "Qualifying" substitute "Certain".

40   (1) Section 1101 (non-qualifying distributions etc: returns and information) is amended as follows.

    (2) In subsection (1) (duty to make return), for "which is not a qualifying distribution" substitute "to which section 1100 does not apply".

    (3) In subsection (4) (duty to make return where not clear whether distribution is non-qualifying), for "which is not a qualifying distribution" substitute "to which section 1100 does not apply".

    (4) In the heading, and in the heading of section 1102, for "Non-qualifying" substitute "Other".

41   In section 1103 (regulations about information about non-qualifying distributions)—

    (a) in subsection (2) (purpose for which sections 1101 and 1102 may be rewritten), for "which are not qualifying distributions" substitute "to which section 1100 does not apply",

    (b) in subsection (4) (special arrangements about matters specified in subsection (5)), for "matters" substitute "matter", and

    (c) in subsection (5)—

        (i) for "Those matters are" substitute "That matter is", and

        (ii) omit paragraph (b) (tax credits), and the "and" preceding it.

42 (1) Section 1106 (interpretation of sections 1104 and 1105) is amended as follows.

  (2) In subsection (4) (meaning of "tax certificate")—

    (a) after paragraph (a) insert "and", and

    (b) omit paragraph (c) (tax credits), and the "and" preceding it.

  (3) Omit subsections (5) and (6) (interpretation of subsection (4)(c)).

43   Omit sections 1110 and 1111 (recovery of overpaid tax credits etc).

44 (1) Section 1115 (meaning of "new consideration" in Part 23) is amended as follows.

  (2) In subsections (5)(a) and (6)(b) for "qualifying" substitute "non-CD".

  (3) After subsection (6) insert—

    "(7) In this section "non-CD distribution" means any distribution other than one which is a distribution for the purposes of the Corporation Tax Acts only because it falls within paragraph C or D in section 1000(1) (redeemable share capital or security issued as bonus in respect of shares in, or securities of, the company)."

45   In section 1119 (definitions for the purposes of the Corporation Tax Acts) omit the entries for "franked investment income", "qualifying distribution" and "tax credit".

46   Omit section 1126 (meaning of "franked investment income").

47   Omit section 1136 (meaning of "qualifying distribution").

48   Omit section 1139(4) ("relief" includes tax credit).

49   In Schedule 2 (transitionals and savings etc) omit paragraph 106(1) (operation of sections 1026 and 1027 in relation to share capital issued before 7 April 1973).

50   In Schedule 4 (index of defined expressions) omit the entries for "franked investment income", "qualifying distribution" and "tax credit".

Other amendments

51 (1) TMA 1970 is amended as follows.

  (2) In section 8(1AA)(b) (payable income tax is chargeable amount less tax deducted at source and tax credits) omit the words after "source".

(3) In section 8A(1AA)(b) (payable income tax is chargeable amount less tax deducted at source and tax credits) omit the words after "source".

(4) In section 9(1) (self-assessment) —

    (a) in paragraph (b) (payable income tax is assessed amount less tax deducted at source and tax credits) omit the words after "source", and

    (b) in the words after paragraph (b) omit ", 400(2), 414(1), 421(1)".

(5) In section 12AA(1A)(b) (partner's payable income tax is chargeable amount less tax deducted at source and tax credits) omit the words after "source".

(6) In section 12AB (partnership statement in partnership return) —

    (a) in subsection (1)(a) —

        (i) after sub-paragraph (ia) insert "and", and

        (ii) omit sub-paragraph (iii) (tax credits), and the "and" preceding it,

    (b) in subsection (1)(b) for ", tax or credit" substitute "or tax", and

    (c) in subsection (5) omit the definition of "tax credit".

(7) In section 12B(4A)(a)(i) (statements themselves must be preserved if of amount of qualifying distribution and tax credit), after "amount" insert "of distribution, formerly amount".

(8) In section 59A(8)(b) (amounts included in annual total of deductions at source) omit "or are tax credits to which section 397(1) or 397A(1) of ITTOIA 2005 applies,".

(9) In section 59B (payment of income tax and capital gains tax) —

    (a) in subsection (1) omit ", 400(2), 414(1), 421(1)", and

    (b) in subsection (2)(b) omit "or is a tax credit to which section 397(1) or 397A(1) of ITTOIA 2005 applies,".

(10) Omit section 87A(5) (interest on assessments under section 1110 of CTA 2010 on overpaid tax credits etc).

(11) In section 98 (special returns), in the first column of the table omit the entry for section 1109 of CTA 2010.

52 (1) ICTA is amended as follows.

(2) Omit section 231B (arrangements to pass on value of tax credit).

(3) Omit section 824(2) (repayment supplements: tax credits).

(4) In section 824(4A) omit paragraph (b) (repayment supplements: tax credit treated as income tax deducted at source), and the "and" preceding it.

(5) In section 825(1) (repayment supplements: companies) omit paragraph (c) (tax credits comprised in franked investment income), and the "or" preceding it.

(6) In section 826 (interest on tax overpaid by companies) —

    (a) in subsection (1) omit paragraph (c) (tax credits), including the "or" at the end, and

    (b) in subsection (3) —

        (i) omit "or a payment of the whole or part of a tax credit falling within subsection (1)(c) above", and

        (ii) omit "or, as the case may be, the franked investment income referred to in subsection (1)(c) above".

53   In FA 1988, in Schedule 13 omit paragraph 7(c) (post-consolidation amendment of section 824(2) of ICTA).

54   In FA 1989—
  (a) omit section 115 (double taxation: tax credits), and
  (b) in section 179(1)(b)(i) (amendments of provisions of TMA 1970 including section 87A(1) and (5)) omit "and (5)".

55   In FA 1993 omit section 171(2B) (which excludes entitlement to tax credits).

56   In FA 1994 omit section 219(4B) (which excludes entitlement to tax credits).

57 (1) F(No.2)A 1997 is amended as follows.

    (2) Omit section 22(1) (which inserted section 171(2B) of FA 1993).

    (3) Omit section 28 (which inserted section 231B of ICTA).

    (4) Omit section 30(9) and (10) (effect of double taxation arrangements in relation to tax credits).

    (5) In Schedule 6 (repeal of provisions relating to foreign income dividends), in paragraph 23 (transitional provision for certain foreign income dividends paid before 6 April 1999 but received on or after that date) omit—
  (a) "qualifying", and
  (b) "nine tenths of".

58 (1) FA 1998 is amended as follows.

    (2) Omit section 76(3) (regulations about tax credits where non-UK residents have invested in individual savings accounts).

    (3) In Schedule 18 (company tax returns etc)—
  (a) omit paragraph 9(3) (certain claims by companies for payment of tax credits),
  (b) in paragraphs 22(3)(a)(i) and 23(3)(a)(i) (which relate to a statement as to amount of qualifying distribution and tax credit), after "amount" insert "of distribution, but formerly amount", and
  (c) in paragraph 52(2)(a) omit "or payment of a tax credit".

59   In the Commonwealth Development Corporation Act 1999, in Schedule 3 omit paragraph 6(2)(b) (provisions about tax credits do not apply in relation to distributions by the Corporation).

60   In the Financial Services and Markets Act 2000 (Consequential Amendments) (Taxes) Order 2001 (S.I. 2001/3629)—
  (a) omit article 82(a), and
  (b) in article 87(a) omit "and (4B)".

61 (1) ITEPA 2003 is amended as follows.

    (2) Omit sections 58(6) and 61H(6) (tax credits to be reduced in line with reductions in distributions).

    (3) In Part 2 of Schedule 1 (index of defined expressions) omit the entry for "tax credit".

62   In ITTOIA 2005, in Schedule 1 (minor and consequential amendments) omit paragraphs 116, 331(2), 359, 360, 361(a), 363, 364, 376, 377(3), 464(3), 496, 503 and 510(2).

63 (1) ITA 2007 is amended as follows.

    (2) In section 26(1)(b) (list of provisions giving tax reductions), in the entry for section 401 of ITTOIA 2005, for "qualifying distribution after linked non-qualifying distribution" substitute "distribution repaying shares or security issued in earlier distribution".

    (3) In section 31 (calculation of total income) —
        (a) omit subsection (3) (dividend etc treated as increased by amount of tax credit), and
        (b) in subsection (4), for "Subsections (2) and (3) apply" substitute "Subsection (2) applies".

    (4) In section 425(5) (deductions in calculating total amount of income tax for gift aid purposes) —
        (a) in paragraph (a) —
            (i) in sub-paragraph (i) omit "or 400(2)", and
            (ii) omit sub-paragraphs (ii) and (iii),
        (b) after paragraph (a) insert "and",
        (c) in paragraph (b), for "680(3)(b) or (4)" substitute "680(4)", and
        (d) omit paragraph (c), and the "and" before it.

    (5) In section 482 (types of amount charged at special rates for trustees), in the entry for Type 1 amounts, omit "qualifying".

    (6) In section 487(6) (non-UK resident trustees: disregarded income which is not included in untaxed income) —
        (a) after paragraph (a) insert "or", and
        (b) omit paragraph (c) (income in respect of which there is a tax credit), and the "or" preceding it.

    (7) In section 498 (discretionary payments by trustees: types of tax to be included in trustees' tax pool) —
        (a) in subsection (1) —
            (i) in Type 1 (tax at special rates for trustees on income not attracting tax credits), omit "2, 3 or",
            (ii) omit Types 2 and 3 (tax at dividend trust rate on income attracting dividend tax credits), and
           (iii) in Type 4 (tax charged at basic rate as a result of section 491), omit "at the basic rate", and
        (b) omit subsection (2) (interpretation of Types 2 and 3).

    (8) In section 502(3) (non-UK resident beneficiaries: disregarded income which is not included in untaxed income) —
        (a) after paragraph (a) insert "or", and
        (b) omit paragraph (c) (income in respect of which there is a tax credit), and the "or" preceding it.

    (9) In section 614ZD (treatment of recipient of manufactured payment) —
        (a) in subsection (3), for "to (6)" substitute "and (5)", and
        (b) omit subsection (6) (which excludes entitlement to tax credits).

(10) In section 687 (transactions in securities: meaning of "income tax advantage") —

    (a) omit "qualifying" in each place, and

    (b) in subsection (4), after "In this section" insert "—

        (a) "distribution" does not include a distribution which is a distribution for the purposes of the Corporation Tax Acts only because it falls within paragraph C or D in section 1000(1) of CTA 2010 (redeemable share capital or security issued as bonus in respect of shares in, or securities of, the company), and

        (b) ".

(11) In section 713 (interpretation of Chapter 1 (transactions in securities)) —

    (a) the existing text becomes subsection (1),

    (b) in that subsection, in the definition of "dividends", omit "qualifying", and

    (c) after that subsection insert—

        "(2) In the definition of "dividends" given by subsection (1), "other distributions" does not include a distribution which is a distribution for the purposes of the Corporation Tax Acts only because it falls within paragraph C or D in section 1000(1) (redeemable share capital or security issued as bonus in respect of shares in, or securities of, the company)."

(12) In section 745(1) (transfer of assets abroad: same rate of tax not to be charged twice) —

    (a) after "at the basic rate," insert "or", and

    (b) omit "or the dividend ordinary rate".

(13) In section 809S(4) (meaning of "income tax advantage") omit the words after paragraph (d).

(14) In section 811(4) (limit on liability to income tax of non-UK residents) —

    (a) after paragraph (a) insert "and", and

    (b) omit paragraph (c) (tax credits), and the "and" preceding it.

(15) In section 815(3) (limit on liability to income tax of non-UK resident companies) —

    (a) after paragraph (a) insert "and", and

    (b) omit paragraph (c) (tax credits), and the "and" preceding it.

(16) In section 989 (definitions for the purposes of the Income Tax Acts) omit the entries for "qualifying distribution" and "tax credit".

(17) In section 1026 ("non-qualifying income" includes income on which tax treated as paid) —

    (a) in paragraph (a) (deemed payment under sections 399 and 400 of ITTOIA 2005) —

        (i) omit "or 400(2)", and

        (ii) for "from UK resident companies on which there is no tax credit" substitute "to non-UK resident persons", and

    (b) omit paragraphs (b) and (c) (deemed payment under sections 414 and 421 of ITTOIA 2005).

(18) In Schedule 1 (minor and consequential amendments) omit paragraphs 26, 245(2)(a) and (3), 446(27), 515(3), 516, 517(2), 520 and 522.

(19) In Schedule 4 (index of defined expressions) omit the entries for "qualifying distribution" and "tax credit".

64   In FA 2008, in Schedule 12 (amendments relating to tax credits) omit paragraphs 3, 5, 6, 8 to 16, 19, 20, 24(b) and 31.

65 (1) CTA 2009 is amended as follows.

(2) In section 1222 (company with investment business: amount deductible for management expenses to be reduced by income from sources not charged to tax) —

   (a) in subsection (1) (UK resident company), for paragraph (c) (franked investment income does not reduce deductibles) substitute —

      "(c) the income does not consist of exempt ABGH distributions.",

   (b) in subsection (2) (non-UK resident company), for paragraph (d) (franked investment income does not reduce deductibles) substitute —

      "(d) the income does not consist of exempt ABGH distributions.", and

   (c) after subsection (3) insert —

      "(4) In this section "exempt ABGH distribution" means a distribution which —

         (a) is a distribution for the purposes of the Corporation Tax Acts only because it falls within paragraph A, B, G or H in section 1000(1) of CTA 2010, and

         (b) is exempt for the purposes of Part 9A (company distributions)."

(3) Omit section 1266(3) (partnerships with foreign element: entitlement to tax credit).

(4) In Schedule 4 (index of defined expressions) omit the entry for "qualifying distribution".

66 (1) FA 2009 is amended as follows.

(2) In Schedule 19 (amendments relating to tax credits) omit paragraphs 2(2) and (3), 3, 5, 6(2)(a), (3) and (4), 7, 9, 10(a), 11, 12 and 13(c).

(3) In paragraph 14 of Schedule 19 (amendments made by the Schedule have effect in relation to distributions etc arising or paid on or after 22 April 2009), after sub-paragraph (2) insert —

      "(3) Section 873(4) of ITTOIA 2005 (inserted by paragraph 8), so far as relating to any order or regulations made after the passing of FA 2016 under any provision of ITTOIA 2005 other than section 397BA of that Act, has effect as if sub-paragraph (1) did not apply in relation to it."

(4) In Schedule 53 (late payment interest) omit —

   (a) paragraph 6 (late payment interest start date in relation to assessments of overpaid tax credits etc under section 1110 of CTA 2010), and

      (b)   the italic heading preceding it.

  (5) In paragraph 9B of Schedule 54 (repayment interest start date: companies: income tax and certain tax credits) —

      (a)   in sub-paragraph (1) omit paragraph (b) (tax credit comprised in franked investment income), and the "and" preceding it, and

      (b)   in sub-paragraph (2) —

          (i)   omit "or payment", and

          (ii)   omit "or the franked investment income mentioned in sub-paragraph (1)(b)".

  (6) In paragraph 14 of Schedule 54 (interpretation) omit paragraph (b) (tax deducted at source treated as including tax credits), and the "and" preceding it.

67   In Schedule 1 to CTA 2010 (minor and consequential amendments) omit paragraphs 19, 153, 156(3), 282, 303(2), 456, 562(7), 704(27) and 722.

68 (1) TIOPA 2010 is amended as follows.

  (2) In section 6(2) (effect of double taxation arrangements) —

      (a)   after paragraph (e) insert "or", and

      (b)   omit paragraph (g) (tax credits), and the "or" preceding it.

  (3) In section 187A (excess interest treated as a qualifying distribution), in subsection (2), and the heading, omit "qualifying".

  (4) Omit section 234(2) ("relief" includes tax credit).

  (5) In Schedule 8 (minor and consequential amendments) omit paragraphs 38, 51, 52, 66 and 67.

69   In FA 2011 —

      (a)   in Part 6 of Schedule 23 (consequential provisions) omit paragraph 64(3), and

      (b)   in Schedule 26 omit paragraph 1(2)(a)(i) (which amended section 231B of ICTA), including the "and" at the end.

70   In FA 2012, in section 169(2) (payments by certain friendly societies treated as qualifying distributions) omit "qualifying".

71   In FA 2013 —

      (a)   in paragraph 6(2) of Schedule 19 (which amends section 549 of CTA 2010), for "subsections (2) and" substitute "subsection", and

      (b)   in Part 3 of Schedule 29 (manufactured dividends: consequential etc amendments) omit paragraphs 13, 14(a) and 44(3).

72   In FA 2015, in section 19 —

      (a)   in subsection (1), for "credits etc" substitute "treated as paid", and

      (b)   omit subsections (5) and (6) (which insert sections 397(5A) and 399(5A) of ITTOIA 2005).

Commencement

73 (1) Subject to the following sub-paragraphs of this paragraph, the amendments made by this Schedule have effect in relation to dividends paid or arising (or

treated as paid), and other distributions made (or treated as made), in the tax year 2016-17 or at any later time.

(2) The following have effect for the tax year 2016-17 and subsequent tax years —

    (a)   the amendments in sections 8 to 9, 12AA and 59B of TMA 1970,

    (b)   the amendments in section 854(6) of ITTOIA 2005,

    (c)   the amendments in section 425 except the amendment in section 425(5)(b), and the amendments in sections 498, 745 and 1026, of ITA 2007,

    (d)   the repeals of paragraphs 359, 360, 361(a), 363 and 377(3) of Schedule 1 to ITTOIA 2005,

    (e)   the repeals of paragraphs 8 to 11 and 14 of Schedule 12 to FA 2008, and

    (f)   the repeals of the following provisions of Schedule 19 to FA 2009 —

        (i)   paragraph 9(a) and (b),

        (ii)   paragraph 9(c) so far as relating to section 12AA of TMA 1970, and

        (iii)   paragraph 9(d) so far as relating to section 59B of TMA 1970.

(3) The amendment in paragraph 23 of Schedule 6 to F(No.2)A 1997 has effect in relation to foreign income dividends received on or after 6 April 2016.

(4) The amendments in sections 393 and 406 of ITTOIA 2005, and the repeal of paragraph 19 of Schedule 12 to FA 2008, have effect in relation to cash dividends paid over in the tax year 2016-17 or at any later time.

(5) The amendment in section 396A of ITTOIA 2005 has effect in relation to things received on or after 6 April 2016 (even if the choice to receive them was made before that date).

(6) The amendments in section 401 of ITTOIA 2005 have effect where the subsequent distribution is made in the tax year 2016-17 or at any later time, even if the prior distribution is made before 6 April 2016.

(7) The amendments in sections 411 and 414 of ITTOIA 2005, and the repeal of paragraph 520 of Schedule 1 to ITA 2007, have effect in relation to stock dividend income treated as arising in the tax year 2016-17 or at any later time.

(8) The amendments in sections 651 to 680A of ITTOIA 2005 (but not the repeal of section 680(3)(a) of that Act) and the amendment in section 425(5)(b) of ITA 2007 —

    (a)   so far as they relate to income within section 664(2)(c) of ITTOIA 2005 (stock dividends), have effect in relation to stock dividend income treated as arising in the tax year 2016-17 or at any later time, and

    (b)   so far as they relate to income within section 664(2)(d) of ITTOIA 2005 (release of loans), have effect in relation to amounts released or written off in the tax year 2016-17 or at any later time.

(9) The amendments in Chapter 6 of Part 4 of ITTOIA 2005 and in section 463 of CTA 2010, and the repeal of paragraph 522 of Schedule 1 to ITA 2007, have effect in relation to amounts released or written off in the tax year 2016-17 or at any later time.

(10) The amendments in section 614ZD of ITA 2007 have effect in relation to manufactured payments made on or after 6 April 2016.

(11) The amendments in section 687 of ITA 2007 have effect where the relevant consideration is received in the tax year 2016-17 or at any later time.

(12) The amendments in section 1222 of CTA 2009 have effect in relation to income arising in the tax year 2016-17 or at any later time.

(13) The amendment in section 1026(1) of CTA 2010 has effect where the bonus share capital is issued on or after 6 April 2016.

(14) Sub-paragraph (1) does not apply in relation to —
   (a)   the amendments in section 401B of ITTOIA 2005;
   (b)   the amendment in paragraph 14 of Schedule 19 to FA 2009.

SCHEDULE 2

SPORTING TESTIMONIAL PAYMENTS

Section 12

Income tax: sporting testimonial payments treated as earnings

1   After section 226D of ITEPA 2003 (shareholder or connected person having material interest in company) insert —

"Sporting testimonial payments

226E Sporting testimonial payments

(1) This section applies in relation to an individual who is or has been employed as a professional sportsperson ("S").

(2) In this section "sporting testimonial" means —
   (a)   a series of relevant events or activities which each have the same controller, or
   (b)   a single relevant event or activity not forming part of such a series.

(3) An event or activity is (subject to subsection (4)(b)) a relevant event or activity if —
   (a)   its purpose (or one of its purposes) is to raise money for or for the benefit of S, and
   (b)   the only or main reason for doing that is to recognise S's service as a professional sportsperson who is or has been employed as such.

(4) An activity that meets the conditions in subsection (3)(a) and (b) and consists solely of inviting and collecting donations for or for the benefit of S —
   (a)   is a relevant activity if it is one of a series of relevant events or activities for the purposes of subsection (2)(a), but
   (b)   is not a relevant activity for the purposes of subsection (2)(b) so long as both conditions in subsection (5) are met while the activity takes place.

(5) The conditions are—

    (a) that any person who is responsible (alone or with others) for collecting the donations or who is the controller (or a member of a committee which is the controller) of the activity is not—

        (i) S,

        (ii) a person who is (or has been) the controller of any other relevant event or activity for or for the benefit of S,

        (iii) a person connected with S or a person mentioned in sub-paragraph (ii),

        (iv) a person acting for or on behalf of a person mentioned in sub-paragraphs (i) to (iii), and

    (b) that the donations collected do not include any sums paid (directly or indirectly) out of money raised by any other relevant event or activity.

(6) A "sporting testimonial payment" is a payment made by (or on behalf of) the controller of a sporting testimonial out of money raised for or for the benefit of S which—

    (a) is made to S, to a member of S's family or household, to a prescribed person, to S's order or otherwise for S's benefit, and

    (b) does not (apart from this section) constitute earnings from an employment.

(7) A sporting testimonial payment is to be treated as earnings of S from the employment or former employment to which the sporting testimonial is most closely linked.

(8) For the purposes of this section if at any material time S is dead—

    (a) anything done for or for the benefit of S's estate is to be regarded as done for or for the benefit of S; and

    (b) a payment made to S's personal representatives or to their order is to be treated as a payment to S or to S's order.

(9) In this section—

    "controller", in relation to an event or activity which meets the conditions in subsection (3)(a) and (b), means the person who controls the disbursement of any money raised for or for the benefit of S from that event or activity,

    "money" includes money's worth and "payment" includes the transfer of money's worth or the provision of any benefit,

    "prescribed person" means a person prescribed in regulations made by the Treasury.

(10) Section 993 of ITA 2007 (meaning of "connected" persons) has effect for the purposes of this section."

Income tax: limited exemption for sporting testimonial payments

2   After section 306A of ITEPA 2003 (exemption for carers) insert—

Professional sportspersons

306B Limited exemption for sporting testimonial payments

  (1) This section applies to any sporting testimonial payments which are—

      (a) made out of money raised by a sporting testimonial ("the sporting testimonial"), and

      (b) treated by virtue of section 226E as earnings of a person ("S").

  (2) No liability to income tax arises in respect of sporting testimonial payments to which this section applies.

  (3) Subsection (2) has effect subject to and in accordance with the following provisions.

  (4) It only applies—

      (a) if the controller of the relevant event or activity (or of all the relevant events or activities in a series) constituting the sporting testimonial is an independent person,

      (b) if S has not already benefitted from an exemption under this section in relation to one or more sporting testimonial payments made out of money raised by another sporting testimonial, and

      (c) where the sporting testimonial consists of a series of relevant events or activities taking place over more than a year, if the sporting testimonial payment is made out of money raised by events or activities taking place within the period of one year beginning with the day on which the first event or activity in the series took place.

  (5) It only applies to the first £100,000 of sporting testimonial payments made out of money raised by the sporting testimonial.

  (6) If sporting testimonial payments are made (out of money raised by the sporting testimonial) in two or more tax years, any part of the exempt amount that is not used in the first of those years is to be carried forward to the next tax year (and so on).

  (7) This section applies to sporting testimonial payments made to or to the order of the personal representatives of S (where S has died) but only if the payments are made within the period of 24 months beginning with the date of death.

  (8) In subsection (4)(a) "independent person" means a person who is not (or where the controller is a committee, a committee none of whose members are)—

      (a) S or a person connected with S,

      (b) an employer or former employer of S or a person connected with an employer or former employer of S, or

      (c) a person acting for or on behalf of a person mentioned in paragraph (a) or (b).

(9) If the first relevant event or activity in a series took place before 6 April 2017, subsection (4)(c) has effect as if it referred to the year beginning with 6 April 2017.

(10) Section 993 of ITA 2007 (meaning of "connected" persons) has effect for the purposes of this section.

(11) Terms used in this section and section 226E have the same meaning as in that section."

Corporation tax: deductions from total profits for sporting testimonial payments and associated payments

3   After section 996 of CTA 2010 (miscellaneous provisions: use of different accounting periods within a group of companies) insert—

"Sporting testimonial payments and associated payments

996A Deductions from total profits for sporting testimonial payments and associated payments

(1) This section applies where a company, in any accounting period—
   (a) is the controller of a relevant event or activity that constitutes or is part of a sporting testimonial, and
   (b) makes a relevant sporting testimonial payment out of money raised by the sporting testimonial.

(2) In this section "relevant sporting testimonial payment" means a sporting testimonial payment that is (or so much of it as is) made out of proceeds of a relevant event or activity which are brought into account in determining the company's total profits or any component of its total profits.

(3) In calculating the amount of corporation tax chargeable for the accounting period, an amount equal to the aggregate of the following amounts is allowed as a deduction from the company's total profits—
   (a) so much of the relevant sporting testimonial payment as is paid to or for the benefit of the sportsperson to whom the sporting testimonial relates,
   (b) any income tax or employee's national insurance contributions deducted at source from that payment, and
   (c) any employer's national insurance contributions relating to that payment.

(4) The amount is deducted—
   (a) from the company's total profits for the accounting period in which the relevant sporting testimonial payment is made, and
   (b) if a claim by the company for relief so requires, previous accounting periods.

(5) A claim under subsection (4)(b) must be made within 2 years after the end of the accounting period in which the relevant sporting testimonial payment is made.

(6) If for an accounting period deductions under subsection (4) are to be made for relevant sporting testimonial payments made in more than one accounting period, the deductions are to be made in the order in which the payments were made (starting with the earliest of them).

(7) The amount of the deduction to be made under subsection (4) for an accounting period is the amount that cannot be deducted under that subsection for a subsequent accounting period.

(8) The amount of the deduction to be made for any accounting period is limited to the amount that reduces the company's taxable total profits for that period to nil.

(9) The deduction is only available if and to the extent that the amount mentioned in subsection (3) is not otherwise deductible in calculating the company's total profits or any component of its total profits.

(10) Terms used in this section and in section 226E of ITEPA 2003 have the same meaning as in that section."

Application of this Schedule

4 (1) The amendments made by this Schedule have effect in relation to a sporting testimonial payment made out of money raised by a sporting testimonial if—

(a) the sporting testimonial was made public on or after 25 November 2015, and

(b) the payment is made out of money raised by one or more relevant events or activities which take place on or after 6 April 2017.

(2) Terms used in sub-paragraph (1) and section 226E of ITEPA 2003 (as inserted by paragraph 1) have the same meaning as in that section.

SCHEDULE 3 Section 16

EMPLOYEE SHARE SCHEMES: MINOR AMENDMENTS

Enterprise management incentives and employee ownership trusts

1 (1) In section 534 of ITEPA 2003 (disqualifying events relating to relevant company), at the end insert—

"(7) Subsection (1)(a) and (b) do not apply where the relevant company is subject to an employee-ownership trust (within the meaning of paragraph 27(4) to (6) of Schedule 2)."

(2) The amendment made by this paragraph is treated as having come into force on 1 October 2014.

Share incentive plans

2 (1) Schedule 2 to ITEPA 2003 (share incentive plans) is amended as follows.

(2) In paragraph 1 (introduction), after sub-paragraph (4) insert—

"(5) Sub-paragraph (A1) is also subject to Part 10A of this Schedule (disqualifying events)."

(3) After Part 10 insert—

"PART 10A

DISQUALIFYING EVENTS

85A (1) A SIP ceases to be a Schedule 2 SIP if (and with effect from the time when) a disqualifying event occurs.

(2) The following are disqualifying events—
   (a) an alteration being made in—
      (i) the share capital of a company any of whose shares are subject to the plan trust, or
      (ii) the rights attaching to any shares of such a company,
      that materially affects the value of the shares that are subject to the plan trust;
   (b) shares of a class of shares that is subject to the plan trust receiving different treatment in any respect from the other shares of that class.

(3) Sub-paragraph (2)(b) applies in particular to different treatment in respect of—
   (a) the dividend payable,
   (b) repayment, or
   (c) any offer of substituted or additional shares, securities or rights of any description in respect of the shares.

(4) Sub-paragraph (2)(b) does not however apply where the difference in treatment arises from—
   (a) a key feature of the plan, or
   (b) any of the participants' shares being subject to any restriction.

(5) Nor does sub-paragraph (2)(b) apply as a result only of the fact that shares which have been newly issued receive, in respect of dividends payable with respect to a period beginning before the date on which they were issued, treatment less favourable than that accorded to shares issued before that date.

(6) For the purposes of this paragraph a "key feature" of a plan is a provision of it that is necessary to meet the requirements of this Schedule.

(7) This paragraph does not affect the operation of the SIP code in relation to shares awarded to participants in the plan before the disqualifying event occurred."

(4) The amendments made by this paragraph have effect in relation to disqualifying events occurring on or after the day on which this Act is passed.

Notification of plans and schemes to HMRC

3   (1) In Schedule 2 to ITEPA 2003 (share incentive plans), Part 10 (notification of plans etc) is amended as follows.

     (2) In paragraph 81A (notice of SIP to be given to HMRC), after sub-paragraph (5) insert—

             "(5A) Sub-paragraph (5) does not apply if the company satisfies HMRC (or, on an appeal under paragraph 81K, the tribunal) that there is a reasonable excuse for failing to give notice on or before the initial notification deadline.

             (5B) Paragraph 81C(9) (what constitutes a reasonable excuse) applies for the purposes of sub-paragraph (5A).

             (5C) Where HMRC are required under sub-paragraph (5A) to consider whether there was a reasonable excuse, HMRC must notify the company of their decision within the period of 45 days beginning with the day on which HMRC received the company's request to consider the excuse.

             (5D) Where HMRC are required to notify the company as specified in sub-paragraph (5C) but do not do so—
                   (a) HMRC are to be treated as having decided that there was no reasonable excuse, and
                   (b) HMRC must notify the company of the decision which they are treated as having made."

     (3) In paragraph 81K (appeals)—
           (a) at the beginning insert—

                 "(A1) The company may appeal against a decision of HMRC under paragraph 81A(5A) that there was no reasonable excuse for its failure to give notice on or before the initial notification deadline.";
           (b) in sub-paragraph (6), before paragraph (a) insert—
                 "(za) in the case of an appeal under sub-paragraph (A1), notice of HMRC's decision is given to the company;";
           (c) in sub-paragraph (7), after "sub-paragraph" insert "(A1),".

     (4) The amendments made by this paragraph have effect in relation to notices given under paragraph 81A of Schedule 2 to ITEPA 2003 on or after 6 April 2016.

4   (1) In Schedule 3 to ITEPA 2003 (SAYE option schemes), Part 8 (notification of schemes etc) is amended as follows.

     (2) In paragraph 40A (notice of scheme to be given to HMRC), after sub-paragraph (5) insert—

             "(5A) Sub-paragraph (5) does not apply if the scheme organiser satisfies HMRC (or, on an appeal under paragraph 40K, the tribunal) that there is a reasonable excuse for the failure to give notice on or before the initial notification deadline.

      (5B) Paragraph 40C(9) (what constitutes a reasonable excuse) applies for the purposes of sub-paragraph (5A).

      (5C) Where HMRC are required under sub-paragraph (5A) to consider whether there was a reasonable excuse, HMRC must notify the scheme organiser of their decision within the period of 45 days beginning with the day on which HMRC received the scheme organiser's request to consider the excuse.

      (5D) Where HMRC are required to notify the scheme organiser as specified in sub-paragraph (5C) but do not do so—

          (a) HMRC are to be treated as having decided that there was no reasonable excuse, and

          (b) HMRC must notify the scheme organiser of the decision which they are treated as having made."

  (3) In paragraph 40K (appeals)—

    (a) at the beginning insert—

      "(A1) The scheme organiser may appeal against a decision of HMRC under paragraph 40A(5A) that there was no reasonable excuse for the failure to give notice on or before the initial notification deadline.";

    (b) in sub-paragraph (5), before paragraph (a) insert—

      "(za) in the case of an appeal under sub-paragraph (A1), notice of HMRC's decision is given to the scheme organiser;";

    (c) in sub-paragraph (6), after "sub-paragraph" insert "(A1),".

  (4) The amendments made by this paragraph have effect in relation to notices given under paragraph 40A of Schedule 3 to ITEPA 2003 on or after 6 April 2016.

5   (1) In Schedule 4 to ITEPA 2003 (CSOP schemes), Part 7 (notification of schemes etc) is amended as follows.

    (2) In paragraph 28A (notice of scheme to be given to HMRC), after sub-paragraph (5) insert—

      "(5A) Sub-paragraph (5) does not apply if the scheme organiser satisfies HMRC (or, on an appeal under paragraph 28K, the tribunal) that there is a reasonable excuse for the failure to give notice on or before the initial notification deadline.

      (5B) Paragraph 28C(9) (what constitutes a reasonable excuse) applies for the purposes of sub-paragraph (5A).

      (5C) Where HMRC are required under sub-paragraph (5A) to consider whether there was a reasonable excuse, HMRC must notify the scheme organiser of their decision within the period of 45 days beginning with the day on which HMRC received the scheme organiser's request to consider the excuse.

      (5D) Where HMRC are required to notify the scheme organiser as specified in sub-paragraph (5C) but do not do so—

          (a) HMRC are to be treated as having decided that there was no reasonable excuse, and

        (b)   HMRC must notify the scheme organiser of the decision which they are treated as having made."

   (3) In paragraph 28K (appeals) —

       (a)   at the beginning insert—

          "(A1) The scheme organiser may appeal against a decision of HMRC under paragraph 28A(5A) that there was no reasonable excuse for the failure to give notice on or before the initial notification deadline.";

       (b)   in sub-paragraph (5), before paragraph (a) insert—

          "(za)   in the case of an appeal under sub-paragraph (A1), notice of HMRC's decision is given to the scheme organiser;";

       (c)   in sub-paragraph (6), after "sub-paragraph" insert "(A1),".

   (4) The amendments made by this paragraph have effect in relation to notices given under paragraph 28A of Schedule 4 to ITEPA 2003 on or after 6 April 2016.

Price for acquisition of shares under share option

6   (1) In Schedule 3 to ITEPA 2003 (SAYE option schemes), paragraph 28 (requirements as to price for acquisition of shares) is amended as follows.

   (2) In sub-paragraph (1) —

       (a)   in paragraph (b), for "at that time" substitute "—

          (i)   at that time, or

          (ii)   at such earlier time as may be determined in accordance with guidance issued by the Commissioners for Her Majesty's Revenue and Customs."

       (b)   for "sub-paragraphs (2) and (3)" substitute "sub-paragraph (3)".

   (3) Omit sub-paragraph (2).

7   (1) In Schedule 4 to ITEPA 2003 (CSOP schemes), paragraph 22 (requirements as to price for acquisition of shares) is amended as follows.

   (2) In sub-paragraph (1) —

       (a)   in paragraph (b), for "at the time when the option is granted" substitute "—

          (i)   at the time when the option is granted, or

          (ii)   at such earlier time as may be determined in accordance with guidance issued by the Commissioners for Her Majesty's Revenue and Customs.";

       (b)   for "sub-paragraphs (2) and (3)" substitute "sub-paragraph (3)".

   (3) Omit sub-paragraph (2).

Tag-along rights

8   (1) In Schedule 5 to ITEPA 2003 (enterprise management incentives), in paragraph 39 (company reorganisations: introduction), in sub-paragraph (2)(c), after "982" insert "or 983 to 985".

(2) The amendment made by this paragraph is treated as having come into force on 17 July 2013.

Exercise of EMI options

9   (1) In section 238A of TCGA 1992 (share schemes and share incentives), in subsection (2), omit paragraph (d) and the preceding "and".

      (2) In Schedule 7D to TCGA 1992 (share schemes and share incentives), omit Part 4.

      (3) In section 527 of ITEPA 2003 (enterprise management incentives: qualifying options), in subsection (3) —

          (a) after paragraph (a) insert "and";

          (b) omit paragraph (c) and the preceding "and".

      (4) The amendments made by this paragraph do not affect —

          (a) the application of paragraph 14(4) of Schedule 7D to TCGA 1992 in relation to a disqualifying event occurring before 6 April 2016, or

          (b) the application of paragraph 16 of that Schedule in relation to an allotment for payment mentioned in section 126(2)(a) of that Act taking place before 6 April 2016.

SCHEDULE 4   Section 19

PENSIONS: LIFETIME ALLOWANCE: TRANSITIONAL PROVISION

PART 1

"FIXED PROTECTION 2016"

The protection

1   (1) Sub-paragraph (2) applies at any particular time on or after 6 April 2016 in the case of an individual if —

          (a) each of the conditions specified in paragraph 2 is met,

          (b) there is no protection-cessation event (see paragraph 3) in the period beginning with 6 April 2016 and ending with the particular time,

          (c) paragraph 1(2) of Schedule 6 to FA 2014 ("individual protection 2014") does not apply in the individual's case at the particular time, and

          (d) at the particular time or any later time, the individual has a reference number (see Part 3 of this Schedule) for the purposes of sub-paragraph (2).

      (2) Part 4 of FA 2004 has effect in relation to the individual as if the standard lifetime allowance were the greater of the standard lifetime allowance and £1,250,000.

The initial conditions

2   The conditions mentioned in paragraph 1(1)(a) are —

Finance Act 2016 (c. 24)
Schedule 4 — Pensions: lifetime allowance: transitional provision
Part 1 — "Fixed protection 2016"

341

   (a)   that, on 6 April 2016, the individual has one or more arrangements under—

      (i)   a registered pension scheme, or

      (ii)   a relieved non-UK pension scheme of which the individual is a relieved member,

   (b)   that paragraph 7 of Schedule 36 to FA 2004 (primary protection) does not make provision for a lifetime allowance enhancement factor in relation to the individual,

   (c)   that paragraph 12 of that Schedule (enhanced protection) does not apply in the individual's case on 6 April 2016,

   (d)   that paragraph 14 of Schedule 18 to FA 2011 (transitional provision relating to new standard lifetime allowance for the tax year 2012-13) does not apply in the individual's case on 6 April 2016, and

   (e)   that paragraph 1 of Schedule 22 to FA 2013 ("fixed protection 2014" relating to new standard lifetime allowance for the tax year 2014-15) does not apply in the individual's case on 6 April 2016.

Protection-cessation events

3   There is a protection-cessation event if—

   (a)   there is benefit accrual in relation to the individual under an arrangement under a registered pension scheme,

   (b)   there is an impermissible transfer into any arrangement under a registered pension scheme relating to the individual,

   (c)   a transfer of sums or assets held for the purposes of, or representing accrued rights under, any such arrangement is made that is not a permitted transfer, or

   (d)   an arrangement relating to the individual is made under a registered pension scheme otherwise than in permitted circumstances.

Protection-cessation events: interpretation: "benefit accrual"

4   (1)   For the purposes of paragraph 3(a) there is benefit accrual in relation to the individual under an arrangement—

   (a)   in the case of a money purchase arrangement that is not a cash balance arrangement, if a relevant contribution is paid under the arrangement on or after 6 April 2016,

   (b)   in the case of a cash balance arrangement or defined benefits arrangement, if there is an increase in the value of the individual's rights under the arrangement at any time on or after that date (but subject to sub-paragraph (5)), and

   (c)   in the case of a hybrid arrangement—

      (i)   where the benefits that may be provided to or in respect of the individual under the arrangement include money purchase benefits other than cash balance benefits, if a relevant contribution is paid under the arrangement on or after 6 April 2016, and

      (ii)   in any case, if there is an increase in the value of the individual's rights under the arrangement at any time on or after that date (but subject to sub-paragraph (5)).

342

Finance Act 2016 (c. 24)
Schedule 4 — Pensions: lifetime allowance: transitional provision
Part 1 — "Fixed protection 2016"

(2) For the purposes of sub-paragraphs (1)(b) and (c)(ii) and (5) whether there is an increase in the value of the individual's rights under an arrangement (and its amount if there is) is to be determined —

    (a)   in the case of a cash balance arrangement (or a hybrid arrangement under which cash balance benefits may be provided to or in respect of the individual under the arrangement), by reference to whether there is an increase in the amount that would, on the valuation assumptions, be available for the provision of benefits to or in respect of the individual (and, if there is, the amount of the increase), and

    (b)   in the case of a defined benefits arrangement (or a hybrid arrangement under which defined benefits may be provided to or in respect of the individual under the arrangement), by reference to whether there is an increase in the benefits amount.

(3) For the purposes of sub-paragraph (2)(b) "the benefits amount" is —

$$(P \times RVF) + LS$$

where —

    LS is the lump sum to which the individual would, on the valuation assumptions, be entitled under the arrangement (otherwise than by commutation of pension),

    P is the annual rate of the pension which would, on the valuation assumptions, be payable to the individual under the arrangement, and

    RVF is the relevant valuation factor.

(4) Paragraph 14 of Schedule 36 to FA 2004 (when a relevant contribution is paid under an arrangement) applies for the purposes of sub-paragraph (1)(a) and (c)(i).

(5) Increases in the value of the individual's rights under an arrangement are to be ignored for the purposes of sub-paragraph (1)(b) or (c)(ii) if in no tax year do they exceed the relevant percentage.

(6) The relevant percentage, in relation to a tax year, means —

    (a)   where the arrangement (or a predecessor arrangement) includes provision for the value of the rights of the individual to increase during the tax year at an annual rate specified in the rules of the pension scheme (or a predecessor registered pension scheme) on 9 December 2015 —

        (i)   that percentage (or, where more than one arrangement includes such provision, the higher or highest of the percentages specified), plus

        (ii)   the relevant statutory increase percentage;

    (b)   otherwise —

        (i)   the percentage by which the consumer prices index for the month of September in the previous tax year is higher than it was for the September before that (or 0% if it is not higher), or

        (ii)   if higher, the relevant statutory increase percentage.

(7) In sub-paragraph (6)(a) —

    "predecessor arrangement", in relation to an arrangement, means another arrangement (under the same or another registered pension scheme) from which some or all of the sums or assets held for the purposes of the arrangement directly or indirectly derive;

Finance Act 2016 (c. 24)
Schedule 4 — Pensions: lifetime allowance: transitional provision
Part 1 — "Fixed protection 2016"

343

"predecessor registered pension scheme", in relation to a registered pension scheme, means another registered pension scheme from which some or all of the sums or assets held for the purposes of the arrangement under the pension scheme directly or indirectly derive.

(8) In sub-paragraph (6) "the relevant statutory increase percentage", in relation to a tax year, means the percentage increase in the value of the individual's rights under the arrangement during the tax year so far as it is attributable solely to one or more of the following —

  (a) an increase in accordance with section 15 of the Pension Schemes Act 1993 or section 11 of the Pension Schemes (Northern Ireland) Act 1993 (increase of guaranteed minimum where commencement of guaranteed minimum pension postponed);

  (b) a revaluation in accordance with section 16 of the Pension Schemes Act 1993 or section 12 of the Pension Schemes (Northern Ireland) Act 1993 (early leavers: revaluation of earnings factors);

  (c) a revaluation in accordance with Chapter 2 of Part 4 of the Pension Schemes Act 1993 or the Pension Schemes (Northern Ireland) Act 1993 (early leavers: revaluation of accrued benefits);

  (d) a revaluation in accordance with Chapter 3 of Part 4 of the Pension Schemes Act 1993 or the Pension Schemes (Northern Ireland) Act 1993 (early leavers: protection of increases in guaranteed minimum pensions);

  (e) the application of section 67 of the Equality Act 2010 (sex equality rule for occupational pension schemes).

(9) Sub-paragraph (10) applies in relation to a tax year if —

  (a) the arrangement is a defined benefits arrangement which is under an annuity contract treated as a registered pension scheme under section 153(8) of FA 2004,

  (b) the contract provides for the value of the rights of the individual to be increased during the tax year at an annual rate specified in the contract, and

  (c) the contract limits the annual rate to the percentage increase in the retail prices index over a 12 month period specified in the contract.

(10) Sub-paragraph (6)(b)(i) applies as if it referred instead to the annual rate of the increase in the value of the rights during the tax year.

(11) For the purposes of sub-paragraph (9)(c) the 12 month period must end during the 12 month period preceding the month in which the increase in the value of the rights occurs.

Protection-cessation events: interpretation: "impermissible transfer"

5   Paragraph 17A of Schedule 36 to FA 2004 (impermissible transfers) applies for the purposes of paragraph 3(b) but as if —

  (a) the references to a relevant existing arrangement were to the arrangement, and

  (b) the reference in sub-paragraph (2) to 5 April 2006 were to 5 April 2016.

Protection-cessation events: interpretation: "permitted transfer"

6   Sub-paragraphs (7) to (8B) of paragraph 12 of Schedule 36 to FA 2004 (when there is a permitted transfer) apply for the purposes of paragraph 3(c).

Protection-cessation events: interpretation: "permitted circumstances"

7   Sub-paragraphs (2A) to (2C) of paragraph 12 of Schedule 36 to FA 2004 ("permitted circumstances") apply for the purposes of paragraph 3(d).

Protection-cessation events: interpretation: relieved non-UK pension schemes

8   (1) Subject to sub-paragraphs (2) to (4), paragraph 3 applies in relation to an individual who is a relieved member of a relieved non-UK pension scheme as if the relieved non-UK pension scheme were a registered pension scheme; and the other paragraphs of this Part of this Schedule apply accordingly.

     (2) Sub-paragraphs (3) and (4) apply for the purposes of paragraph 3(a) (instead of paragraph 4(1)) in determining if there is benefit accrual in relation to an individual under an arrangement under a relieved non-UK pension scheme of which the individual is a relieved member.

     (3) There is benefit accrual in relation to the individual under the arrangement if there is a pension input amount under sections 230 to 237 of FA 2004 (as applied by Schedule 34 to that Act) greater than nil in respect of the arrangement for a tax year; and, in such a case, the benefit accrual is treated as occurring at the end of the tax year.

     (4) There is also benefit accrual in relation to the individual under the arrangement if—
          (a) in a tax year there occurs a benefit crystallisation event in relation to the individual (whether in relation to the arrangement or to any other arrangement under any pension scheme or otherwise), and
          (b) had the tax year ended immediately before the benefit crystallisation event, there would have been a pension input amount under sections 230 to 237 of FA 2004 greater than nil in respect of the arrangement for the tax year,
          and, in such a case, the benefit accrual is treated as occurring immediately before the benefit crystallisation event.

PART 2

"INDIVIDUAL PROTECTION 2016"

The protection

9   (1) Sub-paragraph (2) applies at any particular time on or after 6 April 2016 in the case of an individual if—
          (a) the individual has one or more relevant arrangements (see sub-paragraph (3)) on 5 April 2016,
          (b) the individual's relevant amount at the particular time is greater than £1,000,000 (see sub-paragraphs (4) and (7)),
          (c) paragraph 7 of Schedule 36 to FA 2004 (primary protection) does not make provision for a lifetime allowance enhancement factor in relation to the individual,

Finance Act 2016 (c. 24)
Schedule 4 — Pensions: lifetime allowance: transitional provision
Part 2 — "Individual protection 2016"

345

      (d)   none of the provisions listed in sub-paragraph (5) applies in the individual's case at the particular time, and

      (e)   at the particular time or any later time, the individual has a reference number (see Part 3 of this Schedule) for the purposes of sub-paragraph (2).

(2) Part 4 of FA 2004 has effect in relation to the individual as if the standard lifetime allowance were—

      (a)   if the individual's relevant amount at the particular time is greater than £1,250,000, the greater of the standard lifetime allowance and £1,250,000, or

      (b)   otherwise, the greater of the individual's relevant amount at the particular time and the standard lifetime allowance.

(3) "Relevant arrangement", in relation to an individual, means an arrangement relating to the individual under—

      (a)   a registered pension scheme of which the individual is a member, or

      (b)   a relieved non-UK pension scheme of which the individual is a relieved member.

(4) An individual's "relevant amount" is the sum of amounts A, B, C and D (see paragraphs 10 to 13, but see also sub-paragraph (7)).

(5) The provisions mentioned in sub-paragraph (1)(d) are—

      (a)   paragraph 12 of Schedule 36 to FA 2004 (enhanced protection);

      (b)   paragraph 14 of Schedule 18 to FA 2011 (fixed protection 2012);

      (c)   paragraph 1 of Schedule 22 to FA 2013 (fixed protection 2014);

      (d)   paragraph 1(2) of Schedule 6 to FA 2014 (individual protection 2014);

      (e)   paragraph 1(2) of this Schedule (fixed protection 2016).

(6) Sub-paragraph (7) applies if rights of an individual under a relevant arrangement become subject to a pension debit where the transfer day falls on or after 6 April 2016.

(7) For the purpose of applying sub-paragraph (2) in the case of the individual on and after the transfer day, the individual's relevant amount is reduced (or further reduced) by the following amount—

$$X - (Y \times Z)$$

where—

    X is the appropriate amount,

    Y is 5% of X, and

    Z is the number of tax years beginning after 5 April 2016 and ending on or before the transfer day.

    (If the formula gives a negative amount, it is to be taken to be nil.)

(8) In sub-paragraphs (6) and (7) "appropriate amount" and "transfer day", in relation to a pension debit, have the same meaning as in section 29 of WRPA 1999 or Article 26 of WRP(NI)O 1999 (as the case may be).

Amount A (pre-6 April 2006 pensions in payment)

10   (1) To determine amount A—

346

Finance Act 2016 (c. 24)
Schedule 4 – Pensions: lifetime allowance: transitional provision
Part 2 – "Individual protection 2016"

(a) apply sub-paragraph (2) if a benefit crystallisation event has occurred in relation to the individual during the period beginning with 6 April 2006 and ending with 5 April 2016;

(b) otherwise, apply sub-paragraph (6).

(2) If this sub-paragraph is to be applied, amount A is—

$$25 \times ARP \times \frac{£1,250,000}{SLT}$$

where—

ARP is (subject to sub-paragraph (3)) an amount equal to—

(a) the annual rate at which any relevant existing pension was payable to the individual at the time immediately before the benefit crystallisation event occurred, or

(b) if more than one relevant existing pension was payable to the individual at that time, the sum of the annual rates at which each of the relevant existing pensions was so payable, and

SLT is an amount equal to what the standard lifetime allowance was at the time the benefit crystallisation event occurred.

(3) Paragraph 20(4) of Schedule 36 to FA 2004 applies for the purposes of the definition of "ARP" in sub-paragraph (2) (and, for this purpose, in paragraph 20(4) any reference to "the time" is to be read as a reference to the time immediately before the benefit crystallisation event occurred).

(4) If the time immediately before the benefit crystallisation event occurred falls before 6 April 2015, in sub-paragraph (3) references to paragraph 20(4) are to be read as references to that provision as it had effect in relation to benefit crystallisation events occurring at the time immediately before the benefit crystallisation event occurred.

(5) If more than one benefit crystallisation event has occurred, in sub-paragraphs (2) to (4) references to the benefit crystallisation event are to be read as references to the first benefit crystallisation event.

(6) If this sub-paragraph is to be applied, amount A is—

$$25 \times ARP$$

where ARP is (subject to sub-paragraph (7)) an amount equal to—

(a) the annual rate at which any relevant existing pension is payable to the individual at the end of 5 April 2016, or

(b) if more than one relevant existing pension is payable to the individual at the end of 5 April 2016, the sum of the annual rates at which each of the relevant existing pensions is so payable.

(7) Paragraph 20(4) of Schedule 36 to FA 2004 applies for the purposes of the definition of "ARP" in sub-paragraph (6) (and, for this purpose, in paragraph 20(4) any reference to "the time" is to be read as a reference to 5 April 2016).

(8) In this paragraph "relevant existing pension" means (subject to sub-paragraph (9)) a pension, annuity or right—

(a) which was, at the end of 5 April 2006, a "relevant existing pension" as defined by paragraph 10(2) and (3) of Schedule 36 to FA 2004, and

(b) to the payment of which the individual had, at the end of 5 April 2006, an actual (rather than a prospective) right.

Finance Act 2016 (c. **24**)
Schedule 4 — Pensions: lifetime allowance: transitional provision
Part 2 — "Individual protection 2016"

347

(9) If—

    (a) before 6 April 2016, there was a recognised transfer of sums or assets representing a relevant existing pension, and

    (b) those sums or assets were, after the transfer, applied towards the provision of a scheme pension ("the new scheme pension"),

the new scheme pension is also to be a "relevant existing pension" (including for the purposes of this sub-paragraph).

Amount B (pre-6 April 2016 benefit crystallisation events)

11 (1) To determine amount B—

    (a) identify each benefit crystallisation event that has occurred in relation to the individual during the period beginning with 6 April 2006 and ending with 5 April 2016,

    (b) determine the amount that was crystallised by each of those benefit crystallisation events (applying paragraph 14 of Schedule 34 to FA 2004 if relevant), and

    (c) multiply each crystallised amount by the following fraction—

$$\frac{1{,}250{,}000}{\text{SLT}}$$

where SLT is an amount equal to what the standard lifetime allowance was at the time when the benefit crystallisation event in question occurred.

(2) Amount B is the sum of the crystallised amounts determined under sub-paragraph (1)(b) as adjusted under sub-paragraph (1)(c).

Amount C (uncrystallised rights at end of 5 April 2016 under registered pension schemes)

12 Amount C is the total value of the individual's uncrystallised rights at the end of 5 April 2016 under arrangements relating to the individual under registered pension schemes of which the individual is a member as determined in accordance with section 212 of FA 2004.

Amount D (uncrystallised rights at end of 5 April 2016 under relieved non-UK schemes)

13 (1) To determine amount D—

    (a) identify each relieved non-UK pension scheme of which the individual is a relieved member at the end of 5 April 2016, and

    (b) in relation to each such scheme—

        (i) assume that a benefit crystallisation event occurs in relation to the individual at the end of 5 April 2016, and

        (ii) in accordance with paragraph 14 of Schedule 34 to FA 2004, determine what the untested portion of the relevant relieved amount would be immediately before the assumed benefit crystallisation event.

(2) Amount D is the sum of the untested portions determined under sub-paragraph (1)(b)(ii).

348

Finance Act 2016 (c. **24**)
Schedule 4 — Pensions: lifetime allowance: transitional provision
Part 3 — Reference numbers etc

PART 3

REFERENCE NUMBERS ETC

Issuing of reference numbers for fixed or individual protection 2016

14   (1)   An individual has a reference number for the purposes of paragraph 1(2), or for the purposes of paragraph 9(2), if a reference number —

    (a)   has been issued by or on behalf of the Commissioners in respect of the individual for the purposes concerned, and

    (b)   has not been withdrawn.

  (2)   Such a reference number —

    (a)   may include, or consist of, characters other than figures, and

    (b)   may be issued only if a valid application for its issue is received by or on behalf of the Commissioners.

  (3)   A valid application is an application —

    (a)   made by or on behalf of the individual concerned,

    (b)   made on or after 6 April 2016,

    (c)   made by means of a digital service provided for the purpose by or on behalf of the Commissioners, or by other means authorised in a particular case by an officer of Revenue and Customs,

    (d)   containing —

      (i)   the following details for the individual and, where the individual is not the applicant, also for the applicant: title, full name, full postal address and e-mail address,

      (ii)   the individual's date of birth,

      (iii)   the individual's national insurance number, or the reason why the individual does not qualify for a national insurance number, and

      (iv)   a declaration that everything stated in the application is true and complete to the best of the applicant's knowledge and belief,

    (e)   containing also in the case of an application for a reference number for the purposes of paragraph 1(2) —

      (i)   a declaration that the conditions specified in paragraph 2 are met in the individual's case, and

      (ii)   a declaration that there has been no protection-cessation event (see paragraph 3) in the individual's case in the period beginning with 6 April 2016 and ending with the making of the application, and

    (f)   containing also in the case of an application for a reference number for the purposes of paragraph 9(2) —

      (i)   the individual's relevant amount (see paragraph 9(4) and (7)),

      (ii)   amounts A, B, C and D for the individual (see paragraphs 10 to 13),

      (iii)   if rights of the individual under a relevant arrangement have become subject to a relevant pension debit, the appropriate amount and transfer day for each such pension debit,

Finance Act 2016 (c. 24)
Schedule 4 — Pensions: lifetime allowance: transitional provision
Part 3 — Reference numbers etc

349

      (iv)   a declaration that the condition in paragraph 9(1)(c) is met in the individual's case, and

      (v)   a declaration that paragraph 1(2) of Schedule 6 to FA 2014 ("individual protection 2014") does not apply in the individual's case.

(4) Where an application for a reference number for the purposes of paragraph 1(2) or 9(2) is unsuccessful, or is successful on a dormant basis, that must be notified to the applicant by or on behalf of the Commissioners.

(5) In sub-paragraph (3)(f)(iii) and this sub-paragraph—

    "relevant arrangement" has the meaning given by paragraph 9(3);

    "relevant pension debit", in relation to an application for a reference number, means a pension debit where—

      (a)   the transfer day falls on or after 6 April 2016 and before the day on which the application is made, and

      (b)   the individual has, before the day on which the application is made, received notice under regulation 8(2) or (3) of the Pensions on Divorce etc. (Provision of Information) Regulations 2000 (S.I. 2000/1048) relating to discharge of liability in respect of the pension credit corresponding to the pension debit;

    "appropriate amount" and "transfer day", in relation to a pension debit, have the same meaning as in paragraph 9(6) and (7) (see paragraph 9(8)).

(6) Sub-paragraph (3)(c) is not to be read as requiring a digital service to be provided and available for the purpose referred to.

(7) For the purposes of this Part of this Schedule, an application for a reference number for the purposes of paragraph 1(2) is successful on a dormant basis if the decision on the application is that—

      (a)   the application would have been unconditionally successful but for the fact that paragraph 1(2) of Schedule 6 to FA 2014 ("individual protection 2014") applies in the case of the individual concerned, and

      (b)   a reference number for the purposes of paragraph 1(2) will be issued in response to the application but only when paragraph 1(2) of Schedule 6 to FA 2014 does not apply in the individual's case.

(8) For the purposes of this Part of this Schedule, an application for a reference number for the purposes of paragraph 9(2) is successful on a dormant basis if the decision on the application is that—

      (a)   the application would have been unconditionally successful but for the fact that a prior provision applies in the case of the individual concerned, and

      (b)   a reference number for the purposes of paragraph 9(2) will be issued in response to the application but only when no prior provision applies in the individual's case.

(9) For the purposes of sub-paragraph (8), the prior provisions are—

      (a)   paragraph 12 of Schedule 36 to FA 2004 (enhanced protection),

      (b)   paragraph 14 of Schedule 18 to FA 2011 (fixed protection 2012),

      (c)   paragraph 1 of Schedule 22 to FA 2013 (fixed protection 2014), and

      (d)   paragraph 1(2) of this Schedule (fixed protection 2016).

350

Finance Act 2016 (c. 24)
Schedule 4 — Pensions: lifetime allowance: transitional provision
Part 3 — Reference numbers etc

Withdrawal of reference numbers

15   (1)   This paragraph applies where a reference number for the purposes of paragraph 1(2) or 9(2) has been issued by or on behalf of the Commissioners in respect of an individual.

(2)   The number may be withdrawn by an officer of Revenue and Customs.

(3)   The number may be withdrawn only if —
      (a)   something contained in the application for the number was incorrect, or
      (b)   where the number was for the purposes of paragraph 1(2) —
            (i)   there has been a protection-cessation event (see paragraph 3) in the individual's case since the making of the application, or
            (ii)   paragraph 1(2) of Schedule 6 to FA 2014 has come to apply in the individual's case, or
      (c)   where the number was for the purposes of paragraph 9(2) —
            (i)   a provision listed in paragraph 9(5) has come to apply in the individual's case, or
            (ii)   paragraph 9(2) has ceased to apply in the individual's case as a result of the operation of paragraph 9(7), or
      (d)   the individual —
            (i)   has been given a notice under paragraph 1 of Schedule 36 to FA 2008 (information and inspection powers: taxpayer notice) in connection with (as the case may be) Part 1 or 2 of this Schedule, and
            (ii)   fails to comply with the notice within the period specified in the notice.

(4)   Where the number is withdrawn —
      (a)   notice of the withdrawal, and
      (b)   reasons for the withdrawal,
      are to be given by an officer of Revenue and Customs to the individual.

(5)   Where the number is withdrawn, the effect of the withdrawal is as follows —
      (a)   in the case of withdrawal in reliance on sub-paragraph (3)(a), the number is treated as never having been issued,
      (b)   in the case of withdrawal in reliance on paragraph (b) or (c) of sub-paragraph (3), the number is treated as having been withdrawn at the time of the event mentioned in sub-paragraph (i) or (ii) of that paragraph, and
      (c)   in the case of withdrawal in reliance on sub-paragraph (3)(d), the number is treated as having been withdrawn at the time specified in the notice of the withdrawal as the effective time of the withdrawal, which may be any time not earlier than the time of issue of the number.

Appeals against non-issue or withdrawal of reference numbers

16   (1)   Where —
      (a)   an application is made for a reference number for the purposes of paragraph 1(2) or 9(2) in respect of an individual, and

Finance Act 2016 (c. 24)
Schedule 4 — Pensions: lifetime allowance: transitional provision
Part 3 — Reference numbers etc

351

      (b)   the application is unsuccessful (see sub-paragraph (9)),
the individual may appeal against the decision on the application.

(2) Where a reference number issued in respect of an individual for the purposes of paragraph 1(2) or 9(2) is withdrawn, the individual may appeal against the withdrawal.

(3) Where a reference number issued in respect of an individual for the purposes of paragraph 1(2) or 9(2) is withdrawn in reliance on paragraph 15(3)(d), the individual may appeal against the time specified (in the notice of the withdrawal) as the effective time of the withdrawal.

(4) Where an appeal under sub-paragraph (1) is notified to the tribunal, the tribunal—
    (a)   must allow the appeal if satisfied—
        (i)   that the application was a valid application,
        (ii)   that everything in the application was correct, and
        (iii)   that, at the time of deciding the appeal, paragraph 15(3)(b), (c) or (d) does not authorise withdrawal of the requested number (assuming it had been issued), and
    (b)   must otherwise dismiss the appeal.

(5) Where an appeal under sub-paragraph (2) is notified to the tribunal, the tribunal—
    (a)   must allow the appeal if satisfied that the withdrawal was not authorised by paragraph 15(3), and
    (b)   must otherwise dismiss the appeal.

(6) Where an appeal under sub-paragraph (3) is notified to the tribunal, the tribunal must decide whether it was just and reasonable to specify the particular time specified and—
    (a)   if the tribunal decides that it was, the tribunal must dismiss the appeal, and
    (b)   otherwise—
        (i)   the tribunal must decide what time it would have been just and reasonable to specify, and
        (ii)   the withdrawal has effect as if the notice of the withdrawal had specified the time decided by the tribunal.

(7) Notice of an appeal under this paragraph must be given to Her Majesty's Revenue and Customs before the end of 30 days beginning with the date on which notice under paragraph 14(4) or 15(4) (as the case may be) is given.

(8) In this paragraph "the tribunal" means the First-tier Tribunal or, where determined by or under Tribunal Procedure Rules, the Upper Tribunal.

(9) The references in sub-paragraph (1) and paragraph 17(3)(b)(ii) to an application being unsuccessful do not include a case where an application for a reference number for the purposes of paragraph 1(2) or 9(2) is successful on a dormant basis (see paragraph 14(7) and (8)).

Notification of subsequent protection-cessation events

17   (1) Sub-paragraph (2) applies if, in the case of an individual, there is a protection-cessation event (see paragraphs 3 to 8) at a time when—

352

Finance Act 2016 (c. 24)
Schedule 4 — Pensions: lifetime allowance: transitional provision
Part 3 — Reference numbers etc

  (a) the individual has a reference number for the purposes of paragraph 1(2),

  (b) there is a pending application for a reference number for those purposes in respect of the individual, or

  (c) an appeal under paragraph 16(2) or (3) is in progress in connection with withdrawal of a reference number issued for those purposes in respect of the individual.

(2) The individual —

  (a) must notify the Commissioners of the event, and

  (b) must do so —

    (i) before the end of 90 days beginning with the day on which the individual could first reasonably be expected to have known that the event had occurred, and

    (ii) by means of a digital service provided for the purpose by or on behalf of the Commissioners, or by other means authorised in a particular case by an officer of Revenue and Customs.

(3) For the purposes of this paragraph —

  (a) an application is pending if —

    (i) it has been made,

    (ii) no reference number has been issued in response to the application, and

    (iii) the applicant has not been notified that the application has been unsuccessful;

  (b) an application is also pending if —

    (i) it has been made,

    (ii) it has been unsuccessful, and

    (iii) an appeal under paragraph 16(1) is in progress against the decision on the application;

  (c) an appeal under paragraph 16(1), (2) or (3) is in progress until one of the following happens —

    (i) it, or any further appeal, is withdrawn, or

    (ii) it and any further appeal brought have been determined, and there is no prospect of further appeal.

Notification of subsequent pension debits

18 (1) Sub-paragraph (2) applies if an individual receives a discharge notice related to a pension debit at a time when —

  (a) the individual has a reference number for the purposes of paragraph 9(2),

  (b) there is a pending application for a reference number for those purposes in respect of the individual, or

  (c) an appeal under paragraph 16(2) or (3) is in progress in connection with withdrawal of a reference number issued for those purposes in respect of the individual.

(2) The individual —

  (a) must notify the Commissioners of the appropriate amount and transfer day for the pension debit, and

Finance Act 2016 (c. 24)
Schedule 4 — Pensions: lifetime allowance: transitional provision
Part 3 — Reference numbers etc

353

  (b) must do so—

    (i) before the end of 60 days beginning with the date of the discharge notice related to the pension debit, and

    (ii) by means of a digital service provided for the purpose by or on behalf of the Commissioners, or by other means authorised in a particular case by an officer of Revenue and Customs.

 (3) For the purposes of this paragraph—

  (a) a notice is a discharge notice related to a pension debit if it is notice under regulation 8(2) or (3) of the Pensions on Divorce etc. (Provision of Information) Regulations 2000 (S.I. 2000/1048) relating to discharge of liability in respect of the pension credit corresponding to the pension debit;

  (b) an application is pending if—

    (i) it has been made,

    (ii) no reference number has been issued in response to the application,

    (iii) the applicant has not been notified that the application has been unsuccessful, and

    (iv) the applicant has not been notified that the application has been successful on a dormant basis (see paragraph 14(8));

  (c) an application is also pending if—

    (i) it has been made,

    (ii) it has been unsuccessful, and

    (iii) an appeal under paragraph 16(1) is in progress against the decision on the application;

  (d) an appeal under paragraph 16(1), (2) or (3) is in progress until one of the following happens—

    (i) it, or any further appeal, is withdrawn, or

    (ii) it and any further appeal brought have been determined, and there is no prospect of further appeal.

Personal representatives

19 If an individual dies—

  (a) anything which could have been done under or by virtue of this Part of this Schedule by the individual may be done by the individual's personal representatives,

  (b) paragraph 14(3)(d)(ii) has effect in relation to an application made in respect of the individual after the individual's death as if it also required a valid application to contain the individual's date of death, and

  (c) any notice or reasons given under paragraph 15(4) after the individual's death are to be given to the individual's personal representatives.

Penalties for non-supply, or fraudulent etc supply, of information under paragraph 17 or 18

20 In column 2 of the Table in section 98 of TMA 1970 (provisions about information where non-compliance etc attracts penalties), at the appropriate place insert—

354

Finance Act 2016 (c. 24)
Schedule 4 — Pensions: lifetime allowance: transitional provision
Part 3 — Reference numbers etc

"paragraph 17 or 18 of Schedule 4
to FA 2016;".

PART 4

INFORMATION

Preservation of records in connection with individual protection 2016

21   If an individual is issued with a reference number for the purposes of paragraph 9(2), the individual must preserve, for the period of 6 years beginning with the date the application for the reference number was made, all such records as were required for the purpose of enabling the individual's relevant amount (see paragraph 9), and amounts A, B, C and D for the individual (see paragraphs 10 to 13), to be correctly calculated.

Amendments of regulations

22   (1) The Registered Pension Schemes (Provision of Information) Regulations 2006 (S.I. 2006/567) are amended in accordance with paragraphs 23 to 26.

   (2) The amendments made by those paragraphs are to be treated as having been made by the Commissioners under such of the powers cited in the instrument containing the Regulations as are applicable.

23   In regulation 2(1) (interpretation)—
   (a)   after the entry for "fixed protection 2014" insert—
            ""fixed protection 2016" means protection under paragraph 1(2) of Schedule 4 to FA 2016;", and
   (b)   after the entry for "individual protection 2014" insert—
            ""individual protection 2016" means protection under paragraph 9(2) of Schedule 4 to FA 2016;".

24   (1) In the table in regulation 3(1) (provision of event reports by scheme administrators to HM Revenue and Customs), the entry for reportable event 6 (report where benefit crystallisation event occurs in relation to member of scheme) is amended as follows.

   (2) In column 1 of the entry, in paragraph (b)—
   (a)   omit the "or" at the end of sub-paragraph (iv), and
   (b)   after sub-paragraph (v) insert ", or
            (vi)   fixed protection 2016 or individual protection 2016."

   (3) In column 2 of the entry—
   (a)   in the words before paragraph (a), before "the Commissioners" insert "or on behalf of",
   (b)   omit the "or" at the end of paragraph (c), and
   (c)   after paragraph (d) insert ", or
            (e)   Schedule 4 to the Finance Act 2016 (where the member relies on fixed protection 2016 or individual protection 2016)."

    (4) In the heading of the entry, for the words after "Benefit crystallisation events and" substitute "non-standard lifetime allowances".

25   (1) Regulation 11 (information provided to scheme administrator by member intending to rely on transitional protection in connection with lifetime allowance) is amended as follows.

    (2) In paragraph (1) —

        (a)   omit the "or" at the end of sub-paragraph (b),

        (b)   after sub-paragraph (c) (but before the closing words of paragraph (1)) insert ", or

            (d)   fixed protection 2016 by virtue of Part 1 of Schedule 4 to the Finance Act 2016,", and

        (c)   in those closing words —

            (i)   before "the Commissioners" insert "or on behalf of", and

            (ii)   before "in respect of that entitlement" insert "or Schedule 4 to the Finance Act 2016".

    (3) After paragraph (2) insert —

       "(3)   If the member of a registered pension scheme intends to rely on individual protection 2016 by virtue of Part 2 of Schedule 4 to the Finance Act 2016, the member must notify the scheme administrator of —

        (a)   the reference number in respect of the member issued by or on behalf of the Commissioners for the purposes of paragraph 9(2) of that Schedule, and

        (b)   the member's relevant amount calculated in accordance with Part 2 of that Schedule."

    (4) In the heading —

        (a)   for the "or" substitute a comma, and

        (b)   at the end insert ", fixed protection 2016 or individual protection 2016".

26   After regulation 14B insert —

"14C Individual protection 2016: provision of information by scheme administrator to member on request

    (1)   Where —

        (a)   an individual is a member of a registered pension scheme on 5 April 2016,

        (b)   the individual makes a written request to the scheme administrator for the information mentioned in paragraph (2), and

        (c)   the request is received by the scheme administrator before 6 April 2020,

    the scheme administrator must provide the individual with the information within 3 months following receipt of the request.

    (2)   The information is such information relating to the member's rights under the scheme as is necessary for calculating, in accordance with Part 2 of Schedule 4 to the Finance Act 2016 (individual protection 2016), the member's relevant amount for the purposes of paragraph 9(2) of that Schedule."

27   In consequence of paragraph 24(4), in each of —

    (a)   the Registered Pension Schemes (Provision of Information) (Amendment) Regulations 2013 (S.I. 2013/1742), and

    (b)   the Registered Pension Schemes (Provision of Information) (Amendment) Regulations 2014 (S.I. 2014/1843),

omit regulation 4(2)(a).

PART 5

AMENDMENTS IN CONNECTION WITH PROTECTION OF PRE-6 APRIL 2006 RIGHTS

28   (1) In Part 1 of Schedule 29 to FA 2004 (pension schemes: interpretation of the lump sum rule), in paragraph 2 (permitted maximum amount of pension commencement lump sums, calculated in certain cases by deducting adjusted value of previously crystallised amounts from current standard lifetime allowance), in sub-paragraph (10) (modified adjustments where member has protection under paragraph 7 or 12 of Schedule 36 by reference to pre-6 April 2006 rights), after "have effect" insert " —

    (a)   where the member becomes entitled to the lump sum on or after 6 April 2014, as if PSLA in the case of any previous benefit crystallisation event which occurs on or after 6 April 2014 were £1,500,000 if that is greater than PSLA in that case, and

    (b)   ".

(2) In paragraph 28(3) of Schedule 36 to FA 2004 (transitional provision for pre-6 April 2006 rights: modified version of paragraph 2 of Schedule 29 that applies in certain cases), in the sub-paragraph (7) treated as substituted in paragraph 2 of Schedule 29 to FA 2004, in the definition of "PSLA", after "became entitled to the lump sum" insert "if that occurred before 6 April 2012 but, if that occurred on or after 6 April 2012, PSLA is the greater of £1,800,000 and the standard lifetime allowance at the time the individual became entitled to the lump sum".

(3) The amendment made by sub-paragraph (1) is treated as having come into force on 6 April 2014.

(4) The amendment made by sub-paragraph (2) is treated as having come into force on 6 April 2012.

PART 6

INTERPRETATION AND REGULATIONS

Interpretation of Parts 1, 2 and 3

29   (1) Expressions used in Part 1, 2 or 3 of this Schedule, and in Part 4 of FA 2004 (pension schemes), have the same meaning in that Part of this Schedule as in that Part of that Act.

(2) In particular, references to a relieved non-UK pension scheme or a relieved member of such a scheme are to be read in accordance with paragraphs 13(3) and (4) and 18 of Schedule 34 to FA 2004 (application of lifetime allowance charge provisions to members of overseas pension schemes).

*Finance Act 2016 (c. **24**)*
Schedule 4 — Pensions: lifetime allowance: transitional provision
Part 6 — Interpretation and regulations

357

Interpretation of Parts 3 and 4 and this Part

30   In Parts 3 and 4, and this Part, of this Schedule "the Commissioners" means the Commissioners for Her Majesty's Revenue and Customs.

Regulations

31   (1) The Commissioners may by regulations amend Part 1, 2 or 3 of this Schedule.

      (2) Regulations under this paragraph may (for example) —

          (a) add to the cases in which paragraph 1(2) is to apply or is to cease to apply;

          (b) add to the cases in which paragraph 9(2) is to apply.

      (3) Regulations under this paragraph may include provision having effect in relation to a time before the regulations are made, but—

          (a) the time must not be earlier than 6 April 2016, and

          (b) the provision must not increase any person's liability to tax.

      (4) Regulations under this paragraph may include —

          (a) supplementary or incidental provision;

          (b) consequential amendments of the Table in section 98 of TMA 1970 (information requirements: penalties).

      (5) Power to make regulations under this paragraph is exercisable by statutory instrument.

      (6) A statutory instrument containing regulations under this paragraph is subject to annulment in pursuance of a resolution of the House of Commons.

SCHEDULE 5

Section 22

PENSION FLEXIBILITY

Serious ill-health lump sums

1   (1) Part 4 of FA 2004 (registered pension schemes etc) is amended as follows.

      (2) Omit section 205A (serious ill-health lump sum charge on payment to member who has reached 75).

      (3) In Part 1 of Schedule 29 (interpretation of lump sum rule), paragraph 4 (serious ill-health lump sums) is amended in accordance with sub-paragraphs (4) and (5).

      (4) In sub-paragraph (1) (meaning of "serious ill-heath lump sum") —

          (a) at the end of paragraph (b) insert "and", and

          (b) for paragraphs (c) and (d) substitute —

                "(ca) either—

                        (i) it is paid in respect of an uncrystallised arrangement, and it extinguishes the member's entitlement to benefits under the arrangement, or

           (ii)   it is paid in respect of uncrystallised rights of the member under an arrangement other than an uncrystallised arrangement, and it extinguishes the member's uncrystallised rights under the arrangement."

    (5) After sub-paragraph (2) insert—

       "(2A) In subsection (1)(ca)(ii) "uncrystallised rights", in relation to the member, means rights of the member that are uncrystallised rights as defined by section 212(1) and (2)."

2   (1) Section 636A of ITEPA 2003 (exemption for certain lump sums under registered pension schemes) is amended as follows.

    (2) In the heading, for "Exemption" substitute "Exemptions and liabilities".

    (3) For subsection (3A) (serious ill-health lump sum paid to member who has reached 75 is taxed only under section 205A of FA 2004) substitute—

       "(3A) Section 579A applies in relation to a serious ill-health lump sum which is paid under a registered pension scheme to a member who has reached the age of 75 as it applies to any pension under a registered pension scheme."

3   (1) In consequence of the amendment made by paragraph 1(2), in Part 4 of FA 2004—

       (a)   in section 164(2)(b) omit ", the serious ill-health lump sum charge",

       (b)   omit section 272A(7)(a)(ii),

       (c)   in section 280(2) omit the entry for "serious ill-health lump sum charge", and

       (d)   in Schedule 34—

           (i)   omit paragraph 1(3)(ca), and

          (ii)   in paragraph 5 omit ", serious ill-health lump sum charge".

    (2) In consequence of the amendment made by paragraph 1(2), in section 30(1) of ITA 2007 omit the entry for section 205A of FA 2004.

    (3) In consequence of the amendments made by paragraphs 1 and 2 and sub-paragraphs (1) and (2)—

       (a)   in Schedule 16 to FA 2011, omit paragraphs 28(2)(a), 40, 42(3), 63, 77(4), 81(2) and (4)(b) and 83, and

       (b)   omit section 2(4) of the Taxation of Pensions Act 2014.

4   The amendments made by paragraphs 1 to 3 have effect in relation to lump sums paid after the day on which this Act is passed.

Charity lump sum death benefits

5   (1) In paragraph 18(1A) of Schedule 29 to FA 2004 (when lump sum paid out of uncrystallised funds is charity lump sum death benefit), omit paragraph (a) (member must have died after reaching 75).

    (2) The amendment made by sub-paragraph (1) has effect in relation to lump sums paid after the day on which this Act is passed.

Dependants' flexi-access drawdown funds

6   (1) Part 2 of Schedule 28 to FA 2004 (interpretation of pension death benefit rules) is amended as follows.

   (2) In paragraph 15 (meaning of "dependant"), after sub-paragraph (2) insert—

   "(2A) A child of the member is a dependant of the member if the child —
       (a)   has reached the age of 23, and
       (b)   is not within sub-paragraph (2)(b).

   (2B) But this paragraph, so far as it has effect for the purpose of determining the meaning of "dependant"—
       (a)   in paragraphs 16 to 17 and 27A, and
       (b)   in paragraph 18 of Schedule 29,
   has effect with the omission of sub-paragraph (2A)."

   (3) In paragraph 22 (meaning of "dependant's drawdown pension fund")—
       (a)   in sub-paragraph (2)(a) and (aa) omit "to the dependant", and
       (b)   in sub-paragraph (3), after "representing a" insert "person's".

   (4) The amendments made by this paragraph come into force on the day after the day on which this Act is passed.

   (5) The sub-paragraphs inserted by sub-paragraph (2)—
       (a)   apply for the purpose of determining whether a payment of an annuity is a payment of a dependants' short-term annuity only if the annuity is purchased after the day on which this Act is passed, and
       (b)   apply for the purpose of determining whether a payment to a person is a payment of dependants' income withdrawal if, but only if, the person reaches the age of 23 after the day on which this Act is passed.

   (6) In sub-paragraph (5) "dependants' short-term annuity" and "dependants' income withdrawal" have the same meaning as in Part 4 of FA 2004.

Trivial commutation lump sum

7   (1) Paragraph 7 of Schedule 29 to FA 2004 (interpretation of lump sum rule: meaning of "trivial commutation lump sum") is amended as follows.

   (2) In sub-paragraph (1)(aa) (sum must be paid in respect of a defined benefits arrangement), after "arrangement," insert "or in respect of a scheme pension payable by the scheme administrator to which the member has become entitled under a money purchase arrangement (an "in-payment money-purchase in-house scheme pension"), or partly in respect of the former and partly in respect of the latter,".

   (3) In sub-paragraph (1)(d) (sum must extinguish member's entitlement to defined benefits under the scheme), after "defined benefits" insert ", and any entitlement to payments of in-payment money-purchase in-house scheme pensions,".

8   (1) Section 636B of ITEPA 2003 (taxation of trivial commutation, and winding-up, lump sums) is amended as follows.

   (2) In subsection (3) (taxation of lump sum where member has uncrystallised rights under the pension scheme)—

      (a)   in the words before paragraph (a) omit "(within the meaning of section 212 of FA 2004)", and

      (b)   in paragraph (b), for "the uncrystallised rights calculated in accordance with that section" substitute "any uncrystallised rights extinguished by the lump sum".

   (3) After subsection (4) insert—

      "(5) In this section "uncrystallised rights" has the same meaning as in section 212 of FA 2004; and the value for the purposes of this section of any uncrystallised rights is to be calculated in accordance with that section."

9   The amendments made by paragraphs 7 and 8 have effect in relation to lump sums paid after the day on which this Act is passed.

Top-up of dependants' death benefits

10 (1) In paragraph 15 of Schedule 29 to FA 2004 (uncrystallised funds lump sum death benefits), after sub-paragraph (2) insert—

     "(2A) Where—

      (a)   the arrangement is a cash balance arrangement,

      (b)   under the arrangement, a dependant of the member is entitled to be paid after the member's death an amount by way of a lump sum,

      (c)   the dependant's entitlement to a lump sum of that amount under the arrangement comes into being at a time no later than the member's death,

      (d)   such of the sums and assets held for the purposes of the arrangement immediately after the member's death as are held for the purpose of meeting the liability to pay the lump sum are insufficient for that purpose (including where that is because none are held for that purpose), and

      (e)   a person who was an employer in relation to the member pays a contribution to the scheme—

          (i)   for or towards making good that insufficiency, and

         (ii)   of no more than is needed for making good the insufficiency,

the sums and assets held for the purposes of the arrangement that represent the contribution are to be treated as "relevant uncrystallised funds" for the purposes of this paragraph."

   (2) The amendment made by sub-paragraph (1) has effect in relation to contributions paid after the day on which this Act is passed.

Inheritance tax as respects cash alternatives to annuities for dependants etc

11 (1) In section 152 of the Inheritance Tax Act 1984 (where annuity payable on person' death to dependant etc, person treated as not beneficially entitled to sum that could have been paid to personal representatives instead of being used for annuity), for "or dependant" substitute ", dependant or nominee".

   (2) The amendment made by sub-paragraph (1)—

      (a)   is to be treated as having come into force on 6 April 2015, and

(b)   has effect where the person on whose death an annuity is payable dies on or after that date.

SCHEDULE 6   Section 39

DEDUCTION OF INCOME TAX AT SOURCE

PART 1

ABOLITION OF DUTY TO DEDUCT TAX FROM INTEREST ON CERTAIN INVESTMENTS

1   In Chapter 2 of Part 15 of ITA 2007 (deduction of income tax at source by deposit-takers and building societies) omit—

    (a)   section 851 (duty to deduct when making payment of interest on relevant investment), and

    (b)   the italic heading preceding it.

PART 2

DEDUCTION OF TAX FROM YEARLY INTEREST: EXCEPTION FOR DEPOSIT-TAKERS

2   In section 876 of ITA 2007 (interest paid by deposit-takers), for subsections (1) and (2) substitute—

    "(1)   The duty to deduct a sum representing income tax under section 874 does not apply to a payment of interest on an investment if—

        (a)   the payment is made by a deposit-taker, and

        (b)   when the payment is made, the investment is a relevant investment.

    (1A)   In this section "deposit-taker", "investment" and "relevant investment" have the meaning given by Chapter 2."

PART 3

AMENDMENTS OF OR RELATING TO CHAPTER 2 OF PART 15 OF ITA 2007

Amendments of Chapter 2 of Part 15 of ITA 2007

3   Chapter 2 of Part 15 of ITA 2007 (deduction of income tax at source by deposit-takers and building societies) is amended in accordance with paragraphs 4 to 18.

4   For the Chapter heading substitute "Meaning of "relevant investment" for purposes of section 876".

5   (1) Section 850 (overview of Chapter) is amended as follows.

    (2)   For subsection (1) substitute—

    "(1)   This Chapter has effect for the purposes of section 876 (duty under section 874 to deduct tax from payments of yearly interest: exception for deposit-takers)."

    (3)   Omit subsection (2) (which introduces sections 851 and 852).

362

Finance Act 2016 (c. 24)
Schedule 6 — Deduction of income tax at source
Part 3 — Amendments of or relating to Chapter 2 of Part 15 of ITA 2007

      (4) In subsection (4)(b) (which introduces sections 858 to 870), for "858" substitute "863".

      (5) In subsection (5) (which introduces sections 871 to 873), for "871 to" substitute "872 and".

      (6) In subsection (6) (interpretation), for the words from "Chapter—" to "crediting" substitute "Chapter, crediting".

6   Omit section 852 (power to disapply section 851).

7   In section 853(1) (meaning of "deposit-taker"), after "In this Chapter" insert "and section 876".

8   In section 854(3) (meaning of "relevant investment" in section 851(1)(b)), for "851(1)(b)" substitute "876(1)(b)".

9   For section 855(1) (meaning of "investment") substitute—

      "(1) In this Chapter, and section 876, "investment" means a deposit with a deposit-taker."

10 (1) Section 856 (meaning of "relevant investment") is amended as follows.

      (2) In subsection (1), for "this Chapter" substitute "section 876".

      (3) In subsection (2) (exceptions), for "858" substitute "863".

11   In section 857 (treating investments as being or not being relevant investments) omit "or building society" in each place.

12   Omit—
      (a) sections 858 to 861 (investments which are not relevant investments and in relation to which duty under section 874 does not apply), and
      (b) the italic heading preceding section 858.

13   In the italic heading preceding section 863, for "Other investments" substitute "Investments".

14   In sections 863, 864, 865 and 868(4) (investments with deposit-takers or building societies) omit "or building society" in each place.

15   Omit sections 868(3), 869 and 870(2) (investments with building societies).

16   Omit section 871 (power to make regulations to give effect to Chapter).

17   In section 872 (power to amend Chapter)—
      (a) in subsection (2) (different provision for different deposit-takers)—
         (i) for "which amends this Chapter in its application to deposit-takers may do so" substitute "may amend this Chapter", and
         (ii) in each of paragraphs (a) and (b), for "relation" substitute "its application", and
      (b) omit subsections (4) and (5) (which refer to provisions repealed by this Act).

18   Omit section 873(3) to (6) (interpretation of section 861).

Finance Act 2016 (c. 24)
Schedule 6 — Deduction of income tax at source
Part 3 — Amendments of or relating to Chapter 2 of Part 15 of ITA 2007

363

Amendments relating to Chapter 2 of Part 15 of ITA 2007

19   In Schedule 12 to FA 1988 (transfer of building society's business to a company), in paragraph 6(1) (treatment for tax purposes of benefits conferred in connection with a transfer) omit—

      (a)   "either", and

      (b)   paragraph (b) (benefit not to be subject to deduction of tax under Chapter 2 of Part 15 of ITA 2007), and the "or" preceding it.

20   (1) In section 564Q(1) of ITA 2007 (alternative finance return: deduction of income tax at source under Chapter 2 of Part 15)—

      (a)   after "Chapter 2 of Part 15" insert "and section 876",

      (b)   for "deduction by deposit-takers and building societies" substitute "exception for deposit-takers", and

      (c)   after "Chapter 2 of that Part" insert "and section 876".

    (2) In section 564Q(5) of ITA 2007 (alternative finance return: deduction of income tax at source under Chapters 3 to 5 of Part 15)—

      (a)   after "of Part 15" insert "except section 876", and

      (b)   for "those Chapters" substitute "those provisions".

21   In section 847 of ITA 2007 (overview of Part 15)—

      (a)   in subsection (2) omit paragraph (a) (which introduces Chapter 2), and

      (b)   in subsection (5) (which introduces Chapters containing provision connected with the duties to deduct), before paragraph (a) insert—

            "(za)   Chapter 2 (interpretation of section 876 in Chapter 3: exception for deposit-takers),".

22   In section 946 of ITA 2007 (collection of tax deducted at source: payments to which Chapter applies) omit paragraph (a) (payments from which deductions required to be made under section 851).

23   In Schedule 2 to ITA 2007 omit paragraphs 154 to 156 (transitional provisions related to Chapter 2 of Part 15 of ITA 2007).

24   In Schedule 4 to ITA 2007 (index of defined expressions)—

      (a)   omit the entry for "beneficiary under a discretionary or accumulation settlement (in Chapter 2 of Part 15)",

      (b)   in the entry for "deposit-taker (in Chapter 2 of Part 15)", after "Part 15" insert "and section 876",

      (c)   omit the entry for "dividend (in Chapter 2 of Part 15)",

      (d)   in the entry for "investment (in Chapter 2 of Part 15)", after "Part 15" insert "and section 876", and

      (e)   omit the entry for "relevant investment (in Chapter 2 of Part 15)".

25   In consequence of the amendments made by Part 1 of this Schedule and the preceding provisions of this Part of this Schedule—

      (a)   in Schedule 1 to ITA 2007 omit paragraph 277,

      (b)   in Schedule 1 to FA 2008 omit paragraph 25,

      (c)   in Schedule 46 to FA 2013—

            (i)   in paragraph 68(1) omit paragraph (a) including the "and" at the end,

364

Finance Act 2016 (c. 24)
Schedule 6 — Deduction of income tax at source
Part 3 — Amendments of or relating to Chapter 2 of Part 15 of ITA 2007

      (ii)   in paragraph 69(1) omit paragraph (a) including the "and" at the end,

      (iii)   omit paragraph 70(1), and

      (iv)   in paragraph 71(3) omit paragraph (b) and the "and" preceding it, and

  (d)   in FA 2014 omit section 3(4).

PART 4

DEDUCTION OF TAX FROM UK PUBLIC REVENUE DIVIDENDS

26   In section 877 of ITA 2007 (duty to deduct under section 874: exception relating to UK public revenue dividends)—

  (a)   for "in respect of" substitute "that is", and

  (b)   after "dividend" insert "(as defined by section 891)".

27 (1) Chapter 5 of Part 15 of ITA 2007 (deduction from payments of UK public revenue dividends) is amended as follows.

  (2) In section 893(2) (securities which are gross-paying government securities)—

    (a)   before the "or" at the end of paragraph (a) insert—

       "(aa) securities, so far as they are not gilt-edged securities, issued or treated as issued under—

          (i)   the National Loans Act 1939, or

          (ii) the National Loans Act 1968,", and

    (b)   in paragraph (b), for "894(1) or (3)" substitute "894(3)".

  (3) In section 894 (power to direct that securities are gross-paying government securities)—

    (a)   omit subsections (1) and (2) (power in relation to securities within the new section 893(2)(aa)), and

    (b)   in subsection (5) omit "(1) or".

PART 5

COMMENCEMENT

28 (1) The amendments made by Parts 1 and 3 of this Schedule have effect in relation to—

    (a)   interest paid or credited on or after 6 April 2016, and

    (b)   dividends or other distributions paid by a building society on or after that date.

  (2) Sub-paragraph (1) does not apply to—

    (a)   the repeals in Schedule 12 to FA 1988;

    (b)   the amendments in section 564Q of ITA 2007;

    (c)   the repeal of paragraph 277 of Schedule 1 to ITA 2007.

  (3) The repeals mentioned in sub-paragraph (2)(a) and (c) have effect in relation to benefits conferred on or after 6 April 2016.

  (4) The amendments mentioned in sub-paragraph (2)(b) have effect in relation to alternative finance return paid on or after 6 April 2016.

(5) The amendments made by Part 2 of this Schedule, and the amendments made by this Schedule in sections 893 and 894 of ITA 2007, have effect in relation to interest paid on or after 6 April 2016.

SCHEDULE 7

Section 49

LOAN RELATIONSHIPS AND DERIVATIVE CONTRACTS

Introductory

1   CTA 2009 is amended as follows.

Non-market loans

2   In Chapter 15 of Part 5 (loan relationships: tax avoidance), after section 446 insert—

"*Non-market loans*

446A Non-market loans

(1)   This section applies as respects any accounting period if—
    (a)   a company has a debtor relationship in the period,
    (b)   the amount recognised in the company's accounts in respect of the debt at the time the company became party to the debtor relationship was less than the transaction price,
    (c)   credits in respect of the whole or part of the discount were not brought into account for the purposes of this Part, and
    (d)   in a case where the creditor is a company, the non-qualifying territory condition is met.

(2)   The debits which are to be brought into account for the accounting period for the purposes of this Part by the debtor company in respect of the loan relationship are not to include debits relating to the relevant discount amount, to the extent that that amount is referable to the accounting period.

(3)   In this section "relevant discount amount" means—
    (a)   in a case where credits in respect of the whole of the discount were not brought into account for the purposes of this Part, an amount equal to the whole discount, and
    (b)   in a case where credits in respect of part of the discount were not brought into account for the purposes of this Part, an amount equal to that part of the discount.

(4)   The non-qualifying territory condition referred to in subsection (1)(d) is that the creditor company is—
    (a)   resident for tax purposes in a non-qualifying territory at any time in the accounting period, or
    (b)   effectively managed in a non-taxing non-qualifying territory at any such time.

(5)   In this section—

"discount" means the difference between the two amounts referred to in subsection (1)(b);

"non-qualifying territory" has the meaning given in section 173 of TIOPA 2010;

"non-taxing non-qualifying territory" means a non-qualifying territory under whose law companies are not liable to tax by reason of domicile, residence or place of management;

"resident for tax purposes" means liable, under the law of the non-qualifying territory, to tax there by reason of domicile, residence or place of management."

Transfer pricing

3   In section 446 (loan relationships: bringing transfer-pricing adjustments into account), after subsection (7) insert—

"(8)   No credit is to be brought into account for the purposes of this Part to the extent that it corresponds to an amount which, as a result of the preceding provisions of this section, has not previously been brought into account as a debit."

4   In section 693 (derivative contracts: bringing transfer-pricing adjustments into account), after subsection (5) insert—

"(6)   No credit is to be brought into account for the purposes of this Part to the extent that it corresponds to an amount which, as a result of the preceding provisions of this section, has not previously been brought into account as a debit."

Exchange gains and losses

5   In section 447 (exchange gains and losses on debtor relationships: loans disregarded under Part 4 of TIOPA 2010), after subsection (4) insert—

"(4A)   If the debtor relationship is to any extent matched, subsections (2) and (3) apply to leave out of account only the lesser of—
        (a)   the amount of the exchange gain or loss (in the case of subsection (2)) or the proportion of the exchange gain or loss (in the case of subsection (3)) which would be left out of account apart from this subsection, and
        (b)   the amount of the exchange gain or loss arising in respect of a liability representing the debtor relationship to the extent that the debtor relationship is unmatched (an amount which may be nil)."

6   In section 448 (exchange gains and losses on debtor relationships: equity notes where holder associated with issuer), after subsection (2) insert—

"(3)   If the debtor relationship is to any extent matched, subsection (2) applies to leave out of account only the amount of the exchange gain or loss arising in respect of a liability representing the debtor relationship to the extent that the debtor relationship is unmatched (an amount which may be nil)."

7   In section 449 (exchange gains and losses on creditor relationships: no

corresponding debtor relationship), after subsection (4) insert—

"(4A) If the creditor relationship is to any extent matched, subsection (2) applies to leave out of account only the amount of the exchange gain or loss arising in respect of an asset representing the creditor relationship to the extent that the creditor relationship is unmatched (an amount which may be nil)."

8   In section 451 (exception to section 449 where loan exceeds arm's length amount), after subsection (4) insert—

"(4A) If the creditor relationship is to any extent matched, subsections (3) and (4) apply to leave out of account only the lesser of—

(a)   the proportion of the exchange gain or loss which would be left out of account apart from this subsection, and

(b)   the amount of the exchange gain or loss arising in respect of an asset representing the creditor relationship to the extent that the creditor relationship is unmatched (an amount which may be nil)."

9   (1) Section 452 (exchange gains and losses where loan not on arm's length terms) is amended as follows.

(2) For subsection (3) substitute—

"(3)   Subsections (4) and (5) apply if, because of a claim made under section 192(1) of TIOPA 2010, or because of the claim that is assumed to be made under subsection (2)—

(a)   one company is treated for any purpose as having a debtor relationship, or

(b)   more than one company is treated for any purpose as having a debtor relationship represented by the same liability."

(3) In subsection (4)—

(a)   after "exchange gains" insert "from that debtor relationship (in a subsection (3)(a) case) or";

(b)   after "those debtor relationships" insert "(in a subsection (3)(b) case)";

(c)   for the words from "debits" to the end substitute "exchange gains or the proportion of the exchange gains to be left out of account under section 447 by the issuing company in respect of the loan relationship".

(4) In subsection (5)—

(a)   after "exchange losses" insert "from that debtor relationship (in a subsection (3)(a) case) or";

(b)   after "those debtor relationships" insert "(in a subsection (3)(b) case)";

(c)   for the words from "credits" to the end substitute "exchange losses or the proportion of the exchange losses to be left out of account under section 447 by the issuing company in respect of the loan relationship".

(5) After subsection (5) insert—

"(5A) In this section "issuing company" is to be construed in accordance with section 191(1)(a) of TIOPA 2010."

10   After section 475A insert—

"Meaning of "matched"

475B Meaning of "matched"

    (1)   This section applies for the purposes of this Part.

    (2)   A loan relationship of a company is matched if and to the extent that—

        (a)   it is in a matching relationship with another loan relationship or a derivative contract of the company, or

        (b)   exchange gains or losses arising in relation to an asset or liability representing the loan relationship are excluded from being brought into account under regulations under section 328(4),

    and "unmatched" is to be construed accordingly.

    (3)   A loan relationship is in a matching relationship with another loan relationship or derivative contract if one is intended by the company to act to eliminate or substantially reduce the economic risk of the other.

    (4)   In this section "economic risk" means a risk which can be attributed to fluctuations in exchange rates between currencies over a period of time.

    (5)   In this section "derivative contract" has the same meaning as in Part 7 (see section 576)."

11   (1)   Section 694 (derivative contracts: exchange gains and losses) is amended as follows.

    (2)   After subsection (3) insert—

    "(3A)   If the contract is to any extent matched, subsection (3) applies to leave out of account only the amount of the exchange gains or losses arising to the company in relation to the contract to the extent that the contract is unmatched (an amount which may be nil)."

    (3)   After subsection (7) insert—

    "(7A)   Subsections (5) to (7) apply only to the extent that the contract is unmatched."

    (4)   After subsection (10) insert—

    "(11)   For the purposes of this section a derivative contract of a company is matched if and to the extent that—

        (a)   it is in a matching relationship with another derivative contract or loan relationship of the company, or

        (b)   exchange gains or losses arising in relation to the derivative contract are excluded from being brought into account under regulations under section 606(4)(b),

    and "unmatched" is to be construed accordingly.

    (12)   A derivative contract is in a matching relationship with another derivative contract or loan relationship if one is intended by the

company to act to eliminate or substantially reduce the economic risk of the other.

(13) In this section "economic risk" means a risk which can be attributed to fluctuations in exchange rates between currencies over a period of time.

(14) In this section "loan relationship" has the same meaning as in Part 5 (see section 302)."

Commencement

12 (1) The amendments made by this Schedule have effect in relation to accounting periods beginning on or after 1 April 2016.

(2) For the purposes of sub-paragraph (1), where the accounting period of a company begins before 1 April 2016 and ends on or after that date (the "straddling period"), so much of the straddling period as falls before that date, and so much of the straddling period as falls on or after that date, are to be treated as separate accounting periods.

SCHEDULE 8

Section 54

TAX RELIEF FOR PRODUCTION OF ORCHESTRAL CONCERTS

PART 1

AMENDMENT OF CTA 2009

1 After Part 15C of CTA 2009 insert—

"PART 15D

ORCHESTRA TAX RELIEF

CHAPTER 1

INTRODUCTION

Overview

1217P Overview

(1) This Part is about the production of orchestral concerts, and applies for corporation tax purposes.

(2) This Chapter explains what is meant by "orchestral concert" and how a company comes to be treated as the production company in relation to a concert.

(3) Chapter 2 is about the taxation of the activities of a production company and includes—

(a) provision for the company's activities in relation to its concert, or its concert series, to be treated as a separate trade, and

370

Finance Act 2016 (c. 24)
Schedule 8 — Tax relief for production of orchestral concerts
Part 1 — Amendment of CTA 2009

      (b)   provision about the calculation of the profits and losses of that trade.

  (4) Chapter 3 is about relief (called "orchestra tax relief") which may be given to a production company in relation to its concert or concert series —

      (a)   by way of additional deductions to be made in calculating the profits or losses of the company's separate trade, or

      (b)   by way of a payment (an "orchestra tax credit") to be made on the company's surrender of losses from that trade,

and describes the conditions a company must meet to qualify for orchestra tax relief.

  (5) Chapter 4 contains provision about the use of losses of the separate trade (including provision about relief for terminal losses).

  (6) Chapter 5 provides —

      (a)   for relief under Chapters 3 and 4 to be given on a provisional basis, and

      (b)   for such relief to be withdrawn if it turns out that conditions that must be met for such relief to be given are not actually met.

Interpretation

1217PA "Orchestral concert"

  (1) In this Part "orchestral concert" means a concert by an orchestra, ensemble, group or band consisting wholly or mainly of instrumentalists who are the primary focus of the concert.

  (2) But a concert is not an orchestral concert if —

      (a)   the main purpose, or one of the main purposes, of the concert is to advertise or promote any goods or services,

      (b)   the concert is to consist of or include a competition or contest, or

      (c)   the making of a relevant recording is the main object of the production company's activities in relation to the concert.

  (3) A recording of a concert is a "relevant recording" if the recording is made for the purpose of using it (or an edited version of it) in any of the following ways —

      (a)   broadcast, at the time of the concert or later, to the general public;

      (b)   release, at the time of the concert or later, to the paying public (by digital or other means);

      (c)   use as a soundtrack (or part of a soundtrack) to a television, radio, theatre, video game or similar production for broadcast, exhibition or release to the general public;

      (d)   use in a film (or part of a film) for exhibition to the paying public at the commercial cinema.

  (4) In this section —

      "broadcast" means broadcast by any means (including television, radio or the internet);

Finance Act 2016 (c. 24)
Schedule 8 — Tax relief for production of orchestral concerts
Part 1 — Amendment of CTA 2009

371

"film" has the same meaning as in Part 15 (see section 1181).

1217PB Production company

(1) A company is the production company in relation to a concert if the company (acting otherwise than in partnership) —

    (a) is responsible for putting on the concert from the start of the production process to the finish, including employing or engaging the performers,

    (b) is actively engaged in decision-making in relation to the concert,

    (c) makes an effective creative, technical and artistic contribution to the concert, and

    (d) directly negotiates for, contracts for and pays for rights, goods and services in relation to the concert.

(2) No more than one company can be the production company in relation to a concert.

(3) If more than one company meets the conditions in subsection (1) in relation to a concert, the company that is most directly engaged in the activities mentioned in that subsection is the production company.

(4) If no company meets the conditions in subsection (1), there is no production company in relation to the concert.

CHAPTER 2

TAXATION OF ACTIVITIES OF PRODUCTION COMPANY

Separate orchestral trade

1217Q Separate orchestral trade

(1) Subsection (2) applies to a company in relation to a concert if —

    (a) the company qualifies for orchestra tax relief in relation to the production of the concert (see section 1217RA(2)), and

    (b) the concert is not included in a concert series in relation to which the company has made an election under subsection (4).

(2) The company's activities in relation to the production of the concert are treated as a trade separate from any other activities of the company (including activities in relation to the production of any other concert).

(3) Subsections (4) and (5) apply to a company in relation to concerts in a series if the conditions in section 1217RA(4)(a), (b), (c) and (d) are met in relation to the company and the concert series.

(4) The company may, for the purposes of this Part, make an election in relation to the concert series.
See section 1217QA for provision about making an election.

(5) Where the company makes an election in relation to a concert series (and accordingly qualifies for orchestra tax relief in relation to the

372

Finance Act 2016 (c. 24)
Schedule 8 — Tax relief for production of orchestral concerts
Part 1 — Amendment of CTA 2009

production of the series), the company's activities in relation to the production of the concert series are treated as a trade separate from any other activities of the company (including activities in relation to the production of any other concert).

(6) In this Part the separate trade mentioned in subsection (2) or (5) is called the "separate orchestral trade".

(7) If the separate orchestral trade relates to a single concert, the company is treated as beginning to carry on that trade—

    (a) at the beginning of the pre-performance stage of the concert, or

    (b) if earlier, at the time of the first receipt by the company of any income from the production of the concert.

1217QA Election for concert series

(1) An election under section 1217Q(4) must be made by the company by notice in writing to an officer of Her Majesty's Revenue and Customs before the date of the first concert in the series.

(2) An election has effect in relation to the orchestral concerts specified in it, and must also specify which of those concerts (if any) are not to be qualifying orchestral concerts (see section 1217RA(3)).

(3) An election—

    (a) may have effect in relation to concerts in two or more accounting periods, and

    (b) is irrevocable.

(4) If the separate orchestral trade relates to a concert series, the company is treated as beginning to carry on that trade—

    (a) at the beginning of the pre-performance stage of the first concert in the series, or

    (b) if earlier, at the time of the first receipt by the company of any income from the production of the concert series.

Profits and losses of separate orchestral trade

1217QB Calculation of profits or losses of separate orchestral trade

(1) This section applies for the purpose of calculating the profits or losses of the separate orchestral trade.

(2) For the first period of account during which the separate orchestral trade is carried on, the following are brought into account—

    (a) as a debit, the costs of the production of the concert or concert series incurred to date;

    (b) as a credit, the proportion of the estimated total income from that production treated as earned at the end of that period.

(3) For subsequent periods of account the following are brought into account—

    (a) as a debit, the difference between the amount ("C") of the costs of the production of the concert or concert series incurred to date and the amount corresponding to C for the previous period, and

      (b)   as a credit, the difference between the proportion ("PI") of the estimated total income from that production treated as earned at the end of that period and the amount corresponding to PI for the previous period.

(4)   The proportion of the estimated total income treated as earned at the end of a period of account is—

$$\frac{C}{T} \times I$$

where—

    C is the total to date of costs incurred;

    T is the estimated total cost of the production of the concert or concert series;

    I is the estimated total income from the production of the concert or concert series.

1217QC Income from the production

(1)   References in this Chapter to income from a production of a concert or concert series are to any receipts by the company in connection with the production or exploitation of the concert or concert series.

(2)   This includes—

      (a)   receipts from the sale of tickets or of rights in the concert or concert series;

      (b)   royalties or other payments for use of the concert or concert series;

      (c)   payments for rights to produce merchandise;

      (d)   receipts by the company by way of a profit share agreement.

(3)   Receipts that (apart from this subsection) would be regarded as being of a capital nature are treated as being of a revenue nature.

1217QD Costs of the production

(1)   References in this Chapter to the costs of a production of a concert or concert series are to expenditure incurred by the company on—

      (a)   activities involved in developing and putting on the concert or concert series, or

      (b)   activities with a view to exploiting the concert or concert series.

(2)   This is subject to any provision of the Corporation Tax Acts prohibiting the making of a deduction, or restricting the extent to which a deduction is allowed, in calculating the profits of a trade.

(3)   Expenditure which, apart from this subsection, would be regarded as being of a capital nature only because it is incurred on the creation of an asset (the concert or concert series) is treated as being of a revenue nature.

1217QE When costs are taken to be incurred

(1)   For the purposes of this Chapter, the costs that have been incurred on a production of a concert or concert series at a given time do not

374

Finance Act 2016 (c. 24)
Schedule 8 — Tax relief for production of orchestral concerts
Part 1 — Amendment of CTA 2009

include any amount that has not been paid unless it is the subject of an unconditional obligation to pay.

(2) Where an obligation to pay an amount is linked to income being earned from the production of the concert or concert series, the obligation is not treated as having become unconditional unless an appropriate amount of income is or has been brought into account under section 1217QB.

1217QF Pre-trading expenditure

(1) This section applies if, before the company begins to carry on the separate orchestral trade, it incurs expenditure on activities falling within section 1217QD(1)(a).

(2) The expenditure may be treated as expenditure of the separate orchestral trade and as if incurred immediately after the company begins to carry on that trade.

(3) If expenditure so treated has previously been taken into account for other tax purposes, the company must amend any relevant company tax return accordingly.

(4) Any amendment or assessment necessary to give effect to subsection (3) may be made despite any limitation on the time within which an amendment or assessment may normally be made.

1217QG Estimates

Estimates for the purposes of section 1217QB must be made as at the balance sheet date for each period of account, on a just and reasonable basis taking into consideration all relevant circumstances.

CHAPTER 3

ORCHESTRA TAX RELIEF

Introduction

1217R Overview of orchestra tax relief

(1) Relief under this Chapter ("orchestra tax relief") is given by way of —
    (a) additional deductions (see sections 1217RD to 1217RF), and
    (b) orchestra tax credits (see sections 1217RG to 1217RJ).

(2) See Schedule 18 to FA 1998 (in particular, Part 9D) for provision about the procedure for making claims for orchestra tax relief.

Companies qualifying for orchestra tax relief

1217RA Companies qualifying for orchestra tax relief

(1) Subsection (2) applies in the case of an orchestral concert which is not included in a concert series in relation to which an election has been made under section 1217Q(4).

(2) A company qualifies for orchestra tax relief in relation to the production of a concert if —

       (a)   the concert is a qualifying orchestral concert,

       (b)   the company is the production company in relation to the concert,

       (c)   the company intends that the concert should be performed live—

           (i)   before the paying public, or

           (ii)   for educational purposes, and

       (d)   the EEA expenditure condition is met in relation to the concert (see section 1217RB).

(3)   In this Part "qualifying orchestral concert" means an orchestral concert—

       (a)   in which the instrumentalists number at least 12, and

       (b)   in which none of the musical instruments to be played, or a minority of those instruments, is electronically or directly amplified.

(4)   A company qualifies for orchestra tax relief in relation to the production of a concert series if—

       (a)   the concert series is a qualifying orchestral concert series,

       (b)   the company is the production company in relation to every concert in the series,

       (c)   the company intends that all or a high proportion of the concerts in the series should be performed live—

           (i)   before the paying public, or

           (ii)   for educational purposes,

       (d)   the EEA expenditure condition is met in relation to the series, and

       (e)   the company has made an election under section 1217Q(4) in relation to the series.

(5)   In this section "qualifying orchestral concert series" means two or more orchestral concerts, all or a high proportion of which are qualifying orchestral concerts.

(6)   For the purposes of this section a concert is "live" if it is to an audience before whom the musicians are actually present.

(7)   A concert is not regarded as performed for educational purposes if the production company is, or is associated with, a person who—

       (a)   has responsibility for the beneficiaries, or

       (b)   is otherwise connected with the beneficiaries (for instance, by being their employer).

(8)   For the purposes of subsection (7), a production company is associated with a person ("P") if—

       (a)   P controls the production company, or

       (b)   P is a company which is controlled by the production company or by a person who also controls the production company.

(9)   In this section—

        "the beneficiaries" means persons for whose benefit the concert will or may be performed;

376

Finance Act 2016 (c. 24)
Schedule 8 — Tax relief for production of orchestral concerts
Part 1 — Amendment of CTA 2009

"control" has the same meaning as in Part 10 of CTA 2010 (see section 450 of that Act).

(10) There is further related provision in section 1217RL (tax avoidance arrangements).

1217RB The EEA expenditure condition

(1) The "EEA expenditure condition" is that at least 25% of the core expenditure on the production of the concert or concert series incurred by the company is EEA expenditure.

(2) In this Part "EEA expenditure" means expenditure on goods or services that are provided from within the European Economic Area.

(3) Any apportionment of expenditure as between EEA and non-EEA expenditure for the purposes of this Part is to be made on a just and reasonable basis.

(4) The Treasury may by regulations—
   (a) amend the percentage specified in subsection (1);
   (b) amend subsection (2).

(5) See also sections 1217T and 1217TA (which are about the giving of relief provisionally on the basis that the EEA expenditure condition will be met).

1217RC "Core expenditure"

(1) In this Part "core expenditure", in relation to the production of a concert or concert series, means expenditure on the activities involved in producing the concert or concert series.

(2) The reference in subsection (1) to "expenditure on the activities involved in producing the concert or concert series" includes expenditure on travel to and from a venue which is not a usual venue for concerts produced by the company.

(3) But that reference does not include—
   (a) expenditure on any matters not directly involved with putting on the concert or concerts (for instance, financing, marketing, legal services or storage),
   (b) speculative expenditure on activities not involved with putting on the concert or concerts, and
   (c) expenditure on the actual performance or performances (for instance, payments to musicians for their performances in the concert or concert series).

Additional deduction

1217RD Claim for additional deduction

(1) A company which qualifies for orchestra tax relief in relation to the production of a concert or concert series may claim an additional deduction in relation to the production.

(2) A claim under subsection (1) is made with respect to an accounting period.

(3)   Where a company has made a claim, the company is entitled to make an additional deduction, in accordance with section 1217RE, in calculating the profit or loss of the separate orchestral trade for the accounting period concerned.

(4)   Where the company tax return in which a claim is made is for an accounting period later than that in which the company begins to carry on the separate orchestral trade, the company must make any amendments of company tax returns for earlier periods that may be necessary.

(5)   Any amendment or assessment necessary to give effect to subsection (4) may be made despite any limitation on the time within which an amendment or assessment may normally be made.

1217RE Amount of additional deduction

(1)   The amount of an additional deduction to which a company is entitled as a result of a claim under section 1217RD is calculated as follows.

(2)   For the first period of account during which the separate orchestral trade is carried on, the amount of the additional deduction is E, where E is—

    (a)   so much of the qualifying expenditure incurred to date as is EEA expenditure, or

    (b)   if less, 80% of the total amount of qualifying expenditure incurred to date.

(3)   For any period of account after the first, the amount of the additional deduction is—

$$E - P$$

where E is—

    (a)   so much of the qualifying expenditure incurred to date as is EEA expenditure, or

    (b)   if less, 80% of the total amount of qualifying expenditure incurred to date, and

P is the total amount of the additional deductions given for previous periods.

(4)   The Treasury may by regulations amend the percentage specified in subsection (2) or (3).

1217RF "Qualifying expenditure"

(1)   In this Chapter "qualifying expenditure", in relation to the production of a concert or concert series, means core expenditure (see section 1217RC) on the production that—

    (a)   falls to be taken into account under sections 1217QB to 1217QG in calculating the profit or loss of the separate orchestral trade for tax purposes, and

    (b)   is not expenditure which is otherwise relievable.

378

Finance Act 2016 (c. 24)
Schedule 8 — Tax relief for production of orchestral concerts
Part 1 — Amendment of CTA 2009

(2) For the purposes of this section expenditure is otherwise relievable if it is expenditure in respect of which (assuming a claim were made) the company would be entitled to—

    (a) film tax relief under Chapter 3 of Part 15,

    (b) television tax relief under Chapter 3 of Part 15A,

    (c) video games tax relief under Chapter 3 of Part 15B,

    (d) an additional deduction under Part 15C (theatrical productions), or

    (e) a theatre tax credit under Part 15C.

Orchestra tax credits

1217RG Orchestra tax credit claimable if company has surrenderable loss

(1) A company which qualifies for orchestra tax relief in relation to the production of a concert or concert series may claim an orchestra tax credit in relation to the production for an accounting period in which the company has a surrenderable loss.

(2) Section 1217RH sets out how to calculate the amount of any surrenderable loss that the company has in the accounting period.

(3) A company making a claim may surrender the whole or part of its surrenderable loss in the accounting period.

(4) The amount of the orchestra tax credit to which a company making a claim is entitled for the accounting period is 25% of the amount of the loss surrendered.

(5) The company's available loss for the accounting period (see section 1217RH(2)) is reduced by the amount surrendered.

1217RH Amount of surrenderable loss

(1) The company's surrenderable loss in the accounting period is—

    (a) the company's available loss for the period in the separate orchestral trade (see subsections (2) and (3)), or

    (b) if less, the available qualifying expenditure for the period (see subsections (4) and (5)).

(2) The company's available loss for an accounting period is—

$$L + RUL$$

where—

    L is the amount of the company's loss for the period in the separate orchestral trade, and

    RUL is the amount of any relevant unused loss of the company (see subsection (3)).

(3) The "relevant unused loss" of a company is so much of any available loss of the company for the previous accounting period as has not been—

    (a) surrendered under section 1217RG, or

    (b) carried forward under section 45 of CTA 2010 and set against profits of the separate orchestral trade.

(4) For the first period of account during which the separate orchestral trade is carried on, the available qualifying expenditure is the amount that is E for that period for the purposes of section 1217RE(2).

(5) For any period of account after the first, the available qualifying expenditure is—

$$E - S$$

where—

E is the amount that is E for that period for the purposes of section 1217RE(3), and

S is the total amount previously surrendered under section 1217RG.

(6) If a period of account of the separate orchestral trade does not coincide with an accounting period, any necessary apportionments are to be made by reference to the number of days in the periods concerned.

1217RI Payment in respect of orchestra tax credit

(1) If a company—
   (a) is entitled to an orchestra tax credit for an accounting period, and
   (b) makes a claim,
the Commissioners for Her Majesty's Revenue and Customs ("the Commissioners") must pay the amount of the credit to the company.

(2) An amount payable in respect of—
   (a) an orchestra tax credit, or
   (b) interest on an orchestra tax credit under section 826 of ICTA,
may be applied in discharging any liability of the company to pay corporation tax.
To the extent that it is so applied the Commissioners' liability under subsection (1) is discharged.

(3) If the company's company tax return for the accounting period is enquired into by the Commissioners, no payment in respect of an orchestra tax credit for that period need be made before the Commissioners' enquiries are completed (see paragraph 32 of Schedule 18 to FA 1998).
In those circumstances the Commissioners may make a payment on a provisional basis of such amount as they consider appropriate.

(4) No payment need be made in respect of an orchestra tax credit for an accounting period before the company has paid to the Commissioners any amount that it is required to pay for payment periods ending in that accounting period—
   (a) under PAYE regulations,
   (b) under section 966 of ITA 2007 (visiting performers), or
   (c) in respect of Class 1 national insurance contributions under Part 1 of the Social Security Contributions and Benefits Act 1992 or Part 1 of the Social Security Contributions and Benefits (Northern Ireland) Act 1992.

380

Finance Act 2016 (c. 24)
Schedule 8 — Tax relief for production of orchestral concerts
Part 1 — Amendment of CTA 2009

(5)   A payment in respect of an orchestra tax credit is not income of the company for any tax purpose.

1217RJ Limit on State aid

In accordance with Commission Regulation (EU) No. 651/2014 of 17 June 2014 declaring certain categories of aid compatible with the internal market, the total amount of orchestra tax credits payable under section 1217RI in the case of any undertaking is not to exceed 50 million euros per year.

1217RK No account to be taken of amount if unpaid

(1)   In determining for the purposes of this Chapter the amount of costs incurred on a production of a concert or concert series at the end of a period of account, ignore any amount that has not been paid 4 months after the end of that period.

(2)   This is without prejudice to the operation of section 1217QE (when costs are taken to be incurred).

Anti-avoidance etc

1217RL Tax avoidance arrangements

(1)   A company does not qualify for orchestra tax relief in relation to the production of a concert or concert series if there are any tax avoidance arrangements relating to the production.

(2)   Arrangements are "tax avoidance arrangements" if their main purpose, or one of their main purposes, is the obtaining of a tax advantage.

(3)   In this section—

"arrangements" includes any scheme, agreement or understanding, whether or not legally enforceable;

"tax advantage" has the meaning given by section 1139 of CTA 2010.

1217RM Transactions not entered into for genuine commercial reasons

(1)   A transaction is to be ignored for the purpose of determining orchestra tax relief so far as the transaction is attributable to arrangements (other than tax avoidance arrangements) entered into otherwise than for genuine commercial reasons.

(2)   In this section "arrangements" and "tax avoidance arrangements" have the same meaning as in section 1217RL.

CHAPTER 4

LOSSES OF SEPARATE ORCHESTRAL TRADE

1217S Application of sections 1217SA to 1217SC

(1)   Sections 1217SA to 1217SC apply to a company which is treated under section 1217Q(2) or (5) as carrying on a separate trade in relation to the production of a concert or concert series.

(2) In those sections —

    (a) "the completion period" means the accounting period in which the company ceases to carry on the separate orchestral trade;

    (b) "loss relief" includes any means by which a loss might be used to reduce the amount in respect of which a company, or any other person, is chargeable to tax.

1217SA Restriction on use of losses before completion period

(1) Subsection (2) applies if a loss is made by the company in the separate orchestral trade in an accounting period preceding the completion period.

(2) The loss is not available for loss relief, except to the extent that the loss may be carried forward under section 45 of CTA 2010 to be set against profits of the separate orchestral trade in a subsequent period.

1217SB Use of losses in the completion period

(1) Subsection (2) applies if a loss made in the separate orchestral trade is carried forward under section 45 of CTA 2010 to the completion period.

(2) So much (if any) of the loss as is not attributable to orchestra tax relief (see subsection (4)) may be treated for the purposes of loss relief as if it were a loss made in the completion period.

(3) If a loss is made in the separate orchestral trade in the completion period, the amount of the loss that may be —

    (a) deducted from total profits of the same or an earlier period under section 37 of CTA 2010, or

    (b) surrendered as group relief under Part 5 of that Act,

is restricted to the amount (if any) that is not attributable to orchestra tax relief (see subsection (4)).

(4) The amount of a loss in any period that is attributable to orchestra tax relief is found by —

    (a) calculating what the amount of the loss would have been if there had been no additional deduction under Chapter 3 in that or any earlier period, and

    (b) deducting that amount from the total amount of the loss.

(5) This section does not apply to loss surrendered, or treated as carried forward, under section 1217SC (terminal losses).

1217SC Terminal losses

(1) This section applies if —

    (a) the company ceases to carry on the separate orchestral trade, and

    (b) if the company had not ceased to carry on that trade, it could have carried forward an amount under section 45 of CTA 2010 to be set against profits of that trade in a later period ("the terminal loss").

382

Finance Act 2016 (c. 24)
Schedule 8 — Tax relief for production of orchestral concerts
Part 1 — Amendment of CTA 2009

Below in this section the company is referred to as "company A" and the separate orchestral trade is referred to as "trade 1".

(2) If company A—

    (a) is treated under section 1217Q(2) or (5) as carrying on a separate trade in relation to the production of another concert or concert series ("trade 2"), and

    (b) is carrying on trade 2 when it ceases to carry on trade 1,

company A may (on making a claim) make an election under subsection (3).

(3) The election is to have the terminal loss (or a part of it) treated as if it were a loss brought forward under section 45 of CTA 2010 to be set against the profits of trade 2 of the first accounting period beginning after the cessation and so on.

(4) Subsection (5) applies if—

    (a) another company ("company B") is treated under section 1217Q(2) or (5) as carrying on a separate trade ("company B's trade") in relation to the production of another concert or concert series,

    (b) company B is carrying on that trade when company A ceases to carry on trade 1, and

    (c) company B is in the same group as company A for the purposes of Part 5 of CTA 2010 (group relief).

(5) Company A may surrender the loss (or a part of it) to company B.

(6) On the making of a claim by company B the amount surrendered is treated as if it were a loss brought forward by company B under section 45 of CTA 2010 to be set against the profits of company B's trade of the first accounting period beginning after the cessation and so on.

(7) The Treasury may by regulations make administrative provision in relation to the surrender of a loss under subsection (5) and the resulting claim under subsection (6).

(8) "Administrative provision" means provision corresponding, subject to such adaptations or other modifications as appear to the Treasury to be appropriate, to that made by Part 8 of Schedule 18 to FA 1998 (company tax returns: claims for group relief).

CHAPTER 5

PROVISIONAL ENTITLEMENT TO RELIEF

1217T Provisional entitlement to relief

(1) In relation to a company and the production of a concert or concert series, "interim accounting period" means any accounting period that—

    (a) is one in which the company carries on a separate orchestral trade, and

    (b) precedes the accounting period in which it ceases to do so.

(2) A company is not entitled to orchestra tax relief for an interim accounting period unless—

    (a) its company tax return for the period states the amount of planned core expenditure on the production of the concert or concert series that is EEA expenditure (see section 1217RB(2)), and

    (b) that amount is such as to indicate that the EEA expenditure condition (see section 1217RB) will be met in relation to the production.

If those requirements are met, the company is provisionally treated in relation to that period as if the EEA expenditure condition were met.

1217TA Clawback of provisional relief

(1) If a statement is made under section 1217T(2) but it subsequently appears that the EEA expenditure condition will not be met on the company's ceasing to carry on the separate orchestral trade, the company—

    (a) is not entitled to orchestra tax relief for any period for which its entitlement depended on such a statement, and

    (b) must amend accordingly its company tax return for any such period.

(2) When a company ceases to carry on the separate orchestral trade, the company's company tax return for the period in which that cessation occurs must—

    (a) state that the company has ceased to carry on the separate orchestral trade, and

    (b) be accompanied by a final statement of the amount of the core expenditure on the production of the concert or concert series that is EEA expenditure.

(3) If that statement shows that the EEA expenditure condition is not met—

    (a) the company is not entitled to orchestra tax relief or to relief under section 1217SC (transfer of terminal losses) for any period, and

    (b) must amend accordingly its company tax return for any period for which such relief was claimed.

(4) Any amendment or assessment necessary to give effect to this section may be made despite any limitation on the time within which an amendment or assessment may normally be made.

CHAPTER 6

INTERPRETATION

1217U Interpretation

In this Part—

    "company tax return" has the same meaning as in Schedule 18 to FA 1998 (see paragraph 3(1) of that Schedule);

    "core expenditure" has the meaning given by section 1217RC;

384

Finance Act 2016 (c. 24)
Schedule 8 — Tax relief for production of orchestral concerts
Part 1 — Amendment of CTA 2009

"costs", in relation to a concert or concert series, has the meaning given by section 1217QD;

"EEA expenditure" has the meaning given by section 1217RB(2);

"EEA expenditure condition" has the meaning given by section 1217RB;

"income", in relation to a concert or concert series, has the meaning given by section 1217QC;

"orchestra tax relief" is to be read in accordance with Chapter 3 (see in particular section 1217R(1));

"orchestral concert" has the meaning given by section 1217PA;

"production company" has the meaning given by section 1217PB;

"qualifying expenditure" has the meaning given by section 1217RF;

"qualifying orchestral concert" has the meaning given by section 1217RA(3);

"qualifying orchestral concert series" has the meaning given by section 1217RA(5);

the "separate orchestral trade" is to be read in accordance with section 1217Q."

PART 2

CONSEQUENTIAL AMENDMENTS

ICTA

2   (1)   Section 826 of ICTA (interest on tax overpaid) is amended as follows.

   (2)   In subsection (1), after paragraph (fc) insert—

   "(fd)   a payment of orchestra tax credit falls to be made to a company; or".

   (3)   In subsection (3C), for "or theatre tax credit" substitute ", theatre tax credit or orchestra tax credit".

   (4)   In subsection (8A)—

   (a)   in paragraph (a), for "or (fc)" substitute ", (fc) or (fd)", and

   (b)   in paragraph (b)(ii), after "theatre tax credit" insert "or orchestra tax credit".

   (5)   In subsection (8BA), after "theatre tax credit" (in both places) insert "or orchestra tax credit".

FA 1998

3   Schedule 18 to FA 1998 (company tax returns, assessments and related matters) is amended as follows.

4   In paragraph 10 (other claims and elections to be included in return), in sub-paragraph (4), for "or 15C" substitute ", 15C or 15D".

5   (1)   Paragraph 52 (recovery of excessive repayments etc) is amended as follows.

(2) In sub-paragraph (2), after paragraph (bg) insert—

> "(bh)   orchestra tax credit under Part 15D of that Act,".

(3) In sub-paragraph (5)—

    (a)   after paragraph (ai) insert—

> "(aj)   an amount of orchestra tax credit paid to a company for an accounting period,", and

    (b)   in the words after paragraph (b), after "(ai)" insert ", (aj)".

6   In Part 9D (certain claims for tax relief)—

    (a)   in the heading, for "or 15C" substitute ", 15C or 15D", and

    (b)   in paragraph 83S (introduction), after sub-paragraph (e) insert—

> "(f)   orchestra tax relief."

CAA 2001

7   In Schedule A1 to CAA 2001 (first-year tax credits), in paragraph 11(4), omit the "and" at the end of paragraph (e) and after paragraph (f) insert ", and

> (g)   Chapter 3 of Part 15D of that Act (orchestra tax credits)."

FA 2007

8   In Schedule 24 to FA 2007 (penalties for errors), in paragraph 28(fa) (meaning of "corporation tax credit"), omit the "or" at the end of paragraph (ivc) and after that paragraph insert—

> "(ivd)   an orchestra tax credit under Chapter 3 of Part 15D of that Act, or".

CTA 2009

9   In Part 8 of CTA 2009 (intangible fixed assets), in Chapter 10 (excluded assets), after section 808C insert—

> **"808D Assets representing expenditure incurred in course of separate orchestral trade**
>
> (1)   This Part does not apply to an intangible fixed asset held by an orchestral concert production company so far as the asset represents expenditure on an orchestral concert or orchestral concert series that is treated under Part 15D as expenditure of a separate trade (see particularly sections 1217Q and 1217QF).
>
> (2)   In this section—
>
> > "orchestral concert" has the same meaning as in Part 15D (see section 1217PA);
> >
> > "orchestral concert production company" means a company which, for the purposes of that Part, is the production company in relation to a concert (see section 1217PB)."

10   In section 1310 of CTA 2009 (orders and regulations), in subsection (4), after paragraph (em) insert—

> "(en)   section 1217RB (EEA expenditure condition),
>
> (eo)   section 1217RE (amount of additional deduction),".

386

Finance Act 2016 (c. 24)
Schedule 8 — Tax relief for production of orchestral concerts
Part 2 — Consequential amendments

11   In Schedule 4 to CTA 2009 (index of defined expressions), insert at the appropriate places—

"company tax return (in Part 15D)	section 1217U"
"core expenditure (in Part 15D)	section 1217RC"
"costs, in relation to a concert or concert series (in Part 15D)	section 1217QD"
"EEA expenditure (in Part 15D)	section 1217RB(2)"
"EEA expenditure condition (in Part 15D)	section 1217RB"
"income, in relation to a concert or concert series (in Part 15D)	section 1217QC"
"orchestra tax relief (in Part 15D)	section 1217R(1)"
"orchestral concert (in Part 15D)	section 1217PA"
"production company (in Part 15D)	section 1217PB"
"qualifying expenditure (in Part 15D)	section 1217RF"
"qualifying orchestral concert (in Part 15D)	section 1217RA(3)"
"qualifying orchestral concert series (in Part 15D)	section 1217RA(5)"
"separate orchestral trade (in Part 15D)	section 1217Q".

FA 2009

12   In Schedule 54A to FA 2009 (which is prospectively inserted by F(No. 3)A 2010 and contains provision about the recovery of certain amounts of interest paid by HMRC), in paragraph 2—

    (a)   in sub-paragraph (2), omit the "or" at the end of paragraph (g) and after paragraph (h) insert ", or

           (i)   a payment of orchestra tax credit under Chapter 3 of Part 15D of CTA 2009 for an accounting period.";

    (b)   in sub-paragraph (4), for "(h)" substitute "(i)".

CTA 2010

13   In Part 8B of CTA 2010 (trading profits taxable at Northern Ireland rate), in section 357H(7) (introduction), after "Chapter 14 for provision about theatrical productions;" insert "Chapter 14A for provision about orchestra tax relief;".

Finance Act 2016 (c. 24)
Schedule 8 — Tax relief for production of orchestral concerts
Part 2 — Consequential amendments

387

14   In Part 8B of CTA 2010, after section 357UI insert—

"CHAPTER 14A

ORCHESTRA TAX RELIEF

Introductory

357UJ Introduction and interpretation

(1)   This Chapter makes provision about the operation of Part 15D of CTA 2009 (orchestra tax relief) in relation to expenditure incurred by a company in an accounting period in which it is a Northern Ireland company.

(2)   In this Chapter—

    (a)   "Northern Ireland expenditure" means expenditure incurred in a trade to the extent that the expenditure forms part of the Northern Ireland profits or Northern Ireland losses of the trade;

    (b)   the "separate orchestral trade" has the same meaning as in Part 15D of CTA 2009 (see section 1217Q(6) of that Act);

    (c)   "qualifying expenditure" has the same meaning as in Chapter 3 of that Part (see section 1217RF of that Act).

(3)   References in Part 15D of CTA 2009 to "orchestra tax relief" include relief under this Chapter.

Orchestra tax relief

357UK Northern Ireland additional deduction

(1)   In this Chapter "a Northern Ireland additional deduction" means so much of a deduction under section 1217RD of CTA 2009 (claim for additional deduction) as is calculated by reference to qualifying expenditure that is Northern Ireland expenditure.

(2)   A Northern Ireland additional deduction forms part of the Northern Ireland profits or Northern Ireland losses of the separate orchestral trade.

357UL Northern Ireland supplementary deduction

(1)   This section applies where—

    (a)   a company is entitled under section 1217RD of CTA 2009 to an additional deduction in calculating the profit or loss of the separate orchestral trade in an accounting period,

    (b)   the company is a Northern Ireland company in the period,

    (c)   the additional deduction is wholly or partly a Northern Ireland additional deduction, and

    (d)   any of the following conditions is met—

        (i)   the company does not have a surrenderable loss in the accounting period;

        (ii)   the company has a surrenderable loss in the accounting period, but does not make a claim under section 1217RG of CTA 2009 (orchestra tax credit

388

Finance Act 2016 (c. 24)
Schedule 8 — Tax relief for production of orchestral concerts
Part 2 — Consequential amendments

claimable if company has surrenderable loss) for the period;

    (iii) the company has a surrenderable loss in the accounting period and makes a claim under that section for the period, but the amount of Northern Ireland losses surrendered on the claim is less than the Northern Ireland additional deduction.

(2) The company is entitled to make another deduction ("a Northern Ireland supplementary deduction") in respect of qualifying expenditure.

(3) See section 357UM for provision about the amount of the Northern Ireland supplementary deduction.

(4) The Northern Ireland supplementary deduction—

    (a) is made in calculating the profit or loss of the separate orchestral trade, and

    (b) forms part of the Northern Ireland profits or Northern Ireland losses of the separate orchestral trade.

(5) In this section "surrenderable loss" has the meaning given by section 1217RH of CTA 2009.

357UM Northern Ireland supplementary deduction: amount

(1) This section contains provision for the purposes of section 357UL(2) about the amount of the Northern Ireland supplementary deduction.

(2) If the accounting period falls within only one financial year, the amount of the Northern Ireland supplementary deduction is—

$$(A - B) \times \left(\frac{(MR - NIR)}{NIR} \right)$$

where—

A is the amount of the Northern Ireland additional deduction brought into account in the accounting period;

B is the amount of Northern Ireland losses surrendered in any claim under section 1217RG of CTA 2009 for the accounting period;

MR is the main rate for the financial year;

NIR is the Northern Ireland rate for the financial year.

(3) If the accounting period falls within more than one financial year, the amount of the Northern Ireland supplementary deduction is determined by taking the following steps.

    Step 1

    Calculate, for each financial year, the amount that would be the Northern Ireland supplementary deduction for the accounting period if it fell within only that financial year (see subsection (2)).

    Step 2

    Multiply each amount calculated under step 1 by the proportion of the accounting period that falls within the financial year for which it is calculated.

Step 3

Add together each amount found under step 2.

357UN Orchestra tax credit: Northern Ireland supplementary deduction ignored

For the purpose of determining the available loss of a company under section 1217RH of CTA 2009 (amount of surrenderable loss) for any accounting period, any Northern Ireland supplementary deduction made by the company in the period (and any Northern Ireland supplementary deduction made in any previous accounting period) is to be ignored.

Losses of separate orchestral trade

357UO Restriction on use of losses before completion period

(1) Section 1217SA of CTA 2009 (restriction on use of losses before completion period) has effect subject as follows.

(2) The reference in subsection (1) of that section to a loss made in the separate orchestral trade in an accounting period preceding the completion period is, if the company is a Northern Ireland company in that period, a reference to—

(a) any Northern Ireland losses of the trade of the period, or

(b) any mainstream losses of the trade of the period;

and references to losses in subsection (2) of that section are to be read accordingly.

(3) Subsection (4) applies if a Northern Ireland company has, in an accounting period preceding the completion period—

(a) both Northern Ireland losses of the trade and mainstream profits of the trade, or

(b) both mainstream losses of the trade and Northern Ireland profits of the trade.

(4) The company may make a claim under section 37 (relief for trade losses against total profits) for relief for the losses mentioned in subsection (3)(a) or (b).

(5) But relief on such a claim is available only—

(a) in the case of a claim for relief for Northern Ireland losses, against mainstream profits of the trade of the same period;

(b) in the case of a claim for relief for mainstream losses, against Northern Ireland profits of the trade of the same period.

(6) In this section "the completion period" has the same meaning as in section 1217SA of CTA 2009 (see section 1217S(2) of that Act).

357UP Use of losses in the completion period

(1) Section 1217SB of CTA 2009 (use of losses in the completion period) has effect subject as follows.

(2) The reference in subsection (1) of that section to a loss made in the separate orchestral trade is, in relation to a loss made in a period in which the company is a Northern Ireland company, a reference to—

390

Finance Act 2016 (c. 24)
Schedule 8 — Tax relief for production of orchestral concerts
Part 2 — Consequential amendments

    (a)   any Northern Ireland losses of the trade of the period, or

    (b)   any mainstream losses of the trade of the period;

and references to losses in subsections (2) and (4) of that section are to be read accordingly.

    (3)   The references in subsection (3) of that section to a loss made in the separate orchestral trade in the completion period are, where the company is a Northern Ireland company in the period, references to—

    (a)   any Northern Ireland losses of the trade of the period, or

    (b)   any mainstream losses of the trade of the period;

and references to losses in subsection (4) of that section are to be read accordingly.

    (4)   Subsection (4) of that section has effect, in relation to Northern Ireland losses, as if the reference to an additional deduction under Chapter 3 of Part 15D of CTA 2009 included a reference to a Northern Ireland supplementary deduction under this Chapter.

357UQ Terminal losses

    (1)   Section 1217SC of CTA 2009 (terminal losses) has effect subject as follows.

    (2)   Where—

    (a)   a company makes an election under subsection (3) of that section (election to treat terminal loss as loss brought forward of different trade) in relation to all or part of a terminal loss, and

    (b)   the terminal loss is a Northern Ireland loss,

that subsection has effect as if the reference in it to a loss brought forward were to a Northern Ireland loss brought forward.

    (3)   Where—

    (a)   a company makes a claim under subsection (6) of that section (claim to treat terminal loss as loss brought forward by different company) in relation to part or all of a terminal loss, and

    (b)   the terminal loss is a Northern Ireland loss,

that subsection has effect as if the reference in it to a loss brought forward were to a Northern Ireland loss brought forward."

15   (1)   Schedule 4 to CTA 2010 (index of defined expressions) is amended as follows.

    (2)   In the entry for "Northern Ireland expenditure"—

    (a)   for "14" substitute "14A", and

    (b)   for "and 357U(2)" substitute ", 357U(2) and 357UJ(2)".

    (3)   Insert at the appropriate places—

"qualifying expenditure (in Chapter 14A of Part 8B)	section 357UJ(2)"

Finance Act 2016 (c. **24**)
Schedule 8 — Tax relief for production of orchestral concerts
Part 2 — Consequential amendments

391

| "the separate orchestral trade (in Chapter 14A of | section 357UJ(2)". |
| Part 8B) | |

PART 3

COMMENCEMENT

16   Any power to make regulations conferred on the Treasury by virtue of this Schedule comes into force on the day on which this Act is passed.

17   (1)   The amendments made by the following provisions of this Schedule have effect in relation to accounting periods beginning on or after 1 April 2016 —

    (a)   Part 1, and

    (b)   in Part 2, paragraphs 2 to 12.

  (2)   Sub-paragraph (3) applies where a company has an accounting period beginning before 1 April 2016 and ending on or after that date ("the straddling period").

  (3)   For the purposes of Part 15D of CTA 2009 —

    (a)   so much of the straddling period as falls before 1 April 2016, and so much of that period as falls on or after that date, are separate accounting periods, and

    (b)   any amounts brought into account for the purposes of calculating for corporation tax purposes the profits of a trade for the straddling period are apportioned to the two separate accounting periods on such basis as is just and reasonable.

18   (1)   The amendments made by paragraphs 13 to 15 of this Schedule have effect in relation to accounting periods beginning on or after the first day of the financial year appointed by the Treasury by regulations under section 5(3) of the Corporation Tax (Northern Ireland) Act 2015 ("the commencement day").

  (2)   Sub-paragraph (3) applies where a company has an accounting period beginning before the commencement day and ending on or after that day ("the straddling period").

  (3)   For the purposes of Chapter 14A of Part 8B of CTA 2010 —

    (a)   so much of the straddling period as falls before the commencement day, and so much of that period as falls on or after that day, are separate accounting periods, and

    (b)   any amounts brought into account for the purposes of calculating for corporation tax purposes the profits of a trade for the straddling period are apportioned to the two separate accounting periods on such basis as is just and reasonable.

SCHEDULE 9   Section 64

PROFITS FROM THE EXPLOITATION OF PATENTS ETC: CONSEQUENTIAL

1   CTA 2010 is amended in accordance with this Schedule.

2   In section 357B (meaning of "qualifying company"), in subsection (3)(b)(ii), for "section 357A" substitute "section 357A(1)".

3   In the heading of Chapter 3 of Part 8A, after "profits" insert ": cases mentioned in section 357A(7): no income from new IP".

4   (1) Section 357C (relevant IP profits) is amended as follows.

      (2) Before subsection (1) insert—

           "(A1)   This section applies for the purposes of determining the relevant IP profits of a trade of a company for an accounting period in a case where—
                   (a)   the accounting period began before 1 July 2021,
                   (b)   the company is not a new entrant (see section 357A(11)), and
                   (c)   none of the amounts of relevant IP income brought into account as credits in calculating the profits of the trade for the accounting period is properly attributable to a new qualifying IP right (see section 357BP).
                   But see also section 357D (alternative method of calculating relevant IP profits in such a case)."

      (3) In subsection (1)—
                   (a)   in the words before Step 1, omit "of a trade of a company for an accounting period",
                   (b)   in Step 2, for "357CC and 357CD" substitute "357BH to 357BHC",
                   (c)   in Step 4, after "routine return figure" insert "in relation to the trade for the accounting period",
                   (d)   in Step 5, for "elected" substitute "made an election under section 357CL", and
                   (e)   in Step 6, after "marketing assets return figure" insert "in relation to the trade for the accounting period".

5   In section 357CA (total gross income of a trade), in subsection (2), for "section 357CB" substitute "section 357BG".

6   Omit sections 357CB to 357CF.

7   (1) Section 357CG (adjustments in calculating profits of trade) is amended as follows.

      (2) In subsection (1) after "determining" insert "under section 357C".

      (3) In subsection (4), in the words after paragraph (b), for "section 357CB" substitute "section 357BG".

      (4) In subsection (6), in paragraph (a)(ii) of the definition of "relevant accounting period", for "section 357A" substitute "section 357A(1)".

8   In section 357CI (routine return figure), in Step 1 in subsection (1), for "sections 357CJ and 357CK" substitute "sections 357BJA and 357BJB".

9   Omit sections 357CJ and 357CK.

10   (1) Section 357CL (companies eligible to elect for small claims treatment) is amended as follows.

      (2) In subsection (1) for "elect" substitute "make an election under this section".

    (3) In subsection (6) for "section 357A" substitute "section 357A(1)".

11   In section 357CM (small claims amount), in subsection (1), for "elects" substitute "makes an election under section 357CL".

12   (1) Section 357D (alternative method of calculating relevant IP profits: "streaming") is amended as follows.

    (2) In subsection (1) at the end insert "in a case where—

        (a)   the accounting period began before 1 July 2021,

        (b)   the company is not a new entrant (see section 357A(11)), and

        (c)   none of the amounts of relevant IP income brought into account as credits in calculating the profits of the trade for the accounting period is properly attributable to a new qualifying IP right (see section 357BP)."

    (3) For subsection (4) substitute—

        "(4) A company must apply section 357DA (instead of section 357C) for the purposes of determining the relevant IP profits of a trade of the company for an accounting period in a case mentioned in subsection (1) if any of the mandatory streaming conditions in section 357DC is met in relation to the trade for the period."

13   (1) Section 357DA (relevant IP profits) is amended as follows.

    (2) In subsection (1)—

        (a)   in Step 1—

            (i)   for "section 357CB" substitute "section 357BG", and

            (ii)   for "sections 357CC and 357CD" substitute "sections 357BH to 357BHC",

        (b)   in Step 4, after "routine return figure" insert "in relation to the trade for the accounting period",

        (c)   in Step 5, for "elected" substitute "made an election under section 357CL", and

        (d)   in Step 6, after "marketing assets return figure" insert "in relation to the trade for the accounting period".

    (3) In subsection (4), in the words after paragraph (b), for "sections 357CJ and 357CK" substitute "sections 357BJA and 357BJB".

14   (1) Section 357DC (the mandatory streaming conditions) is amended as follows.

    (2) In subsection (8)(a) for "section 357CC" substitute "section 357BH".

    (3) In subsection (9)(a) for "section 357CC(6)" substitute "section 357BH(6)".

15   In section 357EB (allocation of set-off amount within a group) in subsection (3)(a) for "section 357A" substitute "section 357A(1)".

16   In section 357ED (company ceasing to carry on trade etc) in subsection (2)(c) for "section 357A" substitute "section 357A(1)".

17   In section 357FA (incorporation of qualifying items), in subsection (2), for "357CC(2)" substitute "357BH(2)".

18   In section 357FB (tax advantage schemes) in subsection (4)(b) for "section 357A" substitute "section 357A(1)".

19 (1) Section 357G (making an election under section 357A) is amended as follows.

    (2) In the heading, for "section 357A" substitute "section 357A(1) or (11)(b)".

    (3) In subsection (1) for "section 357A" substitute "section 357A(1) or (11)(b)".

20 (1) Section 357GA (revocation of election made under section 357A) is amended as follows.

    (2) In the heading, for "section 357A" substitute "section 357A(1)".

    (3) In subsection (1) for "section 357A" substitute "section 357A(1)".

    (4) In subsection (5) for "section 357A" substitute "section 357A(1)".

21 (1) Section 357GB (application of Part 8A in relation to partnerships) is amended as follows.

    (2) In subsection (11) —
        (a) in the words before paragraph (a), after "Sections" insert "357BK, 357BKA", and
        (b) in paragraph (a) after "section" insert "357BK or".

    (3) In subsection (12) for "section 357CB(1)(c)" substitute "section 357BG(1)(c)".

22   In section 357GC (application of Part 8A in relation to cost-sharing arrangements), in subsection (3), for "section 357CB(1)(c)" substitute "section 357BG(1)(c)".

23 (1) Section 357GE (other interpretation) is amended as follows.

    (2) In subsection (1) —
        (a) at the appropriate place insert —
                ""payment" includes payment in money's worth.", and
        (b) omit the definition of "qualifying residual profit".

    (3) After subsection (1) insert —

        "(1A) In Chapters 3 and 4 of this Part "qualifying residual profit" of a trade, in relation to any accounting period, is the amount obtained by the application of Steps 1 to 4 in section 357C or (as the case may be) section 357DA in relation to the trade for the accounting period."

24   In Schedule 4 (index of defined expressions) —
        (a) for the entry for "finance income (in Part 8A)" substitute —

"finance income (in Part 8A)	section 357BG",

        (b) after the entry for "new consideration (in Part 23)" insert —

"new entrant (in Part 8A)	section 357A(11)",

        (c) in the entry for "qualifying residual profit of a trade (in Part 8A)", in the left hand column, after "in" insert "Chapters 3 and 4 of", and

(d)   for the entry for "relevant IP income (in Part 8A)" substitute −

| "relevant IP income (in Part 8A) | section 357BH". |

SCHEDULE 10   Section 66

HYBRID AND OTHER MISMATCHES

PART 1

MAIN PROVISIONS

1   In TIOPA 2010, after Part 6 insert −

"PART 6A

HYBRID AND OTHER MISMATCHES

CHAPTER 1

INTRODUCTION

259A Overview of Part

(1)   This Part has effect for the purposes of counteracting certain cases that it is reasonable to suppose would otherwise give rise to −
    (a)   a deduction/non-inclusion mismatch, or
    (b)   a double deduction mismatch.

(2)   A deduction/non-inclusion mismatch arises where an amount is deductible from a person's income −
    (a)   without a corresponding amount of ordinary income arising to another person, or
    (b)   where an amount of ordinary income does arise to a person but is under taxed.

(3)   A double deduction mismatch arises where −
    (a)   an amount is deductible from more than one person's income, or
    (b)   an amount is deductible from a person's income for the purposes of more than one tax.

(4)   The cases with which this Part is concerned involve −
    (a)   payments or quasi-payments under or in connection with financial instruments or repos, stock lending arrangements or other transfers of financial instruments,
    (b)   hybrid entities,
    (c)   companies with permanent establishments, or
    (d)   dual resident companies.

(5) This Part counteracts mismatches that would otherwise arise by making certain adjustments to a person's treatment for corporation tax purposes.

(6) Chapter 2 contains some key definitions for the purposes of this Part, see in particular —

    (a) section 259B which provides that "tax" means income tax, corporation tax on income, the diverted profits tax, the CFC charge, foreign tax or a foreign CFC charge,

    (b) section 259BB which defines "payment", "quasi-payment", "payment period", "relevant deduction", "payer", "payee", and "payee jurisdiction",

    (c) section 259BC which defines "ordinary income" and "taxable profits", in relation to taxes other than the CFC charge and foreign CFC charges,

    (d) section 259BD which contains corresponding provision for the CFC charge and foreign CFC charges,

    (e) section 259BE which defines "hybrid entity" and other related terms, and

    (f) section 259BF which defines "permanent establishment".

(7) Chapter 3 contains provision for the counteraction of certain deduction/non-inclusion mismatches arising from payments or quasi-payments under, or in connection with, financial instruments.

(8) Chapter 4 contains provision for the counteraction of certain deduction/non-inclusion mismatches arising from payments or quasi-payments and involving certain repos, stock lending arrangements or other arrangements for, or relating to, transfers of financial instruments.

(9) Chapter 5 contains provision for the counteraction of certain deduction/non-inclusion mismatches arising from payments or quasi-payments in relation to which the payer is a hybrid entity.

(10) Chapter 6 contains provision for the counteraction of certain deduction/non-inclusion mismatches arising in relation to internal transfers of money or money's worth made, or treated as made, by a multinational company's permanent establishment in the United Kingdom to the territory in which the company is resident for tax purposes.

(11) Chapter 7 contains provision for the counteraction of certain deduction/non-inclusion mismatches arising from payments or quasi-payments in relation to which a payee is a hybrid entity.

(12) Chapter 8 contains provision for the counteraction of certain deduction/non-inclusion mismatches arising from payments or quasi-payments in relation to which a payee is a multinational company.

(13) Chapter 9 contains provision for the counteraction of certain double deduction mismatches arising from a company being a hybrid entity.

(14) Chapter 10 contains provision for the counteraction of certain double deduction mismatches involving dual resident companies or relevant multinational companies.

(15) Chapter 11 contains provision about imported mismatches.

(16) Chapter 12 contains provision—

    (a) for adjustments to be made where a reasonable supposition made for the purposes of this Part turns out to be mistaken or otherwise ceases to be reasonable, and

    (b) for deductions from taxable total profits to be made where a relevant deduction has been denied under certain provisions of this Part and amounts of ordinary income arise later than is permitted.

(17) Chapter 13 contains anti-avoidance provision.

(18) Chapter 14 contains definitions and other provision about the interpretation of this Part.

(19) Each of Chapters 3 to 10 contains provision specifying that some or all of this Part (and any corresponding provision under the law of a territory outside the United Kingdom) is to be disregarded when determining whether a mismatch arises for the purposes of that Chapter and, if so, in what amount, see—

    (a) section 259CA(4) and (5),

    (b) section 259DA(5),

    (c) section 259EA(5) and (6),

    (d) section 259FA(4), (5) and (6),

    (e) section 259GA(5) and (6),

    (f) section 259HA(6) and (7),

    (g) section 259IA(2) and (3), and

    (h) section 259JA(5).

(20) The effect of the provisions mentioned in subsection (19) is that Chapters 3 to 10 (or any corresponding provision under the law of a territory outside the United Kingdom) have effect in the following sequence—

    (a) Chapter 4,

    (b) Chapter 3,

    (c) Chapter 5,

    (d) Chapter 6,

    (e) Chapter 7,

    (f) Chapter 8,

    (g) Chapter 9, and

    (h) Chapter 10.

CHAPTER 2

KEY DEFINITIONS

Meaning of "tax"

259B "Tax" means certain taxes on income and includes foreign tax etc

(1) In this Part "tax" means—

    (a) income tax,

   (b)   the charge to corporation tax on income,

   (c)   diverted profits tax,

   (d)   the CFC charge,

   (e)   foreign tax, or

   (f)   a foreign CFC charge.

(2)   In subsection (1) "foreign tax" means a tax chargeable under the law of a territory outside the United Kingdom so far as it—

   (a)   is charged on income and corresponds to United Kingdom income tax, or

   (b)   is charged on income and corresponds to the United Kingdom charge to corporation tax on income.

(3)   A tax is not outside the scope of subsection (2) by reason only that it—

   (a)   is chargeable under the law of a province, state or other part of a country, or

   (b)   is levied by or on behalf of a municipality or other local body.

(4)   In this Part—

   "CFC" and "the CFC charge" have the same meaning as in Part 9A (see section 371VA);

   "foreign CFC charge" means a charge (by whatever name known) under the law of a territory outside the United Kingdom which is similar to the CFC charge (and reference to a "foreign CFC" is to be read accordingly).

Equivalent provision to this Part under foreign law

259BA References to equivalent provision to this Part under the law of a territory outside the United Kingdom

(1)   A reference in this Part to provision under the law of a territory outside the United Kingdom that is equivalent to—

   (a)   this Part, or

   (b)   a provision of this Part,

is to be read in accordance with subsection (2).

(2)   The reference is to provision under the law of a territory outside the United Kingdom that it is reasonable to suppose—

   (a)   is based on the Final Report on Neutralising the Effects of Hybrid Mismatch Arrangements published by the Organisation for Economic Cooperation and Development ("OECD") on 5 October 2015 or any replacement or supplementary publication, and

   (b)   has effect for the same, or similar, purposes to this Part or (as the case may be) the provision of this Part.

(3)   In paragraph (a) of subsection (2) "replacement or supplementary publication" means any document that is approved and published by the OECD in place of, or to update or supplement, the report mentioned in that paragraph (or any replacement of, or supplement to, it).

Payments and quasi-payments etc

259BB Meaning of "payment", "quasi-payment", "payer", "payee" etc

(1) In this Part "payment" means any transfer—

    (a) of money or money's worth directly or indirectly from one person ("the payer") to one or more other persons, and

    (b) in relation to which (disregarding this Part and any equivalent provision under the law of a territory outside the United Kingdom) an amount (a "relevant deduction") may be deducted from the payer's income for a taxable period (the "payment period") for the purposes of calculating the payer's taxable profits.

(2) For the purposes of this Part, there is a "quasi-payment", in relation to a taxable period (the "payment period") of a person ("the payer"), if (disregarding this Part and any equivalent provision under the law of a territory outside the United Kingdom)—

    (a) an amount (a "relevant deduction") may be deducted from the payer's income for that period for the purposes of calculating the payer's taxable profits, and

    (b) making the assumptions in subsection (4), it would be reasonable to expect an amount of ordinary income to arise to one or more other persons as a result of the circumstances giving rise to the relevant deduction.

(3) But a quasi-payment does not arise under subsection (2) if—

    (a) the relevant deduction is an amount that is deemed, under the law of the payer jurisdiction, to arise for tax purposes, and

    (b) the circumstances giving rise to the relevant deduction do not include any economic rights, in substance, existing between the payer and a person mentioned in subsection (2)(b).

(4) The assumptions are that (so far as would not otherwise be the case)—

    (a) any question as to whether an entity is a distinct and separate person from the payer is determined in accordance with the law of the payer jurisdiction,

    (b) any persons to whom amounts arise, or potentially arise, as a result of the circumstances giving rise to the relevant deduction adopt the same approach to accounting for those circumstances as the payer, and

    (c) any persons to whom amounts arise, or potentially arise, as a result of those circumstances—

        (i) are, under the law of the payer jurisdiction, resident in that jurisdiction for tax purposes, and

        (ii) carry on a business, in connection with which those circumstances arise, in the payer jurisdiction.

(5) In this Part—

    (a) references to a quasi-payment include all the circumstances giving rise to the relevant deduction mentioned in subsection (2)(a), and

    (b) references to a quasi-payment being made are to those circumstances arising.

(6) In this Part "payee" means—
  (a) in the case of a payment, any person—
      (i) to whom the transfer is made as mentioned in subsection (1)(a), or
      (ii) to whom an amount of ordinary income arises as a result of the payment, and
  (b) in the case of a quasi-payment, any person—
      (i) to whom it would be reasonable to expect an amount of ordinary income to arise as mentioned in subsection (2)(b), or
      (ii) to whom an amount of ordinary income arises as a result of the quasi-payment.

(7) For the purposes of this Part, in the case of a quasi-payment, the payer is "also a payee" if—
  (a) an entity is not a distinct and separate person from the payer for the purposes of a tax charged under the law of the United Kingdom,
  (b) that entity is a distinct and separate person from the payer for the purposes of a tax charged under the law of the payer jurisdiction, and
  (c) it would be reasonable to expect an amount of ordinary income to arise to that entity as mentioned in subsection (2)(b).

(8) In this section "payer jurisdiction" means the jurisdiction under the law of which the relevant deduction may (disregarding this Part and any equivalent provision under the law of a territory outside the United Kingdom) be deducted.

(9) In this Part "payee jurisdiction", in relation to a payee, means a territory in which—
  (a) the payee is resident for tax purposes under the law of that territory, or
  (b) the payee has a permanent establishment.

Ordinary income

259BC The basic rules

(1) This section has effect for the purposes of this Part.

(2) "Ordinary income" means income that is brought into account, before any deductions, for the purposes of calculating the income or profits on which a relevant tax is charged ("taxable profits").

(3) But an amount of income is not brought into account for those purposes to the extent that it is excluded, reduced or offset by any exemption, exclusion, relief or credit—
  (a) that applies specifically to all or part of the amount of income (as opposed to ordinary income generally), or
  (b) that arises as a result of, or otherwise in connection with, a payment or quasi-payment that gives rise to the amount of income.

(4) If all the relevant tax charged on taxable profits is, or falls to be, refunded, none of the income brought into account in calculating those taxable profits is "ordinary income".

(5) If a proportion of the relevant tax charged on taxable profits is, or falls to be, refunded, the amount of any income brought into account in calculating those taxable profits that is "ordinary income" is proportionally reduced.

(6) For the purposes of subsections (4) and (5) an amount of relevant tax is refunded if and to the extent that—

  (a) any repayment of relevant tax, or any payment in respect of a credit for relevant tax, is made to any person, and

  (b) that repayment or payment is directly or indirectly in respect of the whole or part of the amount of relevant tax,

but an amount refunded is to be ignored if and to the extent that it results from qualifying loss relief.

(7) In subsection (6) "qualifying loss relief" means—

  (a) any means by which a loss might be used for corporation tax or income tax purposes to reduce the amount in respect of which a person is liable to tax, or

  (b) any corresponding means by which a loss corresponding to a relevant tax loss might be used for the purposes of a relevant tax other than corporation tax or income tax to reduce the amount in respect of which a person is liable to tax,

(and in paragraph (b) "relevant tax loss" means a loss that might be used as mentioned in paragraph (a)).

(8) References to an amount of ordinary income being "included in" taxable profits are to that amount being brought into account for the purposes of calculating those profits.

(9) In this section "relevant tax" means a tax other than the CFC charge or a foreign CFC charge.

(10) Section 259BD contains provision for ordinary income to arise to chargeable companies by virtue of the CFC charge or a foreign CFC charge.

259BD Chargeable companies in respect of CFCs and foreign CFCs

(1) This section has effect for the purposes of this Part.

(2) Subsections (3) to (7) apply where an amount of income arises to an entity ("C") that is a CFC, a foreign CFC or both and all or part of that amount (the "relevant income")—

  (a) is not ordinary income of C under section 259BC, or

  (b) arises as a result of a payment or quasi-payment under, or in connection with, a financial instrument or hybrid transfer arrangement and—

    (i) is (disregarding subsection (4)) ordinary income of C under section 259BC for a taxable period, but

    (ii) under taxed.

(3) The following steps determine whether, and to what extent, the relevant income is "ordinary income" of a chargeable company in relation to the CFC charge or a foreign CFC charge.

Step 1

Determine—

(a) whether any of the relevant income is brought into account in calculating C's chargeable profits for the purposes of the CFC charge or a foreign CFC charge, and

(b) if so, the amount of the relevant income that is so brought into account for the purposes of each relevant charge.

If none of the relevant income is so brought into account, then none of it is "ordinary income" of a chargeable company and no further steps are to be taken.

See subsections (10) to (12) for further provision about how this step is to be taken.

For the purposes of this section—

"relevant chargeable profits" are chargeable profits in relation to the calculation of which, for the purposes of the CFC charge or a foreign CFC charge, any of the relevant income is brought into account;

"relevant charge" means a charge in relation to which any of the relevant income is brought into account in calculating chargeable profits.

Step 2

In relation to each relevant charge, determine the proportion of C's relevant chargeable profits, for the purposes of that charge, that is apportioned to each chargeable company.

For the purposes of this section, each chargeable company to which 25% or more of C's relevant chargeable profits for the purposes of a relevant charge are apportioned is a "relevant chargeable company".

If there are no relevant chargeable companies in relation to any relevant charges, then none of the relevant income is "ordinary income" of a chargeable company and no further steps are to be taken.

Step 3

In relation to each relevant chargeable company, determine what is the appropriate proportion of the relevant income brought into account in calculating relevant chargeable profits, for the purposes of the relevant charge concerned.

That proportion of that income is "ordinary income" of that company for the taxable period for which that charge is charged on it by reference to those profits.

For the purposes of this step, the "appropriate proportion", in relation to a relevant chargeable company, is the same as the proportion of the relevant chargeable profits that is apportioned to it for the purposes of the relevant charge.

(4)   An amount of relevant income that is ordinary income of a relevant chargeable company in accordance with subsection (3) is not ordinary income of C (so far as it otherwise would be).

(5)   Relevant chargeable profits apportioned to a relevant chargeable company for the purposes of a relevant charge are "taxable profits" of that company for the taxable period for which the charge is charged on it by reference to those profits.

(6)   The amount of the relevant income that is ordinary income of that relevant chargeable company under subsection (3), by virtue of being brought into account in calculating those relevant chargeable profits, is "included in" those taxable profits.

(7)   References to tax charged on taxable profits include a relevant charge charged by reference to relevant chargeable profits that are taxable profits under subsection (5).

(8)   For the purposes of subsection (2)(b), an amount of ordinary income is "under taxed" if the highest rate at which tax is charged, for C's taxable period, on the taxable profits in which the amount is included, taking into account on a just and reasonable basis any credit for underlying tax, is less than C's full marginal rate for that period.

(9)   In subsection (8) —
      (a)   C's "full marginal rate" means the highest rate at which the tax that is chargeable on those taxable profits could be charged on taxable profits, of C for the taxable period, which include ordinary income that arises from, or in connection with, a financial instrument, and
      (b)   "credit for underlying tax" means a credit or relief given to reflect tax charged on profits that are wholly or partly used to fund (directly or indirectly) the payment or quasi-payment mentioned in subsection (2)(b).

(10) For the purposes of step 1 in subsection (3), section 259BC(3) applies for the purposes of determining the extent to which an amount of relevant income is brought into account in calculating chargeable profits as it applies for the purposes of determining the extent to which an amount of income is brought into account for the purposes of calculating taxable profits.

(11) Subsection (12) applies for the purposes of step 1 in subsection (3), if —
      (a)   the amount of income arising to C mentioned in subsection (2) —
            (i)   is not all relevant income, and
            (ii)   is only partly brought into account in calculating chargeable profits for the purposes of the CFC charge or a foreign CFC charge, and
      (b)   accordingly, it falls to be determined whether, and to what extent, the relevant income is brought into account in calculating those profits for the purposes of the charge concerned.

(12) The relevant income is to be taken to be brought into account (if at all) only to the extent that the total amount of income mentioned in subsection (2) that is brought into account exceeds the amount of income mentioned in that subsection that is not relevant income.

(13) In this section—

"chargeable company"—

    (a) in relation to the CFC charge, has the same meaning as in Part 9A (see section 371VA), and

    (b) in relation to a foreign CFC charge, means an entity (by whatever name known) corresponding to a chargeable company within the meaning of that Part;

"chargeable profits"—

    (a) in relation to the CFC charge, has the same meaning as in that Part (see that section), and

    (b) in relation to a foreign CFC charge, means the concept (by whatever name known) corresponding to chargeable profits within the meaning of that Part;

"hybrid transfer arrangement" has the meaning given by section 259DB.

Hybrid entity etc

259BE Meaning of "hybrid entity", "investor" and "investor jurisdiction"

(1) For the purposes of this Part, an entity is "hybrid" if it meets conditions A and B.

(2) Condition A is that the entity is regarded as being a person for tax purposes under the law of any territory.

(3) Condition B is that—

    (a) some or all of the entity's income or profits are treated (or would be if there were any) for the purposes of a tax charged under the law of any territory, as the income or profits of a person or persons other than the person mentioned in subsection (2), or

    (b) under the law of a territory other than the one mentioned in subsection (2), the entity is not regarded as a distinct and separate person to an entity or entities that are distinct and separate persons under the law of the territory mentioned in that subsection.

(4) For the purposes of this Part—

    (a) where subsection (3)(a) applies, a person who is treated as having the income or profits of the hybrid entity is an "investor" in it,

    (b) where subsection (3)(b) applies, an entity that—

        (i) is regarded as a distinct and separate person to the hybrid entity under the law of the territory mentioned in subsection (2), but

        (ii) is not regarded as a distinct and separate person to the hybrid entity under the law of another territory,

    is an "investor" in the hybrid entity, and

      (c)   any territory under the law of which an investor is within the charge to a tax is an "investor jurisdiction" in relation to that investor.

Permanent establishments

259BF Meaning of "permanent establishment"

(1)   In this Part "permanent establishment" means anything that is—

      (a)   a permanent establishment of a company within the meaning of the Corporation Tax Acts (see section 1119 of CTA 2010), or

      (b)   within any similar concept under the law of a territory outside the United Kingdom.

(2)   A concept is not outside the scope of subsection (1)(b) by reason only that it is not based on Article 5 of a Model Tax Convention on Income and Capital published by the Organisation for Economic Cooperation and Development.

CHAPTER 3

HYBRID AND OTHER MISMATCHES FROM FINANCIAL INSTRUMENTS

Introduction

259C Overview of Chapter

(1)   This Chapter contains provision that counteracts hybrid or otherwise impermissible deduction/non-inclusion mismatches that it is reasonable to suppose would otherwise arise from payments or quasi-payments under, or in connection with, financial instruments.

(2)   The Chapter counteracts mismatches where the payer or a payee is within the charge to corporation tax and does so by altering the corporation tax treatment of the payer or a payee.

(3)   Section 259CA contains the conditions that must be met for this Chapter to apply.

(4)   Section 259CB defines "hybrid or otherwise impermissible deduction/non-inclusion mismatch" and provides how the amount of the mismatch is to be calculated.

(5)   Section 259CC contains definitions of certain terms used in section 259CB.

(6)   Section 259CD contains provision that counteracts the mismatch where the payer is within the charge to corporation tax for the payment period.

(7)   Section 259CE contains provision that counteracts the mismatch where a payee is within the charge to corporation tax and neither section 259CD nor any equivalent provision under the law of a territory outside the United Kingdom fully counteracts the mismatch.

(8)   See also—

> (a) section 259BB for the meaning of "payment", "quasi-payment", "payment period", "relevant deduction", "payer" and "payee", and
>
> (b) section 259N for the meaning of "financial instrument".

Application of Chapter

259CA Circumstances in which the Chapter applies

(1) This Chapter applies if conditions A to D are met.

(2) Condition A is that a payment or quasi-payment is made under, or in connection with, a financial instrument.

(3) Condition B is that—

> (a) the payer is within the charge to corporation tax for the payment period, or
>
> (b) a payee is within the charge to corporation tax for an accounting period some or all of which falls within the payment period.

(4) Condition C is that it is reasonable to suppose that, disregarding the provisions mentioned in subsection (5), there would be a hybrid or otherwise impermissible deduction/non-inclusion mismatch in relation to the payment or quasi-payment (see section 259CB).

(5) The provisions are—

> (a) this Chapter and Chapters 5 to 10, and
>
> (b) any equivalent provision under the law of a territory outside the United Kingdom.

(6) Condition D is that—

> (a) it is a quasi-payment that is made as mentioned in subsection (2) and the payer is also a payee (see section 259BB(7)),
>
> (b) the payer and a payee are related (see section 259NC) at any time in the period—
>
> > (i) beginning with the day on which any arrangement is made by the payer or a payee in connection with the financial instrument, and
> >
> > (ii) ending with the last day of the payment period, or
>
> (c) the financial instrument, or any arrangement connected with it, is a structured arrangement.

(7) The financial instrument, or an arrangement connected with it, is a "structured arrangement" if it is reasonable to suppose that—

> (a) the financial instrument, or arrangement, is designed to secure a hybrid or otherwise impermissible deduction/non-inclusion mismatch, or
>
> (b) the terms of the financial instrument or arrangement share the economic benefit of the mismatch between the parties to the instrument or arrangement or otherwise reflect the fact that the mismatch is expected to arise.

(8) The financial instrument or arrangement may be designed to secure a hybrid or otherwise impermissible deduction/non-inclusion

mismatch despite also being designed to secure any commercial or other objective.

(9)   Sections 259CD (cases where the payer is within the charge to corporation tax for the payment period) and 259CE (cases where a payee is within the charge to corporation tax) contain provision for the counteraction of the hybrid or otherwise impermissible deduction/non-inclusion mismatch.

259CB Hybrid or otherwise impermissible deduction/non-inclusion mismatches and their extent

(1)   There is a "hybrid or otherwise impermissible deduction/non-inclusion mismatch", in relation to a payment or quasi-payment, if either or both of case 1 or 2 applies.

(2)   Case 1 applies where—
  (a)   the relevant deduction exceeds the sum of the amounts of ordinary income that, by reason of the payment or quasi-payment, arise to each payee for a permitted taxable period, and
  (b)   all or part of that excess arises by reason of the terms, or any other feature, of the financial instrument.

(3)   So far as the excess arises by reason of a relevant debt relief provision, it is to be taken not to arise by reason of the terms, or any other feature, of the financial instrument (whether or not it would have arisen by reason of the terms, or any other feature, of the financial instrument regardless of the relevant debt relief provision).

(4)   Subject to that and subsection (9), for the purposes of subsection (2)(b)—
  (a)   it does not matter whether the excess or part arises for another reason as well as the terms, or any other feature, of the financial instrument (even if it would have arisen for that other reason regardless of the terms, or any other feature, of the financial instrument), and
  (b)   an excess or part of an excess is to be taken to arise by reason of the terms, or any other feature, of the financial instrument (so far as would not otherwise be the case) if, on making such of the relevant assumptions in relation to each payee as apply in relation to that payee (see subsections (5) and (6)), it could arise by reason of the terms, or any other feature, of the financial instrument.

(5)   These are the "relevant assumptions"—
  (a)   where a payee is not within the charge to a tax under the law of a payee jurisdiction because the payee benefits from an exclusion, immunity, exemption or relief (however described) under that law, assume that the exclusion, immunity, exemption or relief does not apply;
  (b)   where an amount of income is not included in the ordinary income of a payee for the purposes of a tax charged under the law of a payee jurisdiction because the payment or quasi-payment is not made in connection with a business carried on

by the payee in that jurisdiction, assume that the payment or quasi-payment is made in connection with such a business;

   (c)   where a payee is not within the charge to a tax under the law of any territory because there is no territory where the payee is —

      (i)   resident for the purposes of a tax charged under the law of that territory, or

      (ii)   within the charge to a tax under the law of that territory as a result of having a permanent establishment in that territory,

assume that the payee is a company that is resident for tax purposes, and carries on a business in connection with which the payment or quasi-payment is made, in the United Kingdom.

(6) Where the relevant assumption in subsection (5)(c) applies in relation to a payee the following provisions are to be disregarded in relation to that payee for the purposes of subsection (4)(b) —

   (a)   section 441 of CTA 2009 (loan relationships for unallowable purposes);

   (b)   section 690 of that Act (derivative contracts for unallowable purposes);

   (c)   Part 4 (transfer pricing);

   (d)   this Part;

   (e)   Part 7 (tax treatment of financing costs and income).

(7) Case 2 applies where there are one or more amounts of ordinary income ("under-taxed amounts") that —

   (a)   arise, by reason of the payment or quasi-payment, to a payee for a permitted taxable period, and

   (b)   are under taxed by reason of the terms, or any other feature, of the financial instrument.

(8) Subject to subsection (9), for the purposes of subsection (7)(b) it does not matter whether an amount of ordinary income is under taxed for another reason as well as the terms, or any other feature, of the financial instrument (even if it would have been under taxed for that other reason regardless of the terms, or any other feature, of the financial instrument).

(9) For the purposes of this section disregard —

   (a)   any excess or part of an excess mentioned in subsection (2), and

   (b)   any under-taxed amount,

that arises as a result of a payee being a relevant investment fund (see section 259NA).

(10) Where case 1 applies, the amount of the hybrid or otherwise impermissible deduction/non-inclusion mismatch is equal to the excess that arises as mentioned in subsection (2)(b).

(11) Where case 2 applies, the amount of the hybrid or otherwise impermissible deduction/non-inclusion mismatch is equal to the

sum of the amounts given in respect of each under-taxed amount by —

$$\frac{(UTA \times (FMR - R))}{FMR}$$

where —

"UTA" is the under-taxed amount;

"FMR" is the payee's full marginal rate (expressed as a percentage) for the permitted taxable period for which the under-taxed amount arises;

"R" is the highest rate (expressed as a percentage) at which tax is charged on the taxable profits in which the under-taxed amount is included, taking into account on a just and reasonable basis the effect of any credit for underlying tax.

(12) Where cases 1 and 2 both apply, the amount of the hybrid or otherwise impermissible deduction/non-inclusion mismatch is the sum of the amounts given by subsections (10) and (11).

(13) See section 259CC for the meaning of "permitted taxable period", "relevant debt relief provision" and "under taxed".

259CC Interpretation of section 259CB

(1) This section has effect for the purposes of section 259CB.

(2) A taxable period of a payee is "permitted" in relation to an amount of ordinary income that arises as a result of the payment or quasi-payment if —

    (a) the period begins before the end of 12 months after the end of the payment period, or

    (b) where the period begins after that —

        (i) a claim has been made for the period to be a permitted period in relation to the amount of ordinary income, and

        (ii) it is just and reasonable for the amount of ordinary income to arise for that taxable period rather than an earlier period.

(3) Each of these is a "relevant debt relief provision" —

    (a) section 322 of CTA 2009 (release of debts: cases where credits not required to be brought into account),

    (b) section 357 of that Act (insolvent creditors),

    (c) section 358 of that Act (exclusion of credits on release of connected companies' debts: general),

    (d) section 359 of that Act (exclusion of credits on release of connected companies' debts during creditor's insolvency),

    (e) section 361C of that Act (the equity-for-debt exception),

    (f) section 361D of that Act (corporate rescue: debt released shortly after acquisition), and

    (g) section 362A of that Act (corporate rescue: debt released shortly after connection arises).

(4) An amount of ordinary income of a payee, for a permitted taxable period, is "under taxed" if the highest rate at which tax is charged on

the taxable profits of the payee in which the amount is included, taking into account on a just and reasonable basis the effect of any credit for underlying tax, is less than the payee's full marginal rate for that period.

(5) The payee's "full marginal rate" means the highest rate at which the tax that is chargeable on the taxable profits mentioned in subsection (4) could be charged on taxable profits, of the payee for the permitted taxable period, which include ordinary income that arises from, or in connection with, a financial instrument.

(6) A "credit for underlying tax" means a credit or relief given to reflect tax charged on profits that are wholly or partly used to fund (directly or indirectly) the payment or quasi-payment.

Counteraction

259CD Counteraction where the payer is within the charge to corporation tax for the payment period

(1) This section applies where the payer is within the charge to corporation tax for the payment period.

(2) For corporation tax purposes, the relevant deduction that may be deducted from the payer's income for the payment period is reduced by an amount equal to the hybrid or otherwise impermissible deduction/non-inclusion mismatch mentioned in section 259CA(4).

259CE Counteraction where a payee is within the charge to corporation tax

(1) This section applies in relation to a payee where—
    (a) the payee is within the charge to corporation tax for an accounting period some or all of which falls within the payment period, and
    (b) it is reasonable to suppose that—
        (i) neither section 259CD nor any equivalent provision under the law of a territory outside the United Kingdom applies, or
        (ii) a provision of the law of a territory outside the United Kingdom that is equivalent to section 259CD applies, but does not fully counteract the hybrid or otherwise impermissible deduction/non-inclusion mismatch mentioned in section 259CA(4).

(2) A provision of the law of a territory outside the United Kingdom that is equivalent to section 259CD does not fully counteract that mismatch if (and only if)—
    (a) it does not reduce the relevant deduction by the full amount of the mismatch, and
    (b) the payer is still able to deduct some of the relevant deduction from income in calculating taxable profits.

(3) In this section "the relevant amount" is—
    (a) in a case where subsection (1)(b)(i) applies, an amount equal to the hybrid or otherwise impermissible deduction/non-inclusion mismatch mentioned in section 259CA(4), or

      (b)   in a case where subsection (1)(b)(ii) applies, the lesser of—

          (i)   the amount by which that mismatch exceeds the amount by which it is reasonable to suppose the relevant deduction is reduced by a provision under the law of a territory outside the United Kingdom that is equivalent to section 259CD, and

          (ii)   the amount of the relevant deduction that may still be deducted as mentioned in subsection (2)(b).

(4)   If the payee is the only payee, the relevant amount is to be treated as income arising to the payee for the counteraction period.

(5)   If there is more than one payee, an amount equal to the payee's share of the relevant amount is to be treated as income arising to the payee for the counteraction period.

(6)   The payee's share of the relevant amount is to be determined by apportioning that amount between all the payees on a just and reasonable basis, having regard (in particular)—

      (a)   to any arrangements as to profit sharing that may exist between some or all of the payees,

      (b)   to whom any under-taxed amounts (within the meaning given by section 259CB(7)) arise, and

      (c)   to whom any amounts of ordinary income that it would be reasonable to expect to arise as a result of the payment or quasi-payment, but that do not arise, would have arisen.

(7)   An amount of income that is treated as arising under subsection (4) or (5) is chargeable under Chapter 8 of Part 10 of CTA 2009 (income not otherwise charged) (despite section 979(2) of that Act).

(8)   The "counteraction period" means—

      (a)   if an accounting period of the payee coincides with the payment period, that accounting period, or

      (b)   otherwise, the first accounting period of the payee that is wholly or partly within the payment period.

CHAPTER 4

HYBRID TRANSFER DEDUCTION/NON-INCLUSION MISMATCHES

Introduction

259D Overview of Chapter

(1)   This Chapter contains provision that counteracts deduction/non-inclusion mismatches that it is reasonable to suppose would otherwise arise from payments or quasi-payments as a consequence of hybrid transfer arrangements.

(2)   The Chapter counteracts mismatches where the payer or a payee is within the charge to corporation tax and does so by altering the corporation tax treatment of the payer or a payee.

(3)   Section 259DA contains the conditions that must be met for this Chapter to apply.

(4) Section 259DB defines "hybrid transfer arrangement".

(5) Section 259DC defines "hybrid transfer deduction/non-inclusion mismatch" and provides how the amount of the mismatch is to be calculated.

(6) Section 259DD contains definitions of certain terms used in section 259DC.

(7) Section 259DE contains provision in connection with excluding mismatches from counteraction by the Chapter where they arise as a consequence of the tax treatment of a financial trader.

(8) Section 259DF contains provision that counteracts the mismatch where the payer is within the charge to corporation tax for the payment period.

(9) Section 259DG contains provision that counteracts the mismatch where a payee is within the charge to corporation tax and neither section 259DF nor any equivalent provision under the law of a territory outside the United Kingdom fully counteracts the mismatch.

(10) See also section 259BB for the meaning of "payment", "quasi-payment", "payment period", "relevant deduction", "payer" and "payee".

Application of Chapter

259DA Circumstances in which the Chapter applies

(1) This Chapter applies if conditions A to E are met.

(2) Condition A is that there is a hybrid transfer arrangement in relation to an underlying instrument (see section 259DB).

(3) Condition B is that a payment or quasi-payment is made under or in connection with—
    (a) the hybrid transfer arrangement, or
    (b) the underlying instrument.

(4) Condition C is that—
    (a) the payer is within the charge to corporation tax for the payment period, or
    (b) a payee is within the charge to corporation tax for an accounting period some or all of which falls within the payment period.

(5) Condition D is that it is reasonable to suppose that, disregarding this Part and any equivalent provision under the law of a territory outside the United Kingdom, there would be a hybrid transfer deduction/non-inclusion mismatch in relation to the payment or quasi-payment (see section 259DC).

(6) Condition E is that—
    (a) it is a quasi-payment that is made as mentioned in subsection (3) and the payer is also a payee (see section 259BB(7)),

    (b)   the payer and a payee are related (see section 259NC) at any time in the period —

        (i)   beginning with the day on which the hybrid transfer arrangement is made, and

        (ii) ending with the last day of the payment period, or

    (c)   the hybrid transfer arrangement is a structured arrangement.

(7)   The hybrid transfer arrangement is a "structured arrangement" if it is reasonable to suppose that —

    (a)   the hybrid transfer arrangement is designed to secure a hybrid transfer deduction/non-inclusion mismatch, or

    (b)   the terms of the hybrid transfer arrangement share the economic benefit of the mismatch between the parties to the arrangement or otherwise reflect the fact that the mismatch is expected to arise.

(8)   The hybrid transfer arrangement may be designed to secure a hybrid transfer deduction/non-inclusion mismatch despite also being designed to secure any commercial or other objective.

(9)   Sections 259DF (cases where the payer is within the charge to corporation tax for the payment period) and 259DG (cases where a payee is within the charge to corporation tax) make provision for the counteraction of the hybrid transfer deduction/non-inclusion mismatch.

259DB Meaning of "hybrid transfer arrangement", "underlying instrument" etc

(1)   This section has effect for the purposes of this Chapter.

(2)   A "hybrid transfer arrangement" means —

    (a)   a repo,

    (b)   a stock lending arrangement, or

    (c)   any other arrangement,

that is an arrangement within subsection (3).

(3)   An arrangement is within this subsection if it provides for, or relates to, the transfer of a financial instrument ("the underlying instrument") and —

    (a)   the dual treatment condition is met in relation to the arrangement, or

    (b)   a substitute payment could be made under the arrangement.

(4)   The dual treatment condition is met in relation to the arrangement if —

    (a)   in relation to a person, for the purposes of a tax —

        (i)   the arrangement is regarded as equivalent, in substance, to a transaction for the lending of money at interest, and

        (ii) a payment or quasi-payment made under, or in connection with, the arrangement or the underlying instrument could be treated so as to reflect the fact the arrangement is so regarded, and

      (b)   in relation to another person, for the purposes of a tax (whether or not the same one), such a payment or quasi-payment would not be treated so as to reflect the arrangement being regarded as equivalent, in substance, to a transaction for the lending of money at interest.

(5)   A payment or quasi-payment is a "substitute payment" if—

      (a)   it consists of or involves—

          (i)   an amount being paid, or

          (ii)   a benefit being given (including the release of the whole or part of any liability to pay an amount),

      (b)   that amount, or the value of that benefit, is representative of a return of any kind ("the underlying return") that arises on, or in connection with, the underlying instrument, and

      (c)   the amount is paid, or the benefit is given, to someone other than the person to whom the underlying return arises.

(6)   For the purposes of subsection (3) where there is an arrangement, to which a person ("P") and another person ("Q") are party, under which—

      (a)   a financial instrument ("the first instrument") ceases to be owned by P (whether or not because it ceases to exist), and

      (b)   Q comes to own a financial instrument ("the second instrument") under which Q has the same, or substantially the same, rights and liabilities as P had under the first instrument,

the second instrument is to be treated as being transferred from P to Q.

259DC Hybrid transfer deduction/non-inclusion mismatches and their extent

(1)   There is a "hybrid transfer deduction/non-inclusion mismatch", in relation to a payment or quasi-payment, if either or both of case 1 or 2 applies.

(2)   Case 1 applies where—

      (a)   the relevant deduction exceeds the sum of the amounts of ordinary income that, by reason of the payment or quasi-payment, arise to each payee for a permitted taxable period, and

      (b)   all or part of that excess arises for a reason mentioned in subsection (8).

(3)   Subject to subsection (9), for the purposes of subsection (2)(b)—

      (a)   it does not matter whether the excess or part arises for another reason as well (even if it would have arisen for that other reason regardless of any reasons mentioned in subsection (8)), and

      (b)   an excess or part of an excess is to be taken to arise for a reason mentioned in subsection (8) (so far as would not otherwise be the case) if, on making such of the relevant assumptions in relation to each payee as apply in relation to that payee (see subsections (4) and (5))), it could arise for a reason mentioned in subsection (8).

(4) These are the "relevant assumptions"—

   (a) where a payee is not within the charge to a tax under the law of a payee jurisdiction because the payee benefits from an exclusion, immunity, exemption or relief (however described) under that law, assume that the exclusion, immunity, exemption or relief does not apply;

   (b) where an amount of income is not included in the ordinary income of a payee for the purposes of a tax charged under the law of a payee jurisdiction because the payment or quasi-payment is not made in connection with a business carried on by the payee in that jurisdiction, assume that the payment or quasi-payment is made in connection with such a business;

   (c) where a payee is not within the charge to a tax under the law of any territory because there is no territory where the payee is—

      (i) resident for the purposes of a tax charged under the law of that territory, or

      (ii) within the charge to a tax under the law of that territory as a result of having a permanent establishment in that territory,

      assume that the payee is a company that is resident for tax purposes, and carries on a business in connection with which the payment or quasi-payment is made, in the United Kingdom.

(5) Where the relevant assumption in subsection (4)(c) applies in relation to a payee the following provisions are to be disregarded in relation to that payee for the purposes of subsection (3)(b)—

   (a) section 441 of CTA 2009 (loan relationships for unallowable purposes);

   (b) Part 4 (transfer pricing);

   (c) this Part;

   (d) Part 7 (tax treatment of financing costs and income).

(6) Case 2 applies where there are one or more amounts of ordinary income ("under-taxed amounts") that—

   (a) arise, by reason of the payment or quasi-payment, to a payee for a permitted taxable period, and

   (b) are under taxed for a reason mentioned in subsection (8).

(7) Subject to subsection (9), for the purposes of subsection (6)(b) it does not matter whether an amount of ordinary income is under taxed for another reason as well (even if it would have been under taxed for that other reason regardless of any reason mentioned in subsection (8)).

(8) The reasons are—

   (a) the dual treatment condition being met in relation to a hybrid transfer arrangement under, or in connection with, which the payment or quasi-payment is made (see section 259DB(4));

   (b) the payment or quasi-payment being a substitute payment.

(9) For the purposes of this section, disregard—

(a) any excess or part of an excess mentioned in subsection (2), and

(b) any under-taxed amount,

in relation to which the financial trader exclusion applies (see section 259DE) or that arises as a result of a payee being a relevant investment fund (see section 259NA).

(10) Where case 1 applies, the amount of the hybrid transfer deduction/non-inclusion mismatch is equal to the excess that arises as mentioned in subsection (2)(b).

(11) Where case 2 applies, the amount of the hybrid transfer deduction/non-inclusion mismatch is equal to the sum of the amounts given in respect of each under-taxed amount by—

$$\frac{(UTA \times (FMR - R))}{FMR}$$

where—

"UTA" is the under-taxed amount;

"FMR" is the payee's full marginal rate (expressed as a percentage) for the permitted taxable period for which the under-taxed amount arises;

"R" is the highest rate (expressed as a percentage) at which tax is charged on the taxable profits in which the under-taxed amount is included, taking into account on a just and reasonable basis the effect of any credit for underlying tax.

(12) Where cases 1 and 2 both apply, the amount of the hybrid transfer deduction/non-inclusion mismatch is the sum of the amounts given by subsections (10) and (11).

(13) See section 259DD for the meaning of "permitted taxable period" and "under taxed".

259DD Interpretation of section 259DC

(1) This section has effect for the purposes of section 259DC.

(2) A taxable period of a payee is "permitted" in relation to an amount of ordinary income that arises as a result of the payment or quasi-payment if—

(a) the period begins before the end of 12 months after the end of the payment period, or

(b) where the period begins after that—

(i) a claim has been made for the period to be a permitted period in relation to the amount of ordinary income, and

(ii) it is just and reasonable for the amount of ordinary income to arise for that taxable period rather than an earlier period.

(3) An amount of ordinary income of a payee, for a permitted taxable period, is "under taxed" if the highest rate at which tax is charged on the taxable profits of the payee in which the amount is included, taking into account on a just and reasonable basis the effect of any credit for underlying tax, is less than the payee's full marginal rate for that period.

(4)   The payee's "full marginal rate" means the highest rate at which the tax that is chargeable on the taxable profits mentioned in subsection (3) could be charged on taxable profits, of the payee for the permitted taxable period, which include ordinary income that arises from, or in connection with, a financial instrument.

(5)   A "credit for underlying tax" means a credit or relief given to reflect tax charged on profits that are wholly or partly used to fund (directly or indirectly) the payment or quasi-payment.

259DE The financial trader exclusion

(1)   This section has effect for the purposes of section 259DC(9).

(2)   The financial trader exclusion applies, in relation to an excess or part of an excess mentioned in section 259DC(2) or an under-taxed amount, where conditions A to C are met.

(3)   Condition A is that the excess or part arises, or the under-taxed amount is under taxed, because the payment or quasi-payment—
    (a)   is a substitute payment,
    (b)   is treated, for the purposes of tax charged on a person, so as to reflect the fact that it is representative of the underlying return, and
    (c)   is brought into account by another person ("the financial trader") in calculating the profits of a trade under—
        (i)   Part 3 of CTA 2009 (trading income), or
        (ii)   an equivalent provision of the law of a territory outside the United Kingdom.

(4)   Condition B is that the financial trader also brings any associated payments into account as mentioned in subsection (3)(c).

(5)   In subsection (4) "associated payment" means a payment or quasi-payment—
    (a)   in relation to which the financial trader is the payer or a payee, and
    (b)   that is made under, or in connection with, the underlying instrument or an arrangement that relates to the underlying instrument.

(6)   Condition C is that—
    (a)   if the underlying return were to arise, and be paid directly, to the payee or payees in relation to the substitute payment, neither Chapter 3 (hybrid and other mismatches from financial instruments) nor any equivalent provision under the law of a territory outside the United Kingdom would apply, and
    (b)   the hybrid transfer arrangement under, or in connection with, which the substitute payment is made is not a structured arrangement (within the meaning given by section 259DA(7) and (8)).

Counteraction

259DF Counteraction where the payer is within the charge to corporation tax for the payment period

(1) This section applies where the payer is within the charge to corporation tax for the payment period.

(2) For corporation tax purposes, the relevant deduction that may be deducted from the payer's income for the payment period is reduced by an amount equal to the hybrid transfer deduction/non-inclusion mismatch mentioned in section 259DA(5).

259DG Counteraction where a payee is within the charge to corporation tax

(1) This section applies in relation to a payee where —
   (a) the payee is within the charge to corporation tax for an accounting period some or all of which falls within the payment period, and
   (b) it is reasonable to suppose that —
      (i) neither section 259DF nor any equivalent provision under the law of a territory outside the United Kingdom applies, or
      (ii) a provision of the law of a territory outside the United Kingdom that is equivalent to section 259DF applies, but does not fully counteract the hybrid transfer deduction/non-inclusion mismatch mentioned in section 259DA(5).

(2) A provision of the law of a territory outside the United Kingdom that is equivalent to section 259DF does not fully counteract that mismatch if (and only if) —
   (a) it does not reduce the relevant deduction by the full amount of the mismatch, and
   (b) the payer is still able to deduct some of the relevant deduction from income in calculating taxable profits.

(3) In this section "the relevant amount" is —
   (a) in a case where subsection (1)(b)(i) applies, an amount equal to the hybrid transfer deduction/non-inclusion mismatch mentioned in section 259DA(5), or
   (b) in a case where subsection (1)(b)(ii) applies, the lesser of —
      (i) the amount by which that mismatch exceeds the amount by which it is reasonable to suppose the relevant deduction is reduced by a provision under the law of a territory outside the United Kingdom that is equivalent to section 259DF, and
      (ii) the amount of the relevant deduction that may still be deducted as mentioned in subsection (2)(b).

(4) If the payee is the only payee, the relevant amount is to be treated as income arising to the payee for the counteraction period.

(5) If there is more than one payee, an amount equal to the payee's share of the relevant amount is to be treated as income arising to the payee for the counteraction period.

(6) The payee's share of the relevant amount is to be determined by apportioning that amount between all the payees on a just and reasonable basis, having regard (in particular)—

   (a) to any arrangements as to profit sharing that may exist between some or all of the payees,

   (b) to whom any under-taxed amounts (within the meaning given by section 259DC(6)) arise, and

   (c) to whom any amounts of ordinary income that it would be reasonable to expect to arise as a result of the payment or quasi-payment, but that do not arise, would have arisen.

(7) An amount of income that is treated as arising under subsection (4) or (5) is chargeable under Chapter 8 of Part 10 of CTA 2009 (income not otherwise charged) (despite section 979(2) of that Act).

(8) The "counteraction period" means—

   (a) if an accounting period of the payee coincides with the payment period, that accounting period, or

   (b) otherwise, the first accounting period of the payee that is wholly or partly within the payment period.

CHAPTER 5

HYBRID PAYER DEDUCTION/NON-INCLUSION MISMATCHES

Introduction

259E Overview of Chapter

(1) This Chapter contains provision that counteracts deduction/non-inclusion mismatches that it is reasonable to suppose would otherwise arise from payments or quasi-payments because the payer is a hybrid entity.

(2) The Chapter counteracts mismatches where the payer or a payee is within the charge to corporation tax and does so by altering the corporation tax treatment of the payer or a payee.

(3) Section 259EA contains the conditions that must be met for this Chapter to apply.

(4) Section 259EB defines "hybrid payer deduction/non-inclusion mismatch" and provides how the amount of the mismatch is to be calculated.

(5) Section 259EC contains provision that counteracts the mismatch where the payer is within the charge to corporation tax for the payment period.

(6) Section 259ED contains provision that counteracts the mismatch where a payee is within the charge to corporation tax and the mismatch is not fully counteracted by provision under the law of a territory outside the United Kingdom that is equivalent to section 259EC.

(7) See also—

    (a)   section 259BB for the meaning of "payment", "quasi-payment", "payment period", "relevant deduction", "payer" and "payee", and

    (b)   section 259BE for the meaning of "hybrid entity", "investor" and "investor jurisdiction".

Application of Chapter

259EA Circumstances in which the Chapter applies

(1)   This Chapter applies if conditions A to E are met.

(2)   Condition A is that a payment or quasi-payment is made under, or in connection with, an arrangement.

(3)   Condition B is that the payer is a hybrid entity ("the hybrid payer").

(4)   Condition C is that—

    (a)   the hybrid payer is within the charge to corporation tax for the payment period, or

    (b)   a payee is within the charge to corporation tax for an accounting period some or all of which falls within the payment period.

(5)   Condition D is that it is reasonable to suppose that, disregarding the provisions mentioned in subsection (6), there would be a hybrid payer deduction/non-inclusion mismatch in relation to the payment or quasi-payment (see section 259EB).

(6)   The provisions are—

    (a)   this Chapter and Chapters 6 to 10, and

    (b)   any equivalent provision under the law of a territory outside the United Kingdom.

(7)   Condition E is that—

    (a)   it is a quasi-payment that is made as mentioned in subsection (2) and the hybrid payer is also a payee (see section 259BB(7)),

    (b)   the hybrid payer and a payee are in the same control group (see section 259NB) at any time in the period—

        (i)   beginning with the day on which the arrangement mentioned in subsection (2) is made, and

        (ii)   ending with the last day of the payment period, or

    (c)   that arrangement is a structured arrangement.

(8)   The arrangement is "structured" if it is reasonable to suppose that—

    (a)   the arrangement is designed to secure a hybrid payer deduction/non-inclusion mismatch, or

    (b)   the terms of the arrangement share the economic benefit of the mismatch between the parties to the arrangement or otherwise reflect the fact that the mismatch is expected to arise.

(9)   The arrangement may be designed to secure a hybrid payer deduction/non-inclusion mismatch despite also being designed to secure any commercial or other objective.

(10) Sections 259EC (cases where the hybrid payer is within the charge to corporation tax for the payment period) and 259ED (cases where a payee is within the charge to corporation tax) contain provision for the counteraction of the hybrid payer deduction/non-inclusion mismatch.

259EB Hybrid payer deduction/non-inclusion mismatches and their extent

(1) There is a "hybrid payer deduction/non-inclusion mismatch", in relation to a payment or quasi-payment, if—

    (a) the relevant deduction exceeds the sum of the amounts of ordinary income that, by reason of the payment or quasi-payment, arise to each payee for a permitted taxable period, and

    (b) all or part of that excess arises by reason of the hybrid payer being a hybrid entity.

(2) The amount of the hybrid payer deduction/non-inclusion mismatch is equal to the excess that arises as mentioned in subsection (1)(b).

(3) For the purposes of subsection (1)(b)—

    (a) it does not matter whether the excess or part arises for another reason as well (even if it would have arisen for that other reason regardless of whether the hybrid payer is a hybrid entity), and

    (b) an excess or part of an excess is to be taken to arise by reason of the hybrid payer being a hybrid entity (so far as would not otherwise be the case) if, on making such of the relevant assumptions in relation to each payee as apply in relation to that payee (see subsection (4)), it could arise by reason of the hybrid payer being a hybrid entity.

(4) These are the "relevant assumptions"—

    (a) where a payee is not within the charge to a tax under the law of a payee jurisdiction because the payee benefits from an exclusion, immunity, exemption or relief (however described) under that law, assume that the exclusion, immunity, exemption or relief does not apply;

    (b) where an amount of income is not included in the ordinary income of a payee for the purposes of a tax charged under the law of a payee jurisdiction because the payment or quasi-payment is not made in connection with a business carried on by the payee in that jurisdiction, assume that the payment or quasi-payment is made in connection with such a business.

(5) A taxable period of a payee is "permitted" in relation to an amount of ordinary income that arises as a result of the payment or quasi-payment if—

    (a) the period begins before the end of 12 months after the end of the payment period, or

    (b) where the period begins after that—

        (i) a claim has been made for the period to be a permitted period in relation to the amount of ordinary income, and

(ii)   it is just and reasonable for the amount of ordinary income to arise for that taxable period rather than an earlier period.

Counteraction

259EC Counteraction where the hybrid payer is within the charge to corporation tax for the payment period

(1)   This section applies where the hybrid payer is within the charge to corporation tax for the payment period.

(2)   For corporation tax purposes, the relevant deduction so far as it does not exceed the hybrid payer deduction/non-inclusion mismatch mentioned in section 259EA(5) ("the restricted deduction") may not be deducted from the hybrid payer's income for the payment period unless it is deducted from dual inclusion income for that period.

(3)   So much of the restricted deduction (if any) as, by virtue of subsection (2), cannot be deducted from the payer's income for the payment period —
    (a)   is carried forward to subsequent accounting periods of the payer, and
    (b)   for corporation tax purposes, may be deducted from dual inclusion income for any such period (and not from any other income), so far as it cannot be deducted under this paragraph for an earlier period.

(4)   In this section "dual inclusion income" of the payer for an accounting period means an amount that arises in connection with the arrangement mentioned in section 259EA(2) and is both —
    (a)   ordinary income of the payer for that period for corporation tax purposes, and
    (b)   ordinary income of an investor in the payer for a permitted taxable period for the purposes of any tax charged under the law of an investor jurisdiction.

(5)   A taxable period of an investor is "permitted" for the purposes of paragraph (b) of subsection (4) if —
    (a)   the period begins before the end of 12 months after the end of the accounting period mentioned in paragraph (a) of that subsection, or
    (b)   where the period begins after that —
        (i)   a claim has been made for the period to be a permitted period in relation to the amount of ordinary income, and
        (ii)   it is just and reasonable for the amount of ordinary income to arise for that taxable period rather than an earlier period.

259ED Counteraction where a payee is within the charge to corporation tax

(1)   This section applies in relation to a payee where —
    (a)   the payee is within the charge to corporation tax for an accounting period some or all of which falls within the payment period, and

      (b)   it is reasonable to suppose that—

          (i)   no provision under the law of a territory outside the United Kingdom that is equivalent to section 259EC applies, or

          (ii)   such a provision does apply, but does not fully counteract the hybrid payer deduction/non-inclusion mismatch mentioned in section 259EA(5).

(2)   A provision of the law of a territory outside the United Kingdom that is equivalent to section 259EC does not fully counteract that mismatch if (and only if)—

      (a)   the amount of the relevant deduction that the provision prevents from being deducted from income of the hybrid payer, for the payment period, other than dual inclusion income, is less than the amount of the mismatch, and

      (b)   the hybrid payer is still able to deduct some of the relevant deduction from income, for the payment period, that is not dual inclusion income.

(3)   In this section "the relevant amount" is—

      (a)   in a case where subsection (1)(b)(i) applies, an amount equal to the hybrid payer deduction/non-inclusion mismatch mentioned in section 259EA(5), or

      (b)   in a case where subsection (1)(b)(ii) applies, the lesser of—

          (i)   the amount by which that mismatch exceeds the amount of the relevant deduction that it is reasonable to suppose is prevented, by a provision of the law of a territory outside the United Kingdom that is equivalent to section 259EC, from being deducted from income of the hybrid payer, for the payment period, other than dual inclusion income, and

          (ii)   the amount of the relevant deduction that may still be deducted as mentioned in subsection (2)(b).

(4)   If the payee is the only payee, an amount equal to—

      (a)   the relevant amount, less

      (b)   any dual inclusion income,

is to be treated as income arising to the payee for the counteraction period.

(5)   If there is more than one payee, an amount equal to—

      (a)   the payee's share of the relevant amount, less

      (b)   the relevant proportion of any dual inclusion income,

is to be treated as income arising to the payee for the counteraction period.

(6)   The payee's share of the relevant amount is to be determined by apportioning that amount between all the payees on a just and reasonable basis, having regard (in particular)—

      (a)   to any arrangements as to profit sharing that may exist between some or all of the payees, and

      (b)   to whom any amounts of ordinary income that it would be reasonable to expect to arise as a result of the payment or quasi-payment, but that do not arise, would have arisen.

(7) The "relevant" proportion of any dual inclusion income for the payment period is the same as the proportion of the relevant amount apportioned to the payee in accordance with subsection (6).

(8) An amount of income that is treated as arising under subsection (4) or (5) is chargeable under Chapter 8 of Part 10 of CTA 2009 (income not otherwise charged) (despite section 979(2) of that Act).

(9) In this section—
   "counteraction period" means—
      (a) if an accounting period of the payee coincides with the payment period, that accounting period, or
      (b) otherwise, the first accounting period of the payee that is wholly or partly within the payment period;
   "dual inclusion income" means an amount that arises in connection with the arrangement mentioned in section 259EA(2) and is both—
      (a) ordinary income of the payer for the payment period, and
      (b) ordinary income of an investor in the payer for a permitted taxable period for the purposes of a tax charged under the law of an investor jurisdiction.

(10) A taxable period of an investor is "permitted" for the purposes of subsection (9) if—
      (a) the period begins before the end of 12 months after the end of the payment period, or
      (b) where the period begins after that—
         (i) a claim has been made for the period to be a permitted period in relation to the amount of ordinary income, and
         (ii) it is just and reasonable for the amount of ordinary income to arise for that taxable period rather than an earlier period.

CHAPTER 6

DEDUCTION/NON-INCLUSION MISMATCHES RELATING TO TRANSFERS BY PERMANENT ESTABLISHMENTS

Introduction

259F Overview of Chapter

(1) This Chapter contains provision that counteracts certain excessive deductions that arise in relation to transfers of money or money's worth made, or taken to be made, by a multinational company's permanent establishment in the United Kingdom to the company in the parent jurisdiction.

(2) The Chapter counteracts such deductions by altering the corporation tax treatment of the company.

(3) Section 259FA contains the conditions that must be met for this Chapter to apply.

(4)   Subsection (3) of that section defines "multinational company" and "the parent jurisdiction".

(5)   Subsection (8) of that section defines "the excessive PE deduction".

(6)   Section 259FB contains provision for the counteraction of the excessive PE deduction.

(7)   See also section 259BF for the meaning of "permanent establishment".

Application of Chapter

259FA Circumstances in which the Chapter applies

(1)   This Chapter applies if conditions A to C are met.

(2)   Condition A is that a company is a multinational company.

(3)   For the purposes of this Chapter, a company is a multinational company if —

    (a)   it is resident in a territory outside the United Kingdom ("the parent jurisdiction") for the purposes of a tax charged under the law of that territory, and

    (b)   it is within the charge to corporation tax because it carries on a business in the United Kingdom through a permanent establishment in the United Kingdom.

(4)   Condition B is that, disregarding the provisions mentioned in subsection (5), there is an amount ("the PE deduction") that —

    (a)   may (in substance) be deducted from the company's income for the purposes of calculating the company's taxable profits for an accounting period ("the relevant PE period") for corporation tax purposes, and

    (b)   is in respect of a transfer of money or money's worth from the company in the United Kingdom to the company in the parent jurisdiction that —

        (i)   is actually made, or

        (ii)   is (in substance) treated as being made for corporation tax purposes.

(5)   The provisions are —

    (a)   this Chapter and Chapters 7 to 10, and

    (b)   any equivalent provision under the law of a territory outside the United Kingdom.

(6)   Condition C is that it is reasonable to suppose that, disregarding the provisions mentioned in subsection (5) —

    (a)   the circumstances giving rise to the PE deduction will not result in —

        (i)   an increase in the taxable profits of the company for any permitted taxable period, or

        (ii)   a reduction of a loss made by the company for any permitted taxable period,

    for the purposes of a tax charged under the law of the parent jurisdiction, or

    (b) those circumstances will result in such an increase or reduction for one or more permitted taxable periods, but the PE deduction exceeds the aggregate effect on taxable profits.

(7) "The aggregate effect on taxable profits" is the sum of—

    (a) any increases, resulting from the circumstances giving rise to the PE deduction, in the taxable profits of the company, for a permitted taxable period, for the purposes of a tax charged under the law of the parent jurisdiction, and

    (b) any amounts by which a loss made by the company, for a permitted taxable period, for the purposes of a tax charged under the law of the parent jurisdiction, is reduced as a result of the circumstances giving rise to the PE deduction.

(8) In this Chapter "the excessive PE deduction" means—

    (a) where paragraph (a) of subsection (6) applies, the PE deduction, or

    (b) where paragraph (b) of subsection (6) applies, the PE deduction so far as it is reasonable to suppose that it exceeds the aggregate effect on taxable profits.

(9) For the purposes of subsections (6) and (7) a taxable period of the company, for the purposes of a tax charged under the law of the parent jurisdiction, is "permitted" if—

    (a) the period begins before the end of 12 months after the end of the relevant PE period, or

    (b) where the period begins after that—

        (i) a claim has been made for the period to be a permitted period for the purposes of subsections (6) and (7), and

        (ii) it is just and reasonable for the circumstances giving rise to the PE deduction to affect the profits or loss made for that period rather than an earlier period.

(10) Section 259FB contains provision for counteracting the excessive PE deduction.

Counteraction

259FB Counteraction of the excessive PE deduction

(1) For corporation tax purposes, the excessive PE deduction may not be deducted from the company's income for the relevant PE period unless it is deducted from dual inclusion income for that period.

(2) So much of the excessive PE deduction (if any) as, by virtue of subsection (1), cannot be deducted from the company's income for the relevant PE period—

    (a) is carried forward to subsequent accounting periods of the company, and

    (b) for corporation tax purposes, may be deducted from dual inclusion income of the company for any such period (and not from any other income), so far as it cannot be deducted under this paragraph for an earlier period.

(3) In this section "dual inclusion income" of the company for an accounting period means an amount that is both—

      (a)   ordinary income of the company for that period for corporation tax purposes, and

      (b)   ordinary income of the company for a permitted taxable period for the purposes of a tax charged under the law of the parent jurisdiction.

(4)   A taxable period of the company is "permitted" for the purposes of paragraph (b) of subsection (3) if—

      (a)   the period begins before the end of 12 months after the end of the accounting period mentioned in paragraph (a) of that subsection, or

      (b)   where the period begins after that—

            (i)   a claim has been made for the period to be a permitted period in relation to the amount of ordinary income, and

            (ii)   it is just and reasonable for the amount of ordinary income to arise for that taxable period rather than an earlier period.

CHAPTER 7

HYBRID PAYEE DEDUCTION/NON-INCLUSION MISMATCHES

Introduction

259G Overview of Chapter

(1)   This Chapter contains provision that counteracts deduction/non-inclusion mismatches that it is reasonable to suppose would otherwise arise from payments or quasi-payments because a payee is a hybrid entity.

(2)   The Chapter counteracts mismatches by—

      (a)   altering the corporation tax treatment of the payer for the payment period,

      (b)   treating income chargeable to corporation tax as arising to an investor who is within the charge to corporation tax, or

      (c)   treating income chargeable to corporation tax as arising to a payee that is a hybrid entity and a limited liability partnership.

(3)   Section 259GA contains the conditions that must be met for this Chapter to apply.

(4)   Section 259GB defines "hybrid payee deduction/non-inclusion mismatch" and provides how the amount of the mismatch is to be calculated.

(5)   Section 259GC contains provision that counteracts the mismatch where the payer is within the charge to corporation tax for the payment period.

(6)   Section 259GD contains provision that counteracts the mismatch where an investor in the payee is within the charge to corporation tax and the mismatch is not fully counteracted by section 259GC or an

equivalent provision under the law of a territory outside the United Kingdom.

(7) Section 259GE contains provision that counteracts the mismatch where a payee is a hybrid entity and limited liability partnership and the mismatch is not otherwise fully counteracted.

(8) See also—

    (a) section 259BB for the meaning of "payment", "quasi-payment", "payment period", "relevant deduction", "payer" and "payee";

    (b) section 259BE for the meaning of "hybrid entity", "investor" and "investor jurisdiction".

Application of Chapter

259GA Circumstances in which the Chapter applies

(1) This Chapter applies if conditions A to E are met.

(2) Condition A is that a payment or quasi-payment is made under, or in connection with, an arrangement.

(3) Condition B is that a payee is a hybrid entity (a "hybrid payee").

(4) Condition C is that—

    (a) the payer is within the charge to corporation tax for the payment period,

    (b) an investor in a hybrid payee is within the charge to corporation tax for an accounting period some or all of which falls within the payment period, or

    (c) a hybrid payee is a limited liability partnership.

(5) Condition D is that it is reasonable to suppose that, disregarding the provisions mentioned in subsection (6), there would be a hybrid payee deduction/non-inclusion mismatch in relation to the payment or quasi-payment (see section 259GB).

(6) The provisions are—

    (a) this Chapter and Chapters 8 to 10, and

    (b) any equivalent provision under the law of a territory outside the United Kingdom.

(7) Condition E is that—

    (a) it is a quasi-payment that is made as mentioned in subsection (2) and the payer is also a hybrid payee (see section 259BB(7)),

    (b) the payer and a hybrid payee or an investor in a hybrid payee are in the same control group (see section 259NB) at any time in the period—

        (i) beginning with the day on which the arrangement mentioned in subsection (2) is made, and

        (ii) ending with the last day of the payment period, or

    (c) that arrangement is a structured arrangement.

(8) The arrangement is "structured" if it is reasonable to suppose that—

    (a)   the arrangement is designed to secure a hybrid payee deduction/non-inclusion mismatch, or

    (b)   the terms of the arrangement share the economic benefit of the mismatch between the parties to the arrangement or otherwise reflect the fact that the mismatch is expected to arise.

(9)   The arrangement may be designed to secure a hybrid payee deduction/non-inclusion mismatch despite also being designed to secure any commercial or other objective.

(10)   The following provisions contain provision for the counteraction of the hybrid payee deduction/non-inclusion mismatch—

    (a)   section 259GC (cases where the payer is within the charge to corporation tax for the payment period),

    (b)   section 259GD (cases where an investor in a hybrid payee is within the charge to corporation tax), and

    (c)   section 259GE (cases where a hybrid payee is a limited liability partnership).

259GB Hybrid payee deduction/non-inclusion mismatches and their extent

(1)   There is a "hybrid payee deduction/non-inclusion mismatch", in relation to a payment or quasi-payment, if—

    (a)   the relevant deduction exceeds the sum of the amounts of ordinary income that, by reason of the payment or quasi-payment, arise to each payee for a permitted taxable period, and

    (b)   all or part of that excess arises by reason of one or more payees being hybrid entities.

(2)   The extent of the hybrid payee deduction/non-inclusion mismatch is equal to the excess that arises as mentioned in subsection (1)(b).

(3)   A relevant amount of the excess is to be taken (so far as would not otherwise be the case) to arise as mentioned in subsection (1)(b) where—

    (a)   a payee is a hybrid entity,

    (b)   there is no territory—

        (i)   where that payee is resident for the purposes of a tax charged under the law of that territory, or

        (ii)   under the law of which ordinary income arises to that payee, by reason of the payment or quasi-payment, for the purposes of a tax that is charged on that payee by virtue of that payee having a permanent establishment in that territory, and

    (c)   no income arising to that payee, by reason of the payment or quasi-payment, is brought into account in calculating chargeable profits for the purposes of the CFC charge or a foreign CFC charge.

(4)   For the purposes of subsection (3), the "relevant amount" of the excess is the lesser of—

    (a)   the amount of the excess, and

     (b)   an amount equal to the amount of ordinary income that it is reasonable to suppose would, by reason of the payment or quasi-payment, arise to the payee for corporation tax purposes, if—

        (i)   the payee were a company, and

        (ii)   the payment or quasi-payment were made in connection with a trade carried on by the payee in the United Kingdom through a permanent establishment in the United Kingdom.

(5)   In subsection (3)(c) "chargeable profits"—

     (a)   in relation to the CFC charge, has the same meaning as in Part 9A (see section 371VA), and

     (b)   in relation to a foreign CFC charge, means the concept (by whatever name known) corresponding to chargeable profits within the meaning of that Part.

(6)   A taxable period of a payee is "permitted" in relation to an amount of ordinary income that arises as a result of the payment or quasi-payment if—

     (a)   the period begins before the end of 12 months after the end of the payment period, or

     (b)   where the period begins after that—

        (i)   a claim has been made for the period to be a permitted period in relation to the amount of ordinary income, and

        (ii)   it is just and reasonable for the amount of ordinary income to arise for that taxable period rather than an earlier period.

Counteraction

259GC Counteraction where the payer is within the charge to corporation tax for the payment period

(1)   This section applies where the payer is within the charge to corporation tax for the payment period.

(2)   For corporation tax purposes, the relevant deduction that may be deducted from the payer's income for the payment period is reduced by an amount equal to the hybrid payee deduction/non-inclusion mismatch mentioned in section 259GA(5).

259GD Counteraction where the investor is within the charge to corporation tax

(1)   This section applies in relation to an investor in a hybrid payee where—

     (a)   the investor is within the charge to corporation tax for an accounting period some or all of which falls within the payment period, and

     (b)   it is reasonable to suppose that—

        (i)   neither section 259GC nor any equivalent provision under the law of a territory outside the United Kingdom applies, or

   (ii) a provision of the law of a territory outside the United Kingdom that is equivalent to section 259GC applies, but does not fully counteract the hybrid payee deduction/non-inclusion mismatch mentioned in section 259GA(5).

(2) A provision of the law of a territory outside the United Kingdom that is equivalent to section 259GC does not fully counteract that mismatch if (and only if) —

  (a) it does not reduce the relevant deduction by the full amount of the mismatch, and

  (b) the payer is still able to deduct some of the relevant deduction from income in calculating taxable profits.

(3) In this section "the relevant amount" is —

  (a) in a case where subsection (1)(b)(i) applies, an amount equal to the hybrid payee deduction/non-inclusion mismatch, or

  (b) in a case where subsection (1)(b)(ii) applies, the lesser of —

   (i) the amount by which that mismatch exceeds the amount by which it is reasonable to suppose the relevant deduction is reduced by a provision of the law of a territory outside the United Kingdom that is equivalent to section 259GC, and

   (ii) the amount of the relevant deduction that may still be deducted as mentioned in subsection (2)(b).

(4) If the investor is the only investor in the hybrid payee, the appropriate proportion of the relevant amount is to be treated as income arising to the investor for the counteraction period.

(5) If there is more than one investor in the hybrid payee, an amount equal to the investor's share of the appropriate proportion of the relevant amount is to be treated as income arising to the investor for the counteraction period.

(6) For the purposes of subsections (4) and (5) the "appropriate proportion of the relevant amount" —

  (a) if the hybrid payee is the only hybrid payee, is all of the relevant amount, or

  (b) if there is more than one hybrid payee, is the proportion of the relevant amount apportioned to the hybrid payee upon an apportionment of that amount between all the hybrid payees on a just and reasonable basis having regard (in particular) to —

   (i) any arrangements as to profit sharing that may exist between some or all of the payees, and

   (ii) the extent to which it is reasonable to suppose that the hybrid payee deduction/non-inclusion mismatch mentioned in section 259GA(5) arises by reason of each hybrid payee being a hybrid entity.

(7) The investor's share of the appropriate proportion of the relevant amount is to be determined by apportioning that proportion of that amount between all the investors in the hybrid payee on a just and reasonable basis, having regard (in particular) to any arrangements

as to profit sharing that may exist between some or all of those investors.

(8) An amount of income that is treated as arising under subsection (4) or (5) is chargeable under Chapter 8 of Part 10 of CTA 2009 (income not otherwise charged) (despite section 979(23) of that Act).

(9) The "counteraction period" means—

    (a) if an accounting period of the investor coincides with the payment period, that accounting period, or

    (b) otherwise, the first accounting period of the investor that is wholly or partly within the payment period.

259GE Counteraction where a hybrid payee is an LLP

(1) This section applies in relation to a hybrid payee where the hybrid payee is a limited liability partnership and it is reasonable to suppose that—

    (a) none of the following provisions applies—

        (i) section 259GC;

        (ii) section 259GD;

        (iii) any provision under the law of a territory outside the United Kingdom that is equivalent to either of those sections, or

    (b) one or more of those provisions apply, but the hybrid payee deduction/non-inclusion mismatch mentioned in section 259GA(5) is not fully counteracted.

(2) The mismatch is not fully counteracted if (and only if), after the application of such of those provisions as apply—

    (a) the relevant deduction is not reduced by the full amount of the mismatch,

    (b) the payer is still able to deduct some of the relevant deduction from income in calculating taxable profits, and

    (c) the lesser of—

        (i) the difference between the amount of the mismatch and the amount by which it is reasonable to suppose the relevant deduction is reduced, and

        (ii) the amount of the relevant deduction that may still be deducted,

    exceeds the sum of any amounts of income treated as arising under section 259GD or any equivalent provision under the law of a territory outside the United Kingdom.

(3) In this section "the relevant amount" is—

    (a) in a case where subsection (1)(a) applies, an amount equal to the hybrid payee deduction/non-inclusion mismatch mentioned in section 259GA(5), or

    (b) in a case where subsection (1)(b) applies, an amount equal to the excess mentioned in subsection (2)(c).

(4) If the hybrid payee is the only hybrid payee, an amount equal to the relevant amount is to be treated as income arising to the hybrid payee on the last day of the payment period.

(5)   If there is more than one hybrid payee, an amount equal to the hybrid payee's share of the relevant amount is to be treated as income arising to the hybrid payee on the last day of the payment period.

(6)   The hybrid payee's share of the relevant amount is to be determined by apportioning that amount between all the hybrid payees on a just and reasonable basis, having regard (in particular) to—

   (a)   any arrangements as to profit sharing that may exist between some or all of the payees, and

   (b)   the extent to which it is reasonable to suppose that the hybrid payee deduction/non-inclusion mismatch mentioned in section 259GA(5) arises by reason of each hybrid payee being a hybrid entity.

(7)   An amount of income that is treated as arising under subsection (4) or (5) is chargeable to corporation tax on the hybrid payee (as opposed to being chargeable to tax on any of its members) under Chapter 8 of Part 10 of CTA 2009 (income not otherwise charged) (despite section 979(2) of that Act).

(8)   Section 863 of ITTOIA 2005 (treatment of certain limited liability partnerships for income tax purposes) and section 1273 of CTA 2009 (treatment of certain limited liability partnerships for corporation tax purposes) are disapplied in relation to the hybrid payee to the extent necessary for the purposes of subsection (7).

(9)   This section is to be disregarded for the purposes of determining whether the hybrid payee is within the charge to corporation tax for the purposes of any other provision of this Part, except section 259M (anti-avoidance).

CHAPTER 8

MULTINATIONAL PAYEE DEDUCTION/NON-INCLUSION MISMATCHES

Introduction

259H Overview of Chapter

(1)   This Chapter contains provision that counteracts deduction/non-inclusion mismatches that it is reasonable to suppose would otherwise arise from payments or quasi-payments, where the payer is within the charge to corporation tax, because a payee is multinational company.

(2)   The Chapter counteracts mismatches by altering the corporation tax treatment of the payer.

(3)   Section 259HA contains the conditions that must be met for this Chapter to apply.

(4)   Subsection (4) of that section defines "multinational company", "parent jurisdiction" and "PE jurisdiction".

(5) Section 259HB defines "multinational payee deduction/non-inclusion mismatch" and provides how the amount of the mismatch is to be calculated.

(6) Section 259HC contains provision that counteracts the mismatch.

(7) See also —

    (a) section 259BB for the meaning of "payment", "quasi-payment", "payment period", "relevant deduction", "payer" and "payee";

    (b) section 259BF for the meaning of "permanent establishment".

Application of Chapter

259HA Circumstances in which the Chapter applies

(1) This Chapter applies if conditions A to E are met.

(2) Condition A is that a payment or quasi-payment is made under, or in connection with, an arrangement.

(3) Condition B is that a payee is a multinational company.

(4) For the purposes of this Chapter, a company is a "multinational company" if —

    (a) it is resident in a territory ("the parent jurisdiction") for tax purposes under the law of that territory, and

    (b) it is regarded as carrying on a business in another territory ("the PE jurisdiction") through a permanent establishment in that territory (whether it is so regarded under the law of the parent jurisdiction, the PE jurisdiction or any other territory).

(5) Condition C is that the payer is within the charge to corporation tax for the payment period.

(6) Condition D is that it is reasonable to suppose that, disregarding the provisions mentioned in subsection (7), there would be a multinational payee deduction/non-inclusion mismatch in relation to the payment or quasi-payment (see section 259HB).

(7) The provisions are —

    (a) this Chapter and Chapters 9 and 10, and

    (b) any equivalent provision under the law of a territory outside the United Kingdom.

(8) Condition E is that —

    (a) it is a quasi-payment that is made as mentioned in subsection (2) and the payer is also a payee (see section 259BB(7)),

    (b) the payer and the multinational company are in the same control group (see section 259NB) at any time in the period —

        (i) beginning with the day on which the arrangement mentioned in subsection (2) is made, and

        (ii) ending with the last day of the payment period, or

    (c) that arrangement is a structured arrangement.

(9) The arrangement is "structured" if it is reasonable to suppose that —

> > (a) the arrangement is designed to secure a multinational company deduction/non-inclusion mismatch, or
> >
> > (b) the terms of the arrangement share the economic benefit of the mismatch between the parties to the arrangement or otherwise reflect the fact that the mismatch is expected to arise.
>
> (10) The arrangement may be designed to secure a multinational payee deduction/non-inclusion mismatch despite also being designed to secure any commercial or other objective.
>
> (11) Section 259HC contains provision for the counteraction of the multinational payee deduction/non-inclusion mismatch.

259HB Multinational payee deduction/non-inclusion mismatches and their extent

> (1) There is a "multinational payee deduction/non-inclusion mismatch", in relation to a payment or quasi-payment, if—
>
> > (a) the relevant deduction exceeds the sum of the amounts of ordinary income that, by reason of the payment or quasi-payment, arise to each payee for a permitted taxable period, and
> >
> > (b) all or part of that excess arises by reason of one or more payees being multinational companies.
>
> (2) The extent of the multinational payee deduction/non-inclusion mismatch is equal to the excess that arises as mentioned in subsection (1)(b).
>
> (3) For the purposes of subsection (1)(b)—
>
> > (a) where the law of a PE jurisdiction in relation to a payee that is a multinational company makes no provision for charging tax on any companies, so much of the excess as arises as a result is to be taken not to arise by reason of that payee being a multinational company, but
> >
> > (b) subject to that, it does not matter whether the excess or part arises for another reason as well as one or more payees being multinational companies (even if it would have arisen for that other reason regardless of whether any payees are multinational companies).
>
> (4) A taxable period of a payee is "permitted" in relation to an amount of ordinary income that arises as a result of the payment or quasi-payment if—
>
> > (a) the period begins before the end of 12 months after the end of the payment period, or
> >
> > (b) where the period begins after that—
> >
> > > (i) a claim has been made for the period to be a permitted period in relation to the amount of ordinary income, and
> > >
> > > (ii) it is just and reasonable for the amount of ordinary income to arise for that taxable period rather than an earlier period.

Counteraction

259HC Counteraction of the multinational payee deduction/non-inclusion mismatch

For corporation tax purposes, the relevant deduction that may be deducted from the payer's income for the payment period is reduced by an amount equal to the multinational payee deduction/non-inclusion mismatch mentioned in section 259HA(6).

CHAPTER 9

HYBRID ENTITY DOUBLE DEDUCTION MISMATCHES

Introduction

259I Overview of Chapter

(1) This Chapter contains provision that counteracts double deduction mismatches that it is reasonable to suppose would otherwise arise by reason of a person being a hybrid entity.

(2) The Chapter counteracts mismatches where the hybrid entity, or an investor in the hybrid entity, is within the charge to corporation tax and does so by altering the corporation tax treatment of the entity or investor.

(3) Section 259IA contains the conditions that must be met for this Chapter to apply.

(4) Subsection (4) of that section defines "hybrid entity double deduction amount".

(5) Section 259IB contains provision that counteracts the mismatch where an investor in the hybrid entity is within the charge to corporation tax.

(6) Section 259IC contains provision that, in certain circumstances, counteracts the mismatch where the hybrid entity is within the charge to corporation tax and the mismatch is not fully counteracted by provision under the law of a territory outside the United Kingdom that is equivalent to section 259IB.

(7) See also section 259BE for the meaning of "hybrid entity", "investor" and "investor jurisdiction".

Application of Chapter

259IA Circumstances in which the Chapter applies

(1) This Chapter applies if conditions A to C are met.

(2) Condition A is that there is an amount or part of an amount that, disregarding the provisions mentioned in subsection (3), it is reasonable to suppose—

    (a) could be deducted from the income of a hybrid entity for the purposes of calculating the taxable profits of that entity for a taxable period ("the hybrid entity deduction period"), and

        (b) could also be deducted, under the law of the investor jurisdiction, from the income of an investor in the hybrid entity for the purposes of calculating the taxable profits of that investor for a taxable period ("the investor deduction period").

(3) The provisions are—

        (a) this Chapter and Chapter 10, and

        (b) any equivalent provision under the law of a territory outside the United Kingdom.

(4) In this Chapter the amount or part of an amount mentioned in subsection (2) is referred to as "the hybrid entity double deduction amount".

(5) Condition B is that—

        (a) the investor is within the charge to corporation tax for the investor deduction period, or

        (b) the hybrid entity is within the charge to corporation tax for the hybrid entity deduction period.

(6) Condition C is that—

        (a) the hybrid entity and any investor in it are related (see section 259NC) at any time—

                (i) in the hybrid entity deduction period, or

                (ii) in the investor deduction period, or

        (b) an arrangement, to which the hybrid entity or any investor in it is party, is a structured arrangement.

(7) An arrangement is "structured" if it is reasonable to suppose that—

        (a) the arrangement is designed to secure the hybrid entity double deduction amount, or

        (b) the terms of the arrangement share the economic benefit of that amount being deductible by both the hybrid entity and the investor between the parties to the arrangement or otherwise reflect the fact that the amount is expected to arise.

(8) The arrangement may be designed to secure the hybrid entity double deduction amount despite also being designed to secure any commercial or other objective.

(9) Sections 259IB (cases where the investor is within the charge to corporation tax for the investor deduction period) and 259IC (cases where the hybrid entity is within the charge to corporation tax for the hybrid entity deduction period) contain provision for the counteraction of the hybrid entity double deduction amount.

Counteraction

259IB Counteraction where the investor is within the charge to corporation tax

(1) This section applies in relation to the investor in the hybrid entity where the investor is within the charge to corporation tax for the investor deduction period.

(2) For corporation tax purposes, the hybrid entity double deduction amount may not be deducted from the investor's income for the investor deduction period unless it is deducted from dual inclusion income of the investor for that period.

(3) So much of the hybrid entity double deduction amount (if any) as, by virtue of subsection (2), cannot be deducted from the investor's income for the investor deduction period—

    (a) is carried forward to subsequent accounting periods of the investor, and

    (b) for corporation tax purposes, may be deducted from dual inclusion income of the investor for any such period (and not from any other income), so far as it cannot be deducted under this paragraph for an earlier period.

(4) If the Commissioners are satisfied that the investor will have no dual inclusion income—

    (a) for an accounting period after the investor deduction period ("the relevant period"), nor

    (b) for any accounting period after the relevant period,

any of the hybrid entity double deduction amount that has not been deducted from dual inclusion income for an accounting period before the relevant period in accordance with subsection (2) or (3) ("the stranded deduction") may be deducted at step 2 in section 4(2) of CTA 2010 in calculating the investor's taxable total profits of the relevant period.

(5) So much of the stranded deduction (if any) as cannot be deducted, in accordance with subsection (4), at step 2 in section 4(2) of CTA 2010 in calculating the investor's taxable total profits of the relevant period—

    (a) is carried forward to subsequent accounting periods of the investor, and

    (b) may be so deducted for any such period, so far as it cannot be deducted under this paragraph for an earlier period.

(6) Subsection (7) applies if it is reasonable to suppose that all or part of the hybrid entity double deduction amount is (in substance) deducted ("the illegitimate overseas deduction"), under the law of a territory outside the United Kingdom, from income of any person, for a taxable period, that is not dual inclusion income of the investor for an accounting period.

(7) For the purposes of determining how much of the hybrid entity double deduction amount may be deducted (if any) for the accounting period of the investor in which the taxable period mentioned in subsection (6) ends, and any subsequent accounting periods of the investor, an amount of it equal to the illegitimate overseas deduction is to be taken to have already been deducted for a previous accounting period of the investor.

(8) In this section "dual inclusion income" of the investor for an accounting period means an amount that is both—

    (a) ordinary income of the investor for that period for corporation tax purposes, and

        (b)   ordinary income of the hybrid entity for a permitted taxable period for the purposes of any tax under the law of a territory outside the United Kingdom.

  (9)   A taxable period of the hybrid entity is "permitted" for the purposes of paragraph (b) of subsection (8) if—

        (a)   the period begins before the end of 12 months after the end of the accounting period of the investor mentioned in paragraph (a) of that subsection, or

        (b)   where the period begins after that—

            (i)   a claim has been made for the period to be a permitted period in relation to the amount of ordinary income, and

            (ii)   it is just and reasonable for the amount of ordinary income to arise for that taxable period rather than an earlier period.

259IC Counteraction where the hybrid entity is within the charge to corporation tax

  (1)   This section applies where—

        (a)   the hybrid entity is within the charge to corporation tax for the hybrid entity deduction period,

        (b)   it is reasonable to suppose that—

            (i)   no provision under the law of an investor jurisdiction that is equivalent to section 259IB applies, or

            (ii)   such a provision does apply, but the hybrid entity double deduction amount exceeds the amount that, under that provision, cannot be deducted from income, for the investor deduction period, other than dual inclusion income of the hybrid entity for the hybrid entity deduction period, and

        (c)   the secondary counteraction condition is met.

  (2)   The secondary counteraction condition is met if—

        (a)   the hybrid entity and any investor in it are in the same control group (see section 259NB) at any time in—

            (i)   the hybrid entity deduction period, or

            (ii)   the investor deduction period, or

        (b)   there is an arrangement, to which the hybrid entity or any investor in it is party, that is a structured arrangement (within the meaning given by section 259IA(7) and (8)).

  (3)   In this section "the restricted deduction" means—

        (a)   in a case where subsection (1)(b)(i) applies, the hybrid entity double deduction amount, or

        (b)   in a case where subsection (1)(b)(ii) applies, the hybrid entity double deduction amount so far as it exceeds the amount that it is reasonable to suppose, under a provision of the law of a territory outside the United Kingdom that is equivalent to section 259IB, cannot be deducted from income, for the investor deduction period, other than dual inclusion income of the hybrid entity for the hybrid entity deduction period.

(4) For corporation tax purposes, the restricted deduction may not be deducted from the hybrid entity's income for the hybrid entity deduction period unless it is deducted from dual inclusion income for that period.

(5) So much of the restricted deduction (if any) as, by virtue of subsection (4), cannot be deducted from the hybrid entity's income for the hybrid entity deduction period —

   (a) is carried forward to subsequent accounting periods of the hybrid entity, and

   (b) for corporation tax purposes, may be deducted from dual inclusion income of the hybrid entity for any such period (and not from any other income), so far as it cannot be deducted under this paragraph for an earlier period.

(6) If the Commissioners are satisfied that the hybrid entity will have no dual inclusion income —

   (a) for an accounting period after the hybrid entity deduction period ("the relevant period"), nor

   (b) for any accounting period after the relevant period,

   any of the restricted deduction that has not been deducted from dual inclusion income for an accounting period before the relevant period in accordance with subsection (4) or (5) ("the stranded deduction") may be deducted at step 2 in section 4(2) of CTA 2010 in calculating the hybrid entity's taxable total profits of the relevant period.

(7) So much of the stranded deduction (if any) as cannot be deducted, in accordance with subsection (6), at step 2 in section 4(2) of CTA 2010 in calculating the hybrid entity's taxable total profits of the relevant period —

   (a) is carried forward to subsequent accounting periods of the hybrid entity, and

   (b) may be so deducted for any such period, so far as it cannot be deducted under this paragraph for an earlier period.

(8) Subsection (9) applies if it is reasonable to suppose that all or part of the hybrid entity double deduction amount is (in substance) deducted ("the illegitimate overseas deduction"), under the law of a territory outside the United Kingdom, from income of any person, for a taxable period, that is not dual inclusion income of the hybrid entity for an accounting period.

(9) For the purposes of determining how much of the hybrid entity double deduction amount may be deducted (if any) for the accounting period of the hybrid entity in which the taxable period mentioned in subsection (8) ends, and any subsequent accounting periods of the hybrid entity, an amount of it equal to the illegitimate overseas deduction is to be taken to have already been deducted for a previous accounting period of the hybrid entity.

(10) In this section "dual inclusion income" of the hybrid entity for an accounting period means an amount that is both —

   (a) ordinary income of the hybrid entity for that period for corporation tax purposes, and

        (b)   ordinary income of an investor in the hybrid entity for a permitted taxable period for the purposes of any tax charged under the law of an investor jurisdiction.

  (11)   A taxable period of an investor is "permitted" for the purposes of paragraph (b) of subsection (10) if—

        (a)   the period begins before the end of 12 months after the end of the accounting period mentioned in paragraph (a) of that subsection, or

        (b)   where the period begins after that—

            (i)   a claim has been made for the period to be a permitted period in relation to the amount of ordinary income, and

            (ii)   it is just and reasonable for the amount of ordinary income to arise for that taxable period rather than an earlier period.

CHAPTER 10

DUAL TERRITORY DOUBLE DEDUCTION CASES

Introduction

259J Overview of Chapter

  (1)   This Chapter contains provision that counteracts double deduction mismatches that it is reasonable to suppose would otherwise arise as a result of a company—

        (a)   being a dual resident company, or

        (b)   being a relevant multinational company.

  (2)   The counteraction operates by altering the corporation tax treatment of the company.

  (3)   Section 259JA contains the conditions that must be met for this Chapter to apply.

  (4)   Subsection (3) of that section defines "dual resident company".

  (5)   Subsection (4) of that section defines "relevant multinational company", "parent jurisdiction" and "PE jurisdiction".

  (6)   Subsection (5) of that section defines "dual territory double deduction amount".

  (7)   Section 259JB contains provision that counteracts the mismatch where the company is a dual resident company.

  (8)   Section 259JC contains provision that counteracts the mismatch where the company is a multinational company and the United Kingdom is the parent jurisdiction.

  (9)   Section 259JD contains provision that counteracts the mismatch where the company is a relevant multinational company, the United Kingdom is the PE jurisdiction and the mismatch is not counteracted under a provision of the law of a territory outside the United Kingdom that is equivalent to section 259JC.

(10) See also section 259BF for the meaning of "permanent establishment".

Application of Chapter

259JA Circumstances in which the Chapter applies

(1) This Chapter applies if conditions A and B are met.

(2) Condition A is that a company is a—
   (a) dual resident company, or
   (b) relevant multinational company.

(3) For the purposes of this Chapter a company is a "dual resident company" if—
   (a) it is UK resident, and
   (b) it is also within the charge to a tax under the law of a territory outside the United Kingdom because—
      (i) it derives its status as a company from that law,
      (ii) its place of management is in that territory, or
      (iii) it is for some other reason treated under that law as resident in that territory for the purposes of that tax.

(4) For the purposes of this Chapter a company is a "relevant multinational company" if—
   (a) it is within the charge to a tax, under the law of a territory ("the PE jurisdiction") in which it is not resident for tax purposes, because it carries on business in that territory through a permanent establishment in that territory, and
   (b) either—
      (i) the PE jurisdiction is the United Kingdom, or
      (ii) the territory in which the company is resident for tax purposes ("the parent jurisdiction") is the United Kingdom.

(5) Condition B is that there is an amount ("the dual territory double deduction amount") that, disregarding this Chapter and any equivalent provision under the law of a territory outside the United Kingdom, it is reasonable to suppose could, by reason of the company being a dual resident company or a relevant multinational company—
   (a) be deducted from the company's income for an accounting period ("the deduction period") for corporation tax purposes, and
   (b) also be deducted from the company's income for a taxable period ("the foreign deduction period") for the purposes of a tax charged under the law of a territory outside the United Kingdom.

(6) The following provisions provide for the counteraction of the dual territory double deduction amount—
   (a) section 259JB (cases where a company is dual resident),

> (b) section 259JC (cases where a company is a relevant multinational and the United Kingdom is the parent jurisdiction), and
>
> (c) section 259JD (cases where a company is a relevant multinational, the United Kingdom is the PE jurisdiction and the amount is not counteracted in the parent jurisdiction).

Counteraction

259JB Counteraction where mismatch arises because of a dual resident company

(1) This section applies where the dual territory double deduction amount arises by reason of the company being a dual resident company.

(2) For corporation tax purposes, the dual territory double deduction amount may not be deducted from the company's income for the deduction period unless it is deducted from dual inclusion income of the company for that period.

(3) So much of the dual territory double deduction amount (if any) as, by virtue of subsection (2), cannot be deducted from the company's income for the deduction period —

> (a) is carried forward to subsequent accounting periods of the company, and
>
> (b) for corporation tax purposes, may be deducted from dual inclusion income of the company for any such period (and not from any other income), so far as it cannot be deducted under this paragraph for an earlier period.

(4) If the Commissioners are satisfied that the company has ceased to be a dual resident company, any of the dual territory double deduction amount that has not been deducted from dual inclusion income in accordance with subsection (2) or (3) ("the stranded deduction") may be deducted at step 2 in section 4(2) of CTA 2010 in calculating the company's taxable total profits of the accounting period in which it ceased to be a dual resident company.

(5) So much of the stranded deduction (if any) as cannot be deducted, in accordance with subsection (4), at step 2 in section 4(2) of CTA 2010 in calculating the company's taxable total profits of the accounting period in which the company ceased to be a dual resident company —

> (a) is carried forward to subsequent accounting periods of the company, and
>
> (b) may be so deducted for any such period, so far as it cannot be deducted under this paragraph for an earlier period.

(6) Subsection (7) applies if it is reasonable to suppose that all or part of the dual territory double deduction amount is (in substance) deducted ("the illegitimate overseas deduction"), under the law of a territory outside the United Kingdom, from income of any person, for a taxable period, that is not dual inclusion income of the company for an accounting period.

(7)   For the purposes of determining how much of the dual territory double deduction amount may be deducted (if any) for the accounting period of the company in which the taxable period mentioned in subsection (6) ends, and any subsequent accounting periods of the company, an amount of it equal to the illegitimate overseas deduction is to be taken to have already been deducted for a previous accounting period of the company.

(8)   In this section "dual inclusion income" of the company for an accounting period means an amount that is both—

   (a)   ordinary income of the company for that period for corporation tax purposes, and

   (b)   ordinary income of the company for a permitted taxable period for the purposes of a tax charged under the law of a territory outside the United Kingdom.

(9)   A taxable period of the company is "permitted" for the purposes of paragraph (b) of subsection (8) if—

   (a)   the period begins before the end of 12 months after the end of the accounting period mentioned in paragraph (a) of that subsection, or

   (b)   where the period begins after that—

      (i)   a claim has been made for the period to be a permitted period in relation to the amount of ordinary income, and

      (ii)   it is just and reasonable for the amount of ordinary income to arise for that taxable period rather than an earlier period.

259JC Counteraction where mismatch arises because of a relevant multinational and the UK is the parent jurisdiction

(1)   This section applies where—

   (a)   the dual territory double deduction amount arises by reason of the company being a relevant multinational company, and

   (b)   the United Kingdom is the parent jurisdiction.

(2)   If some or all of the dual territory double deduction amount is (in substance) deducted ("the impermissible overseas deduction"), for the purposes of a tax under the law of a territory outside the United Kingdom, from the income of any person, for any taxable period, that is not dual inclusion income of the company—

   (a)   the dual territory double deduction amount that may be deducted, for corporation tax purposes, from the company's income for the deduction period is reduced by the amount of the impermissible overseas deduction, and

   (b)   such just and reasonable adjustments (if any) as are required to give effect to that reduction, for corporation tax purposes, are to be made.

(3)   Any adjustment required to be made under subsection (2) may be made (whether or not by an officer of Revenue and Customs)—

   (a)   by way of an assessment, the modification of an assessment, amendment or disallowance of a claim, or otherwise, and

   (b)   despite any time limit imposed by or under any enactment.

(4) In this section "dual inclusion income" of the company means an amount that is both—

    (a) ordinary income of the company for an accounting period for corporation tax purposes, and

    (b) ordinary income of the company for a permitted taxable period for the purposes of a tax charged under the law of a territory outside the United Kingdom.

(5) A taxable period is "permitted" for the purposes of paragraph (b) of subsection (4) if—

    (a) the period begins before the end of 12 months after the end of the accounting period of the company mentioned in paragraph (a) of that subsection, or

    (b) where the period begins after that—

        (i) a claim has been made for the period to be a permitted period in relation to the amount of ordinary income, and

        (ii) it is just and reasonable for the amount of ordinary income to arise for that taxable period rather than an earlier period.

259JD Counteraction where mismatch arises because of a relevant multinational and is not counteracted in the parent jurisdiction

(1) This section applies where—

    (a) the dual territory double deduction amount arises as a result of the company being a relevant multinational company,

    (b) the United Kingdom is the PE jurisdiction, and

    (c) it is reasonable to suppose that no provision of the law of the parent jurisdiction that is equivalent to section 259JC applies.

(2) For corporation tax purposes, the dual territory double deduction amount may not be deducted from the company's income for the deduction period unless it is deducted from dual inclusion income of the company for that period.

(3) So much of the dual territory double deduction amount (if any) as, by virtue of subsection (2), cannot be deducted from the company's income for the deduction period—

    (a) is carried forward to subsequent accounting periods of the company, and

    (b) for corporation tax purposes, may be deducted from dual inclusion income of the company for any such period (and not from any other income), so far as it cannot be deducted under this paragraph for an earlier period.

(4) If the Commissioners are satisfied that the company has ceased to be a relevant multinational company, any of the dual territory double deduction amount that has not been deducted from dual inclusion income in accordance with subsection (2) or (3) ("the stranded deduction") may be deducted at step 2 in section 4(2) of CTA 2010 in calculating the company's taxable total profits of the accounting period in which it ceased to be a relevant multinational company.

(5) So much of the stranded deduction (if any) as cannot be deducted, in accordance with subsection (4), at step 2 in section 4(2) of CTA 2010

in calculating the company's taxable total profits of the accounting period in which the company ceased to be a relevant multinational company—

    (a)   is carried forward to subsequent accounting periods of the company, and

    (b)   may be so deducted for any such period, so far as it cannot be deducted under this paragraph for an earlier period.

(6)   Subsection (7) applies if it is reasonable to suppose that all or part of the dual territory double deduction amount is (in substance) deducted ("the illegitimate overseas deduction"), under the law of a territory outside the United Kingdom, from income of any person, for a taxable period, that is not dual inclusion income of the company for an accounting period.

(7)   For the purposes of determining how much of the dual territory double deduction amount may be deducted (if any) for the accounting period of the company in which the taxable period mentioned in subsection (6) ends, and any subsequent accounting periods of the company, an amount of it equal to the illegitimate overseas deduction is to be taken to have already been deducted for a previous accounting period of the company.

(8)   In this section "dual inclusion income" of the company for an accounting period means an amount that is both—

    (a)   ordinary income of the company for that period for corporation tax purposes, and

    (b)   ordinary income of the company for a permitted taxable period for the purposes of a tax charged under the law of a territory outside the United Kingdom.

(9)   A taxable period of the company is "permitted" for the purposes of paragraph (b) of subsection (8) if—

    (a)   the period begins before the end of 12 months after the end of the accounting period mentioned in paragraph (a) of that subsection, or

    (b)   where the period begins after that—

        (i)   a claim has been made for the period to be a permitted period in relation to the amount of ordinary income, and

        (ii)   it is just and reasonable for the amount of ordinary income to arise for that taxable period rather than an earlier period.

CHAPTER 11

IMPORTED MISMATCHES

Introduction

259K Overview of Chapter

(1)   This Chapter contains provision denying deductions in connection with payments or quasi-payments that are made under, or in

connection with, imported mismatch arrangements where the payer is within the charge to corporation tax for the payment period.

(2) Section 259KA contains the conditions that must be met for this Chapter to apply and defines "imported mismatch payment" and "imported mismatch arrangement".

(3) Section 259KB defines "dual territory double deduction", "excessive PE deduction" and "PE jurisdiction".

(4) Section 259KC contains provision for denying some or all of a relevant deduction in relation to an imported mismatch payment.

(5) See also section 259BB for the meaning of "payment", "quasi-payment", "relevant deduction", "payment period" and "payer".

Application of Chapter

259KA Circumstances in which the Chapter applies

(1) This Chapter applies if conditions A to G are met.

(2) Condition A is that a payment or quasi-payment ("the imported mismatch payment") is made under, or in connection with, an arrangement ("the imported mismatch arrangement").

(3) Condition B is that, in relation to the imported mismatch payment, the payer ("P") is within the charge to corporation tax for the payment period.

(4) Condition C is that the imported mismatch arrangement is one of a series of arrangements.

(5) A "series of arrangements" means a number of arrangements that are each entered into (whether or not one after the other) in pursuance of, or in relation to, another arrangement ("the over-arching arrangement").

(6) Condition D is that—
    (a) under an arrangement in the series other than the imported mismatch arrangement, there is a payment or quasi-payment ("the mismatch payment") in relation to which it is reasonable to suppose that there is or will be—
        (i) a hybrid or otherwise impermissible deduction/non-inclusion mismatch (see section 259CB),
        (ii) a hybrid transfer deduction/non-inclusion mismatch (see section 259DC),
        (iii) a hybrid payer deduction/non-inclusion mismatch (see section 259EB),
        (iv) a hybrid payee deduction/non-inclusion mismatch (see section 259GB),
        (v) a multinational payee deduction/non-inclusion mismatch (see section 259HB),
        (vi) a hybrid entity double deduction amount (see section 259IA(4)), or
        (vii) a dual territory double deduction (see section 259KB), or

    (b)   as a consequence of an arrangement in the series other than the imported mismatch arrangement, there is or will be an excessive PE deduction (see section 259KB),

and in this Chapter "the relevant mismatch" means the mismatch, amount or deduction concerned.

(7)   Condition E is that it is reasonable to suppose —

    (a)   where subsection (6)(a) applies, that no provision of any of Chapters 3 to 5 or 7 to 10 nor any equivalent provision under the law of a territory outside the United Kingdom applies, or will apply, in relation to the tax treatment of any person in respect of the mismatch payment, or

    (b)   where subsection (6)(b) applies, that no provision of Chapter 6 nor any equivalent provision under the law of a territory outside the United Kingdom applies, or will apply, in relation to the tax treatment of the company in relation to which the excessive PE deduction arises.

(8)   Condition F is that —

    (a)   subsection (6)(a) applies and it is reasonable to suppose that a provision of any of Chapters 3 to 5 or 7 to 10, or an equivalent provision under the law of a territory outside the United Kingdom, would apply in relation to the tax treatment of P if —

        (i)   P were the payer in relation to the mismatch payment,

        (ii)   P were a payee in relation to the mismatch payment, or

        (iii)   where the relevant mismatch is a hybrid payee deduction/non-inclusion mismatch or a hybrid entity double deduction amount, P were an investor in the hybrid entity concerned, or

    (b)   the relevant mismatch is an excessive PE deduction.

(9)   Condition G is that —

    (a)   subsection (6)(a) applies and P is in the same control group (see section 259NB) as the payer, or a payee, in relation to the mismatch payment, at any time in the period —

        (i)   beginning with the day the over-arching arrangement is made, and

        (ii)   ending with the last day of the payment period in relation to the imported mismatch payment,

    (b)   subsection (6)(b) applies and P is in the same control group as the company in relation to whom the excessive PE deduction arises at any time in that period, or

    (c)   the imported mismatch arrangement, or the over-arching arrangement, is a structured arrangement.

(10)   The imported mismatch arrangement, or the over-arching arrangement, is a "structured arrangement" if it is reasonable to suppose that —

    (a)   the arrangement concerned is designed to secure the relevant mismatch, or

    (b)   the terms of the arrangement concerned share the economic benefit of the relevant mismatch between the parties to that arrangement or otherwise reflect the fact that the relevant mismatch is expected to arise.

(11) An arrangement may be designed to secure the relevant mismatch despite also being designed to secure any commercial or other objective.

(12) Section 259KC contains provision for denying all or part of the relevant deduction in relation to the imported mismatch payment by reference to the relevant mismatch.

259KB Meaning of "dual territory double deduction", "excessive PE deduction" and "PE jurisdiction"

(1) This section has effect for the purposes of this Chapter.

(2) A "dual territory double deduction" means an amount that can be deducted by a company both—

   (a) from income for the purposes of a tax charged under the law of one territory, and

   (b) from income for the purposes of a tax charged under the law of another territory.

(3) A "PE deduction" is an amount that—

   (a) may (in substance) be deducted from a company's income for the purposes of calculating the company's taxable profits, for a taxable period, for the purposes of a tax that is charged on the company, under the law of a territory ("the PE jurisdiction"), by virtue of the company having a permanent establishment in that territory, and

   (b) is in respect of a transfer of money or money's worth, from the company in the PE jurisdiction to the company in another territory ("the parent jurisdiction") in which it is resident for the purposes of a tax, that—

      (i) is actually made, or

      (ii) is (in substance) treated as being made for tax purposes.

(4) A PE deduction is "excessive" so far as it exceeds the sum of—

   (a) any increases, resulting from the circumstances giving rise to the PE deduction, in the taxable profits of the company, for a permitted taxable period, for the purposes of a tax charged under the law of the parent jurisdiction, and

   (b) any amounts by which a loss made by the company, for a permitted taxable period, for the purposes of a tax charged under the law of the parent jurisdiction, is reduced as a result of the circumstances giving rise to the PE deduction.

(5) A taxable period of the company is "permitted" for the purposes of subsection (4) if—

   (a) the period begins before the end of 12 months after the end of the taxable period mentioned in subsection (3)(a), or

   (b) where the period begins after that—

      (i) a claim has been made for the period to be a permitted period for the purposes of subsection (4), and

    (ii)   it is just and reasonable for the circumstances giving rise to the PE deduction to affect the profits or loss made for that period rather than an earlier period.

Counteraction

259KC Denial of the relevant deduction in relation to the imported mismatch payment

(1)   If, in addition to the imported mismatch payment, there are, or will be, one or more relevant payments in relation to the relevant mismatch, subsection (3) applies.

(2)   Otherwise, for corporation tax purposes, in relation to the imported mismatch payment, the relevant deduction that may be deducted from P's income for the payment period is to be reduced by the amount of the relevant mismatch.

(3)   For corporation tax purposes, where this subsection applies, in relation to the imported mismatch payment, the relevant deduction that may be deducted from P's income for the payment period is to be reduced by P's share of the relevant mismatch.

(4)   P's share of the relevant mismatch is to be determined by apportioning the relevant mismatch between P and every payer in relation to a relevant payment on a just and reasonable basis—

    (a)   where subsection (6)(a) applies, having regard (in particular) to the extent to which the imported mismatch payment and each relevant payment funds (directly or indirectly) the mismatch payment, or

    (b)   where the relevant mismatch is an excessive PE deduction, having regard (in particular) to—

        (i)   if the transfer of money or money's worth mentioned in section 259KB(3)(b) is actually made, the extent to which the imported mismatch payment and each relevant payment funds (directly or indirectly) the transfer, or

        (ii)   if the transfer of money or money's worth mentioned in section 259KB(3)(b) is (in substance) treated as being made, the extent to which the imported mismatch payment and each relevant payment would have funded (directly or indirectly) the transfer if it had actually been made.

(5)   For the purposes of subsection (4)(a) and (b)(i), the imported mismatch payment is to be taken to fund the mismatch payment or transfer to the extent that the mismatch payment or transfer cannot be shown instead to be funded (directly or indirectly) by one or more relevant payments.

(6)   For the purposes of subsection (4)(b)(ii), it is to be assumed that the imported mismatch payment would have funded the transfer if it had actually been made to the extent that it cannot be shown by P that, if it had been made, the transfer would have instead been funded (directly or indirectly) by one or more relevant payments.

(7) For the purposes of this section, a payment or quasi-payment, other than the imported mismatch payment or any mismatch payment, is a "relevant payment" in relation to the relevant mismatch if it is made under an arrangement in the series of arrangements mentioned in section 259KA(4) and—

   (a) where subsection (6)(a) applies, it funds (directly or indirectly) the mismatch payment,

   (b) where the relevant mismatch is an excessive PE deduction and the transfer of money or money's worth mentioned in section 259KB(3)(b) is actually made, it funds (directly or indirectly) that transfer, or

   (c) where the relevant mismatch is an excessive PE deduction and the transfer of money or money's worth mentioned in section 259KB(3)(b) is (in substance) treated as being made, it would have funded (directly or indirectly) that transfer had that transfer actually been made.

(8) In proceedings before a court or tribunal in connection with this section—

   (a) in relation to subsection (1), it is for P to show that, in addition to the imported mismatch payment, there are one or more relevant payments in relation to the relevant mismatch, and

   (b) in relation to subsection (5), it is for P to show that the mismatch payment or transfer is funded (directly or indirectly) by one or more relevant payments instead of by the imported mismatch payment.

CHAPTER 12

ADJUSTMENTS IN LIGHT OF SUBSEQUENT EVENTS ETC

259L Adjustments where suppositions cease to be reasonable

(1) Where—

   (a) a reasonable supposition is made for the purposes of any provision of this Part, and

   (b) the supposition turns out to be mistaken or otherwise ceases to be reasonable,

such consequential adjustments as are just and reasonable may be made.

(2) The adjustments may be made (whether or not by an officer of Revenue and Customs) by way of an assessment, the modification of an assessment, amendment or disallowance of a claim, or otherwise.

(3) But the power to make adjustments by virtue of this section is subject to any time limit imposed by or under any enactment other than this Part.

(4) No adjustment is to be made under this section on the basis that an amount of ordinary income arises, as a result of a payment or quasi-payment, to a payee after that payee's last permitted taxable period in relation to the payment or quasi-payment (see section 259LA, which makes provision about certain such cases).

259LA Deduction from taxable total profits where an amount of ordinary income arises late

(1) This section applies where—

    (a) a relevant deduction in respect of a payment or quasi-payment is reduced by section 259CD, 259DF, 259GC or 259HC or by more than one of those sections,

    (b) no other provision of this Part, or any equivalent provision of the law of a territory outside the United Kingdom, applies or will apply to the tax treatment of any person in respect of the payment or quasi-payment,

    (c) the section or sections had effect because it was reasonable to suppose that the relevant deduction exceeded, or would exceed, the sum of the amounts of ordinary income arising, by reason of the payment or quasi-payment, to each payee for a permitted taxable period, and

    (d) an amount of ordinary income ("the late income") arises—

        (i) by reason of the payment or quasi-payment, but

        (ii) not as a consequence of any provision of this Part or any equivalent provision of the law of a territory outside the United Kingdom,

    to a payee for a taxable period ("the late period") that is not a permitted taxable period.

(2) An amount equal to the late income may be deducted at step 2 in section 4(2) of CTA 2010 in calculating the payer's taxable total profits of the accounting period in which the late period ends.

(3) So much of that amount (if any) as cannot be deducted, in accordance with subsection (2), at step 2 in section 4(2) of CTA 2010 in calculating the taxable total profits of the accounting period in which the late period ends—

    (a) is carried forward to subsequent accounting periods of the payer, and

    (b) may be so deducted for any such period, so far as it cannot be deducted under this paragraph for an earlier period.

(4) But the total amount deducted from taxable total profits under this section, in relation to a payment or quasi-payment, may not exceed the total amount by which the relevant deduction is reduced as mentioned in (1)(a).

(5) In this section "permitted taxable period"—

    (a) where the relevant deduction was reduced under section 259CD, has the meaning given by section 259CC(2),

    (b) where the relevant deduction was reduced under section 259DF, has the meaning given by section 259DD(2),

    (c) where the relevant deduction was reduced under section 259GC, has the meaning given by section 259GB(6),

    (d) where the relevant deduction was reduced under section 259HC, has the meaning given by section 259HB(4), or

    (e) where the relevant deduction was reduced under two or more of the sections mentioned in the preceding paragraphs of this subsection, includes any taxable period that is a permitted period under a provision mentioned in the paragraphs concerned.

CHAPTER 13

ANTI-AVOIDANCE

259M Countering the effect of avoidance arrangements

(1) This section applies where—

    (a) relevant avoidance arrangements exist,

    (b) as a result of those arrangements, any person (whether party to the arrangements or not) would, apart from this section, obtain a relevant tax advantage, and

    (c) that person is—

        (i) within the charge to corporation tax at the time the person would obtain the relevant tax advantage, or

        (ii) would be within the charge to corporation tax at that time but for the relevant avoidance arrangements.

(2) The relevant tax advantage is to be counteracted by making such adjustments to the person's treatment for corporation tax purposes as are just and reasonable.

(3) Any adjustments required to be made under this section (whether or not by an officer of Revenue and Customs) may be made by way of an assessment, the modification of an assessment, amendment or disallowance of a claim, or otherwise.

(4) A person obtains a "relevant tax advantage" if—

    (a) the person avoids, to any extent, any provision of this Part, or any equivalent provision of the law of a territory outside the United Kingdom, restricting whether or how that person may make a deduction from income for the purposes of calculating taxable profits, or

    (b) the person avoids, to any extent, an amount being treated as income of that person under any provision of this Part or any equivalent provision of the law of a territory outside the United Kingdom.

(5) "Relevant avoidance arrangements" means arrangements the main purpose, or one of the main purposes, of which is to enable any person to obtain a relevant tax advantage.

(6) But arrangements are not "relevant avoidance arrangements" if the obtaining of the relevant tax advantage can reasonably be regarded as consistent with the principles on which the provisions of this Part, or the equivalent provisions under the law of a territory outside the United Kingdom, that are relevant to the arrangements are based (whether express or implied) and the policy objectives of those provisions.

(7) For the purposes of determining the principles and policy objectives mentioned in subsection (6), regard may, where appropriate, be had to the Final Report on Neutralising the Effects of Hybrid Mismatch Arrangements published by the Organisation for Economic

Cooperation and Development ("OECD") on 5 October 2015 or any replacement or supplementary publication.

(8) In subsection (7) "replacement or supplementary publication" means any document that is approved and published by the OECD in place of, or to update or supplement, the report mentioned in that subsection (or any replacement of, or supplement to, it).

CHAPTER 14

INTERPRETATION

Financial instruments

259N Meaning of "financial instrument"

(1) A "financial instrument" means —

    (a) an arrangement profits or deficits arising from which would, on the assumption that the person to whom they arise is within the charge to corporation tax, fall to be brought into account for corporation tax purposes in accordance with Part 5 or 6 of CTA 2009 (loan relationships and relationships treated as loan relationships),

    (b) a contract profits or losses arising from which would, on the assumption that the person to whom they arise is within the charge to corporation tax, fall to be brought into account for corporation tax purposes in accordance with Part 7 of CTA 2009 (derivative contracts),

    (c) a type 1, type 2 or type 3 finance arrangement for the purposes of Chapter 2 of Part 16 of CTA 2010 (factoring of income etc: finance arrangements),

    (d) a share forming part of a company's issued share capital or any arrangement that provides a person with economic rights corresponding to those provided by holding such a share, or

    (e) anything else that is a financial instrument.

(2) In subsection (1)(e) "financial instrument" has the meaning that it has for the purposes of UK generally accepted accounting practice.

(3) But "financial instrument" does not include —

    (a) a hybrid transfer arrangement (within the meaning given by section 259DB), or

    (b) anything that is a regulatory capital security for the purposes of the Taxation of Regulatory Capital Securities Regulations 2013 (S.I. 2013/3209) (as amended from time to time).

(4) Subsection (3)(b) is subject to any provision to the contrary that may be made by regulations under section 221 of FA 2012 (tax consequences of financial sector regulation).

Relevant investment funds

259NA Meaning of "relevant investment fund"

(1) "Relevant investment fund" means—

    (a) an open-ended investment company within the meaning of section 613 of CTA 2010,

    (b) an authorised unit trust within the meaning of section 616 of that Act, or

    (c) an offshore fund within the meaning of section 354 of this Act (see section 355),

which meets the genuine diversity of ownership condition (whether or not a clearance has been given to that effect).

(2) "The genuine diversity of ownership condition" means—

    (a) in the case of an offshore fund, the genuine diversity of ownership condition in regulation 75 of the Offshore Funds (Tax) Regulations 2009 (S.I. 2009/3001), and

    (b) in the case of an open-ended investment company or an authorised unit trust, the genuine diversity of ownership condition in regulation 9A of the Authorised Investment Funds (Tax) Regulations 2006 (S.I. 2006/964).

Control groups and related persons

259NB Control groups

(1) A person ("A") is in the same control group as another person ("B")—

    (a) throughout any period for which they are consolidated for accounting purposes,

    (b) on any day on which the participation condition is met in relation to them, or

    (c) on any day on which the 50% investment condition is met in relation to them.

(2) A and B are consolidated for accounting purposes for a period if—

    (a) their financial results for the period are required to be comprised in group accounts,

    (b) their financial results for the period would be required to be comprised in group accounts but for the application of an exemption, or

    (c) their financial results for the period are in fact comprised in group accounts.

(3) In subsection (2), "group accounts" means accounts prepared under—

    (a) section 399 of the Companies Act 2006, or

    (b) any corresponding provision of the law of a territory outside the United Kingdom.

(4) The participation condition is met in relation to A and B ("the relevant parties") on a day if, within the period of 6 months beginning with the day—

    (a) one of the relevant parties directly or indirectly participates in the management, control or capital of the other, or

(b)   the same person or persons directly or indirectly participate in the management, control or capital of each of the relevant parties.

(5)   For the interpretation of subsection (4), see sections 157(1), 158(4), 159(1) and 160(1) (which have the effect that references in subsection (4) to direct or indirect participation are to be read in accordance with provisions of Chapter 2 of Part 4).

(6)   The 50% investment condition is met in relation to A and B if—

(a)   A has a 50% investment in B, or

(b)   a third person has a 50% investment in each of A and B.

(7)   Section 259ND applies for the purposes of determining whether a person has a "50% investment" in another person.

259NC Related persons

(1)   Two persons are "related" on any day that—

(a)   they are in the same control group (see section 259NB), or

(b)   the 25% investment condition is met in relation to them.

(2)   The 25% investment condition is met in relation to a person ("A") and another person ("B") if—

(a)   A has a 25% investment in B, or

(b)   a third person has a 25% investment in each of A and B.

(3)   Section 259ND applies for the purposes of determining whether a person has a "25% investment" in another person.

259ND Meaning of "50% investment" and "25% investment"

(1)   Where this section applies for the purposes of determining whether a person has a "50% investment" in another person for the purposes of section 259NB(6), references in this section to X% are to be read as references to 50%.

(2)   Where this section applies for the purposes of determining whether a person has a "25% investment" in another person for the purposes of section 259NC(2), references in this section to X% are to be read as references to 25%.

(3)   A person ("P") has an X% investment in a company ("C") if it is reasonable to suppose that—

(a)   P possesses or is entitled to acquire X% or more of the share capital or issued share capital of C,

(b)   P possesses or is entitled to acquire X% or more of the voting power in C, or

(c)   if the whole of C's share capital were disposed of, P would receive (directly or indirectly and whether at the time of disposal or later) X% or more of the proceeds of the disposal.

(4)   A person ("P") has an X% investment in another person ("Q") if it is reasonable to suppose that—

(a)   if the whole of Q's income were distributed, P would receive (directly or indirectly and whether at the time of the distribution or later) X% or more of the distributed amount, or

    (b) in the event of a winding-up of Q or in any other circumstances, P would receive (directly or indirectly and whether or not at the time of the winding-up or other circumstances or later) X% or more of Q's assets which would then be available for distribution.

(5) In this section, references to a person receiving any proceeds, amount or assets include references to the proceeds, amount or assets being applied (directly or indirectly) for that person's benefit.

(6) For the purposes of subsections (3) and (4), in determining what percentage investment a person ("P") has in another person ("U"), where P acts together with a third person ("T") in relation to U, P is to be taken to have all of T's rights and interests in relation to U.

(7) P is to be taken to "act together" with T in relation to U if (and only if) —

    (a) P and T are connected (within the meaning given by section 163),

    (b) for the purposes of influencing the conduct of U's affairs —

        (i) P is able to secure that T acts in accordance with P's wishes,

        (ii) T can reasonably be expected to act, or typically acts, in accordance with P's wishes,

        (iii) T is able to secure that P acts in accordance with T's wishes, or

        (iv) P can reasonably be expected to act, or typically acts, in accordance with T's wishes,

    (c) P and T are party to any arrangement that —

        (i) it is reasonable to suppose is designed to affect the value of any of T's rights or interests in relation to U, or

        (ii) relates to the exercise of any of T's rights in relation to U, or

    (d) the same person manages —

        (i) some or all of P's rights or interests in relation to U, and

        (ii) some or all of T's rights or interests in relation to U.

(8) But P does not "act together" with T in relation to U under paragraph (d) of subsection (7) where —

    (a) the person who manages the rights or interests of P mentioned in sub-paragraph (i) of that paragraph, does so as the operator of a collective investment scheme,

    (b) that person manages the rights or interests of T mentioned in sub-paragraph (ii) of that paragraph as the operator of a different collective investment scheme, and

    (c) the Commissioners are satisfied that the management of the schemes is not coordinated for the purpose of influencing the conduct of U 's affairs.

(9) In subsection (8) "collective investment scheme" and "operator" have the same meaning as in Part 17 of the Financial Services and Markets Act 2000 (see sections 235 and 237 of that Act).

Partnerships

259NE Treatment of a person who is a member of a partnership

(1) This section applies where a person is a member of a partnership.

(2) Any reference in this Part to income, profits or an amount of the person includes a reference to the person's share of (as the case may be) income, profits or an amount of the partnership.

(3) For this purpose "the person's share" of income, profits or an amount is determined by apportioning the income, profits or amount between the partners on a just and reasonable basis.

(4) In this section—

(a) "partnership" includes an entity established under the law of a territory outside the United Kingdom of a similar character to a partnership, and

(b) "member" of a partnership is to be read accordingly.

Definitions

259NF Definitions

In this Part—

"arrangement" includes any agreement, understanding, scheme, transaction or series of transactions (whether or not legally enforceable);

"CFC" and "CFC charge" have the meaning given by section 259B(4);

"the Commissioners" means the Commissioners for Her Majesty's Revenue and Customs;

"control group" has the meaning given by section 259NB;

"financial instrument" has the meaning given by section 259N;

"foreign CFC" and "foreign CFC charge" have the meaning given by section 259B(4);

"hybrid entity" has the meaning given by section 259BE;

"investor", in relation to a hybrid entity, has the meaning given by section 259BE(4);

"investor jurisdiction" has the meaning given by section 259BE(4);

"ordinary income" is to be read in accordance with sections 259BC and 259BD;

"payee"—

(a) in relation to a payment, has the meaning given by section 259BB(6)(a), and

(b) in relation to a quasi-payment, has the meaning given by section 259BB(6)(b);

"payee jurisdiction" has the meaning given by 259BB(9);

"payer"—

> (a) in relation to a payment, has the meaning given by section 259BB(1)(a), and
>
> (b) in relation to a quasi-payment, has the meaning given by section 259BB(2);
>
> "payment" has the meaning given by section 259BB(1);
>
> "payment period"—
>
> (a) in relation to a payment, has the meaning given by section 259BB(1)(b), and
>
> (b) in relation to a quasi-payment, has the meaning given by section 259BB(2);
>
> "permanent establishment" has the meaning given by section 259BF;
>
> "quasi-payment" has the meaning given by section 259BB(2) to (5);
>
> "related" has the meaning given by section 259NC;
>
> "relevant deduction"—
>
> (a) in relation to a payment, has the meaning given by section 259BB(1)(b), and
>
> (b) in relation to a quasi-payment, has the meaning given by section 259BB(2)(a);
>
> "relevant investment fund" has the meaning given by section 259NA;
>
> "tax" has the meaning given by section 259B;
>
> "taxable period" means—
>
> (a) in relation to corporation tax, an accounting period,
>
> (b) in relation to income tax, a tax year,
>
> (c) in relation to the CFC charge, a relevant corporation tax accounting period (within the meaning given by section 371BC(3)),
>
> (d) in relation to a foreign CFC charge, a period (by whatever name known) that corresponds to a relevant corporation tax accounting period, and
>
> (e) in relation to any other tax, a period for which the tax is charged;
>
> "taxable profits" is to be read in accordance with sections 259BC(2) and 259BD(5)."

PART 2

CONSEQUENTIAL AMENDMENTS

FA 1998

2   Schedule 18 to FA 1998 (company tax returns) is amended as follows.

3   In paragraph 25(3)—

    (a) insert "or" at the end of paragraph (b), and

    (b) omit paragraph (d) and the "or" preceding it.

4   In paragraph 42(4)—

    (a) insert "or" at the end of paragraph (a), and

    (b) omit paragraph (c) and the "or" preceding it.

CTA 2009

5   In section A1 of CTA 2009 (overview of the Corporation Tax Acts), in subsection (2) —
       (a)   omit paragraph (h), and
       (b)   after that paragraph insert —
              "(ha)   Part 6A of that Act (hybrid and other mismatches),".

CTA 2010

6   CTA 2010 is amended as follows.

7   In section 938N (group mismatch schemes: priority) —
       (a)   omit paragraph (d), and
       (b)   after that paragraph insert —
              "(da)   Part 6A of that Act (hybrid and other mismatches);".

8   In section 938V (tax mismatch schemes: priority) —
       (a)   omit paragraph (c), and
       (b)   after that paragraph insert —
              "(ca)   Part 6A of TIOPA 2010 (hybrid and other mismatches);".

TIOPA 2010

9   TIOPA 2010 is amended as follows.

10   In section 1 (overview of Act), in subsection (1) —
       (a)   omit paragraph (c), and
       (b)   after that paragraph insert —
              "(ca)   Part 6A (hybrid and other mismatches),".

11   In section 157 (direct participation), in subsection (1) —
       (a)   omit the "and" at the end of paragraph (b), and
       (b)   after paragraph (c) insert ", and
              (d)   in Part 6A, section 259NB(4)."

12   In section 158 (indirect participation: defined by sections 159 to 162), in subsection (4) —
       (a)   omit the "and" at the end of paragraph (b), and
       (b)   after paragraph (c) insert ", and
              (d)   in Part 6A, section 259NB(4),".

13   In section 159 (indirect participation: potential direct participant), in subsection (1) —
       (a)   omit the "and" at the end of paragraph (b), and
       (b)   after paragraph (c) insert ", and
              (d)   in Part 6A, section 259NB(4)."

14   In section 160 (indirect participation: one of several major participants), in subsection (1) —
       (a)   omit the "and" at the end of paragraph (b), and

        (b)   after paragraph (c) insert ", and

               (d)   in Part 6A, section 259NB(4)."

15   Omit Part 6 (tax arbitrage).

16   Omit Part 4 of Schedule 11 (tax arbitrage: index of defined expressions used in Part 6).

17   After that Part of that Schedule insert—

"PART 4A

HYBRID AND OTHER MISMATCHES: INDEX OF DEFINED EXPRESSIONS USED IN PART 6A

arrangement (in Part 6A)	section 259NF
CFC and CFC charge (in Part 6A)	section 259B(4)
the Commissioners (in Part 6A)	section 259NF
control group (in Part 6A)	section 259NB
deduction period (in Chapter 10 of Part 6A)	section 259JA(5)(a)
dual resident company (in Chapter 10 of Part 6A)	section 259JA(3)
dual territory double deduction amount (in Chapter 10 of Part 6A)	section 259JA(5)
dual territory double deduction (in Chapter 11 of Part 6A)	section 259KB
excessive PE deduction (in Chapter 6 of Part 6A)	section 259FA(8)
excessive PE deduction (in Chapter 11 of Part 6A)	section 259KB
financial instrument (in Part 6A)	section 259N
foreign CFC and foreign CFC charge (in Part 6A)	section 259B(4)
foreign deduction period (in Chapter 10 of Part 6A)	section 259JA(5)(b)
hybrid entity (in Part 6A)	section 259BE
hybrid entity deduction period (in Chapter 9 of Part 6A)	section 259IA(2)(a)
hybrid entity double deduction amount (in Chapter 9 of Part 6A)	section 259IA(4)

hybrid or otherwise impermissible deduction/non-inclusion mismatch (in Chapter 3 of Part 6A)	section 259CB
hybrid payee (in Chapter 7 of Part 6A)	section 259GA(3)
hybrid payee deduction/non-inclusion mismatch (in Chapter 7 of Part 6A)	section 259GB
hybrid payer (in Chapter 5 of Part 6A)	section 259EA(3)
hybrid payer deduction/non-inclusion mismatch (in Chapter 5 of Part 6A)	section 259EB
hybrid transfer arrangement (in Chapter 4 of Part 6A)	section 259DB
hybrid transfer deduction/non-inclusion mismatch (in Chapter 4 of Part 6A)	section 259DC
imported mismatch payment (in Chapter 11 of Part 6A)	section 259KA(2)
imported mismatch arrangement (in Chapter 11 of Part 6A)	section 259KA(2)
investor (in Part 6A)	section 259BE(4)
investor deduction period (in Chapter 9 of Part 6A)	section 259IA(2)(b)
investor jurisdiction (in Part 6A)	section 259BE(4)
mismatch payment (in Chapter 11 of Part 6A)	section 259KA(6)
multinational company (in Chapter 6 of Part 6A)	section 259FA(3)
multinational company (in Chapter 8 of Part 6A)	section 259HA(4)
multinational payee deduction/non-inclusion mismatch (in Chapter 8 of Part 6A)	section 259HB
ordinary income (in Part 6A)	sections 259BC and 259BD
over-arching arrangement (in Chapter 11 of Part 6A)	section 259KA(5)
P (in Chapter 11 of Part 6A)	section 259KA(3)

parent jurisdiction (in Chapter 6 of Part 6A)	section 259FA(3)(a)
parent jurisdiction (in Chapter 8 of Part 6A)	section 259HA(4)(a)
parent jurisdiction (in Chapter 10 of Part 6A)	section 259JA(4)(b)(ii)
payee (in Part 6A)	section 259BB(6)
payee jurisdiction (in Part 6A)	section 259BB(9)
payer (in Part 6A)	section 259BB(1)(a) or (2)
payment (in Part 6A)	section 259BB(1)
payment period (in Part 6A)	section 259BB(1)(b) or (2)
PE jurisdiction (in Chapter 8 of Part 6A)	section 259HA(4)(b)
PE jurisdiction (in Chapter 10 of Part 6A)	section 259JA(4)(a)
PE jurisdiction (in Chapter 11 of Part 6A)	section 259KB(3)(a)
permanent establishment (in Part 6A)	section 259BF
quasi-payment (in Part 6A)	section 259BB(2) to (5)
related (in Part 6A)	section 259NC
relevant deduction (in Part 6A)	section 259BB(1)(b) or (2)(a)
relevant investment fund (in Part 6A)	section 259NA
relevant mismatch (in Chapter 11 of Part 6A)	section 259KA(6)
relevant multinational company (in Chapter 10 of Part 6A)	section 259JA(4)
relevant PE period (in Chapter 6 of Part 6A)	section 259FA(4)
series of arrangements (in Chapter 11 of Part 6A)	section 259KA(5)
substitute payment (in Chapter 4 of Part 6A)	section 259DB(5)
tax (in Part 6A)	section 259B
taxable period (in Part 6A)	section 259NF
taxable profits (in Part 6A)	sections 259BC(2) and 259BD(5)

| underlying instrument (in Chapter 4 of Part 6A) | section 259DB(3) |
| underlying return (in Chapter 4 of Part 6A) | section 259DB(5)(b)" |

PART 3

COMMENCEMENT

18   Chapters 3 to 5 and 7 and 8 of Part 6A of TIOPA 2010 (counteraction of deduction/non-inclusion mismatches arising from payments and quasi-payments) have effect in relation to—

    (a)   payments made on or after the commencement date, and

    (b)   quasi-payments in relation to which the payment period begins on or after the commencement date.

19   Chapter 6 of Part 6A of TIOPA 2010 (counteraction of deduction/non-inclusion mismatches relating to intra-company transfers from permanent establishments) has effect in relation to excessive PE deductions in relation to which the relevant PE period begins on or after the commencement date.

20   Chapters 9 and 10 of Part 6A of TIOPA 2010 (counteraction of double deduction mismatches) have effect for accounting periods beginning on or after the commencement date.

21   Chapter 11 of Part 6A of TIOPA 2010 (imported mismatch payments) has effect in relation to imported mismatch payments that are—

    (a)   payments made on or after the commencement date, or

    (b)   quasi-payments in relation to which the payment period begins on or after the commencement date.

22   The following provisions of this Schedule have effect in relation to accounting periods beginning on or after the commencement date—

    (a)   paragraphs 2 to 4, and

    (b)   paragraphs 5(a), 7(a), 8(a), 10(a), 15 and 16.

23   For the purposes of paragraph 18 and 21, where a payment period begins before the commencement date and ends on or after that date ("the straddling period")—

    (a)   so much of the straddling period as falls before the commencement date, and so much of that period as falls on or after that date, are to be treated as separate taxable periods, and

    (b)   where it is necessary to apportion an amount for the straddling period to the two separate taxable periods, it is to be apportioned—

        (i)   on a time basis according to the respective length of the separate taxable periods, or

        (ii)   if that method would produce a result that is unjust or unreasonable, on a just and reasonable basis.

24   For the purposes of paragraphs 19, 20 and 22(b), where a company has an accounting period beginning before the commencement date and ending on or after that date ("the straddling period")—

      (a)   so much of the straddling period as falls before the commencement date, and so much of the straddling period as falls on or after that date, are to be treated as separate accounting periods, and

      (b)   where it is necessary to apportion an amount for the straddling period to the two separate accounting periods, it is to be apportioned —

            (i)   in accordance with section 1172 of CTA 2010 (time basis), or

            (ii)   if that method would produce a result that is unjust or unreasonable, on a just and reasonable basis.

25   In this Part of this Schedule "the commencement date" means 1 January 2017.

SCHEDULE 11

Section 83

DISPOSALS OF NON-UK RESIDENTIAL PROPERTY INTERESTS

1   TCGA 1992 is amended in accordance with this Schedule.

2   In section 14B(1) (meaning of "non-resident CGT disposal"), in paragraph (a) after "disposal of a UK residential property interest" insert "(within the meaning given by Schedule B1)".

3   Omit section 14C (which introduces Schedule B1 and is superseded by the section 4BB inserted by section 83 of this Act).

4   In Schedule B1 (disposals of UK residential property interests), in paragraph 1 —

      (a)   in sub-paragraph (4) for "6 April 2015" substitute "the relevant date";

      (b)   after that sub-paragraph insert —

          "(4A) In sub-paragraph (4) "the relevant date" means —

            (a)   for the purpose of determining whether a disposal is a non-resident CGT disposal, 6 April 2015;

            (b)   for any other purpose, 31 March 1982."

5   After Schedule B1 insert —

"SCHEDULE BA1

Section 4BB.

DISPOSALS OF NON-UK RESIDENTIAL PROPERTY INTERESTS

Meaning of "disposal of a non-UK residential property interest"

1   (1)   For the purposes of this Act, the disposal by a person ("P") of an interest in non-UK land (whether made before or after this Schedule comes into force) is a "disposal of a non-UK residential property interest" if the first or second condition is met.

    (2)   The first condition is that —

      (a)   the land has at any time in the relevant ownership period consisted of or included a dwelling, or

(b) the interest in non-UK land subsists for the benefit of land that has at any time in the relevant ownership period consisted of or included a dwelling.

(3) The second condition is that the interest in non-UK land subsists under a contract for an off-plan purchase.

(4) In sub-paragraph (2) "relevant ownership period" means the period—

    (a) beginning with the day on which P acquired the interest in non-UK land or 31 March 1982 (whichever is later), and

    (b) ending with the day before the day on which the disposal occurs.

(5) If the interest in non-UK land disposed of by P as mentioned in sub-paragraph (1) results from interests in non-UK land which P has acquired at different times ("the acquired interests"), P is regarded for the purposes of sub-paragraph (4)(a) as having acquired the interest when P first acquired any of the acquired interests.

(6) In this paragraph—

    "contract for an off-plan purchase" means a contract for the acquisition of land consisting of, or including, a building or part of a building that is to be constructed or adapted for use as a dwelling;

    "dwelling" is to be read in accordance with paragraph 4.

(7) Paragraphs 6 and 20 of Schedule 4ZZC contain further provision about interests under contracts for off-plan purchases.

"Interest in non-UK land"

2   (1) In this Schedule "interest in non-UK land" means—

    (a) an estate, interest, right or power in or over land outside the United Kingdom, or

    (b) the benefit of an obligation, restriction or condition affecting the value of any such estate, interest, right or power,

other than an excluded interest.

(2) The following are excluded interests—

    (a) any security interest;

    (b) a licence to use or occupy land.

(3) In sub-paragraph (2) "security interest" means an interest or right held for the purpose of securing the payment of money or the performance of any other obligation.

(4) The Treasury may by regulations—

    (a) provide that any other description of interest or right in relation to land outside the United Kingdom is an excluded interest;

    (b) exclude from sub-paragraph (2) such interests or rights as may be prescribed in the regulations.

(5) Regulations under sub-paragraph (4) may make incidental, consequential, supplementary or transitional provision or savings.

Grants of options

3 (1) Sub-paragraph (2) applies where—

(a) a person ("P") grants at any time an option binding P to sell an interest in non-UK land, and

(b) a disposal by P of that interest in non-UK land at that time would be a disposal of a non-UK residential property interest by virtue of paragraph 1.

(2) The grant of the option is regarded for the purposes of this Schedule as the disposal of an interest in the land in question (if it would not be so regarded apart from this paragraph).

(3) Nothing in this paragraph affects the operation of section 144 in relation to the grant of the option (or otherwise).

(4) Subsection (6) of section 144 (interpretation of references to "sale" etc) applies for the purposes of this paragraph as it applies for the purposes of that section.

Meaning of "dwelling"

4 (1) Paragraph 4 of Schedule B1 (meaning of "dwelling"), read with paragraphs 6 to 10 of that Schedule, applies for the purposes of this Schedule as it applies for the purposes of Schedule B1, but as if—

(a) in paragraph 4, sub-paragraphs (5) and (6) were omitted,

(b) in paragraphs 6 and 8—

(i) any reference to an interest in UK land were to an interest in non-UK land within the meaning of this Schedule, and

(ii) any reference to paragraph 1(4) of that Schedule were a reference to paragraph 1(4) of this Schedule, and

(c) in paragraphs 7 to 9 any reference to planning permission or development consent were to any permission or consent corresponding to planning permission or development consent within the meaning of that Schedule.

(2) In paragraph 5 of Schedule B1 (power to amend), the reference to paragraph 4 includes paragraph 4 as applied by this paragraph.

(3) The Treasury may by regulations under this sub-paragraph make provision changing or clarifying the cases where a building outside the United Kingdom counts as a dwelling for the purposes of this Schedule (and sub-paragraph (1) has effect subject to any such regulations).

(4) Provision made under sub-paragraph (3) may include provision corresponding to paragraph 4(5) of Schedule B1.

Interpretation

5   In this Schedule "land" includes a building."

SCHEDULE 12   Section 83

DISPOSALS OF RESIDENTIAL PROPERTY INTERESTS: GAINS AND LOSSES

1   TCGA 1992 is amended in accordance with this Schedule.

2   In section 57A(3) (gains and losses on relevant high value disposals: interaction with other provisions) —
         (a)   the words from "Part 4" to the end become paragraph (a), and
         (b)   after that paragraph insert "or,
                        (b)   Part 3 of Schedule 4ZZC applies (other disposals of residential property interests which are or involve relevant high value disposals)."

3   After section 57B insert —

"CHAPTER 7

COMPUTATION OF GAINS AND LOSSES: DISPOSALS OF RESIDENTIAL PROPERTY INTERESTS

57C   Gains and losses on disposals of residential property interests

         Schedule 4ZZC makes provision about the computation of —
         (a)   residential property gains or losses, and
         (b)   other gains or losses,
         on disposals of residential property interests which are not non-resident CGT disposals."

4   In Schedule B1 (disposals of UK residential property interests), in paragraph 1(7) after "Schedule 4ZZB" insert "and paragraphs 6 and 20 of Schedule 4ZZC".

5   After Schedule 4ZZB insert —

"SCHEDULE 4ZZC   Section 57C

DISPOSALS OF RESIDENTIAL PROPERTY INTERESTS: GAINS AND LOSSES

PART 1

INTRODUCTION AND INTERPRETATION

Introduction

1   (1)   In this Schedule "RPI disposal" means a disposal of a residential property interest which is not a non-resident CGT disposal.

         (2)   This Schedule applies for the purpose of determining, in relation to an RPI disposal —
                (a)   whether a residential property gain or loss accrues on the disposal, and the amount of any such gain or loss, and

(b) whether a gain or loss other than a residential property gain or loss accrues on the disposal, and the amount of any such gain or loss.

(3) In this Schedule—

(a) Part 2 contains the main rules for computing the gains and losses;

(b) Part 3 contains the rules for computing the gains and losses in a case where the RPI disposal is, or involves, a relevant high value disposal (as defined in section 2C).

Interpretation

2 (1) For the purposes of this Schedule, a relevant high value disposal is "comprised in" an RPI disposal if—

(a) the RPI disposal is treated for the purposes of section 2C and Schedule 4ZZA as two or more disposals, and

(b) the relevant high value disposal is one of those.

(2) In this Schedule—

"chargeable interest" has the same meaning as in Part 3 of the Finance Act 2013 (annual tax on enveloped dwellings) (see section 107 of that Act);

"dwelling" has the meaning given by —

(a) paragraph 4 of Schedule B1, in relation to a disposal of a UK residential property interest;

(b) paragraph 4 of Schedule BA1, in relation to a disposal of a non-UK residential property interest;

"subject-matter", in relation to an interest in land (or a chargeable interest) means the land to which the interest relates.

PART 2

RPI DISPOSALS NOT INVOLVING RELEVANT HIGH VALUE DISPOSALS

Application of Part

3 (1) This Part of this Schedule applies where a person ("P") makes an RPI disposal of (or of part of) an interest in land.

(2) But this Part of this Schedule does not apply if the disposal is—

(a) a relevant high value disposal, or

(b) a disposal in which a relevant high value disposal is comprised.

(3) In this Part of this Schedule "the disposed of interest" means—

(a) the interest in land, or

(b) if the disposal is of part of that interest, the part disposed of.

Computation of residential property gains and losses

4   (1) The residential property gain or loss accruing on the disposal is computed as follows.

Step 1

Determine the amount of the gain or loss that accrues to P.

(For the purpose of determining the amount of that gain or loss, no account is taken of section 57C or this Schedule.)

Step 2

The residential property gain or loss accruing on the disposal is an amount equal to the relevant fraction of that gain or loss (but see Step 3).

Step 3

If there has been mixed use of the subject matter of the disposed of interest on one or more days in the relevant ownership period, the residential property gain or loss accruing on the disposal is equal to the appropriate fraction of the amount given by Step 2.

(2) In Step 2 "the relevant fraction" means —

$$\frac{RD}{TD}$$

where —

"RD" is the number of days in the relevant ownership period on which the subject matter of the disposed of interest consists wholly or partly of a dwelling;

"TD" is the total number of days in the relevant ownership period.

(3) For the purposes of Step 3 there is "mixed use" of land on any day on which the land consists partly, but not exclusively, of one or more dwellings.

(4) In Step 3 "the appropriate fraction" means the fraction that is, on a just and reasonable apportionment, attributable to the dwelling or dwellings.

(5) In this paragraph the "relevant ownership period" means the period —

   (a) beginning with the day on which P acquired the disposed of interest or, if later, 31 March 1982, and

   (b) ending with the day before the day on which the disposal occurs.

Computation of balancing gains and loses

5   The gain or loss accruing on the disposal which is not a residential property gain or loss is computed as follows.

Step 1

In a case where there is a gain under Step 1 of paragraph 4(1), determine the amount of that gain remaining after the deduction of the residential property gain determined under that paragraph.

That remaining gain is the gain accruing on the disposal which is not a residential property gain.

Step 2

In a case where there is a loss under Step 1 of paragraph 4(1), determine the amount of that loss remaining after the deduction of the residential property loss determined under that paragraph.

That remaining loss is the loss accruing on the disposal which is not a residential property loss.

Interest subsisting under contract for off-plan purchase

6   (1) This paragraph applies where the disposal referred to in paragraph 3(1) is a disposal of a residential property interest only because of—

(a)   the second condition in paragraph 1 of Schedule B1, or

(b)   the second condition in paragraph 1 of Schedule BA1,

(interest subsisting under a contract for the acquisition of land that consists of, or includes, a building that is to be constructed for use as a dwelling).

(2) The land that is the subject of the contract concerned is treated for the purposes of this Part of this Schedule as consisting of (or, as the case requires, including) a dwelling throughout P's period of ownership of the disposed of interest.

PART 3

RPI DISPOSALS INVOLVING RELEVANT HIGH VALUE DISPOSALS

Application of Part

7   (1) This Part of this Schedule applies where—

(a)   a person (other than an excluded person) ("P") makes an RPI disposal of (or of part of) an interest in land, and

(b)   that disposal ("the disposal of land") is a relevant high value disposal or a relevant high value disposal is comprised in it.

(2) "Excluded person" has the meaning given by section 2B(2).

Interpretation of Part

8   (1) This paragraph applies for the interpretation of this Part of this Schedule.

(2) "The asset", in relation to a relevant high value disposal, means the chargeable interest which (or a part of which) is the subject of that disposal.

(3) "The disposed of interest", in relation to a relevant high value disposal, means the asset or, if only part of the asset is the subject of the relevant high value disposal, that part of the asset.

(4) A day is a "residential property chargeable day" in relation to a relevant high value disposal if—

(a)   it is a day on which the subject matter of the disposed of interest consists wholly or partly of a dwelling, but

(b)   it is not an ATED chargeable day (as defined in paragraph 3 of Schedule 4ZZA).

Computation of residential property gains or losses on the RPI disposal

9   (1)   The residential property gain or loss accruing on the disposal of land is computed as follows.

Step 1

Determine in accordance with paragraphs 10 to 15 the amount of the residential property gain or loss accruing on each relevant high value disposal.

Step 2

Add together the amounts of any gains or losses determined under Step 1 (treating any amount which is a loss as a negative amount).

(2)   If the result is a positive amount, that amount is the residential property gain on the disposal of land.

(3)   If the result is a negative amount, that amount (expressed as a positive number) is the residential property loss on the disposal of land.

Computation of residential property gains or losses on relevant high value disposal not within Case 1, 2 or 3 (or where an election is made)

10   (1)   This paragraph applies to a relevant high value disposal where—
(a)   the disposal does not fall within any of Cases 1, 2 or 3 in paragraph 2 of Schedule 4ZZA, or
(b)   P has made an election under paragraph 5 of that Schedule in respect of the asset.

(2)   The residential property gain or loss accruing on the relevant high value disposal is computed as follows—

Step 1

Determine the amount of gain or loss which accrues to P.

(For the purpose of determining the amount of that gain or loss, no account is taken of section 57C or this Schedule.)

Step 2

The residential property gain or loss accruing on the relevant high value disposal is equal to the special fraction of that gain or loss.

(3)   The "special fraction" is—

$$\frac{SD}{TD}$$

where—

"SD" is the number of residential property chargeable days in the relevant ownership period;

"TD" is the total number of days in the relevant ownership period.

(4) "Relevant ownership period" means the period —

    (a) beginning with the day on which P acquired the disposed of interest or, if later, 31 March 1982, and

    (b) ending with the day before the day on which the relevant high value disposal occurs.

Computation of residential property gains and losses on relevant high value disposal within Case 1, 2 or 3 (and no election made)

11 (1) This paragraph applies to a relevant high value disposal where —

    (a) the disposal falls within Case 1, 2 or 3 in paragraph 2 of Schedule 4ZZA, and

    (b) P has not made an election under paragraph 5 of that Schedule in respect of the asset.

(2) The residential property gain or loss accruing on the relevant high value disposal is computed in accordance with paragraphs 12 to 15.

(3) In those paragraphs "the relevant year" means —

    (a) where the relevant high value disposal falls within Case 1 in paragraph 2 of Schedule 4ZZA, 2013,

    (b) where it falls within Case 2 in that paragraph, 2015, and

    (c) where it falls within Case 3 in that paragraph, 2016.

12 (1) Take the following steps —

Step 1
Determine the amount equal to the special fraction of the notional pre-ATED gain or loss (as the case may be) (see paragraph 13).

Step 2
Determine the amount equal to the special fraction of the notional post-ATED gain or loss (as the case may be) (see paragraph 14).

Step 3
Add (treating any amount which is a loss as a negative amount) —

    (a) the amount of any gain or loss determined under Step 1, and

    (b) the amount of any gain or loss determined under Step 2.

(2) If the result is a positive amount, that amount is the residential property gain on the relevant high value disposal.

(3) If the result is a negative amount, that amount (expressed as a positive number) is the residential property loss on the relevant high value disposal.

13 (1) This paragraph applies for the purposes of Step 1 in paragraph 12.

(2) "Notional pre-ATED gain or loss" means the gain or loss which would have accrued on 5 April of the relevant year had the disposed of interest been disposed of for a consideration equal to the market value of the interest on that date.

(3) The "special fraction" is—

$$\frac{SD}{TD}$$

where—

"SD" is the number of residential property chargeable days in the relevant ownership period;

"TD" is the total number of days in the relevant ownership period.

(4) The "relevant ownership period" is the period—

(a) beginning with the day on which P acquired the disposed of interest or, if later, 31 March 1982, and

(b) ending with 5 April of the relevant year.

14 (1) This paragraph applies for the purposes of Step 2 in paragraph 12.

(2) "Notional post-ATED gain or loss" means the gain or loss which would have accrued on the relevant high value disposal had P acquired the disposed of interest on 5 April of the relevant year for a consideration equal to its market value on that date (and see paragraph 15).

(3) The "special fraction" is—

$$\frac{SD}{TD}$$

where—

"SD" is the number of residential property chargeable days in the relevant ownership period;

"TD" is the total number of days in the relevant ownership period.

(4) The "relevant ownership period" is the period beginning with 6 April of the relevant year and ending with the day before the day on which the relevant high value disposal occurs.

15 (1) This paragraph applies for the purposes of computing the notional post-ATED gain or loss for the purposes of Step 2 in paragraph 12.

(2) In determining whether the asset which is the subject of the relevant high value disposal is a wasting asset (as defined for the purposes of Chapter 2 of Part 2), ignore the assumption that the asset was acquired on 5 April of the relevant year.

(3) Sections 41 (restriction of losses by reference to capital allowances and renewals allowances) and 47 (wasting assets subject to capital allowances) apply in relation to any capital allowance or renewals allowance made in respect of the expenditure actually incurred by P in acquiring or providing the asset as if that allowance were made in respect of the expenditure treated as incurred by P on 5 April of the relevant year.

Computation of balancing gains or losses on the RPI disposal

16 (1) The gain or loss on the disposal of land which is neither ATED-related nor a residential property gain or loss ("the balancing gain or loss") is computed as follows.

Step 1

Determine in accordance with paragraphs 17 and 18 the amount of the gain or loss accruing on each relevant high value disposal which is neither ATED-related nor a residential property gain or loss.

This is the "balancing" gain or loss for each disposal.

Step 2

Add together the amounts of any balancing gains or losses determined under Step 1 (treating any amount which is a loss as a negative amount).

(2) If the result is a positive amount, that amount is the balancing gain on the disposal of land.

(3) If the result is a negative amount, that amount (expressed as a positive number) is the balancing loss on the disposal of land.

Computation of balancing gains or losses on relevant high value disposal not within Case 1, 2 or 3 (or where an election is made)

17 (1) In the case of a relevant high value disposal to which paragraph 10 applies, the amount of the balancing gain or loss is determined as follows.

(2) Determine the number of balancing days in the relevant ownership period.

(3) "Balancing day" means a day which is neither—
     (a) a residential property chargeable day, nor
     (b) an ATED chargeable day (as defined in paragraph 3 of Schedule 4ZZA).

(4) The balancing gain or loss on the disposal is equal to the balancing fraction of the amount of the gain or (as the case may be) loss determined under Step 1 of paragraph 10(2).

(5) The "balancing fraction" is—
$$\frac{BD}{TD}$$
where—
     "BD" is the number of balancing days in the relevant ownership period;
     "TD" is the total number of days in the relevant ownership period.

(6) In this paragraph "relevant ownership period" has the same meaning as in paragraph 10.

Computation of balancing gains or losses on relevant high value disposal within Case 1, 2 or 3 (and no election made)

18 (1) The amount of the balancing gain or loss on a relevant high value disposal to which paragraph 11 applies is found by adding—

   (a) the amount of the balancing gain or loss belonging to the notional pre-ATED gain or loss, and

   (b) the amount of the balancing gain or loss belonging to the notional post-ATED gain or loss,

   (treating any amount which is a loss as a negative amount).

   (2) If the result is a positive amount, that amount is the balancing gain on the relevant high value disposal.

   (3) If the result is a negative amount, that amount (expressed as a positive number) is the balancing loss on the relevant high value disposal.

   (4) The balancing gain or loss belonging to the notional pre-ATED gain or loss is equal to the balancing fraction of the notional pre-ATED gain or loss.

   (5) The balancing gain or loss belonging to the notional post-ATED gain or loss is equal to the balancing fraction of the notional post-ATED gain or loss.

   (6) The balancing fraction is—

$$\frac{BD}{TD}$$

   where—

   "BD" is the number of balancing days in the appropriate ownership period;

   "TD" is the total number of days in the appropriate ownership period.

   (7) "Balancing day" means a day which is neither—

   (a) a residential property chargeable day, nor

   (b) an ATED chargeable day (as defined in paragraph 3 of Schedule 4ZZA).

   (8) The appropriate ownership period is—

   (a) for the purpose of computing the balancing gain or loss belonging to the notional pre-ATED gain or loss, the relevant ownership period mentioned in paragraph 13(4);

   (b) for the purpose of computing the balancing gain or loss belonging to the notional post-ATED gain or loss, the relevant ownership period mentioned in paragraph 14(4).

   (9) In this paragraph—

   "notional pre-ATED gain or loss" means the same as in paragraph 13(2);

   "notional post-ATED gain or loss" means the same as in paragraph 14(2).

Relevant high value disposal and "other" disposal are comprised in the disposal of land

19 (1) This paragraph applies where the disposals comprised in the disposal of land include a disposal (the "non-ATED related disposal") which is not a relevant high value disposal.

  (2) This Part of this Schedule (apart from this paragraph) applies in relation to the non-ATED related disposal as if it were a relevant high value disposal.

  (3) Sub-paragraph (4) applies if there has, at any time in the relevant ownership period, been mixed use of the subject matter of the disposed of interest.

  (4) The amount of any residential property gain or loss on the non-ATED related disposal computed under this Part of this Schedule is taken to be the appropriate fraction of the amount that it would otherwise be.

  (5) In sub-paragraph (4) "the appropriate fraction" means the fraction that is, on a just and reasonable apportionment, attributable to the dwelling or dwellings.

  (6) In this paragraph the "relevant ownership period" means—
     (a) where paragraph 10 applies, the relevant ownership period as defined in paragraph 10(4), or
     (b) where paragraph 11 applies, the relevant ownership period as defined in paragraphs 13(4) and 14(4).

Interest subsisting under contract for off-plan purchase

20 (1) This paragraph applies where the RPI disposal made by P is a disposal of a residential property interest only because of—
     (a) the second condition in paragraph 1 of Schedule B1, or
     (b) the second condition in paragraph 1 of Schedule BA1,
     (interest subsisting under a contract for the acquisition of land that consists of, or includes, a building that is to be constructed for use as a dwelling).

  (2) The land that is the subject of the contract concerned is treated for the purposes of this Part of this Schedule as consisting of (or, as the case requires, including) a dwelling throughout P's period of ownership of the interest in land."

SCHEDULE 13

Section 86

ENTREPRENEURS' RELIEF: "TRADING COMPANY" AND "TRADING GROUP"

1 TCGA 1992 is amended as follows.

2 In section 169H(7) (introduction), for "Section 169S contains" substitute "Sections 169S and 169SA contain".

3 In section 169S (interpretation of Chapter), subsection (4A) is treated as never having had effect, and is omitted accordingly.

4   After section 169S insert—

"169SA Meaning of "trading company" and "trading group"

Schedule 7ZA gives the meaning in this Chapter of "trading company" and "trading group"."

5   After Schedule 7 insert—

"SCHEDULE 7ZA   Section 169SA

ENTREPRENEURS' RELIEF: "TRADING COMPANY" AND "TRADING GROUP"

PART 1

MEANING OF "TRADING COMPANY" AND "TRADING GROUP"

1   (1) This paragraph gives the meaning of "trading company" and "trading group" where used in the following provisions of Chapter 3 of Part 5 (entrepreneurs' relief)—

(a)   in section 169I (material disposal of business assets)—

(i)   paragraphs (a) and (b) of subsection (6) (which apply for the purposes of conditions A and B in that section), and

(ii)   sub-paragraphs (i) and (ii) of subsection (7A)(c) (which apply for the purposes of conditions C and D in that section), and

(b)   section 169J(4) (disposal of trust business assets).

(2) "Trading company" and "trading group" have the same meaning as in section 165 (see section 165A), but as modified by Part 2 of this Schedule.

(3) "Trading activities" (see section 165A(4) and (9)) is to be read in accordance with Part 3 of this Schedule.

2   In provisions of Chapter 3 of Part 5 not mentioned in paragraph 1(1), "trading company" and "trading group" have the same meaning as in section 165 (see section 165A), except that subsections (7) and (12) of section 165A are to be disregarded.

PART 2

JOINT VENTURE COMPANIES

Attribution of activities of a joint venture company

3   In relation to a disposal of assets consisting of (or of interests in) shares in or securities of a company ("company A"), activities of a joint venture company are to be attributed to a company under subsections (7) and (12) of section 165A only if P—

(a)   passes the shareholding test in relation to the joint venture company (see paragraphs 5 to 8), and

(b)   passes the voting rights test in relation to the joint venture company (see paragraphs 9 to 12).

Meaning of "investing company"

4 (1) For the purposes of this Part, a company is an "investing company" in relation to P and a joint venture company if it meets conditions 1 and 2.

   (2) Condition 1 is that —
       (a) the company is company A (see paragraph 3), or
       (b) P directly owns some portion of the ordinary share capital of the company.

   (3) Condition 2 is that the company owns some portion of the ordinary share capital of the joint venture company (whether it is owned directly, indirectly, or partly directly and partly indirectly).

   (4) In sub-paragraph (3) the reference to a company owning share capital indirectly is to be read in accordance with section 1155 of CTA 2010.

Shareholding test

5 P passes the shareholding test in relation to a joint venture company if, throughout the relevant period, the sum of the percentages given by paragraphs (a) and (b) is at least 5% —
   (a) the percentage of the ordinary share capital of the joint venture company that is owned directly by P, and
   (b) P's indirect shareholding percentage (see paragraph 6).

6 P's "indirect shareholding percentage" is found by —
   (a) calculating the percentage of the ordinary share capital of the joint venture company that is owned indirectly by P through a particular investing company (see paragraph 7), and
   (b) where there are two or more investing companies, adding those percentages together.

7 The percentage of the ordinary share capital of a joint venture company that is owned indirectly by P through a particular investing company ("company IC") at a particular time is given by —

$$R \times S \times 100$$

where —
   R is the fraction of company IC's ordinary share capital that is owned by P at that time, and
   S is the fraction of the joint venture company's ordinary share capital that is owned by company IC at that time (whether it is owned directly, indirectly, or partly directly and partly indirectly) (see paragraph 8).

8 (1) The fraction of the joint venture company's ordinary share capital that is owned indirectly by company IC is calculated —
       (a) by applying sections 1156 and 1157 of CTA 2010, as read with section 1155 of that Act, and

    (b)   on the assumptions specified in sub-paragraph (2).

  (2) The assumptions are —

    (a)   where company IC directly owns more than 50% of the ordinary share capital of a company, company IC is taken to own the whole of the ordinary share capital of that company;

    (b)   where a company other than company IC ("company B") directly owns more than 50% of the ordinary share capital of another company ("company C") which is a member of a group of companies of which company IC is a member, company B is taken to own the whole of the ordinary share capital of company C.

Voting rights test

9   P passes the voting rights test in relation to a joint venture company if, throughout the relevant period, the sum of the percentages given by paragraphs (a) and (b) is at least 5% —

    (a)   the percentage of the voting rights that P holds directly in the joint venture company, and

    (b)   P's indirect voting rights percentage (see paragraph 10).

10   P's "indirect voting rights percentage" is found by —

    (a)   calculating the percentage of the voting rights in the joint venture company that P holds indirectly through a particular investing company (see paragraph 11), and

    (b)   where there are two or more investing companies, adding those percentages together.

11   The percentage of the voting rights in a joint venture company that P holds indirectly through a particular investing company ("company IC") at a particular time is given by —

$$T \times U \times 100$$

where —

     T is the fraction of the voting rights in company IC that is held by P at that time, and

     U is the fraction of the voting rights in the joint venture company that is held by company IC at that time (whether the voting rights are held directly, indirectly, or partly directly and partly indirectly) (see paragraph 12).

12 (1) The fraction of the voting rights in the joint venture company that is held indirectly by company IC is calculated —

    (a)   by applying sections 1156 and 1157 of CTA 2010, as read with section 1155 of that Act, as if references in those sections to owning the ordinary share capital of a company were references to holding voting rights in a company, and

    (b)   on the assumptions specified in sub-paragraph (2).

  (2) The assumptions are —

(a) where company IC directly holds more than 50% of the voting rights in a company, company IC is taken to hold all the voting rights in that company;

(b) where a company other than company IC ("company B") directly holds more than 50% of the voting rights in another company ("company C") which is a member of a group of companies of which company IC is a member, company B is taken to hold all the voting rights in company C.

PART 3

PARTNERSHIPS

Activities of a company as a member of a partnership

13 (1) In relation to a disposal of assets consisting of (or of interests in) shares in or securities of a company ("company A"), activities carried on by a company as a member of a partnership are to be treated as not being trading activities of the company (see section 165A(4) and (9)) if P fails either or both of the following—

    (a) the profits and assets test in relation to the partnership (see paragraphs 15 to 20);

    (b) the voting rights test in relation to the partnership (see paragraphs 21 to 23).

    (2) In relation to such a disposal, activities carried on by a company as a member of a partnership are also to be treated as not being trading activities of the company if the company is not a member of the partnership throughout the relevant period.

Meaning of "direct interest company" and "relevant corporate partner"

14 (1) This paragraph applies for the purposes of this Part.

    (2) A company is a "direct interest company" in relation to P if—

       (a) it is company A (see paragraph 13(1)), or

       (b) P directly owns some portion of the ordinary share capital of the company.

    (3) A company is a "relevant corporate partner" in relation to P and a partnership if—

       (a) a direct interest company in relation to P ("company DIC") owns some portion of the ordinary share capital of the company (whether it is owned directly, indirectly or partly directly and partly indirectly),

       (b) the company is a member of a group of companies of which company DIC is a member, and

       (c) the company is a member of the partnership.

    (4) In sub-paragraph (3) the reference to a company owning share capital indirectly is to be read in accordance with section 1155 of CTA 2010.

482   *Finance Act 2016 (c. 24)*

Schedule 13 — Entrepreneurs' relief: "trading company" and "trading group"

Profits and assets test

15   P passes the profits and assets test in relation to a partnership if, throughout the relevant period, the sum of the percentages given by paragraphs (a), (b) and (c) is at least 5% —

    (a) the percentage which is P's direct interest in the assets of the partnership,

    (b) the percentage which is P's share of the partnership through direct interest companies that are members of the partnership (see paragraph 16), and

    (c) the percentage which is P's share of the partnership through direct interest companies and relevant corporate partners in the partnership (see paragraph 18).

16   P's "share of the partnership through direct interest companies that are members of the partnership" is found by —

    (a) calculating the percentage which is P's indirect share of the partnership through each direct interest company that is a member of the partnership (see paragraph 17), and

    (b) where there are two or more direct interest companies that are members of the partnership, adding those percentages together.

17   The percentage which is P's indirect share of the partnership through a particular direct interest company that is a member of the partnership ("company DICP") at a particular time is given by —

$$R \times V \times 100$$

where —

  R is the fraction of company DICP's ordinary share capital that is owned by P at that time, and

  V is the lower of —

    (a) the fraction of the profits of the partnership in which company DICP has an interest at that time, and

    (b) the fraction of the assets of the partnership in which company DICP has an interest at that time.

18   P's "share of the partnership through direct interest companies and relevant corporate partners in the partnership" is found by —

    (a) calculating the percentage which is P's indirect share of the partnership through each direct interest company and each relevant corporate partner in the partnership (see paragraph 19), and

    (b) where there are two or more direct interest companies or two or more relevant corporate partners, or both, adding those percentages together.

19   The percentage which is P's indirect share of the partnership through a particular direct interest company ("company DIC")

and a particular relevant corporate partner in the partnership ("company CP") at a particular time is given by—

$$R \times V \times W \times 100$$

where—

R is the fraction of company DIC's ordinary share capital that is owned by P at that time,

V is the lower of—

  (a) the fraction of the profits of the partnership in which company CP has an interest at that time, and

  (b) the fraction of the assets of the partnership in which company CP has an interest at that time, and

W is the fraction of company CP's ordinary share capital that is owned by company DIC at that time (whether it is owned directly, indirectly, or partly directly and partly indirectly) (see paragraph 20).

20 (1) The fraction of a company's ordinary share capital that is owned indirectly by company DIC is calculated—

  (a) by applying sections 1156 and 1157 of CTA 2010, as read with section 1155 of that Act, and

  (b) on the assumptions specified in sub-paragraph (2).

  (2) The assumptions are—

  (a) where company DIC directly owns more than 50% of the ordinary share capital of a company, company DIC is taken to own the whole of the ordinary share capital of that company;

  (b) where a company other than company DIC ("company B") directly owns more than 50% of the ordinary share capital of another company ("company C") which is a member of a group of companies of which company DIC is a member, company B is taken to own the whole of the ordinary share capital of company C.

Voting rights test

21 (1) P passes the voting rights test in relation to a partnership if, throughout the relevant period, the sum of P's direct voting rights percentage and P's indirect voting rights percentage is at least 5%.

  (2) P's "direct voting rights percentage" is found by—

  (a) taking the percentage of the voting rights that P holds directly in each direct interest company that is a member of the partnership, and

  (b) where P directly holds voting rights in two or more direct interest companies that are members of the partnership, adding those percentages together.

  (3) P's "indirect voting rights percentage" is found by—

  (a) calculating the percentage which is P's indirect holding of voting rights in each relevant corporate partner in the partnership through each direct interest company (see paragraph 22), and

 (b) where there are two or more relevant corporate partners or two or more direct interest companies, or both, adding those percentages together.

22 The percentage which is P's indirect holding of voting rights in a particular relevant corporate partner in the partnership ("company CP") through a particular direct interest company ("company DIC") at a particular time is given by—

$$T \times X \times 100$$

where—

 T is the fraction of the voting rights in company DIC that is held by P at that time, and

 X is the fraction of the voting rights in company CP that is held by company DIC at that time (whether the voting rights are held directly, indirectly, or partly directly and partly indirectly) (see paragraph 23).

23 (1) The fraction of the voting rights in a company that is held indirectly by company DIC is calculated—

  (a) by applying sections 1156 and 1157 of CTA 2010, as read with section 1155 of that Act, as if references in those sections to owning the ordinary share capital of a company were references to holding voting rights in a company, and

  (b) on the assumptions specified in sub-paragraph (2).

 (2) The assumptions are—

  (a) where company DIC directly holds more than 50% of the voting rights in a company, company DIC is taken to hold all the voting rights in that company;

  (b) where a company other than company DIC ("company B") directly holds more than 50% of the voting rights in another company ("company C") which is a member of a group of companies of which company DIC is a member, company B is taken to hold all the voting rights in company C.

PART 4

INTERPRETATION OF THIS SCHEDULE

Meaning of "P"

24 (1) In the case of a material disposal of business assets, "P" means the individual making the disposal.

 (2) In the case of a disposal of trust business assets—

  (a) "P" means any relevant beneficiary, but

  (b) in any reference to P passing or failing the tests mentioned in paragraphs 3 and 13(1), P is to be read as being a single body consisting of all the relevant beneficiaries (so that, for the purposes of determining if those tests are met, percentages are to be calculated in respect of each relevant beneficiary and then aggregated).

(3) The following are "relevant beneficiaries"—

(a) the qualifying beneficiary in relation to the disposal (see section 169J(3)), and

(b) any other beneficiary who is, in relation to the disposal, a beneficiary mentioned in section 169O(1).

Meaning of "relevant period"

25   "The relevant period" means—

(a) for the purposes of conditions A and C in section 169I, the period of 1 year ending with the date of the disposal,

(b) for the purposes of conditions B and D in section 169I, the period of 1 year ending with the date mentioned in subsection (7)(a) or (b) or (7O)(a) or (b) of that section, and

(c) for the purposes of section 169J(4), a period of 1 year ending not earlier than 3 years before the date of the disposal.

Other interpretation provisions

26   (1) Terms used in this Schedule which are defined in subsection (14) of section 165A have the same meaning as they have in that subsection.

(2) References to a person holding voting rights include references to a person who has the ability to control the exercise of voting rights by another person.

(3) For the purposes of Part 3 of this Schedule, the assets of—

(a) a Scottish partnership, or

(b) a partnership under the law of any other country or territory under which assets of a partnership are regarded as held by or on behalf of the partnership as such,

are to be treated as held by the members of the partnership in the proportions in which they are entitled to share in the capital profits of the partnership.

References in Part 3 to a person's interest in the assets of a partnership are to be construed accordingly."

6   (1) The amendments made by this Schedule (except paragraph 3) have effect in relation to disposals made on or after 18 March 2015, but only for the purposes of determining what is a trading company or trading group at times on or after that date.

(2) In conditions B and D in section 169I of TCGA 1992 (material disposal of business assets)—

(a) a reference to a company ceasing to be a trading company does not include a case where, as a result of the coming into force of the amendments made by this Schedule, a company which was a trading company immediately before 18 March 2015 is treated as ceasing on that day to be a trading company, and

    (b)   a reference to a company ceasing to be a member of a trading group does not include a case where, as a result of the coming into force of the amendments made by this Schedule, a company which was a member of a trading group immediately before 18 March 2015 is treated as ceasing on that day to be a member of a trading group.

(3)   Sub-paragraph (2) is without prejudice to the operation of section 43(4) of FA 2015.

SCHEDULE 14   Section 87

INVESTORS' RELIEF

1   (1)   In the heading to Part 5 of TGCA 1992, after "ASSETS" insert ", ENTREPRENEURS' RELIEF AND INVESTORS' RELIEF".

    (2)   In the heading to Chapter 1 of that Part, before "GENERAL PROVISIONS" insert "TRANSFER OF BUSINESS ASSETS:"

2   In Part 5 of TCGA 1992, after section 169V insert—

"CHAPTER 5

INVESTORS' RELIEF

Overview

169VA Overview of Chapter

    (1)   This Chapter provides for a relief, in the form of a lower rate of capital gains tax, in respect of disposals of (and disposals of interests in) certain ordinary shares in unlisted companies.

    (2)   Section 169VB defines "qualifying shares", "potentially qualifying shares" and "excluded shares".

    (3)   Section 169VC creates the relief, and relief under that section is to be known as "investors' relief".

    (4)   Section 169VD makes provision about disposals from holdings consisting partly of qualifying shares.

    (5)   Sections 169VE to 169VG contain rules for cases where there have been previous disposals from a holding, to determine which shares remain in the holding.

    (6)   Sections 169VH and 169VI make provision about disposals by trustees of a settlement.

    (7)   Section 169VJ makes provision about disposals of interests in shares.

    (8)   Sections 169VK and 169VL provide for a cap on the amount of investors' relief that can be claimed.

    (9)   Section 169VM makes provision about claims for investors' relief.

(10)   Sections 169VN to 169VT make provision about how investors' relief applies following a company's reorganisation of its share capital, an exchange of shares or securities or a scheme of reconstruction.

(11)   Sections 169VU to 169VY contain definitions for the purposes of this Chapter.

Qualifying shares

169VB Qualifying shares, potentially qualifying shares and excluded shares

(1)   Where there is a disposal of all or part of (or of an interest in) a holding of shares in a company, this section applies to determine whether a share which is in the holding at the time immediately before the disposal ("the relevant time") is for the purposes of this Chapter—

    (a)   a qualifying share,

    (b)   a potentially qualifying share, or

    (c)   an excluded share.

(2)   The share is a "qualifying share" at the relevant time if—

    (a)   the share was subscribed for, within the meaning given by section 169VU, by the person making the disposal ("the investor"),

    (b)   the investor has held the share continuously for the period beginning with the issue of the share and ending with the relevant time ("the share-holding period"),

    (c)   the share was issued on or after 17 March 2016,

    (d)   at the time the share was issued, none of the shares or securities of the company that issued it were listed on a recognised stock exchange,

    (e)   the share was an ordinary share when issued and is an ordinary share at the relevant time,

    (f)   the company that issued the share—

        (i)   was a trading company or the holding company of a trading group (as defined by section 169VV) when the share was issued, and

        (ii)   has been so throughout the share-holding period,

    (g)   at no time in the share-holding period was the investor or a person connected with the investor a relevant employee in respect of that company (within the meaning given by section 169VW), and

    (h)   the period beginning with the date the share was issued and ending with the date of the disposal is at least 3 years.

(3)   The share is a "potentially qualifying share" at the relevant time if—

    (a)   the conditions in subsection (2)(a) to (g) are met, but

    (b)   the period beginning with the date the share was issued and ending with the date of the disposal is less than 3 years.

(4)   The share is an "excluded share" at the relevant time if it is, at that time—

    (a)   not a qualifying share, and

    (b)   not a potentially qualifying share.

(5) This section is subject to Schedule 7ZB (disqualification of share where value received by investor).

(6) In relation to a share issued on or after 17 March 2016 but before 6 April 2016, any reference in subsection (2)(h) or (3) to "3 years" is to be read as a reference to the minimum period.

(7) In subsection (6) "the minimum period" means the period of 3 years extended by a period equal in length to the period beginning with the date the share was issued and ending with 5 April 2016.

The relief

169VC Investors' relief

(1) This section applies where—
    (a) a qualifying person disposes of a holding, or part of a holding, of shares in a company, and
    (b) immediately before that disposal some or all of the shares in the holding are qualifying shares.

(2) If—
    (a) a chargeable gain accrues to the qualifying person on the disposal, and
    (b) a claim for relief under this section is made,
the rate of capital gains tax in respect of the relevant gain is 10 per cent.

(3) In subsection (2) "the relevant gain" means—
    (a) where immediately before the disposal all the shares in the holding are qualifying shares, the chargeable gain on the disposal;
    (b) where at that time only some of the shares in the holding are qualifying shares, the appropriate part of that chargeable gain (defined by section 169VD).

(4) In this section—
    (a) subsection (1) is subject to section 169VH (disposals by trustees of a settlement: further conditions for relief), and
    (b) subsection (2) is subject to—
        section 169VI (reduction of relief for certain disposals by trustees of a settlement), and
        sections 169VK and 169VL (cap on investors' relief).

(5) A reference in subsection (3) to the chargeable gain on the disposal, or to the appropriate part of that gain, is a reference to that chargeable gain, or (as the case may be) that part, after any deduction of allowable losses which is made in accordance with this Act from that chargeable gain or from that part.

(6) For the application of this section to disposals of interests in shares, see section 169VJ.

(7) In this Chapter a "qualifying person" means—
    (a) an individual, or
    (b) the trustees of a settlement.

169VD Disposal where holding consists partly of qualifying shares

(1) This section applies where—

    (a) a disposal ("the disposal concerned") is made as mentioned in section 169VC(1), and

    (b) at the time immediately before the disposal, only some of the shares in the holding are qualifying shares.

(2) Where this section applies, for the purposes of section 169VC(3) "the appropriate part" of the chargeable gain on the disposal is so much of that chargeable gain as is found by multiplying it by the appropriate fraction.

(3) The appropriate fraction is—

$$\frac{Q}{T}$$

where—

    Q is the number of qualifying shares found under subsection (4), and

    T is the total number of shares disposed of in the disposal concerned.

(4) The number of qualifying shares found under this subsection is—

    (a) all the qualifying shares in the holding at the time immediately before the disposal concerned, or

    (b) if less, such number of those qualifying shares as equals the number of shares disposed of in that disposal.

169VE Which shares are in holding immediately before disposal

(1) This section applies where—

    (a) a particular disposal is made as mentioned in section 169VC(1)(a) ("the current disposal"),

    (b) there have been one or more previous disposals of shares from the holding mentioned in section 169VC(1) before the current disposal, and

    (c) it is necessary to determine for the purposes of this Chapter which shares are to be treated as in the holding immediately before the current disposal (and, accordingly, which shares are to be treated as having been disposed of in those previous disposals).

(2) In the case of a previous disposal as regards which investors' relief has been claimed or is being claimed, the shares to be treated as disposed of in that previous disposal are to be determined in accordance with the rules in section 169VF.

(3) In the case of a previous disposal not falling within subsection (2), the shares to be treated as disposed of in that previous disposal are to be determined in accordance with the rules in section 169VG.

169VF Shares treated as disposed of in previous disposal where claim made

(1) The rules referred to in section 169VE(2) are as follows; and in this section "the disposal concerned" means the previous disposal mentioned in section 169VE(2).

(2) There are to be treated as having been disposed of in the disposal concerned —

    (a) all the qualifying shares in the holding at the time immediately before that disposal ("the material time"), or

    (b) if less, such number of those qualifying shares as equals the number of shares disposed of in that disposal.

(3) If—

    (a) the number of qualifying shares in the holding at the material time was less than the total number of shares disposed of, and

    (b) excluded shares were in the holding at the material time,

the available excluded shares are also to be treated as having been disposed of.

(4) "The available excluded shares" means—

    (a) all the excluded shares in the holding at the material time, or

    (b) if less, such number of those excluded shares as is equal to the difference between—

        (i) the total number of shares disposed of, and

        (ii) the number of qualifying shares in the holding at the material time.

(5) If the number of shares treated under subsections (2) to (4) as disposed of in the disposal concerned is less than the total number of shares disposed of, such number of the potentially qualifying shares in the holding at the material time as is equal to the difference are also to be treated as having been disposed of.

(6) Where the number of potentially qualifying shares in the holding at the material time exceeds the difference mentioned in subsection (5), under that subsection potentially qualifying shares acquired later are to be treated as disposed of in preference to ones acquired earlier.

(7) In this section "disposed of" (without more) means disposed of in the disposal concerned.

169VG Shares treated as disposed of in previous disposal: no claim made

(1) The rules referred to in section 169VE(3) are as follows; and in this section "the disposal concerned" means the previous disposal mentioned in section 169VE(3).

(2) If any excluded shares were in the holding at the time immediately before the disposal concerned ("the material time"), the maximum number of excluded shares are to be treated as having been disposed of in the disposal concerned.

(3) "The maximum number of excluded shares" means—

    (a) all the excluded shares in the holding at the material time, or

      (b)   if less, such number of those excluded shares as is equal to the number of shares disposed of.

(4)   If—

      (a)   there were no excluded shares in the holding at the material time, or the number of such shares was less than the total number of shares disposed of, and

      (b)   potentially qualifying shares were in the holding at the material time,

the available potentially qualifying shares are to be treated as having been disposed of.

(5)   "The available potentially qualifying shares" means—

      (a)   all the potentially qualifying shares in the holding at the material time, or

      (b)   if less, such number of those potentially qualifying shares as is equal to the difference between—

          (i)   the total number of shares disposed of, and

          (ii)   the number of excluded shares in the holding at the material time.

(6)   Where the number of potentially qualifying shares in the holding at the material time exceeds the difference mentioned in subsection (5), potentially qualifying shares acquired later are to be treated as disposed of in preference to ones acquired earlier.

(7)   If the number of shares treated under subsections (2) to (5) as disposed of in the disposal concerned is less than the total number of shares disposed of, such number of the qualifying shares in the holding at the material time as is equal to the difference are to be treated as having been disposed of.

(8)   In this section "disposed of" (without more) means disposed of in the disposal concerned.

Trustees of a settlement: special provision

169VH Disposals by trustees: further conditions for relief

(1)   Where a disposal falling within section 169VC(1)(a) and (b) is made by the trustees of a settlement, section 169VC does not apply to the disposal unless there is at least one individual who is an eligible beneficiary in respect of the disposal.

(2)   For the purposes of this section, an individual is an "eligible beneficiary" in respect of the disposal if—

      (a)   at the time immediately before the disposal, the individual has under the settlement an interest in possession in settled property that includes or consists of the holding of shares mentioned in section 169VC(1),

      (b)   the individual has had such an interest in possession under the settlement throughout the period of 3 years ending with the date of the disposal,

      (c)   at no time in that period has the individual been a relevant employee in respect of the company that issued the shares (within the meaning given by section 169VW), and

(d)   the individual has (by the time of the claim under section 169VC in respect of the disposal) elected to be treated as an eligible beneficiary in respect of the disposal.

(3)   For the purposes of subsection (2)(d), an individual elects to be treated as an eligible beneficiary in respect of a disposal if the individual tells the trustees (by whatever means) that he or she wishes to be so treated; and an election under subsection (2)(d) may be withdrawn by the individual at any time until the claim is made.

(4)   In this section "interest in possession" does not include an interest in possession for a fixed term.

(5)   In relation to a disposal made by the trustees of a settlement, any reference in section 169VB(2)(g) to the investor is to be read as a reference to any trustee of the settlement.

169VI Disposals by trustees: relief reduced in certain cases

(1)   Subsection (2) applies where—
    (a)   a disposal falling within section 169VC(1)(a) and (b) is made by the trustees of a settlement,
    (b)   section 169VC applies to the disposal by reason of there being at least one individual who is an eligible beneficiary in respect of the disposal (see section 169VH), and
    (c)   at the time immediately before the disposal, there are two or more persons each of whom has under the settlement an interest in possession in the settled property.

(2)   In such a case the reference in section 169VC(2) to the relevant gain is to be read as a reference—
    (a)   to the eligible beneficiary's share of the relevant gain (see subsections (3) to (6)), or
    (b)   if there is more than one individual who is an eligible beneficiary in respect of the disposal, to so much of the relevant gain as is equal to the aggregate of the eligible beneficiaries' shares of that gain.

(3)   In this section—
        "eligible beneficiary" has the meaning given by section 169VH(2);
        "relevant gain" has the meaning given by section 169VC(3);
        "the settled property" means settled property that includes or consists of the holding of shares mentioned in section 169VC(1).

(4)   Subsection (5) applies to determine for the purposes of this Chapter, in relation to any individual who is an eligible beneficiary in respect of a disposal within section 169VC(1) made by the trustees of a settlement, that individual's share of the relevant gain.

(5)   That individual's share of the relevant gain on the disposal is so much of the relevant gain on the disposal as bears to the whole of that gain the same proportion as X bears to Y, where—
        X is the interest in possession (other than for a fixed term) which, at the time immediately before the disposal, that

individual has under the settlement in the income from the holding of shares mentioned in section 169VC(1), and

Y is all the interests in that income that persons (including that individual) with interests in possession in that holding have under the settlement at that time.

Disposals of interests in shares

169VJ Disposals of interests in shares: joint holdings etc

(1) In section 169VC(1)(a), the reference to the case where a qualifying person disposes of a holding, or part of a holding, of shares in a company includes the case where a qualifying person disposes of an interest in a relevant holding.

(2) In this section a "relevant holding" means either —

    (a) a number of shares in a company which are of the same class and were acquired in the same capacity jointly by the same two or more persons including the qualifying person, or

    (b) a number of shares in a company which are of the same class and were acquired in the same capacity by the qualifying person solely.

(3) In this section —

    (a) "an interest" in a relevant holding means any interests of the qualifying person, in any of the shares in the relevant holding, which are by virtue of section 104 to be regarded as a single asset, and

    (b) references to an interest include part of an interest.

(4) Where section 169VC(1) applies by reason of this section, section 169VD(3) and (4) have effect as if any reference to the number of shares disposed of were a reference to the number of shares an interest in which is disposed of.

(5) In relation to a disposal by the trustees of a settlement of an interest in a relevant holding falling within subsection (2)(a), sections 169VH(2) and 169VI(3) and (5) have effect as if any reference to the holding of shares mentioned in section 169VC(1) were to the interest disposed of.

(6) In accordance with subsection (1) —

    (a) in sections 169VN(1)(d), 169VP(1)(d) and 169VS(1)(d) (reorganisations), any reference to a disposal of all or part of a holding includes a disposal by the qualifying person of an interest in the holding, and

    (b) the reference in section 169VT(2) to a disposal of the original shares is to be read, in relation to a case where the original shares fall within subsection (2)(a) above, as a reference to a disposal of the qualifying person's interest in those shares.

Cap on relief

169VK Cap on relief for disposal by an individual

(1) This section applies if, on a disposal within section 169VC(1) made by an individual ("the individual concerned"), the aggregate of —

    (a)   the amount of the relevant gain on the disposal ("the gain in question"),

    (b)   the total amount of any gains that, in relation to earlier disposals by the individual concerned, were charged at the rate in section 169VC(2), and

    (c)   the total amount of any reckonable trust gains that, on any previous trust disposals in respect of which the individual concerned was an eligible beneficiary, were charged at the rate in section 169VC(2),

exceeds £10 million.

(2)   The rate in section 169VC(2) applies only to so much (if any) of the gain in question as, when added to the aggregate of the total amounts mentioned in subsection (1)(b) and (c), does not exceed £10 million.

(3)   Section 4 (rates of capital gains tax) applies to so much of the gain in question as is not subject to the rate in section 169VC(2).

(4)   In this section—

    "eligible beneficiary", in relation to a disposal, is to be read in accordance with section 169VH(2);

    "reckonable trust gain", in relation to a trust disposal in respect of which the individual concerned was an eligible beneficiary, means—

        (a)   if section 169VI(1)(c) applied in relation to the disposal, that individual's share of the relevant gain on that disposal, within the meaning given by section 169VI(4) and (5);

        (b)   otherwise, the relevant gain on that disposal;

    "the relevant gain", in relation to a disposal, has the meaning given by section 169VC(3);

    "trust disposal" means a disposal by the trustees of a settlement.

169VL Cap on relief for disposal by trustees of a settlement

(1)   This section applies where—

    (a)   a disposal ("the disposal in question") is made by the trustees of a settlement,

    (b)   that disposal is within section 169VC(1), and

    (c)   there is an excess amount in relation to an individual who is an eligible beneficiary in respect of the disposal in question ("the individual concerned").

(2)   For the purposes of this section there is an "excess amount" in relation to the individual concerned if the aggregate of—

    (a)   the amount of the current gain,

    (b)   the total amount of any gains that, in relation to earlier disposals made by the individual concerned, were charged at the rate in section 169VC(2), and

    (c)   the total amount of any reckonable trust gains that, on any previous trust disposals in respect of which the individual concerned was an eligible beneficiary, were charged at the rate in section 169VC(2), exceeds £10 million.

(3) The rate in section 169VC(2) applies to the current gain only to the extent (if any) that the current gain when added to the aggregate of the total amounts mentioned in subsection (2)(b) and (c) does not exceed £10 million.

(4) Section 4 (rates of capital gains tax) applies to so much of the current gain as is not subject to the rate in section 169VC(2).

(5) In this section—

"the current gain" means the reckonable trust gain on the disposal in question;

"eligible beneficiary", in relation to a disposal, is to be read in accordance with section 169VH(2);

"reckonable trust gain", in relation to any trust disposal in respect of which the individual concerned is an eligible beneficiary, means—

   (a) if section 169VI(1)(c) applies in relation to the disposal, that individual's share of the relevant gain on that disposal, within the meaning given by section 169VI(4) and (5);

   (b) otherwise, the relevant gain on that disposal;

"the relevant gain", in relation to a disposal, has the meaning given by section 169VC(3);

"trust disposal" means a disposal by the trustees of a settlement.

Claims for relief

169VM Claims for relief

(1) Any claim for investors' relief must be made—

   (a) in the case of a disposal by an individual, by that individual;

   (b) in the case of a disposal by the trustees of a settlement, jointly by—

      (i) the trustees, and

      (ii) the eligible beneficiary in respect of the disposal, within the meaning given by section 169VH(2) (or, if more than one, all those eligible beneficiaries).

(2) Any claim for investors' relief in respect of a disposal must be made on or before the first anniversary of the 31 January following the tax year in which the disposal is made.

Reorganisations

169VN Reorganisations where no consideration given

(1) This section applies where—

   (a) there is a reorganisation within the meaning of section 126,

   (b) immediately before the reorganisation, a qualifying person holds ordinary shares which, in relation to that reorganisation, are original shares within the meaning of section 126,

    (c)   on the reorganisation that person does not give or become liable to give any consideration for, or for any part of, a new holding, and

    (d)   at a time after the reorganisation, there is a disposal of all or part of a new holding.

(2)   In this section a "new holding" means—

    (a)   the holding that immediately after the reorganisation is (in relation to the original shares) the new holding within the meaning of section 126, or

    (b)   where the new holding within the meaning of section 126 consists of two or more actual holdings, any of those actual holdings.

(3)   Subsections (4) and (5) apply for the purposes of determining (for any purpose of this Chapter) the status of shares that immediately before the disposal mentioned in subsection (1)(d) are in the new holding mentioned there ("the new holding concerned").

(4)   Where a number of the original shares were—

    (a)   subscribed for by the qualifying person,

    (b)   issued on a particular date ("the relevant issue date"), and

    (c)   held continuously by that person for a particular period ending immediately before the reorganisation ("the period concerned"),

the following assumption is to be made.

(5)   That assumption is that an appropriate number of the new shares were—

    (a)   subscribed for by the qualifying person,

    (b)   issued on the relevant issue date, and

    (c)   had by the time immediately after the reorganisation already been held continuously by that person for the period concerned.

(6)   In subsections (4) and (5)—

    "the appropriate number" has the meaning given by section 169VO;

    "the original shares" means the shares held by the qualifying person immediately before the reorganisation that were original shares in relation to the reorganisation;

    "the new shares" means the shares that immediately after the reorganisation were in the new holding concerned (including such, if any, of the original shares as remained after the reorganisation and were in that holding).

(7)   In this section a reference to the "status" of a share is to whether it is qualifying, potentially qualifying or excluded.

(8)   Section 169VE applies to determine, for the purposes of this Chapter, which shares are included in a holding immediately before a reorganisation as it applies for the purposes of determining which shares are included in a holding immediately before a particular disposal.

(9) References in this section to consideration are to be read in accordance with section 128(2).

169VO The appropriate number

(1) The "appropriate number" for the purposes of section 169VN(5) is the number found by multiplying the number of shares that are in the new holding concerned immediately after the reorganisation by the fraction −

$$\frac{A}{B}$$

where −

A is the number of the original shares that were −

    (a) subscribed for by the qualifying person,

    (b) issued on the relevant issue date, and

    (c) continuously held by that person for the period concerned, and

B is the total number of the original shares.

(2) In this section −

"the new holding concerned" has the meaning given by section 169VN(3);

"the original shares" has the meaning given by section 169VN(6);

"the relevant issue date" has the meaning given by section 169VN(4);

"the period concerned" has the meaning given by section 169VN(4).

169VP Reorganisations where consideration given

(1) This section applies where −

    (a) there is a reorganisation within the meaning of section 126,

    (b) immediately before the reorganisation, a qualifying person holds ordinary shares which, in relation to that reorganisation, are original shares within the meaning of section 126,

    (c) on the reorganisation that person gives or becomes liable to give consideration for shares ("shares issued for consideration") which −

        (i) are issued to that person on the reorganisation, and

        (ii) immediately after the reorganisation are in a new holding, and

    (d) at a time after the reorganisation, there is a disposal of all or part of that new holding.

(2) In this section a "new holding" means −

    (a) the holding that immediately after the reorganisation is (in relation to the original shares) the new holding within the meaning of section 126, or

    (b)   where the new holding within the meaning of section 126 consists of two or more actual holdings, any of those actual holdings.

(3)   In determining, for any purpose of this Chapter, the status of shares that immediately before the disposal mentioned in subsection (1)(d) are in the new holding mentioned there—

    (a)   the date of issue of the shares issued for consideration is to be taken to be their actual date of issue (rather than the date of issue of any of the original shares), and

    (b)   in relation to any part of the new holding for which consideration was not given, sections 169VN(3) to (6) and 169VO apply but as if any reference to the new holding concerned were to that part of the new holding.

(4)   Section 169VN(3) to (6) and 169VO also apply in relation to any other holding which is a new holding in relation to the reorganisation and as respects which the person did not, on the reorganisation, give or become liable to give any consideration.

(5)   In this section a reference to the "status" of a share is to whether it is qualifying, potentially qualifying or excluded.

(6)   References in this section to consideration are to be read in accordance with section 128(2).

169VQ Exchange of shares for those in another company

(1)   This section applies where section 135 applies in relation to an issue of shares in a company ("company B") in exchange for shares in another company ("company A").

(2)   For the purposes of sections 169VN to 169VP—

    (a)   companies A and B are to be treated as if they were the same company, and

    (b)   the exchange of shares is to be treated as if it were a reorganisation of that company's share capital.

169VR New shares issued on scheme of reconstruction

(1)   This section applies where—

    (a)   section 136 applies in relation to an arrangement between a company ("company A") and the persons holding shares, or any class of shares, in company A, under which another company ("company B") issues shares to those persons, and

    (b)   under section 136(2)(a) those persons are treated as exchanging shares in company A for the shares held by them in consequence of the arrangement.

(2)   For the purposes of sections 169VN to 169VP—

    (a)   companies A and B are to be treated as if they were the same company, and

    (b)   the exchange of shares is to be treated as if it were a reorganisation of that company's share capital.

(3) In the following provisions of this Chapter, any reference to an exchange of shares includes anything that section 136(2)(a) treats as an exchange of shares.

169VS Modification of conditions for being a qualifying share

(1) This section applies where—

    (a) an ordinary share ("the original share") is subscribed for by a qualifying person ("the investor");

    (b) the conditions in section 169VB(2)(c) and (d) are met in relation to the original share,

    (c) the share is involved in an exchange of shares treated under section 169VQ or 169VR as a reorganisation of share capital, and accordingly is included in the original shares within the meaning of section 169VN(6), and

    (d) subsequently there is a disposal of all or part of a holding of shares that in relation to that exchange is a new holding within the meaning given by section 169VN(2).

(2) As respects a share which is in that holding immediately before that disposal, the conditions in section 169VB(2)(f) and (g) are to be regarded as met if (and only if)—

    (a) in relation to the period beginning with the issue of the original share and ending with the exchange of shares, those conditions were met by the original share, and

    (b) in relation to the period beginning with the exchange of shares and ending with the disposal, those conditions were met by a share representing the original share.

(3) Accordingly—

    (a) in section 169VB(2)(f) and (g) as they apply to the original share, any reference to the share-holding period is to be read as to the period mentioned in subsection (2)(a) above, and

    (b) in section 169VB(2)(f) and (g) as they apply to a share representing the original share, any reference to the share-holding period is to be read as to the period mentioned in subsection (2)(b) above.

(4) In subsection (1)(c) "the share" includes a share that, following a reorganisation or following an exchange of shares in relation to which section 169VQ or 169VR applies, represents the original share, and subsections (2) and (3) apply in such a case with the necessary modifications.

169VT Election to disapply section 127

(1) This section applies where—

    (a) there is—

        (i) a reorganisation (within the meaning of section 126), or

        (ii) an exchange of shares which is treated as such a reorganisation by virtue of section 135 or 136, and

    (b) the original shares and the new holding would fall to be treated by virtue of section 127 as the same asset.

(2)   If an election is made under this section, a claim for investors' relief may be made as if the reorganisation or exchange of shares involved a disposal of the original shares; and if such a claim is made section 127 and sections 169VN to 169VS do not apply.

(3)   Any election under this section must be made −
    (a)   if the reorganisation or exchange of shares would (apart from section 127) involve a disposal by the trustees of a settlement, jointly by −
        (i)   the trustees, and
        (ii)   the person who if the disposal were made would be the eligible beneficiary in respect of the disposal, within the meaning given by section 169VH(2) (or, if more than one, all the persons who would be such eligible beneficiaries);
    (b)   otherwise, by the individual concerned.

(4)   Any election under this section must be made on or before the first anniversary of the 31 January following the tax year in which the reorganisation or exchange of shares takes place.

(5)   In this section "the original shares" and "the new holding" have the meaning given by section 126.

Supplemental

169VU "Subscribe" etc

(1)   For the purposes of this Chapter (other than this subsection) a person "subscribes for" a share in a company if −
    (a)   that person subscribes for the share,
    (b)   the share is issued to that person by the company for consideration consisting wholly of cash,
    (c)   the share is fully paid up at the time it is issued,
    (d)   the share is subscribed for, and issued, for genuine commercial reasons and not as part of arrangements the main purpose, or one of the main purposes, of which is to secure a tax advantage to any person, and
    (e)   the share is subscribed for, and issued, by way of a bargain at arm's length.

(2)   In subsection (1) "arrangements" and "tax advantage" have the same meaning as in section 16A.

(3)   If −
    (a)   an individual ("A") subscribed for, or is treated under this subsection as having subscribed for, any shares,
    (b)   A transferred the shares to another individual ("B") during their lives, and
    (c)   A was living together with B as B's spouse or civil partner at the time of the transfer,
B is to be treated for the purposes of this Chapter as having subscribed for the shares.

(4)   Accordingly, for the purposes of this Chapter any period for which A held the shares continuously is to be added to, and treated as part of, the period for which B held the shares continuously.

(5)   In this Chapter, apart from subsections (3) and (4), references to a person's having subscribed for a share include the person's having subscribed for the share jointly with any other person (and references to a person's holding a share or to a share being issued to a person are to be read accordingly).

169VV "Trading company" etc

(1)   In this Chapter "trading company" and "the holding company of a trading group" have the same meaning as in section 165 (see section 165A).

(2)   For the purposes of this Chapter a company is not to be regarded as ceasing to be a trading company, or the holding company of a trading group, merely because of anything done in consequence of —

    (a)   the company, or any of its subsidiaries, being in administration or receivership, or

    (b)   a resolution having been passed, or an order made, for the winding up of the company or any of its subsidiaries.

(3)   But subsection (2) applies only if —

    (a)   the entry into administration or receivership, or the resolution or order for winding up, and

    (b)   everything done as a result of the company concerned being in administration or receivership, or as a result of that resolution or order,

is for genuine commercial reasons and is not part of a scheme or arrangement the main purpose or one of the main purposes of which is the avoidance of tax.

169VW "Relevant employee"

(1)   This section applies to determine for the purposes of —

    (a)   section 169VB(2)(g), or

    (b)   section 169VH(2)(c),

whether a particular person has at any time in the relevant period been a "relevant employee" in respect of the issuing company.

(2)   A person who has at any time in the relevant period been an officer or employee of —

    (a)   the issuing company, or

    (b)   a connected company,

is to be regarded as having at that time been a relevant employee in respect of the issuing company, but this is subject to subsections (3) and (5).

(3)   If —

    (a)   a person is an unremunerated director of the issuing company or a connected company at any time in the relevant period, and

    (b)   the condition in subsection (4) is met,

the fact that the person holds that directorship at that time does not make the person a relevant employee in respect of the issuing company at that time.

(4)   The condition referred to in subsection (3) is that at no time before the relevant period had the person mentioned in that subsection, or a person connected with that person, been—

    (a)   connected with the issuing company, or

    (b)   involved in carrying on (whether on the person's own account or as a partner, director or employee) the whole or any part of the trade, business or profession carried on by the issuing company or a company connected with that company.

(5)   If—

    (a)   a person becomes an employee of the issuing company or a connected company at a time which is—

        (i)   within the relevant period, but

        (ii)   not within the first 180 days of that period,

    (b)   at the beginning of the relevant period, there was no reasonable prospect that the person would become such an employee within the relevant period, and

    (c)   the person is not at any time in the relevant period a director of the issuing company or a connected company,

that employment of the person does not make the person a relevant employee in respect of the issuing company at any time in the relevant period.

(6)   For the purposes of subsection (5) there is a "reasonable prospect" of a thing if it is more likely than not.

(7)   In this section—

    "director" is to be read in accordance with section 452 of CTA 2010,

    "connected company" means a company which at any time in the relevant period is connected with the issuing company (and it does not matter for this purpose whether that time is a time when the person in question is an officer or employee of either company);

    "the issuing company" means the company mentioned in (as the case may be) section 169VB(2)(g) or section 169VH(2)(c);

    "the relevant period" means the period mentioned in (as the case may be) section 169VB(2)(g) or section 169VH(2)(c);

    "unremunerated director" has the meaning given by section 169VX.

169VX   "Unremunerated director"

(1)   For the purposes of section 169VW a person ("the person concerned") is an "unremunerated director" of the issuing company or a connected company at a particular time in the relevant period if that person is a director of that company at that time and—

    (a)   does not receive in the relevant period any disqualifying payment from the issuing company or a related person, and

      (b)   is not entitled to receive any such payment in respect of that period or any part of it.

  (2) In this section "disqualifying payment" means any payment other than—

      (a)   a payment or reimbursement of travelling or other expenses wholly, exclusively and necessarily incurred by the person concerned in the performance of his or her duties as a director,

      (b)   any interest which represents no more than a reasonable commercial return on money lent to the issuing company or a related person,

      (c)   any dividend or other distribution which does not exceed a normal return on the investment to which the dividend or distribution relates,

      (d)   any payment for the supply of goods which does not exceed their market value,

      (e)   any payment of rent for any property occupied by the issuing company or a related person which does not exceed a reasonable and commercial rent for the property, or

      (f)   any necessary and reasonable remuneration which is—

         (i)   paid for qualifying services that are provided to the issuing company or a related person in the course of a trade or profession carried on wholly or partly in the United Kingdom, and

        (ii)   taken into account in calculating for tax purposes the profits of that trade or profession.

  (3) In this section a "related person" means—

      (a)   a connected company of which the person concerned is a director, or

      (b)   any person connected with the issuing company or with a company within paragraph (a).

  (4) In this section any reference to a payment to the person concerned includes a payment made to that person indirectly or to that person's order or for that person's benefit.

  (5) In this section "qualifying services" means services which are—

      (a)   not secretarial or managerial services, and

      (b)   not services of a kind provided by the person to whom they are provided.

  (6) In this section the following expressions have the same meaning as in section 169VW—

      "connected company";

      "director";

      "issuing company";

      "relevant period".

169VY General definitions

In this Chapter—

      "employee" (except in the expression "relevant employee", which is to be read in accordance with section 169VW) has the meaning given by section 4 of ITEPA 2003;

      "employment" has the meaning given by section 4 of ITEPA 2003;

      "exchange of shares" is to be read in accordance with section 169VR(3);

      "excluded share" has the meaning given by section 169VB;

      a "holding" of shares in a company means a holding of such shares which by virtue of section 104(1) is to be regarded as a single asset;

      "investors' relief" has the meaning given by section 169VA(3);

      "office" has the meaning given by section 5(3) of ITEPA 2003;

      "ordinary shares", in relation to a company, means any shares forming part of the company's ordinary share capital (within the meaning given by section 989 of ITA 2007);

      "potentially qualifying share" has the meaning given by section 169VB;

      "qualifying person" has the meaning given by section 169VC(7);

      "qualifying share" has the meaning given by section 169VB;

      "subscribe" is to be read in accordance with section 169VU;

      "trading company" and "the holding company of a trading group" are to be read in accordance with section 169VV."

3   After Schedule 7ZA of TCGA 1992 (inserted by Schedule 13) insert—

"SCHEDULE 7ZB   Section 169VB

INVESTORS' RELIEF: DISQUALIFICATION OF SHARES

Disqualification of shares where value received in period of restriction

1   (1) Sub-paragraph (2) applies where—

      (a) shares in a company are issued to a qualifying person ("the investor") on a particular date,

      (b) any of those shares would, apart from this Schedule, be or be treated as being qualifying shares or potentially qualifying shares at a particular time ("the relevant time"), and

      (c) the investor receives any value, other than insignificant value, from the company at any time in the period of restriction.

    (2) The shares in question are to be treated for the purposes of this Chapter as being excluded shares at the relevant time.

    (3) Where—

      (a) the investor receives value ("the relevant receipt") from the company during the period of restriction,

      (b) the investor has received from the company one or more receipts of insignificant value at a time or times—

         (i) during that period, but

         (ii) not later than the time of the relevant receipt, and

       (c)   the aggregate amount of the value of the receipts within paragraphs (a) and (b) is not an amount of insignificant value,

the investor is to be treated for the purposes of this Schedule as if the relevant receipt had been a receipt of an amount equal to that aggregate amount.

For this purpose a receipt does not fall within paragraph (b) in relation to the shares if it has previously been aggregated under this sub-paragraph in relation to them.

(4) In this Schedule "the period of restriction" means the period −

       (a)   beginning one year before the date the shares are issued, and

       (b)   ending immediately before the third anniversary of the date the shares are issued.

(5) In sub-paragraphs (3) and (4) and in the following provisions of this Schedule references to "the shares" are to the shares referred to in sub-paragraph (1)(a).

(6) This paragraph is subject to paragraph 4.

"Receives value"

2   (1) For the purposes of this Schedule the investor receives value from the company if the company −

       (a)   repays, redeems or repurchases any of its share capital or securities which belong to the investor or makes any payment to the investor for giving up a right to any of the company's share capital or any security on its cancellation or extinguishment,

       (b)   repays, in pursuance of any arrangements for or in connection with the acquisition of the shares, any debt owed to the investor other than a debt which was incurred by the company −

           (i)   on or after the date of issue of the shares, and

           (ii)   otherwise than in consideration of the extinguishment of a debt incurred before that date,

       (c)   makes to the investor any payment for giving up the investor's right to any debt on its extinguishment,

       (d)   releases or waives any liability of the investor to the company or discharges, or undertakes to discharge, any liability of the investor to a third person,

       (e)   makes a loan or advance to the investor which has not been repaid in full before the issue of the shares,

       (f)   provides a benefit or facility for the investor,

       (g)   disposes of an asset to the investor for no consideration or for a consideration which is or the value of which is less than the market value of the asset,

       (h)   acquires an asset from the investor for a consideration which is or the value of which is more than the market value of the asset, or

       (i)   makes any payment to the investor other than a qualifying payment.

(2) For the purposes of sub-paragraph (1)(e) there is to be treated as if it were a loan made by the company to the investor —

   (a) the amount of any debt (other than an ordinary trade debt) incurred by the investor to the company, and

   (b) the amount of any debt due from the investor to a third person which has been assigned to the company.

(3) For the purposes of this paragraph the investor also receives value from the company if any person connected with the company —

   (a) purchases any of its share capital or securities which belong to the investor, or

   (b) makes any payment to the investor for giving up any right in relation to any of the company's share capital or securities.

(4) In this paragraph "qualifying payment" means —

   (a) the payment by any company of such remuneration for service as an officer or employee of that company as may be reasonable in relation to the duties of that office or employment,

   (b) any payment or reimbursement by any company of travelling or other expenses wholly, exclusively and necessarily incurred by the investor to whom the payment is made in the performance of duties as an officer or employee of that company,

   (c) the payment by any company of any interest which represents no more than a reasonable commercial return on money lent to that company,

   (d) the payment by any company of any dividend or other distribution which does not exceed a normal return on any investment in shares in or other securities of that company,

   (e) any payment for the supply of goods which does not exceed their market value,

   (f) any payment for the acquisition of an asset which does not exceed its market value,

   (g) the payment by any company, as rent for any property occupied by the company, of an amount not exceeding a reasonable and commercial rent for the property,

   (h) any reasonable and necessary remuneration which —

      (i) is paid by any company for services rendered to that company in the course of a trade or profession carried on wholly or partly in the United Kingdom; and

      (ii) is taken into account in calculating for tax purposes the profits of that trade or profession, or

   (i) a payment in discharge of an ordinary trade debt.

(5) For the purposes of this paragraph a company is to be treated as having released or waived a liability if the liability is not discharged within 12 months of the time when it ought to have been discharged.

(6) In this paragraph —

    (a) references to a debt or liability do not, in relation to a company, include references to any debt or liability which would be discharged by the making by that company of a qualifying payment, and

    (b) references to a benefit or facility do not include references to any benefit or facility provided in circumstances such that, if a payment had been made of an amount equal to its value, that payment would be a qualifying payment.

(7) In this paragraph and paragraph 3—

    (a) any reference to a payment or disposal to the investor includes a reference to a payment or disposal made to the investor indirectly or to the investor's order or for the investor's benefit;

    (b) any reference to the investor includes an associate of the investor;

    (c) any reference to a company includes a person who at any time in the period of restriction is connected with the company, whether or not that person is connected at the material time.

(8) In this paragraph "ordinary trade debt" means any debt for goods or services supplied in the ordinary course of a trade or business where any credit given—

    (a) does not exceed six months, and

    (b) is not longer than that normally given to customers of the person carrying on the trade or business.

Amount of value

3   (1) For the purposes of paragraph 1, the value received by the investor is—

    (a) in a case within paragraph 2(1)(a), (b) or (c), the amount received by the investor or, if greater, the market value of the share capital, securities or debt in question;

    (b) in a case within paragraph 2(1)(d), the amount of the liability;

    (c) in a case within paragraph 2(1)(e), the amount of the loan or advance reduced by the amount of any repayment made before the issue of the shares;

    (d) in a case within paragraph 2(1)(f), the cost to the company of providing the benefit or facility less any consideration given for it by the investor;

    (e) in a case within paragraph 2(1)(g) or (h), the difference between the market value of the asset and the consideration (if any) given for it;

    (f) in a case within paragraph 2(1)(i), the amount of the payment;

    (g) in a case within paragraph 2(3), the amount received by the investor or, if greater, the market value of the share capital or securities in question.

(2) In this Schedule references to a receipt of insignificant value (however expressed) are references to a receipt of an amount of insignificant value.

This is subject to sub-paragraph (4).

(3) For the purposes of this Schedule "an amount of insignificant value" means an amount of value which does not exceed £1,000.

(4) For the purposes of this Schedule, if at any time in the period —

    (a) beginning one year before the shares are issued, and

    (b) expiring at the end of the issue date,

arrangements are in existence which provide for the investor to receive or to be entitled to receive, at any time in the period of restriction, any value from the company that issued the shares, no amount of value received by the investor is to be treated as a receipt of insignificant value.

(5) In sub-paragraph (4)—

    (a) any reference to the investor includes a reference to any person who, at any time in the period of restriction, is an associate of the investor (whether or not that person is such an associate at the material time), and

    (b) the reference to the company includes a reference to any person who, at any time in the period of restriction, is connected with the company (whether or not that person is so connected at the material time).

Receipt of replacement value

4   (1) Where—

    (a) by reason of a receipt of value within sub-paragraph (1) (other than paragraph (b)) or sub-paragraph (3) of paragraph 2 ("the original value"), any shares would, in the absence of this paragraph, be treated under this Schedule as excluded shares at a particular time,

    (b) at or before that time the original supplier receives value ("the replacement value") from the original recipient by reason of a qualifying receipt, and

    (c) the amount of the replacement value is not less than the amount of the original value,

the receipt of the original value is to be disregarded for the purposes of this Schedule.

(2) This paragraph is subject to paragraph 5.

(3) For the purposes of this paragraph and paragraph 5—

    (a) "the original recipient" means the person who receives the original value, and

    (b) "the original supplier" means the person from whom that value was received.

(4) A receipt of the replacement value is a qualifying receipt for the purposes of sub-paragraph (1) if it arises—

    (a) by reason of the original recipient doing one or more of the following—

          (i)   making a payment to the original supplier, other than a payment which falls within paragraph (c) or to which sub-paragraph (5) applies,

          (ii)   acquiring any asset from the original supplier for a consideration the amount or value of which is more than the market value of the asset,

          (iii) disposing of any asset to the original supplier for no consideration or for a consideration the amount or value of which is less than the market value of the asset,

    (b)   where the receipt of the original value was within paragraph 2(1)(d), by reason of an event the effect of which is to reverse the event which constituted the receipt of the original value, or

    (c)   where the receipt of the original value was within paragraph 2(3), by reason of the original recipient repurchasing the share capital or securities in question, or (as the case may be) reacquiring the right in question, for a consideration the amount or value of which is not less than the amount of the original value.

(5) This sub-paragraph applies to—

    (a)   any payment for any goods, services or facilities, provided (whether in the course of a trade or otherwise) by—

          (i)   the original supplier, or

          (ii)   any other person who, at any time in the period of restriction, is an associate of, or connected with, that supplier (whether or not that person is such an associate, or so connected, at the material time),

       which is reasonable in relation to the market value of those goods, services or facilities,

    (b)   any payment of any interest which represents no more than a reasonable commercial return on money lent to—

          (i)   the original recipient, or

          (ii)   any person who, at any time in the period of restriction, is an associate of the original recipient (whether or not such an associate at the material time),

    (c)   any payment for the acquisition of an asset which does not exceed its market value,

    (d)   any payment, as rent for any property occupied by—

          (i)   the original recipient, or

          (ii)   any person who, at any time in the period of restriction, is an associate of the original recipient (whether or not such an associate at the material time),

       of an amount not exceeding a reasonable and commercial rent for the property,

    (e)   any payment in discharge of an ordinary trade debt (within the meaning of paragraph 2(8)), and

  (f) any payment for shares in or securities of any company in circumstances that do not fall within sub-paragraph (4)(a)(ii).

 (6) For the purposes of this paragraph, the amount of the replacement value is—

  (a) in a case within paragraph (a) of sub-paragraph (4), the aggregate of—

   (i) the amount of any payment within sub-paragraph (i) of that paragraph, and

   (ii) the difference between the market value of any asset within sub-paragraph (ii) or (iii) of that paragraph and the amount or value of the consideration (if any) received for it,

  (b) in a case within sub-paragraph (4)(b), the same as the amount of the original value, and

  (c) in a case within sub-paragraph (4)(c), the amount or value of the consideration received by the original supplier,

and paragraph 3(1) applies for the purposes of determining the amount of the original value.

 (7) In this paragraph any reference to a payment to a person (however expressed) includes a reference to a payment made to the person indirectly or to the person's order or for the person's benefit.

5 (1) The receipt of the replacement value by the original supplier is to be disregarded for the purposes of paragraph 4, as it applies in relation to the shares, to the extent to which that receipt has previously been set (under that paragraph) against any receipts of value which are, in consequence, disregarded for the purposes of paragraph 4 as that paragraph applies in relation to those shares or any other shares subscribed for by the investor.

 (2) The receipt of the replacement value by the original supplier ("the event") is also be disregarded for the purposes of paragraph 4 if—

  (a) the event occurs before the start of the period of restriction, or

  (b) in a case where the event occurs after the time the original recipient receives the original value, it does not occur as soon after that time as is reasonably practicable in the circumstances.

But nothing in paragraph 4 or this paragraph requires the replacement value to be received after the original value.

 (3) In this paragraph "the original value" and "the replacement value" are to be construed in accordance with paragraph 4.

Interpretation

6 In this Schedule—

   "arrangements" includes any scheme, agreement, understanding, transaction or series of transactions (whether or not legally enforceable);

"associate" has the meaning that would be given by section 448 of CTA 2010 if in that section "relative" did not include a brother or sister;

"period of restriction" has the meaning given by paragraph 1(4);

"the shares" has the meaning given by paragraph 1(5)."

SCHEDULE 15

Section 93

INHERITANCE TAX: INCREASED NIL-RATE BAND

1   IHTA 1984 is amended as follows.

2   (1) Section 8D (extra nil-rate band on death if interest in home goes to descendants etc) is amended as follows.

    (2) In subsection (4), after "8G" insert "(and see also section 8M)".

    (3) In subsection (9), before the definition of "tax year" insert—
            ""consumer prices index" means the all items consumer prices index published by the Statistics Board,".

3   (1) Section 8E (residence nil-rate amount: interest in home goes to descendants etc) is amended as follows.

    (2) In subsection (6), after "(7)" insert "and sections 8FC and 8M(2B) to (2E)".

    (3) In subsection (7), for paragraphs (a) and (b) substitute—
        "(a)   the person's residence nil-rate amount is equal to VT,
        (b)   where E is less than or equal to TT, an amount, equal to the difference between VT and the person's default allowance, is available for carry-forward, and
        (c)   where E is greater than TT, an amount, equal to the difference between VT and the person's adjusted allowance, is available for carry-forward."

    (4) In subsection (8)—
        (a)   before the entry for section 8H insert—
                "section 8FC (modifications of this section where there is entitlement to a downsizing addition),", and
        (b)   in the entry for section 8H, after ""qualifying residential interest"" insert ", "qualifying former residential interest" and "residential property interest"".

4   In section 8F(4) (list of other relevant sections)—
        (a)   before the entry for section 8H insert—
                "section 8FD (which applies instead of this section where there is entitlement to a downsizing addition),", and
        (b)   in the entry for section 8H, after ""qualifying residential interest"" insert ", "qualifying former residential interest" and "residential property interest"".

5   After section 8F insert—

"8FA   Downsizing addition: entitlement: low-value death interest in home

(1)   There is entitlement to a downsizing addition in calculating the person's residence nil-rate amount if each of conditions A to F is met (see subsection (8) for the amount of the addition).

(2)   Condition A is that—

    (a)   the person's residence nil-rate amount is given by section 8E(2) or (4), or

    (b)   the person's estate immediately before the person's death includes a qualifying residential interest but none of the interest is closely inherited, and—

        (i)   where E is less than or equal to TT, so much of VT as is attributable to the person's qualifying residential interest is less than the person's default allowance, or

        (ii)   where E is greater than TT, so much of VT as is attributable to the person's qualifying residential interest is less than the person's adjusted allowance.

Section 8E(6) and (7) do not apply, and any entitlement to a downsizing addition is to be ignored, when deciding whether paragraph (a) of condition A is met.

(3)   Condition B is that not all of VT is attributable to the person's qualifying residential interest.

(4)   Condition C is that there is a qualifying former residential interest in relation to the person (see sections 8H(4A) to (4F) and 8HA).

(5)   Condition D is that the value of the qualifying former residential interest exceeds so much of VT as is attributable to the person's qualifying residential interest.

Section 8FE(2) explains what is meant by the value of the qualifying former residential interest.

(6)   Condition E is that at least some of the remainder is closely inherited, where "the remainder" means everything included in the person's estate immediately before the person's death other than the person's qualifying residential interest.

(7)   Condition F is that a claim is made for the addition in accordance with section 8L(1) to (3).

(8)   Where there is entitlement as a result of this section, the addition—

    (a)   is equal to the lost relievable amount (see section 8FE) if that amount is less than so much of VT as is attributable to so much of the remainder as is closely inherited, and

    (b)   otherwise is equal to so much of VT as is attributable to so much of the remainder as is closely inherited.

(9)   Subsection (8) has effect subject to section 8M(2G) (reduction of downsizing addition in certain cases involving conditional exemption).

(10)   See also—

      section 8FC (effect of an addition: section 8E case),

section 8FD (effect of an addition: section 8F case),

section 8H (meaning of "qualifying residential interest", "qualifying former residential interest" and "residential property interest"),

section 8J (meaning of "inherit"),

section 8K (meaning of "closely inherited"), and

section 8M (cases involving conditional exemption).

8FB Downsizing addition: entitlement: no residential interest at death

(1) There is also entitlement to a downsizing addition in calculating the person's residence nil-rate amount if each of conditions G to K is met (see subsection (7) for the amount of the addition).

(2) Condition G is that the person's estate immediately before the person's death ("the estate") does not include a residential property interest.

(3) Condition H is that VT is greater than nil.

(4) Condition I is that there is a qualifying former residential interest in relation to the person (see sections 8H(4A) to (4F) and 8HA).

(5) Condition J is that at least some of the estate is closely inherited.

(6) Condition K is that a claim is made for the addition in accordance with section 8L(1) to (3).

(7) Where there is entitlement as a result of this section, the addition —

   (a) is equal to the lost relievable amount (see section 8FE) if that amount is less than so much of VT as is attributable to so much of the estate as is closely inherited, and

   (b) otherwise is equal to so much of VT as is attributable to so much of the estate as is closely inherited.

(8) Subsection (7) has effect subject to section 8M(2G) (reduction of downsizing addition in certain cases involving conditional exemption).

(9) See also —

section 8FD (effect of an addition: section 8F case),

section 8H (meaning of "qualifying residential interest", "qualifying former residential interest" and "residential property interest"),

section 8J (meaning of "inherit"),

section 8K (meaning of "closely inherited"), and

section 8M (cases involving conditional exemption).

8FC Downsizing addition: effect: section 8E case

(1) Subsection (2) applies if —

   (a) as a result of section 8FA, there is entitlement to a downsizing addition in calculating the person's residence nil-rate amount, and

   (b) the person's residence nil-rate amount is given by section 8E.

(2) Section 8E has effect as if, in subsections (2) to (5) of that section, each reference to NV/100 were a reference to the total of −

    (a) NV/100, and

    (b) the downsizing addition.

8FD   Downsizing addition: effect: section 8F case

(1) This section applies if −

    (a) as a result of section 8FA or 8FB, there is entitlement to a downsizing addition in calculating the person's residence nil-rate amount, and

    (b) apart from this section, the person's residence nil-rate amount is given by section 8F.

(2) Subsections (3) to (6) apply instead of section 8F.

(3) The person's residence nil-rate amount is equal to the downsizing addition.

(4) Where −

    (a) E is less than or equal to TT, and the downsizing addition is equal to the person's default allowance, or

    (b) E is greater than TT, and the downsizing addition is equal to the person's adjusted allowance,

no amount is available for carry-forward.

(5) Where −

    (a) E is less than or equal to TT, and

    (b) the downsizing addition is less than the person's default allowance,

an amount, equal to the difference between the downsizing addition and the person's default allowance, is available for carry-forward.

(6) Where −

    (a) E is greater than TT, and

    (b) the downsizing addition is less than the person's adjusted allowance,

an amount, equal to the difference between the downsizing addition and the person's adjusted allowance, is available for carry-forward.

8FE   Calculation of lost relievable amount

(1) This section is about how to calculate the person's lost relievable amount for the purposes of sections 8FA(8) and 8FB(7).

(2) For the purposes of this section and section 8FA(5), the value of the person's qualifying former residential interest is the value of the interest at the time of completion of the disposal of the interest.

(3) In this section, the person's "former allowance" is the total of −

    (a) the residential enhancement at the time of completion of the disposal of the qualifying former residential interest,

    (b) any brought-forward allowance that the person would have had if the person had died at that time, having regard to the circumstances of the person at that time (see section 8G as applied by subsection (4)), and

        (c)   if the person's allowance on death includes an amount of brought-forward allowance which is greater than the amount of brought-forward allowance given by paragraph (b), the difference between those two amounts.

(4) For the purposes of calculating any brought-forward allowance that the person ("P") would have had as mentioned in subsection (3)(b)−

        (a)   section 8G (brought-forward allowance) applies, but as if references to the residential enhancement at P's death were references to the residential enhancement at the time of completion of the disposal of the qualifying former residential interest, and

        (b)   assume that a claim for brought-forward allowance was made in relation to an amount available for carry-forward from a related person's death if, on P's death, a claim was in fact made in relation to the amount.

(5) For the purposes of subsection (3)(c), where the person's allowance on death is equal to the person's adjusted allowance, the amount of brought-forward allowance included in the person's allowance on death is calculated as follows.

Step 1

Express the person's brought-forward allowance as a percentage of the person's default allowance.

Step 2

Multiply−

$$\frac{E - TT}{2}$$

by the percentage given by step 1.

Step 3

Reduce the person's brought-forward allowance by the amount given by step 2.

The result is the amount of brought-forward allowance included in the person's allowance on death.

(6) If completion of the disposal of the qualifying former residential interest occurs before 6 April 2017−

        (a)   for the purposes of subsection (3)(a), the residential enhancement at the time of completion of the disposal is treated as being £100,000, and

        (b)   for the purposes of subsection (3)(b), the amount of brought-forward allowance that the person would have had at that time is treated as being nil.

(7) In this section, the person's "allowance on death" means−

        (a)   where E is less than or equal to TT, the person's default allowance, or

        (b)   where E is greater than TT, the person's adjusted allowance.

(8) For the purposes of this section, "completion" of the disposal of a residential property interest occurs at the time of the disposal or, if the disposal is under a contract which is completed by a conveyance, at the time when the interest is conveyed.

(9)   Where, as a result of section 8FA, there is entitlement to a downsizing addition in calculating the person's residence nil-rate amount, take the following steps to calculate the person's lost relievable amount.

Step 1

Express the value of the person's qualifying former residential interest as a percentage of the person's former allowance, but take that percentage to be 100% if it would otherwise be higher.

Step 2

Express QRI as a percentage of the person's allowance on death, where QRI is so much of VT as is attributable to the person's qualifying residential interest, but take that percentage to be 100% if it would otherwise be higher.

Step 3

Subtract the percentage given by step 2 from the percentage given by step 1, but take the result to be 0% if it would otherwise be negative. The result is P%.

Step 4

The person's lost relievable amount is equal to P% of the person's allowance on death.

(10)   Where, as a result of section 8FB, there is entitlement to a downsizing addition in calculating the person's residence nil-rate amount, take the following steps to calculate the person's lost relievable amount.

Step 1

Express the value of the person's qualifying former residential interest as a percentage of the person's former allowance, but take that percentage to be 100% if it would otherwise be higher.

Step 2

Calculate that percentage of the person's allowance on death.
The result is the person's lost relievable amount."

6   In section 8G (meaning of "brought-forward allowance"), in subsection (3)(a), for "and 8F" substitute ", 8F and 8FD".

7   (1) Section 8H (meaning of "qualifying residential interest") is amended as follows.

(2) In the heading, at the end insert ", "qualifying former residential interest" and "residential property interest"".

(3) In subsection (1), for "and 8F" substitute "to 8FE and section 8M".

(4) In subsection (2), for "In this section" substitute "A".

(5) After subsection (4) insert—

"(4A)   Subsection (4B) or (4C) applies where—

    (a) a person disposes of a residential property interest in a dwelling-house on or after 8 July 2015 (and before the person dies), and

    (b) the person's personal representatives nominate—

        (i) where there is only one such dwelling-house, that dwelling-house, or

            (ii)   where there are two or more such dwelling-houses, one (and only one) of those dwelling-houses.

(4B)   Where—

    (a)   the person—

        (i)   disposes of a residential property interest in the nominated dwelling-house at a post-occupation time, or

        (ii)   disposes of two or more residential property interests in the nominated dwelling-house at the same post-occupation time or at post-occupation times on the same day, and

    (b)   the person does not otherwise dispose of residential property interests in the nominated dwelling-house at post-occupation times,

the interest disposed of is, or the interests disposed of are, a qualifying former residential interest in relation to the person.

(4C)   Where—

    (a)   the person disposes of residential property interests in the nominated dwelling-house at post-occupation times on two or more days, and

    (b)   the person's personal representatives nominate one (and only one) of those days,

the interest or interests disposed of at post-occupation times on the nominated day is or are a qualifying former residential interest in relation to the person.

(4D)   For the purposes of subsections (4A) to (4C)—

    (a)   a person is to be treated as not disposing of a residential property interest in a dwelling-house where the person disposes of an interest in the dwelling-house by way of gift and the interest is, in relation to the gift and the donor, property subject to a reservation within the meaning of section 102 of the Finance Act 1986 (gifts with reservation), and

    (b)   a person is to be treated as disposing of a residential property interest in a dwelling-house if the person is treated as making a potentially exempt transfer of the interest as a result of the operation of section 102(4) of that Act (property ceasing to be subject to a reservation).

(4E)   Where—

    (a)   a transfer of value by a person is a conditionally exempt transfer of a residential property interest, and

    (b)   at the time of the person's death, no chargeable event has occurred with respect to that interest,

that interest may not be, or be included in, a qualifying former residential interest in relation to the person.

(4F)   In subsections (4B) and (4C) "post-occupation time" means a time—

    (a)   on or after 8 July 2015,

    (b)   after the nominated dwelling-house first became the person's residence, and

      (c)   before the person dies.

  (4G)   For the purposes of subsections (4A) to (4C), if the disposal is under a contract which is completed by a conveyance, the disposal occurs at the time when the interest is conveyed."

8   After section 8H insert—

"8HA "Qualifying former residential interest": interests in possession

  (1)   This section applies for the purposes of determining whether certain interests may be, or be included in, a qualifying former residential interest in relation to a person (see section 8H(4A) to (4C)).

  (2)   This section applies where—
      (a)   a person ("P") is beneficially entitled to an interest in possession in settled property, and
      (b)   the settled property consists of, or includes, an interest in a dwelling-house.

  (3)   Subsection (4) applies where—
      (a)   the trustees of the settlement dispose of the interest in the dwelling-house to a person other than P,
      (b)   P's interest in possession in the settled property subsists immediately before the disposal, and
      (c)   P's interest in possession—
          (i)   falls within subsection (7) throughout the period beginning with P becoming beneficially entitled to it and ending with the disposal, or
         (ii)   falls within subsection (8).

  (4)   The disposal is to be treated as a disposal by P of the interest in the dwelling-house to which P is beneficially entitled as a result of the operation of section 49(1).

  (5)   Subsection (6) applies where—
      (a)   P disposes of the interest in possession in the settled property, or P's interest in possession in the settled property comes to an end in P's lifetime,
      (b)   the interest in the dwelling-house is, or is part of, the settled property immediately before the time when that happens, and
      (c)   P's interest in possession—
          (i)   falls within subsection (7) throughout the period beginning with P becoming beneficially entitled to it and ending with the time mentioned in paragraph (b), or
         (ii)   falls within subsection (8).

  (6)   The disposal, or (as the case may be) the coming to an end of P's interest in possession, is to be treated as a disposal by P of the interest in the dwelling-house to which P is beneficially entitled as a result of the operation of section 49(1).

  (7)   An interest in possession falls within this subsection if—

     (a)   P became beneficially entitled to it before 22 March 2006 and section 71A does not apply to the settled property; or

     (b)   P becomes beneficially entitled to it on or after 22 March 2006 and the interest is —

         (i)   an immediate post-death interest,

         (ii)   a disabled person's interest, or

         (iii)   a transitional serial interest.

    (8)   An interest in possession falls within this subsection if P becomes beneficially entitled to it on or after 22 March 2006 and it falls within section 5(1B)."

9   In section 8J (meaning of "inherited"), in subsection (1), for "and 8F" substitute ", 8F, 8FA, 8FB and 8M".

10   In section 8K (meaning of "closely inherited"), in subsection (1), for "and 8F" substitute ", 8F, 8FA, 8FB and 8M".

11   In section 8L (claims for brought-forward allowance) —

     (a)   in the heading, at the end insert "and downsizing addition", and

     (b)   in subsection (1), after "(see section 8G)" insert "or for a downsizing addition for a person (see sections 8FA to 8FD)".

12 (1)   Section 8M (residence nil-rate amount: cases involving conditional exemption) is amended as follows.

    (2)   For subsections (1) and (2) substitute —

    "(1)   This section applies where —

     (a)   a person ("D") dies on or after 6 April 2017,

     (b)   ignoring the application of this section, D's residence nil-rate amount is greater than nil, and

     (c)   some or all of the transfer of value under section 4 on D's death is a conditionally exempt transfer of property consisting of, or including, any of the following —

        (i)   some or all of a qualifying residential interest;

        (ii)   some or all of a residential property interest, at least some portion of which is closely inherited, and which is not, and is not included in, a qualifying residential interest;

        (iii)   one or more closely inherited assets that are not residential property interests.

    (2)   Subsections (2B) to (2E) apply for the purposes of sections 8E to 8FD if —

     (a)   ignoring the application of this section, D's residence nil-rate amount is given by section 8E, and

     (b)   some or all of the transfer of value under section 4 is a conditionally exempt transfer of property mentioned in subsection (1)(c)(i).

(2A)   In subsections (2B) to (2E), but subject to subsection (3)(a), "the exempt percentage of the QRI" is given by —

$$\frac{X}{QRI} \times 100$$

where —

X is the attributable portion of the value transferred by the conditionally exempt transfer,

QRI is the attributable portion of the value transferred by the transfer of value under section 4, and

"the attributable portion" means the portion (which may be the whole) attributable to the qualifying residential interest.

(2B)   If —

(a)   the exempt percentage of the QRI is 100%, and

(b)   D has no entitlement to a downsizing addition,

D's residence nil-rate amount and amount available for carry-forward are given by section 8F(2) and (3) (instead of section 8E).

(2C)   If —

(a)   the exempt percentage of the QRI is 100%, and

(b)   D has an entitlement to a downsizing addition,

D's residence nil-rate amount and amount available for carry-forward are given by section 8FD(3) to (6) (instead of section 8E as modified by section 8FC(2)).

See also subsection (2G).

(2D)   If —

(a)   the exempt percentage of the QRI is less than 100%, and

(b)   D has no entitlement to a downsizing addition,

D's residence nil-rate amount and amount available for carry-forward are given by section 8E but as if, in subsections (2) to (5) of that section, each reference to NV/100 were a reference to NV/100 multiplied by the percentage that is the difference between 100% and the exempt percentage of the QRI.

(2E)   If —

(a)   the exempt percentage of the QRI is less than 100%, and

(b)   D has an entitlement to a downsizing addition,

D's residence nil-rate amount and amount available for carry-forward are given by section 8E as modified by section 8FC(2), but as if the reference to NV/100 in section 8FC(2)(a) were a reference to NV/100 multiplied by the percentage that is the difference between 100% and the exempt percentage of the QRI.

See also subsection (2G).

(2F)   Subsection (2G) applies for the purposes of sections 8FA to 8FD if —

(a)   some or all of the transfer of value under section 4 is a conditionally exempt transfer of property mentioned in subsection (1)(c)(ii) or (iii) (or both),

(b)   D has an entitlement to a downsizing addition, and

(c)   DA exceeds Y (see subsection (2H)).

(2G) Subject to subsection (3)(aa) and (ab), the amount of the downsizing addition is treated as reduced by whichever is the smaller of—

   (a) the difference between DA and Y, and

   (b) Z.

(2H) In subsections (2F) and (2G)—

   DA is the amount of the downsizing addition to which D has an entitlement (ignoring the application of subsection (2G));

   Y is so much (if any) of the value transferred by the transfer of value under section 4 as—

   (a) is not transferred by a conditionally exempt transfer, and

   (b) is attributable to—

      (i) the closely inherited portion (which may be the whole) of any residential property interests that are not, and are not included in, a qualifying residential interest, or

      (ii) closely inherited assets that are not residential property interests;

   Z is the total of—

   (a) the closely inherited conditionally exempt values of all residential property interests mentioned in subsection (1)(c)(ii), and

   (b) so much of the value transferred by the conditionally exempt transfer as is attributable to property mentioned in subsection (1)(c)(iii).

(2I) For the purposes of the definition of "Z", "the closely inherited conditionally exempt value" of a residential property interest means—

   (a) so much of the value transferred by the conditionally exempt transfer as is attributable to the interest, multiplied by

   (b) the percentage of the interest which is closely inherited."

(3) In subsection (3), for the words before paragraph (b) substitute—

   "(3) For the purposes of calculating tax chargeable under section 32 or 32A by reference to a chargeable event related to property forming the subject-matter of the conditionally exempt transfer where D is the relevant person for the purposes of section 33—

   (a) where subsections (2B) to (2E) apply and the chargeable event relates to property mentioned in subsection (1)(c)(i), in calculating the exempt percentage of the QRI, X is calculated as if the attributable portion of the value transferred by the conditionally exempt transfer had not included the portion (which may be the whole) of the qualifying residential interest on which the tax is chargeable,

   (aa) where subsection (2G) applies and the chargeable event relates to property mentioned in subsection (1)(c)(ii), Z is calculated as if it had not included the portion (which may be the whole) of the closely inherited conditionally exempt value of the residential property interest on which the tax is chargeable, (ab)   where subsection (2G) applies and the chargeable event relates to an asset mentioned in subsection (1)(c)(iii) ("the taxable asset"), Z is calculated as if it had not included so much of the value transferred by the conditionally exempt transfer as is attributable to the taxable asset,".

(4) In subsection (3) —

      (a) at the beginning of paragraph (b) insert "in the cases mentioned in paragraphs (a), (aa) and (ab),",

      (b) at the end of paragraph (b) omit "and",

      (c) in paragraph (c), for "less" substitute "reduced (but not below nil) by", and

      (d) after paragraph (c) insert ", and

             (d) where the chargeable event relates to property mentioned in subsection (1)(c)(i) and subsections (2B) to (2E) do not apply, section 33 has effect as if in subsection (1)(b)(ii) after "in accordance with" there were inserted "section 8D(2) and (3) above and".".

(5) In subsection (5), for "the qualifying residential interest which" substitute "property which forms the subject-matter of the conditionally exempt transfer where the chargeable event".

(6) In subsection (6), for "the qualifying residential interest which" substitute "property which forms the subject-matter of the conditionally exempt transfer and the chargeable event".

(7) In subsection (7), for "the qualifying residential interest" substitute "property which forms the subject-matter of the conditionally exempt transfer".

SCHEDULE 16

Section 133

PROPERTY AUTHORISED INVESTMENT FUNDS AND CO-OWNERSHIP AUTHORISED CONTRACTUAL SCHEMES

PART 1

CO-OWNERSHIP AUTHORISED CONTRACTUAL SCHEMES

1   In FA 2003, after section 102 insert —

"102A Co-ownership authorised contractual schemes

(1) This section has effect for the purposes of this Part.

(2) This Part, with the exception of Schedule 7 (see subsection (10)), applies in relation to a co-ownership authorised contractual scheme as if —

      (a) the scheme were a company, and

      (b) the rights of the participants were shares in the company.

(3) An "umbrella COACS" means a co-ownership authorised contractual scheme —

Finance Act 2016 (c. 24)   523
Schedule 16 — Property authorised investment funds and co-ownership authorised contractual schemes
Part 1 — Co-ownership authorised contractual schemes

    (a)   whose arrangements provide for separate pooling of the contributions of the participants and the profits or income out of which payments are made to them ("pooling arrangements"), and

    (b)   under which the participants are entitled to exchange rights in one pool for rights in another.

(4)   A "sub-scheme", in relation to an umbrella COACS, means such of the pooling arrangements as relate to a separate pool.

(5)   Each of the sub-schemes of an umbrella COACS is regarded as a separate co-ownership authorised contractual scheme, and the umbrella COACS as a whole is not so regarded.

(6)   In relation to a sub-scheme of an umbrella COACS—

    (a)   references to chargeable interests are references to such of the chargeable interests as under the pooling arrangements form part of the separate pool to which the sub-scheme relates, and

    (b)   references to the scheme documents are references to such parts of the documents as apply to the sub-scheme.

(7)   References to a co-ownership authorised contractual scheme are treated as including a collective investment scheme which—

    (a)   is constituted under the law of an EEA State other than the United Kingdom by a contract,

    (b)   is managed by a body corporate incorporated under the law of an EEA State, and

    (c)   is authorised under the law of the EEA State mentioned in paragraph (a) in a way which makes it, under that law, the equivalent of a co-ownership authorised contractual scheme as defined in subsection (8),

provided that, apart from this section, no charge to tax is capable of arising to the scheme under this Part.

(8)   Subject to any regulations under subsection (9)—

"co-ownership authorised contractual scheme" means a co-ownership scheme which is authorised for the purposes of FSMA 2000 by an authorisation order in force under section 261D(1) of that Act;

"co-ownership scheme" has the same meaning as in FSMA 2000 (see section 235A of that Act).

(9)   The Treasury may by regulations provide that a scheme of a description specified in the regulations is to be treated as not being a co-ownership authorised contractual scheme for the purposes of this Part.

Any such regulations may contain such supplementary and transitional provisions as appear to the Treasury to be necessary or expedient.

(10)   A co-ownership authorised contractual scheme is not to be treated as a company for the purposes of Schedule 7 (group relief, reconstruction relief or acquisition relief).

(11)   In relation to a land transaction in respect of which a co-ownership authorised contractual scheme is treated as the purchaser by virtue

524   *Finance Act 2016 (c. 24)*

Schedule 16 — Property authorised investment funds and co-ownership authorised contractual schemes
Part 1 — Co-ownership authorised contractual schemes

of this section, references to the purchaser in the following provisions are to be read as references to the operator of the scheme —

 (a) sections 76, 80, 81, 81A and 108(2) and Schedule 10 (provisions about land transaction returns and further returns, enquiries, assessments and related matters),

 (b) section 85 (liability for tax), and

 (c) section 90 (application to defer payment in case of contingent or unascertained consideration).

(12) In this section —

  "collective investment scheme" has the meaning given by section 235 of FSMA 2000;

  "FSMA 2000" means the Financial Services and Markets Act 2000;

  "operator" —

   (a) in relation to a co-ownership authorised contractual scheme constituted under the law of the United Kingdom, has the meaning given by section 237(2) of FSMA 2000, and

   (b) in relation to a collective investment scheme treated as a co-ownership authorised contractual scheme by virtue of subsection (7) (equivalent EEA schemes), means the corporate body responsible for the management of the scheme (however described);

  "participant" is to be read in accordance with section 235 of FSMA 2000."

PART 2

SEEDING RELIEF FOR PROPERTY AUTHORISED INVESTMENT FUNDS AND CO-OWNERSHIP AUTHORISED CONTRACTUAL SCHEMES

2 FA 2003 is amended in accordance with this Part.

3 After section 65 insert —

"65A PAIF seeding relief and COACS seeding relief

(1) Schedule 7A provides for relief from stamp duty land tax.

(2) In that Schedule —

 (a) Part 1 makes provision for relief for property authorised investment funds (PAIF seeding relief), and

 (b) Part 2 makes provision for relief for co-ownership authorised contractual schemes (COACS seeding relief).

(3) Any relief under that Schedule must be claimed in a land transaction return or an amendment of such a return, and must be accompanied by a notice to HMRC referring to the claim.

(4) In the case of a claim for PAIF seeding relief, the notice must confirm that the purchaser is —

 (a) a property AIF as defined in paragraph 2(2) of Schedule 7A, or

Finance Act 2016 (c. 24)   525

Schedule 16 — Property authorised investment funds and co-ownership authorised contractual schemes
Part 2 — Seeding relief for property authorised investment funds and co-ownership authorised contractual schemes

     (b)   a company treated as a property AIF by virtue of paragraph 2(5) of Schedule 7A (equivalent EEA funds).

(5)   In the case of a claim for COACS seeding relief, the notice must confirm that the purchaser is—

     (a)   a co-ownership authorised contractual scheme as defined in section 102A(8), or

     (b)   an entity treated as a co-ownership authorised contractual scheme by virtue of section 102A(7) (equivalent EEA schemes).

(6)   The notice must be in such form, and contain such further information, as HMRC may require."

4   After Schedule 7 insert—

"SCHEDULE 7A   Section 65A

PAIF SEEDING RELIEF AND COACS SEEDING RELIEF

PART 1

PROPERTY AUTHORISED INVESTMENT FUNDS

PAIF seeding relief

1   (1)   A land transaction is exempt from charge if conditions A to D are met.

Relief under this paragraph is referred to in this Part of this Act as "PAIF seeding relief".

(2)   Condition A is that the purchaser is a property AIF (see paragraph 2).

(3)   Condition B is that the main subject-matter of the transaction consists of a major interest in land.

(4)   Condition C is that the only consideration for the transaction is the issue of units in the property AIF to a person who is the vendor.

(5)   Condition D is that the effective date of the transaction is a day within the seeding period (see paragraph 3).

(6)   This paragraph is subject to paragraph 4 (restrictions on availability of relief) and paragraphs 5 to 8 (withdrawal of relief).

Meaning of "property AIF"

2   (1)   This paragraph has effect for the purposes of this Schedule.

(2)   A "property AIF" is an open-ended investment company to which Part 4A of the AIF (Tax) Regulations applies.

(3)   In sub-paragraph (2) "open-ended investment company" is to be read in accordance with regulation 7(1) and (2) of those Regulations (part of an umbrella company is regarded as an open-ended investment company).

526   *Finance Act 2016 (c. 24)*
Schedule 16 — Property authorised investment funds and co-ownership authorised contractual schemes
Part 2 — Seeding relief for property authorised investment funds and co-ownership authorised contractual schemes

(4) Regulation 7(3)(a) of those Regulations applies for the purposes of this Schedule as it applies for the purposes of those Regulations but as if references to investments and scheme property were a reference to chargeable interests.

(5) References to a property AIF are treated as including a collective investment scheme which —

    (a) is a company incorporated under the law of an EEA State other than the United Kingdom, and

    (b) is authorised under the law of that EEA State in a way which makes it, under that law, the equivalent of a property AIF as defined in sub-paragraph (2).

(6) In sub-paragraph (5) "collective investment scheme" has the meaning given by section 235 of FSMA 2000.

Meaning of "seeding period"

3   (1) In this Part of this Schedule, subject to sub-paragraph (2), the "seeding period" means —

    (a) the period beginning with the first property seeding date and ending with the date of the first external investment into the property AIF, or

    (b) if shorter, the period of 18 months beginning with the first property seeding date.

(2) The property AIF may elect to bring the seeding period to an end sooner than it would otherwise end under sub-paragraph (1).

Where an election is made, the seeding period is the period beginning with the first property seeding date and ending with the date specified in the election.

(3) An election under sub-paragraph (2) may be made —

    (a) by being included in a notice accompanying a claim for PAIF seeding relief (see section 65A), or

    (b) by separate notice in writing to HMRC.

(4) In sub-paragraphs (1) and (2), "the first property seeding date" means the earliest effective date of a transaction in respect of which conditions A to C in paragraph 1 are met.

(5) In this paragraph —

"external investment" means a non-land transaction in which the vendor is an external investor;

"external investor" means a person other than a person who has been a vendor in a transaction —

    (a) the effective date of which is on or before the date of the non-land transaction, and

    (b) in respect of which conditions A to C in paragraph 1 are met;

"non-land transaction" means a transaction by which the property AIF acquires assets which do not consist of or include a chargeable interest.

Finance Act 2016 (c. 24)   527
Schedule 16 — Property authorised investment funds and co-ownership authorised contractual schemes
Part 2 — Seeding relief for property authorised investment funds and co-ownership authorised contractual schemes

Restrictions on availability of relief

4   (1) This paragraph restricts the availability of PAIF seeding relief for a transaction in respect of which conditions A to D in paragraph 1 are met.

   (2) PAIF seeding relief is not available unless, at the effective date of the transaction, the property AIF has arrangements in place requiring a person who is the vendor to notify the authorised corporate director of the property AIF of the following matters —

   (a) the identity of the beneficial owner of the units in the property AIF received in consideration of the transaction, and

   (b) any disposal of units in the property AIF on or after the effective date of that transaction by that owner (or, where that person is a company, by a group company) which is or could be a relevant disposal (see paragraph 7).

   In paragraph (b) "group company" means a company which is a member of the same group of companies as the person mentioned in paragraph (a) for the purposes mentioned in paragraph 1(2) of Schedule 7 (group relief).

   (3) PAIF seeding relief is not available if at the effective date of the transaction there are arrangements in existence by virtue of which, at that or some later time, a person who is the vendor makes or could make a disposal of units in the property AIF which is or could be a relevant disposal (see paragraph 7).

   (4) PAIF seeding relief is not available if the transaction —

   (a) is not effected for bona fide commercial reasons, or

   (b) forms part of arrangements of which the main purpose, or one of the main purposes, is the avoidance of liability to tax.

   "Tax" here means stamp duty, income tax, corporation tax, capital gains tax or tax under this Part.

Withdrawal of relief: ceasing to be property AIF

5   (1) Where PAIF seeding relief has been allowed in respect of a transaction ("the relevant transaction"), and the purchaser ceases to be a property AIF —

   (a) at any time after the effective date of that transaction but within the seeding period,

   (b) at any time in the control period (see paragraph 21), or

   (c) in pursuance of, or in connection with, arrangements made before the end of the control period,

   then, subject to sub-paragraph (2), the relief, or an appropriate proportion of it, is withdrawn, and tax is chargeable in accordance with this paragraph.

   (2) Relief is withdrawn only if, at the time when the purchaser ceases to be a property AIF, the purchaser holds —

   (a) the chargeable interest that was acquired by the purchaser under the relevant transaction, or

528   *Finance Act 2016 (c. 24)*
Schedule 16 — Property authorised investment funds and co-ownership authorised contractual schemes
Part 2 — Seeding relief for property authorised investment funds and co-ownership authorised contractual schemes

    (b)   a chargeable interest that is derived from that interest.

(3) The amount chargeable is the amount that would have been chargeable in respect of the relevant transaction but for PAIF seeding relief or, as the case may be, an appropriate proportion of the tax that would have been so chargeable.

(4) In sub-paragraphs (1) and (3) an "appropriate proportion" means an appropriate proportion having regard to the subject-matter of the relevant transaction and what is held by the purchaser at the time it ceases to be a property AIF.

Withdrawal of relief: portfolio test not met

6   (1) Where PAIF seeding relief has been allowed in respect of a transaction, and the portfolio test is not met immediately before the end of the seeding period, the relief is withdrawn and tax is chargeable in accordance with sub-paragraph (2).
See sub-paragraph (7) for the meaning of "portfolio test".

(2) The amount chargeable is the amount that would have been chargeable in respect of the transaction but for PAIF seeding relief.

(3) Where PAIF seeding relief has been allowed in respect of a transaction ("the relevant transaction"), and the portfolio test is met immediately before the end of the seeding period, but is not met—
    (a)   at a time in the control period, or
    (b)   at a time after the end of the control period, where the failure is pursuant to or in connection with arrangements made before the end of that period,
then, subject to sub-paragraph (4), the relief, or an appropriate proportion of it, is withdrawn, and tax is chargeable in accordance with sub-paragraph (5).

(4) The requirement to meet the portfolio test at a time mentioned in sub-paragraph (3)(a) or (b) applies only to times when the property AIF holds—
    (a)   the chargeable interest that was acquired by the property AIF under the relevant transaction, or
    (b)   a chargeable interest that is derived from that interest.

(5) The amount chargeable is the amount that would have been chargeable in respect of the relevant transaction but for PAIF seeding relief or, as the case may be, an appropriate proportion of the tax that would have been so chargeable.

(6) In sub-paragraphs (3) and (5) an "appropriate proportion" means an appropriate proportion having regard to the subject-matter of the relevant transaction and what is held by the property AIF at the time when the portfolio test is not met.

(7) The portfolio test is a requirement that the property AIF meets—
    (a)   the non-residential portfolio test (see sub-paragraph (8)), or
    (b)   the residential portfolio test (see sub-paragraph (9)).

Finance Act 2016 (c. **24**)

Schedule 16 — *Property authorised investment funds and co-ownership authorised contractual schemes*
Part 2 — *Seeding relief for property authorised investment funds and co-ownership authorised contractual schemes*

529

(8) The "non-residential portfolio test" is met at any time if—

    (a) the property AIF holds at least 10 seeded interests at that time,

    (b) so much of the total chargeable consideration as is attributable to all the seeded interests held by the property AIF at that time ("the seeded portfolio") is at least £100 million, and

    (c) so much of the total chargeable consideration as is attributable to so many of those seeded interests as are interests in or over residential property (if any) does not exceed 10% of the seeded portfolio.

(9) The "residential portfolio test" is met at any time if—

    (a) so much of the total chargeable consideration as is attributable to all the seeded interests held by the property AIF at that time is at least £100 million, and

    (b) at least 100 of the seeded interests held by the property AIF at that time are interests in or over residential property.

(10) In sub-paragraphs (8) and (9)—

    "seeded interest" means a chargeable interest acquired by the property AIF in a transaction for which PAIF seeding relief is allowed (whether or not relief is subsequently withdrawn to any extent) (a "seeding transaction"), and

    "total chargeable consideration" means the total of the chargeable consideration for all seeding transactions.

(11) For the purposes of this paragraph, section 116(7) does not apply (modification of what counts as residential property).

Withdrawal of relief: units disposed of

7   (1) This paragraph applies where—

    (a) a person ("V") makes a relevant disposal of one or more units in a property AIF—

        (i) at any time in the seeding period,

        (ii) at any time in the control period, or

        (iii) in pursuance of, or in connection with, arrangements made before the end of the control period, and

    (b) there is, in relation to that disposal, a relevant seeding transaction (see sub-paragraph (6)).

(2) In respect of a transaction which is, in relation to the relevant disposal, a relevant seeding transaction—

    (a) PAIF seeding relief is withdrawn to the extent set out in this paragraph, and

    (b) tax is chargeable in accordance with this paragraph.

(3) V's disposal of units in a property AIF is a "relevant disposal" for the purposes of this paragraph if, in relation to the disposal, A exceeds B.

(4) In this paragraph—

    "A" means—

530   *Finance Act 2016 (c. 24)*
Schedule 16 — Property authorised investment funds and co-ownership authorised contractual schemes
Part 2 — Seeding relief for property authorised investment funds and co-ownership authorised contractual schemes

(a)   where the value of V's investment in the property AIF immediately before the disposal is equal to or greater than the total of the chargeable consideration for all relevant seeding transactions, the total of the chargeable consideration for all relevant seeding transactions, or

(b)   where the value of V's investment in the property AIF immediately before the disposal is less than the total of the chargeable consideration for all relevant seeding transactions, the value of V's investment in the property AIF immediately before the disposal, and

"B" means the value of V's investment in the property AIF immediately after the disposal.

(5)   The amount chargeable in respect of a relevant seeding transaction ("RST") is —

$$\frac{C}{CCRST} \times SDLT$$

where —

"C" means the difference between A and B;

"CCRST" means the total of the chargeable consideration for all relevant seeding transactions;

"SDLT" means the amount of tax that would have been chargeable in respect of RST but for PAIF seeding relief, ignoring any amount of tax that has been charged under this paragraph in respect of RST in relation to an earlier disposal of units by V.

(6)   In this paragraph —

"group company" means (where V is a company) a company which is a member of the same group of companies as V for the purposes mentioned in paragraph 1(2) of Schedule 7 (group relief);

"relevant seeding transaction", in relation to a disposal of units by V in a property AIF, means a seeding transaction —

(a)   the effective date of which is, or is before, the date of the disposal,

(b)   in which that property AIF is the purchaser, and

(c)   in which a vendor is —

(i)   V, or

(ii)   (where V is a company) a company which is a group company at the time of the disposal;

"seeding transaction" means a transaction in respect of which PAIF seeding relief is allowed (whether or not relief is subsequently withdrawn to any extent);

"the value of V's investment in the property AIF" at a particular time means the market value of all units in the property AIF held at that time by —

(a)   V, and

Finance Act 2016 (c. 24)   531

Schedule 16 — Property authorised investment funds and co-ownership authorised contractual schemes
Part 2 — Seeding relief for property authorised investment funds and co-ownership authorised contractual schemes

        (b)   (where V is a company) a company which—

           (i)   is a group company at that time, and

           (ii)   before that time, has been a vendor in one or more seeding transactions in which the property AIF was the purchaser.

(7) For the purposes of this paragraph, the "market value" on a particular date of units in the property AIF is an amount equal to the buying price (that is, the lower price) published by the authorised corporate director on that date (or, if no such price is published on that date, on the latest date before).

Withdrawal of relief: dwelling occupied by non-qualifying individual

8   (1) This paragraph applies to a transaction ("the relevant transaction") if—

        (a)   PAIF seeding relief has been allowed in respect of the transaction,

        (b)   the main subject-matter of the transaction consists of a chargeable interest in or over land which is or includes a dwelling, and

        (c)   a non-qualifying individual (see paragraph 9) is permitted to occupy the dwelling at any time on or after the effective date of the transaction.

    The dwelling which a non-qualifying individual is permitted to occupy is referred to as "the disqualifying dwelling".

(2) The relief, or an appropriate proportion of it, is withdrawn, and tax is chargeable in accordance with this paragraph.

    This is subject to sub-paragraphs (3) and (4).

(3) Relief is withdrawn only if, at the time a non-qualifying individual is permitted to occupy the disqualifying dwelling, the property AIF holds a chargeable interest in or over that dwelling—

        (a)   that was acquired by the property AIF under the relevant transaction, or

        (b)   that is derived from an interest so acquired.

(4) Where a non-qualifying individual is first permitted to occupy the disqualifying dwelling at a time after the end of the control period, relief is withdrawn only if, at that time, the purchaser in the relevant transaction fails to meet the genuine diversity of ownership condition set out in regulation 9A of the AIF (Tax) Regulations.

    For the purposes of this sub-paragraph, regulation 9A(2)(a) of those Regulations is to be read as if the words "throughout the accounting period" were omitted.

(5) The amount chargeable is the amount that would have been chargeable in respect of the relevant transaction but for PAIF seeding relief or, as the case may be, an appropriate proportion of the tax that would have been so chargeable.

(6) In sub-paragraphs (2) and (5), an "appropriate proportion" means an appropriate proportion having regard to the extent to which

532   Finance Act 2016 (c. 24)
Schedule 16 — Property authorised investment funds and co-ownership authorised contractual schemes
Part 2 — Seeding relief for property authorised investment funds and co-ownership authorised contractual schemes

the subject-matter of the relevant transaction was an interest in or over land other than the disqualifying dwelling.

9   (1)   In paragraph 8 "non-qualifying individual", in relation to a land transaction and a property AIF, means any of the following —

(a)   an individual who is a major participant in the property AIF;

(b)   an individual who is connected with a major participant in the property AIF;

(c)   an individual who is connected with the property AIF;

(d)   a relevant settlor;

(e)   the spouse or civil partner of an individual falling within paragraph (b), (c) or (d);

(f)   a relative of an individual falling within paragraph (b), (c) or (d), or the spouse or civil partner of a relative of an individual falling within paragraph (b), (c) or (d);

(g)   a relative of the spouse or civil partner of an individual falling within paragraph (b), (c) or (d);

(h)   the spouse or civil partner of an individual falling within paragraph (g).

(2)   An individual who participates in a property AIF is a "major participant" in it if the individual —

(a)   is entitled to a share of at least 50% either of all the profits or income arising from the property AIF or of any profits or income arising from it that may be distributed to participants, or

(b)   would in the event of the winding up of the property AIF be entitled to 50% or more of the assets of the property AIF that would then be available for distribution among the participants.

(3)   The reference in sub-paragraph (2)(a) to profits or income arising from the property AIF is to profits or income arising from the acquisition, holding, management or disposal of the property subject to the property AIF.

(4)   In this paragraph —

"relative" means brother, sister, ancestor or lineal descendant;

"relevant settlor", in relation to a land transaction, means an individual who is a settlor in relation to a relevant settlement (as defined in sub-paragraph (5));

"settlement" has the same meaning as in Chapter 5 of Part 5 of ITTOIA 2005 (see section 620 of that Act).

(5)   Where a person, in the capacity of trustee of a settlement, is connected with a person who is the purchaser under a land transaction, that settlement is a "relevant settlement" in relation to the transaction.

(6)   In sub-paragraph (5) "trustee" is to be read in accordance with section 1123(3) of CTA 2010 ("connected" persons: supplementary).

Finance Act 2016 (c. 24)   533
Schedule 16 — Property authorised investment funds and co-ownership authorised contractual schemes
Part 2 — Seeding relief for property authorised investment funds and co-ownership authorised contractual schemes

(7) Section 1122 of CTA 2010 (connected persons) has effect for the purposes of this paragraph, but for those purposes, subsections (7) and (8) of that section (application of rules about connected persons to partnerships) are to be disregarded.

PART 2

CO-OWNERSHIP AUTHORISED CONTRACTUAL SCHEMES

COACS seeding relief

10   (1) A land transaction is exempt from charge if conditions A to D are met.

Relief under this paragraph is referred to in this Part of this Act as "COACS seeding relief".

(2) Condition A is that the purchaser is a co-ownership authorised contractual scheme (see section 102A).

(3) Condition B is that the main subject-matter of the transaction consists of a major interest in land.

(4) Condition C is that the only consideration for the transaction is the issue of units in the co-ownership authorised contractual scheme to a person who is the vendor.

(5) Condition D is that the effective date of the transaction is a day within the seeding period (see paragraph 11).

(6) This paragraph is subject to paragraph 12 (restrictions on availability of relief) and paragraphs 13, 14, 16, 17 and 18 (withdrawal of relief).

Meaning of "seeding period"

11   (1) In this Part of this Schedule, subject to sub-paragraph (2), the "seeding period" means—
   (a) the period beginning with the first property seeding date and ending with the date of the first external investment into the co-ownership authorised contractual scheme, or
   (b) if shorter, the period of 18 months beginning with the first property seeding date.

(2) The co-ownership authorised contractual scheme may elect to bring the seeding period to an end sooner than it would otherwise end under sub-paragraph (1).

Where an election is made, the seeding period is the period beginning with the first property seeding date and ending with the date specified in the election.

(3) An election under sub-paragraph (2) may be made—
   (a) by being included in a notice accompanying a claim for COACS seeding relief (see section 65A), or
   (b) by separate notice in writing to HMRC.

534   *Finance Act 2016 (c. 24)*
Schedule 16 — Property authorised investment funds and co-ownership authorised contractual schemes
Part 2 — Seeding relief for property authorised investment funds and co-ownership authorised contractual schemes

(4) In sub-paragraphs (1) and (2), "the first property seeding date" means the earliest effective date of a transaction in respect of which conditions A to C in paragraph 10 are met.

(5) In this paragraph—

"external investment" means a non-land transaction in which the vendor is an external investor;

"external investor" means a person other than a person who has been a vendor in a transaction—

(a) the effective date of which is on or before the date of the non-land transaction, and

(b) in respect of which conditions A to C in paragraph 10 are met;

"non-land transaction" means a transaction by which the scheme acquires assets which do not consist of or include a chargeable interest.

Restrictions on availability of relief

12 (1) This paragraph restricts the availability of COACS seeding relief for a transaction in respect of which conditions A to D in paragraph 10 are met.

(2) COACS seeding relief is not available unless, at the effective date of the transaction, the arrangements constituting the co-ownership authorised contractual scheme require a person who is the vendor to notify the operator of the scheme of the following matters—

(a) the identity of the beneficial owner of the units in the scheme received in consideration of the transaction, and

(b) any disposal of units in the scheme on or after the effective date of that transaction by that owner (or, where that person is a company, by a group company) which is or could be a relevant disposal (see paragraph 17).

In paragraph (b) "group company" means a company which is a member of the same group of companies as the person mentioned in paragraph (a) for the purposes mentioned in paragraph 1(2) of Schedule 7 (group relief).

(3) COACS seeding relief is not available if at the effective date of the transaction there are arrangements in existence by virtue of which, at that or some later time, a person who is the vendor makes or could make a disposal of units in the co-ownership authorised contractual scheme which is or could be a relevant disposal (see paragraph 17).

(4) COACS seeding relief is not available if the transaction—

(a) is not effected for bona fide commercial reasons, or

(b) forms part of arrangements of which the main purpose, or one of the main purposes, is the avoidance of liability to tax.

"Tax" here means stamp duty, income tax, corporation tax, capital gains tax or tax under this Part.

Finance Act 2016 (c. 24)   535
Schedule 16 — Property authorised investment funds and co-ownership authorised contractual schemes
Part 2 — Seeding relief for property authorised investment funds and co-ownership authorised contractual schemes

Withdrawal of relief: ceasing to be co-ownership authorised contractual scheme

13   (1)   Where COACS seeding relief has been allowed in respect of a transaction ("the relevant transaction"), and the purchaser ceases to be a co-ownership authorised contractual scheme—

        (a)   at any time after the effective date of that transaction but within the seeding period,

        (b)   at any time in the control period (see paragraph 21), or

        (c)   in pursuance of, or in connection with, arrangements made before the end of the control period,

        then, subject to sub-paragraph (2), the relief, or an appropriate proportion of it, is withdrawn, and tax is chargeable in accordance with this paragraph.

     (2)   Relief is withdrawn only if, at the time when the purchaser ceases to be a co-ownership authorised contractual scheme, the purchaser holds—

        (a)   the chargeable interest that was acquired by the purchaser under the relevant transaction, or

        (b)   a chargeable interest that is derived from that interest.

     (3)   The amount chargeable is the amount that would have been chargeable in respect of the relevant transaction but for COACS seeding relief or, as the case may be, an appropriate proportion of the tax that would have been so chargeable.

     (4)   In sub-paragraphs (1) and (3) an "appropriate proportion" means an appropriate proportion having regard to the subject-matter of the relevant transaction and what is held by the purchaser at the time it ceases to be a co-ownership authorised contractual scheme.

Withdrawal of relief: genuine diversity of ownership condition not met

14   (1)   Where COACS seeding relief has been allowed in respect of a transaction ("the relevant transaction"), and the genuine diversity of ownership condition (see paragraph 15) is not met—

        (a)   immediately before the end of the seeding period,

        (b)   at a time in the control period, or

        (c)   at a time after the end of the control period, where the failure is pursuant to or in connection with arrangements made before the end of that period,

        then, subject to sub-paragraph (2), the relief, or an appropriate proportion of it, is withdrawn, and tax is chargeable in accordance with this paragraph.

     (2)   The requirement to meet the genuine diversity of ownership condition at a time mentioned in sub-paragraph (1) applies only to times when the co-ownership authorised contractual scheme holds—

        (a)   the chargeable interest that was acquired by the scheme under the relevant transaction, or

        (b)   a chargeable interest that is derived from that interest.

     (3)   The amount chargeable is the amount that would have been chargeable in respect of the relevant transaction but for COACS

536   *Finance Act 2016 (c. 24)*

Schedule 16 — Property authorised investment funds and co-ownership authorised contractual schemes
Part 2 — Seeding relief for property authorised investment funds and co-ownership authorised contractual schemes

seeding relief or, as the case may be, an appropriate proportion of the tax that would have been so chargeable.

(4) In sub-paragraphs (1) and (3) an "appropriate proportion" means an appropriate proportion having regard to the subject-matter of the relevant transaction and what is held by the scheme at the time when the genuine diversity of ownership condition is not met.

(5) For the purposes of this paragraph, the operator of a co-ownership authorised contractual scheme may apply to HMRC in writing for clearance that the scheme meets the genuine diversity of ownership condition, and where an application is made, HMRC must notify the scheme of its decision within 28 days of the receipt of all the information that is needed to make the decision.

(6) Any such clearance has effect only for so long as the information on which HMRC relies in granting clearance is materially unchanged and the scheme is operated in accordance with it (including, in particular, continuing to operate in accordance with condition C of the genuine diversity of ownership condition).

Genuine diversity of ownership condition

15 (1) This paragraph has effect for the purposes of paragraphs 14 and 18(4).

(2) A co-ownership authorised contractual scheme meets the genuine diversity of ownership condition at any time when it meets conditions A to C.

(3) Condition A is that the scheme documents, which are available to investors and to HMRC, contain —

    (a) a statement specifying the intended categories of investor,

    (b) an undertaking that units in the scheme will be widely available, and

    (c) an undertaking that units in the scheme will be marketed and made available in accordance with the requirements of sub-paragraph (6)(a).

(4) Condition B is that —

    (a) the specification of the intended categories of investor does not have a limiting or deterrent effect, and

    (b) any other terms or conditions governing participation in the scheme do not have a limiting or deterrent effect.

(5) In sub-paragraph (4) "limiting or deterrent effect" means an effect which —

    (a) limits investors to a limited number of specific persons or specific groups of connected persons, or

    (b) deters a reasonable investor falling within one of (what are specified as) the intended categories of investor from investing in the scheme.

(6) Condition C is that —

    (a) units in the scheme are marketed and made available —

      (i)   sufficiently widely to reach the intended categories of investors, and

      (ii)   in a manner appropriate to attract those categories of investors, and

   (b)   a person who falls within one of the intended categories of investors can, upon request to the operator of the scheme, obtain information about the scheme and acquire units in it.

(7) A scheme is not regarded as failing to meet condition C at any time by reason of the scheme's having, at that time, no capacity to receive additional investments, unless—

   (a)   the capacity of the scheme to receive investments in it is fixed by the scheme documents (or otherwise), and

   (b)   a pre-determined number of specific persons or specific groups of connected persons make investments in the scheme which collectively exhaust all, or substantially all, of that capacity.

(8) A co-ownership authorised contractual scheme also meets the genuine diversity of ownership condition at any time when—

   (a)   there is a feeder fund in relation to the scheme (see paragraph 20), and

   (b)   conditions A to C are met in relation to the scheme after taking into account—

      (i)   the scheme documents relating to the feeder fund, and

      (ii)   the intended investors in the feeder fund.

(9) Section 1122 of CTA 2010 (connected persons) has effect for the purposes of this paragraph.

Withdrawal of relief: portfolio test not met

16   (1) Where COACS seeding relief has been allowed in respect of a transaction, and the portfolio test is not met immediately before the end of the seeding period, the relief is withdrawn and tax is chargeable in accordance with sub-paragraph (2).

See sub-paragraph (7) for the meaning of "portfolio test".

(2) The amount chargeable is the amount that would have been chargeable in respect of the transaction but for COACS seeding relief.

(3) Where COACS seeding relief has been allowed in respect of a transaction ("the relevant transaction"), and the portfolio test is met immediately before the end of the seeding period, but is not met—

   (a)   at a time in the control period, or

   (b)   at a time after the end of the control period, where the failure is pursuant to or in connection with arrangements made before the end of that period,

then, subject to sub-paragraph (4), the relief, or an appropriate proportion of it, is withdrawn, and tax is chargeable in accordance with sub-paragraph (5).

538   *Finance Act 2016 (c. 24)*
Schedule 16 — Property authorised investment funds and co-ownership authorised contractual schemes
Part 2 — Seeding relief for property authorised investment funds and co-ownership authorised contractual schemes

(4) The requirement to meet the portfolio test at a time mentioned in sub-paragraph (3)(a) or (b) applies only to times when the co-ownership authorised contractual scheme holds—

   (a) the chargeable interest that was acquired by the scheme under the relevant transaction, or

   (b) a chargeable interest that is derived from that interest.

(5) The amount chargeable is the amount that would have been chargeable in respect of the relevant transaction but for COACS seeding relief or, as the case may be, an appropriate proportion of the tax that would have been so chargeable.

(6) In sub-paragraphs (3) and (5) an "appropriate proportion" means an appropriate proportion having regard to the subject-matter of the relevant transaction and what is held by the scheme at the time when the portfolio test is not met.

(7) The portfolio test is a requirement that the scheme meets—

   (a) the non-residential portfolio test (see sub-paragraph (8)), or

   (b) the residential portfolio test (see sub-paragraph (9)).

(8) The "non-residential portfolio test" is met at any time if—

   (a) the scheme holds at least 10 seeded interests at that time,

   (b) so much of the total chargeable consideration as is attributable to all the seeded interests held by the scheme at that time ("the seeded portfolio") is at least £100 million, and

   (c) so much of the total chargeable consideration as is attributable to so many of those seeded interests as are interests in or over residential property (if any) does not exceed 10% of the seeded portfolio.

(9) The "residential portfolio test" is met at any time if—

   (a) so much of the total chargeable consideration as is attributable to all the seeded interests held by the scheme at that time is at least £100 million, and

   (b) at least 100 of the seeded interests held by the scheme at that time are interests in or over residential property.

(10) In sub-paragraphs (8) and (9)—

   "seeded interest" means a chargeable interest acquired by the scheme in a transaction for which COACS seeding relief is allowed (whether or not relief is subsequently withdrawn to any extent) (a "seeding transaction"), and

   "total chargeable consideration" means the total of the chargeable consideration for all seeding transactions.

(11) For the purposes of this paragraph, section 116(7) does not apply (modification of what counts as residential property).

Withdrawal of relief: units disposed of

17   (1) This paragraph applies where—

Finance Act 2016 (c. 24)   539
Schedule 16 — Property authorised investment funds and co-ownership authorised contractual schemes
Part 2 — Seeding relief for property authorised investment funds and co-ownership authorised contractual schemes

    (a)   a person ("V") makes a relevant disposal of one or more units in a co-ownership authorised contractual scheme—

        (i)   at any time in the seeding period,

        (ii)   at any time in the control period, or

        (iii)   in pursuance of, or in connection with, arrangements made before the end of the control period, and

    (b)   there is, in relation to that disposal, a relevant seeding transaction (see sub-paragraph (6)).

(2) In respect of a transaction which is, in relation to the relevant disposal, a relevant seeding transaction—

    (a)   COACS seeding relief is withdrawn to the extent set out in this paragraph, and

    (b)   tax is chargeable in accordance with this paragraph.

(3) V's disposal of units in a scheme is a "relevant disposal" for the purposes of this paragraph if, in relation to the disposal, A exceeds B.

(4) In this paragraph—

    "A" means—

    (a)   where the value of V's investment in the scheme immediately before the disposal is equal to or greater than the total of the chargeable consideration for all relevant seeding transactions, the total of the chargeable consideration for all relevant seeding transactions, or

    (b)   where the value of V's investment in the scheme immediately before the disposal is less than the total of the chargeable consideration for all relevant seeding transactions, the value of V's investment in the scheme immediately before the disposal, and

    "B" means the value of V's investment in the scheme immediately after the disposal.

(5) The amount chargeable in respect of a relevant seeding transaction ("RST") is—

$$\frac{C}{CCRST} \times SDLT$$

where—

    "C" means the difference between A and B;

    "CCRST" means the total of the chargeable consideration for all relevant seeding transactions;

    "SDLT" means the amount of tax that would have been chargeable in respect of RST but for COACS seeding relief, ignoring any amount of tax that has been charged under this paragraph in respect of RST in relation to an earlier disposal of units by V.

(6) In this paragraph—

540   Finance Act 2016 (c. **24**)

Schedule 16 — Property authorised investment funds and co-ownership authorised contractual schemes
Part 2 — Seeding relief for property authorised investment funds and co-ownership authorised contractual schemes

"group company" means (where V is a company) a company which is a member of the same group of companies as V for the purposes mentioned in paragraph 1(2) of Schedule 7 (group relief);

"relevant seeding transaction", in relation to a disposal of units by V in a co-ownership authorised contractual scheme, means a seeding transaction—

    (a)   the effective date of which is, or is before, the date of the disposal,

    (b)   in which that scheme is the purchaser, and

    (c)   in which a vendor is—

        (i)   V, or

        (ii)   (where V is a company) a company which is a group company at the time of the disposal;

"seeding transaction" means a transaction in respect of which COACS seeding relief is allowed (whether or not relief is subsequently withdrawn to any extent);

"the value of V's investment in the scheme" at a particular time means the market value of all units in the co-ownership authorised contractual scheme held at that time by—

    (a)   V, and

    (b)   (where V is a company) a company which—

        (i)   is a group company at that time, and

        (ii)   before that time, has been a vendor in one or more seeding transactions in which the scheme was the purchaser.

(7) For the purposes of this paragraph, the "market value" on a particular date of units in the scheme is an amount equal to the buying price (that is, the lower price) published by the operator on that date (or, if no such price is published on that date, on the latest date before).

Withdrawal of relief: dwelling occupied by non-qualifying individual

18 (1) This paragraph applies to a transaction ("the relevant transaction") if—

    (a)   COACS seeding relief has been allowed in respect of the transaction,

    (b)   the main subject-matter of the transaction consists of a chargeable interest in or over land which is or includes a dwelling, and

    (c)   a non-qualifying individual (see paragraph 19) is permitted to occupy the dwelling at any time on or after the effective date of the transaction.

The dwelling which a non-qualifying individual is permitted to occupy is referred to as "the disqualifying dwelling".

(2) The relief, or an appropriate proportion of it, is withdrawn, and tax is chargeable in accordance with this paragraph.

This is subject to sub-paragraphs (3) and (4).

Finance Act 2016 (c. 24)   541
Schedule 16 — Property authorised investment funds and co-ownership authorised contractual schemes
Part 2 — Seeding relief for property authorised investment funds and co-ownership authorised contractual schemes

(3) Relief is withdrawn only if, at the time a non-qualifying individual is permitted to occupy the disqualifying dwelling, the co-ownership authorised contractual scheme holds a chargeable interest in or over that dwelling —

    (a) that was acquired by the scheme under the relevant transaction, or

    (b) that is derived from an interest so acquired.

(4) Where a non-qualifying individual is first permitted to occupy the disqualifying dwelling at a time after the end of the control period, relief is withdrawn only if, at that time, the scheme fails to meet the genuine diversity of ownership condition (see paragraph 15).

(5) The amount chargeable is the amount that would have been chargeable in respect of the relevant transaction but for COACS seeding relief or, as the case may be, an appropriate proportion of the tax that would have been so chargeable.

(6) In sub-paragraphs (2) and (5), an "appropriate proportion" means an appropriate proportion having regard to the extent to which the subject-matter of the relevant transaction was an interest in or over land other than the disqualifying dwelling.

19 (1) In paragraph 18 "non-qualifying individual", in relation to a land transaction and a co-ownership authorised contractual scheme, means any of the following —

    (a) an individual who is a major participant in the scheme;

    (b) an individual who is connected with a major participant in the scheme;

    (c) an individual who is connected with the operator of the scheme (see section 102A) or the depositary of the scheme;

    (d) a relevant settlor;

    (e) the spouse or civil partner of an individual falling within paragraph (b), (c) or (d);

    (f) a relative of an individual falling within paragraph (b), (c) or (d), or the spouse or civil partner of a relative of an individual falling within paragraph (b), (c) or (d);

    (g) a relative of the spouse or civil partner of an individual falling within paragraph (b), (c) or (d);

    (h) the spouse or civil partner of an individual falling within paragraph (g).

(2) An individual who participates in a scheme is a "major participant" in it if the individual —

    (a) is entitled to a share of at least 50% either of all the profits or income arising from the scheme or of any profits or income arising from it that may be distributed to participants, or

    (b) would in the event of the winding up of the scheme be entitled to 50% or more of the assets of the scheme that would then be available for distribution among the participants.

(3) The reference in sub-paragraph (2)(a) to profits or income arising from the scheme is to profits or income arising from the

542   Finance Act 2016 (c. 24)
Schedule 16 — Property authorised investment funds and co-ownership authorised contractual schemes
Part 2 — Seeding relief for property authorised investment funds and co-ownership authorised contractual schemes

acquisition, holding, management or disposal of the property subject to the scheme.

(4) In this paragraph—

"depositary", in relation to a co-ownership authorised contractual scheme, means the person to whom the property subject to the scheme is entrusted for safekeeping;

"relative" means brother, sister, ancestor or lineal descendant;

"relevant settlor", in relation to a land transaction, means an individual who is a settlor in relation to a relevant settlement (as defined in sub-paragraph (5));

"settlement" has the same meaning as in Chapter 5 of Part 5 of ITTOIA 2005 (see section 620 of that Act).

(5) Where a person, in the capacity of trustee of a settlement, is connected with a person who is the purchaser under a land transaction, that settlement is a "relevant settlement" in relation to the transaction.

(6) In sub-paragraph (5) "trustee" is to be read in accordance with section 1123(3) of CTA 2010 ("connected" persons: supplementary).

(7) Section 1122 of CTA 2010 (connected persons) has effect for the purposes of this paragraph, but for those purposes, subsections (7) and (8) of that section (application of rules about connected persons to partnerships) are to be disregarded.

PART 3

INTERPRETATION

"Feeder fund" and "units"

20   In this Schedule—

a "feeder fund" of a property AIF means a unit trust scheme—

(a)   one of the main objects of which is investment in the property AIF, and

(b)   which is managed by the same person as the property AIF;

a "feeder fund" of a co-ownership authorised contractual scheme means an open-ended investment company, an offshore fund or a unit trust scheme—

(a)   one of the main objects of which is investment in the co-ownership authorised contractual scheme, and

(b)   which is managed by the same person as the scheme;

"units in the property AIF" means—

(a)   units in the property AIF (and, where the property AIF is a part of an umbrella company as mentioned in regulation 7(1) and (2) of the AIF (Tax) Regulations,

Finance Act 2016 (c. 24)   543
Schedule 16 — Property authorised investment funds and co-ownership authorised contractual schemes
Part 2 — Seeding relief for property authorised investment funds and co-ownership authorised contractual schemes

this means units in the separate pool to which that part of the umbrella company relates), and

(b) units in a feeder fund of the property AIF;

"units in the co-ownership authorised contractual scheme" means—

(a) units in the co-ownership authorised contractual scheme (and, where the co-ownership authorised contractual scheme is a sub-scheme of an umbrella COACS (see section 102A(3) and (4)), this means units in the separate pool to which that sub-scheme relates), and

(b) units in a feeder fund of the scheme;

"units" means the rights or interests (however described) of the participants in the property AIF or the co-ownership authorised contractual scheme.

Interpretation of other terms

21   In this Schedule—

the "AIF (Tax) Regulations" means the Authorised Investment Funds (Tax) Regulations 2006 (S.I. 2006/964);

"arrangements" includes any scheme, agreement or understanding, whether or not legally enforceable;

"attributable" means attributable on a just and reasonable basis;

"authorised corporate director", in relation to a property AIF, has the same meaning as in regulation 8 of the AIF (Tax) Regulations;

"COACS seeding relief" means relief under paragraph 10;

"control period" means the period of 3 years beginning with the day following the last day of the seeding period;

"co-ownership authorised contractual scheme" is to be construed in accordance with section 102A (see in particular subsections (2), (5), (7) and (8) of that section);

"CTA 2010" means the Corporation Tax Act 2010;

"FSMA 2000" means the Financial Services and Markets Act 2000;

the "genuine diversity of ownership condition", in relation to a co-ownership authorised contractual scheme, has the meaning given by paragraph 15;

"ITTOIA 2005" means the Income Tax (Trading and Other Income) Act 2005;

"non-qualifying individual" has the meaning given by paragraph 9 (in relation to a property AIF) and paragraph 19 (in relation to a co-ownership authorised contractual scheme);

"offshore fund" has the meaning given by section 355 of the Taxation (International and Other Provisions) Act 2010;

"open-ended investment company" has the meaning given by section 236 of FSMA 2000;

544   Finance Act 2016 (c. 24)
Schedule 16 — Property authorised investment funds and co-ownership authorised contractual schemes
Part 2 — Seeding relief for property authorised investment funds and co-ownership authorised contractual schemes

"operator", in relation to a co-ownership authorised contractual scheme, has the same meaning as in section 102A;

"PAIF seeding relief" means relief under paragraph 1;

"participant" is to be read in accordance with section 235 of FSMA 2000;

"portfolio test" has the meaning given by paragraph 6(7) (in relation to a property AIF) and paragraph 16(7) (in relation to a co-ownership authorised contractual scheme);

"property AIF" is to be construed in accordance with paragraph 2 (see in particular sub-paragraphs (2), (3) and (5) of that paragraph);

"relevant disposal" has the meaning given by paragraph 7(3) (in relation to a property AIF) and paragraph 17(3) (in relation to a co-ownership authorised contractual scheme);

"seeding period" has the meaning given by paragraph 3 (in relation to a property AIF) and paragraph 11 (in relation to a co-ownership authorised contractual scheme);

"unit trust scheme" has the meaning given by section 237(1) of FSMA 2000."

PART 3

CONSEQUENTIAL AMENDMENTS

5   FA 2003 is amended in accordance with this Part.

6   In section 75C (anti-avoidance: supplemental), in subsection (4), after "Schedule 6A" insert ", 7A".

7   (1) Section 81 (further return where relief withdrawn) is amended as follows.

    (2) In subsection (1) —

        (a)   omit "or" at the end of paragraph (b), and

        (b)   after paragraph (b) insert—

                "(ba)   paragraph 5, 7 or 8 of Schedule 7A (PAIF seeding relief),

                (bb)   paragraph 13, 17 or 18 of Schedule 7A (COACS seeding relief), or".

    (3) In subsection (1A), after "transactions)" insert ", or under paragraph 6 of Schedule 7A (PAIF seeding relief) or paragraph 14 or 16 of Schedule 7A (COACS seeding relief),".

    (4) In subsection (1B), after paragraph (e) insert—

                "(f)   in the case of relief under paragraph 6 of Schedule 7A (PAIF seeding relief: portfolio test) —

                    (i)   where relief is withdrawn under paragraph 6(1), the last day of the seeding period (see paragraph 3 of that Schedule), or

                    (ii)   where relief is withdrawn under paragraph 6(3), the first time mentioned in paragraph 6(3)(a) or (b) at which the portfolio test was not met;

      (g)   in the case of relief under paragraph 14 of Schedule 7A (COACS seeding relief: genuine diversity of ownership condition), the first time mentioned in paragraph 14(1) at which the genuine diversity of ownership condition was not met;

      (h)   in the case of relief under paragraph 16 of Schedule 7A (COACS seeding relief: portfolio test) –

          (i)   where relief is withdrawn under paragraph 16(1), the last day of the seeding period (see paragraph 11 of that Schedule), or

          (ii)   where relief is withdrawn under paragraph 16(3), the first time mentioned in paragraph 16(3)(a) or (b) at which the portfolio test was not met."

(5) In subsection (4), after paragraph (b) insert—

      "(ba)   in relation to the withdrawal of PAIF seeding relief—

          (i)   the purchaser ceasing to be a property AIF as mentioned in paragraph 5 of Schedule 7A,

          (ii)   a person making a relevant disposal of units as mentioned in paragraph 7 of that Schedule, or

          (iii)   the grant of permission to a non-qualifying individual to occupy a dwelling as mentioned in paragraph 8 of that Schedule;

      (bb)   in relation to the withdrawal of COACS seeding relief—

          (i)   the purchaser ceasing to be a co-ownership authorised contractual scheme as mentioned in paragraph 13 of Schedule 7A,

          (ii)   a person making a relevant disposal of units as mentioned in paragraph 17 of that Schedule, or

          (iii)   the grant of permission to a non-qualifying individual to occupy a dwelling as mentioned in paragraph 18 of that Schedule;".

8   In section 86 (payment of tax), in subsection (2) –

    (a)   omit "or" at the end of paragraph (b), and

    (b)   after paragraph (b) insert—

        "(ba)   Part 1 of Schedule 7A (PAIF seeding relief),

        (bb)   Part 2 of Schedule 7A (COACS seeding relief), or".

9   (1) Section 87 (interest on unpaid tax) is amended as follows.

    (2) In subsection (3) –

      (a)   in paragraph (a) –

          (i)   omit "or" at the end of sub-paragraph (ii), and

          (ii)   after sub-paragraph (ii) insert—

             "(iia)   paragraph 5, 7 or 8 of Schedule 7A (PAIF seeding relief),

             (iib)   paragraph 13, 17 or 18 of Schedule 7A (COACS seeding relief), or";

      (b)   after paragraph (aza) insert—

        "(azb)   in the case of an amount payable under paragraph 6(3) of Schedule 7A (PAIF seeding relief: portfolio

546   *Finance Act 2016 (c. 24)*
Schedule 16 — Property authorised investment funds and co-ownership authorised contractual schemes
Part 3 — Consequential amendments

       test), the first time mentioned in paragraph 6(3)(a) or (b) at which the portfolio test was not met;

  (azc) in the case of an amount payable under paragraph 14(1) of Schedule 7A (COACS seeding relief: genuine diversity of ownership condition) because the genuine diversity of ownership condition was not met at a time mentioned in paragraph 14(1)(b) or (c), the first time mentioned in paragraph 14(1)(b) or (c) at which that condition was not met;

  (azd) in the case of an amount payable under paragraph 16(3) of Schedule 7A (COACS seeding relief: portfolio test), the first time mentioned in paragraph 16(3)(a) or (b) at which the portfolio test was not met;".

  (3) In subsection (4), for "means —" to the end substitute "has the same meaning as in section 81(4)."

10 In section 118 (market value) —

  (a) the existing text becomes subsection (1), and

  (b) after subsection (1) insert —

    "(2) This is subject to paragraphs 7(7) and 17(7) of Schedule 7A (which define "market value" for certain purposes of PAIF seeding relief and COACS seeding relief)."

11 In section 122 (index of defined expressions), at the appropriate place insert —

"COACS seeding relief	Schedule 7A, paragraph 10(1)"
"co-ownership authorised contractual scheme	section 102A"
"operator (in relation to a co-ownership authorised contractual scheme)	section 102A"
"PAIF seeding relief	Schedule 7A, paragraph 1(1)".

12 In Schedule 4A (SDLT: higher rate for certain transactions), in paragraph 2(6) —

  (a) omit "and" at the end of paragraph (d),

  (b) after paragraph (d) insert —

    "(da) Schedule 7A (PAIF seeding relief and COACS seeding relief), and", and

  (c) in paragraph (e), for "(d)" substitute "(da)".

13 In Schedule 6B (transfers involving multiple dwellings), in paragraph 2(4)(b), after "Schedule 7" insert ", Schedule 7A".

14 (1) In Schedule 17A (further provisions relating to leases), paragraph 11 (cases where assignment of lease treated as grant of lease) is amended as follows.

(2) In sub-paragraph (3), after paragraph (b) insert—

  "(ba) Part 1 or 2 of Schedule 7A (PAIF seeding relief and COACS seeding relief);".

(3) In sub-paragraph (4), after "acquisition relief" insert ", PAIF seeding relief, COACS seeding relief".

(4) In sub-paragraph (5), after paragraph (b) insert—

  "(ba) in relation to the withdrawal of PAIF seeding relief—

   (i) the purchaser ceasing to be a property AIF as mentioned in paragraph 5 of Schedule 7A,

   (ii) a person making a relevant disposal of units as mentioned in paragraph 7 of that Schedule, or

   (iii) the grant of permission to a non-qualifying individual to occupy a dwelling as mentioned in paragraph 8 of that Schedule;

  (bb) in relation to the withdrawal of COACS seeding relief—

   (i) the purchaser ceasing to be a co-ownership authorised contractual scheme as mentioned in paragraph 13 of Schedule 7A,

   (ii) a person making a relevant disposal of units as mentioned in paragraph 17 of that Schedule, or

   (iii) the grant of permission to a non-qualifying individual to occupy a dwelling as mentioned in paragraph 18 of that Schedule;".

(5) After sub-paragraph (5) insert—

  "(6) This paragraph also does not apply where the relief in question is PAIF seeding relief or COACS seeding relief and is withdrawn as a result of a requirement not being met at a time which is before the effective date of the assignment of the lease.

  (7) For the purposes of sub-paragraph (6), the reference to a requirement not being met is a reference to—

   (a) in relation to the withdrawal of PAIF seeding relief under paragraph 6 of Schedule 7A, the portfolio test not being met (see paragraph 6(7));

   (b) in relation to the withdrawal of COACS seeding relief under paragraph 14 of Schedule 7A, the genuine diversity of ownership condition not being met (see paragraph 15);

   (c) in relation to the withdrawal of COACS seeding relief under paragraph 16 of Schedule 7A, the portfolio test not being met (see paragraph 16(7))."

PART 4

COMMENCEMENT

15 (1) The amendments made by Parts 2 and 3 of this Schedule have effect in relation to any land transaction of which the effective date is, or is after, the date on which this Act is passed.

  (2) But those amendments do not have effect in relation to a transaction if—

548

Finance Act 2016 (c. 24)
Schedule 16 — Property authorised investment funds and co-ownership authorised contractual schemes
Part 4 — Commencement

> (a) the transaction is effected in pursuance of a contract entered into and substantially performed before the date on which this Act is passed, or
>
> (b) the transaction is effected in pursuance of a contract entered into before that date and is not excluded by sub-paragraph (3).

(3) A transaction effected in pursuance of a contract entered into before the date on which this Act is passed is excluded by this sub-paragraph if—

> (a) there is any variation of the contract, or assignment of rights under the contract, on or after that date,
>
> (b) the transaction is effected in consequence of the exercise on or after that date of any option, right of pre-emption or similar right, or
>
> (c) on or after that date there is an assignment, subsale or other transaction relating to the whole or part of the subject-matter of the contract as a result of which a person other than the purchaser under the contract becomes entitled to call for a conveyance.

(4) In this paragraph—

> "purchaser" has the same meaning as in Part 4 of FA 2003 (see section 43(4) of that Act);
>
> "substantially performed", in relation to a contract, has the same meaning as in that Part (see section 44(5) of that Act).

SCHEDULE 17   Section 153

AQUA METHANOL ETC

PART 1

AQUA METHANOL

Introductory

1   HODA 1979 is amended as follows.

Definition

2   After section 2AB insert—

"2AC Aqua methanol

> In this Act "aqua methanol" means a liquid fuel which meets each of the following conditions—
>
> (a) the amount of water it contains is not less than 4.7 per cent and not more than 5.3 per cent by volume,
>
> (b) the amount of methanol it contains is not less than 96 per cent by volume of the remainder of the substance, and
>
> (c) at a temperature of 15°C and under a pressure of 1013.25 millibars, it has a density of not less than 0.81 g/ml and not more than 0.82 g/ml."

3   In section 2A (power to amend definitions), in subsection (1), after

paragraph (b) insert—
> "(ba)   aqua methanol;".

Charging of excise duty

4   After section 6AF insert—

"6AG Excise duty on aqua methanol

(1)   A duty of excise shall be charged on the setting aside for a chargeable use by any person, or (where it has not already been charged under this section) on the chargeable use by any person, of aqua methanol.

(2)   In subsection (1) "chargeable use" means use—
   (a)   as fuel for any engine, motor or other machinery, or
   (b)   as an additive or extender in any substance so used.

(3)   The rate of duty under this section is—
   (a)   in the case of a chargeable use within subsection (2)(a), £0.079 a litre;
   (b)   in the case of a chargeable use within subsection (2)(b), the rate prescribed by order made by the Treasury.

(4)   In exercising their power under subsection (3)(b), the Treasury shall so far as practicable secure that aqua methanol set aside for use or used as an additive or extender in any substance is charged with duty at the same rate as the substance in which it is an additive or extender.

(5)   The power of the Treasury to make an order under this section shall be exercisable by statutory instrument subject to annulment in pursuance of a resolution of the House of Commons.

(6)   An order under this section—
   (a)   may make different provision for different cases, and
   (b)   may prescribe the rate of duty under subsection (3)(b) by reference to the rate of duty under this Act in respect of any other substance.

6AH Application to aqua methanol of provisions relating to hydrocarbon oil

(1)   The Commissioners may by regulations provide for—
   (a)   references in this Act, or specified references in this Act, to hydrocarbon oil to be construed as including references to aqua methanol;
   (b)   references in this Act, or specified references in this Act, to duty on hydrocarbon oil to be construed as including references to duty under section 6AG above;
   (c)   aqua methanol to be treated for the purposes of such of the following provisions of this Act as may be specified as if it fell within a specified description of hydrocarbon oil.

(2)   Where the effect of provision made under subsection (1) above is to extend any power to make regulations, provision made in exercise of the power as extended may be contained in the same statutory instrument as the provision extending the power.

(3) In this section "specified" means specified by regulations under this section.

(4) Regulations under this section may make different provision for different cases.

(5) Paragraph (b) of subsection (1) above shall not be taken as prejudicing the generality of paragraph (a) of that subsection."

5   In section 6A (fuel substitutes), in subsection (1) —
    (a) omit the "or" after paragraph (d), and
    (b) after paragraph (e) insert ", or
          (f) aqua methanol."

Mixing of aqua methanol

6   (1) For the italic heading before section 20A substitute "Mixing".

    (2) After section 20AAB insert —

"20AAC Prohibition on mixing of aqua methanol

(1) Aqua methanol on which duty under section 6AG(3)(a) of this Act has been charged must not be mixed with any relevant substance.

(2) In subsection (1) "relevant substance" means biodiesel, bioethanol, bioblend, bioethanol blend or hydrocarbon oil.

(3) A person commits an offence under this subsection if —
    (a) the person intentionally uses aqua methanol in contravention of subsection (1) above, or
    (b) the person supplies aqua methanol, intending that it will be used in contravention of subsection (1) above.

(4) A person guilty of an offence under subsection (3) above shall be liable —
    (a) on summary conviction in England and Wales —
        (i) to imprisonment for a term not exceeding 12 months (or 6 months, if the offence was committed before the commencement of section 154(1) of the Criminal Justice Act 2003), or
        (ii) to a fine not exceeding £20,000 or (if greater) 3 times the value of the aqua methanol in question,
    or both;
    (b) on summary conviction in Scotland —
        (i) to imprisonment for a term not exceeding 12 months, or
        (ii) to a fine not exceeding the statutory maximum or (if greater) 3 times the value of the aqua methanol in question,
    or both;
    (c) on summary conviction in Northern Ireland —
        (i) to imprisonment for a term not exceeding 6 months, or

        (ii)   to a fine not exceeding the statutory maximum or (if greater) 3 times the value of the aqua methanol in question,

or both;

    (d)   on conviction on indictment, to imprisonment for a term not exceeding 7 years or a fine, or both.

(5)   Any aqua methanol, or any mixture containing aqua methanol, in respect of which an offence under subsection (3) above has been committed shall be liable to forfeiture.

20AAD Mixing of aqua methanol in contravention of prohibition: adjustment of duty

(1)   A duty of excise shall be charged on a mixture which is produced by mixing aqua methanol on which duty under section 6AG(3)(a) of this Act has been charged with a relevant substance.

(2)   In subsection (1) "relevant substance" means biodiesel, bioethanol, bioblend, bioethanol blend or hydrocarbon oil.

(3)   The rate of duty on a mixture under subsection (1) shall be the rate of duty specified in section 6(1A)(c) (general rate for heavy oil).

(4)   The person liable to pay duty charged under this section on production of a mixture is the person producing the mixture.

(5)   Where it appears to the Commissioners—
    (a)   that a person ("P") has produced a mixture on which duty is charged under this section, and
    (b)   that P is the person liable to pay the duty,
they may assess the amount of duty due from P to the best of their judgment and notify that amount to P or P's representative.

(6)   An assessment under subsection (5) above shall be treated as if it were an assessment under section 12(1) of the Finance Act 1994.

(7)   Where duty under a provision of this Act has been paid on an ingredient of a mixture, the duty charged under this section shall be reduced by the amount of any duty which the Commissioners are satisfied has been paid on the ingredient (but not to a negative amount).

(8)   The Commissioners may exempt a person from liability to pay duty under this section in respect of production of a mixture of a kind described in subsection (1) if satisfied that—
    (a)   the liability was incurred accidentally, and
    (b)   in the circumstances the person should be exempted.

Powers to allow reliefs".

Enforcement

7   (1)   Section 22 (prohibition on use of petrol substitutes on which duty has not been paid) is amended as follows.

(2) After subsection (1AB) insert—

"(1AC) Where any person—

    (a) puts any aqua methanol to a chargeable use (within the meaning of section 6AG above), and

    (b) knows or has reasonable cause to believe that there is duty charged under section 6AG above on that aqua methanol which has not been paid and is not lawfully deferred,

his putting the aqua methanol to that use shall attract a penalty under section 9 of the Finance Act 1994 (civil penalties), and any goods in respect of which a person contravenes this section shall be liable to forfeiture."

(3) In subsection (1A), for "or (1AB)" substitute ", (1AB) or (1AC)".

(4) For the heading substitute "Prohibition on use of fuel substitutes on which duty has not been paid".

Consequential amendments

8   In section 23C (warehousing), in subsection (4), after paragraph (d) insert—
"(da) aqua methanol,".

9   In section 27(1) (interpretation), before the definition of "aviation gasoline" insert—

""aqua methanol" has the meaning given by section 2AC above;".

10   In section 16 of FA 1994 (appeals to a tribunal), in subsection (6)(c), before "section 23(1)" insert "or (1AC)".

11   In paragraph 3 of Schedule 41 to FA 2008 (penalties for putting product to use that attracts higher duty), in the Table in sub-paragraph (1), at the appropriate place insert—

"HODA 1979 section 20AAD(5)	Mixtures containing aqua methanol."

PART 2

HYDROCARBON OILS: MISCELLANEOUS AMENDMENTS

HODA 1979

12   In section 20AAA of HODA 1979 (mixing of rebated oil), in subsection (4)(a), for "section 6A(1A)(c)" substitute "section 6(1A)(c)".

FA 1994

13   In section 16 of FA 1994 (appeals to a tribunal), in subsection (6)(c), after "section 22(1)" insert "(1AA), (1AB)".

PART 3

COMMENCEMENT

14   The amendments made by this Schedule come into force —
    (a)   so far as they confer a power to make regulations or an order, on the day on which this Act is passed, and
    (b)   for all other purposes, on 14 November 2016.

SCHEDULE 18   Section 159

SERIAL TAX AVOIDANCE

PART 1

CONTENTS OF SCHEDULE

1   In this Schedule —
    (a)   Part 2 provides for HMRC to give warning notices to persons who incur relevant defeats and includes —
        (i)   provision about the duration of warning periods under warning notices (see paragraph 3), and
        (ii)   definitions of "relevant defeat" and other key terms;
    (b)   Part 3 contains provisions about persons to whom a warning notice has been given, and in particular —
        (i)   imposes a duty to give information notices, and
        (ii)   allows the Commissioners to publish information about such persons in certain cases involving repeated relevant defeats;
    (c)   Part 4 contains provision about the restriction of reliefs;
    (d)   Part 5 imposes liability to penalties on persons who incur relevant defeats in relation to arrangements used in warning periods;
    (e)   Part 6 contains provisions about corporate groups, associated persons and partnerships;
    (f)   Part 7 contains definitions and other supplementary provisions.

PART 2

ENTRY INTO THE REGIME AND BASIC CONCEPTS

Duty to give warning notice

2   (1) This paragraph applies where a person incurs a relevant defeat in relation to any arrangements.

    (2) HMRC must give the person a written notice (a "warning notice").

    (3) The notice must be given within the period of 90 days beginning with the day on which the relevant defeat is incurred.

    (4) The notice must —
        (a)   set out when the warning period begins and ends (see paragraph 3),
        (b)   specify the relevant defeat to which the notice relates, and

554

Finance Act 2016 (c. 24)
Schedule 18 — Serial tax avoidance
Part 2 — Entry into the regime and basic concepts

     (c)   explain the effect of paragraphs 3 and 17 to 46.

(5) A warning notice given by virtue of paragraph 49 must also explain the effect of paragraph 51 (information in certain cases involving partnerships).

(6) In this Schedule "arrangements" includes any agreement, understanding, scheme, transaction or series of transactions (whether or not legally enforceable).

(7) For the meaning of "relevant defeat" and provision about when a relevant defeat is incurred see paragraph 11.

Warning period

3   (1) If a person is given a warning notice with respect to a relevant defeat (and sub-paragraph (2) does not apply) the period of 5 years beginning with the day after the day on which the notice is given is a "warning period" in relation to that person.

    (2) If a person incurs a relevant defeat in relation to arrangements during a period which is a warning period in relation to that person, the warning period is extended to the end of the 5 years beginning with the day after the day on which the relevant defeat occurs.

    (3) In relation to a warning period which has been extended under this Schedule, references in this Schedule (including this paragraph) to the warning period are to be read as references to the warning period as extended.

Meaning of "tax"

4   In this Schedule "tax" includes any of the following taxes —
      (a) income tax,
      (b) corporation tax, including any amount chargeable as if it were corporation tax or treated as if it were corporation tax,
      (c) capital gains tax,
      (d) petroleum revenue tax,
      (e) diverted profits tax,
      (f) apprenticeship levy,
      (g) inheritance tax,
      (h) stamp duty land tax,
      (i) annual tax on enveloped dwellings,
      (j) VAT, and
      (k) national insurance contributions.

Meaning of "tax advantage" in relation to VAT

5   (1) In this Schedule "tax advantage", in relation to VAT, is to be read in accordance with sub-paragraphs (2) to (4).

    (2) A taxable person obtains a tax advantage if —
      (a) in any prescribed accounting period, the amount by which the output tax accounted for by the person exceeds the input tax deducted by the person is less than it would otherwise be,

Finance Act 2016 (c. 24)
Schedule 18 — Serial tax avoidance
Part 2 — Entry into the regime and basic concepts

555

(b)   the person obtains a VAT credit when the person would not otherwise do so, or obtains a larger VAT credit or obtains a VAT credit earlier than would otherwise be the case,

(c)   in a case where the person recovers input tax as a recipient of a supply before the supplier accounts for the output tax, the period between the time when the input tax is recovered and the time when the output tax is accounted for is greater than would otherwise be the case, or

(d)   in any prescribed accounting period, the amount of the person's non-deductible tax is less than it would otherwise be.

(3)   A person who is not a taxable person obtains a tax advantage if the person's non-refundable tax is less than it otherwise would be.

(4)   In sub-paragraph (3) "non-refundable tax", in relation to a person who is not a taxable person, means—

(a)   VAT on the supply to the person of any goods or services,

(b)   VAT on the acquisition by the person from another member State of any goods, and

(c)   VAT paid or payable by the person on the importation of any goods from a place outside the member States,

but excluding (in each case) any VAT in respect of which the person is entitled to a refund from the Commissioners by virtue of any provision of VATA 1994.

Meaning of "non-deductible tax"

6   (1)   In this Schedule "non-deductible tax", in relation to a taxable person, means—

(a)   input tax for which the person is not entitled to credit under section 25 of VATA 1994, and

(b)   any VAT incurred by the person which is not input tax and in respect of which the person is not entitled to a refund from the Commissioners by virtue of any provision of VATA 1994.

(2)   For the purposes of sub-paragraph (1)(b), the VAT "incurred" by a taxable person is—

(a)   VAT on the supply to the person of any goods or services,

(b)   VAT on the acquisition by the person from another member State of any goods, and

(c)   VAT paid or payable by the person on the importation of any goods from a place outside the member States.

"Tax advantage": other taxes

7   In relation to taxes other than VAT, "tax advantage" includes—

(a)   relief or increased relief from tax,

(b)   repayment or increased repayment of tax,

(c)   receipt, or advancement of a receipt, of a tax credit,

(d)   avoidance or reduction of a charge to tax, an assessment of tax or a liability to pay tax,

(e)   avoidance of a possible assessment to tax or liability to pay tax,

556

Finance Act 2016 (c. 24)
Schedule 18 — Serial tax avoidance
Part 2 — Entry into the regime and basic concepts

    (f)   deferral of a payment of tax or advancement of a repayment of tax, and

    (g)   avoidance of an obligation to deduct or account for tax.

"DOTAS arrangements"

8   (1)   For the purposes of this Schedule arrangements are "DOTAS arrangements" at any time if they are notifiable arrangements at the time in question and a person—

        (a)   has provided information in relation to the arrangements under section 308(3), 309 or 310 of FA 2004, or

        (b)   has failed to comply with any of those provisions in relation to the arrangements.

    (2)   But for the purposes of this Schedule "DOTAS arrangements" does not include arrangements in respect of which HMRC has given notice under section 312(6) of FA 2004 (notice that promoters not under duty to notify client of reference number).

    (3)   For the purposes of sub-paragraph (1) a person who would be required to provide information under subsection (3) of section 308 of FA 2004—

        (a)   but for the fact that the arrangements implement a proposal in respect of which notice has been given under subsection (1) of that section, or

        (b)   but for subsection (4A), (4C) or (5) of that section,

    is treated as providing the information at the end of the period referred to in subsection (3) of that section.

    (4)   In this paragraph "notifiable arrangements" has the same meaning as in Part 7 of FA 2004.

"Disclosable VAT arrangements"

9   For the purposes of this Schedule arrangements are "disclosable VAT arrangements" at any time if at that time—

    (a)   a person has complied with paragraph 6 of Schedule 11A to VATA 1994 in relation to the arrangements (duty to notify Commissioners),

    (b)   a person under a duty to comply with that paragraph in relation to the arrangements has failed to do so, or

    (c)   a reference number has been allocated to the scheme under paragraph 9 of that Schedule (voluntary notification of avoidance scheme which is not a designated scheme).

Paragraphs 8 and 9: "failure to comply"

10   (1)   A person "fails to comply" with any provision mentioned in paragraph 8(1) or 9(a) if and only if any of the conditions in sub-paragraphs (2) to (4) is met.

    (2)   The condition in this sub-paragraph is that—

        (a)   the tribunal has determined that the person has failed to comply with the provision concerned,

        (b)   the appeal period has ended, and

        (c)   the determination has not been overturned on appeal.

    (3)   The condition in this sub-paragraph is that—

Finance Act 2016 (c. 24)
Schedule 18 — Serial tax avoidance
Part 2 — Entry into the regime and basic concepts

557

    (a)   the tribunal has determined for the purposes of section 118(2) of TMA 1970 that the person is to be deemed not to have failed to comply with the provision concerned as the person had a reasonable excuse for not doing the thing required to be done,

    (b)   the appeal period has ended, and

    (c)   the determination has not been overturned on appeal.

(4) The condition in this sub-paragraph is that the person admitted in writing to HMRC that the person has failed to comply with the provision concerned.

(5) In this paragraph "the appeal period" means —

    (a)   the period during which an appeal could be brought against the determination of the tribunal, or

    (b)   where an appeal mentioned in paragraph (a) has been brought, the period during which that appeal has not been finally determined, withdrawn or otherwise disposed of.

(6) In this paragraph "the tribunal" means the First-tier tribunal or, where determined by or under Tribunal Procedure Rules, the Upper Tribunal.

"Relevant defeat"

11   (1) A person ("P") incurs a "relevant defeat" in relation to arrangements if any of Conditions A to E is met in relation to P and the arrangements.

    (2) The relevant defeat is incurred when the condition in question is first met.

Condition A

12   (1) Condition A is that —

    (a)   P has been given a notice under paragraph 12 of Schedule 43 to FA 2013 (general anti-abuse rule: notice of final decision), paragraph 8 or 9 of Schedule 43A to that Act (pooling and binding of arrangements: notice of final decision) or paragraph 8 of Schedule 43B to that Act (generic referrals: notice of final decision) stating that a tax advantage arising from the arrangements is to be counteracted,

    (b)   that tax advantage has been counteracted under section 209 of FA 2013, and

    (c)   the counteraction is final.

    (2) For the purposes of this paragraph the counteraction of a tax advantage is "final" when the adjustments made to effect the counteraction, and any amounts arising as a result of those adjustments, can no longer be varied, on appeal or otherwise.

Condition B

13   (1) Condition B is that (in a case not falling within Condition A above) a follower notice has been given to P by reference to the arrangements (and not withdrawn) and —

    (a)   the necessary corrective action for the purposes of section 208 of FA 2014 has been taken in respect of the denied advantage, or

    (b)   the denied advantage has been counteracted otherwise than as mentioned in paragraph (a) and the counteraction of the denied advantage is final.

558

Finance Act 2016 (c. 24)
Schedule 18 — Serial tax avoidance
Part 2 — Entry into the regime and basic concepts

(2) In sub-paragraph (1) the reference to giving a follower notice to P includes a reference to giving a partnership follower notice in respect of a partnership return in relation to which P is a relevant partner (as defined in paragraph 2(5) of Schedule 31 to FA 2014).

(3) For the purposes of this paragraph it does not matter whether the denied advantage has been dealt with—

   (a) wholly as mentioned in one or other of paragraphs (a) and (b) of sub-paragraph (1), or

   (b) partly as mentioned in one and partly as mentioned in the other of those paragraphs.

(4) In this paragraph "the denied advantage" has the same meaning as in Chapter 2 of Part 4 of FA 2014 (see section 208(3) of and paragraph 4(3) of Schedule 31 to that Act).

(5) For the purposes of this paragraph the counteraction of a tax advantage is "final" when the adjustments made to effect the counteraction, and any amounts arising as a result of those adjustments, can no longer be varied, on appeal or otherwise.

(6) In this Schedule "follower notice" means a follower notice under Chapter 2 of Part 4 of FA 2014.

(7) For the purposes of this paragraph a partnership follower notice is given "in respect of" the partnership return mentioned in paragraph (a) or (b) of paragraph 2(2) of Schedule 31 to FA 2014.

Condition C

14 (1) Condition C is that (in a case not falling within Condition A or B)—

   (a) the arrangements are DOTAS arrangements,

   (b) P has relied on the arrangements (see sub-paragraph (2))—

   (c) the arrangements have been counteracted, and

   (d) the counteraction is final.

(2) For the purposes of sub-paragraph (1), P "relies on the arrangements" if—

   (a) P makes a return, claim or election, or a partnership return is made, on the basis that a relevant tax advantage arises, or

   (b) P fails to discharge a relevant obligation ("the disputed obligation") and there is reason to believe that P's failure to discharge that obligation is connected with the arrangements.

(3) For the purposes of sub-paragraph (2) "relevant tax advantage" means a tax advantage which the arrangements might be expected to enable P to obtain.

(4) For the purposes of sub-paragraph (2) an obligation is a "relevant obligation" if the arrangements might be expected to have the result that the obligation does not arise.

(5) For the purposes of this paragraph the arrangements are "counteracted" if—

   (a) adjustments, other than taxpayer emendations, are made in respect of P's tax position—

      (i) on the basis that the whole or part of the relevant tax advantage mentioned in sub-paragraph (2)(a) does not arise, or

Finance Act 2016 (c. 24)
Schedule 18 — Serial tax avoidance
Part 2 — Entry into the regime and basic concepts

559

          (ii)   on the basis that the disputed obligation does (or did) arise, or

      (b)   an assessment to tax other than a self-assessment is made, or any other action is taken by HMRC, on the basis mentioned in paragraph (a)(i) or (ii) (otherwise than by way of an adjustment).

(6) For the purposes of this paragraph a counteraction is "final" when the assessment, adjustments or action in question, and any amounts arising from the assessment, adjustments or action, can no longer be varied, on appeal or otherwise.

(7) For the purposes of sub-paragraph (1) the time at which it falls to be determined whether or not the arrangements are DOTAS arrangements is when the counteraction becomes final.

(8) The following are "taxpayer emendations" for the purposes of sub-paragraph (5) —

      (a)   an adjustment made by P at a time when P had no reason to believe that HMRC had begun or were about to begin enquiries into P's affairs relating to the tax in question;

      (b)   an adjustment (by way of an assessment or otherwise) made by HMRC with respect to P's tax position as a result of a disclosure made by P which meets the conditions in sub-paragraph (9).

For the purposes of paragraph (a) a payment in respect of a liability to pay national insurance contributions is not an adjustment unless it is a payment in full.

(9) The conditions are that the disclosure —

      (a)   is a full and explicit disclosure of an inaccuracy in a return or other document or of a failure to comply with an obligation, and

      (b)   was made at a time when P had no reason to believe that HMRC were about to begin enquiries into P's affairs relating to the tax in question.

(10) For the purposes of this paragraph a contract settlement which HMRC enters into with P is treated as an assessment to tax (other than a self-assessment); and in relation to contract settlements references in sub-paragraph (5) to the basis an which any assessment or adjustments are made, or any other action is taken, are to be read with any necessary modifications.

Condition D

15 (1) Condition D is that —

      (a)   P is a taxable person;

      (b)   the arrangements are disclosable VAT arrangements to which P is a party,

      (c)   P has relied on the arrangements (see sub-paragraph (2));

      (d)   the arrangements have been counteracted, and

      (e)   the counteraction is final.

(2) For the purposes of sub-paragraph (1) P "relies on the arrangements" if —

      (a)   P makes a return or claim on the basis that a relevant tax advantage arises, or

560

Finance Act 2016 (c. 24)
Schedule 18 – Serial tax avoidance
Part 2 – Entry into the regime and basic concepts

      (b)   P fails to discharge a relevant obligation ("the disputed obligation") and there is reason to believe that P's failure to discharge that obligation is connected with those arrangements.

(3) For the purposes of sub-paragraph (2) "relevant tax advantage" means a tax advantage which the arrangements might be expected to enable P to obtain.

(4) For the purposes of sub-paragraph (2) an obligation is a "relevant obligation" if the arrangements might be expected to have the result that the obligation does not arise.

(5) For the purposes of this paragraph the arrangements are "counteracted" if—

      (a)   adjustments, other than taxpayer emendations, are made in respect of P's tax position—

            (i)   on the basis that the whole or part of the relevant tax advantage mentioned in sub-paragraph (2)(a) does not arise, or

            (ii)   on the basis that the disputed obligation does (or did) arise, or

      (b)   an assessment to tax is made, or any other action is taken by HMRC, on the basis mentioned in paragraph (a)(i) or (ii) (otherwise than by way of an adjustment).

(6) For the purposes of this paragraph a counteraction is "final" when the assessment, adjustments or action in question, and any amounts arising from the assessment, adjustments or action, can no longer be varied, on appeal or otherwise.

(7) For the purposes of sub-paragraph (1) the time at which it falls to be determined whether or not the arrangements are disclosable VAT arrangements is when the counteraction becomes final.

(8) The following are "taxpayer emendations" for the purposes of sub-paragraph (5)—

      (a)   an adjustment made by P at a time when P had no reason to believe that HMRC had begun or were about to begin enquiries into P's affairs relating to VAT;

      (b)   an adjustment made by HMRC with respect to P's tax position (by way of an assessment or otherwise) as a result of a disclosure made by P which meets the conditions in sub-paragraph (9).

(9) The conditions are that the disclosure—

      (a)   is a full and explicit disclosure of an inaccuracy in a return or other document or of a failure to comply with an obligation, and

      (b)   was made at a time when P had no reason to believe that HMRC were about to begin enquiries into P's affairs relating to VAT.

Condition E

16 (1) Condition E is that the arrangements are disclosable VAT arrangements to which P is a party and—

      (a)   the arrangements relate to the position with respect to VAT of a person other than P ("S") who has made supplies of goods or services to P,

      (b)   the arrangements might be expected to enable P to obtain a tax advantage in connection with those supplies of goods or services,

Finance Act 2016 (c. 24)
Schedule 18 — Serial tax avoidance
Part 2 — Entry into the regime and basic concepts

561

       (c)   the arrangements have been counteracted, and

       (d)   the counteraction is final.

(2) For the purposes of this paragraph the arrangements are "counteracted" if—

       (a)   HMRC assess S to tax or take any other action on a basis which prevents P from obtaining (or obtaining the whole of) the tax advantage in question, or

       (b)   adjustments, other than taxpayer emendations, are made in relation to S's VAT affairs on a basis such as is mentioned in paragraph (a).

(3) For the purposes of this paragraph a counteraction is "final" when the assessment, adjustments or action in question, and any amounts arising from the assessment, adjustments or action, can no longer be varied, on appeal or otherwise.

(4) For the purposes of sub-paragraph (1) the time when it falls to be determined whether or not the arrangements are disclosable VAT arrangements is when the counteraction becomes final.

(5) The following are "taxpayer emendations" for the purposes of sub-paragraph (2)—

       (a)   an adjustment made by S at a time when neither P nor S had reason to believe that HMRC had begun or were about to begin enquiries into the affairs of S or P relating to VAT;

       (b)   an adjustment (by way of an assessment or otherwise) made by HMRC with respect to S's tax position as a result of a disclosure made by S which meets the conditions in sub-paragraph (6).

(6) The conditions are that the disclosure—

       (a)   is a full and explicit disclosure of an inaccuracy in a return or other document or of a failure to comply with an obligation, and

       (b)   was made at a time when neither S nor P had reason to believe that HMRC were about to begin enquiries into the affairs of S or P relating to VAT.

PART 3

ANNUAL INFORMATION NOTICES AND NAMING

Annual information notices

17 (1) A person ("P") who has been given a warning notice under this Schedule must give HMRC a written notice (an "information notice") in respect of each reporting period in the warning period (see sub-paragraph (11)).

    (2) An information notice must be given not later than the 30th day after the end of the reporting period to which it relates.

    (3) An information notice must state whether or not P—

       (a)   has in the reporting period delivered a return, or made a claim or election, on the basis that a relevant tax advantage arises, or has since the end of the reporting period delivered on that basis a return which P was required to deliver before the end of that period,

       (b)   has in the reporting period failed to take action which P would be required to take under or by virtue of an enactment relating to tax

562

Finance Act 2016 (c. 24)
Schedule 18 — Serial tax avoidance
Part 3 — Annual information notices and naming

but for particular DOTAS arrangements or disclosable VAT arrangements to which P is a party,

    (c)   has in the reporting period become a party to arrangements which—

        (i)   relate to the position with respect to VAT of another person ("S") who has made supplies of goods or services to P, and

        (ii)   might be expected to enable P to obtain a relevant tax advantage ("the expected tax advantage") in connection with those supplies of goods or services,

    (d)   has failed to deliver a return which P was required to deliver by a date falling in the reporting period.

(4) In this paragraph "relevant tax advantage" means a tax advantage which particular DOTAS arrangements or disclosable VAT arrangements enable, or might be expected to enable, P to obtain.

(5) If P has, in the reporting period concerned, made a return, claim or election on the basis mentioned in sub-paragraph (3)(a) or failed to take action as mentioned in sub-paragraph (3)(b) the information notice must—

    (a)   explain (on the assumptions made by P in so acting or failing to act) how the DOTAS arrangements or disclosable VAT arrangements enable P to obtain the tax advantage, or (as the case may be) have the result that P is not required to take the action in question, and

    (b)   state (on the same assumptions) the amount of the relevant tax advantage mentioned in sub-paragraph (3)(a) or (as the case may be) the amount of any tax advantage which arises in connection with the absence of a requirement to take the action mentioned in sub-paragraph (3)(b).

(6) If P has, in the reporting period, become a party to arrangements such as are mentioned in sub-paragraph (3)(c), the information notice—

    (a)   must state whether or not it is P's view that the expected tax advantage arises to P, and

    (b)   if that is P's view, must explain how the arrangements enable P to obtain the tax advantage and state the amount of the tax advantage.

(7) If the time by which P must deliver a return falls within a reporting period and P fails to deliver the return by that time, HMRC may require P to give HMRC a written notice (a "supplementary information notice") setting out any matters which P would have been required to set out in an information notice had P delivered the return in that reporting period.

(8) A requirement under sub-paragraph (7) must be made by a written notice which states the period within which P must comply with the notice.

(9) If P fails to comply with a requirement of (or imposed under) this paragraph HMRC may by written notice extend the warning period to the end of the period of 5 years beginning with—

    (a)   the day by which the information notice or supplementary information notice should have been given (see sub-paragraphs (2) and (8)) or, as the case requires,

    (b)   the day on which P gave the defective information notice or supplementary information notice to HMRC,

or, if earlier, the time when the warning period would have expired but for the extension.

*Finance Act 2016 (c. **24**)*
Schedule 18 − Serial tax avoidance
Part 3 − Annual information notices and naming

563

(10) HMRC may permit information notices given by members of the same group of companies (as defined in paragraph 46(9)) to be combined.

(11) For the purposes of this paragraph−

    (a) the first reporting period in any warning period begins with the first day of the warning period and ends with a day specified by HMRC ("the specified day"),

    (b) the remainder of the warning period is divided into further reporting periods each of which begins immediately after the end of the preceding reporting period and is twelve months long or (if that would be shorter) ends at the end of the warning period.

Naming

18 (1) The Commissioners may publish information about a person if the person−

    (a) incurs a relevant defeat in relation to arrangements which the person has used in a warning period, and

    (b) has been given at least two warning notices in respect of other defeats of arrangements which were used in the same warning period.

(2) Information published for the first time under sub-paragraph (1) must be published within the 12 months beginning with the day on which the most recent of the warning notices falling within that sub-paragraph has been given to the person.

(3) No information may be published (or continue to be published) after the end of the period of 12 months beginning with the day on which it is first published.

(4) The information that may be published is−

    (a) the person's name (including any trading name, previous name or pseudonym),

    (b) the person's address (or registered office),

    (c) the nature of any business carried on by the person,

    (d) information about the fiscal effect of the defeated arrangements (had they not been defeated), for instance information about total amounts of tax understated or total amounts by which claims, or statements of losses, have been adjusted,

    (e) the amount of any penalty to which the person is liable under paragraph 30 in respect of the relevant defeat of any defeated arrangements,

    (f) the periods in which or times when the defeated arrangements were used, and

    (g) any other information the Commissioners may consider it appropriate to publish in order to make clear the person's identity.

(5) If the person mentioned in sub-paragraph (1) is a member of a group of companies (as defined in paragraph 46(9)), the information which may be published also includes−

    (a) any trading name of the group, and

    (b) information about other members of the group of the kind described in sub-paragraph (4)(a), (b) or (c).

564

Finance Act 2016 (c. 24)
Schedule 18 — Serial tax avoidance
Part 3 — Annual information notices and naming

(6) If the person mentioned in sub-paragraph (1) is a person carrying on a trade or business in partnership, the information which may be published also includes—

    (a) any trading name of the partnership, and

    (b) information about other members of the partnership of the kind described in sub-paragraph (4)(a) or (b).

(7) The information may be published in any manner the Commissioners may consider appropriate.

(8) Before publishing any information the Commissioners—

    (a) must inform the person that they are considering doing so, and

    (b) afford the person reasonable opportunity to make representations about whether or not it should be published.

(9) Arrangements are "defeated arrangements" for the purposes of sub-paragraph (4) if the person used them in the warning period mentioned in sub-paragraph (1) and a warning notice specifying the defeat of those arrangements has been given to the person before the information is published.

(10) If a person has been given a single warning notice in relation to two or more relevant defeats, the person is treated for the purposes of this paragraph as having been given a separate warning notice in relation to each of those relevant defeats.

(11) Nothing in this paragraph prevents the power under sub-paragraph (1) from being exercised on a subsequent occasion in relation to arrangements used by the person in a different warning period.

PART 4

RESTRICTION OF RELIEFS

Duty to give a restriction relief notice

19 (1) HMRC must give a person a written notice (a "restriction of relief notice") if—

    (a) the person incurs a relevant defeat in relation to arrangements which the person has used in a warning period,

    (b) the person has been given at least two warning notices in respect of other relevant defeats of arrangements which were used in that same warning period, and

    (c) the defeats mentioned in paragraphs (a) and (b) meet the conditions in sub-paragraph (2).

(2) The conditions are—

    (a) that each of the relevant defeats is by virtue of Condition A, B or C,

    (b) that each of the relevant defeats relates to the misuse of a relief (see sub-paragraph (5)), and

    (c) in the case of each of the relevant defeats, either—

        (i) that the relevant counteraction (see sub-paragraph (7)) was made on the basis that a particular avoidance-related rule applies in relation to a person's affairs, or

        (ii) that the misused relief is a loss relief.

*Finance Act 2016 (c. **24**)*
Schedule 18 — Serial tax avoidance
Part 4 — Restriction of reliefs

565

(3) In sub-paragraph (2)(c)—

    (a) the "misused relief" means the relief mentioned in sub-paragraph (5), and

    (b) "loss relief" means any relief under Part 4 of ITA 2007 or Part 4 or 5 of CTA 2010.

(4) A restriction of relief notice must—

    (a) explain the effect of paragraphs 20, 21 and 22, and

    (b) set out when the restricted period is to begin and end.

(5) For the purposes of this Part of this Schedule, a relevant defeat by virtue of Condition A, B or C "relates to the misuse of a relief" if—

    (a) the tax advantage in question, or part of the tax advantage in question, is or results from (or would but for the counteraction be or result from) a relief or increased relief from tax, or

    (b) it is reasonable to conclude that the making of a particular claim for relief, or the use of a particular relief, is a significant component of the arrangements in question.

(6) In sub-paragraph (5) "the tax advantage in question" means—

    (a) in relation to a defeat by virtue of Condition A, the tax advantage mentioned in paragraph 12(1)(a),

    (b) in relation to a defeat by virtue of Condition B, the denied advantage (as defined in paragraph 13(4)), or

    (c) in relation to a defeat by virtue of Condition C—

        (i) the tax advantage mentioned in paragraph 14(2)(a), or, as the case requires,

        (ii) the absence of the relevant obligation (as defined in paragraph 14(4)).

(7) In this paragraph "the relevant counteraction", in relation to a relevant defeat means—

    (a) in the case of a defeat by virtue of Condition A, the counteraction referred to in paragraph 12(1)(c);

    (b) in the case of a defeat by virtue of Condition B, the action referred to in paragraph 13(1);

    (c) in the case of a defeat by virtue of Condition C, the counteraction referred to in paragraph 14(1)(d).

(8) If a person has been given a single warning notice in relation to two or more relevant defeats, the person is treated for the purposes of this paragraph as having been given a separate warning notice in relation to each of those relevant defeats.

Restriction of relief

20 (1) Sub-paragraphs (2) to (15) have effect in relation to a person to whom a relief restriction notice has been given.

    (2) The person may not, in the restricted period, make any claim for relief.

    (3) Sub-paragraph (2) does not have effect in relation to—

        (a) a claim for relief under Schedule 8 to FA 2003 (stamp duty land tax: charities relief);

566

Finance Act 2016 (c. 24)
Schedule 18 — Serial tax avoidance
Part 4 — Restriction of reliefs

    (b)   a claim for relief under Chapter 3 of Part 8 of ITA 2007 (gifts of shares, securities and real property to charities etc);

    (c)   a claim for relief under Part 10 of ITA 2007 (special rules about charitable trusts etc);

    (d)   a claim for relief under double taxation arrangements;

    (e)   an election under section 426 of ITA 2007 (gift aid: election to treat gift as made in previous year).

(4)   Claims under the following provisions in Part 4 of FA 2004 (registered pension schemes: tax reliefs etc) do not count as claims for relief for the purposes of this paragraph—

    section 192(4) (increase of basic rate limit and higher rate limit);

    section 193(4) (net pay arrangements: excess relief);

    section 194(1) (relief on making of a claim).

(5)   The person may not, in the restricted period, surrender group relief under Part 5 of CTA 2010.

(6)   No deduction is to be made under section 83 of ITA 2007 (carry forward against subsequent trade profits) in calculating the person's net income for a relevant tax year.

(7)   No deduction is to be made under section 118 of ITA 2007 (carry-forward property loss relief) in calculating the person's net income for a relevant tax year.

(8)   The person is not entitled to relief under section 448 (annual payments: relief for individuals) or 449 (annual payments: relief for other persons) of ITA 2007 for any payment made in the restricted period.

(9)   No deduction of expenses referable to a relevant accounting period is to be made under section 1219(1) of CTA 2009 (expenses of management of a company's investment business).

(10)   No reduction is to be made under section 45(4) of CTA 2010 (carry-forward of trade loss relief) in calculating the profits for a relevant accounting period of a trade carried on by the person.

(11)   In calculating the total amount of chargeable gains accruing to a person in a relevant tax year (or part of a relevant tax year), no losses are to be deducted under subsections (2) to (2B) of section 2 of TCGA 1992 (persons and gains chargeable to capital gains tax, and allowable losses).

(12)   In calculating the total amount of ATED-related chargeable gains accruing to a person in a relevant tax year, no losses are to be deducted under subsection (3) of section 2B of TCGA 1992 (persons chargeable to capital gains tax on ATED-related gains).

(13)   In calculating the total amount of chargeable NRCGT gains accruing to a person in a relevant tax year on relevant high value disposals, no losses are to be deducted under subsection (2) of section 14D of TCGA 1992 (persons chargeable to capital gains tax on NRCGT gains).

(14)   If the person is a company, no deduction is to be made under section 62 of CTA 2010 (relief for losses made in UK property business) from the company's total profits of a relevant accounting period.

*Finance Act 2016 (c. **24**)*
Schedule 18 — Serial tax avoidance
Part 4 — Restriction of reliefs

567

(15) No deduction is to be made under regulation 18 of the Unauthorised Unit Trusts (Tax) Regulations 2013 (S.I. 2013/2819) (relief for deemed payments by trustees of an exempt unauthorised unit trust) in calculating the person's net income for a relevant tax year.

(16) In this paragraph "relevant tax year" means any tax year the first day of which is in the restricted period.

(17) In this paragraph "relevant accounting period" means an accounting period the first day of which is in the restricted period.

(18) In this paragraph "double taxation arrangements" means arrangements which have effect under section 2(1) of TIOPA 2010 (double taxation relief by agreement with territories outside the UK).

The restricted period

21 (1) In paragraphs 19 and 20 (and this paragraph) "the restricted period" means the period of 3 years beginning with the day on which the relief restriction notice is given.

(2) If during the restricted period (or the restricted period as extended under this sub-paragraph) the person to whom a relief restriction notice has been given incurs a further relevant defeat meeting the conditions in sub-paragraph (4), HMRC must give the person a written notice (a "restricted period extension notice").

(3) A restricted period extension notice extends the restricted period to the end of the period of 3 years beginning with the day on which the further relevant defeat occurs.

(4) The conditions mentioned in sub-paragraph (2) are that—
   (a) the relevant defeat is incurred by virtue of Condition A, B or C in relation to arrangements which the person used in the warning period mentioned in paragraph 19(1)(a), and
   (b) the warning notice given to the person in respect of the relevant defeat relates to the misuse of a relief.

(5) If the person to whom a relief restriction notice has been given incurs a relevant defeat which meets the conditions in sub-paragraph (4) after the restricted period has expired but before the end of a concurrent warning period, HMRC must give the person a restriction of relief notice.

(6) In sub-paragraph (5) "concurrent warning period" means a warning period which at some time ran concurrently with the restricted period.

Reasonable excuse

22 (1) If a person who has incurred a relevant defeat satisfies HMRC or, on an appeal under paragraph 24, the First-tier Tribunal or Upper Tribunal that the person had a reasonable excuse for the matters to which that relevant defeat relates, then—
   (a) for the purposes of paragraph 19(1)(a) and 21(2) and (5), the person is treated as not having incurred that relevant defeat, and
   (b) for the purposes of paragraph 19(1)(b) and (c) any warning notice given to the person which relates to that relevant defeat is treated as not having been given to the person.

568   *Finance Act 2016 (c. 24)*
Schedule 18 — Serial tax avoidance
Part 4 — Restriction of reliefs

(2) For the purposes of this paragraph, in the case of a person ("P") —

    (a) an insufficiency of funds is not a reasonable excuse unless attributable to events outside P's control,

    (b) where P relies on another person to do anything, that is not a reasonable excuse unless P took reasonable care to avoid the relevant failure, and

    (c) where P had reasonable excuse for the relevant failure but the excuse had ceased, P is to be treated as having continued to have the excuse if the failure is remedied without unreasonable delay after the excuse ceased.

(3) In determining for the purposes of this paragraph whether or not a person ("P") had a reasonable excuse for any action, failure or inaccuracy, reliance on advice is to be taken automatically not to constitute a reasonable excuse if the advice is addressed to, or was given to, a person other than P or takes no account of P's individual circumstances.

(4) In this paragraph "relevant failure", in relation to a relevant defeat, is to be interpreted in accordance with sub-paragraphs (2) to (7) of paragraph 43.

Mitigation of restriction of relief

23   (1) The Commissioners may mitigate the effects of paragraph 20 in relation to a person ("P") so far as it appears to them that there are exceptional circumstances such that the operation of that paragraph would otherwise have an unduly serious impact with respect to the tax affairs of P or another person.

    (2) For the purposes of sub-paragraph (1) the Commissioners may modify the effects of paragraph 20 in any way they think appropriate, including by allowing P access to the whole or part of a relief to which P would otherwise not be entitled as a result of paragraph 20.

Appeal

24   (1) A person may appeal against —

    (a) a relief restriction notice, or

    (b) a restricted period extension notice.

    (2) An appeal under this paragraph must be made within the period of 30 days beginning with the day on which the notice is given.

    (3) An appeal under this paragraph is to be treated in the same way as an appeal against an assessment to income tax (including by the application of any provision about bringing the appeal by notice to HMRC, about HMRC's review of the decision or about determination of the appeal by the First-tier Tribunal or Upper Tribunal).

    (4) On an appeal the tribunal may —

    (a) cancel HMRC's decision, or

    (b) affirm that decision with or without any modifications in accordance with sub-paragraph (5).

    (5) On an appeal the tribunal may rely on paragraph 23 (mitigation of restriction of relief) —

Finance Act 2016 (c. 24)
Schedule 18 — Serial tax avoidance
Part 4 — Restriction of reliefs

569

    (a)   to the same extent as HMRC (which may mean applying the same mitigation as HMRC to a different starting point), or

    (b)   to a different extent, but only if the tribunal thinks that HMRC's decision in respect of the application of paragraph 23 was flawed.

(6) In this paragraph "tribunal" means the First-tier Tribunal or Upper Tribunal (as appropriate by virtue of sub-paragraph (3)).

Meaning of "avoidance-related rule"

25 (1) In this Part of this Schedule "avoidance-related rule" means a rule in Category 1 or 2.

(2) A rule is in Category 1 if it refers (in whatever terms)—

    (a)   to the purpose or main purpose or purposes of a transaction, arrangements or any other action or matter, and

    (b)   to whether or not the purpose in question is or involves the avoidance of tax or the obtaining of any advantage in relation to tax (however described).

(3) A rule is also in Category 1 if it refers (in whatever terms) to—

    (a)   expectations as to what are, or may be, the expected benefits of a transaction, arrangements or any other action or matter, and

    (b)   whether or not the avoidance of tax or the obtaining of any advantage in relation to tax (however described) is such a benefit.

For the purposes of paragraph (b) it does not matter whether the reference is (for instance) to the "sole or main benefit" or "one of the main benefits" or any other reference to a benefit.

(4) A rule falls within Category 2 if as a result of the rule a person may be treated differently for tax purposes depending on whether or not purposes referred to in the rule (for instance the purposes of an actual or contemplated action or enterprise) are (or are shown to be) commercial purposes.

(5) For example, a rule in the following form would fall within Category 1 and within Category 2—

> **"Example rule**
> Section X does not apply to a company in respect of a transaction if the company shows that the transaction meets Condition A or B.
>
> Condition A is that the transaction is effected—
>> (a) for genuine commercial reasons, or
>> (b) in the ordinary course of managing investments.
>
> Condition B is that the avoidance of tax is not the main object or one of the main objects of the transaction."

Meaning of "relief"

26   The following are "reliefs" for the purposes of this Part of this Schedule—

    (a)   any relief from tax (however described) which must be claimed, or which is not available without making an election,

    (b)   relief under section 1219 of CTA 2009 (expenses of management of a company's investment business),

570

Finance Act 2016 (c. 24)
Schedule 18 — Serial tax avoidance
Part 4 — Restriction of reliefs

(c) any relief (not falling within paragraph (a)) under Part 4 of ITA 2007 (loss relief) or Part 4 or 5 of CTA 2010 (loss relief and group relief), and

(d) any relief (not falling within paragraph (a) or (b)) under a provision listed in section 24 of ITA 2007 (reliefs deductible at Step 2 of the calculation of income tax liability).

"Claim" for relief

27   In this Part of this Schedule "claim for relief" includes any election or other similar action which is in substance a claim for relief.

VAT

28   In this Part of this Schedule "tax" does not include VAT.

Power to amend

29 (1) The Treasury may by regulations—

   (a) amend paragraph 20;

   (b) amend paragraph 26.

(2) Regulations under sub-paragraph (1)(a) may, in particular, alter the application of paragraph 20 in relation to any relief, exclude any relief from its application or extend its application to further reliefs.

(3) Regulations under sub-paragraph (1)(b) may amend the meaning of "relief" in any way (including by extending or limiting the meaning).

(4) Regulations under this paragraph may—

   (a) make supplementary, incidental and consequential provision;

   (b) make transitional provision.

(5) Regulations under this paragraph are to be made by statutory instrument.

(6) A statutory instrument containing regulations under this paragraph may not be made unless a draft of the instrument has been laid before and approved by a resolution of the House of Commons.

PART 5

PENALTY

Penalty

30 (1) A person is liable to pay a penalty if the person incurs a relevant defeat in relation to any arrangements which the person has used in a warning period.

(2) The penalty is 20% of the value of the counteracted advantage if neither sub-paragraph (3) nor sub-paragraph (4) applies.

(3) The penalty is 40% of the value of the counteracted advantage if before the relevant defeat is incurred the person has been given, or become liable to be given, one (but not more than one) relevant prior warning notice.

(4) The penalty is 60% of the value of the counteracted advantage if before the current defeat is incurred the person has been given, or become liable to be given, two or more relevant prior warning notices.

(5) In this paragraph "relevant prior warning notice" means a warning notice in relation to the defeat of arrangements which the person has used in the warning period mentioned in sub-paragraph (1).

(6) For the meaning of "the value of the counteracted advantage" see paragraphs 32 to 37.

Simultaneous defeats etc

31 (1) If a person incurs simultaneously two or more relevant defeats in relation to different arrangements, sub-paragraphs (2) to (4) of paragraph 30 have effect as if the relevant defeat with the lowest value was incurred last, the relevant defeat with the next lowest value immediately before it, and so on.

(2) For this purpose the "value" of a relevant defeat is taken to be equal to the value of the counteracted advantage.

(3) If a person has been given a single warning notice in relation to two or more relevant defeats, the person is treated for the purposes of paragraph 30 as having been given a separate warning notice in relation to each of those relevant defeats.

Value of the counteracted advantage: basic rule for taxes other than VAT

32 (1) In relation to a relevant defeat incurred by virtue of Condition A, B or C, the "value of the counteracted advantage" is —
   (a) in the case of a relevant defeat incurred by virtue of Condition A, the additional amount due or payable in respect of tax as a result of the counteraction mentioned in paragraph 12(1)(c);
   (b) in the case of a relevant defeat incurred by virtue of Condition B, the additional amount due or payable in respect of tax as a result of the action mentioned in paragraph 13(1);
   (c) in the case of a relevant defeat incurred by virtue of Condition C, the additional amount due or payable in respect of tax as a result of the counteraction mentioned in paragraph 14(1)(d).

(2) The reference in sub-paragraph (1) to the additional amount due and payable includes a reference to —
   (a) an amount payable to HMRC having erroneously been paid by way of repayment of tax, and
   (b) an amount which would be repayable by HMRC if the counteraction mentioned in paragraph (a) or (c) of sub-paragraph (1) were not made or the action mentioned in paragraph (b) of that sub-paragraph were not taken (as the case may be).

(3) The following are ignored in calculating the value of the counteracted advantage —
   (a) group relief, and
   (b) any relief under section 458 of CTA 2010 (relief in respect of repayment etc of loan) which is deferred under subsection (5) of that section.

(4) This paragraph is subject to paragraphs 33 and 34.

Value of counteracted advantage: losses for purposes of direct tax

33 (1) This paragraph has effect in relation to relevant defeats incurred by virtue of Condition A, B or C.

(2) To the extent that the counteracted advantage (see paragraph 35) has the result that a loss is wrongly recorded for the purposes of direct tax and the loss has been wholly used to reduce the amount due or payable in respect of tax, the value of the counteracted advantage is determined in accordance with paragraph 32.

(3) To the extent that the counteracted advantage has the result that a loss is wrongly recorded for purposes of direct tax and the loss has not been wholly used to reduce the amount due or payable in respect of tax, the value of the counteracted advantage is—
    (a) the value under paragraph 32 of so much of the counteracted advantage as results from the part (if any) of the loss which is used to reduce the amount due or payable in respect of tax, plus
    (b) 10% of the part of the loss not so used.

(4) Sub-paragraphs (2) and (3) apply both—
    (a) to a case where no loss would have been recorded but for the counteracted advantage, and
    (b) to a case where a loss of a different amount would have been recorded (but in that case sub-paragraphs (2) and (3) apply only to the difference between the amount recorded and the true amount).

(5) To the extent that a counteracted advantage creates or increases an aggregate loss recorded for a group of companies—
    (a) the value of the counteracted advantage is calculated in accordance with this paragraph, and
    (b) in applying paragraph 32 in accordance with sub-paragraphs (2) and (3), group relief may be taken into account (despite paragraph 32(3)).

(6) To the extent that the counteracted advantage results in a loss, the value of it is nil where, because of the nature of the loss or the person's circumstances, there is no reasonable prospect of the loss being used to support a claim to reduce a tax liability (of any person).

Value of counteracted advantage: deferred tax

34 (1) To the extent that the counteracted advantage (see paragraph 35) is a deferral of tax (other than VAT), the value of that advantage is—
    (a) 25% of the amount of the deferred tax for each year of the deferral, or
    (b) a percentage of the amount of the deferred tax, for each separate period of deferral of less than a year, equating to 25% per year,
    or, if less, 100% of the amount of the deferred tax.

(2) This paragraph does not apply to a case to the extent that paragraph 33 applies.

Meaning of "the counteracted advantage" in paragraphs 33 and 34

35 (1) In paragraphs 33 and 34 "the counteracted advantage" means—

    (a)   in relation to a relevant defeat incurred by virtue of Condition A, the tax advantage mentioned in paragraph 12(1)(b);

    (b)   in relation to a relevant defeat incurred by virtue of Condition B, the denied advantage in relation to which the action mentioned in paragraph 13(1) is taken;

    (c)   in relation to a relevant defeat incurred by virtue of Condition C, means any tax advantage in respect of which the counteraction mentioned in paragraph 14(1)(c) is made.

(2) In sub-paragraph (1)(c) "counteraction" is to be interpreted in accordance with paragraph 14(5).

Value of the counteracted advantage: Conditions D and E

36 (1) In relation to a relevant defeat incurred by a person by virtue of Condition D or E, the "value of the counteracted advantage" is equal to the sum of any counteracted tax advantages determined under sub-paragraphs (3) to (6).
But see also paragraph 37.

(2) In this paragraph "the counteraction" means the counteraction mentioned in paragraph 15(1) or 16(1) (as the case may be).

(3) If the amount of VAT due or payable by the person in respect of any prescribed accounting period (X) exceeds the amount (Y) that would have been so payable but for the counteraction, the amount by which X exceeds Y is a counteracted tax advantage.

(4) If the person obtains no VAT credit for a particular prescribed accounting period, the amount of any VAT credit which the person would have obtained for that period but for the counteraction is a counteracted tax advantage.

(5) If for a prescribed accounting period the person obtains a VAT credit of an amount (Y) which is less than the amount (X) of the VAT credit which the person would have obtained but for the counteraction, the amount by which X exceeds Y is a counteracted tax advantage.

(6) If the amount (X) of the person's non-deductible tax for any prescribed accounting period is greater than Y, where Y is what would be the amount of the person's non-deductible tax for that period but for the counteraction, then the amount by which X exceeds Y is a counteracted tax advantage, but only to the extent that amount is not represented by a corresponding amount which is the whole or part of a counteracted tax advantage by virtue of sub-paragraphs (3) to (5).

(7) In this paragraph "non-deductible tax", in relation to the person who incurred the relevant defeat, means—

    (a)   input tax for which the person is not entitled to credit under section 25 of VATA 1994, and

    (b)   any VAT incurred by the person which is not input tax and in respect of which the person is not entitled to a refund from the Commissioners by virtue of any provision of VATA 1994.

(8) For the purposes of sub-paragraph (7)(b) the VAT "incurred" by a taxable person is—

    (a)   VAT on the supply to the person of any goods or services,

    (b)   VAT on the acquisition by the person from another member State of any goods;

    (c)   VAT on the importation of any goods from a place outside the member States.

(9)   References in sub-paragraph (3) to amounts due and payable by the person in respect of a prescribed accounting period include references to—

    (a)   amounts payable to HMRC having erroneously been paid by way of repayment of tax, and

    (b)   amounts which would be repayable by HMRC if the counteraction mentioned in sub-paragraph (3) were not made.

Value of counteracted advantage: delayed VAT

37   (1)   Sub-paragraph (3) of paragraph 36 has effect as follows so far as the tax advantage which is counteracted as mentioned in that sub-paragraph is in the nature of a delay in relation to the person's obligations with respect to VAT.

    (2)   That sub-paragraph has effect as if for "the amount by which X exceeds Y is a counteracted tax advantage" there were substituted, "there is a counteracted tax advantage of—

        (d)   25% of the amount of the delayed VAT for each year of the delay, or

        (e)   a percentage of the amount of the delayed VAT, for each separate period of delay of less than a year, equating to 25% per year,

    or, if less, 100% of the amount of the delayed VAT".

Assessment of penalty

38   (1)   Where a person is liable for a penalty under paragraph 30, HMRC must assess the penalty.

    (2)   Where HMRC assess the penalty, HMRC must—

    (a)   notify the person who is liable for the penalty, and

    (b)   state in the notice a tax period in respect of which the penalty is assessed.

    (3)   A penalty under this paragraph must be paid before the end of the period of 30 days beginning with the day on which the person is notified of the penalty under sub-paragraph (2).

    (4)   An assessment—

    (a)   is to be treated for procedural purposes as if it were an assessment to tax,

    (b)   may be enforced as if it were an assessment to tax, and

    (c)   may be combined with an assessment to tax.

    (5)   An assessment of a penalty under this paragraph must be made before the end of the period of 12 months beginning with the date of the defeat mentioned in paragraph 30(1).

Alteration of assessment of penalty

39　(1)　After notification of an assessment has been given to a person under paragraph 38(2), the assessment may not be altered except in accordance with this paragraph or on appeal.

　　(2)　A supplementary assessment may be made in respect of a penalty if an earlier assessment operated by reference to an underestimate of the value of the counteracted advantage.

　　(3)　An assessment may be revised as necessary if operated by reference to an overestimate of the value of the counteracted advantage.

Aggregate penalties

40　(1)　The amount of a penalty for which a person is liable under paragraph 30 is to be reduced by the amount of any other penalty incurred by the person, or any surcharge for late payment of tax imposed on the person, if the amount of the penalty or surcharge is determined by reference to the same tax liability.

　　(2)　In sub-paragraph (1) "any other penalty" does not include a penalty under section 212A of FA 2013 (GAAR penalty) or Part 4 of FA 2014 (penalty where corrective action not taken after follower notice etc).

　　(3)　In the application of section 97A of TMA 1970 (multiple penalties) no account shall be taken of a penalty under paragraph 30.

Appeal against penalty

41　(1)　A person may appeal against a decision of HMRC that a penalty is payable under paragraph 30.

　　(2)　A person may appeal against a decision of HMRC as to the amount of a penalty payable by P under paragraph 30.

　　(3)　An appeal under this paragraph must be made within the period of 30 days beginning with the day on which notification of the penalty is given under paragraph 38.

　　(4)　An appeal under this paragraph is to be treated in the same way as an appeal against an assessment to the tax concerned (including by the application of any provision about bringing the appeal by notice to HMRC, about HMRC's review of the decision or about determination of the appeal by the First-tier Tribunal or Upper Tribunal).

　　(5)　Sub-paragraph (4) does not apply—
　　　　(a)　so as to require a person to pay a penalty before an appeal against the assessment of the penalty is determined, or
　　　　(b)　in respect of any other matter expressly provided for by this Part of this Schedule.

　　(6)　On an appeal under sub-paragraph (1) or (2) the tribunal may—
　　　　(a)　affirm HMRC's decision, or
　　　　(b)　substitute for HMRC's decision another decision that HMRC has power to make.

(7) In this paragraph "tribunal" means the First-tier Tribunal or Upper Tribunal (as appropriate by virtue of sub-paragraph (4)).

Penalties: reasonable excuse

42 (1) A person is not liable to a penalty under paragraph 30 in respect of a relevant defeat if the person satisfies HMRC or (on appeal) the First-tier Tribunal or Upper Tribunal that the person had a reasonable excuse for the relevant failure to which that relevant defeat relates (see paragraph 43).

(2) Sub-paragraph (3) applies if—

   (a)   a person has incurred a relevant defeat in respect of which the person is liable to a penalty under paragraph 30, and

   (b)   before incurring that defeat the person had been given, or become liable to be given, an excepted warning notice.

(3) The person is treated for the purposes of sub-paragraphs (2) to (4) of paragraph 30 (rate of penalty) as not having been given, and not having become liable to be given, the excepted notice (so far as it relates to the relevant defeat in respect of which the person had a reasonable excuse).

(4) A warning notice is "excepted" for the purposes of this paragraph if the person was not liable to a penalty in respect of the defeat specified in it because the person had a reasonable excuse for the relevant failure in question.

(5) For the purposes of this paragraph, in the case of a person ("P")—

   (a)   an insufficiency of funds is not a reasonable excuse unless attributable to events outside P's control,

   (b)   where P relies on another person to do anything, that is not a reasonable excuse unless P took reasonable care to avoid the relevant failure, and

   (c)   where P had a reasonable excuse for the relevant failure but the excuse had ceased, P is to be treated as having continued to have the excuse if the failure is remedied without unreasonable delay after the excuse ceased.

(6) In determining for the purposes of this paragraph whether or not a person ("P") had a reasonable excuse for any action, failure or inaccuracy, reliance on advice is to be taken automatically not to constitute a reasonable excuse if the advice is addressed to, or was given to, a person other than P or takes no account of P's individual circumstances.

Paragraph 42: meaning of "the relevant failure"

43 (1) In paragraph 42 "the relevant failure", in relation to a relevant defeat, is to be interpreted in accordance with sub-paragraphs (2) to (7).

(2) In relation to a relevant defeat incurred by virtue of Condition A, "the relevant failure" means the failures or inaccuracies as a result of which the counteraction under section 209 of FA 2013 was necessary

(3) In relation to a relevant defeat incurred by virtue of Condition B, "the relevant failure" means the failures or inaccuracies in respect of which the action mentioned in paragraph 13(1) was taken.

(4) In relation to a relevant defeat incurred by virtue of Condition C, "the relevant failure" means the failures of inaccuracies as a result of which the adjustments, assessments, or other action mentioned in paragraph 14(5) are required.

(5) In relation to a relevant defeat incurred by virtue of Condition D, "the relevant failure" means the failures or inaccuracies as a result of which the adjustments, assessments or other action mentioned in paragraph 15(5) are required.

(6) In relation to a relevant defeat incurred by virtue of Condition E, "the relevant failure" means P's actions (and failures to act), so far as they are connected with matters in respect of which the counteraction mentioned in paragraph 16(1) is required.

(7) In sub-paragraph (6) "counteraction" is to be interpreted in accordance with paragraph 16(2).

Mitigation of penalties

44 (1) The Commissioners may in their discretion mitigate a penalty under paragraph 30, or stay or compound any proceedings for such a penalty.

(2) They may also, after judgment, further mitigate or entirely remit the penalty.

PART 6

CORPORATE GROUPS, ASSOCIATED PERSONS AND PARTNERSHIPS

Representative member of a VAT group

45 (1) Where a body corporate ("R") is the representative member of a group (and accordingly is treated for the purposes of this Schedule as mentioned in section 43(1) of VATA 1994), anything which has been done by or in relation to another body corporate ("B") in B's capacity as representative member of that group is treated for the purposes of this Schedule as having been done by or in relation to R in R's capacity as representative member of the group. Accordingly paragraph 3 (warning period) operates as if the successive representative members of a group were a single person.

(2) This Schedule has effect as if the representative member of a group, so far as acting in its capacity as such, were a different person from that body corporate so far as acting in any other capacity.

(3) In this paragraph the reference to a "group" is to be interpreted in accordance with sections 43A to 43D of VATA 1994.

Corporate groups

46 (1) Sub-paragraphs (2) and (3) apply if HMRC has a duty under paragraph 2 to give a warning notice to a company ("C") which is a member of a group.

(2) That duty has effect as a duty to give a warning notice to each current group member (see sub-paragraph (8)).

(3) Any warning notice which has been given (or is treated as having been given) previously to any current group member is treated as having been given to each current group member (and any provision in this Schedule

578

Finance Act 2016 (c. 24)
Schedule 18 — Serial tax avoidance
Part 6 — Corporate groups, associated persons and partnerships

which refers to a "warning period" in relation to a person is to be interpreted accordingly).

But see sub-paragraphs (4) and (5).

(4) In relation to a company which incurs a relevant defeat, paragraph 19(1) (duty to give relief restriction notice) does not have effect unless the warning period mentioned in that sub-paragraph would be a warning period in relation to the company regardless of sub-paragraph (3).

(5) A company which incurs a relevant defeat is not liable to pay a penalty under paragraph 30 unless the warning period mentioned in sub-paragraph (1) of that paragraph would be a warning period in relation to the company regardless of sub-paragraph (3).

(6) HMRC may discharge any duty to give a warning notice to a current group member in accordance with sub-paragraph (2) by delivering the notice to C (and if it does so may combine one or more warning notices in a single notice).

(7) If a company ceases to be a member of a group, and —

   (a) immediately before it ceases to be a member of the group, a warning period has effect in relation to the company, but

   (b) no warning period would have effect in relation to the company at that time but for sub-paragraph (2) or (3),

   that warning period ceases to have effect in relation to the company when it ceases to be a member of that group.

(8) In this paragraph "current group member" means a company which is a member of the group concerned at the time when the warning notice mentioned in sub-paragraph (1) is given.

(9) For the purposes of this paragraph two companies are members of the same group of companies if —

   (a) one is a 75% subsidiary of the other, or

   (b) both are 75% subsidiaries of a third company.

(10) In this paragraph "75% subsidiary" has the meaning given by section 1154 of CTA 2010.

(11) In this paragraph "company" has the same meaning as in the Corporation Tax Acts (see section 1121 of CTA 2010).

Associated persons treated as incurring relevant defeats

47 (1) Sub-paragraph (2) applies if a person ("P") incurs a relevant defeat in relation to any arrangements (otherwise than by virtue of this paragraph).

   (2) Any person ("S") who is associated with P at the relevant time is also treated for the purposes of paragraphs 2 (duty to give warning notice) and 3(2) (warning period) as having incurred that relevant defeat in relation to those arrangements (but see sub-paragraph (3)).

   For the meaning of "associated" see paragraph 48.

   (3) Sub-paragraph (2) does not apply if P and S are members of the same group of companies (as defined in paragraph 46(9)).

Finance Act 2016 (c. 24)
Schedule 18 – Serial tax avoidance
Part 6 – Corporate groups, associated persons and partnerships

579

(4) In relation to a warning notice given to S by virtue of sub-paragraph (2), paragraph 2(4)(c) (certain information to be included in warning notice) is to be read as referring only to paragraphs 3, 17 and 18.

(5) A warning notice which is given to a person by virtue of sub-paragraph (2) is treated for the purposes of paragraphs 19(1) (duty to give relief restriction notice) and 30 (penalty) as not having been given to that person.

(6) In sub-paragraph (2) "the relevant time" means the time when P is given a warning notice in respect of the relevant defeat.

Meaning of "associated"

48 (1) For the purposes of paragraph 47 two persons are associated with one another if —
   (a)   one of them is a body corporate which is controlled by the other, or
   (b)   they are bodies corporate under common control.

(2) Two bodies corporate are under common control if both are controlled —
   (a)   by one person,
   (b)   by two or more, but fewer than six, individuals, or
   (c)   by any number of individuals carrying on business in partnership.

(3) For the purposes of this section a body corporate ("H") is taken to control another body corporate ("B") if —
   (a)   H is empowered by statute to control B's activities, or
   (b)   H is B's holding company within the meaning of section 1159 of and Schedule 6 to the Companies Act 2006.

(4) For the purposes of this section an individual or individuals are taken to control a body corporate ("B") if the individual or individuals, were they a body corporate, would be B's holding company within the meaning of those provisions.

Partners treated as incurring relevant defeats

49 (1) Where paragraph 50 applies in relation to a partnership return, each relevant partner is treated for the purposes of this Schedule as having incurred the relevant defeat mentioned in paragraph 50(1)(b), (2) or (3)(b) (as the case may be).

(2) In this paragraph "relevant partner" means any person who was a partner in the partnership at any time during the relevant reporting period (but see sub-paragraph (3)).

(3) The "relevant partners" do not include —
   (a)   the person mentioned in sub-paragraph (1)(b), (2) or (3)(b) (as the case may be) of paragraph 50, or
   (b)   any other person who would, apart from this paragraph, incur a relevant defeat in connection with the subject matter of the partnership return mentioned in sub-paragraph (1).

(4) In this paragraph the "relevant reporting period" means the period in respect of which the partnership return mentioned in sub-paragraph (1), (2) or (3) of paragraph 50 was required.

580

Finance Act 2016 (c. 24)
Schedule 18 — Serial tax avoidance
Part 6 — Corporate groups, associated persons and partnerships

Partnership returns to which this paragraph applies

50 (1) This paragraph applies in relation to a partnership return if—

    (a) that return has been made on the basis that a tax advantage arises to a partner from any arrangements, and

    (b) that person has incurred, in relation to that tax advantage and those arrangements, a relevant defeat by virtue of Condition A (final counteraction of tax advantage under general anti-abuse rule).

    (2) Where a person has incurred a relevant defeat by virtue of sub-paragraph (2) of paragraph 13 (Condition B: case involving partnership follower notice) this paragraph applies in relation to the partnership return mentioned in that sub-paragraph.

    (3) This paragraph applies in relation to a partnership return if—

    (a) that return has been made on the basis that a tax advantage arises to a partner from any arrangements, and

    (b) that person has incurred, in relation to that tax advantage and those arrangements, a relevant defeat by virtue of Condition C (return, claim or election made in reliance on DOTAS arrangements).

    (4) The references in this paragraph to a relevant defeat do not include a relevant defeat incurred by virtue of paragraph 47(2).

Partnerships: information

51 (1) If paragraph 50 applies in relation to a partnership return, the appropriate partner must give HMRC a written notice (a "partnership information notice") in respect of each sub-period in the information period.

    (2) The "information period" is the period of 5 years beginning with the day after the day of the relevant defeat mentioned in paragraph 50.

    (3) If, in the case of a partnership, a new information period (relating to another partnership return) begins during an existing information period, those periods are treated for the purposes of this paragraph as a single period (which includes all times that would otherwise fall within either period).

    (4) An information period under this paragraph ends if the partnership ceases.

    (5) A partnership information notice must be given not later than the 30th day after the end of the sub-period to which it relates.

    (6) A partnership information notice must state—

    (a) whether or not any relevant partnership return which was, or was required to be, delivered in the sub-period has been made on the basis that a relevant tax advantage arises, and

    (b) whether or not there has been a failure to deliver a relevant partnership return in the sub-period.

    (7) In this paragraph—

    (a) "relevant partnership return" means a partnership return in respect of the partnership's trade, profession or business;

    (b) "relevant tax advantage" means a tax advantage which particular DOTAS arrangements enable, or might be expected to enable, a person who is or has been a partner in the partnership to obtain.

Finance Act 2016 (c. 24)
Schedule 18 — Serial tax avoidance
Part 6 — Corporate groups, associated persons and partnerships

581

(8) If a partnership information notice states that a relevant partnership return has been made on the basis mentioned in sub-paragraph (6)(a) the notice must—

    (a) explain (on the assumptions made for the purposes of the return) how the DOTAS arrangements enable the tax advantage concerned to be obtained, and

    (b) describe any variation in the amounts required to be stated in the return under section 12AB(1) of TMA 1970 which results from those arrangements.

(9) HMRC may require the appropriate partner to give HMRC a notice (a "supplementary information notice") setting out further information in relation to a partnership information notice.

In relation to a partnership information notice "further information" means information which would have been required to be set out in the notice by virtue of sub-paragraph (6)(a) or (8) had there not been a failure to deliver a relevant partnership return.

(10) A requirement under sub-paragraph (9) must be made by a written notice and the notice must state the period within which the notice must be complied with.

(11) If a person fails to comply with a requirement of (or imposed under) this paragraph, HMRC may by written notice extend the information period concerned to the end of the period of 5 years beginning with—

    (a) the day by which the partnership information notice or supplementary information notice was required to be given to HMRC or, as the case requires,

    (b) the day on which the person gave the defective notice to HMRC,

or, if earlier, the time when the information period would have expired but for the extension.

(12) For the purposes of this paragraph—

    (a) the first sub-period in an information period begins with the first day of the information period and ends with a day specified by HMRC,

    (b) the remainder of the information period is divided into further sub-periods each of which begins immediately after the end of the preceding sub-period and is twelve months long or (if that would be shorter) ends at the end of the information period.

(13) In this paragraph "the appropriate partner" means the partner in the partnership who is for the time being nominated by HMRC for the purposes of this paragraph.

Partnerships: special provision about taxpayer emendations

52 (1) Sub-paragraph (2) applies if a partnership return is amended at any time under section 12ABA of TMA 1970 (amendment of partnership return by representative partner etc) on a basis that—

    (a) results in an increase or decrease in, or

    (b) otherwise affects the calculation of,

any amount stated under subsection (1)(b) of section 12AB of that Act (partnership statement) as a partner's share of any income, loss, consideration, tax or credit for any period.

582

*Finance Act 2016 (c. **24**)*
Schedule 18 — Serial tax avoidance
Part 6 — Corporate groups, associated persons and partnerships

(2) For the purposes of paragraph 14 (Condition C: counteraction of DOTAS arrangements), the partner is treated as having at that time amended —

    (a)   the partner's return under section 8 or 8A of TMA 1970, or

    (b)   the partner's company tax return,

so as to give effect to the amendments of the partnership return.

(3) Sub-paragraph (4) applies if a partnership return is amended at any time by HMRC as a result of a disclosure made by the representative partner or that person's successor on a basis that —

    (a)   results in an increase or decrease in, or

    (b)   otherwise affects the calculation of,

any amount stated under subsection (1)(b) of section 12AB of TMA 1970 (partnership statement) as the share of a particular partner (P) of any income, loss, consideration, tax or credit for any period.

(4) If the conditions in sub-paragraph (5) are met, P is treated for the purposes of paragraph 14 as having at that time amended —

    (a)   P's return under section 8 or 8A of TMA 1970, or

    (b)   P's company tax return,

so as to give effect to the amendments of the partnership return.

(5) The conditions are that the disclosure —

    (a)   is a full and explicit disclosure of an inaccuracy in the partnership return, and

    (b)   was made at a time when neither the person making the disclosure nor P had reason to believe that HMRC was about to begin enquiries into the partnership return.

Supplementary provision relating to partnerships

53   (1) In paragraphs 49 to 52 and this paragraph —

       "partnership" is to be interpreted in accordance with section 12AA of TMA 1970 (and includes a limited liability partnership);

       "the representative partner", in relation to a partnership return, means the person who was required by a notice served under or for the purposes of section 12AA(2) or (3) of TMA 1970 to deliver the return;

       "successor", in relation to a person who is the representative partner in the case of a partnership return, has the same meaning as in TMA 1970 (see section 118(1) of that Act).

   (2) For the purposes of this Part of this Schedule a partnership is treated as the same partnership notwithstanding a change in membership if any person who was a member before the change remains a member after the change.

PART 7

SUPPLEMENTAL

Meaning of "adjustments"

54   (1) In this Schedule "adjustments" means any adjustments, whether by way of an assessment, the modification of an assessment or return, amendment or disallowance of a claim, a payment, the entering into of a contract settlement, or otherwise (and references to "making" adjustments

accordingly include securing that adjustments are made by entering into a contract settlement).

(2) "Adjustments" also includes a payment in respect of a liability to pay national insurance contributions.

Time of "use" of defeated arrangements

55　(1) With reference to a particular relevant defeat incurred by a person in relation to arrangements, the person is treated as having "used" the arrangements on the dates set out in this paragraph.

(2) If the person incurs the relevant defeat by virtue of Condition A, the person is treated as having "used" the arrangements on the following dates —

   (a) the filing date of any return made by the person on the basis that the tax advantage mentioned in paragraph 12(1)(a) arises from the arrangements;

   (b) the date on which the person makes any claim or election on that basis;

   (c) the date of any relevant failure by the person to comply with an obligation.

(3) For the purposes of sub-paragraph (2) a failure to comply with an obligation is a "relevant failure" if the whole or part of the tax advantage mentioned in paragraph 12(1)(b) arose as a result of, or in connection with, that failure.

(4) If the person incurs the relevant defeat by virtue of Condition B, the person is treated as having "used" the arrangements on the following dates —

   (a) the filing date of any return made by the person on the basis that the asserted advantage (see section 204(3) of FA 2014) results from the arrangements,

   (b) the date on which any claim is made by the person on that basis,

   (c) the date of any failure by the person to comply with a relevant obligation.

In this sub-paragraph "relevant obligation" means an obligation which would not have fallen on the person (or might have been expected not to do so), had the denied advantage arisen (see section 208(3) of FA 2014).

(5) If the person incurs the relevant defeat by virtue of Condition C, the person is treated as having "used" the arrangements on the following dates —

   (a) the filing date of any return made by the person on the basis mentioned in paragraph 14(2)(a);

   (b) the date on which the person makes any claim or election on that basis;

   (c) the date of any failure by the person to comply with a relevant obligation (as defined in paragraph 14(4)).

(6) If the person incurs the relevant defeat by virtue of Condition D, the person is treated as having "used" the arrangements on the following dates —

   (a) the filing date of any return made by the person on the basis mentioned in paragraph 15(2)(a);

   (b) the date on which the person makes any claim on that basis;

   (c) the date of any failure by the person to comply with a relevant obligation (as defined in paragraph 15(4)).

(7) If the person incurs the relevant defeat by virtue of Condition E, the person is treated as having "used" the arrangements on the following dates—

    (a)   the filing date of any return made by S to which the counteraction mentioned in paragraph 16(1)(c) relates;

    (b)   the date on which S made any claim to which that counteraction relates;

    (c)   the date of any relevant failure by S to which that counteraction relates.

(8) In sub-paragraph (7) "relevant failure" means a failure to comply with an obligation relating to VAT.

(9) In this paragraph "filing date", in relation to a return, means the earlier of—

    (a)   the day on which the return is delivered, or

    (b)   the last day of the period within which the return must be delivered.

(10) References in this paragraph to the date on which a person fails to comply with an obligation are to the date on which the person is first in breach of the obligation.

Inheritance tax

56   (1) In the case of inheritance tax, each of the following is treated as a return for the purposes of this Schedule—

    (a)   an account delivered by a person under section 216 or 217 of IHTA 1984 (including an account delivered in accordance with regulations under section 256 of that Act);

    (b)   a statement or declaration which amends or is otherwise connected with such an account produced by the person who delivered the account;

    (c)   information or a document provided by a person in accordance with regulations under section 256 of that Act;

and such a return is treated as made by the person in question.

(2) In this Schedule (except where the context requires otherwise) "assessment", in relation to inheritance tax, includes a determination.

National insurance contributions

57   (1) In this Schedule references to an assessment to tax include a NICs decision relating to a person's liability for relevant contributions.

(2) In this Schedule a reference to a provision of Part 7 of FA 2004 (disclosure of tax avoidance schemes) (a "DOTAS provision") includes a reference to—

    (a)   that DOTAS provision as applied by regulations under section 132A of the Social Security Administration Act 1992 (disclosure of contributions avoidance arrangements);

    (b)   any provision of regulations under that section that corresponds to that DOTAS provision,

whenever the regulations are made.

(3) Regulations under section 132A of that Act may disapply, or modify the effect of, sub-paragraph (2).

    (4) In this paragraph "NICs decision" means a decision under section 8 of the Social Security Contributions (Transfer of Functions, etc) Act 1999 or Article 7 of the Social Security Contributions (Transfer of Functions, etc) (Northern Ireland) Order 1999 (S.I. 1999/671).

General interpretation

58   (1) In this Schedule—

    "arrangements" has the meaning given by paragraph 2(6);

    "the Commissioners" means the Commissioners for Her Majesty's Revenue and Customs;

    "contract settlement" means an agreement in connection with a person's liability to make a payment to the Commissioners under or by virtue of an enactment;

    "disclosable VAT arrangements" is to be interpreted in accordance with paragraph 9;

    "DOTAS arrangements" is to be interpreted in accordance with paragraph 8 (and see also paragraph 57(2));

    "follower notice" has the meaning given by paragraph 13(6);

    "HMRC" means Her Majesty's Revenue and Customs;

    "national insurance contributions" means contributions under Part 1 of the Social Security Contributions and Benefits Act 1992 or Part 1 of the Social Security Contributions and Benefits (Northern Ireland) Act 1992;

    "net income" has the meaning given by section 23 of ITA 2007 (see Step 2 of that section);

    "partnership follower notice" has the meaning given by paragraph 2(2) of Schedule 31 to FA 2014;

    "partnership return" means a return under section 12AA of TMA 1970;

    "relevant contributions" means the following contributions under Part 1 of the Social Security Contributions and Benefits Act 1992 or Part 1 of the Social Security Contributions and Benefits (Northern Ireland) Act 1992—

        (a) Class 1 contributions;

        (b) Class 1A contributions;

        (c) Class 1B contributions;

        (d) Class 2 contributions which must be paid but in relation to which section 11A of the Act in question (application of certain provisions of the Income Tax Acts in relation to Class 2 contributions under section 11(2) of that Act) does not apply;

    "relevant defeat" is to be interpreted in accordance with paragraph 11;

    "tax" has the meaning given by paragraph 4;

    "tax advantage" has the meaning given by paragraph 7;

    "warning notice" has the meaning given by paragraph 2.

    (2) In this Schedule an expression used in relation to VAT has the same meaning as in VATA 1994.

    (3) In this Schedule (except where the context requires otherwise) references, however expressed, to a person's affairs in relation to tax include the person's position as regards deductions or repayments of, or of sums

representing, tax that the person is required to make by or under an enactment.

(4) For the purposes of this Schedule a partnership return is regarded as made on the basis that a particular tax advantage arises to a person from particular arrangements if —

    (a)   it is made on the basis that an increase or reduction in one or more of the amounts mentioned in section 12AB(1) of TMA 1970 (amounts in the partnership statement in a partnership return) results from those arrangements, and

    (b)   that increase or reduction results in that tax advantage for the person.

Consequential amendments

59   In section 103ZA of TMA 1970 (disapplication of sections 100 to 103 in the case of certain penalties) —

    (a)   omit "or" at the end of paragraph (ga), and

    (b)   after paragraph (h) insert "or

        (i)   Part 5 of Schedule 18 to the Finance Act 2016 (serial tax avoidance)."

60   In section 212 of FA 2014 (follower notices: aggregate penalties), in subsection (4) —

    (a)   omit "or" at the end of paragraph (b), and

    (b)   after paragraph (c) insert ", or

        (d)   Part 5 of Schedule 18 to FA 2016 (serial tax avoidance)."

61   (1) The Social Security Contributions and Benefits Act 1992 is amended as follows.

   (2) In section 11A (application of certain provisions of the Income Tax Acts in relation to Class 2 contributions under section 11(2)), in subsection (1), at the end of paragraph (e) insert —

        "(ea)   the provisions of Schedule 18 to the Finance Act 2016 (serial tax avoidance);".

   (3) In section 16 (application of Income Tax Acts and destination of Class 4 contributions), in subsection (1), at the end of paragraph (d) insert "and

        "(e)   the provisions of Schedule 18 to the Finance Act 2016 (serial tax avoidance),".

62   In the Social Security Contributions and Benefits (Northern Ireland) Act 1992, in section 11A (application of certain provisions of the Income Tax Acts in relation to Class 2 contributions under section 11(2)), in subsection (1), at the end of paragraph (e) insert —

        "(ea)   the provisions of Schedule 18 to the Finance Act 2016 (serial tax avoidance);".

Commencement

63   Subject to paragraphs 64 and 65, paragraphs 1 to 62 of this Schedule have effect in relation to relevant defeats incurred after the day on which this Act is passed.

64 (1) A relevant defeat is to be disregarded for the purposes of this Schedule if it is incurred before 6 April 2017 in relation to arrangements which the person has entered into before the day on which this Act is passed.

(2) A relevant defeat incurred on or after 6 April 2017 is to be disregarded for the purposes of this Schedule if—

(a) the person entered into the arrangements concerned before the day on which this Act is passed, and

(b) before 6 April 2017—

(i) the person incurring the defeat fully discloses to HMRC the matters to which the relevant counteraction relates, or

(ii) that person gives HMRC notice of a firm intention to make a full disclosure of those matters and makes such a full disclosure within any time limit set by HMRC.

(3) In sub-paragraph (2) "the relevant counteraction" means—

(a) in a case within Condition A, the counteraction mentioned in paragraph 12(1)(c);

(b) in a case within Condition B, the action mentioned in paragraph 13(1);

(c) in a case within Condition C, the counteraction mentioned in paragraph 14(1)(c);

(d) in a case within Condition D, the counteraction mentioned in paragraph 15(1)(d);

(e) in a case within Condition E, the counteraction mentioned in paragraph 16(1)(c).

(4) In sub-paragraph (3)—

(a) in paragraph (c) "counteraction" is to be interpreted in accordance with paragraph 14(5);

(b) in paragraph (d) "counteraction" is to be interpreted in accordance with paragraph 15(5);

(c) in paragraph (e) "counteraction" is to be interpreted in accordance with paragraph 16(2).

(5) See paragraph 11(2) for provision about when a relevant defeat is incurred.

65 (1) A warning notice given to a person is to be disregarded for the purposes of—

(a) paragraph 18 (naming), and

(b) Part 4 of this Schedule (restriction of reliefs),

if the relevant defeat specified in the notice relates to arrangements which the person has entered into before the day on which this Act is passed.

(2) Where a person has entered into any arrangements before the day on which this Act is passed—

(a) a relevant defeat incurred by a person in relation to the arrangements, and

(b) any warning notice specifying such a relevant defeat,

is to be disregarded for the purposes of paragraph 30 (penalty).

SCHEDULE 19   Section 161

LARGE BUSINESSES: TAX STRATEGIES AND SANCTIONS

PART 1

INTERPRETATION

Purpose of Part 1

1   This Part defines terms for the purposes of this Schedule.

"Relevant body"

2   (1) "Relevant body" means a UK company or any other body corporate
           (wherever incorporated), but does not include a limited liability partnership.

      (2) A relevant body is a "foreign" relevant body (or member of a group or sub-
           group) if it is incorporated outside the United Kingdom.

"UK company"

3   (1) "UK company" means a company which is (or is treated as if it is) formed
           and registered under the Companies Act 2006, unless it falls within sub-
           paragraph (2).

      (2) The term "UK company" does not include a company which is—
           (a) an open-ended investment company within the meaning of section
                613 of CTA 2010, or
           (b) an investment trust within the meaning of section 1158 of CTA 2010.

"UK permanent establishment"

4   (1) "UK permanent establishment" means a permanent establishment in the
           United Kingdom of a foreign relevant body.

      (2) In sub-paragraph (1) "permanent establishment" has the same meaning as it
           has for the purposes of the Corporation Tax Acts (see section 1141 to 1144 of
           CTA 2010).

"Qualifying company"

5   (1) A UK company is a "qualifying company" in any financial year (subject to
           any regulations under sub-paragraph (5)) if sub-paragraph (2) or (3) applies
           to it.

      (2) This sub-paragraph applies to the company if, at the end of the previous
           financial year—
           (a) it satisfied the qualification test for a UK company, and
           (b) was not a member of a UK group or a UK sub-group.

      (3) This sub-paragraph applies to the company if, at the end of the previous
           financial year—
           (a) it was a member of a foreign group,
           (b) the group met the qualification test for a group, and
           (c) it was not a member of a UK sub-group of that foreign group.

(4) The qualification test for a UK company is that the company satisfied either or both of the following conditions (by reference to the previous financial year) —

1. The company's turnover	More than £200 million
2. The company's balance sheet total	More than £2 billion.

(5) The Treasury may by regulations provide that a company of a description specified in the regulations is not a qualifying company for the purposes of this Schedule (or any such purpose specified in the regulations).

(6) For the purposes of this paragraph a UK permanent establishment of a foreign relevant body is to be treated as if it were —

    (a)   a UK company, and

    (b)   if the foreign relevant body is a member of a UK group or a UK sub-group, a member of that group or sub-group.

"Group" and related expressions

6   (1)   "Group" means two or more relevant bodies which together constitute —

    (a)   an MNE Group (see paragraph 7), or

    (b)   a group other than an MNE group (see paragraph 8).

    (2)   "UK group" means a group whose head is a relevant body incorporated in the United Kingdom.

    (3)   "Foreign group" means a group whose head is a foreign relevant body.

    (4)   For the purposes of sub-paragraphs (2) and (3) it is immaterial where other members of the group are incorporated.

7   (1)   "MNE Group" has the same meaning (subject to sub-paragraph (2) below) as in the OECD Model Legislation in the OECD Country-by-Country Reporting Implementation Package as contained in the OECD's Guidance on Transfer Pricing Documentation and Country-by-Country Reporting published in 2014.

    (2)   Paragraph (ii) (excluded MNE Group) of the Implementation Package is not part of the definition applied by sub-paragraph (1) above for the purposes of this Schedule.

    (3)   In sub-paragraph (1) "OECD" means the Organisation for Economic Co-operation and Development.

8   (1)   A "group other than an MNE group" means a group consisting of two or more relevant bodies —

    (a)   each of which is a member of the group by virtue of sub-paragraph (3) or (4),

    (b)   at least two of which are UK companies,

which is not an MNE Group.

    (2)   For the purposes of the condition in sub-paragraph (1)(b) a UK permanent establishment of a foreign member of a group is to be treated as if it were a UK company and a member of the group.

(3) A relevant body is a member of a group if—
    (a) another relevant body is its 51% subsidiary, or
    (b) it is a 51% subsidiary of another relevant body.

(4) Two relevant bodies are members of the same group if—
    (a) one is a 51% subsidiary of the other, or
    (b) both are 51% subsidiaries of another relevant body.

(5) Chapter 3 of Part 24 of CTA 2010 (meaning of 51% subsidiary) applies for the purposes of this Schedule as it applies for the purposes of the Corporation Tax Acts (but with the modification in sub-paragraph (6)).

(6) It applies as if references to a body corporate were references to a relevant body.

9   A group is headed by whichever relevant body within the group is not a 51% subsidiary of another relevant body within the group (and "head", in relation to the group, means that body).

"Qualifying group"

10 (1) A group is a "qualifying group" in any financial year if, at the end of the previous financial year—
    (a) in the case of a group other than an MNE Group, the group satisfied the qualification test for such a group (subject to any regulations under sub-paragraph (6)), or
    (b) in the case of an MNE Group—
        (i) there was a mandatory reporting requirement in respect of the group under regulations made under section 122 of FA 2015 (country-by-country reporting), or
        (ii) there would have been such a requirement if the head of the group were resident in the United Kingdom for tax purposes.

(2) The qualification test for a group other than an MNE Group is that the group satisfied either or both of the following conditions (by reference to the previous financial year)—

1. Group turnover	More than £200 million
2. Group balance sheet total	More than £2 billion.

(3) In sub-paragraph (2)—
    (a) "group turnover" means the aggregate turnover of the UK companies that are members of the group at the end of the previous financial year, and
    (b) "group balance sheet total", means the aggregate balance sheet totals for all those UK companies.

(4) Where the financial year of a UK company within in the group does not end on the same day as the previous financial year of the head of the group, the figures from the company that are to be included in the aggregate figures are those for the company's financial year ending last before the end of the previous financial year of the head of the group.

(5) For the purposes of assessing the turnover or balance sheet total of the group, sub-paragraphs (3) and (4) apply as if a UK permanent establishment of a foreign member of the group were a UK company and a member of the group.

(6) The Treasury may by regulations provide—

    (a) that a group other than an MNE Group which is of a specified description is not a qualifying group for the purposes, or any specified purpose, of this Schedule, or

    (b) that a relevant body, or a UK permanent establishment, of a specified description is to be disregarded in determining whether the qualification test is satisfied by a group other than an MNE Group;

and in this sub-paragraph "specified" means specified in the regulations.

(7) In this paragraph "financial year", in relation to a group, means a financial year of the head of the group.

"UK sub-group" and "head" (in relation to a UK sub-group)

11 (1) A "UK sub-group" consists of two or more relevant bodies that would be a UK group, but for the fact that they are members of a larger group headed by a relevant body incorporated outside the United Kingdom.

(2) A UK sub-group is headed by the company or other relevant body incorporated in the United Kingdom that is not a 51% subsidiary of another member of the UK sub-group (and "head", in relation to the sub-group, means that company or body).

"UK partnership", "qualifying partnership" and "representative partner"

12 (1) "UK partnership" means a body of any of the following descriptions which is carrying on a trade, business or profession with a view to profit—

    (a) a partnership within the meaning of the Partnership Act 1890,

    (b) a limited partnership registered under the Limited Partnerships Act 1907, or

    (c) a limited liability partnership incorporated in the United Kingdom.

(2) A UK partnership is a "qualifying partnership" in a financial year, if it satisfied the qualification test for a UK partnership at the end of the previous financial year (subject to any regulations under sub-paragraph (4)).

(3) The qualification test for a UK partnership is that the partnership satisfied either or both of the following conditions (by reference to the previous financial year)—

1. The partnership's turnover	More than £200 million
2. The partnership's balance sheet total	More than £2 billion.

(4) The Treasury may by regulations provide that a UK partnership of a description specified in the regulations is not a qualifying partnership for

the purposes of this Schedule (or any such purpose specified in the regulations).

(5) "Representative partner", in relation to a UK partnership, means the partner who is required by a notice served under or by virtue of section 12AA(2) or (3) of TMA 1970 to make and deliver returns to an officer of HMRC.

"Financial year"

13   "Financial year"—

(a)   in relation to a UK company, has the meaning given by the Companies Act 2006 (see section 390 of that Act),

(b)   in relation to any other relevant body, means any period in respect of which a profit and loss account for the body's undertaking is required to be made up (whether by its constitution or by the law under which it is established), whether that period is a year or not,

(c)   in relation to a UK partnership, means any period of account for which its representative partner has provided or is required to provide a partnership statement under a return issued under section 12AB TMA 1970.

"Turnover" and "balance sheet total"

14   (1) "Turnover"—

(a)   in relation to a UK company, has the same meaning as in Part 15 of the Companies Act 2006 (see section 474 of that Act), and

(b)   in relation to a UK partnership or a UK permanent establishment, has a corresponding meaning.

(2) "Balance sheet total", in relation to a UK company, UK partnership or UK permanent establishment and a financial year, means the aggregate of the amounts shown as assets in its balance sheet at the end of the financial year.

"UK taxation"

15   (1) "UK taxation" means —

(a)   income tax,

(b)   corporation tax, including any amount assessable or chargeable as if it were corporation tax or treated as if it were corporation tax,

(c)   value added tax,

(d)   amounts for which the company is accountable under PAYE regulations,

(e)   diverted profits tax,

(f)   insurance premium tax,

(g)   annual tax on enveloped dwellings,

(h)   stamp duty land tax,

(i)   stamp duty reserve tax,

(j)   petroleum revenue tax;

(k)   customs duties,

(l)   excise duties,

(m)   national insurance contributions.

(2) In relation to a tax strategy required to be published by Part 2, "UK taxation" refers to the taxes or duties mentioned above so far as relating to or affecting the bodies or body to which the required tax strategy relates.

PART 2

PUBLICATION OF TAX STRATEGIES

Qualifying UK groups: duty to publish a group tax strategy

16 (1) This paragraph applies in relation to a UK group which is a qualifying group in any financial year ("the current financial year").

(2) The head of the group must ensure that a group tax strategy for the group, containing the information required by paragraph 17, is prepared and published on behalf of the group in accordance with this paragraph.

(3) The group tax strategy—
   (a)   must be published before the end of the current financial year, and
   (b)   if the group was a qualifying group in the previous financial year, must not be published more than 15 months after the day on which its previous group tax strategy was published.

(4) The group tax strategy—
   (a)   must be published on the internet by any of the UK companies that are members of the group so as to be accessible to the public free of charge (whether or not it is also published in any other way), and
   (b)   may be published as a separate document or as a self-contained part of a wider document.

(5) The head of the group must ensure that the group tax strategy published on the internet remains accessible to the public free of charge—
   (a)   if a group tax strategy for the group's next financial year is required by this paragraph to be published, until that tax strategy is published, or
   (b)   if paragraph (a) does not apply, for at least one year.

(6) For the purposes of this paragraph—
   (a)   a group tax strategy is published when it is first published on the internet as mentioned in paragraph (4)(a),
   (b)   the identity of the group is not to be regarded as altered by any change in its membership during the current financial year resulting from a relevant body—
      (i)   becoming a 51% subsidiary of a member of the group, or
      (ii)   ceasing to be a 51% subsidiary of another member of the group; and
   (c)   if the group becomes a UK sub-group of a foreign group during the current financial year, it is to be treated for the rest of that year as if it were still a UK group.

(7) In this paragraph and paragraph 17 "financial year", in relation to a UK group, means a financial year of the head of the group.

594

Finance Act 2016 (c. 24)
Schedule 19 — Large businesses: tax strategies and sanctions
Part 2 — Publication of tax strategies

Content of group tax strategy

17 (1) A group tax strategy required to be published on behalf of a UK group by paragraph 16 must set out—

    (a) the approach of the group to risk management and governance arrangements in relation to UK taxation,

    (b) the attitude of the group towards tax planning (so far as affecting UK taxation),

    (c) the level of risk in relation to UK taxation that the group is prepared to accept, and

    (d) the approach of the group towards its dealings with HMRC.

  (2) The group tax strategy may—

    (a) include other information relating to taxation (whether UK taxation or otherwise), and

    (b) deal with a matter mentioned in sub-paragraph (1) by reference to the group as a whole or to individual members of the group (or to both).

  (3) The information required by sub-paragraph (1) to be included in the group tax strategy does not include any information about activities of any member of the group that consists of the provision of tax advice or related professional services to persons who are not members of the group.

  (4) The publication of information as the group tax strategy does not constitute publication of the strategy for the purposes of paragraph 16 unless the UK company publishing it makes clear (in a way that will be readily apparent to anyone accessing the information online) that the company regards its publication as complying with the duty under paragraph 16(2) in the current financial year.

  (5) For the purposes of this paragraph a UK permanent establishment of a foreign member of the group is to be treated as if it were a member of the group.

  (6) The Treasury may by regulations require the group tax strategy to include a country-by-country report.

  (7) In this paragraph "country-by-country report" has the meaning given by the Taxes (Base Erosion and Profit Shifting) (Country-by-Country Reporting) Regulations 2016.

Penalty for non-compliance with paragraph 16

18 (1) This paragraph applies where paragraph 16 requires a group tax strategy to be published for a UK group in any financial year of the head of the UK group.

  (2) The head of the group is liable to a penalty of £7,500 if—

    (a) there is a failure to publish a group tax strategy for the group that complies with paragraph 16(2), or

    (b) where a group tax strategy has been published, there is a failure to comply with paragraph 16(5).

Finance Act 2016 (c. 24) 595
Schedule 19 — Large businesses: tax strategies and sanctions
Part 2 — Publication of tax strategies

(3) Subject to sub-paragraph (5) the head of the group is only liable to one penalty by virtue of sub-paragraph (2) in respect of a group tax strategy required for the financial year in question.

(4) Sub-paragraph (5) applies where—

    (a) the head of the group is liable to a penalty under this paragraph in respect of a failure mentioned in sub-paragraph (2)(a), and

    (b) no group tax strategy for the group that complies with paragraph 16(2) (disregarding paragraph 16(3)) is published within the period of 6 months after the last day on which the duty under paragraph 16(2) could have been complied with.

(5) At the end of that period, the head of the group—

    (a) is liable to a further penalty of £7,500, and

    (b) where the failure mentioned in sub-paragraph (4)(b) continues, is liable to a further penalty of £7,500 at the end of each subsequent month in which no such group tax strategy is published.

UK sub-groups: duty to publish a sub-group tax strategy

19 (1) This paragraph applies to a UK sub-group of a foreign group if in any financial year ("the current financial year") the foreign group is a qualifying group.

(2) The head of the sub-group must ensure that a sub-group tax strategy for the sub-group, giving the information required by paragraph 20, is prepared and published in accordance with this paragraph.

(3) The sub-group tax strategy—

    (a) must be published before the end of the current financial year, and

    (b) if the group of which the sub-group is part was a qualifying group in the previous financial year, must not be published more than 15 months after the day on which its sub-group tax strategy for that year was published;

(4) The sub-group tax strategy—

    (a) must be published on the internet by any of the UK companies that are members of the foreign group so as to be accessible to the public free of charge (whether or not it is also published in any other way), and

    (b) may be published as a separate document or as a self-contained part of a wider document.

(5) The head of the sub-group must ensure that the sub-group tax strategy published on the internet remains accessible to the public free of charge—

    (a) if a sub-group tax strategy for the sub-group's next financial year is required by this paragraph to be published, until that tax strategy is published, or

    (b) if paragraph (a) does not apply, for at least one year.

(6) For the purposes of this paragraph—

    (a) a sub-group tax strategy is published when it is first published on the internet as mentioned in sub-paragraph (4)(a),

    (b) the identity of the sub-group is not affected by any change in its membership in the current financial year resulting from a relevant

596

Finance Act 2016 (c. 24)
Schedule 19 – Large businesses: tax strategies and sanctions
Part 2 – Publication of tax strategies

body becoming or ceasing to be a 51% subsidiary of a member of the sub-group, and

    (c)   if the sub-group becomes a UK sub-group of another foreign group during the current financial year, for the rest of that year it is to be treated as if it were still a UK sub-group of the original foreign group (but only a UK company within the sub-group may publish a sub-group tax strategy for the sub-group after that change).

(7)   In this paragraph "financial year", in relation to a UK sub-group, means a financial year of the head of the group of which it is a sub-group.

Content of a sub-group tax strategy

20   (1)   Paragraph 17 applies in relation to a sub-group tax strategy required to be published on behalf of a UK sub-group by paragraph 19 as it applies to a group tax strategy required to be published by a qualifying UK group.

    (2)   In the application of paragraph 17 to a sub-group tax strategy, references to the group or members of the group are to be read as references to the UK sub-group or members of the UK sub-group.

    (3)   In the application of paragraph 17 as modified by this paragraph to a sub-group tax strategy, a UK permanent establishment of a foreign member of the UK sub-group is to be treated as if it were a member of the sub-group.

Penalty for non-compliance with requirements of paragraph 19

21   (1)   This paragraph applies where paragraph 19 requires a sub-group tax strategy to be published for a UK sub-group in any financial year of the head of the sub-group.

    (2)   The head of the sub-group is liable to a penalty of £7,500 if —
        (a)   there is a failure to publish a sub-group tax strategy for the sub-group that complies with paragraph 19(2), or
        (b)   where a sub-group tax strategy has been published, there is a failure to comply with paragraph 19(5).

    (3)   Subject to sub-paragraph (5), the head of the sub-group is only liable to one penalty by virtue of sub-paragraph (2) in respect of a sub-group tax strategy required for the financial year in question.

    (4)   Sub-paragraph (5) applies where —
        (a)   the head of the sub-group is liable to a penalty under this paragraph in respect of a failure mentioned in sub-paragraph (2)(a), and
        (b)   no sub-group tax strategy for the sub-group that complies with paragraph 19(2) (disregarding paragraph 19(3)) is published within the period of 6 months after the last day on which the duty under paragraph 19(2) could have been complied with.

    (5)   At the end of that period, the head of the sub-group is liable —
        (a)   to a further penalty of £7,500, and
        (b)   where the failure mentioned in sub-paragraph (4)(b) continues, to a further penalty of £7,500 at the end of each subsequent month in which no such sub-group tax strategy is published.

Finance Act 2016 (c. 24)   597
Schedule 19 – Large businesses: tax strategies and sanctions
Part 2 – Publication of tax strategies

Qualifying companies: duty to publish a company tax strategy

22 (1) This paragraph applies in relation to a UK company which in any financial year ("the current financial year") is a qualifying company.

(2) The company must prepare and publish a company tax strategy, containing the information required by paragraph 23, in accordance with this paragraph.

(3) The duty under sub-paragraph (2) applies even if the company becomes a member of a UK group or a UK sub-group during the current financial year.

(4) The company tax strategy—
    (a) must be published by the company before the end of the current financial year, and
    (b) if the company was a qualifying company in the previous financial year, must not be published more than 15 months after the day on which its company tax strategy was published in the previous financial year.

(5) The company tax strategy—
    (a) must be published on the internet so as to be accessible to the public free of charge (whether or not published in any other way), and
    (b) may be published as a separate document or a self- contained part of a wider document.

(6) The company must ensure that the company tax strategy published on the internet remains accessible to the public free of charge—
    (a) if a company tax strategy for the next financial year is required by this paragraph to be published, until that tax strategy is published, or
    (b) if paragraph (a) does not apply, for at least one year.

(7) For the purposes of this paragraph a company tax strategy is published when it is first published as mentioned in sub-paragraph (5)(a).

(8) A UK permanent establishment which in any financial year is by virtue of paragraph 5(6) to be treated as a qualifying company is to be treated for the purposes of this paragraph and paragraphs 23 and 24 as if it were a UK company which in that financial year is a qualifying company.

Content of a company tax strategy

23 (1) The company tax strategy must set out—
    (a) the company's approach to risk management and governance arrangements in relation to UK taxation,
    (b) the company's attitude towards tax planning (so far as affecting UK taxation),
    (c) the level of risk in relation to UK taxation that the company is prepared to accept,
    (d) the company's approach towards its dealings with HMRC.

(2) The company tax strategy may include other information relating to taxation (whether UK taxation or otherwise).

(3) The information required by sub-paragraph (1) to be included in a company tax strategy does not include any information about activities of the

598

Finance Act 2016 (c. 24)
Schedule 19 – Large businesses: tax strategies and sanctions
Part 2 – Publication of tax strategies

company that consist of the provision of tax advice or related professional services to other persons.

(4) The publication of information as a company tax strategy does not constitute publication of the strategy for the purposes of paragraph 22 unless the company makes clear (in a way that will be readily apparent to anyone accessing the information online) that the company regards its publication as complying with the duty under paragraph 22(2) in the current financial year.

Penalty for non-compliance with paragraph 22

24 (1) This paragraph applies where paragraph 22 requires a company tax strategy to be published for a UK company in any financial year.

(2) The company is liable to a penalty of £7,500 if —

    (a) there is a failure to publish a company tax strategy for the company that complies with paragraph 22(2), or

    (b) where a company tax strategy has been published, there is a failure to comply with paragraph 22(6).

(3) Subject to sub-paragraph (5), the company is only liable to one penalty by virtue of sub-paragraph (2) in respect of a company tax strategy required for the financial year in question.

(4) Sub-paragraph (5) applies where —

    (a) a penalty is imposed under this paragraph in respect of a failure mentioned in sub-paragraph (2)(a), and

    (b) no company tax strategy that complies with paragraph 22(2) (disregarding paragraph 22(4)) is published within the period of 6 months after the last day on which the duty under paragraph 22(2) could have been complied with.

(5) At the end of that period, the company is liable —

    (a) to a further penalty of £7,500, and

    (b) where the failure mentioned in sub-paragraph (4)(b) continues, to a further penalty of £7,500 at the end of each subsequent month in which no such company tax strategy is published.

Qualifying partnerships: duty to publish a partnership tax strategy

25 (1) Paragraphs 22 to 24 apply in relation to a UK partnership which is (in any financial year of the partnership) a qualifying partnership as they apply to a UK company which is (in any financial year of the company) a qualifying company.

(2) Those paragraphs have effect in their application to a qualifying partnership —

    (a) with the omission of paragraph 22(3) and (8),

    (b) as if for "company tax strategy" (in each place) there were substituted "partnership tax strategy", and

    (c) as if for "company" and "company's" (in each place) there were substituted respectively "partnership" and "partnership's".

Finance Act 2016 (c. 24) 599
Schedule 19 – Large businesses: tax strategies and sanctions
Part 2 – Publication of tax strategies

Penalties under this Part: general provisions

26 (1) Paragraphs 27 to 33 apply in relation to the liability of any person to a penalty under this Part and, accordingly, in those paragraphs—

"failure", in relation to a liability for a penalty, means a failure which could give rise to that liability,

"liability to a penalty" means a liability under paragraph 18, 21 or 24 (including paragraph 24 as applied to a qualifying UK partnership), and

"penalty" means a penalty under any of those paragraphs.

(2) In those paragraphs "tribunal" means the First-tier Tribunal or, where determined by or under the Tribunal Procedure Rules, the Upper Tribunal.

Failure to comply with a time limit

27 A failure to do anything required by this Part to be done within a limited period of time goes not give rise to liability to a penalty if it is done within such further time (if any) as an officer of Revenue and Customs may have allowed.

Reasonable excuse

28 (1) Liability to a penalty for a failure does not arise if the person who would otherwise be liable to that penalty satisfies HMRC or (on an appeal notified to the tribunal) the tribunal that the person had a reasonable excuse for that failure.

(2) For the purposes of this paragraph—

 (a) an insufficiency of funds is not a reasonable excuse unless attributable to events outside the person's control,

 (b) where the person relies on another person to do anything, that cannot be a reasonable excuse—

  (i) unless the first person took reasonable care to avoid the failure, or

  (ii) if the first person is a UK group or UK sub-group, where the person relied on is another member of the group or sub-group,

 (c) where the person had a reasonable excuse but the excuse has ceased, the person is to be treated as having continued to have the excuse if the failure is remedied without unreasonable delay after the excuse ceased.

Assessment of penalties

29 (1) Where a person becomes liable to a penalty—

 (a) HMRC may assess the penalty, and

 (b) if they do so, HMRC must notify the person of the assessment.

(2) An assessment of a penalty may not be made—

 (a) more than 6 months after the failure first comes to the attention of an officer of Revenue and Customs, or

600

Finance Act 2016 (c. 24)
Schedule 19 – Large businesses: tax strategies and sanctions
Part 2 – Publication of tax strategies

     (b)   more than 6 years after the end of the financial year in which the tax strategy to which the failure relates was (or was originally) required to be published.

Appeal

30 (1) A person may appeal against a decision of HMRC that a penalty is payable by that person.

    (2) Notice of an appeal must be given—
        (a)   in writing,
        (b)   before the end of the period of 30 days beginning with the date on which the notification under paragraph 29(1)(b) was issued,

    (3) Notice of an appeal must state the grounds of appeal.

    (4) On an appeal that is notified to the tribunal, the tribunal may confirm or cancel the decision.

    (5) Subject to this paragraph and paragraph 31, the provisions of Part 5 of TMA 1970 relating to appeals have effect in relation to appeals under this Schedule as they have effect in relation to an appeal against an assessment to income tax.

Enforcement

31 (1) A penalty must be paid—
        (a)   before the end of the period of 30 days beginning with the date on which the notification under paragraph 29(1)(b) was issued, or
        (b)   if a notice of appeal is given, before the end of 30 days beginning with the day on which the appeal is determined or withdrawn.

    (2) A penalty may be enforced as if it were corporation tax charged in an assessment and due and payable.

Power to change amount of penalties

32 (1) If it appears to the Treasury that there has been a change in the value of money since the last relevant date, they may by regulations substitute for any sums for the time being specified in paragraph 18, 21 or 24 such other sum as appear to them to be justified by the change.

    (2) In sub-paragraph (1) "relevant date" means—
        (a)   the date on which this Act is passed, and
        (b)   each date on which the power conferred by that sub-paragraph has been exercised.

    (3) Regulations under this paragraph do not apply to a failure that occurs in respect of a financial year (of the body or partnership responsible for the failure) that begins before the date on which they come into force.

Application of provisions of TMA 1970

33   Subject to the provisions of this Part, the following provisions of TMA 1970 apply for the purposes of this Part as they apply for the purposes of the Taxes Acts—

Finance Act 2016 (c. 24)
Schedule 19 — Large businesses: tax strategies and sanctions
Part 2 — Publication of tax strategies

601

    (a)   section 108 (responsibility of company officers),

    (b)   section 114 (want of form), and

    (c)   section 115 (delivery and service of documents).

Meaning of "tax strategy"

34   In this Part "tax strategy" means—

    (a)   a group tax strategy (see paragraphs 16 to 18),

    (b)   a sub-group tax strategy (see paragraphs 19 to 21),

    (c)   a company tax strategy (see paragraphs 22 to 24), or

    (d)   a partnership tax strategy (see paragraph 25).

PART 3

SANCTIONS FOR PERSISTENTLY UNCO-OPERATIVE LARGE BUSINESSES

Large groups falling within Part 3

35   A UK group falls within this Part of this Schedule ("this Part") if—

    (a)   the group has persistently engaged in unco-operative behaviour (see paragraphs 36 to 38),

    (b)   some or all of the unco-operative behaviour has caused there to be, or contributed to there being, two or more significant tax issues in respect of the group or members of the group which are unresolved (see paragraph 39), and

    (c)   there is a reasonable likelihood of further instances of the group engaging in unco-operative behaviour in a manner which causes there to be, or contributes to there being, significant tax issues in respect of the group or members of the group.

36 (1) A UK group has "engaged in unco-operative behaviour" if—

    (a)   a member of the group has satisfied either or both of the conditions listed in sub-paragraph (2), or

    (b)   two or more of the members of the group, taken together, have satisfied either or both of those conditions.

  (2) Those conditions are—

    (a)   the behaviour condition (see paragraph 37);

    (b)   the arrangements condition (see paragraph 38).

  (3) A UK group has engaged in unco-operative behaviour "persistently" if—

    (a)   a member of the group has done so persistently, or

    (b)   two or more members of the group, taken together, have done so persistently.

  (4) References in this Part to doing something "persistently" include doing it on a sufficient number of occasions for it to be clear that it represents a pattern of behaviour.

37 (1) A member of a UK group has, or two or more members of a UK group (taken together) have, "satisfied the behaviour condition" if it has, or they have, behaved in a manner which has delayed or otherwise hindered HMRC in the exercise of their functions in connection with determining the liability to UK taxation of the group or a member of the group.

602

Finance Act 2016 (c. 24)
Schedule 19 — Large businesses: tax strategies and sanctions
Part 3 — Sanctions for persistently unco-operative large businesses

    (2) Factors which may indicate that a member of a UK group has behaved as described in sub-paragraph (1) include—

       (a) the extent to which HMRC have used statutory powers to obtain information relating to the UK group or members of the group;

       (b) the reasons why those powers have been used;

       (c) the number and seriousness of inaccuracies in, and omissions from, documents given to HMRC by or on behalf of the UK group or members of the group;

       (d) the extent to which, in dealings with HMRC, members of the group (or people acting on their behalf) have relied on interpretations of legislation relating to UK taxation which, at the time, are speculative.

    (3) An interpretation of legislation relating to UK taxation is "speculative" if it is likely that a court or tribunal would disagree with it.

38   (1) A member of a UK group has "satisfied the arrangements condition" if it is a party to a tax avoidance scheme.

    (2) "Tax avoidance scheme" means—

       (a) arrangements in respect of which a notice of final decision has been given under—

          (i) paragraph 12 of Schedule 43 to FA 2013,

          (ii) paragraph 5 or 6 of Schedule 43A to FA 2013, or

          (iii) paragraph 9 of Schedule 43B to FA 2013,

       stating that a tax advantage arising from the arrangements is to be counteracted;

       (b) arrangements which are notifiable arrangements for the purposes of Part 7 of FA 2004 (disclosure of tax avoidance schemes), other than arrangements in relation to which HMRC have given notice under section 312(6) of FA 2004 (notice that promoters not under duty to provide clients with prescribed information);

       (c) a scheme which is a notifiable scheme for the purposes of Schedule 11A to VATA 1994 (disclosure of avoidance schemes).

39   (1) There is a significant tax issue in respect of a UK group or a member of a UK group where—

       (a) there is a disagreement between HMRC and a member of the group about an issue affecting the amount of the liability of the group or a member of the group to UK taxation,

       (b) the issue has been, or could be, referred to a court or tribunal to determine, and

       (c) as regards the amount of the liability, the difference between HMRC's view and the view of the member is, or is likely to be, not less than £2 million.

    (2) The reference in sub-paragraph (1)(a) to circumstances in which there is a disagreement include circumstances in which there is a reasonable likelihood of a disagreement.

    (3) The Treasury may by regulations substitute a higher amount for the amount for the time being specified in sub-paragraph (1)(c).

40   The references in paragraphs 36 to 39 to things done by a member of a UK group ("the group in question")—

Finance Act 2016 (c. 24)
Schedule 19 – Large businesses: tax strategies and sanctions
Part 3 – Sanctions for persistently unco-operative large businesses

603

    (a)   include acts and omissions of a relevant body that is not a member of the group in question if they took place at a time when the relevant body was a member of a group headed by the body that is the head of the group in question;

    (b)   do not include acts or omissions of a relevant body that is a member of the group in question if they took place at a time when the relevant body was not a member of a group headed by the body that is the head of the group in question.

Warning notices

41   (1) A designated HMRC officer may give the head of a UK group a notice under this paragraph (a "warning notice") if the officer considers that the group is a qualifying group that falls within this Part.

    (2) The notice must set out the reasons why the officer considers that the group falls within this Part.

    (3) The notice –

        (a)   may be withdrawn by a designated HMRC officer at any time by giving a further notice to the head of the group, and

        (b)   expires (if not previously withdrawn) at the end of the period of 15 months beginning with the day on which it was given.

    (4) Once a warning notice has been given –

        (a)   it is immaterial for the purposes of this Part whether the group remains a qualifying group,

        (b)   the identity of the group is not to be regarded as altered by any change in its membership resulting from a relevant body –

            (i)   becoming a 51% subsidiary of a member of the group, or

            (ii) ceasing to be a 51% subsidiary of another member of the group; and

        (c)   if the group becomes a UK sub-group of a foreign group it is to be treated as if it were still a UK group.

    (5) Sub-paragraph (4) applies while the group is subject to –

        (a)   the warning notice, or

        (b)   any other notice under this Part issued as a result of the group having been given the warning notice.

Special measures notices

42   (1) This paragraph applies to a UK group if –

        (a)   the head of the group has been given a warning notice in relation to the group that has not been withdrawn,

        (b)   the period of 12 months beginning with the day on which the warning notice was given has elapsed, and

        (c)   the period of 15 months beginning with that day has not elapsed.

    (2) If a designated HMRC officer considers that the group falls within this Part, the officer may give the head of the group a notice under this paragraph (a "special measures notice").

604

Finance Act 2016 (c. 24)
Schedule 19 – Large businesses: tax strategies and sanctions
Part 3 – Sanctions for persistently unco-operative large businesses

(3) When considering whether the group falls within this Part, the officer may take into account any relevant behaviour, whether or not it is mentioned in the warning notice.

(4) When deciding whether to give a special measures notice, the designated HMRC officer must consider any representations made by a member of the group before the end of the period of 12 months beginning with the day on which the warning notice was given.

(5) The special measures notice must set out the reasons why the officer considers that the group falls within this Part.

(6) Paragraph 45 deals with other circumstances in which a UK group may be given a special measures notice.

43 (1) A special measures notice –

    (a) may be withdrawn by a designated HMRC officer at any time by giving a further notice to the head of the UK group, and

    (b) expires, if not previously withdrawn, at the end of the period of 27 months beginning with the relevant day.

(2) "The relevant day" means the later of –

    (a) the day on which the special measures notice was given, and

    (b) the day on which it was last confirmed under paragraph 44.

44 (1) This paragraph applies to a UK group if –

    (a) the head of the group has been given a special measures notice in relation to the group which has not been withdrawn,

    (b) the period of 24 months beginning with the relevant day has elapsed, and

    (c) the period of 27 months beginning with that day has not elapsed.

(2) If a designated HMRC officer considers that the group falls within this Part, the officer may give the head of the group a notice under this paragraph (a "confirmation notice") confirming the special measures notice given in relation to the group.

(3) When considering whether the group falls within this Part, the officer may take into account any relevant behaviour, whether or not it is mentioned in the special measures notice which is to be confirmed, in any previous confirmation notice or in the warning notice.

(4) "The relevant day" has the same meaning as in paragraph 43(2).

(5) The confirmation notice must set out the reasons why the officer considers that the group falls within this Part.

(6) When deciding whether to give a confirmation notice, a designated HMRC officer must consider any representations made by a member of the group before the end of the period of 24 months beginning with the relevant day.

(7) A confirmation notice –

    (a) may be withdrawn by a designated HMRC officer at any time by giving a further notice to the head of the group, and

    (b) expires, if not previously withdrawn, at the end of the period of 27 months beginning with the day on which it is given.

45 (1) This paragraph applies in relation to a UK group where –

Finance Act 2016 (c. 24) 605
Schedule 19 — Large businesses: tax strategies and sanctions
Part 3 — Sanctions for persistently unco-operative large businesses

    (a)   the head of the group has been given a warning notice or a special measures notice in relation to the group, and

    (b)   that notice has expired.

(2) A designated HMRC officer may give the head of a UK group a special measures notice if —

    (a)   it appears to the officer that —

        (i)   during the period of 6 months beginning with the day on which the notice mentioned in sub-paragraph (1)(a) expired ("the expiry day"), the group has engaged in unco-operative behaviour (see paragraphs 36 to 38), and

        (ii)   there is a reasonable likelihood that, if it had engaged in the behaviour before the notice expired, a designated HMRC officer would have considered that the group fell within this Part (so that a special measures notice or confirmation notice could have been given to the head of the group),

    (b)   during the period of 7 months beginning with the expiry day, a designated HMRC officer has notified the head of the group that the power under this paragraph may be exercised in relation to the group, and

    (c)   the period of 9 months beginning with that day has not elapsed.

(3) When deciding whether to give a special measures notice under this paragraph, the officer must consider any representations made by a member of the group before the end of the period of 8 months beginning with the expiry day.

Circumstances in which warning and special measures notices are treated as having been given

46   (1) Sub-paragraphs (2) and (3) apply where —

    (a)   a relevant body ("B1") is given a warning notice, and

    (b)   before the notice ceases to have effect, B1 becomes a member of a group headed by another relevant body ("H1").

(2) H1 is to be treated as having been given a warning notice on the day on which the warning notice was given to B1.

(3) A warning notice treated as given under sub-paragraph (2) is valid whether or not, on the day mentioned in that sub-paragraph, H1 was the head of a qualifying UK group that fell within this Part.

(4) Sub-paragraphs (5) to (7) apply where —

    (a)   a relevant body ("B2") is given a special measures notice, and

    (b)   before the notice ceases to have effect, B2 becomes a member of a group headed by another relevant body ("H2").

(5) H2 is to be treated as having been given a special measures notice on the day on which the special measures notice was given to B2.

(6) A special measures notice treated as given under sub-paragraph (5) is valid whether or not, on the day mentioned in that sub-paragraph, H2 was the head of a qualifying UK group that fell within this Part.

(7) Paragraph 47(1) does not by virtue of sub-paragraphs (5) and (6) of this paragraph apply to an inaccuracy in a document given to HMRC by or on behalf of a person —

606

Finance Act 2016 (c. 24)
Schedule 19 — Large businesses: tax strategies and sanctions
Part 3 — Sanctions for persistently unco-operative large businesses

        (a)   at a time when the person was a member of a group headed by H2, but

        (b)   before the day B2 becomes a member of H2.

  (8) Sub-paragraphs (9) and (10) apply where—

        (a)   a relevant body ("B3") is given a confirmation notice, and

        (b)   before the notice ceases to have effect, B3 becomes a member of a group headed by another relevant body ("H3").

  (9) H3 is to be treated as having been given a confirmation notice on the day on which the confirmation notice was given to B3.

  (10) A confirmation notice treated as given under sub-paragraph (9) is valid whether or not, on the day mentioned in that sub-paragraph, H3 was the head of a qualifying UK group that fell within this Part.

  (11) The Treasury may by regulations make provision for warning notices, special measures notices and confirmation notices to be treated as having been given to relevant bodies in other circumstances described in the regulations.

  (12) Regulations under this paragraph may, in particular—

        (a)   make provision about the validity of notices treated as given by virtue of the regulations;

        (b)   make provision about the effect of paragraph 47(1) in cases involving such notices.

Sanctions: liability for penalties for errors in documents given to HMRC

47 (1) For the purposes of Schedule 24 to FA 2007 (penalties for errors), an inaccuracy in a document given to HMRC by or on behalf of a person is to be treated as being due to failure by the person to take reasonable care if—

        (a)   the document was given to HMRC at a time when the person was a member of a group subject to a special measures notice, and

        (b)   the inaccuracy—

               (i)   relates to a tax avoidance scheme (as defined in paragraph 38) entered into by the person at a time when the person was a member of a group subject to a special measures notice, or

              (ii)   is, entirely or partly, attributable to an interpretation of legislation relating to UK taxation which, at the time the document was given to HMRC, was speculative.

  (2) A group is "subject to a special measures notice" if a special measures notice—

        (a)   has been given to the head of the group in relation to the group, and

        (b)   is in force.

  (3) An interpretation of legislation relating to UK taxation is "speculative" if it is likely that a court or tribunal would disagree with it.

  (4) Sub-paragraph (1) does not apply to an inaccuracy if—

        (a)   it is deliberate on the part of the person or someone acting on the person's behalf,

        (b)   it is in fact due to a failure by the person or someone acting on the person's behalf to take reasonable care, or

Finance Act 2016 (c. 24)
Schedule 19 — Large businesses: tax strategies and sanctions
Part 3 — Sanctions for persistently unco-operative large businesses

607

       (c)   it is treated as due to such a failure by virtue of another enactment.

48   In Schedule 24 to FA 2007 (penalties for errors), at the end of paragraph 3 (meaning of "careless" etc) insert—

> "(3) Paragraph 47 of Schedule 19 to FA 2016 (special measures for persistently unco-operative large businesses) provides for certain inaccuracies to be treated, for the purposes of this Schedule, as being due to a failure by P to take reasonable care."

Sanctions: Commissioners publishing information

49   (1) If a group is subject to a confirmed special measures notice, the Commissioners for Her Majesty's Revenue and Customs ("the Commissioners") may publish the following information—

      (a)   the name of the group, including any previous name;

      (b)   the address or registered office of the head of the group;

      (c)   any other information that the Commissioners consider it appropriate to publish in order to identify the group;

      (d)   the fact that the group is subject to a confirmed special measures notice.

   (2) A group is "subject to a confirmed special measures notice" if sub-paragraph (3) or (4) is satisfied.

   (3) This sub-paragraph is satisfied if—

      (a)   a special measures notice has been given to the head of the group and confirmed under paragraph 44, and

      (b)   the special measures notice is in force.

   (4) This sub-paragraph is satisfied if—

      (a)   a special measures notice has been given to the head of the group and confirmed under paragraph 44,

      (b)   that notice has ceased to have effect,

      (c)   a further special measures notice has been given to the head of the group under paragraph 45 in the period of 9 months beginning with the day on which the special measures notice mentioned in paragraph (a) ceased to have effect, and

      (d)   that notice is in force.

   (5) Before publishing the information, the Commissioners must—

      (a)   inform the head of the group that they are considering doing so, and

      (b)   allow the head of the group a reasonable opportunity to make representations about whether the information should be published.

   (6) If, after information about a group is published under this paragraph, the group ceases to be subject to a confirmed special measures notice, the Commissioners must publish a notice stating that the group is no longer subject to a confirmed special measures notice.

   (7) A notice under sub-paragraph (6) must be published before the end of the period of 30 days beginning with the day on which the special measures notice is withdrawn or has expired.

   (8) The Commissioners may publish information and notices under this paragraph in any manner they consider appropriate.

608

Finance Act 2016 (c. 24)
Schedule 19 – Large businesses: tax strategies and sanctions
Part 3 – Sanctions for persistently unco-operative large businesses

Application of Part 3 to large UK sub-groups

50   (1) A UK sub-group of a foreign group falls within this Part if—

      (a) the sub-group has persistently engaged in unco-operative behaviour (see paragraphs 36 to 38),

      (b) some or all of the unco-operative behaviour has caused there to be, or contributed to there being, two or more significant tax issues in respect of the sub-group or members of the sub-group which are unresolved (see paragraph 39), and

      (c) there is a reasonable likelihood of further instances of the sub-group engaging in unco-operative behaviour in a manner which causes there to be, or contributes to there being, significant tax issues in respect of the sub-group or members of the sub-group.

    (2) Paragraphs 36 to 40 apply in relation to a UK sub-group as they apply in relation to a UK group.

    (3) Paragraphs 41 to 45 apply in relation to the head of a UK sub-group of a foreign group that is a qualifying group at the material time as they apply in relation to the head of a UK group.

    (4) In the application of paragraph 41 in the case of a UK sub-group, sub-paragraph (4) has effect in relation to a UK sub-group as if for paragraphs (b) and (c) there were substituted—

          "(b) the identity of the sub-group is not to be regarded as altered by any change in its membership resulting from a relevant body—

              (i) becoming a 51% subsidiary of a member of the sub-group, or

              (ii) ceasing to be a 51% subsidiary of another member of the sub- group; and

          (c) if the sub-group becomes a UK sub-group of another foreign group, it is to be treated as if it were still a UK sub-group of the original foreign group."

    (5) As applied by this paragraph, paragraphs 36 to 45 have effect as if references to a UK group (including in references to the head of a UK group or members of a UK group) were references to a UK sub-group.

    (6) In paragraphs 40, 41, 46, 47 and 49, references to a group (including in references to the head of a group or members of a group) include a UK sub-group.

    (7) In paragraph 46, references to the head of a UK group include the head of a UK sub-group.

Application of Part 3 to large companies

51   (1) A UK company falls within this Part if—

      (a) the company has persistently engaged in unco-operative behaviour (see paragraphs 36 to 38),

      (b) some or all of the unco-operative behaviour has caused there to be, or contributed to there being, two or more significant tax issues in respect of the company which are unresolved (see paragraph 39), and

Finance Act 2016 (c. 24)
Schedule 19 — Large businesses: tax strategies and sanctions
Part 3 — Sanctions for persistently unco-operative large businesses

609

    (c)   there is a reasonable likelihood of further instances of the company engaging in unco-operative behaviour in a manner which causes there to be, or contributes to there being, significant tax issues in respect of the company.

(2) Paragraphs 36 to 39 apply in relation to a company as they apply in relation to a UK group.

(3) Paragraphs 41 to 45 apply in relation to a company as they apply in relation to the head of a UK group.

(4) As applied by this paragraph, paragraphs 36 to 39 and 41 to 45 have effect as if references to a UK group, the head of a UK group or a member of a UK group were references to a company.

(5) Paragraph 47 applies in relation to a company as it applies in relation to a member of a group.

(6) Paragraph 49 applies in relation to a company as it applies in relation to a group.

(7) As applied by this paragraph, paragraphs 47 and 49 have effect as if references to a group, the head of a group or a member of a group were references to a company.

Application of Part 3 to large partnerships

52   (1)   A UK partnership falls within this Part if—

    (a)   the partnership has persistently engaged in unco-operative behaviour (see paragraphs 36 to 38),

    (b)   some or all of the unco-operative behaviour has caused there to be, or contributed to there being, two or more significant tax issues in respect of the partnership which are unresolved (see paragraph 39), and

    (c)   there is a reasonable likelihood of further instances of the partnership engaging in unco-operative behaviour in a manner which causes there to be, or contributes to there being, significant tax issues in respect of the partnership.

(2) Paragraphs 36 to 39 of this Schedule apply in relation to a UK partnership as they apply in relation to a UK group.

(3) Paragraphs 41 to 45 of this Schedule apply in relation to the representative partner of a UK partnership as they apply in relation to the head of a UK group.

(4) As applied by this paragraph, paragraphs 36 to 39 and 41 to 45 have effect as if—

    (a)   references to a UK group were references to a UK partnership;

    (b)   references to the head of a UK group were references to the representative partner of a UK partnership;

    (c)   references to a member of a UK group were references to a partner of a UK partnership, acting in the person's capacity as such.

(5) The Treasury may by regulations make provision for warning notices, special measures notices and confirmation notices to be treated as having

610

Finance Act 2016 (c. 24)
Schedule 19 — Large businesses: tax strategies and sanctions
Part 3 — Sanctions for persistently unco-operative large businesses

been given to the representative partner of a UK partnership in circumstances described in the regulations.

(6) Paragraph 46(12) applies to regulations under this paragraph.

(7) Paragraph 47 applies in relation to an inaccuracy in a document given to HMRC by a partner of a UK partnership, acting in the person's capacity as such, as if—

    (a) references to a group were references to a partnership;

    (b) references to the head of a group were references to the representative partner of a partnership;

    (c) references to a member of a group were references to a partner of a partnership.

(8) Paragraph 47 applies in relation to an inaccuracy in any other document given to HMRC on behalf of a UK partnership as if—

    (a) references to a person included a UK partnership;

    (b) references to a group, or a member of a group, were references to a UK partnership;

    (c) references to the head of a group were references to the representative partner of a UK partnership.

(9) Paragraph 49 applies in relation to a UK partnership as it applies in relation to a group.

(10) As applied by this paragraph, paragraph 49 has effect as if—

    (a) references to a group were references to a UK partnership;

    (b) references to the head of a group were references to the representative partner of a UK partnership.

Meaning of "designated HMRC officer"

53   In this Part "designated HMRC officer" means an officer of Revenue and Customs who has been designated by the Commissioners for Her Majesty's Revenue and Customs for the purposes of this Part.

PART 4

SUPPLEMENTARY

Amendment of power under section 122 of FA 2015

54   The power to make regulations under section 122(6)(c) of FA 2015 (country-by-country reporting: incidental etc provision that may be included in regulations) includes power to amend paragraph 7 above.

Regulations

55 (1) Regulations under this Schedule are to be made by statutory instrument.

    (2) A statutory instrument containing regulations under this Schedule is subject to annulment in pursuance of a resolution of the House of Commons.

Terms defined for purposes of more than one paragraph of this Schedule

Term	Paragraph
balance sheet total	paragraph 14(2)
confirmation notice (in Part 3)	paragraph 44
designated HMRC officer (in Part 3)	paragraph 53
engaged in unco-operative behaviour (in Part 3)	paragraph 36
failure (in paragraphs 27 to 33)	paragraph 26(1)
financial year (in relation to a UK group) (in paragraphs 16 and 17)	paragraph 16(7)
foreign (in relation to a relevant body)	paragraph 2(2)
foreign (in relation to a group)	paragraph 6(3)
group	paragraph 6(1)
group other than an MNE Group	paragraph 8
head (in relation to a group)	paragraph 9
head (in relation to a UK sub-group)	paragraph 11(2)
"liability to a penalty" (in paragraphs 27 to 33)	paragraph 26(1)
MNE Group	paragraph 7(1)
member (in relation to a group)	paragraph 8(2) and (3)
penalty (in paragraphs 27 to 33)	paragraph 26(1)
qualifying company	paragraph 5
qualifying group	paragraph 10
qualifying UK partnership	paragraph 12(2)
relevant body	paragraph 2(1)
representative partner	paragraph 12(5)
satisfied the arrangements condition (in Part 3)	paragraph 38
satisfied the behaviour condition (in Part 3)	paragraph 37
special measures notice	paragraphs 42 and 45
tax strategy (in Part 2)	paragraph 34
tribunal (in paragraphs 27 to 33)	paragraph 26(2)
turnover	paragraph 14(1)
UK company	paragraph 3
UK group	paragraph 6(2)
UK partnership	paragraph 12(1)
UK permanent establishment	paragraph 4(1)

Term	Paragraph
UK sub-group	paragraph 11(1)
UK taxation	paragraph 15
warning notice	paragraph 41.

SCHEDULE 20   Section 162

PENALTIES FOR ENABLERS OF OFFSHORE TAX EVASION OR NON-COMPLIANCE

PART 1

LIABILITY FOR PENALTY

Liability for penalty

1   (1)   A penalty is payable by a person (P) who has enabled another person (Q) to carry out offshore tax evasion or non-compliance, where conditions A and B are met.

(2)   For the purposes of this Schedule —
   (a)   Q carries out "offshore tax evasion or non-compliance" by —
      (i)   committing a relevant offence, or
      (ii)   engaging in conduct that makes Q liable (if the applicable conditions are met) to a relevant civil penalty,
      where the tax at stake is income tax, capital gains tax or inheritance tax, and
   (b)   P "has enabled" Q to carry out offshore tax evasion or non-compliance if P has encouraged, assisted or otherwise facilitated conduct by Q that constitutes offshore tax evasion or non-compliance.

(3)   The relevant offences are-
   (a)   an offence of cheating the public revenue involving offshore activity, or
   (b)   an offence under section 106A of TMA 1970 (fraudulent evasion of income tax) involving offshore activity,
   (c)   an offence under section 106B, 106C or 106D of TMA 1970 (offences relating to certain failures to comply with section 7 or 8 by a taxpayer chargeable to income tax or capital gains tax on or by reference to offshore income, assets or liabilities).

(4)   The relevant civil penalties are —
   (a)   a penalty under paragraph 1 of Schedule 24 to FA 2007 (errors in taxpayer's document) involving an offshore matter or an offshore transfer (within the meaning of that Schedule),
   (b)   a penalty under paragraph 1 of Schedule 41 to FA 2008 (failure to notify etc) in relation to a failure to comply with section 7(1) of TMA 1970 involving offshore activity,
   (c)   a penalty under paragraph 6 of Schedule 55 to FA 2009 (failure to make return for 12 months) involving offshore activity,

Finance Act 2016 (c. **24**)   613
Schedule 20 – *Penalties for enablers of offshore tax evasion or non-compliance*
Part 1 – *Liability for penalty*

(d) a penalty under paragraph 1 of Schedule 21 to FA 2015 (penalties in connection with relevant offshore asset moves).

(5) Condition A is that P knew when P's actions were carried out that they enabled, or were likely to enable, Q to carry out offshore tax evasion or non-compliance.

(6) Condition B is that—

    (a) in the case of offshore tax evasion or non-compliance consisting of the commission of a relevant offence, Q has been convicted of the offence and the conviction is final, or

    (b) in the case of offshore tax evasion or non-compliance consisting of conduct that makes Q liable to a relevant penalty—

        (i) Q has been found to be liable to such a penalty, assessed and notified, and the penalty is final, or

        (ii) a contract has been made between the Commissioners for Her Majesty's Revenue and Customs and Q under which the Commissioners undertake not to assess the penalty or (if it has been assessed) not to take proceedings to recover it.

(7) For the purposes of sub-paragraph (6)(a)—

    (a) "convicted of the offence" means convicted of the full offence (and not for example of an attempt), and

    (b) a conviction becomes final when the time allowed for bringing an appeal against it expires or, if later, when any appeal against conviction has been determined.

(8) For the purposes of sub-paragraph (6)(b)(i) a penalty becomes final when the time allowed for any appeal or further appeal relating to it expires or, if later, any appeal or final appeal relating to it is determined.

(9) It is immaterial for the purposes of condition B that—

    (a) any offence of which Q was convicted, or

    (b) any penalty for which Q was found to be liable,

relates also to other tax evasion or non-compliance by Q.

(10) In this Schedule "other tax evasion or non-compliance by Q" means conduct by Q that—

    (a) constitutes an offence of cheating the public revenue or an offence of fraudulent evasion of tax, or

    (b) makes Q liable to a penalty under any provision of the Taxes Acts,

but does not constitute offshore tax evasion or non-compliance.

(11) Nothing in condition B affects the law of evidence as to the relevance if any of a conviction, assessment of a penalty or contract mentioned in sub-paragraph (6) for the purpose of proving that condition A is met in relation to P.

(12) In this Schedule "conduct" includes a failure to act.

Meaning of "involving offshore activity" and related expressions

2   (1) This paragraph has effect for the purposes of this Schedule.

    (2) Conduct involves offshore activity if it involves—

        (a) an offshore matter,

614

Finance Act 2016 (c. 24)
Schedule 20 — Penalties for enablers of offshore tax evasion or non-compliance
Part 1 — Liability for penalty

     (b)   an offshore transfer, or

     (c)   a relevant offshore asset move.

(3) Conduct involves an offshore matter if it results in a potential loss of revenue that is charged on or by reference to—

     (a)   income arising from a source in a territory outside the United Kingdom,

     (b)   assets situated or held in a territory outside the United Kingdom,

     (c)   activities carried on wholly or mainly in a territory outside the United Kingdom, or

     (d)   anything having effect as if it were income, assets or activities of the kind described above.

(4) Where the tax at stake is inheritance tax, assets are treated for the purposes of sub-paragraph (3) as situated or held in a territory outside the United Kingdom if they are so held or situated immediately after the transfer of value by reason of which inheritance tax becomes chargeable.

(5) Conduct involves an offshore transfer if—

     (a)   it does not involve an offshore matter,

     (b)   it is deliberate (whether or not concealed) and results in a potential loss of revenue,

     (c)   the condition set out in paragraph 4AA of Schedule 24 to FA 2007 is satisfied.

(6) Conduct involves a relevant offshore asset move if at a time when Q is the beneficial owner of an asset ("the qualifying time")—

     (a)   the asset ceases to be situated or held in a specified territory and becomes situated or held in a non-specified territory,

     (b)   the person who holds the asset ceases to be resident in a specified territory and becomes resident in a non-specified territory, or

     (c)   there is a change in the arrangements for the ownership of the asset,

and Q remains the beneficial owner of the asset, or any part of it, immediately after the qualifying time.

(7) Paragraphs 4(2) to (4) of Schedule 21 to FA 2015 apply for the purposes of sub-paragraph (6) above as they apply for purposes of paragraph 4 of that Schedule.

(8) In sub-paragraph (6) above, "specified territory" has the same meaning as in paragraph 4(5) of Schedule 21 to FA 2015.

Amount of penalty

3   (1) The penalty payable under paragraph 1 is (except in a case mentioned in sub-paragraph (2)) the higher of—

     (a)   100% of the potential lost revenue, or

     (b)   £3,000.

(2) In a case where P has enabled Q to engage in conduct which makes Q liable to a penalty under paragraph 1 of Schedule 21 to FA 2015, the penalty payable under paragraph 1 is the higher of—

     (a)   50% of the potential lost revenue in respect of the original tax non-compliance, and

     (b)   £3,000.

Finance Act 2016 (c. **24**)   615
Schedule 20 – Penalties for enablers of offshore tax evasion or non-compliance
Part 1 – Liability for penalty

(3) In sub-paragraph (2)(a) "the original tax non-compliance" means the conduct that incurred the original penalty and "the potential lost revenue" (in respect of that non-compliance) is—

    (a) the potential lost revenue under Schedule 24 to FA 2007,

    (b) the potential lost revenue under Schedule 41 to FA 2008, or

    (c) the liability to tax which would have been shown on the return (within the meaning of Schedule 55 to FA 2009),

according to whether the original penalty was incurred under paragraph 1 of Schedule 24, paragraph 1 of Schedule 41 or paragraph 6 of Schedule 55.

Potential lost revenue: enabling Q to commit relevant offence

4   (1) The potential lost revenue in a case where P is liable to a penalty under paragraph 1 for enabling Q to commit a relevant offence is the same amount as the potential lost revenue applicable for the purposes of the corresponding relevant civil penalty (determined in accordance with the relevant sub-paragraph of paragraph 5).

    (2) Where Q's offending conduct is—

      (a) an offence of cheating the public revenue involving offshore activity, or

      (b) an offence under section 106A of TMA 1970 involving offshore activity,

the corresponding relevant civil penalty is the penalty which Q is liable for as a result of that offending conduct.

    (3) Where Q's offending conduct is an offence under section 106B, 106C or 106D of TMA 1970, the corresponding relevant civil penalty is—

      (a) for an offence under section 106B of TMA 1970, a penalty under paragraph 1 of Schedule 41 to FA 2008,

      (b) for an offence under section 106C of TMA 1970, a penalty under paragraph 6 of Schedule 55 to FA 2009, and

      (c) for an offence under section 106D of TMA 1970, a penalty under paragraph 1 of Schedule 24 to FA 2007.

    (4) In determining any amount of potential lost revenue for the purposes of this paragraph, the fact Q has been prosecuted for the offending conduct is to be disregarded.

Potential lost revenue: enabling Q to engage in conduct incurring relevant civil penalty

5   (1) The potential lost revenue in a case where P is liable to a penalty under paragraph 1 for enabling Q to engage in conduct that makes Q liable (if the applicable conditions are met) to a relevant civil penalty is to be determined as follows.

    (2) In the case of a penalty under paragraph 1 of Schedule 24 to FA 2007 involving an offshore matter or an offshore transfer, the potential lost revenue is the amount that under that Schedule is the potential lost revenue in respect of Q's conduct.

    (3) In the case of a penalty under paragraph 1 of Schedule 41 to FA 2008 in relation to a failure to comply with section 7(1) of TMA 1970 involving offshore activity, the potential lost revenue is the amount that under that Schedule is the potential lost revenue in respect of Q's conduct.

616

Finance Act 2016 (c. 24)
Schedule 20 — Penalties for enablers of offshore tax evasion or non-compliance
Part 1 — Liability for penalty

(4) In the case of a penalty under paragraph 6 of Schedule 55 to FA 2009 involving offshore activity, the potential lost revenue is the liability to tax which would have been shown in the return in question (within the meaning of that Schedule).

Treatment of potential lost revenue attributable to both offshore tax evasion or non-compliance and other tax evasion or non-compliance

6   (1) This paragraph applies where any amount of potential lost revenue in a case falling within paragraph 4 or 5 is attributable not only to Q's offshore tax evasion or non-compliance but also to any other tax evasion or non-compliance by Q.

(2) In that case the potential lost revenue in respect of Q's offshore tax evasion or non-compliance is to be taken for the purposes of assessing the penalty to which P is liable as being or (as the case may be) including such share as is just and reasonable of the amount mentioned in sub-paragraph (1).

Reduction of penalty for disclosure etc by P

7   (1) If P (who would otherwise be liable to a penalty under paragraph 1) —

   (a) makes a disclosure to HMRC of —

      (i) a matter relating to an inaccuracy in a document, a supply of false information or a failure to disclose an under-assessment,

      (ii) P's enabling of actions by Q that constituted (or might constitute) a relevant offence or that made (or might make) Q liable to a relevant penalty, or

      (iii) any other matter HMRC regard as assisting them in relation to the assessment of P's liability to a penalty under paragraph 1, or

   (b) assists HMRC in any investigation leading to Q being charged with a relevant offence or found liable to a relevant penalty,

   HMRC must reduce the penalty to one that reflects the quality of the disclosure or assistance.

(2) But the penalty may not be reduced —

   (a) in the case of unprompted disclosure or assistance, below whichever is the higher of —

      (i) 10% of the potential lost revenue, or

      (ii) £1,000, or

   (b) in the case of prompted disclosure or assistance, below whichever is the higher of —

      (i) 30% of the potential lost revenue, or

      (ii) £3,000.

8   (1) This paragraph applies for the purposes of paragraph 7.

(2) P discloses a matter by —

   (a) telling HMRC about it,

   (b) giving HMRC reasonable help in relation to the matter (for example by quantifying an inaccuracy in a document, an inaccuracy attributable to the supply of false information or withholding of information or an under-assessment), and

Finance Act 2016 (c. 24)
Schedule 20 — Penalties for enablers of offshore tax evasion or non-compliance
Part 1 — Liability for penalty

617

> > (c) allowing HMRC access to records for any reasonable purpose connected with resolving the matter (for example for the purpose of ensuring that an inaccuracy in a document, an inaccuracy attributable to the supply of false information or withholding of information or an under-assessment is fully corrected).
>
> (3) P assists HMRC in relation to an investigation leading to Q being charged with a relevant offence or found liable to a relevant penalty by—
>
> > (a) assisting or encouraging Q to disclose all relevant facts to HMRC,
> >
> > (b) allowing HMRC access to records, or
> >
> > (c) any other conduct which HMRC considers assisted them in investigating or assessing Q's liability to such a penalty.
>
> (4) Disclosure or assistance by P—
>
> > (a) is "unprompted" if made at a time when P has no reason to believe that HMRC have discovered or are about to discover Q's offshore tax evasion or non-compliance (including any inaccuracy in a document, supply of false information or withholding of information, or under-assessment), and
> >
> > (b) otherwise is "prompted".
>
> (5) In relation to disclosure or assistance, "quality" includes timing, nature and extent.

9 (1) If they think it right because of special circumstances, HMRC may reduce a penalty under paragraph 1.

> (2) In sub-paragraph 1 "special circumstances" does not include—
>
> > (a) ability to pay, or
> >
> > (b) the fact that a potential loss of revenue from one taxpayer is balanced by a potential overpayment by another.
>
> (3) In sub-paragraph (1) the reference to reducing a penalty includes a reference to—
>
> > (a) staying a penalty, or
> >
> > (b) agreeing a compromise in relation to proceedings for a penalty.

Procedure for assessing penalty, etc

10 (1) Where a person is found liable for a penalty under paragraph 1 HMRC must—

> > (a) assess the penalty,
> >
> > (b) notify the person, and
> >
> > (c) state in the notice the period in respect of which the penalty is assessed.
>
> (2) A penalty must be paid before the end of the period of 30 days beginning with the day on which notification of the penalty is issued.
>
> (3) An assessment of a penalty—
>
> > (a) is to be treated for procedural purposes in the same way as an assessment to tax (except in respect of a matter expressly provided for by this Schedule), and
> >
> > (b) may be enforced as if it were an assessment to tax.

618

Finance Act 2016 (c. 24)
Schedule 20 — Penalties for enablers of offshore tax evasion or non-compliance
Part 1 — Liability for penalty

(4) A supplementary assessment may be made in respect of a penalty if an earlier assessment operated by reference to an underestimate of the liability to tax that would have been shown in a return.

(5) Sub-paragraph (6) applies if —

    (a) an assessment in respect of a penalty is based on a liability to tax that would have been shown on a return, and

    (b) that liability is found by HMRC to have been excessive.

(6) HMRC may amend the assessment so that it is based upon the correct amount.

(7) But an amendment under sub-paragraph (6) —

    (a) does not affect when the penalty must be paid, and

    (b) may be made after the last day on which the assessment in question could have been made under paragraph 11.

11   An assessment of a person as liable to a penalty under paragraph 1 may not take place more than 2 years after the fulfilment of the conditions mentioned in paragraph 1(1) (in relation to that person) first came to the attention of an officer of Revenue and Customs.

Appeals

12   A person may appeal against —

    (a) a decision of HMRC that a penalty under paragraph 1 is payable by that person, or

    (b) a decision of HMRC as to the amount of a penalty under paragraph 1 payable by the person.

13 (1) An appeal under paragraph 12 is to be treated in the same way as an appeal against an assessment to the tax at stake (including by the application of any provision about bringing the appeal by notice to HMRC, about HMRC review of the decision or about determination of the appeal by the First-tier Tribunal or Upper Tribunal).

    (2) Sub-paragraph (1) does not apply —

        (a) so as to require the person bringing the appeal to pay a penalty before an appeal against the assessment of the penalty is determined,

        (b) in respect of any other matter expressly provided for by this Schedule.

14 (1) On an appeal under paragraph 12(a) that is notified to the tribunal, the tribunal may affirm or cancel HMRC's decision.

    (2) On an appeal under paragraph 12(b) that is notified to the tribunal, the tribunal may —

        (a) affirm HMRC's decision, or

        (b) substitute for that decision another decision that HMRC had power to make.

    (3) If the tribunal substitutes its own decision for HMRC's, the tribunal may rely on paragraph 7 or 9 (or both) —

        (a) to the same extent as HMRC (which may mean applying the same percentage reduction as HMRC to a different starting point),

Finance Act 2016 (c. 24)
Schedule 20 — Penalties for enablers of offshore tax evasion or non-compliance
Part 1 — Liability for penalty

619

       (b)   to a different extent, but only if the tribunal thinks that HMRC's decision in respect of the application of that paragraph was flawed.

  (4) In sub-paragraph (3)(b) "flawed" means flawed when considered in the light of the principles applicable in proceedings for judicial review.

  (5) In this paragraph "tribunal" means the First-tier Tribunal or Upper Tribunal (as appropriate by virtue of paragraph 13(1).

Double jeopardy

15   A person is not liable to a penalty under paragraph 1 in respect of conduct for which the person —

    (a)   has been convicted of an offence, or

    (b)   has been assessed to a penalty under any provision other than paragraph 1.

Application of provisions of TMA 1970

16   Subject to the provisions of this Part of this Schedule, the following provisions of TMA 1970 apply for the purposes of this Part of this Schedule as they apply for the purposes of the Taxes Acts —

    (a)   section 108 (responsibility of company officers),

    (b)   section 114 (want of form), and

    (c)   section 114 (delivery and service of documents).

Interpretation of Part 1

17 (1) This paragraph applies for the purposes of this Schedule.

  (2) References to an assessment to tax, in relation to inheritance tax, are to a determination.

PART 2

APPLICATION OF SCHEDULE 36 TO FA 2008: INFORMATION POWERS

General application of information and inspection powers to suspected enablers

18 (1) Schedule 36 to FA 2008 (information and inspection powers) applies for the purpose of checking a relevant person's position as regards liability for a penalty under paragraph 1 as it applies for checking a person's tax position, subject to the modifications in paragraphs 19 to 21.

  (2) In this Part of this Schedule "relevant person" means a person an officer of Revenue and Customs has reason to suspect has or may have enabled offshore tax evasion or non-compliance by another person so as to be liable to a penalty under paragraph 1.

General modifications

19   In its application for the purpose mentioned in paragraph 18(1) Schedule 36 to FA 2008 has effect as if —

    (a)   any provisions which can have no application for that purpose, or are specifically excluded by paragraph 20, were omitted,

620

Finance Act 2016 (c. 24)
Schedule 20 — Penalties for enablers of offshore tax evasion or non-compliance
Part 2 — Application of Schedule 36 to FA 2008: information powers

    (b)   references to "the taxpayer" were references to the relevant person whose position as regards liability for a penalty under paragraph 1 is to be checked, and references to "a taxpayer" were references to a relevant person,

    (c)   references to a person's "tax position" are to the relevant person's position as regards liability for a penalty under paragraph 1,

    (d)   references to prejudice to the assessment or collection of tax included a reference to prejudice to the investigation of the relevant person's position as regards liability for a penalty under paragraph 1,

    (e)   references to information relating to the conduct of a pending appeal relating to tax were references to information relating to the conduct of a pending appeal relating to an assessment of liability for a penalty under paragraph 1.

Specific modifications

20   The following provisions are excluded from the application of Schedule 36 to FA 2008 for the purpose mentioned in paragraph 18(1) —

    (a)   paragraph 24 (exception for auditors),

    (b)   paragraph 25 (exception for tax advisers),

    (c)   paragraphs 26 and 27 (provisions supplementary to paragraphs 24 and 25),

    (d)   paragraphs 50 and 51 (tax-related penalty).

21   In the application of Schedule 36 to FA 2008 for the purpose mentioned in paragraph 18(1), paragraph 10A (power to inspect business premises of involved third parties) has effect as if the reference in sub-paragraph (1) to the position of any person or class of persons as regards a relevant tax were a reference to the position of a relevant person as regards liability for a penalty under paragraph 1.

PART 3

PUBLISHING DETAILS OF PERSONS FOUND LIABLE TO PENALTIES

Naming etc of persons assessed to penalty or penalties under paragraph 1

22   (1)   The Commissioners for Her Majesty's Revenue and Customs ("the Commissioners") may publish information about a person if—

    (a)   in consequence of an investigation the person has been found to have incurred one or more penalties under paragraph 1 (and has been assessed or is the subject of a contract settlement), and

    (b)   the potential lost revenue in relation to the penalty (or the aggregate of the potential lost revenue in relation to each of the penalties) exceeds £25,000.

(2)   The Commissioners may also publish information about a person if the person has been found to have incurred 5 or more penalties under paragraph 1 in any 5 year period.

(3)   The information that may be published is—

    (a)   the person's name (including any trading name, previous name or pseudonym),

    (b)   the person's address (or registered office),

Finance Act 2016 (c. 24)
Schedule 20 – Penalties for enablers of offshore tax evasion or non-compliance
Part 3 – Publishing details of persons found liable to penalties

621

      (c)   the nature of any business carried on by the person,

      (d)   the amount of the penalty or penalties in question,

      (e)   the periods or times to which the actions giving rise to the penalty or penalties relate,

      (f)   any other information that the Commissioners consider it appropriate to publish in order to make clear the person's identity.

(4) The information may be published in any manner that the Commissioners consider appropriate.

(5) Before publishing any information the Commissioners must—

      (a)   inform the person that they are considering doing so, and

      (b)   afford the person the opportunity to make representations about whether it should be published.

(6) No information may be published before the day on which the penalty becomes final or, where more than one penalty is involved, the latest day on which any of the penalties becomes final.

(7) No information may be published for the first time after the end of the period of one year beginning with that day.

(8) No information may be published if the amount of the penalty—

      (a)   is reduced under paragraph 7 to—

           (i)   10% of the potential lost revenue (in a case of unprompted disclosure or assistance), or

           (ii)   30% of potential lost revenue (in a case of prompted disclosure or assistance),

      (b)   would have been reduced to 10% or 30% of potential lost revenue but for the imposition of the minimum penalty,

      (c)   is reduced under paragraph 9 to nil or stayed.

(9) For the purposes of this paragraph a penalty becomes final—

      (a)   if it has been assessed, when the time for any appeal or further appeal relating to it expires or, if later, any appeal or final appeal relating to it is finally determined, and

      (b)   if a contract settlement has been made, at the time when the contract is made.

(10) In this paragraph "contract settlement", in relation to a penalty, means a contract between the Commissioners and the person under which the Commissioners undertake not to assess the penalty or (if it has been assessed) not to take proceedings to recover it.

23   (1) The Treasury may by regulations amend paragraph 22(1) to vary the amount for the time being specified in paragraph (b).

    (2) Regulations under this paragraph are to be made by statutory instrument.

    (3) A statutory instrument under this paragraph is subject to annulment in pursuance of a resolution of the House of Commons.

SCHEDULE 21   Section 163

PENALTIES RELATING TO OFFSHORE MATTERS AND OFFSHORE TRANSFERS

Amendments to Schedule 24 to the Finance Act 2007 (c. 11)

1   Schedule 24 to FA 2007 (penalties for errors) is amended as follows.

2   (1) Paragraph 9 (reductions for disclosure) is amended as follows.

     (2) For sub-paragraph (A1) substitute—

        "(A1) Paragraph 10 provides for reductions in penalties—
              (a) under paragraph 1 where a person discloses an inaccuracy
                   that involves a domestic matter,
              (b) under paragraph 1A where a person discloses a supply of
                   false information or withholding of information, and
              (c) under paragraph 2 where a person discloses a failure to
                   disclose an under-assessment.

         (A2) Paragraph 10A provides for reductions in penalties under
               paragraph 1 where a person discloses an inaccuracy that involves
               an offshore matter or an offshore transfer.

         (A3) Sub-paragraph (1) applies where a person discloses—
              (a) an inaccuracy that involves a domestic matter,
              (b) a careless inaccuracy that involves an offshore matter,
              (c) a supply of false information or withholding of
                   information, or
              (d) a failure to disclose an under-assessment."

     (3) In sub-paragraph (1), in the words before paragraph (a), for the words from
         "an inaccuracy" to "under-assessment" substitute "the matter".

     (4) After sub-paragraph (1) insert—

        "(1A) Sub-paragraph (1B) applies where a person discloses—
              (a) a deliberate inaccuracy (whether concealed or not) that
                   involves an offshore matter, or
              (b) an inaccuracy that involves an offshore transfer.

         (1B) A person discloses the inaccuracy by—
              (a) telling HMRC about it,
              (b) giving HMRC reasonable help in quantifying the
                   inaccuracy,
              (c) allowing HMRC access to records for the purpose of
                   ensuring that the inaccuracy is fully corrected, and
              (d) providing HMRC with additional information.

         (1C) The Treasury must make regulations setting out what is meant by
               "additional information" for the purposes of sub-paragraph
               (1B)(d).

         (1D) Regulations under sub-paragraph (1C) are to be made by statutory
               instrument.

(1E) An instrument containing regulations under sub-paragraph (1C) is subject to annulment in pursuance of a resolution of the House of Commons."

(5) At the end insert—

"(4) Paragraph 4A(4) to (5) applies to determine whether an inaccuracy involves an offshore matter, an offshore transfer or a domestic matter for the purposes of this paragraph."

3   In paragraph 10 (amount of reduction for disclosure), for the Table in sub-paragraph (2) substitute—

"Standard %	Minimum % for prompted disclosure	Minimum % for unprompted disclosure
30%	15%	0%
70%	35%	20%
100%	50%	30%"

4   After paragraph 10 insert—

"10A(1) If a person who would otherwise be liable to a penalty of a percentage shown in column 1 of the Table (a "standard percentage") has made a disclosure, HMRC must reduce the standard percentage to one that reflects the quality of the disclosure.

(2) But the standard percentage may not be reduced to a percentage that is below the minimum shown for it—

(a) in the case of a prompted disclosure, in column 2 of the Table, and

(b) in the case of an unprompted disclosure, in column 3 of the Table.

Standard %	Minimum % for prompted disclosure	Minimum % for unprompted disclosure
30%	15%	0%
37.5%	18.75%	0%
45%	22.5%	0%
60%	30%	0%
70%	45%	30%
87.5%	53.75%	35%
100%	60%	40%

Standard %	Minimum % for prompted disclosure	Minimum % for unprompted disclosure
105%	62.5%	40%
125%	72.5%	50%
140%	80%	50%
150%	85%	55%
200%	110%	70%"

Amendments to Schedule 41 to the Finance Act 2008 (c. 9)

5   Schedule 41 to FA 2008 (penalties: failure to notify etc) is amended as follows.

6   (1) Paragraph 12 (reductions for disclosure) is amended as follows.

(2) For sub-paragraph (1) substitute —

"(1) Paragraph 13 provides for reductions in penalties —
   (a) under paragraph 1 where P discloses a relevant failure that involves a domestic matter, and
   (b) under paragraphs 2 to 4 where P discloses a relevant act or failure.

(1A) Paragraph 13A provides for reductions in penalties under paragraph 1 where P discloses a relevant failure that involves an offshore matter or an offshore transfer.

(1B) Sub-paragraph (2) applies where P discloses —
   (a) a relevant failure that involves a domestic matter,
   (b) a non-deliberate relevant failure that involves an offshore matter, or
   (c) a relevant act or failure giving rise to a penalty under any of paragraphs 2 to 4."

(3) In sub-paragraph (2), for "a" substitute "the".

(4) After sub-paragraph (2) insert —

"(2A) Sub-paragraph (2B) applies where P discloses —
   (a) a deliberate relevant failure (whether concealed or not) that involves an offshore matter, or
   (b) a relevant failure that involves an offshore transfer.

(2B) P discloses the failure by —
   (a) telling HMRC about it,
   (b) giving HMRC reasonable help in quantifying the tax unpaid by reason of it,
   (c) allowing HMRC access to records for the purpose of checking how much tax is so unpaid, and
   (d) providing HMRC with additional information.

     (2C) The Treasury must make regulations setting out what is meant by "additional information" for the purposes of sub-paragraph (2B)(d).

     (2D) Regulations under sub-paragraph (2C) are to be made by statutory instrument.

     (2E) An instrument containing regulations under sub-paragraph (2C) is subject to annulment in pursuance of a resolution of the House of Commons."

  (5) At the end insert—

     "(5) Paragraph 6A(4) to (5) applies to determine whether a failure involves an offshore matter, an offshore transfer or a domestic matter for the purposes of this paragraph.

     (6) In this paragraph "relevant failure" means a failure to comply with a relevant obligation."

7   In paragraph 13 (amount of reduction for disclosure), for the Table in sub-paragraph (3) substitute—

"Standard %	Minimum % for prompted disclosure	Minimum % for unprompted disclosure
30%	case A: 10% case B: 20%	case A: 0% case B: 10%
70%	35%	20%
100%	50%	30%"

8   After paragraph 13 insert—

     "13A(1) If a person who would otherwise be liable to a penalty of a percentage shown in column 1 of the Table (a "standard percentage") has made a disclosure, HMRC must reduce the standard percentage to one that reflects the quality of the disclosure.

     (2) But the standard percentage may not be reduced to a percentage that is below the minimum shown for it—

       (a) for a prompted disclosure, in column 2 of the Table, and

       (b) for an unprompted disclosure, in column 3 of the Table.

     (3) Where the Table shows a different minimum for case A and case B—

       (a) the case A minimum applies if HMRC becomes aware of the failure less than 12 months after the time when the tax first becomes unpaid by reason of the failure;

       (b) otherwise, the case B minimum applies.

Standard %	Minimum % for prompted disclosure	Minimum % for unprompted disclosure
30%	case A: 10% case B: 20%	case A: 0% case B: 10%
37.5%	case A: 12.5% case B: 25%	case A: 0% case B: 12.5%
45%	case A: 15% case B: 30%	case A: 0% case B:15%
60%	case A: 20% case B: 40%	case A: 0% case B: 20%
70%	45%	30%
87.5%	53.75%	35%
100%	60%	40%
105%	62.5%	40%
125%	72.5%	50%
140%	80%	50%
150%	85%	55%
200%	110%	70%"

Amendments to Schedule 55 to the Finance Act 2009 (c.10)

9   Schedule 55 to FA 2009 (penalty for failure to make returns etc) is amended as follows

10   (1) Paragraph 14 (reductions for disclosure) is amended as follows.

      (2) At the beginning insert—

          "(A1) In this paragraph, "relevant information" means information which has been withheld by a failure to make a return."

      (3) In sub-paragraph (1)—
          (a) after "6(3) or (4)" insert "where P discloses relevant information that involves a domestic matter";
          (b) for the words from "information which" to the end substitute "relevant information".

      (4) After sub-paragraph (1) insert—

          "(1A) Paragraph 15A provides for reductions in the penalty under paragraph 6(3) or (4) where P discloses relevant information that involves an offshore matter or an offshore transfer.

          (1B) Sub-paragraph (2) applies where—

      (a)   P is liable to a penalty under paragraph 6(3) or (4) and P discloses relevant information that involves a domestic matter, or

      (b)   P is liable to a penalty under any of the other provisions mentioned in sub-paragraph (1) and P discloses relevant information."

(5) After sub-paragraph (2) insert—

  "(2A) Sub-paragraph (2B) applies where P is liable to a penalty under paragraph 6(3) or (4) and P discloses relevant information that involves an offshore matter or an offshore transfer.

  (2B) P discloses relevant information by—

      (a)   telling HMRC about it,

      (b)   giving HMRC reasonable help in quantifying any tax unpaid by reason of its having been withheld,

      (c)   allowing HMRC access to records for the purpose of checking how much tax is so unpaid, and

      (d)   providing HMRC with additional information.

  (2C) The Treasury must make regulations setting out what is meant by "additional information" for the purposes of sub-paragraph (2B)(d).

  (2D) Regulations under sub-paragraph (2C) are to be made by statutory instrument.

  (2E) An instrument containing regulations under sub-paragraph (2C) is subject to annulment in pursuance of a resolution of the House of Commons."

(6) At the end insert—

  "(5) Paragraph 6A(4) to (5) applies to determine whether relevant information involves an offshore matter, an offshore transfer or a domestic matter for the purposes of this paragraph."

11   In paragraph 15 (amount of reduction for disclosure), for the Table in sub-paragraph (2) substitute—

"Standard %	Minimum % for prompted disclosure	Minimum % for unprompted disclosure
70%	35%	20%
100%	50%	30%"

12   After paragraph 15 insert—

  "15A(1) If a person who would otherwise be liable to a penalty of a percentage shown in column 1 of the Table (a "standard percentage") has made a disclosure, HMRC must reduce the standard percentage to one that reflects the quality of the disclosure.

(2) But the standard percentage may not be reduced to a percentage that is below the minimum shown for it—

    (a) in the case of a prompted disclosure, in column 2 of the Table, and

    (b) in the case of an unprompted disclosure, in column 3 of the Table.

Standard %	Minimum % for prompted disclosure	Minimum % for unprompted disclosure
70%	45%	30%
87.5%	53.75%	35%
100%	60%	40%
105%	62.5%	40%
125%	72.5%	50%
140%	80%	50%
150%	85%	55%
200%	110%	70%

(3) But HMRC must not under this paragraph reduce a penalty below £300."

SCHEDULE 22

Section 165

ASSET-BASED PENALTY FOR OFFSHORE INACCURACIES AND FAILURES

PART 1

LIABILITY FOR PENALTY

Circumstances in which asset-based penalty is payable

1 (1) An asset-based penalty is payable by a person (P) where—

    (a) one or more standard offshore tax penalties have been imposed on P in relation to a tax year (see paragraphs 2 and 3), and

    (b) the potential lost revenue threshold is met in relation to that tax year (see paragraph 4).

(2) But this is subject to paragraph 6 (restriction on imposition of multiple asset-based penalties in relation to the same asset).

Meaning of standard offshore tax penalty

2 (1) A standard offshore tax penalty is a penalty that falls within sub-paragraph (2), (3) or (4).

Finance Act 2016 (c. 24)
Schedule 22 — Asset-based penalty for offshore inaccuracies and failures
Part 1 — Liability for penalty

629

(2) A penalty falls within this sub-paragraph if —

    (a) it is imposed under paragraph 1 of Schedule 24 to FA 2007 (inaccuracy in taxpayer's document),

    (b) the inaccuracy for which the penalty is imposed involves an offshore matter or an offshore transfer,

    (c) it is imposed for deliberate action (whether concealed or not), and

    (d) the tax at stake is (or includes) capital gains tax, inheritance tax or asset-based income tax.

(3) A penalty falls within this sub-paragraph if —

    (a) it is imposed under paragraph 1 of Schedule 41 to FA 2008 (penalty for failure to notify),

    (b) the failure for which the penalty is imposed involves an offshore matter or an offshore transfer,

    (c) it is imposed for a deliberate failure (whether concealed or not), and

    (d) the tax at stake is (or includes) capital gains tax or asset-based income tax.

(4) A penalty falls within this sub-paragraph if —

    (a) it is imposed under paragraph 6 of Schedule 55 to FA 2009 (penalty for failure to make return more than 12 months after filing date),

    (b) it is imposed for the withholding of information involving an offshore matter or an offshore transfer,

    (c) it is imposed for a deliberate withholding of information (whether concealed or not), and

    (d) the tax at stake is (or includes) capital gains tax, inheritance tax or asset-based income tax.

(5) In a case where the inaccuracy, failure or withholding of information for which a penalty is imposed involves both an offshore matter or an offshore transfer and a domestic matter, the standard offshore tax penalty is only that part of the penalty that involves the offshore matter or offshore transfer.

(6) In a case where the tax at stake in relation to a penalty includes a tax other than capital gains tax, inheritance tax or asset-based income tax, the standard offshore tax penalty is only that part of the penalty which relates to capital gains tax, inheritance tax or asset-based income tax.

(7) "Asset-based income tax" means income tax that is charged under any of the provisions mentioned in column 1 of the table in paragraph 13(2).

Tax year to which standard offshore tax penalty relates

3   (1) Where a standard offshore tax penalty is imposed under paragraph 1 of Schedule 24 to FA 2007, the tax year to which that penalty relates is —

    (a) if the tax at stake as a result of the inaccuracy is income tax or capital gains tax, the tax year to which the document containing the inaccuracy relates;

    (b) if the tax at stake as a result of the inaccuracy is inheritance tax, the year, beginning on 6 April and ending on the following 5 April, in which the liability to tax first arose.

    (2) Where a standard offshore tax penalty is imposed under paragraph 1 of Schedule 41 to FA 2008 for a failure to comply with an obligation specified

630

Finance Act 2016 (c. 24)
Schedule 22 — Asset-based penalty for offshore inaccuracies and failures
Part 1 — Liability for penalty

in the table in that paragraph, the tax year to which that penalty relates is the tax year to which the obligation relates.

(3) Where a standard offshore tax penalty is imposed under paragraph 6 of Schedule 55 to FA 2009 for a failure to make a return or deliver a document specified in the table of paragraph 1 of that Schedule, the tax year to which that penalty relates is —

    (a) if the tax at stake is income tax or capital gains tax, the tax year to which the return or document relates;

    (b) if the tax at stake is inheritance tax, the year, beginning on 6 April and ending on the following 5 April, in which the liability to tax first arose.

Potential lost revenue threshold

4 (1) The potential lost revenue threshold is reached where the offshore PLR in relation to a tax year exceeds £25,000.

(2) The Treasury may by regulations change the figure for the time being specified in sub-paragraph (1).

(3) Regulations under sub-paragraph (2) are to be made by statutory instrument.

(4) A statutory instrument containing regulations under sub-paragraph (2) is subject to annulment in pursuance of a resolution of the House of Commons.

(5) Regulations under sub-paragraph (2) —

    (a) may make different provision for different purposes;

    (b) may contain supplemental, incidental, consequential, transitional and transitory provision.

Offshore PLR

5 (1) The offshore PLR, in relation to a tax year, is the total of —

    (a) the potential lost revenue (in the case of a standard offshore tax penalty imposed under Schedule 24 to FA 2007 or Schedule 41 to FA 2008), and

    (b) the liability to tax (in the case of a standard offshore tax penalty imposed under Schedule 55 to FA 2009),

by reference to which all of the standard offshore tax penalties imposed on P in relation to the tax year are assessed.

(2) Sub-paragraphs (3) to (5) apply where —

    (a) a penalty is imposed on P under paragraph 1 of Schedule 24 to FA 2007, paragraph 1 of Schedule 41 to FA 2008 or paragraph 6 of Schedule 55 to FA 2009, and

    (b) the potential lost revenue or liability to tax by reference to which the penalty is assessed relates to a standard offshore tax penalty and one or more other penalties.

In this paragraph, such a penalty is referred to as a "combined penalty".

(3) Only the potential lost revenue or liability to tax relating to the standard offshore tax penalty is to be taken into account in calculating the offshore PLR.

Finance Act 2016 (c. 24)   631
Schedule 22 – Asset-based penalty for offshore inaccuracies and failures
Part 1 – Liability for penalty

(4) Where the calculation of the potential lost revenue or liability to tax by reference to which a combined penalty is assessed depends on the order in which income or gains are treated as having been taxed, for the purposes of calculating the offshore PLR—

    (a) income and gains relating to domestic matters are to be taken to have been taxed before income and gains relating to offshore matters and offshore transfers;

    (b) income and gains relating to taxes that are not capital gains tax, inheritance tax or asset-based income tax are to be taken to have been taxed before income and gains relating to capital gains tax, inheritance tax and asset-based income tax.

(5) In a case where it cannot be determined—

    (a) whether income or gains relate to an offshore matter or offshore transfer or to a domestic matter, or

    (b) whether income or gains relate to capital gains tax, asset-based income tax or inheritance tax or not,

for the purposes of calculating the offshore PLR, the potential lost revenue or liability to tax relating to the standard offshore tax penalty is to be taken to be such share of the total potential lost revenue or liability to tax by reference to which the combined penalty was calculated as is just and reasonable.

(6) Sub-paragraph (7) applies where—

    (a) a standard offshore tax penalty or a combined penalty is imposed on P, and

    (b) there are two or more taxes at stake, including capital gains tax and asset-based income tax.

(7) Where the calculation of the potential lost revenue or liability to tax by reference to which the penalty is assessed depends on the order in which income or gains are treated as having been taxed, for the purposes of calculating the offshore PLR, income and gains relating to asset-based income tax are to be taken to have been taxed before income and gains relating to capital gains tax.

Restriction on imposition of multiple asset-based penalties in relation to the same asset

6   (1) Sub-paragraphs (2) and (3) apply where—

    (a) a standard offshore tax penalty has been imposed on P, and

    (b) the potential lost revenue threshold is met,

in relation to more than one tax year falling within the same investigation period.

(2) Only one asset-based penalty is payable by P in the investigation period in relation to any given asset.

(3) The asset-based penalty is to be charged by reference to the tax year in the investigation period with the highest offshore PLR.

(4) An "investigation period" is—

    (a) the period starting with the day on which this Schedule comes into force and ending with the last day of the last tax year before P was notified of an asset-based penalty in respect of an asset, and

632

Finance Act 2016 (c. 24)
Schedule 22 — Asset-based penalty for offshore inaccuracies and failures
Part 1 — Liability for penalty

(b)   subsequent periods beginning with the day after the previous period ended and ending with the last day of the last tax year before P is notified of a subsequent asset-based penalty in respect of the asset,

and different investigation periods may apply in relation to different assets.

PART 2

AMOUNT OF PENALTY

Standard amount of asset-based penalty

7   (1) The standard amount of the asset-based penalty is the lower of —
    (a)   10% of the value of the asset, and
    (b)   offshore PLR x 10.

   (2) See also —
    (a)   paragraphs 8 and 9, which provide for reductions in the standard amount, and
    (b)   Part 3, which makes provision about the identification and valuation of the asset.

Reductions for disclosure and co-operation

8   (1) HMRC must reduce the standard amount of the asset-based penalty where P does all of the following things —
    (a)   makes a disclosure of the inaccuracy or failure relating to the standard offshore tax penalty;
    (b)   provides HMRC with a reasonable valuation of the asset;
    (c)   provides HMRC with information or access to records that HMRC requires from P for the purposes of valuing the asset.

   (2) A reduction under sub-paragraph (1) must reflect the quality of the disclosure, valuation and information provided (and for these purposes "quality" includes timing, nature and extent).

   (3) The Treasury must make regulations setting out the maximum amount of the penalty reduction under sub-paragraph (1).

   (4) The maximum amount may differ according to whether the case involves only unprompted disclosures or involves prompted disclosures.

   (5) A case involves only unprompted disclosures where —
    (a)   in a case where the asset-based penalty relates to only one standard offshore tax penalty, that standard offshore tax penalty was reduced on the basis of an unprompted disclosure, or
    (b)   in a case where the asset-based penalty relates to more than one standard offshore tax penalty, all of those standard offshore tax penalties were reduced on the basis of unprompted disclosures.

   (6) A case involves prompted disclosures where any of the standard offshore tax penalties to which the asset-based penalty relates was reduced on the basis of a prompted disclosure.

   (7) Regulations under sub-paragraph (3) are to be made by statutory instrument.

Finance Act 2016 (c. 24)
Schedule 22 — Asset-based penalty for offshore inaccuracies and failures
Part 2 — Amount of penalty

633

(8) A statutory instrument containing regulations under sub-paragraph (3) is subject to annulment in pursuance of a resolution of the House of Commons.

(9) Regulations under sub-paragraph (3) —

    (a) may make different provision for different purposes;

    (b) may contain supplemental, incidental, consequential, transitional and transitory provision.

Special reduction

9   (1) If HMRC think it right because of special circumstances, they may reduce the standard amount of the asset-based penalty.

    (2) In sub-paragraph (1) "special circumstances" does not include —

        (a) ability to pay, or

        (b) the fact that a potential loss of revenue from one taxpayer is balanced by a potential over-payment by another.

    (3) In sub-paragraph (1) the reference to reducing a penalty includes a reference to —

        (a) staying a penalty, and

        (b) agreeing a compromise in relation to proceedings for a penalty.

PART 3

IDENTIFICATION AND VALUATION OF ASSETS

Introduction

10   (1) This Part makes provision about the identification and valuation of the asset for the purposes of calculating the amount of the asset-based penalty.

    (2) An asset-based penalty may relate to more than one asset.

    (3) The identification and valuation of the asset is to be determined —

        (a) under paragraph 11 where the principal tax at stake is capital gains tax,

        (b) under paragraph 12 where the principal tax at stake is inheritance tax, and

        (c) under paragraph 13 where the principal tax at stake is asset-based income tax.

    See also paragraph 14 (jointly held assets).

    (4) The principal tax at stake —

        (a) in a case where the standard offshore tax penalty (or penalties) relates to only one type of tax, is the tax to which that standard offshore tax penalty (or penalties) relates;

        (b) in a case where the standard offshore tax penalty (or penalties) relate to more than one type of tax, is the tax which gives rise to the highest offshore PLR value.

    (5) The offshore PLR value, in relation to a type of tax, is the potential lost revenue or liability to tax by reference to which the part of the penalty relating to that type of tax was assessed.

634

Finance Act 2016 (c. 24)
Schedule 22 — Asset-based penalty for offshore inaccuracies and failures
Part 3 — Identification and valuation of assets

(6) The rules in paragraph 5(2) to (7) apply for the purposes of calculating the offshore PLR value, in relation to a type of tax, as they apply for the purposes of calculating the offshore PLR.

Capital gains tax

11 (1) This paragraph applies where the principal tax at stake is capital gains tax.

(2) The asset is the asset that is the subject of the disposal (or deemed disposal) on or by reference to which the capital gains tax to which the standard offshore penalty relates is charged.

(3) For the purposes of calculating the amount of the asset-based penalty, the value of the asset is to be taken to be the consideration for the disposal of the asset that would be used in the computation of the gain under TCGA 1992 (other than in a case where sub-paragraph (4) applies).

(4) In a case where the disposal on or by reference to which the capital gains tax is charged is a part disposal of an asset, the asset-based penalty is to be calculated by reference to the full market value of the asset immediately before the part disposal took place.

(5) Terms used in this paragraph have the same meaning as in TCGA 1992.

Inheritance tax

12 (1) This paragraph applies where the principal tax at stake is inheritance tax.

(2) The asset is the property the disposition of which gave rise to the transfer of value by reason of which the inheritance tax to which the standard offshore penalty relates became chargeable.

(3) For the purposes of calculating the amount of the asset-based penalty, the value of the property is to be the value of the property used by HMRC in assessing the liability to inheritance tax.

(4) Terms used in this paragraph have the same meaning as in IHTA 1984.

Asset-based income tax

13 (1) This paragraph applies where the principal tax at stake is asset-based income tax.

(2) Where the standard offshore tax penalty relates to income tax charged under a provision shown in column 1 of the Table, the asset is the asset mentioned in column 2 of the Table.

Provision under which income tax is charged	*Asset*
Chapters 3, 7 and 10 of Part 3 of ITTOIA 2005 (property businesses)	The estate, interest or right in or over the land that generates the income for the business (see sections 264 to 266 of ITTOIA 2005)

*Finance Act 2016 (c. **24**)*
Schedule 22 — Asset-based penalty for offshore inaccuracies and failures
Part 3 — Identification and valuation of assets

635

Provision under which income tax is charged	*Asset*
Chapter 8 of Part 3 of ITTOIA 2005 (rent receivable in connection with a s.12(4) concern)	The estate, interest or right in or over the land that generates the rent receivable in connection with a UK section 12(4) concern (see sections 335 and 336 of ITTOIA 2005)
Chapters 2 and 2A of Part 4 of ITTOIA 2005 (interest and disguised interest)	The asset that generates the interest
Chapters 3 to 5 of Part 4 of ITTOIA 2005 (dividends etc)	The shares or other securities in relation to which the dividend or distribution is paid
Chapter 7 of Part 4 of ITTOIA 2005 (purchased life annuity payments)	The annuity that gives rise to the payments
Chapter 8 of Part 4 of ITTOIA 2005 (profits from deeply discounted securities)	The deeply discounted securities that are disposed of (see sections 427 to 430 of ITTOIA 2005)
Chapter 9 of Part 4 of ITTOIA 2005 (gains from contracts for life insurance etc)	The policy or contract from which the gain is treated as arising
Chapter 11 of Part 4 of ITTOIA 2005 (transactions in deposits)	The deposit right which is disposed of (see sections 551 and 552 of ITTOIA 2005)
Chapter 2 of Part 5 of ITTOIA 2005 (receipts from intellectual property)	The intellectual property, know-how or patent rights which generate the income (see sections 579, 583 and 587 of ITTOIA 2005)
Chapter 4 of Part 5 of ITTOIA 2005 (certain telecommunication rights: non-trading income)	The relevant telecommunication right from which the income derives (see section 614 of ITTOIA 2005)
Chapter 5 of Part 5 of ITTOIA 2005 (settlements: amounts treated as income of settlor)	The settlement which gives rise to the income or capital sums treated as income of a settlor

(3) For the purposes of calculating the amount of the asset-based penalty, the asset is to be valued as follows.

(4) In a case where the charge to income tax was triggered by a disposal of the asset, the value of the asset is to be taken as its market value on the date of disposal (and in the case of a part disposal, the value of the asset is to be taken as its full market value immediately before the part disposal took place).

636

Finance Act 2016 (c. 24)
Schedule 22 — Asset-based penalty for offshore inaccuracies and failures
Part 3 — Identification and valuation of assets

(5) In any other case—

    (a) where P still owns the asset on the last day of the tax year to which the standard offshore tax penalty relates, the value of the asset is to be taken as its market value on that day;

    (b) where P disposed of the asset during the course of the tax year to which the standard offshore tax penalty relates, the value of the asset is to be taken as its market value on the date of disposal;

    (c) where P disposed of part of the asset during the course of the tax year to which the standard offshore tax penalty relates, the value of the asset is to be taken as the market value of the part disposed on the date (or dates) of disposal plus the market value of the part still owned by the person on the last day of that tax year.

(6) But if the value of the asset, as determined in accordance with sub-paragraphs (4) and (5), does not appear to HMRC to be a fair and reasonable value, then HMRC may value the asset for the purposes of this Schedule in any other way which appears to them to be fair and reasonable.

(7) For the purposes of sub-paragraph (5)—

    (a) P owns an asset if P is liable to asset-based income tax in relation to that asset;

    (b) references to a disposal (and related expressions) have the same meaning as in TCGA 1992.

(8) In this paragraph "market value" has the same meaning as in TCGA 1992 (see section 272 of that Act).

(9) Other terms used in this paragraph have the same meaning as in ITTOIA 2005.

Jointly held assets

14 (1) This paragraph applies where an asset-based penalty is chargeable in relation to an asset that is jointly held by P and another person (A).

(2) The value of the asset is to be taken to be the value of P's share of the asset.

(3) In a case where P and A—

    (a) are married to, or are civil partners of, each other, and

    (b) live together,

the asset is to be taken to be jointly owned by P and A in equal shares, unless it appears to HMRC that this is not the case.

PART 4

PROCEDURE

Assessment

15 (1) Where a person (P) becomes liable for an asset-based penalty under paragraph 1, HMRC must—

    (a) assess the penalty,

    (b) notify P, and

    (c) state in the notice—

        (i) the tax year to which the penalty relates, and

          (ii)   the investigation period within which that tax year falls (see paragraph 6).

(2) A penalty under paragraph 1 must be paid before the end of the period of 30 days beginning with the day on which notification of the penalty is issued.

(3) An assessment—

    (a)   is to be treated for procedural purposes in the same way as an assessment to tax (except in respect of a matter expressly provided for by this Schedule),

    (b)   may be enforced as if it were an assessment to tax, and

    (c)   may be combined with an assessment to tax.

(4) An assessment of an asset-based penalty under paragraph 1 must be made within the period allowed for making an assessment of the standard offshore tax penalty to which the asset-based penalty relates (and where an asset-based penalty relates to more than one standard offshore tax penalty, the assessment must be made within the latest of those periods).

(5) In this Part of this Schedule references to an assessment to tax, in relation to inheritance tax, are to a determination.

Appeal

16   (1) P may appeal against a decision of HMRC that a penalty is payable by P.

     (2) P may appeal against a decision of HMRC as to the amount of a penalty payable by P.

17   (1) An appeal is to be treated in the same way as an appeal against an assessment to the tax concerned (including by the application of any provision about bringing the appeal by notice to HMRC, about HMRC review of the decision or about determination of the appeal by the First-tier Tribunal or the Upper Tribunal).

     (2) Sub-paragraph (1) does not apply—

    (a)   so as to require P to pay a penalty before an appeal against the assessment of the penalty is determined, or

    (b)   in respect of any other matter expressly provided for by this Schedule.

18   (1) On an appeal under paragraph 16(1), the tribunal may affirm or cancel HMRC's decision.

     (2) On an appeal under paragraph 16(2), the tribunal may—

    (a)   affirm HMRC's decision, or

    (b)   substitute for HMRC's decision another decision that HMRC had power to make.

     (3) If the tribunal substitutes its decision for HMRC's, the tribunal may rely on paragraph 9—

    (a)   to the same extent as HMRC (which may mean applying the same percentage reduction as HMRC to a different starting point), or

    (b)   to a different extent, but only if the tribunal thinks that HMRC's decision in respect of the application of paragraph 9 was flawed.

638

Finance Act 2016 (c. 24)
Schedule 22 — Asset-based penalty for offshore inaccuracies and failures
Part 4 — Procedure

(4) In sub-paragraph (3), "flawed" means flawed when considered in the light of the principles applied in proceedings for judicial review.

(5) In this paragraph "tribunal" means the First-tier Tribunal or the Upper Tribunal (as appropriate by virtue of paragraph 17(1)).

PART 5

GENERAL

Interpretation

19 (1) In this Schedule—

"asset" has the same meaning as in TCGA 1992 (but also includes currency in sterling);

"asset-based income tax" has the meaning given in paragraph 2(7);

"HMRC" means Her Majesty's Revenue and Customs;

"investigation period" has the meaning given in paragraph 6(4);

"offshore PLR" has the meaning given in paragraph 5;

"standard amount of the asset-based penalty" has the meaning given in paragraph 7;

"standard offshore tax penalty" has the meaning given in paragraph 2.

(2) Terms used in relation to a penalty imposed under Schedule 24 to FA 2007, Schedule 41 to FA 2008 or Schedule 55 to FA 2009 have the same meaning as in the Schedule under which the penalty was imposed.

(3) References in this Schedule to capital gains tax do not include capital gains tax payable by companies in respect of chargeable gains accruing to them to the extent that those gains are NRCGT gains in respect of which the companies are chargeable to capital gains tax under section 14D or 188D of TCGA 1992 (see section 1(2A)(b) of that Act).

Consequential amendments etc

20 (1) In section 103ZA to TMA 1970 (disapplication of sections 100 to 103 in case of certain penalties), omit the "or" at the end of paragraph (h), and at the end insert ", or

(j) Schedule 22 to the Finance Act 2016 (asset-based penalty)".

(2) In section 107A of that Act (relevant trustees)—

(a) in subsection (2)(a), after "Schedule 55 to the Finance Act 2009" insert "or Schedule 22 to the Finance Act 2016";

(b) after subsection (3)(a) insert—

"(aa) in relation to a penalty under Schedule 22 to the Finance Act 2016, or to interest under section 101 of the Finance Act 2009 on such a penalty, the time when the relevant act or omission occurred;";

(c) in the words after paragraph (c), after "paragraph" insert "(aa) and".

(3) In Schedule 24 to FA 2007 (penalties for errors), in paragraph 12 (interaction with other penalties etc), in sub-paragraph (2A) at the end insert "or Schedule 22 to FA 2016 (asset-based penalty)".

Finance Act 2016 (c. 24)
Schedule 22 — Asset-based penalty for offshore inaccuracies and failures
Part 5 — General

639

(4) In Schedule 41 to FA 2008 (penalties for failure to notify), in paragraph 15 (interaction with other penalties etc), in sub-paragraph (1A) at the end insert "or Schedule 22 to FA 2016 (asset-based penalty)."

(5) In Schedule 55 to FA 2009 (penalty for failure to make return etc), in paragraph 17 (interaction with other penalties etc), in sub-paragraph (2), at the end insert ", or

      (d)   a penalty under Schedule 22 to FA 2016 (asset-based penalty)."

21   Section 97A of TMA 1970 (two or more tax-geared penalties in respect of same tax) does not apply in relation to an asset-based penalty imposed under this Schedule.

SCHEDULE 23 Section 167

SIMPLE ASSESSMENTS

1   TMA 1970 is amended in accordance with paragraphs 2 to 8 of this Schedule.

2   In section 7 (notice of liability to income tax and capital gains tax), after subsection (2) insert—

"(2A)   A person who—
      (a)   falls within subsection (1A) or (1B), and
      (b)   is notified of a simple assessment for the year of assessment,
is not required to give notice under subsection (1) for that year unless the person is chargeable to income tax or capital gains tax for the year of assessment on any income or gain that is not included in the assessment."

3   After section 28G (determination of amount notionally chargeable where no NRCGT return delivered) insert—

"28H Simple assessments by HMRC: personal assessments

(1)   HMRC may make a simple assessment for a year of assessment in respect of a person (other than a person to whom section 28I applies) if, when the assessment is made, the person is not excluded by subsection (2) in relation to that year.

(2)   Subsection (1) does not apply to a person at any time in relation to that year of assessment if—
      (a)   the person has delivered a return under section 8 for that year, or
      (b)   the person is at that time subject to a requirement to make and deliver such a return by virtue of a notice under section 8.
but nothing in this subsection prevents HMRC from giving the person notice of a simple assessment at the same time as a notice withdrawing a notice under section 8.

(3)   A simple assessment is—
      (a)   an assessment of the amounts in which the person is chargeable to income tax and capital gains tax for the year of assessment to which it relates, and

(b) an assessment of the amount payable by the person by way of income tax for that year, that is to say, the difference between the amount in which the person is assessed to income tax under paragraph (a) and the aggregate amount of any income tax deducted at source;

but nothing in this subsection enables an assessment to show as repayable any income tax which any provision of the Income Tax Acts provides is not repayable.

(4) The amounts in which a person is chargeable to income tax and capital gains are net amounts, taking into account any relief or allowance that is applicable.

(5) A simple assessment must be based on information relating to the person that is held by HMRC (whether or not supplied by the person to whom the assessment relates).

(6) The notice of a simple assessment required to be sent to the person by section 30A(3) must (among other things) —

(a) include particulars of the income and gains, and any relief or allowance, taken into account in the assessment, and

(b) state any amount payable by the person by virtue of section 59BA (with particulars of how it may be paid and the date by which it is payable).

(7) The tax to be assessed on a person by a simple assessment does not include any tax which —

(a) is chargeable on the scheme administrator of a registered pension scheme under Part 4 of Finance Act 2004,

(b) is chargeable on the sub-scheme administrator of a sub-scheme under Part 4 of the Finance Act 2004 as modified by the Registered Pension Schemes (Splitting of Schemes) Regulations 2006, or

(c) is chargeable on the person who is (or persons who are) the responsible person in relation to an employer-financed retirement benefits scheme under section 394(2) of ITEPA 2003.

(8) Nothing in this section prevents HMRC issuing more than one simple assessment to the same person in respect of the same year of assessment (whether or not any earlier simple assessment for that year is withdrawn).

(9) In this section references to a simple assessment are to an assessment under this section.

28I   Simple assessments by HMRC: trustees

(1) HMRC may make a simple assessment for a year of assessment in respect of a settlement if, when the assessment is made, the relevant trustees of the settlement are not excluded by subsection (2) in relation to that year.

(2) Subsection (1) does not apply at any time in relation to that year of assessment if —

(a) a return under section 8A has been delivered for that year by the relevant trustees or any of them, or

        (b)   there is at that time a subsisting requirement to make and deliver such a return by virtue of a notice under section 8A;

but nothing in this subsection prevents HMRC from giving notice of a simple assessment at the same time as a notice withdrawing a notice under section 8A.

(3)   A simple assessment is—

        (a)   an assessment of the amounts in which the relevant trustees are chargeable to income tax and capital gains tax for the year of assessment to which it relates, and

        (b)   an assessment of the amount payable by them by way of income tax for that year, that is to say, the difference between the amount in which they are assessed to income tax under paragraph (a) and the aggregate amount of any income tax deducted at source;

but nothing in this subsection enables an assessment to show as repayable any income tax which any provision of the Income Tax Acts provides is not repayable.

(4)   The amounts in which the relevant trustees are chargeable to income tax and capital gains are net amounts, taking into account any relief or allowance that is applicable.

(5)   A simple assessment must be based only on information relating to the settlement that is held by HMRC (whether or not supplied by the relevant trustees).

(6)   The notice of a simple assessment required by section 30A(3) may be given to any one or more of the relevant trustees.

(7)   That notice must (among other things)—

        (a)   include particulars of the income and gains, and any relief or allowance, taken into account in the assessment, and

        (b)   state any amount payable by the relevant trustees by virtue of section 59BA (with particulars of how it may be paid and the date by which it is payable).

(8)   The tax to be assessed by a simple assessment does not include any tax which—

        (a)   is chargeable on the scheme administrator of a registered pension scheme under Part 4 of Finance Act 2004,

        (b)   is chargeable on the sub-scheme administrator of a sub-scheme under Part 4 of the Finance Act 2004 as modified by the Registered Pension Schemes (Splitting of Schemes) Regulations 2006, or

        (c)   is chargeable on the person who is (or persons who are) the responsible person in relation to an employer-financed retirement benefits scheme under section 394(2) of ITEPA 2003.

(9)   Nothing in this section prevents HMRC issuing more than one simple assessment in respect of the same settlement and the same year of assessment (whether or not any earlier simple assessment for that year is withdrawn).

    (10)   In this section references to a "simple assessment" are to an assessment under this section.

    (11)   In this Act references to the person to whom a simple assessment relates are, in relation to one made under this section, to the relevant trustees of the settlement to which it relates.

28J   Power to withdraw a simple assessment

    (1)   HMRC may withdraw a simple assessment by notice to the person to which it relates.

    (2)   An assessment that has been withdrawn ceases to have effect (and is to be taken as never having had any effect)."

4   In section 31 (appeals: right to appeal), before subsection (4) insert—

    "(3A)   In the case of a simple assessment, the right to appeal under subsection (1)(d) does not apply unless and until the person concerned has—

        (a)   raised a query about the assessment under section 31AA, and

        (b)   been given a final response to that query."

5   (1)   Section 31A (appeals: notice of appeal) is amended as follows.

    (2)   In subsection (4), after "this Act" insert "(other than an appeal against a simple assessment)".

    (3)   After subsection (4) insert—

    "(4A)   In relation to an appeal under section 31(1)(d) against a simple assessment—

        (a)   the specified date is the date on which the person concerned is given notice under section 31AA of the final response to the query the person is required by section 31(3A) to make, and

        (b)   the relevant officer of the Board is the officer by whom the notice of assessment was given."

6   After section 31A (notice of appeal) insert—

"31AA   Taxpayer's right to query simple assessment

    (1)   This section applies where a person has been given notice of a simple assessment.

    (2)   The person may query the simple assessment by notifying HMRC of—

        (a)   a belief that the assessment is or may be incorrect, and

        (b)   the reasons for that belief.

    (3)   The person may exercise the power to query the simple assessment at any time within—

        (a)   the period of 60 days after the date on which the notice of assessment was issued, or

        (b)   such longer period as HMRC may allow.

    (4)   If the simple assessment is queried, HMRC must—

        (a)   consider the query and the matters raised by it, and

        (b)   give a final response to the query.

(5) The person may at any time withdraw a query (which terminates HMRC's duties under subsection (4)).

(6) If it appears to HMRC that—
  (a) they need time to consider the matters raised by the query, or
  (b) further information (whether from the person or anyone else) is required,

  HMRC may postpone the simple assessment in whole or part (according to how much of it is being queried by the person).

(7) If the simple assessment is postponed in whole or part, HMRC must notify the person in writing—
  (a) whether the assessment is postponed in whole or part, and
  (b) if it is postponed in part, of the amount that remains payable under the assessment.

(8) While the simple assessment is postponed the person is under no obligation to pay—
  (a) the payable amount specified in the notice of assessment (if the whole assessment is postponed), or
  (b) the postponed part of the payable amount so specified (if the assessment is postponed in part).

(9) After considering the query the final response must be to—
  (a) confirm the simple assessment,
  (b) give the person an amended simple assessment (which supersedes the original assessment), or
  (c) withdraw the simple assessment (without replacing it).

(10) HMRC must notify the person in writing of their final response.

(11) This section does not apply to an amended simple assessment given as a final response to the query.

(12) Nothing in this section affects—
  (a) a person's right to request an explanation from HMRC of a simple assessment or the information on which it is based, or
  (b) HMRC's power to give a person such explanation or information as they consider appropriate,

  whether as part of the querying process under this section or otherwise.

(13) In subsection (12) "person" means a person who has been given notice of a simple assessment".

7 (1) Section 59B (payment of income tax and capital gains tax) is amended as follows.

  (2) In the heading, at end insert "**: assessments other than simple assessments**".

  (3) In subsection (6), after "9" insert ", 28H or 28I".

8   After section 59B insert—

  "59BA Payment of income tax and capital gains tax: simple assessments

    (1) This section applies where a person has been given a simple assessment in relation to a year of assessment.

(2) Subject to subsection (3), the difference between—

    (a) the amount of income tax and capital gains tax for that year contained in the simple assessment, and

    (b) the aggregate of any payments on account made by the person in respect of that year (whether under section 59A or 59AA or otherwise) and any income tax which in respect of that year has been deducted at source,

is payable by that person as mentioned in subsection (4) or (5).

(3) Nothing in subsection (2) is to be read as requiring the repayment of any income tax which any provision of the Income Tax Acts provides is not repayable.

(4) In a case where the person is given notice of the simple assessment after the 31st October next after the year of assessment, the difference is payable at the end of the period of 3 months after the day on which that notice was given.

(5) In any other case the difference is payable on or before the 31st January next after the end of the year of assessment.

(6) Section 59B(7) (which explains references to income tax deducted at source) applies for the purposes of this section.

(7) PAYE regulations may provide that, for the purpose of determining the amount of the difference mentioned in subsection (2), any necessary adjustments in respect of matters prescribed in the regulations shall be made to the amount of tax deducted at source under PAYE regulations."

9 (1) Schedule 56 to FA 2009 (penalty for failure to make payments on time) is amended as follows.

(2) In the Table in paragraph 1, after item 1 insert—

"1A	Income tax or capital gains tax	Amount payable under section 59BA(4) or (5) of TMA 1970	The date falling 30 days after the date specified in section 59BA(4) or (5) of TMA 1970 as the date by which the amount must be paid."

(3) In paragraph 3(1)(a), after "items 1," insert "1A,".

Finance Act 2016 (c. 24)
Schedule 24 — Tax advantages constituting the grant of state aid
Part 1 — Tax advantages to which section 180(2)applies

645

SCHEDULE 24   Section 180(2) and (5)

TAX ADVANTAGES CONSTITUTING THE GRANT OF STATE AID

PART 1

TAX ADVANTAGES TO WHICH SECTION 180(2)APPLIES

Enhanced capital allowances

Tax advantage	*Provision under which tax advantage is given*
Business premises renovation allowances	Part 3A of CAA 2001
Zero-emission goods vehicle allowances	Section 45DA, 45DB and 212T of CAA 2001
Expenditure on plant and machinery for use in designated assisted areas (enhanced capital allowances for enterprise zones)	Sections 45K to 45N and 212U of CAA 2001

Creative tax reliefs

Tax advantage	*Provision under which tax advantage is given*
Film tax relief	Part 15 of CTA 2009
Television tax reliefs	Part 15A of CTA 2009
Theatre relief	Part 15C of CTA 2009
Orchestra tax relief	Part 15D of CTA 2009

Research and development reliefs

Tax advantage	*Provision under which tax advantage is given*
Relief for SMEs: cost of research and development incurred by SME	Chapter 2 of Part 13 of CTA 2009

646

Finance Act 2016 (c. 24)
Schedule 24 — Tax advantages constituting the grant of state aid
Part 1 — Tax advantages to which section 180(2)applies

Tax advantage	Provision under which tax advantage is given
Vaccine research relief	Chapter 7 of Part 13 of CTA 2009

PART 2

TAX ADVANTAGES TO WHICH SECTION 180(5) APPLIES

Tax advantage	Provision under which tax advantage is given to beneficiary	Person liable to receive request under section 180(5)
Reduced rate of climate change levy payable in respect of a reduced rate supply (for supplies covered by climate change agreement)	Paragraphs 42 and 44 of Schedule 6 to FA 2000	The person to whom the reduced rate taxable supply is supplied
Relief granted to investors in a company under the enterprise investment scheme	Part 5 of ITA 2007	The company whose shares are acquired by investors
Relief granted to investors in a venture capital trust under the venture capital trust scheme	Part 6 of ITA 2007	The venture capital trust

SCHEDULE 25

Section 184

OFFICE OF TAX SIMPLIFICATION

Membership

1   (1) The OTS is to consist of not more than eight members.

(2) The members of the OTS must include —
    (a) a chair,
    (b) a tax director (see sub-paragraph (5)),
    (c) a representative of Her Majesty's Revenue and Customs, and
    (d) a representative of the Treasury.

(3) The additional members, if any, are to be nominated by the chair.

(4) The members of the OTS are to be appointed by the Chancellor of the Exchequer.

(5) A person may be appointed as a tax director of the OTS only if the Chancellor of the Exchequer is satisfied that the person has the necessary qualifications and experience to direct the manner in which the OTS discharges its functions.

(6) The Chancellor of the Exchequer must consult the chair of the OTS before appointing a person as a tax director (subject to paragraph 3(3)).

Term of office

2 (1) A person holds and vacates office as a member of the OTS in accordance with the terms of the appointment, subject to the following provisions.

(2) A period of appointment may not exceed 5 years.

(3) A person who ceases to be a member of the OTS is eligible for re-appointment.

Appointment of initial members

3 (1) Sub-paragraphs (2) and (3) apply where a person ("P") appointed under paragraph 1(2)(a) or (b) was, immediately before the appointment, the chair or tax director (as the case may be) of the non-statutory Office of Tax Simplification.

(2) P's period of appointment is to be taken to have begun with the appointment of P as the chair or tax director (as the case may be) of the non-statutory Office of Tax Simplification.

(3) The requirement in paragraph 1(6) does not apply where P was, immediately before P's appointment under paragraph 1(2)(b), the tax director of the non-statutory Office of Tax Simplification.

Termination of appointments

4 A member of the OTS may at any time resign by giving written notice to the Chancellor of the Exchequer.

5 (1) The Chancellor of the Exchequer may terminate the appointment of a member of the OTS by giving the member written notice.

(2) In the case of a member appointed for the purposes of paragraph 1(2)(a) or (b) or (3), the Chancellor of the Exchequer may only terminate the appointment if —
   (a) the member has been absent from meetings of the OTS without the OTS's permission for a period of more than 3 months,
   (b) the member becomes bankrupt (see sub-paragraph (3)),
   (c) the member has failed to comply with the terms of the appointment, or
   (d) the member is, in the opinion of the Chancellor of the Exchequer, unable, unfit or unwilling to carry out the member's functions.

(3) A member becomes bankrupt if —

(a) in England and Wales or Northern Ireland, a bankruptcy order is made in relation to the member;

(b) in Scotland, the member's estate is sequestrated.

Remuneration

6   The Treasury may pay a member of the OTS such remuneration and allowances as the Treasury may determine.

Provision of staff and facilities etc.

7   The Treasury may provide the OTS with such staff, accommodation, services and other facilities as appear to the Treasury to be necessary or expedient for the proper performance by the OTS of its functions.

Validity of proceedings

8   The OTS may regulate its own procedure.

9   The validity of anything done by the OTS is not affected by –
        (a) any vacancy in the membership of the OTS, or
        (b) any defect in the appointment of a member of the OTS.

Supplementary powers

10   The OTS may do anything that appears to it to be necessary or appropriate for the purpose of, or in connection with, the performance of its functions.

Finance

11 (1) The Treasury may make to the OTS such payments out of money provided by Parliament as the Treasury considers appropriate for the purpose of enabling the Office to meet its expenses.

    (2) Payments are to be made at such times, and subject to such conditions, as the Treasury may determine.

Disqualification

12   In Part 2 of Schedule 1 to the House of Commons Disqualification Act 1975 (bodies of which all members are disqualified) insert at the appropriate place –
        "The Office of Tax Simplification."

13   In Part 2 of Schedule 1 to the Northern Ireland Assembly Disqualification Act 1975 (bodies of which all members are disqualified) insert at the appropriate place –
        "The Office of Tax Simplification."

Freedom of information

14   In Part 6 of Schedule 1 to the Freedom of Information Act 2000 (public authorities to which the Act applies) insert at the appropriate place –
        "The Office of Tax Simplification."

Public sector equality duty

15   In Part 1 of Schedule 19 to the Equality Act 2010 (authorities subject to the public sector equality duty) under the heading "Industry, business, finance etc." insert at the appropriate place—

"The Office of Tax Simplification."